"This thought-provoking book provides a th
theory, research, and practical consideratior
our profession. In his third edition of this
incorporated new research, thinking, and illustrative examples. He writes about
complex issues in a conversational manner with helpful summaries provided
throughout the text. He clearly communicates when and how his own views and
motives are reflected in his writing, challenging the reader to self-reflect on their
own values and how those influence their own ethical decision-making. All I-O
psychologists, regardless of career stage or professional role, will find something to
learn here."

Deirdre J. Knapp, *Principal Scientist, Human Resources*
Research Organization (HumRRO), USA

"I don't say this often, but this book is truly important. It cogently, practically,
and clearly brings insight, evidence, theory, and philosophy forward to meaningfully understand ethics and morality at work and in organizations. At the same
time, the book inspires you to be the best human, practitioner, and scholar you
can be and shares approaches and perspectives to help with that journey."

Steven Rogelberg, Ph.D., *Chancellor's Professor and Immediate Past President*
of the Society for Industrial and Organizational Psychology

"Only read this book if you want to get an expanded image of how to think
about, study and help people and organizations be all they can be for the
betterment of them and society. Joel Lefkowitz is amazing in his ability to
meaningfully present the thinking and ideas of the great philosophers and
ethicists—and then he shows with explicit examples how, by adding moral and
ethical values to what we do and how we do it, our lives and the lives of those we
study and work with will be enhanced. And you need not be an I-O Psychologist
to find the book a mind-expanding great read—anyone in HR, OB, OD and so
forth will find new ways to think about what they do and how to do it better for
all. Did I say I loved the book?"

Benjamin Schneider, *Professor Emeritus, University of Maryland. Past President,*
Society for Industrial-Organizational Psychology, USA

VALUES AND ETHICS OF INDUSTRIAL-ORGANIZATIONAL PSYCHOLOGY

This foundational text was one of the first books to integrate work from moral philosophy, developmental/moral psychology, applied psychology, political and social economy, and political science, as well as business scholarship. Twenty years on, this third edition utilizes ideas from the first two to provide readers with a practical model for ethical decision making and includes examples from I-O research and practice, as well as current business events.

The book incorporates diverse perspectives into a "framework for taking moral action" based on learning points from each chapter. Examples and references have been updated throughout, and sections on moral psychology, economic justice, the "replicability crisis," and open science have been expanded and the "radical behavioral challenge" to ethical decision-making is critiqued. In fifteen clearly structured and theory-based chapters, the author also presents a variety of ethical incidents reported by practicing I-O psychologists.

This is the ideal resource for Ethics and I-O courses at the graduate and doctoral level. Academics in Organizational Behavior and Human Resource Management will also benefit from this book, as well as anyone interested in Ethics in Psychology and Business.

Joel Lefkowitz is Professor Emeritus at the Baruch College and the Graduate Center of the City University of New York, USA, where he headed the I-O doctoral program from its inception in 1982 until 2009. He still regularly teaches the doctoral course in Ethical, Professional and Legal Issues for Psychologists, and is a Fellow of the Society for Industrial-Organizational Psychology, The American Psychological Association—Divisions 9 and 14, and the Association for Psychological Science.

Series In Applied Psychology

Jeanette N. Cleveland
Colorado State University Donald Truxillo, Portland State University
Edwin A. Fleishman
Founding Series Editor (1987-2010)
Kevin R. Murphy
Emeritus Series Editor (2010-2018)

Bridging both academic and applied interests, the Applied Psychology Series offers publications that emphasize state-of-the-art research and its application to important issues of human behavior in a variety of societal settings. To date, more than 50 books in various fields of applied psychology have been published in this series.

For more information about this series, please visit: https://www.routledge.com/Applied-Psychology-Series/book-series/SAP

VALUES AND ETHICS OF INDUSTRIAL-ORGANIZATIONAL PSYCHOLOGY

Third Edition

Joel Lefkowitz

Routledge
Taylor & Francis Group

NEW YORK AND LONDON

Cover image: © Fotosearch.com, LLC, Waukesha, WI

First published 2023
by Routledge
605 Third Avenue, New York, NY 10158

and by Routledge
4 Park Square, Milton Park, Abingdon, Oxon, OX14 4RN

Routledge is an imprint of the Taylor & Francis Group, an informa business

© 2023 Joel Lefkowitz

Library of Congress Cataloguing-in-Publication Data
Names: Lefkowitz, Joel, author.
Title: Values and ethics of industrial-organizational psychology / Joel Lefkowitz.
Description: Third edition. | New York, NY : Routledge, 2023. |
Series: Applied psychology series | Previous edition title: Ethics and values in industrial-organizational psychology. | Includes bibliographical references and index.
Identifiers: LCCN 2022039425 (print) | LCCN 2022039426 (ebook) |
ISBN 9781032080253 (hbk) | ISBN 9781032080246 (pbk) |
ISBN 9781003212577 (ebk)
Subjects: LCSH: Psychology, Industrial. | Business ethics.
Classification: LCC HF5548.8 .L3644 2023 (print) | LCC HF5548.8 (ebook) |
DDC 174/.91587--dc23
LC record available at https://lccn.loc.gov/2022039425
LC ebook record available at https://lccn.loc.gov/2022039426

ISBN: 978-1-032-08025-3 (hbk)
ISBN: 978-1-032-08024-6 (pbk)
ISBN: 978-1-003-21257-7 (ebk)

DOI: 10.4324/9781003212577

This book is dedicated to back-office clerks doing data entry
in the financial districts of New York;
goldminers in the dark and the wet and the heat
more than a mile beneath the Black Hills of South Dakota;
a police officer alone in his cruiser at 3:00 a.m.
after several days of street violence in Dayton, Ohio;
young women high school graduates
learning power sewing machine operation for piece rates
in Pennsylvania and New England;
partially literate washers and pressers in a steamy industrial laundry
in rural Louisiana;
aircraft parts production workers in Cleveland;
and many more....
Because they graciously allowed themselves
to be observed, interviewed, surveyed, tested, evaluated or trained,
I came to appreciate what it is like to work in America.

And to Setha, who continues to model so brilliantly the role of
passionate scholar-author.

And in a world seeming heavier and heavier, in appreciation for
the lightness and effervescence of Max, Skye and Gavin.

CONTENTS

FIGURES

TABLES

BOXES

SERIES FOREWORD

The goal of the Applied Psychology Series is to create books that exemplify the use of scientific research, theory, and findings to solve real problems in organizations and society. Lefkowitz's *Values and Ethics of Industrial-Organizational Psychology, Third Ed.*, takes this approach. The current volume updates and significantly expands the second edition, preserving the strengths of previous work while incorporating new material with a slightly new focus.

Lefkowitz introduces a wide-ranging book with thoughtful discussion of the meaning of ethical behavior and of philosophers' long quest to understand the meaning and determinants of ethics. Lefkowitz shares his rationale for the subtle change in the book's title from previous editions, specifically, to emphasize the primacy of "values". He also notes the importance of filling the gap between ethical principles and practice. Following this introductory chapter, the first section of the book ("Moral Philosophy and Psychology"; Chapters 2–7) provides a discussion of the current streams of thought regarding ethics in the long history of western civilization. Lefkowitz pays careful attention to identifying concrete principles that can be applied to help make ethical decisions in organizations. In Part II ("Values"; Chapters 8–12), he builds a detailed and rigorous model for analyzing ethical choices in organizations. In Part III ("The Responsible Conduct of Research"; Chapters 13–14), he applies these principles to understand the ethical conduct of business, as well as the ethical conduct of research in practice in applied psychology. In the concluding section, Lefkowitz provides a detailed strategy for resolving ethical dilemmas at work, making ethical decisions, and taking moral action.

Lefkowitz draws from a broad literature, presenting thoughtful syntheses of a number of disciplines. He makes a strong case for the need to take ethical reasoning seriously. Importantly, the book integrates both the philosophical foundations and the practical implications of the systematic study of ethical behavior in organizations. We welcome the addition of *Values and Ethics of Industrial-Organizational Psychology, Third Ed.*, to the Applied Psychology Series.

1

INTRODUCTION

A successful academic author once told me that an effective book is based primarily on just one good idea—irrespective of how broad the topic or complex the material is. Well, the overarching thesis of this book is that contrary to a widespread view, professional ethics is not an unreasonable set of rules or expectations designed by intrusive idealists to make our lives more difficult.

As psychologists we study human behavior. To do so, we depend on the goodwill and trust of the persons who cooperate with us voluntarily, sometimes revealing their private selves to us, enabling us to do our applied work and research. As industrial and organizational (I-O) psychologists, we further depend on the goodwill of organizational decision-makers who trust us when we say that we can improve the effectiveness of their enterprises. As professionals, we cannot do that work very well, at least not for very long, if we do not treat all of those persons ethically—that is, honestly, fairly and with respect and dignity. It has been observed that

> the idea of dignity as underlying the intrinsic value on human life and liberty has been central to societal progress since the Middle Ages … . Dignity represents a pillar of our moral and political heritage; so much so that even some economic historians argue that the attribution of human dignity was a key success factor of social and economic development in the West.
>
> *(Pirson et al., 2016, p.465)*

Accordingly, it has played a central (albeit sometimes implicit) role in moral philosophy, social science, business ethics and attempts to humanize organizations. And in two recent surveys "Ethical, legal, & professional contexts" was rated 4th-highest among 25 domains of competency by I-O graduate program

DOI: 10.4324/9781003212577-1

directors (Payne et al., 2015) and 2nd-highest among 21 content areas by practicing I-O psychologists (Steiner & Yancey, 2013).[1]

But our motives ought not to be solely instrumental. Indeed, as reviewed in chapters 3 and 5, the hallmark of some moral theories is the rejection of such utilities or "cost-benefit analyses" as a means of judging ethical behavior. As is characteristic of all professionals we assume the responsibility of "the service ideal." As psychologists we carry with us a humanistic tradition that includes a concern for promoting people's welfare, some of which is formalized in our ethical codes. Thus, ethical issues of fairness and justice and of duty and beneficence are central to our core values as professional psychologists. That is also in keeping with contemporary views regarding personal morality: "Living a fully ethical life involves doing the most good we can" (Singer, 2015, p. vii); "the central core of morality [is] to treat others only in ways that could be justified to them" (Scanlon, 1998, p. 361). Similar voices are being raised in academe—e.g., in advocating an expansion of the criteria for hiring, tenure and promotion beyond the traditional ones of research, service and teaching, to a fourth dimension of "doing for the greater good," including intrinsic values like ethical behavior, fostering community well-being, and quality of mentoring (Luthar, 2017; Sternberg, 2016).

Some of the more controversial portions of this book, however, include the criticism that much of I-O psychology drifted rather far from those core values and to a considerable degree replaced them with a narrow version of business values that are not commensurate with psychology's humanistic heritage. I agree with Kelman (2021) that "ultimately a responsible psychologist is a responsible citizen" (p. 3). At their best, they are both guided by the fundamental values of society. And this can be illustrated by the core meta-questions posed in Box 1.1. (Throughout the book I have refrained from offering commentary on the box illustrations—leaving that material for the reader's own reflections and/or group discussion.)

There seem to be essentially four kinds of publications concerned with ethics. Each type is rather different from the others and makes a relatively unique contribution, notwithstanding that there is some inevitable overlap among them. The first category of publications consists of normative guidelines in the form of ethical codes that have been promulgated by governments, professional and trade associations, individual organizations (including business corporations) and others. Such codes are offered as presumably helpful and practical guides to ethical behavior, generally within particular domains such as business management or a particular profession. The Center for the Study of Ethics in the Professions has a collection of more than 2,500 codes from approximately 1,500 organizations! There are, however, frequently problems with ethical codes—such as fuzzy boundaries between what is considered professional behavior (covered by

---

1 However, one wonders whether the inclusion of *legal* concerns as part of the domain may have contributed to a positive rating bias.

BOX 1.1 CORE ISSUES IN NORMATIVE ETHICS—TWO QUESTIONS

Throughout human history—probably starting even earlier among proto-human populations—there has been a core moral domain that can be expressed by just two (non-independent) all-encompassing questions or challenges that have been considered in many moral philosophies.[2]

I. Start with the premise that we each have the right to maintain and enhance our dignity and well-being, self-esteem, and chances to suc-ceed. But there are often good justifications for maintaining and en-hancing the well-being of others in our communities (whether for moral reasons or for reasons that have adaptive advantages for everyone). So we are challenged, whether we like it or not, to consider,

QUESTION I: *What is the appropriate dividing line (or balance) between individual rights and the common good?*[3]

II. Let us recognize that there are always people who, for a multitude of reasons (including circumstances not of their making), are hard-pressed to provide for themselves the adequate means to survive, much less thrive. So we are challenged, whether we like it or not, to consider,

QUESTION II: *What is one's responsibility with regard to the less fortunate?*

Individuals, families, groups, organizations, societies, nations and interna-tional associations have adopted a variety of responses to that question, including simply ignoring it.

Our answers to these questions reflect our individual and collective beliefs about human nature and worth, as well as our valued norms of social organization—expressed in our systems of economics, governance, educa-tion and law—including professional ethics.

Many, perhaps every professional ethical dilemma one faces, no matter how enmeshed it may be in technical matters, complex social relations, and idiosyncratic circumstances, contains a kernel of one or both of those issues.

---

2   This is written from an avowedly Western cultural perspective without explicitly considering, e.g., Buddhist, Confucian, Hindu or Taoist insights.
3   With an appreciative nod to the sociologist Amitai Etzioni's (2015) book title, *The new normal: finding a balance between individual rights and the common good.*

the code) and personal behavior (not covered) (Pipes et al., 2005). It has also been pointed out that a singular reliance solely on a professional code "may lead practitioners to focus on rules so much that they risk harming the quality of their professional relationships" (Knapp et al., 2013).[4] The ethical psychologist will need to think beyond merely being familiar with the 5 aspirational principles and 89 enforceable standards of the American Psychological Association's *Ethical Principles and Code of Conduct* (hereafter, APA Code).

In contrast, the second category of publications consists of highly theoretical and philosophical treatises. Chapters 2, 3, 4 and 5 of this book present a distillation of moral philosophies in which it is my intention to allow the reader to become familiar with some varieties of ethical reasoning. They offer alternative conceptual approaches that may be useful in anticipating, evaluating and resolving ethical dilemmas—even when you cannot find your specific problem described in an ethics code. Different ethical problems, even within a single domain such as business practices, may induce different types of ethical reasoning corresponding to different moral theories (Fritzsche & Becker, 1984).

A third category of publications consists of illustrative casebooks that contribute to our understanding by providing applications of ethical principles and guidelines that may otherwise be ambiguous. But they tend to be limited by the same factors that limit the codes themselves, and no one person or even a small number of persons is likely to have direct experience with enough real cases to represent anywhere near an entire code. Good casebooks, therefore, almost always need to be collaborative enterprises—perhaps developed by members of a professional ethics committee with considerable experience evaluating complaints. New to this 3rd edition are a total of 23 verbatim narrative descriptions of actual ethical situations experienced and reported by members of the Society for Industrial-Organizational Psychology (SIOP) (cf. Tables 6.5 and 15.1).

The last major category of ethics publications consists of books that aim to impact people's lives and, by extension, society by showing how ethical considerations are relevant to everyday affairs, contributing to general well-being and to having a fulfilling life. These books deal with applied ethics, practical ethics or social criticism (from an ethical or moral perspective). Perhaps the two best-known contemporary examples of this genre are both by Peter Singer (2011; 2015): the wide-ranging *Practical Ethics*, which tackles issues like euthanasia, animal killing, environmental degradation, climate change, the distribution of wealth and much more, from a consistent theoretical position (that of *consequentialism,* see Chap. 4), and *The Most Good You*

---

4   The authors are writing about training in clinical psychology, but I believe the point is apt for us as well.

Can Do, explaining the philosophy and social movement of "effective altruism." Other examples are targeted at a specific audience, such as books on business ethics (Schminke, 2014).

With perhaps more than a little hubris, but within the limited domain of professional ethics for I-O psychologists, this book touches at least lightly all four of those bases and emphasizes primarily the ubiquitous, but often unacknowledged, role played by personal and institutional values in shaping moral action.

This is not primarily a book *about* organizational ethics as studied by I-O psychologists and other organizational scholars (e.g., ethical leadership, ethical organizational climate, managerial corruption) although some of that scholarship is presented in chapters 6 and 7 as illustrative of "contemporaneous contextual influences" on ethical behavior. Nor have ethical aspects of recent technological developments been covered, such as research using "big data" (Favaretto et al., 2020); use of Amazon's "Mechanical Turk" as a source of participant data (Buhrmester et al., 2018; Paolacci & Chandler, 2014); or the use of social media as a research tool (Kosinski et al., 2015; Sugiura et al., 2017; Taylor & Pagliari, 2018). Each of those could warrant a separate text.

This book develops a "framework for ethical decision-making," culminating in a model of ethical reasoning for taking moral action. The important role played by the values that underlie our reasoning is emphasized throughout, and there are three broad objectives: to enhance the reader's ability to: (1) recognize and understand the origins and nature of ethical problems and their contemporary determinants; (2) appreciate the role of personal and societal values in shaping ethical dilemmas and our reactions to them; and (3) improve the quality of those reactions—i.e., make better moral choices. Deliberately fostering a broad, open-ended perspective also serves the function of preparing one to engage in ethical issues that may never have been encountered previously.

An explosion of interest in ethics and morality appears to have taken place in many spheres of life. Social scientists (Etzioni, 1996, 2015) and revered religious leaders (e.g., Dalai Lama, 1999, 2011) have felt the need to offer prescriptions for improving the moral dimension of society; psychologists have shown increased interest in morality as a unifying cognitive construct (Brandt & Reyna, 2015); the number of books published on business ethics has soared and professional journals, such as *Ethics & Behavior, The Journal of Business Ethics, Business Ethics Quarterly, The Journal of Religion and Business Ethics, Journal of Business, Peace and Sustainable Development, Business and Society,* and others have flourished; the surefire indicator that a scholarly field has achieved a critical mass of attention—an edited handbook—has existed for a while as well (Cooper, 2001); consultants teaching business ethics or "values clarification" in corporations and "character training" in the schools constitute a growth industry; within our profession the APA (1992) revised its ethical code not all that long ago yet recently revised it again (APA, 2002), and again, even more recently (APA, 2010a, 2017), and as of this writing is in the process of another major revision; in conjunction with the APA, SIOP revised and expanded its casebook on ethics (Lowman et al., 2006); morality and character issues have become preeminent screening criteria for those who wish to serve in public office[5]; and if further mundane demonstration were needed to make the point, the Sunday magazine section of my hometown paper, *The New York Times*, has been publishing an advice column titled "The Ethicist" for more than 15 years for those who find themselves ethically challenged.

But that does not address why attention to ethics and morality has recently increased. I do not know that anyone has provided a fully satisfactory non-metaphysical explanation, but there has been a litany of anxiety-producing, fear-inducing events that may have contributed to people searching for something "better." Briefly, they are:

1. The world has been stunned by biomedical advances such as mapping of the entire human genome (Zimmer, 2021); genetic engineering of food crops and livestock; the cloning to-date of approximately two dozen species of animals since Dolly the sheep in 1996—albeit not yet including humans; the creation of human embryos in order to extract undifferentiated stem cells that can be "directed" into becoming a variety of specialized tissues; a very efficient method of "gene editing" (i.e., altering an organism's heritable DNA); plans to collect genetic data on one million Americans while it remains unclear as to who will "own" that data (Davis, 2016); and most recently, the successful transplantation of the heart of a genetically altered pig into a human (Rabin, 2022). It is not surprising that many have become more than a little concerned by the ethical implications of those achievements (National Human Genome Research Institute, 2015; Pollack, 2015; Wade, 2015; Zimmer, 2015)—and for some, it even recalls the horrific eugenics movement in the U.S. from the 1920s into the 1950s, in which tens of thousands of men and women underwent forced sterilization because of their alleged inferiority (Cohen, 2016; Leonard, 2016). A consortium of four international medical and scientific academies has recently called for a moratorium on gene alteration because of doubts about its moral and medical appropriateness (Wade, 2015b).
2. The globalization of American corporations has led to a growing awareness of differences in what are considered ethically acceptable business practices in other cultures and to the passage and amendment of the Foreign Corrupt Practices Act (U.S. Congress, 1977/1998), as well as to a concern for the

---

5 With some astounding recent exceptions.

extent to which U.S. corporations maintain working conditions and terms of employment in developing-world production facilities that they could not do in the United States. There have been 127 FCPA enforcement actions brought by the Securities and Exchange Commission against American corporations over the past 10 years, 2011–2020, most resulting in fines of many millions of dollars (SEC, 2021).

3. The proliferation of the Internet, access to the World Wide Web and social media have led to grave concerns regarding privacy and confidentiality in business transactions, extortionate hacking of websites, abusive social behavior toward others, as well as paradoxically to a growing sense of anonymity. It is paradoxical because there is growing evidence that many people actually strive to be anonymous, or use a pseudonymous identity on the web; yet even though the incidence of *cyberbullying* and *trolling* on social media is extensive it may not be associated disproportionately with anonymity (Herrman, 2021). There is also evidence that smartphone access and degree of internet usage are associated with loneliness and lower life satisfaction among teenagers worldwide (Twenge et al., in press).

4. There has been a growing fearfulness associated with apparently random street crime since the 1980s; tragic numbers of drug overdoses and deaths; a seemingly ceaseless incidence of highly publicized mass shootings—all of which are viewed by many Americans as evidence of moral failing rather than emotional disturbance or a reflection of socioeconomic and socio-political forces.

5. There has been an extraordinary increase in the power exercised by business corporations over people's lives—virtually tearing up the old implied social contract—as well as the shift from a manufacturing to a service economy with the attendant job losses from the 1980s–2000s, loss of a sense of economic security, and destruction of the sense of commitment and loyalty to a long-term employer. These have all been exacerbated by the financial crisis of 2008 and the subsequent worldwide recession. Interestingly however, although it is too early to draw firm conclusions, the enormous economic dislocations wrought by the Covid-19 pandemic seem to be having a paradoxical effect in empowering workers in the U.S. and elsewhere—labor movements somewhat ironically labeled "the mass resignation."

6. There have been so many high-profile instances of unethical or corrupt behavior on the part of corporate leaders that it has been characterized in the press as a "scourge" (Zipkin, 2000). And it seems to have continued virtually unabated since that discouraging comment was made: unscrupulous mortgage lending practices and corruption in the financial services sector in 2008 and beyond (Sorkin, 2015) in which, e.g., Goldman Sachs (and other banks) "falsely assur[ed] investors that securities it sold were backed by sound mortgages, when it knew that they were full of mortgages that were likely to fail" (Delery, 2016, p. B3); corporate personnel concealing ignition switch

malfunctions responsible for at least 124 deaths in General Motors cars (Ivory et al., 2015; Meier, 2016); corporate sabotaging of emissions control computer software in Volkswagen cars (Hakim et al., 2015); intentionally selling salmonella-tainted peanut butter, resulting in at least 9 deaths and hundreds of cases of food poisoning (Lewis, 2015); disregard of safety regulations at the Upper Big Branch mine in West Virginia, resulting in an explosion killing 29 miners and jail time for the company's CEO (Blinder, 2015, 2016; Stolberg, 2015); and on it goes … .

All of this is taking place amidst a zeitgeist of fearful forces that we seem unable and/or unwilling to deal with effectively: near-cataclysmic events associated with climate change and global warming; a seemingly ever-mutating global pandemic; multiple wars on terrorism; the flourishing of authoritarian governments and decline of democratic pluralism; expanding social and economic inequalities (in wealth, income, education, healthcare, morbidity, etc.); extreme social and political polarization, enhanced by vitriolic social media; and rapidly shifting technology causing traumatic dislocations for workers. No wonder many people have begun to wonder—what is going on? What is the right thing? How can I lead a better life?

Philosophy and Psychology

The relationship between psychology and philosophy is a long and close one. As pointed out by the philosopher K.A. Appiah (2014),

> the canonical philosophers belong as much to the history of what we now call psychology as to the genealogy of philosophy … . And though we typically suppose that psychology calved off from philosophy, you can make a case that it was the other way round. (p. 11)

He goes on to point out that it wasn't until the late 19th century that philosophy "swerved away from psychologism" and became "what the best philosophy has always been: conceptual analysis" (p. 12). So it is not surprising to learn that much of the content of ethical philosophical thought deals with familiar psychological issues. Assumptions about human nature and motivation abound in ethical treatises.

Even to the classical philosophers the plausibility of an ethical theory was a psychological criterion that is implicitly empirical (even if that sounds like an oxymoron). That is, philosophers generally recognize that it makes little sense to advocate a normative ethical model of morality that is based on unrealistic assumptions and expectations about human behavior. In recent years there has been a resurgence of an explicitly empirical approach to the study of philosophy—ethics in particular—with the growth of the interdisciplinary field of *experimental philosophy* (Luetge et al., 2014).

Moreover, Steininger et al. (1984) argued that the several differences that were traditionally advanced as distinguishing between ethics and psychology failed to establish a clear demarcation. For example, one of the primary distinctions has to do with the presumed differences between description and explanation—which is what psychologists do—versus the ethical justification of behavior. But on analysis the differentiation between the [scientific] "causes" of behavior and the [phenomenological] "reasons" for engaging in it turns out to be not so clear-cut. For example, *why* some accountants at Arthur Anderson shredded documents from Enron or *why* some engineers at G.M. did not correct the faulty ignition switches would seem to be different questions from whether they *ought (not) have* done so. But scientific explanations of behavior often involve the actor's own agentic reasons or justifications; and moral justifications generally depend on assumptions about the causes of behavior. "In the domain of human action, it is difficult, perhaps impossible, to explain without assuming or implying values, and the 'why?' often refers to both" (Steininger et al., 1984, p. 262). When someone asks why those accountants shredded the documents, they are probably seeking both the explanation and the justification for the actions.

> *Both the psychologist who tries to explain behavior in morally [i.e., values-] neutral terms and the ethicist who tries to justify judgments about the moral rightness or wrongness of an action independent of any psychological considerations are denying the inevitable overlap of their two disciplines.*
>
> (p. 266, emphasis added)

I-O Psychology, Social Science and Professional Ethics

As I-O psychologists the great bulk of our theoretical and practice concerns focus on individual workers and work groups—especially lower-level employees and managers (Bergman & Jean, 2016). But as scientists we have long known that we cannot fruitfully avoid the economic and sociopolitical antecedents of organizational behavior any more than we could hope to understand the functioning of a company as if it were a closed system, ignoring its cultural history and the social, political and economic environments that influence and set constraints on its policies (Katz & Kahn, 1978). In an analogous fashion, when we consider professional ethics it is even more imperative that we expand our horizons to consider the insights of social historians interested in economic and business institutions, as well as insights from political philosophy, political economy, sociology and, of course, moral philosophy. That is because those realms contribute to the establishment of the values and normative standards of what we consider acceptable/unacceptable, right/wrong, appropriate/inappropriate, just/unjust, etc. An implication of this is that the ethics of what we do are not reasonably separable from the moral standing of the institutions and organizations in which we do it.[6] Consequently, portions of this book are concerned with matters that probably go beyond what some of my colleagues view as the appropriate domain of professional ethics. And that is why the book title has been changed to "Values and ethics *of* Industrial-Organizational Psychology"—emphasizing the primacy of values, and because "of" incorporates "in" but connotes a more inclusive perspective. For example, with respect to employee selection in particular:

> ... doing selection well (i.e., technical competence) is inextricably bound up with doing it right. This approach also opens to reflection the implicit values and moral justification underlying the practice itself, in addition to considering the manner in which its constituent activities are implemented. In other words, the ethics *of* employee selection are as relevant as the ethics *in* employee selection.
>
> *(Lefkowitz & Lowman, 2017, p. 575, emphases in the original)*

One of those "more inclusive" issues pertains to the consequences of organizational actions. For example, I-O psychology studies as legitimate and important facets of individual employees' job performance their organizational citizenship behaviors (OCBs) because such prosocial behaviors contribute to organizational effectiveness, even though they may not be part of the prescribed work role (Podsakoff et al., 2009).[7] By extension, we should not ignore the moral qualities and actions of the organizations to which we devote our efforts—in effect, an *organization's citizenship behavior*—with respect to the society that legitimizes and supports it and in which it functions. Similarly, just as we study employee perceptions of organizational justice vis-a-vis an organization's *internal* human resources activities (Gilliland et al., 2001; Greenberg, 2009), we should also be concerned with the social justice implications of the organization's *external* actions, which characterize the probity of its role in society. This perspective is in keeping with that of other psychologists who have begun to express concern for the way in which professionals carry out *good* work—"work that is both excellent in quality and socially responsible" (Gardner et al., 2001).

---

6 To offer an absurdist example, can a certified public accountant following generally accepted accounting principles, or an I-O psychologist using best practices to develop an employee selection system be considered ethical if their work is in service to a criminal enterprise?

7 Although in recent years a view has begun to take hold that OCB may also have some detrimental effects on individuals (Bolino et al., 2013, 2015; Koopman et al., 2016).

Ethics Education in I-O Psychology

There has been in recent years considerable turmoil about how ethics should be taught—in philosophy departments, in professional and pre-professional programs, and in the sciences, including I-O psychology. Hartner (2015) contrasts

> Two approaches to ethics education. Traditional, or theoretical, ethics might best be understood as the approach to teaching ethics that emphasizes the philosophical roots of ethics … . A more practical approach to teaching ethics, by contrast, generally means drawing heavily from real-world scenarios and cases, putting a focus on relevant empirical and technical details related to the student's future profession. (p. 350)

He observes a movement in academia to largely replace the former with the latter (and argues against it). For example, Bhuyan and Chakroborty (2020) cite the advantage of case studies as requiring students to deal with "irreconcilable dichotomies" (p. 113); Choe-Smith (2020) emphasizes "teaching ethics, not teaching about ethics" (p. 97) and argues for the effectiveness of *service learning*, as opposed to "philosophical reflection," which involves structured *experiential learning* in an applied setting. And systematic investigations of the effectiveness of business school ethics courses (Waples et al., 2009) have yielded conclusions characterized as "a mixed bag" (Naidoo, 2020). I agree with all of them! Realistic experiential learning, even just case discussion, is essential. But discussing ethical problems detached from their moral roots risks devolving into a nearly useless attempt to memorize lists of disembodied "dos and don'ts." Uglietta (2018) has advocated a resolution to the issue by articulating the "middle level of theory" that comprises the "wide gap between abstract moral theories and concrete professional cases." He advocates becoming intimately familiar with and "incorporating the goals, circumstances, customs and other established social practices and compromises of particular professions" (p. 161)—i.e., it would have to include *every* profession to be considered.

My own independent perception of that gap led to virtually the opposite approach. I have suggested that the gap can be bridged usefully by inserting an additional conceptual level, consisting of the *form* or *structure* of ethical dilemmas.

> This relatively 'content-free' structural aspect of ethical dilemmas enables comparisons across different domains (of professions, organizations, demographic groups, age cohorts, etc.) in which the overt idiosyncratic ethical problems experienced are not commensurable. Similarly, it can yield interpretable longitudinal comparisons despite changes in the manifestations of ethical problems encountered over time.
>
> *(Lefkowitz, 2021, p. 297) (cf. Table 6.4)*

BOX 1.2 ETHICAL ISSUES THAT DIDN'T EXIST A FEW YEARS AGO[8]

Most people are aware that Facebook has been dogged with trying to eliminate or control the enormous amount of violent and hateful material that regularly is posted on the social media site. Their first lines of defense are screening algorithms developed by means of artificial intelligence, which catch over 90% of the objectionable posts. Very few people are aware, however, that the remaining highly noxious material—still an enormous amount—is outsourced to other companies and inspected by many thousands of their employees.

Foremost among those companies is the consulting firm Accenture (formerly Anderson Consulting) with almost 6,000 full-time employees doing this "content moderation" in eight cities around the world, including Mountain View, CA. and Austin, TX. The annual fee for this (and other consulting work, as well) is reported to be more than $500 million.

The outsourced employees are tasked with deciding whether to keep a posting or remove it. (For example, testifying at a legal hearing a former moderator in Austin indicated he was required to decide "whether to delete a video of a dog being skinned alive or simply mark it as disturbing.") This work is performed under a strict performance management system in which moderators can be fired for excessive mistakes in implementing Facebook's policies—which are regularly in a state of flux.

The adverse emotional, psychological and physical effects of performing this work are apparently substantial, and at least one class-action lawsuit has been filed against Accenture to protest these conditions. Workers have also pressed for better pay and benefits. There is no indication of any systematic employee selection screening for the job, although the company did prepare a brief realistic job preview that indicates the job has "the potential to negatively impact your emotional or mental health." None of this has directly impacted Facebook because the workers are employees of Accenture.

Here are some questions that come to mind:

- Is Accenture responsible for the nature of the job, and its effects on employees?
- Should the company refuse the consulting contract?

---

8 This narrative is based on the extensive reporting of Adam Satariano and Mike Isaac (2021).

- Isn't the work being performed a societal good?
- Is it Facebook's primary responsibility to not accept the noxious posts to begin with?
- What about the adverse effect of the employees' condition on the company's reputation?
- Is it appropriate to have tight performance management standards with severe consequences for this type of job?
- Could the company benefit from a systematic employee selection system?
- The senior management team at Accenture recently held a meeting to discuss the situation with its lucrative client. As head of H.R. at the company, what is your opinion?

For example, Box 1.2 describes a situation with ethical aspects that came into existence only recently.

Another dimension to the debate is emphasized by Rehwaldt (2019), especially with respect to teaching introductory ethics courses. He believes that such instructors emphasize the exploration of moral theories and "fail to recognize humans as biologically driven, psychologically shaped, and sociologically constrained beings" (p. 35). He argues for greater attention to the role of emotion, unconscious bias, and the influence of social structures on ethical decision-making. This book, since the 1st edition, has attempted to reflect that perspective.

But for our purposes, even more important may be that in the sciences ethics is often taught as "something we unfortunately must require you to do, so let's get it over with as quickly as we can, and then we can move on to the important things" (Zigmond & Fischer, 2014, p. xviii). One could be excused for inferring that something of that sort is also common in I-O psychology graduate/doctoral training in so far as 65% of I-O doctoral programs do not offer a required or even elective course in ethics (Brossoit et al., 2021)—despite the fact that it is an officially recommended area of competence (SIOP, 2016) and that ethics training seems to be effective (Watts et al., 2017). The most common reason given by program directors (70% of them) is that ethics is included in a unit in other courses. But it may be that considering a few particular problems that arise in the research lab, segmented from those that arise while doing employee selection, separate from those encountered on an organizational consultation, distinct from those faced while teaching or supervising students, etc., etc., misses critical meta-issues and other important considerations—such as much of the content of this book, including ethical reasoning.

However, aiding ethical decision-making is just one of the main purposes served by moral theory for professionals such as applied psychologists (Knapp, 1999). The other purposes are to help explain the fundamental moral underpinnings of society and its institutions, to identify and justify the general principles on which our ethical standards and codes are based, to encourage moral behavior, and to assist in the education and self-regulation of the profession by providing a basis for compliance with those standards.

There are other pedagogical, social and moral issues that ought to be considered, as well. Much appropriate professional and ethical behavior is probably taught implicitly by example, role-modeling and other socialization processes on the part of graduate faculty, internship supervisors and early mentors at work—and there are some data indicating that that is also the case in I-O psychology (Brossoit et al., 2021). Hafferty (1998), in writing about curriculum reform in medicine, emphasized the importance of the *informal curriculum* and the *hidden curriculum*, as distinct from a program's formal curriculum. The former is "an unscripted, predominantly ad hoc, and highly interpersonal form of teaching and learning that takes place among and between faculty and students," and the latter refers to "a set of influences that function at the level of organizational structure and culture" (p. 404). In a similar vein, Handelsman et al. (2005) emphasize the acquisition of ethical knowledge and skill as an acculturation process.

It's interesting to note that in I-O psychology informal curricula seem focused primarily on research ethics, whereas hidden curricula have, until very recently, served to socialize or acculturate beginning I-O psychology students into I-O psychology's predominant corporatist value system (Lefkowitz, 2019). But there are also newer, more humanistic and prosocial perspectives emerging in the field to be acknowledged (cf. Carr et al., 2013; Carr et al., 2012; McWha–Herman et al., 2016; Olson-Buchanan et al., 2013; Reichman, 2014). In recognition of that flux one of the objectives of this book is to encourage students to reflect on their core professional identity—by which I mean one's *beliefs, goals, and meta-objectives concerning what it is you intend to accomplish in the organizations with which you work and how you prefer to go about accomplishing them* (Lefkowitz, 2010, p. 294, emphasis in the original). How one answers that question has profound implications for how one views professional ethics and behaves accordingly.

The reader may find one of the moral theories discussed in chapters 2, 3, 4 and 5 more useful or otherwise more compatible than others so that it might be adopted as a consistent perspective within which to approach ethical deliberations. Alternatively, I have found different models with their associated ethical principles to be more or less helpful and appropriate with respect to different types of problems. This accords with the opinion of Bennis et al. (2010a) who, in discussing moral decision-making based on rules versus cost/benefit analyses, assert that "different modes of decision making can be seen as adaptations to particular environments" (p. 187). Either perspective necessitates becoming familiar with the general issues and alternative approaches offered by the various moral philosophies. In fact, I will note the opinions of several scholars who advocate considering simultaneously all three major normative perspectives presented in these pages (deontology, consequentialism and virtue ethics). Consequently, my primary aim in this regard has been to produce a usable synthesis that would be helpful in decision-making, not just for the rare ethical crisis one might face but for the "quiet, steady, day-to-day choices that add up to a career characterized by integrity or moral malaise and/or conflict. It is for the quotidian choices that moral guideposts are most needed and most wanting" (Lowman, 1991, p. 196).

Personal Biases

This book is premised on a number of personal beliefs and concerns about ethics, the profession of psychology, I-O psychology in particular, the contemporary world of business, and the sociopolitical nature of society. Most will become apparent in later chapters, but it is fair to the reader and perhaps constructive to make some of them explicit at this point.

First off, concern about a high level of unethical behavior by I-O psychologists, or even a high incidence of ethical dilemmas in the field, was not among the motives for writing (or revising) this book. In fact, when I was asked some years ago to prepare a talk admonishing I-O psychologists to improve their ethics, I demurred because I felt it was unnecessary and instead focused on criticizing the underlying values of the field (Lefkowitz, 2008). Based on very limited empirical data, self-reported ethical problems in I-O psychology have never seemed to be a prevalent problem (Pope & Vetter, 1992). More recent surveys targeted to I-O psychologists have revealed the wide range of ethical issues we face, but response rates were not adequate to estimate their incidence in the population (Lefkowitz, 2021; Lefkowitz & Watts, 2022).

Despite the critical determinative role played by values in one's experience of and reactions to ethical dilemmas, discussions concerning the foundational values of the field are not well represented in the professional literature of I-O psychology. And so this book is as much or more about values as it is about ethics per se.

Young I-O psychologists and business managers have come of age professionally at a time when the U.S. business world has been marked by momentous displays of greed, self-aggrandizement, and disregard on the part of many leaders for the well-being of customers or clients, workers, the public-at-large and sometimes even shareholders. One of the issues to be considered later is whether this merely represents the actions of a relatively few "bad apples" or whether there may also be systemic influences involved (Kish-Gephart et al., 2010). If the latter, it would be the sort of cultural influence that could contribute to generational differences in the workplace (Constanza & Finkelstein, 2015).

Especially germane to the aims of this book, I have observed a variety of unfortunate adaptations to the prevailing zeitgeist exhibited by many students. Some seem resigned to accepting greed and corruption as natural reflections of the essentially egocentric nature of human beings in a competitive environment. Similarly, some seem to view it as representing merely unfortunate excesses of the free-enterprise system—minor costs to pay as the price for harnessing the enormous productive potential of individual ambition and incentive. Some I-O psychologists appear to be exercising a form of "technocratic denial"—retreating behind the presumably objective-scientific implementation of assessment and selection devices, training modules, quasi-experimental interventions, competency models, performance management systems, etc.—as if the perhaps questionable practices of the enterprises in which these are implemented were none of our concern.

But others hold an alternative view of the possibilities and justification for moral and ethical corporate behavior and the salience of more altruistic concerns. In fact, there is a substantial, albeit loosely organized coalition of business scholars, social critics and progressive business leaders who have been pressing the moral dimension of capitalism and promoting *corporate social responsibility* as well as models of *corporate social performance*. Up until relatively recently I-O psychologists had been conspicuously absent in this alliance. However, as alluded to above, since the first edition of this book appeared in 2003 a number of dramatic and uplifting changes have taken place, marked by the creation of a Global Organization for Humanitarian Work Psychology (GOHWP) as well as the more prosocial perspectives on the field mentioned earlier (Carr et al., 2012; McWha et al., 2015; Olson-Buchanan et al., 2013; Reichman, 2014).[9]

An adequate consideration of professional ethics entails incorporating the border domain it shares at one level with models of personal ethical decision-making—what the father of *utilitarianism* Jeremy Bentham referred to as "private ethics"—and at the macro-level with the moral aspects of institutional decision-making, social policy and political economy. All these levels of activities reflect underlying values concerning interpersonal and group relations and pertain to deliberations about what is appropriate in that regard. And it seems to me that it would be intolerably inconsistent—requiring substantial amounts of rationalization—to accept the primacy of moral standards and the importance of human dignity in one's personal life, but not with respect to one's professional behavior; or to accept those norms personally and professionally, but not to expect and demand such from the organizations in/with which we work; or to accept them at the personal, professional and organizational levels but to not be concerned for the manifestations of economic [in]justice in our society. As Cohen (2002) noted, ethical virtues are expressed not only in the individual's behavior toward others but in the quality of the societies we create; they should be identified with civic virtue. And as mentioned earlier, "ultimately a responsible psychologist is a responsible citizen" (Kelman, 2021, p. 3).

---

9   Information can be obtained from http://gohwp.org/

The existence of cross-domain professional journals like *Business and Society; Journal of Humanistic Management; Philosophy and Public Affairs;* and *Psychology, Public Policy and Law* suggest that a book on values and ethics of I-O psychology should range beyond the specific ethical issues we face in our research and practice. It should include discussions of such topics as business ethics and the morality of corporations and the capitalist system—focusing on the domains in which we conduct our research and practice and the organizations we support.

As I-O psychologists we share with our colleagues in the other sub-specializations of psychology a common heritage regarding what it means to be a psychologist. We have acknowledged and prided ourselves on adhering to some aspects of those traditions (e.g., the epistemic values of empirical science) but have given short shrift to other aspects, such as its humanistic ideals. Chapter 12 explores some of the consequences of having largely abandoned those ideals and offers some suggestions for their redevelopment.

In our role as applied psychologists working in complex social settings we encounter some potential ethical dilemmas that for the most part, do not confront our academic colleagues engaged exclusively in laboratory or basic research. Some of those dilemmas are the result of conflicts between the humanistic value system of psychology noted previously, and the value system of the organizations within which we work—the values of a competitive free-enterprise, profit-driven economic system.

Complicating the situation, but also rendering it more interesting, is the fact that a dominant ideology in I-O psychology is the belief in value-free science and research (e.g., the distinction between the putatively neutral and scientific issue of *test bias* and the value-laden social issue of *test fairness*). This view is advanced by those who believe improbably that the field is entirely objective and scientific despite our service to the highly competitive world of business in which our professional practice and much of even our research agendas are shaped by the values and goals of the corporation and the ideology of the economic system. For some time now I have disagreed with and critiqued aspects of that belief (Lefkowitz, 1990, 2005, 2008, 2009a, 2010a, 2011b, 2012a, 2013a, 2014a, 2016, 2017, 2019). When one's personal value system (such as that of a management-oriented I-O psychologist) is consonant with that of the social systems within which one functions (such as a profit-oriented corporation in a free-market economic system), the absence of conflict or "moral friction" between those values sets can make it seem as if the systems are value-free.

In any event, as noted sagely in the *Canadian Code of Ethics for Psychologists* (Canadian Psychological Association, 2017), "Although it can be argued that science is value-free and impartial, scientists are not" (p. 1). One of the advantages of a single-author book is the opportunity to express a particular point of view—especially so in the realm of applied ethics because real-world moral decisions are value driven. I cannot (and would not wish to) claim that my own values and views regarding a variety of issues have not influenced the content of this book—in choice of topics, opinions expressed, what I have criticized, what I have lauded, and how they impact my ethical analyses. But I have tried to make those values explicit, both here and in the essays cited above, and thereby subject to scrutiny. My hope has always been that this prompts readers to consider the ways in which their own values disagree or are in accord with mine, and—more importantly—how they affect their ethical deliberations. In that way we may together raise the level of discourse, if not necessarily agreement, in moral reasoning and ethical problem-solving among I-O psychologists.

SECTION I

Moral Philosophy and Psychology

2

META-ETHICS

> Despite the efforts of Descartes and his successors to elaborate a method—
> based, in different versions, on clear and distinct ideas, dialectics,
> mathematical logic, phenomenological intuition or conceptual analysis—
> philosophers have never agreed on a way to resolve their disputes. At the
> same time, the area of competence in which they roam has steadily
> diminished, as the natural and then the social sciences developed bodies of
> theory and methods of investigation calling for specific apprenticeships, not
> general wisdom. Philosophers have been left with commentary on the
> sciences and arts, along with musings on morality whose superiority to
> anyone else's, when there is any, is due to a higher degree of self-conscious
> organization of thought rather than to some special knowledge or method.
> —Paul Mattick

Expressing an even more pessimistic view, some moral philosophers (Cross, 2021) argue that "the extent of disagreement in modern moral philosophy prevents moral philosophers from being classified as moral experts (p. 188)" to whom others should defer regarding ethical recommendations. But I believe that Mattick and Cross are being too harsh on their profession and colleagues. First, there is much to be said for a "high degree of self-conscious organization of thought"—especially when it illuminates a domain not well explored by others. As behavioral scientists we are used to refining ambiguous constructs operationally and resolving theoretical contradictions empirically. It is precisely when we enter the realm of values and ethics that we are largely left in the lurch by the scientific method and must call on the "general wisdom" and the "musings on morality" by philosophers to help us light the way. For example, the more optimistic philosopher Alexander Rosenberg (2016) pointed out that philosophy has always addressed the questions that the

DOI: 10.4324/9781003212577-3

sciences cannot answer, such as what ought to be the case as opposed to what is, as well as the epistemological questions concerning why science cannot answer them. Those musings concern questions like "What is the right thing to do in this situation?" "How should I live my life?," "What ought she have done then?" Attempts to provide systematic answers to these questions by defining *right* and *wrong* or *good* and *evil* and justifying rationally what one should or ought to do constitute the substantive matter of ethics or moral philosophy and are referred to as *normative ethics*.[1] Kant (1785) distinguished between natural philosophy (physics) and moral philosophy (ethics) and indicated that the former is affected by "laws according to which everything does happen; the latter, laws according to which everything *ought* to happen" (p. v, emphasis added).

An interesting take on the relationship between philosophy and empirical social science is offered by the recent rejuvenation of an avowedly *experimental ethics* by philosophers, psychologists, economists, cognitive scientists and sociologists. It has been defined as "an experimental approach to research questions traditionally deemed purely philosophical … . the study of moral intuitions, justification, and decision making as well as metatheoretical stances" (Luetge et al., 2014a).

Before embarking on a survey of normative ethics it will be helpful to begin by discussing some of the fundamental issues that provide its underpinnings. What, for example, is the nature of morality or ethics and of ethical theories? How does one go about arriving at the definitions of *right, wrong* or *good?* These concerns are commonly referred to as *meta-ethical issues* and they are embedded at least implicitly in all normative ethical theories. At the end of the chapter, I present a set of conclusions that may be drawn from considering these matters and, therefore, provide us with the beginnings of a **Framework for Ethical Decision Making.**

Two Critical Meta-Ethical Issues

The ancient Greeks dealt with meta-ethics along with their deliberations about the content issues of normative ethics. In contrast, the great 17th, 18th and 19th century "modern" philosophers (e.g., Thomas Hobbes, Immanuel Kant) were primarily concerned with developing normative theories. However, in the 20th century meta-ethical concerns saw something of a revival. Perhaps the most important meta-ethical issue is whether answers to the fundamental ethical questions (e.g., what does it mean when we say something is morally right?) are in some way potentially verifiable objectively. In other words, do morals represent "truths" to be uncovered, or are they entirely subjective? All the classical

---

1   There is frequently a nuanced distinction between the term ethics, which is of Greek origin, and morality, which is Latin: The latter term is often used with a religious implication, whereas ethics is invariably used when referring to professional issues, as with ethical codes of conduct. I follow customary practice by using the terms roughly synonymously.

ethical theories may be categorized as explicitly or implicitly *objectivist* or *subjectivist* in nature. The second major meta-ethical issue concerns the perspective from which the conclusions of right or wrong are made. Here, the issue is a dichotomy between a consideration only of the person who is doing the deciding (e.g., one's own flourishing as the criterion) and a more encompassing perspective (e.g., the well-being of all involved). This is the issue of whether normative ethical theories are *egoistic* or *universalistic* in nature. It is rather remarkable that the roots of both the *subjectivist–objectivist* and the *egoist–universalist* controversies in ethical thinking originate in western thought from the same source—the *Sophists*.

Subjectivist Versus Objectivist Perspectives

Origins of Subjectivism

Approximately 2,500 years ago in Greece a very bright group of itinerant teachers earned their living by helping their fellow citizens be successful politically and commercially. These *Sophists* were generalists, teaching much of what we would call the liberal arts curriculum. But they specialized in teaching public speaking, debate or rhetoric because rhetoric was a critical skill for success in public life. However, they were not well-liked in many quarters because of their emphasis on the arts of persuasion—convincing others or winning an argument rather than on illuminating truth. (To this day the characterization of one's views as "sophistry" is generally meant as an insult.) But some of the Sophists were not only rhetoricians but philosophers who dabbled in the ethical dialogues of 5th century BCE Athens. Their reaction to the criticism was not merely to defend their activities on pragmatic grounds—much like their contemporary counterparts in the fields of public relations, advertising and political consulting may be expected to do. Instead, they took the philosophical offensive by questioning the very existence of objective truth.

They advanced a point of view that thousands of years later psychologists refer to as a *phenomenological perspective*. It maintains that because we each experience the world through our separate perceptual-cognitive systems and interpret it through the filters of our (relatively) unique psycho-social-cultural histories, there is no objectively verifiable truth to be known. How one person experiences the world cannot be the same as another person experiences it. This ultimately leads to a position of *ethical relativism* at the individual level—what is right for me is not necessarily right for you—and of *cultural relativism* at the societal level. The Sophists' growing awareness of diverse social practices and customs among the many societies to which sophisticated Athenians were exposed undoubtedly influenced the development of their notion of cultural relativism. Because all societies have a set of moral conventions—albeit different in each case—morality must simply be a matter of social convention. (As discussed later, this is a rather naïve version of relativism in comparison with contemporary views.)

Objectivist Rejoinders

So, if morality and laws are mere conventions and if, as some Sophists observed, those rules are enacted by the powerful in society (i.e., "might makes right"), there is no moral reason to obey them. But then, how does one know what is correct? What should replace social convention? Their answer was the introduction of the concept of *natural law*—a notion that plays a key ingredient in the philosophies of the "big three" who follow: Socrates, Plato and Aristotle. Obedience to conventional law is supplanted by obedience to natural law, by which they meant human nature—which is simply the pursuit of one's own self-interest, undeterred by conventions. Now, these Sophists were not so naive as to fail to recognize that a society in which everyone pursues only their own self-interests is likely to run into some difficulties concerning a lack of integration and cooperation, frustration of objectives, conflict and aggression. Consequently, they acknowledged the necessity for laws to provide protection against the exploitation of the weak. But, having no inherent value, these laws were to be obeyed only if and when one had to in order to avoid punishment.

The radical Sophists provided Plato and Aristotle with a conceptual point of view called *ethical naturalism,* which they elaborated to refute the subjectivist view that all morality is relative. They reasoned that the best way to live can be inferred from human nature, which is an objective, potentially knowable aspect of the real world. But before Plato and Aristotle there was Socrates, who was no less iconoclastic and as annoying to much of Athenian society as were the Sophists; in fact, his incessant annoying challenges and refutations of accepted conceptions of virtue got him killed.[2]

He, like the Sophists, challenged the conventional morality but did so by poking holes in the customary views of what is meant by moral principles like justice or personal virtues such as honesty. Unlike the Sophists he believed that these virtues were potentially knowable by the good person—indeed, it is such knowledge that renders the person good, because that is all that is necessary to *be* good. Although that seems psychologically naive to us today, ignoring motivational determinants of behavior, the important point is that he laid the groundwork for the importance of logical reasoning in deciding what is justifiably good or right. It is worth noting that attempts to integrate the cognitive dimension of ethics ("what is the right thing to do, and how can I know it?") with the pragmatic motivational dimension ("why should I do what's right?") have plagued moral philosophers for centuries—ever since Socrates simply finessed the

---

2   There is no direct written record of Socrates' views. Virtually all of what we know of his thought is from how he is represented in the writings of Plato, and scholars are uncertain about how much of those representations are Plato's views, not those of Socrates.

question by assuming that knowing what is right is all that is needed in order to do the right thing.

Plato, Socrates' pupil, developed a very modern sounding answer to the questions "What does it mean to be just or good," and "How will we know?" His answer is psychological in nature and also draws on (primitive) sociology and physiology by analogy. Individual physical health reflects the various parts of the body functioning properly and synchronously, and we experience that as pleasurable. By extension therefore the just (moral) person must be one for whom the three aspects of human nature also are in harmonious balance: under the control of *reason* which, with the help of *spirit*, keeps *desire* in check. "Goodness," therefore, becomes the health and harmony of the personality (Norman, 1998). And by further extension, a just society is one in which the three major social classes—guardian, military and economic—perform their functions well so that the society as a whole functions harmoniously. Thus, Plato provided an answer to the problem that Socrates simply defined out of existence. The reason we act in accord with reason and justice is that it is pleasurable to do so.

As a student of Plato's, Aristotle's meta-ethics also represents a version of ethical naturalism and gives a prominent position to the role of reason. But according to Aristotle the ultimate aim of human behavior is happiness. Happiness is taken as an intrinsic human objective needing no explanation or justification. It is the ultimate good that results from acting in accord with all the customary human virtues: honesty, bravery, prudence, etc. In fact, the reason the virtues *are* virtues is that behaving in that manner produces happiness. Although that is the usual closest translation of the Greek *eudaimonia,* the word is generally conceded to include the state of being fulfilled or actualized, as well as simply feeling happy. Frequently used equivalents nowadays include *flourishing* and *the meaning of life.* And it is noteworthy that a great deal of empirical psychological research has focused on exploring the nature, antecedents and consequences of such (cf. Diener, et al., 2015; Diener & Seligman, 2018; King & Hicks, 2021; Myers & Diener, 2018; Ryff, 2018 for summaries). The research has "delineated numerous characteristics of what it means to be mentally healthy, fully developed, purposefully engaged, self-actualized, fully functioning, and mature" (Ryff, 2018, p. 242). And most recently, the adverse impact of the Covid-19 pandemic on subjective well-being has been documented (Zacher & Rudolph, 2020).

Egoism Versus Universalism, Altruism, Cooperation and Compassion

Whether subjectivist or objectivist, the ancient Greek philosophers shared the same meta-ethical position concerning whose interests should be considered in attempting to understand what is good or right: one's self—i.e., it is right/best for everyone to pursue their own well-being. This is reflected in the Sophist's pursuit of self-interest generally and in Aristotle's focus on happiness (one's own). The position is referred to as *ethical egoism* and characterizes relatively few normative ethical theories, although it is well represented in modern economic and political theory and business values. Perhaps the best-known example among the classical moral theories is that of Thomas Hobbes, and among more contemporaneous sources the views of Ayn Rand and Libertarians.[3]

Ethical egoism is in opposition to the more numerous normative ethical theories characterized as *universalist* in nature because they explicitly consider the concerns of a wide array of folks—typically all who may be affected by the actions under consideration. Examples include the theories of Hume, Kant, Mill and Hegel, as well as both Jewish and Christian ethics. For example, one variety of *consequentialist* theory (that of Mill) holds specifically that the most morally defensible action is that which results in the greatest happiness for all those affected. The philosophical tenet of universalism is a realistic normative standard because of the extensive psychological reality of altruism, cooperation and compassion in human behavior.

The beauty of Aristotle's position in this regard is that he simply did not see any conflict between self-interest and morality because the human virtues, even the altruistic and compassionate ones like honesty, sympathy, charity, and so on, represent the reasoned and correct moral choice because they are pleasing to oneself. In fact, there is a considerable amount of evidence to suggest that people are less motivated by self-interest than even they would describe themselves to be (Miller, 1999; also cf. Crocker et al., 2017). In our highly individualistic society, we are often taught that rational self-interest is not only natural but also appropriate and good. Therefore, Miller suggested, we may be more influenced by not violating a social norm of rational self-interest and thereby appearing to be a "do-gooder" or "bleeding heart" than by genuine motives of self-interest.

In fact, it may be entirely natural to be altruistic (Brown et al., 2011; Hare, 2017; Simon, 1990; Stich et al., 2010) and there is a considerable amount of empirical evidence supporting the notion of an "altruistic (or prosocial) personality"—albeit with little yet known about the extent of intraindividual variability (Carlo et al., 2009). Many scholars view altruistic behavior as having evolved by natural selection because of the advantages it conveys to the

---

3 *Ethical egoism* is a meta-ethical view that it is right and proper for each of us to pursue our own selfish interests: morally, that is how we *ought* to behave. This is invariably based on an assumption of *psychological egoism*, which is the view of human nature that we are predominantly if not exclusively motivated by selfish or hedonistic concerns—a view that does not withstand psychological scrutiny. However, one could be a psychological egoist without necessarily being an ethical egoist. Whereas Rand was for the most part what I would call an unqualified or unrestrained ethical egoist, Hobbes was a qualified or enlightened ethical egoist (cf. Chap. 3). *Rational egoism* is a separate construct in moral philosophy, referring to the relatively tenable assertion that it is reasonable or rational to act in accord with one's self-interests, although that may not be the moral thing or necessarily even the best thing to do in any situation.

population (Kurzban et al., 2015; Simon, 1990, 1993). On one hand, some emphasize that what we inherit is only a "selective altruism" enhanced by cultural-developmental processes (Wynn et al., 2018). Conversely, there are those convinced that "modern moral sensibilities have expanded far beyond the standards of past generations" (Crimston et al. 2018, p. 14)—even to the extent of a growing interest in the expression of compassion at work (Dutton et al., 2014). In any event, as Miller (1999) suggested, the extent and preeminence of self-interest motivation may be highly exaggerated in our society, and this is confirmed by the prevalence and rewarding nature of altruistic endeavors and an organized social movement for *effective altruism* (Singer, 2015).[4]

Recent evidence indicates that cooperative behavior in humans appears early in life (Warneken, 2018), is widespread across cultures (Henrich & Muthukrishna, 2021), is probably hard-wired (de Waal, 2009; Rilling et al., 2002; Sober & Wilson, 1998; Whiten, 2017), and may be facilitated by one's "identification with all humanity" (McFarland et al., 2013). And even the notion of compassion has been acknowledged in organizations (Dutton et al., 2014) because people do evidence suffering at work and compassionate reactions from others can reduce anxiety, enhance attachment to the organization and help people feel valued at work.

Rand's (1964) defense of ethical egoism depends in great measure on placing it in opposition to altruism and on the justification that altruism is so self-sacrificing and all-consuming that it precludes the ability to lead a meaningful, productive and independent life. Consequently, a concern solely for one's own interests is promoted as the only morality that respects the integrity of the individual. And so, the welfare of society must always be subordinate to in-dividual self-interest.[5]

But that is a fallacious argument. As noted above, altruism is not the opposite of ethical egoism. Egoism is opposed by universalism, the belief that all persons'

---

4   The more cynical among us may accept the appearance of altruism within one's family as being natural, but when such behavior is directed toward others it is frequently rationalized as mere *reciprocal altruism*—undertaken with an expectation of reciproca-tion, hence not really altruistic at all. Similarly, many take a Hobbesian position that altruistic feelings are merely a version of self-satisfaction. The economist Samuelson (1993) replied: "When the governess of infants caught in a burning building reenters it unobserved in a hopeless mission of rescue, casuists may argue: 'She did it only to get the good feeling of doing it. Because otherwise she wouldn't have done it.' Such argumentation (in Wofgang Pauli's scathing phrase) *is not even wrong*. It is just boring, irrelevant, and in the technical sense of old-fashioned logical positivism 'meaningless'" (p.143, italics in the original).

5   That's a hard argument to understand as I write this in the summer of 2021, witnessing a major increase in hospitalizations and deaths from Covid-19 in the areas of the U.S. in which large numbers of people are contributing to that by refusing to wear masks, socially distance or be vaccinated because it supposedly infringes on their liberty/ freedom (cf. Question I in Box 1.1.)

interests deserve equal consideration—unless there are justifiable reasons to do otherwise. There is no moral theory of which I am aware that posits that one ought to always act in a manner to benefit others, even if it is antagonistic to one's self-interest. Even the burgeoning creed of *effective altruism*—"based on a very simple idea [that] we should do the most good we can ... . [notes that] ... . we should not think of effective altruism as requiring self-sacrifice, in the sense of something necessarily contrary to one's own interests. If doing the most you can for others means that you are also flourishing then that is the best possible outcome for everyone" (Singer, 2015, pp. vii, 5). Perhaps that is what accounts for "our species' unusual levels of cooperation" (Henrik & Muthukrishna, 2021, p. 209).

There is little reason to accept Rand's assumption about the extremity of the consequences of behaving altruistically; concern for others need only be one of several considerations that govern our actions in any instance, along with self-interest; and there seem to be many examples of accomplished, flourishing, autonomous people who nevertheless engage in substantial altruistic, even charitable, activities. (Cf. the well-known example of Zell Kravinsky [Strom, 2003)]—popular professor and successful investor and philanthropist—who has donated a kidney and almost all his considerable fortune to strangers and has considered donating the second kidney, as well.) Bill and Melinda Gates, Warren Buffet and more than 150 other multi-billionaires have taken Mr. Buffett's "giving pledge" to donate at least half of their wealth before they die, or in their wills, to enhance the human condition (Goel & Wingfield, 2015). In fact, of special interest to I-O psychologists is Simon's (1993) observation that economic analyses should pay more attention to the motivational effects of forms of altruism derived from the group and organizational loyalties. Accordingly, Grant and Shandell (2022) emphasize the social forces (e.g., prosocial motives, competition) that influence work motivation. There is empirical evidence that altruism is prompted by subjective well-being (Brethel-Haurwitz & Marsh, 2014), and organizational scholars have begun to study compassion—i.e., the interpersonal processes that attenuate the various forms of suffering that occur in organizations (Dutton et al., 2014).

As Barry and Stephens (1998) summarized, philosophical views such as Rand's (1964) single-minded focus on self-interest have not generally been well-received among modern moral philosophers or as an avowed foundation for applied business ethics. Nevertheless, they are not totally without adherents (Becker, 1998; Locke, 1988; Locke & Becker, 1998; Locke & Woiceshyn, 1995). In general, ethical egoism seems to be endorsed mostly by those who see themselves as holding sufficient social advantage to successfully promote their self-interests even though everyone else is presumably trying to do the same, and by adherents of the narrow classical model of economic behavior emphasizing "rational self-interest" in making choices (*homo economicus*).

Rachels and Rachels (2015) present two arguments that many philosophers believe sink unconditional egoism as a viable meta-ethical position.[6] The first is that a primary objective of ethics is the resolution of interpersonal conflict (as well as intrapersonal). In other words, moral guidance comes into being as a means of reducing conflict and enhancing relations among members of society. This jibes with psychological views that "moral systems are interlocking sets of values, virtues, norms, practices, identities, institutions, technologies, and evolved psychological mechanisms that work together to suppress or regulate selfishness and make cooperative social life possible" (Haidt, 2010, p. 800). And it supports a respect for furthering the common good—i.e., "what we owe one another as members of the same society" (Reich, 2018, p.6). If one accepts all this as a legitimate conceptualization of ethics, it is clear that unqualified ethical egoism provides no basis for contributing to this enterprise; if universally adhered to it would, in fact, exacerbate tensions and conflict. This outcome has been well documented at the macro-level in economics by the *fallacy of composition*—what is best for each person need not be best or even good for all (Samuelson, 1993). Moreover, we currently see the adverse effects of egoism at the macro-level in the form of increasing *nationalism*—at a time when humanity is facing the existential crisis of climate change that requires collective action.

Admittedly, however, we can see in Hobbes' work (cf. Chap. 3) how a cooperative ethical model—the social contract—can be developed within a framework of egoistic assumptions about human behavior.

The second criticism places unrestricted egoism in a class of moral views that makes a priori distinctions among people and views as morally correct the practice of treating people differently based on those distinctions—e.g., racism, sexism, antisemitism, ageism, etc. (I.e., my group versus "them.") In this case, however, the distinction consists of there being just two classes of people—oneself and everyone else. In both cases, of course, there is no a priori morally acceptable justification for treating groups of people (or oneself) as differentially worthy of respect or consideration. It is refuted by the Principle of Equal Treatment (Rachels & Rachels, 2015): *"We should treat people in the same way unless there is a good reason not to"* (p.79, emphasis in the original). In other words, there should be some factual difference between them that is relevant to justifying the difference in treatment. In this context we can understand that the process of stereotyping a group is a spurious attempt to provide such "factual differences" to justify discriminatory treatment. So, this refutation of ethical egoism leads us to acknowledge that there can be no a priori moral basis for

---

6   They do not threaten seriously Hobbes' version of qualified or enlightened egoism (cf. Arrington, 1998; Copleston, 1994; Kymlicka, 1993). And they do not necessarily contradict a benign interpretation of Rand's (1964) views as reflecting mere rational egoism rather than ethical egoism (Locke & Woiceshyn, 1995). Refer to Baier (1993) for a critique of the several versions of egoism.

considering anyone's interests as having precedence over anyone else's. Singer (2011) elaborated these views considerably into a riveting discussion of "equality and its implications." His major point does not concern *factual* equality because individual differences among people are clear, but with *equality of interests*—one's rights and freedoms—that are independent of individual differences in ability, talent, intelligence, and so on.

But now, after having discussed two of the fundamental meta-ethical issues in moral philosophy, we will consider, albeit briefly, some illustrative meta-ethical theories.

Examples of Meta-Ethical Theories

Objectivist Theories

The objectivist perspective is sometimes referred to as *moral realism* (Smith, 1993), and has two basic tenets. First, as with all normative ethics, the focus is the very practical goal of providing the basis for doing what is morally right or making the ethically correct choice. Second, and this is the essence of the issue, objectivist or moral realist theories assume that those right actions and correct choices exist as a body of "moral facts" that are potentially knowable and verifiable, just as are empirical scientific facts. Different objectivist theories entail different ways of presumably knowing and verifying those "facts."

Ethical Naturalism

The earliest version of a naturalist theory in ethics was, as discussed, the model of natural law developed by the ancient Greeks. Aristotle defined the essence of human functioning as our reasoning capacities that, if adopted as the guiding principle of our lives, will result in achieving fulfillment and happiness. The Stoics stipulated that this should mean *right reason* to preclude mere selfishness, and the model is later taken up and systematized further by the Roman Cicero. The theme survives to the Middle Ages at which time it is given perhaps its best-known expression by Thomas Aquinas:

> Whatever is contrary to the order of reason is contrary to the nature of human beings as such; and what is reasonable is in accordance with human nature as such. The good of the human being is being in accord with reason, and human evil is being outside the order of reasonableness … . So human virtue, which makes good both the human person and his works, is in accordance with human nature just in so far as it is in accordance with reason; and vice is contrary to human nature just in so far as it is contrary to the order of reasonableness.
>
> *(Cited in Buckle, 1993, p. 165)*

One of the major difficulties with natural law theory is its ambiguity: Natural law theorists rarely specify just what actions are natural and which are unnatural; when some behaviors are specified as unnatural, the justifications—if any are offered at all—tend to be vague condemnations that they are self-destructive (often without specifying how or in what way). This is true even of the most popular contemporary versions of ethical naturalism—theories of human rights—as developed by John Locke (1689/1988) and culminating in such grand statements as the United Nation's *Universal Declaration of Human Rights* (1948).

Less ambiguous are the versions of natural law employed by some orthodox religious groups in condemning sexual behaviors like homosexuality, masturbation and contraception. The natural law objection (and there are other bases of objection as well) is that these practices are "unnatural" because they violate the basic biological function of sex, which is procreation for species propagation. As Buckle (1993) pointed out, biological function is a very restricted conceptualization of human beings.

Evolutionary psychology

More justifiable is the contemporary naturalist position represented by the field of *sociobiology* (Wilson, 1975/2000)or *evolutionary psychology* (Barkow et al., 1992): the use of evolutionary theory and evolutionary biology to understand human behavior. Although most psychologists do not receive training in this area (cf. Lewis et al., 2017), it has been applied specifically to organizational psychology (Van Vugt, 2017; Van Vugt, Hogan & Anderson, 2008). One of the more interesting features of sociobiology is that it posits an evolutionary origin for intraspecies cooperation, including the prosocial and altruistic actions that characterize what we call ethical or moral behavior. It views altruistic behavior as well as the accompanying thoughts about altruism (i.e., our ethical beliefs) as a human adaptation: our ancestors who thought and acted in that fashion survived and reproduced better than those who did not (Hare, 2017; Ruse, 1993; Whiten, 2017). Contemporary economists have also indicated that altruistic behavior is an underrecognized human motive in social and economic behavior (Samuelson, 1993; Simon, 1993).

Sociobiology or evolutionary psychology as a meta-ethical theory is rightly considered an example of ethical naturalism, positing a biological basis for the very existence of morality itself, and we will return to this topic briefly in the chapters on Moral Psychology. From that empirical standpoint it has been concluded that "In sum, I think the evidence for moral nativism is incomplete, at best" (Prinz, 2008, p. 403), and other critiques have been offered as well (Li et al., 2018; van Vugt, 2017).

At this point in time, it seems to me that not much can be said about it from the standpoint of normative ethics—that is, what the *content* of an ethical theory based on evolutionary psychology might be. The study of moral psychology is a descriptive, scientific enterprise; it does not explicitly offer prescriptive guidance on how one should behave. On the other hand, it now seems clear that humans, along with the four other species of great apes—orangutans, gorillas, chimpanzees and bonobos—are highly social creatures so that even though there exists a great deal of competition among each, there is also a great deal of friendship, co-operation, collaboration, helping and reciprocity (Seyfarth & Cheney, 2012; Tomasello & Vaish, 2013), as is somewhat the case even with lower primates (deWaal, 2008). Nevertheless, Jerome Kagan (2018) suggests that "human morality rests on a combination of cognitive and emotional processes that are missing from the repertoires of other species" (p. 346).

The overarching criticism of ethical naturalism as a moral theory is that its essential nature is a non-sequitur. It is a specific case of the *naturalistic fallacy,* which consists of defining something (a concept—e.g., goodness) by means of the object(s) that possess that thing or ability. It is a conflation of two separate realms of meaning. For example, because reasoning is good, it does not follow that we can define good exclusively as reasoning. Hume (1978) pointed out, in what has become known as Hume's Law, it is a logical fallacy to believe that empirical facts, even if correct, tell us anything about moral judgments. Arrington (1998) summarizes:

> From the fact that human beings are constituted in a certain way and behave in certain ways, nothing follows about how they *ought* to behave and about the character they *ought* to have. Being what they are, human beings may in fact never do or be what they ought (p. 242).

One cannot justifiably infer what ought to be merely from what is.[7]

All of this should not be taken as a blanket criticism of evolutionary psychology's relevance to the study of morality. Investigating the possible hereditary foundations of moral behavior is a perfectly appropriate and valuable enterprise; what is at issue is whether the heritability of an ethically relevant behavior pattern justifies it as moral. I believe de Waal (1996) overstated the case when he asserted that "we seem to be reaching a point at which [biological] science can wrest morality from the hands of philosophers" (p. 218). Twenty years later, and even in light of the burgeoning advances in neuropsychology during that time, not all psychologists accept *eliminative reductionism* (the view that psychological phenomena can be

---

7 Arrington also noted, however, that Hume's famous "is/ought" distinction has not gone unchallenged by other philosophers and that there is considerable controversy over its validity (cf. Flanagan et al., 2008; Sinnott & Armstrong, 2008). For example, Tiberius (2015) points out that the issue(s) are more complex than usually thought, and that scientific facts (what *is*) are relevant to the empirical assumptions made in moral philosophies (about what *ought* to be). She concludes "maybe you can't derive an ought from an is, but it would be a huge mistake to think that what is—particularly what is true about our psychology—doesn't matter for ethics" (p. 219).

explained completely at the biological level) (Schwartz et al., 2016). In fact, one could make the case that there has been in recent years great integration and co-operative synergy between philosophers with psychologists, brain scientists and evolutionary biologists—under the umbrella of *moral psychology* (Sinnott-Armstrong, 2008) and to a lesser degree, *experimental philosophy* (Luetge et al., 2014). But I think it is valuable to keep in mind the still-relevant distinction between normative, i.e., prescriptive, models of moral action and the descriptive scientific study of moral behavior, including its origins. Nevertheless, it is certainly plausible to accept some behaviors (e.g., prosocial-altruistic) as moral if they have an evolutionary basis—i.e., they cannot readily be dismissed as "unnatural."

Yet morality is largely a matter of human values, as defined in the humanities, social sciences and religious teachings. It is in those realms that we forge the essence of morality as the socially constructed meanings of respect, responsibility, dignity, duty, fairness and justice, as well as the qualities of empathy, caring, altruism, honesty, reasoning, susceptibility to community and other social influences, and so on. Admittedly, it is fascinating and important to our conception of human nature to learn that protobehaviors reflecting those qualities are observed in infrahuman species, especially the other great apes, and that there is undoubtedly an evolutionary basis for the expression of those human qualities. But I agree with Malik (2014) that the essence of morality is the distinction between "man [sic] as he happens to be" and "man [sic] as he could be" (p. 336). But it's a moving target: we need to recognize that our understanding of who we "happen to be"—i.e., human nature—changes over time (partly in response to advances in biological and social science) and that, in turn, transforms our notions of who we "could be."

Religion

A position taken by some proponents of religion is that there can be no true morality divorced from religious faith. Or, as Dostoyevsky put it "If God does not exist, everything is permitted" (cited in Malik, 2014, p. vi). The meta-ethical issue concerns the nature of the relation between ethics and religion—whether ethics *depends* on religion.

From an empirical standpoint, there is evidence that religious beliefs are a cultural adaptation with societal benefits (Laurin, 2017) and that participating in religious communities is associated with aspects of flourishing (VanderWeele, 2017). Bloom (2012) concludes that "religion has powerfully good moral effects and powerfully bad moral effects, but these are due to aspects of religion that are shared by other human practices. There is surprisingly little evidence for a moral effect of specifically religious beliefs" (p. 179). Galen (2012) goes even further in observing that "many [prosocial] effects attributed to religious processes can be explained in terms of general nonreligious psychological effects" (p. 876).

According to philosophers such as Berg (1993) and Shafer-Landau (2015) there are three ways in which ethics might be dependent on religion: (a) God as the source of that which is good, which is known as the *divine command theory* of ethics; (b) God as the source of moral knowledge; and (c) God as the source of moral motivation, that is, as the provider of the reason(s) for behaving morally. None of these ideas is very successful at making a case for the indispensable reliance of morality on religion.

Divine command theory

This point of view holds that what is "good" (i.e., moral, just or right) is equivalent to "God's will." There can be no conception of the good without God. The difficulties encountered by this view were elucidated by Plato even before the spread of monotheism: "Do the gods love holiness because it is holy, or is it holy because they love it?" (cited in Berg, 1993, p. 527). If one chooses the first option, that God wills us to be good because it is good, it must mean that there is an independent standard or criterion of "goodness" that is separate from God's will. This would appear to be an unacceptable infringement on the putative omnipotence of God. Conversely, one may believe that it is only by virtue of God's will that what we think of as good is good. But that renders the notion of good extremely arbitrary. If God had willed torture, slavery, and genocide to be good and helping others in need to be bad would we accept that? A religionist rejoinder to that challenge is that God is good and, therefore, could not possibly will those evil things. But that puts one back on the other horn of the dilemma.

God as the source of moral knowledge

Perhaps it can more reasonably be concluded that our knowledge of good and evil and of right and wrong depends on God.[8] But we know that there are plenty of atheists who know right from wrong, and many of them even demonstrate extremely moral behavior; thus, morality cannot depend on knowing or believing in God. Perhaps what is meant by this view is simply that, for each of us, our moral sense is God-given whether we realize it or not. That may be a comforting source of faith for some, but it is not really a justification.

God as the source of moral motivation

This pertains to the distinction between the cognitive aspects of normative ethical theory (knowledge of what one ought to do) and the motivational aspects (why one should do it). The answer traditionally provided by religion to the question

---

8   As Berg (1993) pointed out, this does not refer to the unhelpful belief that God is the source of everything in the universe including whatever it is that we know. The directly relevant issue is whether God is the source of moral knowledge in some special way that is not true for, say, scientific knowledge.

"why be moral?" is so that one can hope for the reward of heaven and avoid divine punishment. This is probably the least justifiable of the three bases considered. It seems apparent that there are many reasonably moral people who do not believe in an afterlife. Clearly, their motivation must have other sources.

These arguments should not be misconstrued as being anti-religion. In fact, a major concern of this book are the ethical issues of justice and care, and religious principles are among the prominent sources supporting concern for economic and social justice (cf. Chap. 8). For example, the National Conference of Catholic Bishops (1986) asked Americans to consider "How do my economic choices contribute … to a sensitivity to those in need?" and "With what care, human kindness and justice do I conduct myself at work?" (Para. 23). It should also be noted that more recently the relationships among religion, morality, intergroup relations and culture have been approached in avowedly scientific and evolutionary perspectives (Cohen, 2015; McKay & Whitehouse, 2014). In that context Haidt (2010) emphasizes the evolutionary basis for religion as enhancing "trust, co-operation, generosity, and solidarity within the moral community" (p. 821).

Subjectivist Theories

Suppose I was to ask you "Aren't affirmative action programs wonderful?" and you reply "Are you kidding? They are awful and destructive." I am expressing a positive attitude about affirmative action, and you are expressing the opposite. But which of us is correct—i.e., are such programs good/right or bad/wrong? Simple *subjectivism* doesn't consider that question. You have your view; I have mine, and "truth" does not enter into it. This is very different from the objectivist belief in the existence of moral facts, however they are defined.

To be sure, each of us may be convinced that we are correct—that we are on the side of truth. But the subjectivist would point out that at the level of known facts you and I are probably in agreement. That is because all that our respective statements mean to the subjectivist is I approve of affirmative action, and you disapprove. Both of those factual statements are true, and each of us would presumably agree to their accuracy. Thus, simple subjectivism trivializes moral expression because it implicitly treats moral judgments merely as factual statements about our attitudes. But there have been subsequent modifications designed to improve the simple version of the theory.

Emotivism and Prescriptivism

Stevenson (1944) developed a partially successful advance over simple subjectivism based on linguistic analysis. He pointed out that language is used for more than merely stating facts—whether they are descriptive facts (e.g., "Since the advent of affirmative action the employment rate of ethnic minorities and women has increased") or facts about attitudes ("I think affirmative action is great"). Moral language is *emotive;* that is, it is used to express attitudes (implicitly, "Thank goodness for affirmative action") and to influence other people's behavior ("You should consider implementing an affirmative action program in your organization"). The contribution over simple subjectivism is that this expressiveness and influence clearly separates the factual from the attitudinal. You and I may agree or disagree about the empirical facts regarding affirmative action and its effects. But even if we agree on most of those facts, emotivism allows we may still disagree in our attitudes. Our disagreement is, according to Stevenson, a moral one—meaning that it is a difference *in* attitude, rather than a disagreement *about* attitudes.

The problem is that even after this elaboration we still are left with the expression of potentially conflicting ethical attitudes with no basis to choose among them. That is because the theory does not concern itself with the processes by which those competing points of view may be evaluated. That's where reason comes in. Contemporary philosophers have refined emotivism by emphasizing that any value judgment, especially moral points of view, must be supported by reasons. (Attitudes about trivial matters of taste require no greater justification than one's preference. E.g., no reason is required for the assertion that you enjoy listening to heavy metal.) Moreover, the explanations should be morally relevant and not merely expressions of self-interest or bias. Recall that this harks back to the Stoics and their emphasis on the right reason. Rachels (1993) pointed out that it is consonant with several contemporary ethical theories, such as the ideal observer theory, which holds that the ethical choice is the one all perfectly rational, impartial, and benevolent observers would make.

By far the best-known of the contemporary elaborations of subjectivism is Hare's (1993) *universal prescriptivism.* In prescriptivism, Hare emphasized that moral statements always contain an implicit action recommendation of what one ought or ought not to do. And it is that recommendation that needs justification. If I cannot produce good answers to your question "Why should my company implement an affirmative action program?" then my advocacy cannot claim to be an ethical position.

According to Hare (1993), the fundamental justification of moral prescriptives is their *universalizability:* If, in a particular situation, I tell you to do such-and-such, my viewpoint can be accepted as an ethical one only if I accept that anyone (including myself) in the same situation ought to do the same thing. The principle of universalizability is reminiscent of the various versions of *The Golden Rule* ("Do unto others only that which you would have them do unto you") that are found in Confucianism (ca. 500 BCE), in the Old and New Testaments, and as reflected in Kant's famous categorical imperative ("Act only on that maxim which you can at the same time will that it should become a universal law"; Cf. Chap. 3). The eminent personality psychologist Erik Erikson (1964) viewed the rule, in all its many cultural versions, as a foundation of morality. It is the universalizable characteristic that makes a particular "ought statement" moral.

Relativism[9]

At the beginning of this chapter the origination of the idea of cultural relativism by the Greek Sophists was noted. It has remained a seductively attractive notion all this time—probably because it seems to fit so well our common experience of the enormous variation in customs, practices and institutions of the world's diverse cultures and even subcultures within pluralistic societies. For example, I am writing this during the 2021 summer Olympic Games in Tokyo. In today's newspaper there is a report of the abject shame felt, tears shed, and heartfelt apologies offered by a number of Japanese athletes who suffered the ignominy (to them) of winning only silver medals in their events (Rich, 2021)—(i.e., signifying being merely the second-best in the world!).

Although at the descriptive level of analysis we are in social science, particularly cultural anthropology and sociology, the relevance for ethics is direct. Isn't it self-evident that what is morally correct varies as a function of what each society deems it to be? However, from within one's own cultural perspectives and biases, most of us find it extremely difficult to accept as normal—much less, moral—customs that we find shocking: "One's own morality lies deeply internalized, and it is not easy to overcome ethnocentric prejudice when confronted by behavior which prima facie offends against it" (Silberbauer, 1993, p. 15). Or more basically, "In one's own culture, it is easy to fail to see that a cultural lens exists and instead to think that there is no lens at all, only reality" (Oyserman, 2017, p. 435).

It has become common for many managers in this age of globalization to encounter foreign business people, government officials and customers whose business practices are not merely different, but seem strange and perhaps even unethical—e.g., distortions of the facts or bluffing, and bribes or side payments in contract negotiations. In any discussion of cultural relativism it is important to keep in mind what sort of behavior is under consideration—mere social conventions, or ethical behavior reflecting moral norms of right and wrong. From a social science perspective, the effects of cultural differences on conventional organizational functioning have been studied extensively (Gelfand et al., 2007; Hofstede, 2004; Hofstede et al., 2010). Although cultural differences have been observed in the content of ethical principles and ethical reasoning processes (Thorne & Saunders, 2002), results are often modest or inconsistent (Weber & Warnell, 2022). But there are those who make the case for there being universal values and virtues across cultures, even in business (Demuijnck, 2015; Sagiv & Schwartz, 2022; Schwartz, 1992, 1994, 1999).

---

9 *Ethical* or *cultural relativism* is one of two major forms of rejecting objectivist theories (Shafer-Landau, 2015); the other is *moral nihilism*—the view that there are no moral truths at all. E.g., that there is no legitimate moral basis for believing that genocide is wrong. I have not explored that view here.

The modern representation of cultural relativism can be traced back to the theory of *functionalism* in sociology developed by Emil Durkheim (1898/1953, 1893/1956), and advanced by his successors in sociology (Talcott Parsons and Robert K. Merton) and anthropology (Bronislaw Malinowski). It starts from the belief that societies fulfill certain functions to survive effectively, and each society develops customs and folkways that reflect those functional accomplishments. Each society's functional adaptations may be unique, and as there is presumably no independent standard of right or wrong each culture's traditions are correct by virtue of their satisfying the society's needs. However, if that's all there were to it there'd be no basis for moral condemnation—e.g., of Nazi Germany during the 1930s and 1940s, of the Soviet Union during Stalin's regime, of South Africa during apartheid—or of conditions of employment in the U.S, prior to the 1964 Civil Rights Act.

That uncertainty has tended to give cultural relativism a bad name. In addition, as Hatch (1983) and many others pointed out, there appears to be an inherent contradiction in the cultural relativist position in so far as it involves the non-relativist values of tolerance and understanding of all cultures. (Are tolerance and understanding "universal" moral values?)

Clearly, notions of relativism warrant some clarification. According to Scanlon (1998) moral relativism is the notion "that there is no single ultimate standard for the moral appraisal of actions, a standard uniquely appropriate for all agents and all moral judges; rather there are many such standards" (pp. 328–329). Note that he doesn't suggest, as some vociferous critics of moral relativism contend, that there are *no* moral standards (as with moral nihilism), but that there are multiple such, each capable of being justified in moral terms by what I have been calling right reasoning: i.e., "if a moral appraisal of an action is to be defensible it must be understood not as a judgment about what is right or wrong absolutely, but only about what is right or wrong relative to one of many possible standards" (Scanlon, 1998, p.332). That means it is possible for two conflicting moral judgments to both be true if there are "good reasons for taking [each] to be worthy of respect" (p. 345).[10]

Recall that objectivism—the view that there exists some independent universal and knowable standard of morality that pertains to all cultures—also does not fare well upon analysis. In fact, even presumably widespread and "basic" moral evaluations such as "the tendency to attribute intentions to negative but not positive outcomes (the side-effect effect)" may depend on the cultural context (Robbins et al., 2017, p. 23).

---

10 Later on, Scanlon admits that such reasons "require us to strive to find terms of justification that others could not reasonably reject. But we are not in a position to say, once and for all, what these terms should be. Working out the terms of moral justification is an unending task" (p. 361).

The anthropologist Clifford Geertz (1973) was rather disparaging of what he referred to as "a hunt for universals in culture," although he acknowledged that it is a scientifically and emotionally appealing position:

> In essence, this is not altogether a new idea. The notion … that there are some things that all men [sic] will be found to agree upon as right, real, just, or attractive and that these things are, therefore, in fact right, real, just, or attractive—was present in the Enlightenment and probably has been present in some form or another in all ages and climes. It is one of those ideas that occur to almost anyone sooner or later. (pp. 38–39)

In the late 19th and early 20th centuries, he observed, this "hunt" took the form of a search "for empirical uniformities that, in the face of the diversity of customs around the world and over time, could be found everywhere in *about the same form*" (p. 38, emphasis added). This approach was largely a failure: The forms (behavioral patterns) are simply different. In modern anthropology beginning in the 1920s, according to Geertz, this hunt adds something new: "It added the notion that … some aspects of culture take their specific forms solely as a result of historical accidents; others are tailored by forces which can properly be designated as a universal" (p. 39). The universals are based on core values embedded in the requirements for developing and maintaining any human society, and/or pre-dispositions we inherited because they are adaptive, whereas some cultural practices do not imply any such core values but merely reflect historical tradition, particular political systems, or environmental factors and the like.

Among the several telling criticisms that Geertz (1973) offered of that view, the most relevant for us is the challenge that even if such substantial universals can be demonstrated (and he by no means concedes the point) the question remains:

> should [those universals] be taken as the central elements in the definition of man [sic], whether a lowest-common-denominator view of humanity is what we want anyway. This is, of course, now a philosophical question, not as such a scientific one; but the notion that the essence of what it means to be human is most clearly revealed in those features of human culture that are universal rather than in those that are distinctive to this people or that is a prejudice we are not necessarily obliged to share. (p. 43)

A rapprochement

The philosopher David B. Wong (1993) observed:

> Almost all polemics against moral relativism are directed at its most extreme versions: those holding that all moralities are equally true (or equally false,

or equally lacking in cognitive content) ... . One reason, in fact, that not much progress has been made in the debate between relativists and universalists is that each side has tended to define the opponent as holding the most extreme position possible. (pp. 446–447)

Wong took as his starting point the view that all human beings have developed some form of moral system. This is so because it serves two universal human needs: regulating interpersonal conflict and regulating intrapersonal conflict due to competing motives. Therefore, some commonality among those systems is likely to exist. Rachels and Rachels (2015) agree as they assert that there is actually less disagreement among cultures than it appears. They explain that the relevant commonalities exist at the level of societies' values, not their overt customs and practices. In particular,

> ... we cannot conclude that two societies differ in values just because they differ in customs. After all, customs may differ for a number of reasons. Thus there may be less moral disagreement across cultures than there appears to be. (p. 22)

Using a variant of Durkheim's societal functions argument Rachels and Rachels (2015) go on to suggest that there are certain values that must be more or less universal because they seem important for the maintenance of virtually any functioning society. These would include objectives such as the care and protection of infants, telling the truth, and prohibiting willful murder—notwithstanding that there may be some exceptions under certain conditions and that the relative importance of each of them may vary. Other scholars believe that there is an even longer list of principles and practices that may be universally represented in virtually all moral codes: keeping promises, protecting the vulnerable, avoiding incest, justice, unprejudiced judgment, reciprocity, and respect for personal property (Shweder et al., 1987). According to this view these shared values represent the core of a more-or-less universal set of moral principles: That is, many (but not all) of these values are shared by many (but not all) societies because they are adaptive. But even so, they may be expressed in rather divergent practices at the behavioral level because overt social practices and customs reflect not only a society's moral values and principles but are also influenced by environmental and contextual factors. Those might include the form and level of economic development, historical and religious beliefs, traditions and folkways, as well as cultural conventions and institutions, such as the political system.

In the field of international business, in which these academic considerations take on a very pragmatic cast, such broad-based normative or ethical principles have been conceived as *hypernorms* that provide the basis for macrolevel social contracts (Donaldson & Dunfee, 1994). The conception still allows room for the existence of more idiosyncratic microlevel social contracts, if they don't contradict the hypernorms. Similarly, Donaldson (1989) presented a common ethical core of 10 fundamental rights to be respected by all corporations wherever they conduct business. Nevertheless, justifications for the existence of hypernorms are still being considered (Scherer, 2016).

The view represented by both Rachels and Rachels (2015) and Wong (1993) is a modified or attenuated version of cultural relativism. (Alternatively, it could be referred to as a modified version of universalism.) They held that all societies develop moral systems because of a need to regulate conflict among their members so that the societies can function. Similarly, they argued that there is a certain degree of similarity in human nature as well. Based on those two sets of constraints, ethical systems are developed that are comprised of a certain number of core values that generalize across cultures but may be expressed in a variety of social practices due to the influence of other antecedent influences such as historical tradition, environmental context, nature of the political system and level of economic development of the society. This view leaves open the question of how much commonality or uniqueness one may find across cultures.

Toward a Framework for Ethical Decision Making

So, where does all this leave us? This brief overview of meta-ethics has yielded six "Learning Points" that provide the beginning of a useful framework for ethical decision-making to which we can add in later chapters.

1. The use of ethical reasoning is critically important. The major meta-ethical issue that we have dealt with is the tension between subjectivist and objectivist views. Rachels and Rachels (2015) warn that we should not fall into the trap of structuring the issue as a dichotomous choice between two extremes: Either (a) there are objective moral facts just like empirical facts in science, or (b) one's moral principles and values are merely reflections of the idiosyncratic subjective feelings and beliefs of each of us. As we have seen there are substantial problems with both stances. They point out the following:

> This overlooks a third possibility. People have not only feelings but reason, and that makes a big difference. It may be that … moral truths are matters of reason; *a moral judgment is true if it is backed by better reasons than the alternatives.*
> *(p. 41, emphasis added)*

In that sense supporting our moral judgments and actions with good reasons, being able to explain why those reasons matter, and showing that the alternative possibilities are not as good, is as close to "proof" as one gets in the realm of normative morals. Although Rachels and Rachels are quick to point out that demonstrating such proof may not necessarily persuade others to accept it—for many reasons of which the psychologically oriented reader is probably well aware.

But that conclusion can seem inadequate to psychologists who are trained in the traditions of empirical science:

> Human cognitive ability is so flexible and creative that every conceivable moral principle generates opposition and counterprinciples … . However, whereas oppositional thought in science is checked by empirical constraints, it goes unimpeded in ethics. Ethics, unlike science, as repeatedly noted, has no extrinsic criterion, shared by all, that can be used to judge the validity of moral principles … . A moral pluralism appears to be a psychological end product of a democratic society whose members are free to express their ethical views … .
>
> *(Kendler, 1999, p. 832)*

But then Kendler went on to discuss the necessity for moral pluralism to be conceived as an ongoing set of guidelines that "require constant evaluation to determine their consequences so that the functional value of moral pluralism will not be endangered either by disruptive moral conflicts or by intolerant restrictions" (p. 832).[11] It seems that what Kendler envisioned as the evaluation of alternative moral principles is akin to the ethical reasoning advocated by the moral philosophers, so there is little distinction between his position and the one advocated here.

Drawing an analogy from the realm of science may be helpful in elucidating the notion of appropriate or "right" moral reasoning from inappropriate. McIntyre (2015), a historian of science, has explained the difference between scientific *skepticism* as opposed to *denialism*. All good scientists are skeptics, i.e., one doesn't accept a scientific theory unless it is well substantiated by empirical evidence, or accept the conclusions of a research study unless it employed rigorous scientific methods. Our scientific beliefs are justified in that way. In contrast, when one refuses to believe something even in the face of compelling evidence, that's denial—usually motivated by ideological, religious and/or political beliefs. Speaking psychologically, McIntyre goes on to point out "The throes of denial must feel a lot like skepticism. The rest of the world 'just doesn't get it.' We are the ones being rigorous" (p. 8). Obvious contemporary examples include the denial of evolution, human-induced global climate change, or the effectiveness of vaccines. Applying that sort of distinction, by analogy, to the realm of moral action we can demand that well-explained and justifiable ethical reasons are

---

11 Kendler's (1999) remarks were written in the context of the ongoing debate regarding the relation between values and science and in defense of the position that psychology must adhere to the model of value-free science. There are many proponents of the alternative view that values are always inherent in the scientific enterprise and that the value-free model of the natural sciences is an ideal that has never characterized science as it is practiced. These matters will be discussed in chap. 10.

required to distinguish a moral choice from one motivated primarily by self-interest or other irrelevant motives.[12]

Nevertheless, we would be poor psychologists if we underestimated both the psychological complexity of logical reasoning and the potentially distorting influences of which humans and even nonhuman primates are capable (Kahneman, 2011; Santos & Rosati, 2015). Decision-making processes can be influenced by emotional arousal integral to the situation at hand, or by "incidental emotions" carried over from other situations (Lerner et al., 2015). Even emotionally neutral rules of logic may yield ambiguous determinations (Rips, 2001). And we know all too well that personality factors and strongly held political, social and religious beliefs and values influence the premises on which our reasoning processes are based. As a consequence of different strongly held attitudes, what seems reasonable (i.e., appropriately reasoned) to me may not appear so to you and vice versa. The best we can do is to be aware of those potentially distorting influences, try to be honest with ourselves by unmasking those hidden blinders, and expose our views to others who are likely to not share the same biases—that is, to attempt always to engage in "right reason." But we will also need to consider contemporary models of morality that view ethical reasoning as playing a decidedly minor role in moral judgments, in comparison with innate moral intuitions and emotions (Haidt, 2001, 2010; Haidt & Joseph, 2004; cf. Chap. 6).

2. An indispensable aspect of moral reasoning is the universalizability of an ethical decision. Most people probably accept this principle implicitly, but it bears being made explicit. I cannot give you advice regarding what to do in a difficult situation and expect it to be considered an ethical recommendation if I would not advise myself similarly in the same situation. Universalizability is responsive to the principle that there should be consistency in what is considered ethical behavior, irrespective of individual personalities.

3. Egoism is rejected in favor of the universalist tradition. Despite how well thought out the basis for one's behavior, it will not in these pages be considered ethical if the justification is entirely self-interest. The position I have adopted is reflected in the moral philosophies reviewed in the next three chapters and is consonant with that of Singer (1995): "Self-interested acts must be shown to be compatible with more broadly based ethical principles if they are to be ethically defensible, for the notion of ethics carries with it the idea of something bigger than the individual" (p. 10). No one's interests and concerns, especially

12 The analogy is not a perfect one. In the realm of science, one cannot be both a skeptic and a denier (about the same phenomena): the latter precludes having the open mind and curiosity necessary for the former. But it is possible for an ethical choice to be both egoistically self-serving and morally justified if it is not *only* or *primarily* self-serving. Paradoxically, however, there is some evidence that actions that produce both personal gain as well as charitable benefits are viewed as worse (less moral or ethical) than equivalent actions that yield no charitable benefits—a *tainted altruism* effect (Newman & Cain, 2014).

one's own, can be held to have a greater a priori moral claim than anyone else's. Beyond the individual level of analysis this principle refers also to the self-interest of one group (e.g., senior executives) over other groups (e.g., shareholders, employees, and/or consumers).

Some scholars believe that there is no antagonism between selfishness and altruism. For social beings self-interest and social-mindedness may be entirely compatible. Some cynics even go so far as to assert that there is no such thing as altruism because doing good is pleasurable, hence completely egoistic. But that seems like tautological wordplay: concluding that altruistic behavior is egoistic because of the presumption that all behavior is egoistic.

4. There is a potential distinction to be acknowledged between moral knowledge and moral action. On one hand, we can agree with *universal prescriptivism* (Hare, 1993) that knowing the correct thing to do in the face of an ethical dilemma always carries with it the implicit commitment to act accordingly. And we can further agree, therefore, that the failure to do so renders our behavior unethical. Nevertheless, as psychologists we know that most behavior is multiply- determined, and we should bear in mind that moral dilemmas can be complicated and stressful, with competing motives. Consequently, if the situation warrants, and if significant harm has not been done, we should be prepared to cut others (as well as ourselves) some slack in terms of the severity of condemnation that an ethical violation deserves. Chapters 6 and 7, which introduce the scientific psychological perspective as distinct from the philosophical, explore further the process of moral reasoning, choice and action.

5. The problem represented by cultural relativism in ethical thinking remains incompletely resolved. The middle-ground position discussed in this chapter may be useful. That is, judgments regarding the degree of similarity or difference among cultures in their ethical standards ought to consider not merely the surface manifestations or social practices of the societies but the meaning of those practices in terms of their implicit moral values. It is to be expected that at the level of values there will be greater cross-cultural similarity than at the level of social customs because customs are determined by a variety of nonmoral antecedents as well as by those values.

6. We should remember Hume's Law. As social scientists we may be especially vulnerable to slipping into the "ought from is" trap. We may be so accustomed to looking to our empirical data as the means of resolving ambiguities, discrepancies and disagreements in our work that we uncritically generalize that procedure to our deliberations regarding ethical matters. Natural phenomena, including even those aspects of human behavior that may have a high genetic component, carry no a priori moral capital by virtue of their naturalness. Ethical reasoning cannot legitimately be co-opted entirely by recourse to scientific facts.

3

NORMATIVE ETHICAL THEORIES: I. DEONTOLOGY

The word philosophy means the love of wisdom, but what philosophers really love is reasoning. They formulate theories and marshal reasons to support them, they consider objections and try to meet these, they construct arguments against other views. Even philosophers who proclaim the limitations of reason—the Greek skeptics, David Hume, doubters of the objectivity of science—all adduce reasons for their views and present difficulties for opposing ones. Proclamations or aphorisms are not considered philosophy unless they also enshrine and delineate reasoning.

—Robert Nozick

The sample of philosophers presented in this chapter illustrates the truth of Nozick's observation with a dazzling variety of forms of moral reasoning. Most contemporary philosophers in the western tradition agree that there are three broad categories of normative ethical theories, albeit with many examples and variations within each: *deontological theories, teleological theories* and *aretaic theories.*[1] *Deontology* derives from the Greek word *deon,* meaning duty, and refers to points of view in which actions are viewed as inherently ethical or not. *Teleology* derives from the Greek *telos,* or goal, and is used to label theories in which what is ethical or moral is determined by the effects or consequences of the actions.

Rawls (1999) explains the conceptual distinction between the two as determined by the way in which a theory defines and relates the two notions of (a) right and wrong and (b) good and evil (or bad). Teleological ethical

---

1 This book is biased by the omission of eastern philosophy such as *Confucianism* and *Buddhism,* even though these have had some prominent application in the business world (cf. Chan, 2008; Schumacher, 1973).

DOI: 10.4324/9781003212577-4

theories—more frequently referred to nowadays as *consequentialist* theories—give primacy to the good: That is, they focus on the good and bad that will result from an act, or from two or more alternatives, and they define the rightness or wrongness of the action(s) in terms of the net amount of goodness that results from each. Deontologists essentially do not deal with notions of good and bad; the rightness or wrongness of an act is intrinsic to the nature of the act, based on whether it violates a moral principle, and is independent of its consequences. Whether or not I may ethically mislead the student–participants in a psychological experiment will depend, for the consequentialist, on the balance of benefits likely to result from the research, in comparison with the possible harms that might ensue from the deception. For the deontologist, deceiving the participants—that is, not providing fully informed consent—is wrong irrespective of how much good might result from the research. The deontologist will view me as having *wronged* those students even if I have not *harmed* them. This perspective has been applied in I-O psychology with the construct of "deontic justice, the view that justice is of value for its own sake" (Cropanzano et al., 2017; also see Gan et al., 2020).

Virtue theorists (cf. Chap. 5) largely reject the dependence on ethical reasoning of either sort, and instead focus on the moral character of the protagonist as determinative. The ethical question to be answered shifts from "what is the right (or best) thing to do?" to "what is the (right) kind of person to be?"

Deontological Theories

Most of the moral rules or principles that constitute a deontological position are phrased in the negative as a proscription. In other words, deontological morality generally has to do with defining what is permissible or impermissible—not what is required.[2] For example, in a treatise on ethical concerns in conducting organizational surveys, 23 ethical principles are promulgated all of which begin "You shall not …" (Sashkin & Prien, 1996). As Davis (1993) pointed out, although the rules might be rephrased in the positive (e.g, "always tell the truth") the negative formulation focusing on the impermissible is not accidental in the deontological perspective. There is both a pragmatic and a theoretical reason for it. The practical reason is that it would be extremely difficult to stipulate everything that a person should do: The possibilities are virtually infinite; specifying what is wrong is a more limited enterprise. The theoretical reason has to do with the distinction that must be maintained by deontologists between intended and unintended effects. Within this view one would violate the proscription against harming others only if one did so intentionally; if our behavior harms others unintentionally, we have not transgressed—even if we anticipated the harmful results of our actions! This is a theoretically necessary aspect of a deontological

---

2 There are exceptions, such as theories that focus on one's affirmative duties.

position because, if it were not, one would come perilously close to adopting a consequentialist position (foreseeing negative consequences is a teleological reason to refrain from carrying out such a bad act).

The sorts of deontological theories I have been alluding to are examples of *rule deontology*. They entail the establishment of general moral rules to be followed. A rule-deontological theory does not assume that following the rule is necessarily the best thing to do in every instance, just that it's the best *general* rule, so that the specifics of any situation are simply not considered. Obviously, basic questions for deontology are "What are those moral rules," and "How are they determined?" The different answers to those questions constitute different normative ethical theories. One of the essential problems for rule deontologists has to do with situations in which the rules are in conflict. Perhaps I feel professionally obligated to advance psychological knowledge and understanding (to contribute to the betterment of society, and as "pay back" for government funding that enabled my education). And I also feel obligated to be open and honest with the cooperating participants in my research projects. What do I do if I am contemplating conducting a study the success of which entails deceiving those participants about aspects of the study? Strict rule deontology has no fully satisfactory answer to this dilemma because all the rules are conceived as absolute moral principles.

However, compromises are possible. For example, one could rank order the principles to establish some prioritization. But that certainly is a lot more complicated to deal with than a simple list of universals that are morally equivalent (e.g., whose preferences will hold sway in determining the rankings?). This approach is illustrated prominently by a rank ordering of the four principles that comprise the organizing structure of the *Canadian Code of Ethics for Psychologists* (Canadian Psychological Association, 2017). Barring exceptions having to do with imminent danger to someone's physical safety, respect for the dignity of persons is expected to take precedence over responsible caring, which in turn is viewed as more important than integrity in relationships, which outweighs responsibility to society.

Another possibility is that the rules could be formulated more narrowly so that the incidence of conflict among them is diminished. This is exactly what has been done for millenia even with respect to the biblical commandment not to kill: It has been interpreted in western civilization as a prohibition only against taking innocent life. Other exceptions are routinely made even by religious people, such as wartime killing. In psychology one might operate under the qualified rule that "it is wrong to deceive research participants unless the study is breaking important new ground." Of course, the difficulties are apparent. "Important" according to whom? By what standards, and to what degree? How new is "new"?

Religious precepts tend to be deontological in nature: They set forth specific rules to follow in a legalistic fashion (Fletcher, 1966). Over the years, however, circumstances change, and empathic motives of sympathy, fairness and justice lead to modifications, exceptions and qualifications to the rules that, in

Chandler's (2001) ironic characterization, take the form of "rules for breaking the rules" (p. 187). The most extreme compromise is called *act deontology* in which each alternative action-response in a particular situation is evaluated in light of the relevant deontological principles, which are treated more as guidelines than absolute rules. The question to be answered is whether following the rule(s) is justified in this instance. But note that the evaluation is supposed to remain within the boundaries of deontological considerations—presumably ignoring the teleological issue concerning the consequences of each contemplated action. However, many consequentialist philosophers are of the opinion that these individual situational act-deontological evaluations inevitably involve a consideration of the relative good or harm associated with the available options, thus constituting a utilitarian justification.

Probably the quintessential deontological theory is that of Immanuel Kant, who ultimately offered a single moral principle that may be said to underlie all others: Do not violate anyone's dignity, respect and autonomy, which are everyone's rights.

Immanuel Kant

Immanuel Kant (1724–1804) wrote about many areas of philosophy, as well as geology and astronomy. He probably has been the most influential philosopher in western culture since Aristotle even though his work has been criticized extensively (cf. Arrington, 1998; O'Neill, 1993). The importance of his work stems from three sources. First, his elaborate theoretical formulations come close to representing an appealing common-sense view of ethics. Kant conceived of moral behavior as answering the call of duty, of doing what one ought to do, despite having motives—what he termed *inclinations*—to the contrary.

Second, he has been so influential because many of the principles he introduced or systematically elaborated have become generally accepted foundations for moral positions that many ethicists and laypeople take for granted. Those include most of the points noted at the conclusion of the previous chapter constituting the beginnings of a general framework for ethical decision-making: (a) the essential role of reasoning or the rational self as the source of morality; (b) the criterion of consistency or universalizability in the application of ethical principles (i.e., that the same moral rules should apply to everyone); (c) the requirement of universalism (i.e., everyone's interests and autonomy must be respected) because of the inherent worth and dignity of all human beings; and in a psychological vein (d) his emphasis on the criticality of the motives for an action in judging its ethicality, not merely the behavior itself or its consequences.

And third, this Kantian perspective has been extended to many related realms of study, such as moral development in psychology—influencing greatly the work of Jean Piaget and Lawrence Kohlberg—and business ethics (Bowie, 2017), in which many believe "that a Kantian point of view is essential to democratic capitalism" (Werhane, 2018, p. 110).

The Centrality of Motivation and the Function of Reason

According to Kant there is only one thing in the world that can be taken as good (i.e., moral, or right) without qualification. That thing is what he called *good will,* or what we might think of as moral motivation. Even Aristotle's criterion of happiness cannot be taken as an unqualified good: A person might be pleased at someone else's misfortune. Because right motives are unqualifiedly good, their moral value does not depend on the person's success in implementing them. If I see a child drowning in the ocean at a nearly deserted beach and I plunge into the surf to rescue her but am too poor a swimmer to reach her before she disappears, my behavior is no less moral for its ineffectiveness. Similarly, suppose I do rescue her but unfortunately, she cannot be revived. My behavior is no less moral because of the negative outcome. This definition of moral behavior independent of its consequences is one of the attributes that clearly renders Kant's philosophy deontological in nature. And it resonates with people's general notions of morality as having to do with good intentions. These intentions or motives—more particularly, the underlying principle(s) that they reflect (e.g., one should try to save an innocent person's life if there is the possibility of doing so)—Kant called a *maxim.* Recent experimental evidence underscores the intuitive importance of motivation, in that people tend to ascribe intentionality to a person's actions when it results in harmful (even if accidental, side) effects, but do not infer intentionality when the side effects are helpful or benign (Wagner, 2014).[3]

None of this emphasis on intentions or maxims would make much sense if Kant didn't assume that we are all autonomous beings free to choose (or not) the correct thing and that we have the reasoning capacity to do so. It is reason that guides the operation of free will. Each of us, as rational agents, prescribes for ourselves what is moral.[4] How that comes about takes us to the next elements in his philosophy.

Duty

Kant was the first to put the notion of duty at the core of an ethical theory. He undoubtedly was influenced by the ideas of the Protestant ethic, which viewed the fulfillment of one's duties in everyday life (e.g., duties as a parent, good citizen, and loyal employee) as the highest calling in life (Norman, 1998). Kant

---

3 However, the theoretical interpretation of this "so-called Knobe effect" is unclear.
4 One might question, "Why should reason be given this preeminence? Why be rational?" However, as Norman (1998) pointed out, one who poses such a question has already accepted the truth of the assertion.

contrasted duties with those aspects of our behavior influenced by our desires, temptations, preferences or what he referred to as our *inclinations*. What makes an act moral is it's being motivated by a sense of duty rather than by our inclinations. The prototypical moral act is one we initiate out of a sense of duty despite feeling compelled by an inclination to do otherwise. And it is not enough for Kant that the action merely is in *accord* with a sense of duty; for it to have moral worth it must actually *be motivated* by a sense of duty rather than inclination.

Therefore, referring to my previous hypothetical encounter with a drowning child, if my motives for attempting her rescue were entirely egoistic (e.g., fantasies about being hailed as a hero) or instrumental (anticipation of a monetary reward) or even a reflection of my basically kind-hearted, generous and altruistic nature, then for Kant my actions are without moral worth. If I had been quaking with fear and wishing I had not come along at just that time, but my concern for the child managed to overcome that trepidation so that I dove into the surf, then my behavior would be morally worthy.

One of the interesting implications of Kant's position is the indeterminacy of judgment in mixed-motive situations in which our inclinations and our duty coincide. Kant did not have a good answer for that. Conversely, he should not be misinterpreted as proposing that any involvement of our inclinations precludes moral value. He was saying only that acting from duty is the necessary condition. Moreover, this perspective seems to be supported by empirical psychological findings that adults (but not young children) view as morally superior someone who does the right thing by overcoming conflicting desires, in comparison with persons who do the [same] right thing without having experienced immoral impulses (Starmans & Bloom, 2016).

Kant went a step further and radicalized the notion of duty as a generalized abstraction requiring adherence for its own sake, without reference to any specific purposes or outcomes. And we can do our duty (i.e., do what we ought to do or what is right) by following the dictates of reason. To summarize, ethical behavior is that which is motivated by good intentions, or the aim of doing one's duty, which is most clearly evidenced when one must overcome contrary inclinations in order to do so. This seems to correspond to findings of empirical socialization studies that societies depend on citizens developing an "obligation to obey the law" (Fine & van Rooij, 2021).

But what does Kant mean by generalized duty? If duties are not to be defined by their descriptions, purposes or consequences, then what are they?

Universal Law and the Categorical Imperative

Kant said that "duty is the necessity to act out of reverence for the [moral] law" (cited in Arrington, 1998, p. 267). This is important because only rational beings can have laws and intentions to follow them, so the highest purpose of reason is to provide the motivation to follow moral law. But, wait a second. Kant seems to have merely shifted the focus without answering the question. If duty consists of obeying moral law, but the content or substance of the duty is undefined, what is this "law"? His answer is brilliant. Because the law, like duty, cannot be defined by its content (which can at best refer only to a qualified good) or by its unreliable consequences, it can only be defined by the formal quality of law itself, which boils down ultimately to its universal nature, or what I have previously referred to as universalizability. For a principle or maxim such as "never tell a lie" or "help others if you can" to qualify as a moral law, it must be one that we can be assured all people should be obliged to obey.

For Kant (as with Hare's universal prescriptivism two centuries later; see Chap. 2) a moral principle or maxim has the nature of a command: "Do this" or, more frequently, "don't do that." The reason that we experience it as an imperative is because we have inclinations that may be in opposition to our duties which need to be overcome. According to Kant an imperative that is conditional on an inclination is a *hypothetical imperative*. For example, "If you want to graduate and receive your PhD degree you must complete your doctoral dissertation"; "The honest thing to do is to return that money." Completing your dissertation and returning the money are imperatives only if you accept the conditional purposes of wanting to graduate and being honest, respectively. In contrast, universal moral laws are expressed as *categorical imperatives*, meaning that they have no conditional purpose(s). Obedience to them is absolute: "Do not lie [ever, under any circumstances]."

"Do not lie" is a categorical imperative because it is universalizable. "It's okay to lie under some circumstances" is not universalizable. That is, if society operated according to that qualified principle no one could know whether or when they were being lied to so no one's word could be accepted, and society could not survive. As is evident from this example the determination of whether a maxim is universalizable is generally hypothetical, imagining what society would be like if everyone always behaved in accord with it. Could there be a viable society in which no one was ever sure whether they were being lied to?[5]

Although there are many maxims that could be formulated as potential categorical imperatives, there is one overall categorical imperative—*The* categorical imperative: "Act only on that maxim whereby you can at the same time will that it should become a universal law." Thus, universalizability is the hallmark of morality; because we are all rational beings, we all will agree on what is universalizable. Kant developed a few other formulations of the categorical imperative that are meant to be expressed in more practical terms. The most important of these is referred to as the *formula of the end in itself*, or the *formula of humanity*.

---

5   It is just this sort of reasoning, however, that leads consequentialists to charge that Kantian deontology, in the process of analyzing the universalizabilty of an imperative, resorts to a utilitarian assessment of consequences, illustrating that deontology cannot stand on its own independent of a consideration of outcomes.

Respect for People as Ends in Themselves

Just as Kant reasoned that there is only one unqualified good (goodwill), he also reasoned that there is only one thing that has absolute, objectively verifiable value: human beings. The value of all other things such as physical objects or even individual qualities of people (e.g., their wit or intelligence) varies; in fact, human beings, through their inclinations, impart value to all other things. Because the values of things vary some things may be perceived and used as *means* of obtaining other valued things. This cannot be true of human beings because their value is absolute; we are *ends* in and of ourselves. Arrington (1998) pointed out that this is consistent with the universalizability of the categorical imperative:

> If all rational beings are ends-in-themselves, we treat them as such only if we refuse to make any arbitrary distinctions among them, distinctions that would demote some of them to the status of mere things to be used by others. We must, that is to say, act consistently toward all rational beings. Hence whatever we conceive to be right for ourselves, we must also conceive to be right for other rational creatures—all of them. And whatever commands to action we give to others, we must also give to ourselves as well; whatever duties we assign to them, we must also impose on ourselves. (p. 277)

Therefore, Kant was led to this revision or corollary of the categorical imperative: "So act as to treat humanity, whether in your own person or in that of any other, never solely as a means but always also as an end." The qualifiers *solely* and *also* are important. Kant recognized that we may, with no adverse moral implications, "use" people as appropriate to the circumstances—to cook a meal for us, drive us to the airport, or mentor the development of our careers. Kant's formula of humanity is generally viewed as one of the most fundamental moral principles ever developed. It dictates that we never lose sight of the view of all human beings as having absolute worth in and of themselves and thus should be treated with dignity and respect. Far from being a trite platitude, the implications of this view, as Norman (1998) articulated, are profound. It suggests that we be concerned for other people's objectives as well as our own. It means recognizing that the pursuit of our own goals is limited by their potential infringement on the rights of others; we should not manipulate or use others merely for our own purposes, regardless of how worthwhile those purposes may be. It implies respect for the liberty and autonomy of others to pursue their own ends freely.

Thomas Hobbes

Suppose you lived in a world in which people were motivated exclusively by their own selfish interests; there was no political, legal or social machinery to enable or enforce cooperative relations so that the predominant attitude with which you and everyone else engaged the world was a mixture of distrust, fear, competition and aggression; most of your existence was focused on the struggle to survive. (Think of the Australian movie franchise of *Mad Max* films.) That is what Thomas Hobbes (1588–1679) envisioned as the natural *state of nature* of humankind without the mechanisms of civilization—what he characterized as a perpetual state of war. His description of the likely devastating consequences of these conditions is one of the most widely quoted passages in all of philosophy:

> In such condition there is no place for industry; because the fruit thereof is uncertain: and consequently no culture of the earth; no navigation, not use of the commodities that may be imported by sea; no commodious building; no instruments of moving and removing such things as require much force; no knowledge of the face of the earth; no account of time; no arts; no letters; no society; and, which is worst of all, continual fear and danger of violent death; and the life of man, solitary, poor, nasty, brutish and short.
>
> *(From* Leviathan, *cited in Arrington, 1998, p. 161)*

What Hobbes meant by "no society," among other things, is an absence of morality or of any sense of good and evil, right and wrong, or justice and injustice. Under these conditions each person would have the *right of nature*—the freedom to do anything they want to protect and enhance their life. Because living under such conditions of continual fear and insecurity is untenable, it is clearly in humankind's self-interest to escape this brutish existence. And this we do, according to Hobbes, by means of the *laws of nature*.

The Laws of Nature and the Idea of the Social Contract

Fortunately, according to Hobbes, we possess the powers of reason that enable us to find a way out of this horrible life. Reason leads us to principles (19 in all) that he referred to as the laws of nature. The first two of these emphasize that it is in our own self-interests to abandon the state of war and to seek peace, and to give up our unlimited freedoms under the right of nature, providing others do so as well. The condition is important: Hobbes was a "psychological egoist" as well as an "ethical egoist." People cannot be expected to relinquish their natural freedom to pursue their exclusive self-interests if others are not abiding by the same ground rules. It is this emphasis on the renunciation of some personal liberty to achieve peaceful conditions allowing all to pursue their limited self-interest that makes Hobbes an *enlightened* ethical egoist.

When people mutually renounce some of their rights, they enter into an agreement that Hobbes referred to as a *contract;* to the extent that the contract entails a commitment to future actions, it is a *covenant.* The third law of nature is that we are required to live up to the obligations incurred by our contracts and covenants with others; otherwise, peace cannot actually be attained. *Justice* entails abiding by these *social contracts* that structure civilized social life; *injustice* is failing to do so.

But given Hobbes' decidedly pessimistic view of human nature, how can he expect people to abide voluntarily by their social contracts? The answer is he does not. Included with the liberties that we relinquish is the establishment of a superordinate agent that we all empowered to enforce the laws and covenants. This agent Hobbes called the *Sovereign,* and it is only because of our fear of punishment by the sovereign for committing an injustice that we achieve a workable social system that he referred to as a *commonwealth.* (The commonwealth may exist in any political form, such as democracy or totalitarianism; Hobbes himself was a staunch monarchist.) Moreover, the security afforded by the commonwealth allows us to temper our potentially unlimited pursuit of self-interest by enabling some expression of altruistic motives. That is a theme developed more fully by Jean Jacques Rousseau in *The Social Contract,* published more than a century after *Leviathan.*

The Relation Between the Individual and Institutional Power

Hobbes' discussion of the powers of the sovereign betrays a rather totalitarian point of view. The powers of the sovereign are virtually unlimited. Hobbes undoubtedly was led to this position by virtue of his rather disquieting view of the nature of human behavior in an unregulated state, as well as by his personal observations of social disorder during the English civil wars (1642–1651). But the purpose of the sovereign is to maintain overall peace and security and the survival and gratification of all members of the commonwealth, so the powers are not completely unlimited. We are absolved from obeying the sovereign (i.e., the laws of the land) if the sovereign is not able to provide the protections that are its reason for being. Moreover, individuals' basic rights to pursue their self-interest (within the limits of the law), the right to self-defense, and protection against self-incrimination (i.e., thwarting one's own self-interests) are never surrendered. This is Hobbes' answer to Question I of the core issues in ethics (cf. Box 1.1).

One of the values of Hobbes' theory is the integration of what is essentially a political philosophy concerning the acquisition and exercise of institutional power, along with morality. Ethical issues surrounding the use and abuse of institutional power are certainly relevant topics for organizational psychologists, notwithstanding our focus on corporations or other social organizations as the institution rather than the state. It is not much of a stretch to cast the modern corporation in the role of sovereign, and its relationship with its employees, as well as the relationships among employees, as governed by social contracts and covenants more familiarly referred to as organizational policies and regulations, employment contracts, collective-bargaining agreements, and other artifacts of organizational culture, as well as implicit psychological contracts (Rousseau, 1995; Rousseau & Schalk, 2000).

When the sovereign is unable to provide the protections or other benefits that are due under the terms of the social contract, it may morally be disobeyed. The rules of the social contract are based on an implied or explicit reciprocity: I give up my freedom to act unilaterally in my own interest in order to obtain the longer-term benefits that will accrue to me by everyone else doing the same. Therefore, at the individual level, if someone violates that reciprocity we are morally released from our obligations (within the limits allowed by law). Similarly, Rachels and Rachels (2015) point out that social contract theory provides a meaningful rationale for explicit group defiance of the law—civil disobedience—under certain circumstances:

> According to The Social Contract Theory, we are obligated to obey the law because we each participate in a social system that promises more benefits than burdens. The benefits are the benefits of social living: We escape the state of nature and live in a society in which we are secure and enjoy basic rights. To gain these benefits, we agree to uphold the institutions that make them possible … .

> But what if some citizens are denied their basic rights? … . Under such circumstances, the social contract is not being honored. By asking the disadvantaged group to obey the law and respect society's institutions, we are asking them to accept the burdens of social living while being denied its benefits. (p. 94)

Critique

It is easy to criticize Hobbes factually and literally. First, we know his view of human nature to be at best a pessimistic unidimensional view that emphasizes a narrow range of self-interest motivation. Second, there is no historical or anthropological record of humans living in a "state of nature," as he visualized it, or of them ever having entered into an actual contract of some sort that marked a transition from the state of nature to civilized society. In fairness to Hobbes, he did not actually advance the latter point as a historical event, but he accepted the social contract as implied by the relatively uniform conventions that characterize a society.

In fact the contemporary study of social psychology, sociology, anthropology, political science and economics all encompass the existence of socialization processes and unarticulated cultural values, assumptions and normative expectations that serve to regulate our interpersonal, commercial and legal interactions without the benefit of formal contractual arrangements or explicit recognition.[6] The contractarian approach is a helpful model by which to understand a range of

---

6   See Danley (1994) for a discussion of the distinctions among actual, tacit and hypothetical contracts.

interpersonal phenomena, especially in organizational settings, without assuming the literal existence of myriad formal contracts. On the other hand, the social contract is not a mere metaphor: There are in fact sets of social rules by which we live our lives, and this arrangement benefits all of us. As Rachels and Rachels (2015) recognize,

> the story of the 'social contract' need not be intended as a description of historical events. Rather, it is a useful analytical tool, based on the idea that we may understand our moral obligations *as if* they had arisen in this way. (p. 96)

Perhaps most important, Hobbes' approach provides the essence of one of the major general conceptions of what is meant by justice: that is, justice as mutual advantage (cf. Barry, 1989). Within the meta-ethical context of ethical egoism, in which each party to an eventual contract is concerned exclusively with maximizing their position, negotiators bargain as best they can to advance their self-interests based on their likely positions of power. The outcome of such bargaining will probably reflect the differential bargaining power of the participants. That seems to be a flawed conception of justice (see section on John Rawls, below).

John Locke and Natural Rights

The key to understanding the significance of any ethical naturalist theory is that it is a reaction against the skeptical or relativist view that morality is essentially a matter of cultural (i.e., local) conventions. Instead, morality consists of universal individual rights (Buckle, 1993) that we expect to be respected by society even though significant compromises may be needed to gain the security that society provides (Schneewind, 1993). Although most rights theorists view human rights as self-justifying—either by divine revelation or reasoning—they are not absolute rights because some potentially conflict with others, and because no one is free to exercise their rights by infringing on those of others.

Although John Locke (1632–1704) extended earlier work concerning human rights and the social contract, he also challenged existing conceptualizations by emphasizing that some of our rights are inalienable and thus may not be abridged by society (i.e., government). This is the origin of the *classical liberal* tradition in political philosophy which influenced the American and French revolutions. And he opposed Hobbes by positing a very different state of nature than the devastating warfare Hobbes envisioned. Recall that for Hobbes the state of nature consists in an absence of society, which meant to him an absence of morality. Morality is achieved only by people agreeing reluctantly to the creation of the commonwealth. But for Locke, morality is based on our natural rights and precedes society. In the state of nature, all are free and equal: "Men living together according to reason, without a common superior on earth with authority to judge between them, is properly the state of nature" (cited in Copleston, 1994, p. 128). And if all people are fundamentally equal, independent and rational, reason clearly indicates that no one should deprive another of life, health, liberty or their possessions; the state should not deprive people as well, except in defense of these liberties on someone's behalf. That is what he meant by the natural moral law. Hence, there are moral limits to what governments may legitimately do.

The fact that Locke emphasized the right to private property is frequently attributed to the fact that he moved among the landed gentry of England, who were his patrons (Copleston, 1994). His views form the kernel of what is characterized as the classical liberal tradition in western political philosophy, especially as applied to economic theory (Danley, 1994). In current political parlance, it is known as libertarian (cf. Chap. 8). What is frequently ignored by libertarians and other contemporary proponents of a minimalist government is that Locke's defense of private property was a limited one. What justifies entitlement to private property is one's labor in producing and enjoying it. Amassing more than one can reasonably use and enjoy personally, especially if it is to the detriment of others, is "more than one's share" and is not justifiable. Also, emphasizing personal rights is not incompatible with notions of overall utility and social responsibility insofar as "the assertion of rights necessarily involves recognition of the rights of others as well as one's own" (Almond, 1993, p. 267), and Locke viewed the primary role of the state as promoting the common good (cf. Question I, Box 1.1). It is here and in his consistent antiauthoritarian themes that we see the seeds of political liberalism in the modern meaning of "progressive."

Most rights-based theories share the flaw of natural law meta-theories on which they are based (cf. Chap. 2). What is the justification for these rights? How were they determined? On what basis do we accept them as the basis for morality? Normative theories of human rights have difficulty answering such questions other than by recourse to religious beliefs of their having been God-given, which most scholars do not accept as a sufficient philosophical or rational justification. Moreover, even if one did accept that explanation, on what basis do we honor Locke's list of rights (or anyone else's) as the correct ones? Locke himself provided no justification. The most frequent justifications have probably been utilitarian (e.g., liberty and justice contribute to human happiness; Almond, 1993), but that breaches the deontological aims of the theory.

John Rawls: A Contemporary Contractarian View

Perhaps the most salient criticism of Hobbes' moral philosophy and its version of the social contract theory is that it is not really a moral theory (Kymlicka, 1993). Although Hobbesian theory contains the notion of justice—living up to one's social obligations—those obligations reflect contracts negotiated by people who likely differ substantially in bargaining power for a variety of (perhaps irrelevant or unjustifiable) reasons. A conception of justice posited entirely on the expression of regulated self-interest, which ignores social inequities, and is enforced in great measure by external authority and the threat of punishment is viewed by some critics as not being about morality at all.

But John Rawls' (1958, 1971, 1999, 2001) contemporary version of social contract theory is in the tradition of universal human rights and Kantian morality. It

> uses the device of a social contract in order to develop, rather than replace, traditional notions of moral obligation; it uses the idea of the contract to express the inherent moral standing of persons, rather than to generate an artificial moral standing.
>
> *(Kymlicka, 1993, p. 191)*

The "inherent moral standing of persons" is reflected in the Kantian and Lockian ideas of universalizability or the moral equality of persons, and respect for people as autonomous "ends in themselves."

The principles of right and justice Rawls develops are done in a manner so that an agreement reached under their conditions will be accepted by all parties because the terms require free and equal opportunity for all. Therefore, in terms probably familiar to the reader, Rawls is largely about *procedural justice*. For Rawls, the social contract reflects the natural duty of justice we owe to one another by virtue of our existence, not the artifice of a mechanism of mutual restraint. Therefore,

> this agreement ... must be entered into under certain conditions if it is to be a valid agreement from the point of view of political justice. In particular, these conditions must situate free and equal persons fairly and must not permit some to have unfair bargaining advantages over others. Further, threats of force and coercion, deception and fraud, and so on must be ruled out.
>
> *(Rawls, 2001, p. 15)*

Rawls uses the contractarian approach as a mechanism to articulate the somewhat vague natural duty of justice. Starting from Hobbes' rather pessimistic and totally egoistic state of nature, he asserted that morality (i.e., justice) can be achieved only if we can obviate the natural inequalities among people because contracts negotiated among parties of unequal power are not likely to be fair. For example, a growing number of companies—estimated at 19% in 1997 by the federal General Accounting Office and 23% by a later survey (Greenhouse, 2001)—require employees to surrender their right to sue their employer (e.g., for employment discrimination, wrongful dismissal or sexual harassment) as a condition of employment, and preclude commercial customers and even medical patients from suing for fraud or malpractice. (Often prohibited by agreement, also, is being able to participate in class-action lawsuits—often the only way individuals can hope to redress grievances against a large, wealthy organization.) Instead, so-called "due process procedures," are required such as arbitration by an internal tribunal of employees and managers or by external arbitrators (who generally have an ongoing relationship with the company).

Although some management scholars view such *alternative dispute resolution* (ADR) programs as effective and safe forums for employees to express grievances (McCabe, 1997), the coercive aspect seems to belie that. More recent investigations suggest that the practice is increasing greatly, to the extent of being characterized as a "privatization of the justice system" (Corkery & Silver-Greenberg, 2015; Silver-Greenberg & Corkery, 2015; Silver-Greenberg & Gebeloff, 2015). Employers have unilaterally applied these due-process rights (which may require many levels of expensive hearings before the employee even reaches the arbitration stage) even to existing employees who had no voice in the implementation of this retroactive condition of employment (Walsh, 2000).[7] As we might expect, there is evidence that the perceived fairness of ADR systems is related more to its procedural justice aspects such as the level of employee input and the composition of the grievance panel, than to outcome (Blancero et al., 2010).

Nevertheless, an even more important issue may be the vast majority of employees who enjoy little due-process job protection at all and work under the dominant model of **at-will employment** in which, with a few exceptions, an employer can hire or fire at will with no explanation required (Werhane, 1999b). Dunford and Devine (1998) provided an overview of the common law history of employment-at-will in the United States.

This issue of power differentials has been a long-recognized weakness of the contractarian model of corporations as voluntary associations of people united by a network of contracts (Hessen, 1979). Kelley (1983) pointed out the following:

> All kinds of organizational agreements are actually 'contracts of adhesion,' that is, agreements containing standardized terms set by dominant parties and only marginally negotiable, if understandable, by weaker parties to a transaction … . In these contracts, terms often have been skillfully designed to minimize the legal liabilities of their authors; and, although the

---

7   The power imbalance in this agreement is reflected in the facts that the employers determine the dispute resolution rules—which may not be questioned as part of the arbitration—and frequently choose the arbitrators as well. They also may have many experiences with the process, whereas a complainant or employee is likely to be going through the process for the first time—an inequality that is exacerbated by the closed-door feature of the arbitrations, in which even the decisions remain unpublished and therefore unavailable to potential future complainants. Thus, it has been reported that the arbitration forum "tends to favor repeat users—management—over individuals who use it only once" (Greenhouse, 2001).

'adhering' party theoretically is free to shop around for a better deal, one finds similar terms offered by competing organizations. (p. 382)

As examples, think about the extent to which you were free and empowered to negotiate the terms of your agreements with your cell phone company, credit card company, internet service provider, cable TV company, your landlord or the bank from which you obtained a home mortgage and/or student loan, or your acceptance of the "terms of use" every time you download or purchase something on-line.

Scanlon (1998) emphasizes that all contractualist moral theories, whether classical (Hobbes) or contemporary like Rawls, Habermas, Hare or himself, are based on the notion that justice or morality requires that all parties to the matter in question find the operative decision principles acceptable. That is, "principles which no one could reasonably reject ... [or] rationally reject" (p. 191).[8] The metaphorical device Rawls created to achieve justice is the *veil of ignorance*. If we designed our social relationships without knowing beforehand our own talents and weaknesses, our personal preferences or our position in society—not even what generation we were part of, Rawls assumed that we would simply have to decide what is best for society impartially. And that, he asserted, would lead to a self-protective attitude in which everyone would favor benefitting those who are the worst off (which might turn out to be oneself). Thus, he conceptualizes justice within the Kantian tradition of fairness, impartiality and universalism based on the assumption of respect for the autonomy of all rational people. Given that (in a Rawlsian just society) all have the same rights and liberties, "social cooperation is guided by publicly recognized rules and procedures which those cooperating accept as appropriate to regulate their conduct" (Rawls, 2001, p. 6). Rawls will come up again in chapter 8.

Georg Wilhelm Friedrich Hegel

It seems fitting to end this sampling of deontological ethical theories primarily with the views of G. W. F. Hegel (1770–1831) and secondarily with some elaborations of Hegelian notions by Karl Marx (1818–1883). That is because (a) Hegel's ethical theory emphasizes greatly the social nature of existence, including our participation in the institutions of society, which is very much in keeping with the points of view expressed throughout this book; and (b) he utilized in his ethical ideology—200 years ago(!)—a number of modern psychological constructs with which professionals in developmental, social, as well as I-O psychology would feel quite comfortable.

---

8 This seems rather close to what might be conditions of procedural justice. In addition, Scanlon makes a big deal of distinguishing between reasonable and rational. We don't need to go there.

The overriding principle that is reflected in Hegel's philosophy is that humans start life in an alienated state; through a series of developmental stages, we ultimately achieve *self-realization* via our intimate engagement in social life—through our families, our civil life (e.g., involvement in local community and our work), and the larger society or state. A necessary component of that approach is acceptance of the social character of the individual. We are born into a family and nurtured by its members and others in the local community. Our cognitive and emotional development occurs in a highly social context, and we continue to expand our relationship to the external world largely through involvement in larger and more varied social organizations and institutions. The implications are that (a) the crux of what we mean by ethics, according to Hegel, has to do with interpersonal relationships, which are based on trust, loyalty, cooperation, emotional commitment and the like, initially just to one's family and then to the wider circle of interdependent social and economic institutions he referred to as *civil society,* including those at work, and ultimately to the state; and (b) these social relations are not merely things we do and peripheral aspects of our personality, but they are intrinsic aspects of our *self-identity*. Thus, when I extend my trust to a close friend, family member or good colleague, it is not because it will increase the overall level of happiness or good in the world (Utilitarianism; cf. Chap. 4) or because it is a dutiful thing for me and everyone else to do (Kant), but because my relationships with these folks are part of my psychological identity and it gives my life meaning to do so.

However, extending this principle to an ever-widening social world—for example, loyalty to fellow employees and one's employer, relations with community members, and identification with one's country—depends on the quality of one's relationships with those people and entities. We do not, according to Hegel, owe blind loyalty irrespective of the worthiness of those people, organizations and institutions.

The Development of Self-Identity[9]

Hegel took a developmental perspective concerning the process whereby we achieve an ethical existence, which he referred to as *self-realization*. Because, as noted, the essence of the ethical sphere is social, self-realization is the realization of the social self. That is the ultimate goal of human development. The developmental process starts with us as mere physical beings until, through interacting with the environment, we begin to be aware of ourselves as conscious and willful beings. The basis for all personality development is this initial undifferentiated self-consciousness and what Hegel called the *imperative of right* associated with it (i.e., the right of all humans to be). Personality—and especially one's sense of

9   This discussion is based largely on analyses by Arrington (1998).

personal freedom—begins to become differentiated through engaging with objects; possessing, using and ultimately exchanging them with others (e.g., think of a young child in a sandbox tightly in possession of his or her pail and shovel, not yet able to share). Hegel placed great store on the notion of private property as the means by whereby we learn to express our individual rights and freedom, as well as how to interact socially.

These exchanges of private property ("My LeBron James trading card for your Derek Jeter?"), which Hegel referred to as *contracts,* are the means whereby we acquire normative notions of right and wrong, which are formalized in the laws and customs of society. From these particularized notions of right and wrong develop a more elaborated sense of morality, which consists of a generalized notion of how one ought to be. And it is a critical point for Hegel that this generalized notion includes the recognition that we share this morality with others; in that way, our identity is transformed from an individual, isolated selfhood to that of a social being. It is at this point in his ethical theory that Hegel's notions of universal subjectivity become rather metaphysical. But we need not be too put off. As explained by Norman (1998) the essence of the concept is that the self which we realize is a social self—not an isolated entity, but the self which develops through one's relations to other selves, the self that one shares with others, as a social being. On this basis, therefore, the substance of morality becomes welfare—clearly not only my own but universalized as that of others as well.

But what does everyone's welfare consist of? How does one know what is the good thing to do? What are one's right duties? Hegel specifically rejected Kant's answer to these questions. Recall that Kant believed that moral law and its attendant duties could not be specified by their substance (which represents only qualified goods at best) or by their consequences (which are unreliable), but only by the formal quality of the law itself—its universalizability, or the categorical imperative. Hegel's answer is very different and is highly susceptible to misinterpretation and distortion (as it was, by European Fascists in the 1920s and 1930s), but it is consistent with his focus on our social character. He asserted that the only possible objective ethical content, free of individual subjective distortions, are the "absolutely valid laws and institutions" of our social existence that are embodied in the family, civil society and the state.

> In an *ethical* community, it is easy to say what a man must do, what are the duties he has to fulfill in order to be virtuous: he has simply to follow the well-known and explicit rules of his own situation. Rectitude is the general character which may be demanded of him by law or custom.
>
> *(cited in Arrington, 1998, p. 309)*

In this regard F. H. Bradley (1935), a foremost interpreter of Hegel, is responsible for publicizing the phrase "my station and its duties." In this way, Hegel defined our ethical obligations in a concrete and specific manner, between the ambiguous and unhelpful abstractions of the moral law on one hand and the potentially biased and self-serving subjectivity of personal conscience on the other hand.

A casual reading of these notions might create the impression that, far from leading to the freedom of self-realization that was Hegel's objective, this is a very conservative and constraining conception of the ethical life: mere reverence to the status quo traditions, obligations and laws of one's society. But that overlooks two matters. First, for Hegel the institutions, work organizations and the state in which we perform our duties are assumed to be ethical ones, by which he meant that these organizations can justify the rationality or validity of their laws and regulations and demonstrate that their functioning is compatible with the personal objectives of their constituents or citizens. (This is reminiscent of Hobbes' view that we are absolved from obeying authority if it cannot provide the individual protections that justify its existence.) Second, contingent on our acceptance of the institutions as ethical, Hegel assumed we do not experience them as coercive or antagonistic. In fact, it is presumed we identify psychologically with them and with our duties; they in part identify who we are—as a family member, a member of the larger society in which our well-being is interwoven with that of others, and a citizen of the state.

Self-Realization

An additional brief word seems in order concerning what Hegel meant by "self-realization." In this regard, he accepted Kant's emphases on respect for the in-dividual and on each of us as an end in our own right, but he rejected Jeremy Bentham's utilitarian ideal of maximizing pleasure as the hallmark of individual actions (cf. Chap. 4).[10] That is because he viewed the utilitarian approach as atomistic, superficial and incomplete, whereas self-realization involves a more inclusive and coherent affirmation of one's whole social being. That coherence is frequently attained by virtue of having a dominant focus in one's life around which all else revolves—it is frequently one's work or career, commitment to a political or religious movement, or family relationships. In all cases, it generally provides a sense of social recognition for the individual and a sense of identity.

Especially apropos is Hegel's focus on the importance of work as a means of self-expression that provides one with a sense of identity. It is in this rich context that we should understand the meaning of "my station and its duties." Bradley (1935) elaborated this Hegelian theme by enunciating the principles of what, many years later, psychologists would refer to under the rubrics of *effectance motivation, activation theory,* and *job enrichment* (e.g., see Deci & Ryan, 1991). That is, the process of self-realization requires action and accomplishment—in particular, accomplishing meaningful and challenging tasks.

---

10 Hegel's familiarity with utilitarianism was limited to his knowledge of Bentham's work. Hegel died when John Stuart Mill was only 25 years old.

Karl Marx

There is an irony about Marx being considered in a work focused on ethics or moral philosophy given his rejection of moral theorizing and the very notion of morality as we conceive it. However, quite a few interpreters of Marx have suggested that Marxist theory itself is rather ironic in this regard because of the highly moralistic nature of its denunciation of capitalism for allegedly stifling human freedom. J.P Sartre (1945) observed, "Anyone who could say whether Marx first chose to be a revolutionary and then a philosopher—or first chose philosophy and then became a revolutionary—would be clever indeed" (p. 56). In any event, there are several reasons for his inclusion, here. Early in his intellectual life Marx was a Hegelian, and several aspects of Hegelian ethics are represented in Marxist theory, including the notions of alienation and the expression of self-identity through work, the interdependence of the individual and society, the objectives of freedom and self-realization, and a rejection of Kant's abstract formalism. As expressed by MacIntyre (1998),

> Like Hegel, Marx envisages freedom in terms of the overcoming of limitations and constraints of one social order by bringing another, less limited social order into being … . What constitutes a social order, what constitutes both its possibilities and its limitations, is the dominant form of work by which its material sustenance is produced. The forms of work vary with the forms of technology; and both the division of labor and the consequent division of masters and laborers are divisive of human society, producing classes and conflicts between them. (p. 203)

Ultimately, of course, Marx rejects Hegel's view of the psychological importance of private property ownership and the rectitude of accepting one's station in life and fulfilling its duties. In addition, Marx was not the first to illustrate that reflections on ethics inevitably lead to a consideration of the social, economic and political institutions by which society regulates the behavior of its members toward one another.

Historical Materialism and the Rejection of Morality

Marx believed, as did the Sophists, that society's laws, customs and morality simply reflect the self-interests of the dominant members of the society. This is elaborated within the larger context of his theory of *historical materialism,* which views history as divided into eras characterized by a particular mode of economic production that is controlled by a particular segment of society, which also is the primary beneficiary of that production. Other segments of society are relegated to other roles. To the extent that each segment of society is represented by relatively organized political and social representation it becomes a *class,* and it almost goes without saying that the class that is in control of the means and rewards of production is highly motivated to maintain that position, and those not in control are motivated to acquire it.

According to Marx, virtually all aspects of culture—religion, art, literature, science and morality—are *ideological,* meaning that they represent and reinforce the class interests of those who are in power at any time. "Morality is a system of ideas which both interprets and regulates people's behavior in ways which are vital for the working of any social order" (Wood, 1993, p. 516). Most people remain unaware of this, even with respect to their own motives and behavior—they lack *self-transparency*—and so remain in a state of "unfreedom." A Marxist might assert, for example, that our ethical notions of universalizability and universalism (i.e., impartiality and equivalence of interests) are an illusion. Given the nature of the class structure—one class that rules at the expense of all others—any apparent impartiality is illusory: It merely furthers the interests of those in power. Similarly, free trade, free competition and freedom of the worker to contract his or her services in the capitalist system are all illusory insofar as they are structured and constricted by the economic system that serves the interests of the ruling class. Therefore, Marx's views in this regard are diametrically opposed to Hegel's and Bradley's focus on "my station and its duties." Note that Marx believed that the self-serving advancement of one's own class interests would be no less characteristic of the motives of the working class if it was in power. That is why the proletarian revolution was conceived as merely a step toward the goal of a classless society, which would accomplish what illusory morality pretends to do, so that ideology would be unnecessary.

Alienation, Realization and Work

Marx believed, as did Hegel and many I-O psychologists today (cf. Dik et al., 2013), that work provides a critical source of self-identity, social recognition and self-realization—when it is meaningful work that allows the expression of some autonomy. This focus on the ideal of a fully realized life through meaningful productivity makes Marx no more radical than Plato, Aristotle, Hegel, Kant or Mill, or the psychologists Maslow (1998), Herzberg et al. (1959) or Hackman and Oldham (1980). However, he further believed, as most I-O psychologists do not, that those objectives are precluded by work as it exists within the capitalist system, namely, *wage labor:* working for others who own the capital and means of production.

Marx borrowed Hegel's notion of alienation to describe the consequences of wage labor. As Norman (1998) summarized, Marx identified four dimensions of *alienated labor:*

1. Alienation from the product of one's labor: That is, the worker has little or no concern for the qualities of the product and does not own it. It is merely a means of earning a wage.
2. Alienation from one's own productive activity: By this he meant working under conditions of external structure and substantial controls with no expression of individual autonomy.
3. Alienation from our distinctly human capacities: such as intelligent, creative functioning.
4. Alienation from others: When work is motivated solely by extrinsic financial reward, especially when based on individual performance, it precludes the social rewards of a cooperative, shared experience.

How is this to be overcome? How is the worker able to move from a state of alienation to self-realization? For Marx, the only solution is bringing the means of production under the ownership and control of the workers themselves. That is the only way in which work can be experienced by workers as putting into effect their own communal aspirations, and be experienced as an enterprise in which each individual finds their own shared identity. As radical as that seems, the restructuring of society can be viewed as merely differing in degree rather than in kind from more modest change projects like work design, job restructuring, revising reinforcement contingencies (e.g., wage rates), organization development interventions, et al. They are all based on a belief in the efficacy of social–structural, contextual and environmental influences on behavior.

Critique

Given the general historical failure of communism as an effective economic and political system for enhancing individual freedom, it seems most useful to focus on the positive features that one can glean from Marxist theory. From our vantage point 1½ centuries later it seems clear that Marx's empirical observations were mostly correct. The importance of people's social and psychological growth needs and the salience of work as a sphere uniquely suited for expressing and gratifying them is widely accepted now. Similarly, his characterization of the stultifying conditions under which most workers labored in the early stages of the industrial age remained widely true for over a century (cf. Walker & Guest, 1952) and, for many workers, remains true today (Mumby, 2019). Moreover, contemporary criticism of the economic and social power and political influence wielded by corporations, especially the precipitate exodus of capital and production facilities from communities that have both supported and come to depend on them to cheap labor markets around the globe, is at least compatible with Marx's views of historical materialism and class divisions. Last, Norman (1998) emphasizes that Marx's recognition that the human good requires action not only at the individual level but also politically remains very important. This is in keeping with the view of many philosophers that ethics consists of both "personal morality" and "a social institution analogous to law … [that] is part of the apparatus of power" (Seckel, 1987, p. 69).

Additions to the **Framework for Ethical Decision-Making** are deferred until after the following chapter so as to integrate suggestions drawn from both deontological and consequentialist views.

4

NORMATIVE ETHICAL THEORIES: II. CONSEQUENTIALISM

> An ethical judgment that is no good in practice must suffer from a theoretical defect as well, for the whole point of ethical judgments is to guide practice.
>
> —Peter Singer

Consequentialist Theories

Singer (2011), a famous contemporary utilitarian philosopher, draws our attention to a point of view taken throughout this book. As noted at the outset of the previous chapter the teleological or consequentialist point of view asserts that the morality of our actions is to be judged by the relative goodness of their effects rather than by their inherent rightness or wrongness. Pragmatists, such as business managers, economists and applied psychologists, who are accustomed to basing their professional choices on their anticipated consequences, have generally felt more comfortable with consequentialism than with deontological theories (Fritzsche & Becker, 1984). For example, a proposed model of ethical decision-making in organizations defines a moral issue entirely in terms of harm or benefit to others (Jones, 1991). The first systematic formulation of this approach, *utilitarianism,* was presented by Jeremy Bentham (although it was suggested earlier by Hume) and it was expanded and refined by his student, John Stuart Mill. The resulting composite of their work is usually referred to as *classical utility theory*, and it has undergone further refinements in response to the self-critiques by Bentham and Mill themselves, as well as by vociferous critics. Contemporary consequentialist theories retain much of the essence of classical utility theory but with several substantial modifications, as I will show. And, as noted by Sison et al. (2012)

DOI: 10.4324/9781003212577-5

utilitarianism … seems to be a particularly appropriate ethical theory for business. Utilitarianism fits well with cost-benefit analysis; it places a high value on the enormous productive power of capitalism; it is consistent with the presuppositions of standard economic theory. (p. 207–208)

Jeremy Bentham

Jeremy Bentham (1748–1832) was a radical who aimed to rid moral philosophy of reliance on what he considered to be irrational notions, mystical and religious justifications, and abstract moral rules such as natural law or natural rights. Moreover, he also hoped to transform English institutions by ridding them of their ill-conceived conventions and traditions which he held responsible for much social injustice and unhappiness. In fact, his major work is entitled "The Principles of Morals *and Legislation*." Both aims were to be accomplished by adherence to the one ultimate moral principle, the principle of utility, which is …

> … that principle which approves or disapproves of every action whatsoever, according to the tendency which it appears to have to augment or diminish the happiness of the party whose interest is in question: or, what is the same thing in other words, to promote or to oppose that happiness.
>
> *(cited in Arrington, 1998, p. 320)*

Bentham, therefore, was a hedonist—a position he arrived at by adherence to his belief in empirical science. That is, we human beings encounter the world through our senses, and our actions are determined entirely by the experience and/or anticipation of pleasure and pain. Realistically, therefore, maximizing pleasure and avoiding pain (i.e., increasing happiness) is the only justifiable moral principle. And the principle is applicable at the individual level with respect to one's private morality as well as at the public level so that legislators ought to design laws in light of people's propensity to promote their own happiness, and all government officials should base their policy decisions on the criterion of maximizing public welfare. Therefore, although Bentham was a psychological egoist (he believed that people tend to act in their own self-interest), he was not an ethical egoist. He believed that moral actions are those that produce the greatest happiness for oneself and others. For Bentham, the great appeal of the principle of utility is that it gives moral philosophy an objective basis. The justification of its ultimate principle does not rely on deontological abstractions or appeals to the revealed word of God but on the objective consideration of real-world consequences. But how is this objective consideration to be accomplished?

The Hedonic Calculus

Bentham meant nothing less than that Utility was a measurable (i.e., quantifiable) construct. Although this was a somewhat radical notion, it was not new: His ideas were based on Bernoulli's (1738/1954) mathematical expression of psychological utilities in decision-making. Bentham conceptualized the construct as multi-dimensional: Each action we take may have a variety of consequences, each of them being relatively pleasurable or painful. And pleasure and pain can be assessed quantitatively by measuring the seven dimensions of which they are comprised. Pleasure and pain vary in:

- *duration*
- *intensity*
- *certainty* or *uncertainty* (the likelihood that the action will result in the sensation)
- *propinquity* or *remoteness* (the immediacy or distal nature of the occurrence of the effect—e.g., contrast the immediacy of the discomfort of a visit to the dentist versus the delayed effects of failing to study for a midterm exam)
- *fecundity* (the probability that the pain or pleasure will be followed by more of the same kind—e.g., the additional ramifications of failing that midterm exam), and
- *purity* (the probability that the pain or pleasure will not be followed by the opposite sensation).

To determine the goodness of an act or the relative goodness of several alternative options, (a) each of the six attributes is to be assessed for each of the consequences of every option: (b) a net effect for each option is calculated as a multiplicative function of the six dimensions, and (c) a seventh dimension should be considered, *extent*, by adding algebraically for each option the net pleasure and pain experienced by all other people affected, as calculated in the same manner. The best—that is, most morally defensible—action is the option whose consequences have the highest overall net pleasure score or the lowest overall net pain score.

Bentham did not presume that this complicated set of psychometric calculations—what Knapp (1999) referred to as *felicific calculus* and a measurement-oriented psychologist might neologize as *ethimetrics*—is carried out prior to every individual action or governmental decision.[1] And it is beyond our purposes here to consider all of the difficult scaling and other measurement issues that would have to be overcome in operationalizing this ethimetric system (see Arrington, 1998, and

---

1 Although something very much like it in principle, cost—benefit analyses are indeed frequently carried out in the process of planning or evaluating social programs. Moreover, to my knowledge, utilitarians do not ordinarily figure in the *opportunity costs* of each choice (the net value of the best alternative not chosen) (cf. Greenberg & Spiller, 2015).

Goodin, 1993, for summaries). Nevertheless, Bentham said that this is just the sort of reasoning that people intuitively approximate when confronted with difficult choices. And he held it up as a model to be achieved if possible because it represents the ideal of a rational underpinning for ethical decision-making. Similarly, Pettit (1993) made the point that consequentialist approaches in general are more validly thought of as a theoretical way of justifying ethical decision-making after the fact than as a blueprint for actual deliberation.[2] However, we know that contemporary behavioral theories of decision-making and gaming in psychology and economics have long made use of subjective expected utility (SEU) as a basis for understanding and predicting choice behavior (Barry, 1989; Mellers, 2000; Savage, 1954), despite evidence suggesting that people's preferences or values are unstable and biased by the particular measurement operations used to estimate them (Kahneman et al., 1982; Slovik et al., 1985).

John Stuart Mill

John Stuart Mill (1806–1873) was the son of James Mill who was a close colleague and collaborator of Bentham. So, John's philosophical education was dominated by utilitarianism, and he maintained an adherence to its basic tenets, such as what he referred to as "the greatest happiness principle." But he also was dissatisfied with several aspects of the theory and so is responsible for having modified and refined it in a few ways. For example, although Bentham did include consideration of others' welfare as well as one's own, Mill emphasized even more the criterion of the greatest overall happiness for everyone, with no person's well-being counting more than anyone else's. Mill's views are a clear example of what I referred to as the universalist tradition in moral theorizing. Most important, he expanded the hedonistic conceptualization of pleasure to include a more complete picture of human nature and thus enlarged the notion of what is meant by the ultimate principle of happiness.

The Pleasures of Swine

Because of his strong preference for empiricism, Bentham's notions of pleasure and pain were limited essentially to the sensual level of experience and so, to Mill, could be considered "a doctrine worthy only of swine." Mill corrected this limitation of the theory by introducing a consideration of higher pleasures—so characterized because he viewed them as superior to the baser pleasures to which Bentham attended. They are superior insofar as they depend on the functioning of the higher human faculties: intellect, abstract thought, aesthetic appreciation, a

---

2   This is very similar to the social intuitionist model (Haidt, 2001), which posits that moral reasoning follows the appearance of automatic moral intuitions. (Cf. Chap. 6.)

sense of freedom and autonomy, personal security, social gratification, and so on. Mill would feel quite comfortable with a consideration of Maslow's hierarchy of human needs stacked on the base of physiological drives or with Hegel's notion of self-realization at the top of the hierarchy. In fact, Mill redefined Bentham's limited conception of happiness into one that is more compatible with Aristotle's *eudaimonia* or fulfillment (cf. Chap. 2).

However, because these pleasures are different in kind from each other and, especially from the lower pleasures, they can be considered only qualitatively, not quantitatively. He did not reject the quantitative hedonic calculus of Bentham (e.g., he continued to consider the *greatest* happiness) but, as Norman (1998) pointed out, Mill tended to exclude consideration of the lower pleasures and so it is unclear how he intended to integrate both the quantitative and qualitative dimensions of the varieties of pleasure. Perhaps this is not such a serious problem considering the general recognition that utilitarian calculations are often implicit and intuitive in any event and thus should be able to accommodate the qualitative considerations. Mill wrote at length about *secondary principles* that represent generalizations and extrapolations regarding the relative benefit to society of various kinds of actions. For example, over the span of civilization we have learned that truthfulness and respecting others are generally beneficial in the long run and that deceitfulness is generally harmful. These sorts of guidelines make it unnecessary for us to engage in elaborate multidimensional ethimetric calculations for each specific decision. Those analyses can be reserved for instances in which two or more secondary principles may conflict.

Contemporary Consequentialism

A variety of consequentialist theories remain popular in ethical thought today. They generally represent modifications of classical utilitarianism developed in response to significant criticisms of the narrowly hedonistic view of the classical Bentham/Mill model, so it makes sense for us to understand them in that context.

Responses to the Limits of Hedonism

Many philosophers have argued that the pursuit of happiness—even Mill's expanded eudaimonic version of the construct—is at least a myopic, if not completely flawed vision of morality. It ignores much of what we view as noble in human behavior—expressions of virtue as well as the many other values that guide people's attempts to do what they perceive as right. Some of these criticisms were made even in Mill's time, and his response is viewed by some philosophers as inadequate. Mill acknowledged that, although virtue is not an intrinsic aspect of hedonistic utilitarianism, it is readily incorporated into the theory to the extent that people who are virtuous behave that way because it pleases them to do so. At least for those folks, then, virtuousness is simply a component of happiness. The reader may recall from chapter 2 that this is essentially Aristotle's position as well. Nevertheless, many view this as an inadequate tautological explanation: i.e., from an initial premise that the pursuit of happiness is the ultimate objective of all behavior, one simply infers inappropriately that anything we do must therefore have been done because it contributes to our happiness.

Early in the 20th century G. E. Moore (1903/1993) gave a more satisfactory answer to this challenge by acknowledging that human beings intuitively recognize the intrinsic value or good of other things like aesthetic beauty, knowledge, and feelings of friendship and love—independent of whatever role they may have in contributing to happiness. His version of *ideal utilitarianism* maintains a utilitarian focus on maximizing the overall good of outcomes, but it permits a wider variety of goods to be included in the calculus. It does little, however, to address another sticky issue for utilitarianism—the need to accurately predict the future in order to compare the consequences associated with each decision option.

The theory of *preference utilitarianism* is similar to the "ideal" version in that it maintains the basic structure of utilitarianism (i.e., the maximization of utility) but sidesteps entirely the definition of what is good. Happiness, virtuous action, loving relationships, the appreciation of beauty—whatever!—can be considered as legitimate preferences for each individual, the relative satisfaction of which is what gets considered in the evaluation of utility. Perhaps more important, preference utilitarianism also obviates the other difficulty for utilitarianism as a system of ethical decision-making: the difficulty in predicting with any certainty or known probability all the consequences of one's potential actions. Therefore, the calculations of the hedonic calculus, whether explicit or implicit, are invariably incomplete and inaccurate when applied to anticipated consequences. In contrast, one's a priori preferences are more readily specified and evaluated; thus, preference utilitarianism is the version most often used by economists in theorizing about political economy (Danley, 1994; cf. Chap. 11) and behavioral economists trying to understand individual choice. But note that both ideal and preference utilitarianism shift the source of effects to be considered from the (relative pleasure) of all those affected by the actions to the (relative preferences) of the actor. This arguably could render the model no longer universalist.[3]

The theory of *welfare utilitarianism* is another variant that considers people's welfare or interests as the basis on which utility should be assessed. Whenever our best interests and conscious preferences coincide there is no difference between those two models. When they do not coincide, the two sets of utility analyses will diverge. Unfortunately, there are many reasons to presume that people's preferences and interests will frequently not be the same, such as when one has

---

3   Although I suppose one could hypothetically try to encompass in the calculus the preferences of all those impacted.

incomplete information about the available options or conflicting motives concerning them. For example, I hope that smoking cigarettes is not high on your list of preferences; it is hardly in your long-term best interests. Similar statements apply re wearing a helmet when riding a motorcycle, or a surgical mask during a deadly pandemic.

These examples bring to mind Mill's classic liberal (in current political parlance, *libertarian,* cf. Chap. 8) statement on the relation between the state and the individual. (Also cf. Box 1.1, Question I.) Recall that this issue seems to arise almost inevitably in the deliberations of many moral philosophers and social thinkers, from Plato to Hobbes, Hegel, Marx and Bertrand Russell. In his essay "On Liberty," Mill expressed his views on personal freedom, independence and autonomy in a utilitarian context: Freedom should be virtually limitless up to the point at which one harms the interests of others. Therefore, at the individual level, self-protection or preventing harm to others is the only justification for interfering with the actions of others. Not even the person's own welfare is a legitimate justification for restricting his or her autonomy. Extrapolating to the state, the only justification for government interference is the prevention of harm to others. This is the classical liberal position regarding civil liberties and provides the basis for the minimal government conceptualization of laissez-faire capitalism. Mill would likely have concluded that we have no ethical right to prevent people from acting against their own interests by smoking cigarettes, not using seat belts in their automobile, a helmet when on their motorcycle, or a mask during a pandemic. (However, the enormous public health costs associated with the long-term effects of smoking, the hospital emergency room treatment of car crash victims and motorcyclists with traumatic brain injury, as well as the millions of flu victims hospitalized in ICUs—and dying—must be weighed in this moral evaluation.)

The Exclusion of Justice, Duties, Rights and Obligations

Other modern criticisms of classical utilitarianism are that it ignores and cannot account for such obvious bases of morality as living up to one's obligations, promises and duties. It betrays this weakness, the criticism holds, because of its teleological nature (i.e., a forward-looking perspective focused on consequences), whereas obligations and promises (e.g., keeping one's word) are what Rachels (1993a) referred to as "backward-looking" (p. 116). Norman (1983) presented the following example:

> Suppose that I have arranged to visit a friend on my bicycle, and have promised my daughter that I will take her with me on the child-seat of the bicycle. As I am about to leave, my son says that he wants to go with me. I cannot take them both. Now suppose that my son and my daughter would equally enjoy going with me, and would be equally disappointed if they

cannot go (and suppose that this is the case, even when we take into account the added disappointment which my daughter will feel as a result of having had her expectation roused). Or suppose that my son will even enjoy it very slightly more than my daughter would. The utilitarian will have to say that if my son would enjoy it even more, I ought to take him; and that if they would both enjoy it equally, it would be equally right for me to take either my son or my daughter. To say this, however, is to deny all significance to what is, in fact, the crucial difference between the two alternatives, the fact that I have made a promise to my daughter, but not to my son. In virtue of that fact it is clear that, even though the consequences might be just as good in either case, I ought to take my daughter. This shows that there is a duty to keep one's promises, quite apart from utilitarian considerations. (p. 134)

Although this criticism may be apropos of classical utilitarianism, it can be rebutted successfully if we think in terms of some combination of ideal and preference utilitarianism, in which one's intentions to live up to one's obligations, responsibilities, and commitments are represented in the utilitarian equation. The satisfaction or fulfillment of those intentions may be included among the benefits, or goods that contribute to one's sense of well-being. All else being equal, Norman will feel better and more righteous if he takes his daughter.

Similar arguments against utilitarianism have been made with respect to the concepts of justice and individual rights. Suppose I am an organizational consultant conducting individual and group on-site interviews with employees of a large department store in connection with the development of an overall competency model for the store. Suppose that during the few days that I spent meeting with people in a particular department, some merchandise was stolen from that area in a manner that could only have been accomplished by some employee. The store is owned by a parent corporation located in another city and they just announced that if the culprit is not identified within two days it will take retributive action against all eight employees who work in that department.

Suppose I have an idea who the likely culprit is. Shouldn't I, if I am a consequentialist, identify that person in order to prevent adverse consequences to all innocent employees? It seems defensible in utilitarian terms. My target will be harmed, but they will probably just lose their job; there won't be enough proof for a criminal charge. And there will be a great deal of offsetting benefit done, likely saving the jobs of seven innocent employees.

Clearly, my behaving as suggested would be wrong. Most people have no difficulty recognizing immediately that I will have violated a moral right of the accused, which would be unjust. In deontological terms, I will have intentionally wronged (as well as harmed) this person, so the utilitarian analysis therefore cannot be correct. This is the sort of argument that is used to illustrate the presumed weakness of utilitarianism in failing to account for values such as rights and justice.[4]

There are two related but distinct criticisms being subsumed in this illustration, and they lead to two more modifications of classical utilitarianism. The first criticism is that because utilitarianism emphasizes the greatest (i.e., aggregate) good for all concerned it ignores potentially relevant distinctions among people. In other words, it doesn't matter who benefits or who is harmed. The classical theory does not deal with the notion that people may differ in the extent to which they deserve the outcomes in question. A research psychologist may decide that the likely aggregate scientific and educational benefits of a research study outweigh the possible harm resulting from deceiving participants about a noxious or emotionally stressful experimental manipulation to be employed. But the benefits accrue to the researcher (and perhaps to society), whereas the harms are visited on only the research participants.

Focusing on the overall level of happiness or well-being also ignores instances in which the injustice has more to do with some people benefitting unjustifiably more than others. This becomes an extremely important consideration when the analysis is elevated to the institutional or societal level. For example, some people have characterized the past few decades as a time of unparalleled economic success for the United States because of the steady growth in *overall* (or average) wealth and earnings. But others point to increasing and unjustifiable *discrepancies* in wealth between the very few fabulously wealthy families on one extreme and the persistently large proportion of very poor, including working poor families, at the other extreme, whose earning power in constant dollars has actually declined over the past generation or so. As will be discussed in chapters 8 and 11, a focus on maximizing the production of aggregate wealth or on issues of its equitable distribution mark two divergent models of political economy with significant social and moral implications for business and its relation to the rest of society and government.

This criticism has led to a transformation in our understanding of the nature of the universalist tradition from its original characterization in classical utilitarianism. In chapter 2's discussion of egoism versus universalism the point was made, following the utilitarian Peter Singer (2011), that a moral perspective does not require treating everyone equally, but that everyone's interests—their rights and freedoms—should be given equal consideration. The quotation from

---

4   Do not get hung up on the extremely unlikely nature of the scenario and the important aspects of the situation that I am not considering, such as the effect of this action on my continuing relationship with this client and its employees, possible actions on the part of the employees, and whether this is a client I want to work with. It is not meant to be a realistic case; I'm trying to illustrate a point. Philosophers (and decision scientists as well as economists) are fond of posing such scenarios under *closed-world assumptions*—i.e., only the facts as given are to be considered.

Rachels and Rachels (2015) bears repeating: "We can justify treating people differently only if we can show that there is some factual difference between them that is relevant to justifying differences in treatment" (p. 79). So, it is simply not true that modern utilitarianism overlooks deserved distinctions among people; it emphasizes the need for a moral justification of those distinctions.

The second criticism implicit in the (unrealistic) store theft illustration is that utilitarianism putatively condones or even requires on occasion that we lie, cheat, steal or engage in other obviously immoral acts if the balance of good over bad consequences is notable. The aspect of Bentham's classical utility theory that renders it susceptible to this criticism is that it is an *act utilitarianism*. That is, it presupposes that the hedonic calculus is applied, even if implicitly, to each contemplated action with moral implications. Mill's response to this criticism involves his conceptualization of "secondary principles" noted earlier. I mentioned this notion previously in the context of Mill's acknowledgment that much of utilitarian ethical reasoning is likely to take place only intuitively and implicitly, using general guidelines, rather than by means of an explicit analysis of each specific situation. According to Mill, these guidelines are developed inductively by a society and learned by its members as part of their culture based on the primary principle of utility. We have learned collectively, for example, that lying is generally likely to have more harmful than beneficial consequences and respecting other people's property is generally likely to yield more positive than negative repercussions. In the language of modern computer software, these secondary principles become ethical "default options," to which exceptions may be applied if and when they are clearly warranted.

Moreover, that is a simplistic and unfair criticism of utilitarianism, as noted by perhaps the best-known contemporary utilitarian:

> breaking moral rules ... seriously harming an innocent person will almost always have worse consequences than following these rules. Even thoroughgoing utilitarians ... are wary of speculative reasoning that suggests we should violate basic human rights today for the sake of some distant future good.
>
> *(Singer, 2015, p. 9–10)*

Similarly, "killing a smaller number of people to avoid killing a greater number of people based on numbers alone is unethical because it disrespects the humanity of the individuals in the smaller-numbered group" (Scharding, 2020, p. 450).

Mill's invocation of secondary principles brings his version of the classical theory close to a *rule utilitarianism* in which the general utilitarian rules are employed as guidelines by which to judge the ethicality of actions. A rule utilitarian will apply an implicit utilitarian analysis to generalized moral principles rather than to the actions possible in a particular situation.[5] It is viewed frequently as a more relevant approach than the original act-based theory (Knapp, 1999), and the two approaches may lead to different ethical conclusions about the same situation (Fritzsche & Becker, 1984). If two or more secondary principles that produce equal aggregate benefit, or are equally preferred, are in conflict (e.g., being truthful to participants in our psychological research and conducting the research in a fashion that will yield unambiguously interpretable findings)—but abiding by the former will preclude the latter—then recourse to the primary principle of act utility and its calculations is called for in this particular situation.[6]

Adding to the Framework for Ethical Decision Making

The brief survey of prominent normative ethical theories presented in this chapter and the previous one suggests that we add the following considerations to the framework begun at the end of chapter 2.

7. Neither deontological nor utilitarian approaches emerge unscathed and intact from analyses by their critics, so we should accept both the principled expressions of rights, duties, justice (and virtues—see Chap. 5), as well as analyses of consequences, as legitimate for ethical consideration. Some ethical dilemmas seem to be more amenable to analysis by one or the other of these paradigms, so we are best served by keeping all doors open. In some situations, right or wrong seems to be a more appropriate and/or salient criterion than the extent of benefit or harm to those involved; for some other situations, the opposite seems to hold. This is consonant with a conclusion reached by White (1993) in the business context: "Although these two outlooks conflict in theory, they complement one another in practice. In the pragmatic challenge of identifying and resolving ethical dilemmas, neither should be ignored; each acts as a check on the limitation of the other" (p.11). And "more generally, different modes of decision-making can be seen as adaptations to particular environments" (Bennis et al., 2010, p. 187).

I am indebted to Cohen (2000) for calling attention to a relatively mundane dilemma that provides a good example of a situation that may be viewed deontologically or as a consequentialist, with a different conclusion resulting from

5   There is considerable disagreement among philosophers over whether Mill is truly a rule utilitarian. (The term was coined long after his death.) The secondary principles appear to indicate that he is, but his acknowledgment of possible exceptions to the rules seems to place him back in the act-utilitarian camp. There has also been a sizable debate concerning whether strict rule utilitarianism—adherence to general principles—is even utilitarianism at all, as it does not involve an assessment of utility for the situation.

6   It is debatable, however, whether the two principles are actually of equal value—that is, are likely to produce the same overall amount of benefit—or are of equal preferential interest to all researchers.

each. How many times have you attended a sporting event or the theater and during intermission or a break in the action moved from your inexpensive seat to a more expensive seat with a better view? Viewed deontologically, it is clearly wrong. You did not pay for the seat. Some might even consider it theft of service. But, from a consequentialist perspective, no one is harmed. In some venues this practice may even have the status of a normative tradition. (I'm assuming that you have accomplished this migration discretely and politely, without disturbing other patrons or performers, and are prepared to graciously surrender your seats to their rightful occupants should they show up late.) If the same action can be viewed as unethical within one of the two normative moral traditions and acceptable by the other, it stands to reason that we ought to be familiar with and able to reason with both of them.

8. Our initial predilections or gut reactions may be unreliable indicators of what is the correct ethical choice.[7] It is sometimes assumed, extrapolating from Kant, that doing the right thing will invariably be experienced as painful, necessitating a struggle against our more selfish interests. That is not necessarily the case. The assumption underestimates the extent to which most of us have introjected society's values—at least as ideals for which to strive. Therefore, sometimes there is no marked conflict between our inclinations and doing the right thing. And the converse is also true. Our conscience is not an infallible indicator of unethical choices to be avoided. In the first place, there is great inter-individual variability in the voice of conscience. Moreover, it is unfortunately true that human beings have an almost unlimited capacity for guilt and anxiety. Some of us, due to the nature of our primary socialization, have grown up with overly restrictive superegos that are not to be entirely trusted as objective moral barometers. As Russell (1987) pointed out, the study of the unconscious has revealed the often-mundane causes of our pangs of conscience; and the emotion of *regret* is a common reaction to decision-making (McCormack et al., 2020). So, what should we do? Which of our reactions are to be trusted? The answer is to return to the advice offered in chapter 2: ethical reasoning. One will always be on surer footing if one can articulate the rationale for one's choices and actions and subject them to impartial scrutiny.

9. A few core values appear to underlie many different normative ethical theories and, therefore, seem worthy of our allegiance. The first two were introduced in chapter 2.

---

7   Although in recent years, through the work of Jonathon Haidt and his colleagues, a perspective emphasizing human morality's dependence on innate, emotional moral intuitions has gained prominence (cf. Chaps. 5 & 6). Chapter 15 also considers the challenge to normative ethical decision-making posed by intuitive "biases and heuristics"—our *bounded awareness* and *bounded ethicality*.

a. *Universalizability* or consistency of judgment. One of the hallmarks of an appropriate ethical decision is that it remains appropriate in the same situation, irrespective of who the actor is, or for the same person in a recurrence of the same situation.

b. *Universalism*: Each person's interests are morally equivalent to everyone else's (unless there is some morally relevant factual basis for treating people differently). As noted in chapter 2, I have rejected the perspective of unqualified ethical egoism in which one's own interests count as more important than the interests of others in one's ethical deliberations. This is reflected in both the universalist utilitarian position that everyone's interests are equal as well as in the deontological concern for fairness, impartiality and justice.

However, there is an unresolved difficulty with this value that needs to be illuminated. Such impartial treatment assumes an impersonality that most of us do not possess or, in many instances, even desire. For example, people will generally not find it at all mystifying or necessarily inappropriate if one cares more about one's own interests than for the interests of others (rational egoism) or if you care more for your family than you do for almost anyone else. As a pragmatic matter we can expect a declining degree of concern as one considers the well-being of one's own family and friends to that of neighbors, colleagues and acquaintances, to that of strangers of the same nationality, to strangers in some distant land, and so forth. Prior to our era of rapid travel around the world, instantaneous global communications, and international connectedness of political and economic institutions, this gradient of (un)concern could be attributed entirely to a combination of ignorance and ineffectualness:

> All men [sic], even those at the greatest distance, are no doubt entitled to our good wishes, and our good wishes we naturally give them. But if, notwithstanding, they should be unfortunate, to give ourselves any anxiety upon that account seems to be no part of our duty. That we should be but little interested, therefore, in the fortune of those whom we can neither serve nor hurt, and who are in every respect so very remote from us, seems wisely ordered by Nature … .
>
> *(Adam Smith, cited in Barry, 1989. p. 5)*

But we now recognize that social relations and social identity are emotionally salient considerations that lead to a declining sense of responsibility and obligation to those further removed from our core identities, irrespective of physical distance. We grow up caring more for those close to us emotionally. Nevertheless, one must acknowledge a potentially slippery slope in this regard. It is not a very far slide from the modestly distasteful practice of nepotism to a host of even more repugnant "isms"—chauvinism, sexism, ageism. ethnocentrism and racism.

I do not believe that there is any fully satisfactory resolution to the incompatible values of impersonal universalism (fairness as impartiality) and personal commitment, duty or obligation based on individual social relations. Situations in which they conflict are likely to be uncomfortable. As stated earlier in chapter 2, "as psychologists we know that most behavior is multiply determined, and we should bear in mind that moral dilemmas can be complicated and stressful, with several competing motives." Moreover, an important point made by psychologist Carol Gilligan is that the motive of interpersonal caring is not outside the domain of morality but should be viewed as another dimension of it, along with the principle of justice. Writing in his newspaper column "The Ethicist," in the aftermath of the destruction of the World Trade Center in New York, Cohen (2001) reflected:

> We are not solitary. We live among others, and we rely on them—on strangers—for society to function, for any kind of life to be possible. Honesty demands that we acknowledge this; ethics demands that we act upon it. As we mature, both physically and morally, we are able to see beyond ourselves and embrace the concerns of a widening circle—family, friends, community and further. No one may be forced to live for others—to donate an organ, for example, let alone a life. But each of us must see the reciprocal ties we rely on every day. Passivity in the face of the current calamity not only weakens these essential communal bonds; it also diminishes our own humanity. (p. 30)

c. *Limited liberty.* The essence of ethics and morality is the right treatment of others, and the overarching principle is that people are to be treated with maximum respect, meaning that our own motives and intentions cannot ethically be realized at the cost of violating the dignity, autonomy or legitimate objectives of others. Whatever moral or political rights or liberties we envision ourselves as possessing are enjoyed equally by others.

d. *The right to flourish.* The attainment of a worthwhile personal identity, social recognition and rewarding personal relationships, as well as the opportunity to engage in meaningful and rewarding work, appear to be extremely widespread if not universal meta-objectives of people that should be facilitated and promoted. I will argue later (in Chap. 8) that, as psychologists, we are especially obligated to take a proactive stance promoting this value and the previous one, not merely be alert for possible barriers. Moreover, the observation that people differ in the strength of their inclinations to fulfill these objectives is of no moral significance with respect to our obligation to promote the availability of conditions enabling their attainment.

10. Ethics is inevitably political. "Ethical beliefs, throughout recorded history, have had two very different sources, one political, the other concerned with personal religious and moral convictions" (Russell, 1987, p. 89). The focus of ethics is on the processes whereby interpersonal relations are most appropriately regulated and controlled for the benefit of all concerned, from the microlevel of individual face-to-face interactions to institutional, governmental and international relations. These activities are conditioned by explicit rules, regulations, policies, laws and agreements, and by implicit values, customs, norms and social contracts—all of which serve to specify the appropriate distribution of expected power relations among individuals and between individuals and organizations. It is in that sense that ethics is political.

11. To the extent that loyally fulfilling one's duties and responsibilities to one's employer is a justifiable ethical requirement, it is contingent on the corresponding ethical behavior of the employer in furthering and not thwarting the legitimate interests of all those who are affected by its actions. Of particular concern to I-O psychologists is the considerable power wielded by business organizations to impact people's economic, social and emotional well-being, along with people's rightful expectations that employers behave responsibly in the exercise of that power.

5

NORMATIVE ETHICAL THEORIES: III. VIRTUE ETHICS

> Being ethical is primarily a matter of being a person of good character, with virtues, emotions, values, and practical intelligence to match … . Ethical progress is a matter of refining and adjusting these values, learning to bring them to bear in making decisions, and protecting them from hostile environments.
> —Edwin M. Hartman

Comparing Rules Versus Consequences, and The Re-Emergence of Virtue Ethics

The preceding chapters have barely hinted at the considerable variety of thought that has characterized moral philosophy over the past few millennia. And much of that thinking has taken the form of pervasive disagreements between competing perspectives: subjectivist versus objectivist, egoist versus universalist, and absolutist versus relativist assumptions; normative theories that are deontological (duty or rule-based) versus those that are consequentialist (outcome-based)—to say nothing about sharp disagreements among philosophers within each of the deontological and consequentialist camps. The epigraph from Hartman (2008) emanates from a third normative perspective, virtue ethics, that is responsive to the putative weaknesses of the first two. As is apparent even in that short quote, this perspective focuses on intra-psychic constructs like values and character. In other words, the emphasis is not only on taking ethical action (and deciding what that should be), but also on being an ethical person.

Comparing Rules versus Consequences

As discussed in the preceding chapters, there are many instances in which particular versions of the deontological and consequentialist modes of thought appear to be

DOI: 10.4324/9781003212577-6

almost indistinguishable, such as when a Kantian assessment of whether a maxim is universalizable seems to rest on implicit utilitarian analyses of its consequences, or when a utilitarian incorporates adherence to duty in the hedonic calculus as a source of preference satisfaction or happiness. The conceptual and pragmatic difficulties experienced by rule deontologists led to modifications that entail (act-based) individual evaluations of the applicability of a general moral rule in a particular situation. Conversely, analogous difficulties experienced by act-utilitarians resulted in the development of (rule-based) general guidelines concerning the anticipated consequences of various actions, obviating the need for situation-specific calculations.

Act-deontological theory is a position that was developed in response to major criticisms of the traditional *rule-deontological* theories. And the *rule-utilitarian* model evolved to meet significant criticisms of the classical *act-utilitarian* model. Theoretically, the dialectic modifications should have worked better for the deontologists than for the consequentialists because an absolute adherence to rules is not an easily defended ethical position, irrespective of context. However, act deontology is not a very popular position—perhaps for psychological reasons. People who are most comfortable with an absolutist principled view may be less disposed to accept the uncertainties of taking into account the particulars of the situation.

Present-day moralists who are uncomfortable with the indefiniteness of act-based ethical analyses often refer to them derisively as *situational ethics* or as exercises in mere expediency. Presumably, the terms are meant to indicate an unprincipled or amoral attitude, which of course is not justified (Fletcher, 1966). These moralists, however, rarely acknowledge in their public admonishments the theoretical inconsistencies and pragmatic difficulties of attempts to adhere to absolutist principles.

Numerous instances can be found of ethical disagreements between those adopting consequentialist positions and those advocating essentially deontological positions. Some of these disagreements are even played out in the political arena. For example, critics of environmental policy in the United States are skeptical of many existing environmental regulations on the basis of their cost-effectiveness. According to these folks cost–benefit analyses indicate that some regulations are astronomically expensive, hence unjustifiable and inappropriate.[1] Conversely, adopting a more deontological point of view,

---

1 Frequently glossed over, however, are the difficulties inherent in trying to quantify some costs and effects—problems in what I have called the *ethimetrics* of the analyses. For example, in evaluating certain Environmental Protection Agency regulations there is a dispute regarding whether one should determine the cost of a regulation per each life saved or for the total years of life saved. The different units of analysis yield very different estimates of program value, hence ethicality (the latter metric "weights" the lives of young people more, and older people less; and yields higher estimates of overall benefits to be had per unit of cost). To my knowledge, utilitarian analyses also generally neglect to factor in *opportunity costs*—the net value of the best alternative not chosen (Greenberg & Spiller, 2015).

the Supreme Court recently upheld a prohibition in the Clean Air Act and other environmental legislation that expressly forbids federal agencies from considering costs as a factor in their decision making, directing that the agencies seek to do everything feasible to protect human health.

(Jehl, 2001, p. 28)

An interesting interplay of deontological rules and utilitarian consequences is offered by *the problem of dirty hands* (Coady, 2009; Walzer, 2006) because it is subject to alternative moral analyses. The problem was first posed in the context of large-scale political action by governments in situations of extreme emergency. "Should political leaders violate the deepest constraints of morality in order to achieve great goods or avoid disasters for their communities?" (Coady, p. 1). Coady goes on to paraphrase an assertion by Walzer:

> An appeal to 'supreme emergency' could not only explain but justify the Allied terror bombing of German cities in the early stages of World War II … . For these early stages … the deliberate massacre of thousands of German non-combatants was required by supreme emergency, even though it was gravely immoral. The prospect and likelihood of a Nazi victory were so dire for the lives and communal values of those facing defeat that the price of severe immorality was worth paying. In the subsequent conduct of the war … the city bombings were simply immoral (as were the city bombings of Japan, including the atomic attacks on Hiroshima and Nagasaki) and could not be justified by supreme emergency. (p. 3)

How is the "dirty hands" situation to be understood? There are at least three possibilities: (a) pragmatic considerations occasioned by dire exigencies might justify ignoring moral principles; (b) although deontological rights may trump utilitarian thinking in ordinary circumstances, even a great *wrong* might be justified in order to avoid cataclysmic *harm*; or (c) rather specific moral principles associated with a particular role (e.g., parents' responsibilities concerning their children; fiduciary duties of managers to company shareholders, of lawyers to clients, of psychologists to their experimental research participants) can be thought to override more general obligations and rights.[2] The problem of dirty hands remains rather contentious among moral philosophers.

---

2   A well-known example of this is the legal precedent (established by the *Tarasoff* case) from which it is now understood that psychologists (among others) have an affirmative duty to violate a client's privacy and confidentiality in order to prevent possible imminent harm to another or oneself (cf. APA Code, Standard 4.05(b)).

The Re-Emergence of Virtue Ethics

As noted above, partisan moral philosophers—depending on their orientation—have long been engaged in pointing out the deficiencies of deontological *or* consequentialist thought. In the last 50 years or so, some philosophers (and, as we shall consider, social scientists as well as organization and management scholars) have expressed dissatisfaction with *both* deontological and utilitarian perspectives because they seem to overlook the person. Now it just so happens that this re-emergence corresponded roughly with a resurgence in the study and rigorous measurement of personality in psychology, and in I-O psychology in particular (cf. Judge & Zapata, 2015). I refer, of course, to the identification of the "big five" personality constructs. It has not been lost on moral philosophers and psychologists that these personality attributes have relevance for understanding the nature of social-moral behavior in human beings:

> Humans have evolved to note variations in these kinds of [social] traits, for these variations have important bearing on adaptation to group life ... . Human beings have been designed by natural selection to detect differences in others with respect to such qualities as how sociable and dominant a person is (*extraversion*), the extent to which a person is caring and cooperative (*agreeableness*), a person's characteristic level of dependability and industrious-ness (*conscientiousness*), level of emotional stability and dysfunction in other people (*neuroticism*), and the extent to which a person may be cognitively flexible or rigid in facing a range of adaptive problems (*openness to experience*).
> *(McAdams, 2009, p. 14)*

In other words, the argument that the critics have is with the notion of ethics as consisting of following moral principles, whether of the deontological or utilitarian variety. The renewed questioning was begun by Anscombe (1958), who resurrected the potential importance of *virtue* as a "third way," so to speak. Yet she admitted that

> the proof that an unjust man is a bad man would require a positive account of justice as a 'virtue.' This part of the subject-matter of ethics is, however, completely closed to us until we have an account of what type of characteristic a virtue is—a problem, not of ethics, but of conceptual analysis. (pp. 4–5)

And so such analyses commenced and have continued until the present, with the influential work of Alasdair MacIntyre (2007), first published in 1981, worth noting. One of the reasons for our considering the topic is that it has become rather popular, in one version or another, in the domains of business ethics and moral psychology, as presented below.

Conceptions of Virtue

Virtue theory responds to a perceived overemphasis in modern western ethical theories on right actions and on the efficacy of ethical reasoning—to the putative exclusion of the moral character of the actor. "It is a deep fault of non-virtue theories that they pay little or no attention to the areas of life which form character" (Pence, 1993, p. 257). By its inclusion the ethical question shifts from a focus on "What shall I do?" to include "Who shall I be?" (Jordan & Meara, 1990). This is not new: recall that for Aristotle and the ancient Greeks the study of ethics had only secondarily to do with questions concerning "what is the right thing to do?" and more to do with "what is the right kind of person to be?" or "what does it mean to be 'good' or 'just'?" Thus, they focused on human nature with particular reference to the so-called virtues (and vices)—i.e., the moral portion of what personality psychologists generally refer to as *character*.[3] They enumerated many virtues, the essence of which could presumably be subsumed by the four cardinal virtues of prudence, temperance, justice and courage (or fortitude). Christian moral theology has added to these natural virtues the theological virtues of faith, hope, charity (or love) and obedience.

Another interesting perspective from virtue theory has to do with a reversal of subject and object. That is, it does not focus on the implied question "What kind of person am I?" but on "What kind of person are you?" Uhlmann et al. (2015) emphasize that we are motivated to evaluate the character of others, and that

> there is growing evidence that when it comes to moral judgment, human beings appear to be best characterized not as intuitive deontologists or consequentialists but as intuitive virtue theorists: individuals who view acts as a rich set of signals about the moral qualities of an agent and not as the endpoint of moral judgment. (p. 73)

In the next chapter I will define character as referring to relatively stable dispositional aspects of personality that account for relatively consistent attitudes and behavioral tendencies across a variety of circumstances. Because of the social nature of morality, it has been observed that it is not enough for one to simply espouse a moral principle on occasion. People with whom we are engaged need to be assured that we truly hold those principles: that is, that we believe them to be correct and right and can be counted on to behave accordingly (Nozick, 1993). Character is the aspect of personality that provides that reassurance, but not all aspects of the character are moral in nature. For example, among the four

---

3   Virtues and vices are generally not opposites; more frequently a virtue represents a middle ground on a continuum anchored by vices on each end. For example, the virtue of being financially prudent lies between irresponsible profligate spending and dysfunctional miserliness.

cardinal virtues only one is unambiguously moral in nature, as is only one of the Christian virtues.

Although religious moralists frequently express their theology in such terms, there is nothing inherently religious about virtue theory. And it seems that the virtues extolled in a conservative religious context by some very vocal proponents are often limited to those having to do with authority and control—such as obedience, politeness, sexual abstinence or fidelity, loyalty and honesty; as opposed to those having to do with beneficence or altruism—such as compassion, kindness, generosity, helpfulness, considerateness and sympathy (cf. Blum, 1987).

The attributes of character that are moral relate to values and behavior concerning justice and welfare, the two traditional irreducible dimensions of morality (Boyd, 1994; Frankena, 1973). Just as values may be thought of as either personal or social in nature, so too are the virtues that relate to them. According to this conception, personal virtues like industriousness, thrift, perseverance, sobriety, and so on have few moral implications. They are what Hume (1978) referred to as *selfish virtues*. They are virtues insofar as they are useful or valuable attributes to their possessor. But "it is only when we are motivated by sentiments favoring our fellow human beings that we enter the realm of morality" (Arrington, 1998, p. 252). The moral virtues, therefore, are comprised of attributes such as generosity, honesty, and integrity—by which I mean adhering consistently to principles of justice and caring despite countervailing pressures. Hume, who wrote a great deal about virtue, was (unlike Rand, 1964) adamant that these are not at all antagonistic to self-interest. He held that acting on these sentiments is in fact more gratifying than the sort of satisfaction derived from accomplishing purely selfish aims.

Admittedly, one of the problems for virtue theory is specifying just what qualifies as a "virtue." MacIntyre (2007) notes "a startling number of differences and incompatibilities" (p. 183) among the virtues offered by Homer, Sophocles, Aristotle, the New Testament, medieval thinkers and Benjamin Franklin, as well as contemporary Western, Eastern and Native American cultures. (Moreover, he notes, they represent at least three different underlying conceptions of a virtue.)[4] Rachels and Rachels (2015) offer a partial list of two dozen attributes; *Forbes* magazine (1996) lists 19; Haidt and Joseph (2004) offer 11; Comte-Sponville (2001) suggests 18; Gini and Green (2013) offer ten—just regarding leadership. From a psychological perspective, Peterson and Seligman (2004) offer six broadband virtues—but those are comprised of 24 subordinate "character strengths,"

---

4 He goes on, however, to develop a "core conception of the virtues which might make a claim for universal allegiance" (p. 186). To both oversimplify and translate into psychological language, a virtue is something the exercise of which produces intrinsic rewards in the process of striving for excellence in some realm of cooperative human activity, referred to as a *practice*. Striving for extrinsic rewards (e.g., money, status) is not virtuous.

many of which also would be labeled as virtues by other scholars. One business coach lists more than 650 (Goodman, 2009)! Sadler-Smith (2012) presented "a comparison of selected systems of virtues from a variety of historical, philosophical, scientific, and cultural traditions" that he believes reveal a similarity across different social settings. It is included here in Table 5.1.

The virtues are all high in what psychologists refer to as *social desirability* (e.g., courage, dependability, fairness, tactfulness, self-reliance, etc.).[5] Accordingly, Rachels and Rachels define a virtue as "a *commendable* trait of character manifested in habitual action" or "*a trait of character, manifested in habitual action, that is good for anyone to have*" (p. 161, emphases in the original). Similarly,

> Virtues are characteristics of a person that are morally praiseworthy ... . Virtues are social skills. To possess a virtue is to have disciplined one's faculties so they are fully and properly responsive to one's local sociomoral context ... . A virtuous person is one who has the proper automatic reactions to ethically relevant events and states of affairs, for example another person's suffering, an unfair distribution of a good, a dangerous but necessary mission.
>
> *(Haidt & Joseph, 2004)*

The reason that any virtue is good or commendable is because, as emphasized by Aristotle, it contributes to a life of eudaimonia, or "flourishing"—the good and satisfying life (cf. Chap. 2). And moral theories focusing on leading a good life—as understood in that way—are referred to as *aretaic* (from the Greek *aretai*, meaning "virtue" or "excellence"), so that we now have three families of normative moral theories: deontological, consequentialist and aretaic.

The relatively new field of *positive psychology* takes such flourishing or happiness as an orienting feature, and the antecedents, consequences and nature of *well-being* (hedonic/subjective satisfaction as well as Eudaimonia) has become a topic of interest in organizational psychology (Sonnentag, 2015). A potentially important finding is that several interventions were found to increase happiness and decrease depressive symptoms over a six-month duration (Seligman et al., 2005). But contrary to Aristotle's assumption, virtuousness may not universally lead to happiness: the effect is conditional on living in a culture that values and respects such action (Stavrova et al., 2013).

---

5 Sadler-Smith enumerated the intuitive "moral modules" indicated by Haidt and Joseph (2004) that "undergird the moral systems that cultures develop" (p. 56) such as the virtues; they did not refer to the virtues themselves. So for example, the (noxious) intuitive ethic module of *suffering* enables the development of the positive moral virtues of kindness and compassion (cf. Table 6.3).

TABLE 5.1 Some Groupings of Virtues and Values

PHILOSOPHICAL Moral Virtues (Aristotle, 1953/2004)	SPIRITUAL Buddhist Eightfold Path (Goenka, 1993)	BIOLOGICAL Moral Modules (Haidt & Joseph, 2004)	PSYCHOLOGICAL Virtue Clusters (Seligman, 2002)	ORGANIZATIONAL Organizational Moral Values (Scott, 2002)	ENVIRONMENTAL Environmental Virtues (van Wensveen, 2005)
Courage	Wisdom: right view and intention	Suffering	Wisdom and knowledge	Organizational justice	Care
Temperance		Hierarchy	Courage	Honest organizational communication	Respect
Liberality		Reciprocity	Humanity and love	Respect for property	Love
Magnificence		Purity	Justice	Respect for life	Compassion
Magnanimity	Ethical conduct: right speech, action and livelihood	Affiliation	Temperance	Respect for religion	Reverence
Proper ambition			Transcendence		Humility
Patience					Creativity
Truthfulness					Hope
Wittiness	Mental development: right effort, mindfulness and concentration				Sensitivity
Friendliness					
Modesty					
Righteous indignation					

Source: Adapted from Sadler-Smith, E. (2012). Before virtue: Biology, brain, behavior, and the "moral sense." *Business Ethics Quarterly*, 22(2), 351–376. Used by permission.

Shafer-Landau (2015) adds that virtue must be learned from experience and that

> Virtues require wisdom about what is important, and why … . In addition
> to routinely acting well, the virtuous person also has a distinctive set of
> perceptions, thoughts, and motives … . Virtuous people are therefore
> defined not just by their deeds, but also by their inner life … . They see
> what's important, know what is right and why it is right, and want to do
> things because they are right. (pp. 260–261)

In other words, moral motivation is critical.[6] Similarly, focusing on the development of virtuousness over time, Weaver (2006) adds "each act performed by a
person is held to contribute to the further development or undermining of that
person's virtue. Thus virtue theories focus on the actor's dispositions and development" (p. 342). Sison and Ferrero (2015) are very concerned with drawing
a distinction between virtue (internal; characterological) and virtuousness (externally verifiable actions).

Also essential to most modern conceptions of ethics (although originating with
Aristotle) is the notion of "practical wisdom" as a kind of meta-virtue that accounts for the so-called unity of the virtues (Tiberius, 2015, p. 110). Similarly,
Melé (2009) observed that "Among human virtues, practical wisdom is particularly important. This virtue helps practical rationality to identify what is good
in each situation" (p. 239). That is also what Shafer-Landau has in mind in the
above quotation when he emphasizes that "virtues require wisdom about what is
important, and why … .," and what Weaver acknowledges in focusing on the
cumulative "development or undermining" of one's virtue. But such putative
"unity" goes to the heart of a critical issue in personality psychology: the degree
to which individual personality/character traits (including the virtues) are manifested consistently across differing situations. We'll return to this issue shortly.

Further clarification is offered by Audi (2012), who suggests that a virtue may
be viewed as having several dimensions:[7]

- *The Domain of Action.* The situation or context to which the virtue in question is
  relevant. The virtue could be very broad (a *comprehensive virtue*)—applicable to
  many areas of human activity (e.g., beneficence)—or more restricted (e.g., a *role-
  specific virtue* such as a salesperson's honesty with clients).
- *The Objective.* Who/what is the aim of the virtuous behavior and/or who are
  its beneficiaries? There are, in fact, virtues that appear to benefit primarily
  oneself—e.g., thrift, diligence, perseverance—and because of that some
  would doubt their claim to virtuousness.

---

6 That is why virtue theorists would not consider a terrorist to be brave or courageous
   despite being willing to die for his ideals in the process of murdering innocents.
7 With apologies to that author I have changed the names of some dimensions and
   collapsed his six into four.

- *Instrumental Knowledge.* The understanding needed in order to express the virtuous behavior successfully. This may be "technical" in nature, such as having learned how to be an effective, just and considerate leader, and it might invoke broad abilities such as "social intelligence."
- *Motivational Grounding.* Virtuous behavior is driven by the intention to be virtuous—an expression of moral character; it is not merely in conformance with action that happens to seem virtuous. This sounds similar to but is the opposite of Kant's admonition that a moral act must be motivated by a sense of duty rather than by our self-serving inclinations, and not simply be in accord with that sense of duty. To be virtuous the behavior in question must be in accord with one's (virtuous) inclinations, not merely with an extrinsic moral principle or rule like a duty.

Alzola (2015) seems to agree with Audi. He describes two conflicting conceptions of what a virtue is, one of which he argues is far superior to the other. The one he disapproves of, and characterizes as *reductive*, is the one used most frequently by psychologists who study virtue and the good life, and by some philosophers as well. A popular contemporary example comes from *positive psychology* (Peterson & Seligman, 2004), and derives from trait psychology, emphasizing the interplay of relatively stable, long-term dispositions (i.e., traits) and the manifestation of consistent actions based on those inclinations as the components of a virtue. One of the problems he finds with this approach is that the moral dispositions are defined in terms of tendencies to act in accord with moral rules (e.g., generosity). In other words, a presumably aretaic theory is actually based inappropriately on deontological or consequentialist principles. He also criticizes the empirical emphasis on the behavioral expressions of the virtuous dispositions, rather than on the virtues themselves:

> the reductive account blurs the very important distinction between character attribution and the evaluation of actions, that is, between the possession of a virtue and an action in conformity with virtue … . Acts that are merely in conformity with virtue may qualify as instances of what [some call] 'virtuousness' …, but they are not genuinely virtuous. For only actions from virtue bespeak a feature of good character. (pp. 300, 301)

For example, the taxonomy used in positive psychology consists of only six virtues (e.g., wisdom; courage), and "these relatively abstract virtues are differentiated from [24] *character strengths*, which are the observable traits manifest in cross-situationally consistent behavior" (Shryack et al., 2010). But the behaviors (indicators of virtuousness) are what get studied, not the virtues themselves.

Alzola views as far superior what he believes to be a more comprehensive, *non-reductive* conceptualization of virtue that he refers to as "real virtue." It is "comprehensive," he asserts, because it is comprised of four separate (albeit interrelated) elements. Using the virtue of justice as an example: it has *intellectual* and *emotional* components—knowledge and beliefs about what is fair and just; a *motivational* disposition to be fair, and for the right reasons; as well as a *behavioral* component indicating that the person typically acts so as to be fair and avoids making unjust decisions. All four must be present:

> A non-reductive account holds that a virtue is not a disposition to behave in accordance with certain rules of action. For an action to be from a state of virtue—for an action to bespeak a mark of good character—it must be expressive of appropriate inner states. The reductive account reduces virtue to its behavioral aspects, thereby neglecting this inner dimension. Virtue ethicists, on the contrary, highlight the understanding of virtue as … integrating the cognitive, the emotional, and the motivational components of virtue … . When we praise a truly virtuous action we do not simply value a reliable tendency to perform the action. Rather, what we value is the state of character that the person displays in his or her action. (Alzola, 2015, p. 301)

The Disposition versus Context Issue

From the foregoing definitions and conceptualizations of virtue, we learn that it is generally thought of as something akin to a relatively stable (albeit modifiable), unitary or comprehensive composite: "virtue is held to require a degree of narrative unity … or continuity … in the life of an individual, a purposeful quest for the good" (Weaver, 2006, p. 344). And some empirical support is had by the observation that personality traits appear to be relatively stable (correlations of moderate effect-size) in childhood through middle-age (Caspi et al., 2005; McAdams & Pal, 2006) and "a considerable body of research speaks to the longitudinal continuity of dispositional traits" (McAdams, 2009, p. 13). Moreover, McAdams adds:

> Personality research suggests that [among the so-called 'big-five'] dispositional traits linked to conscientiousness, agreeableness, and openness to experience have strong moral implications. High scores on conscientiousness and agreeableness have been linked to pro-social behavior, commitment to societal institutions, honesty, integrity, and fewer instances of violating moral norms. At least moderately high levels of openness to experience appear to be a prerequisite for valuing tolerance and diversity in society, for understanding multiple perspectives, and for principled moral reasoning. (pp. 23–24)

And we know from research in I-O psychology on the big five that they are important for success in a wide variety and level of jobs, especially the attributes of conscientiousness and agreeableness (Judge & Zapata, 2015; Sackett & Walmsley, 2014).

Nevertheless, for quite some time it also has been recognized that there is intraindividual variation in the expression of personality traits, including indications of moral behavior and values or character such as honesty (Hartshorne & May, 1928; Murphy, 1993). For example, in our own domain it's been observed that some supervisors are both abusive and known for their prosocial organizational behavior (Johnson, et al., 2021). Such variability typically has been seen as an outcome of competing motives and/or varying contextual influences (Mischel, 1999; Ross & Nisbett, 1991) and led to an emphasis on the salience of the context or situation in the expression of behavior (*situationism*). The analog to this in the realm of moral philosophy was considerable skepticism regarding the notion of virtue, the definition of which generally assumes the consistency of personality such as is indicated by terms like disposition, trait or character (Doris, 2002; Merritt et al., 2010). However, most psychologists nowadays probably accept an *interactionist* perspective of behavior as due to the interplay of dispositional attributes of personality, including character, as well as situational influences (Kenrick & Funder, 1988). This has also been found to be the case with respect to job performance: all big five personality traits "were more predictive of performance for jobs in which the process by which the work was done represented weak situations (e.g., work was unstructured, employee had discretion to make decisions)" (Judge & Zapata, 2015, p. 1149). Some psychologists have even reconceptualized the notion of the consistency of personality to include not only stable individual differences but also "distinctive and stable patterns of situation-behavior relations (e.g., she does X when A but Y when B)" (Mischel et al., 2002, p. 50).

Consequently, despite the focus on character, many versions of virtue theory do not preclude consideration of situational or contextual factors. These sorts of findings have necessitated a somewhat looser conceptualization of virtue (Tiberius, 2015). For example, in the context of a concern for business ethics, Hartman (1998) points out that

> A character trait can be a virtue or a vice depending on the circumstances … . Consider the trait of self-confidence for example. Self-confidence in acting on one's principles despite peer pressure is virtuous … . Self-confidence in acting on one's principles while ignoring good arguments against them is not, for stubbornness is no virtue, even though in some cases stubbornness will lead to a good outcome. (P. 50)

Intuitions as antecedents

An intellectually provocative use of virtue theory has to do with the hypothetical source of human virtues. Haidt's (2001; Haidt & Joseph, 2004) theory posits innate, automatic *intuitions* which, if given appropriate sociocultural learning opportunities, provide the foundation for our morality, expressed as virtue. That is, humans "come equipped with an *intuitive ethics*, an innate preparedness to feel flashes of approval or disapproval toward certain patterns of events involving other human beings" (Haidt & Joseph, 2004, p. 56). They proposed that there are (at least) four moral patterns or modules of innate reactions that constitute our intuitive ethical sense, having to do with *suffering, hierarchy, reciprocity* and *purity*. Table 6.3 in the next chapter presents an outline of how these intuitions relate to the manifest world of morality, especially to virtues, when we delve into this recent theory in Moral Psychology.

Virtue Ethics in Business, I-O Psychology and Organizational Behavior

Business

The literature applying virtue ethics to business enterprises has grown rather vast (Akrivou & Sison, 2016; Moore, 2015, 2017; Sadler-Smith, 2012; Weaver, 2006), and an entire recent special issue of *Business Ethics Quarterly* was devoted to "Virtue and the Common Good in Business and Management" (Sison et al., 2012). Moore (2012) provides a succinct summary of developments while expanding on the work of MacIntyre (2007); and Alzola (2015) discusses positive psychology (Peterson & Seligman, 2004) in relation to his two conceptualizations of virtue. Akrivou and Sison (2016) view a concern for the common good via virtue ethics as leading to a better form of capitalism, and Moore (2017) argues that virtue and successful business enterprises are compatible.

In propounding the value of virtue theory in business ethics Hartman (2008) argues that "Recognizing that principles by themselves do not suffice for ethical guidance and that ethics has something to do with character is a good antidote to cynicism" (p. 316). (He refers to cynicism presumably resulting from the uncertainties and difficulties encountered in attempting to apply moral principles to specific real-world problems.) Indeed, the importance of virtue and personal integrity has provided the framework for comprehensive treatments of business ethics (Petrick & Quinn, 1997; Solomon, 1992). Dyck and Kleysen (2001) operationalized Aristotle's cardinal virtues in a fashion similar to Fayol's familiar functions of management and Mintzberg's managerial roles in an effort to show that the virtues may "provide a useable framework for integrating moral concerns into a holistic view of management" (p. 570).

At the institutional level, a business organization must be successful at its core mission, what the influential theorist Alisdair MacIntyre (2007) calls a *practice*, such as the production of goods or services. To do so it pursues excellence in that productive endeavor, and if successful those involved will experience the intrinsic rewards or *internal goods* that result. But the institution must also attend to the achievement of *external goods* like survival, profit, long-term viability, etc. Moore (2012) notes that the virtuous organization is *not* one which prioritizes the pursuit of internal goods to the exclusion of external goods, but one that maintains an appropriate balance, with the emphasis just on the side of internal goods. Identifying that point of balance is, of course, not a science but will require judgement on behalf of both the practitioner and managers of the organization.

(p. 367, emphasis in the original)

Consequently, as will be discussed later in the context of contemporaneous contextual influences on moral reasoning, it is not surprising to learn that virtue is seen as a particularly important aspect of outstanding leadership (Gini & Green, 2013).

The following quotations impart some of the beliefs and attitudes on the part of management and organization scholars regarding the relevance and usefulness of virtue ethics in business organizations. Most of the concerns focus on the moral character of individuals in the organization; some focus on the moral character of the organization itself:

"When the defenders of the paradigm … of the modern management orthodoxy consider administrative ethics, they most often do so within the framework of a morality of rules, which are attached to organizational positions, and ignore the issue of the moral character of the incumbents. This is intentional, because it corresponds to the cardinal rule of the management orthodoxy that an organization must never allow itself to be dependent upon individuals."

(Hart, 2001, p. 135)

"Understanding how moral people behave and how they become moral requires reference to virtues, some of which are important in business … . Understanding character makes one a better manager from a moral point of view."

(Hartman, 1998, p. 547)

"Organizational field research finds that virtue and vice concepts are necessary to describe what is meant by an excellent manager; his or her productivity and principled-behavior are not sufficient."

(Whetstone, 2001, p. 103)

"… the leaders of human organizations should be chosen only from the ranks of the most experienced and virtuous people."

(Kilburg, 2012, p. 162)

"Work, business, and management are … vital areas for the development of virtues, not the least with a view to human flourishing."

(Sison et al., 2012, p. 207)

"Formal organizations can function like a moral person, and so be considered to possess an institutional character replete with institution-level virtues and vices."

(Duchon & Drake, 2009, p. 302)

Perhaps the essential rationale comes from Audi (2012):

If any question posed by virtue ethics is central in moral practice, it is probably *What kind of person do I want to be?* In Aristotelian terms, this would be closely tied to the question of what excellences I might develop and how the quest for them can lead to a life of flourishing in which I can take pride. We can also ask what kind of *business*persons we want to be—or teachers, lawyers, parents, and so on. But virtue ethics forces us to focus, both in self-direction and in role-modeling, on the most general evaluative terms.

(p. 286, emphasis in the original)

I-O Psychology

Although there does not seem to be a great deal of empirical research in this area, interesting confirmation of those beliefs from the realm of political leadership comes from ten Brinke et al. (2015) who studied the political speeches and influence of U.S. senators after they had been elevated to powerful leadership roles as committee chairs. After coding the nonverbal behaviors displayed in the senators' speeches the authors "found that virtuous senators became more influential after they assumed leadership roles, whereas senators who displayed behaviors consistent with vices—particularly psychopathy—became no more influential or even less influential" (p. 1). The virtues assessed were courage, humanity, justice, wisdom, temperance and transcendence; and the effect of the first three were all independently statistically significant, as was the composite of all six. The vices were Machiavellianism, psychopathy and narcissism. This brings us to one of the most interesting realms of exploration.

It has been more than 30 years since the study of the role of personality was accelerated by the development of the five-factor model of personality and its measurement (Costa & McCrae, 1985; cf. Digman, 1990, for a review of its origins). Although the personality theorists and other psychologists involved never to my knowledge utilized the language of "virtues" they were focused for the most part on positive dispositional attributes and their expression that would fit most definitions of virtue. Ironically, however, the most recent prominent area of study has focused on *negative* attributes of personality that are seen as leading to a variety of adverse individual, team and organizational consequences in organizations. This has particularly marked the study of what has variously been referred to as leadership "derailment," "failure" and "incompetence" (Hogan & Hogan, 2001) or "toxic leadership" (Schyns, 2015). It is viewed as an important issue because there are so many bad managers in most organizations ... [and] bad managers make life miserable for those who must work for them, and there is virtually nothing subordinates can do to defend themselves, except to suffer in silence.

(Hogan & Hogan, 2001, p. 40)

Sometimes, however, employees withdraw from the workplace (cf. special issue of *Journal of Applied Psychology*, 2016).

This has spawned two related lines of research. One has to do with *abusive supervision*, its antecedents in the supervisor's dispositional attributes, such as lack of self-control (Yam et al., 2016); or in the contextual nature of the work situation, such as a supervisor's dependence on subordinates (Walter et al., 2015), or the ways in which cyclical supervisor-subordinate interactions may exacerbate or attenuate the toxic relations (Mitchell et al., 2015; Simon et al., 2015).

The second area focuses more generally on "the dark side" of personality (Hogan & Hogan, 2001), "dark personality" (Schyns, 2015), or "the dark triad" in the workplace (Paulhus & Williams, 2002). The dark triad consists of the three vices measured by ten Brinke et al. (2015) in the study of U.S. senators described above: Machiavellianism, Narcissism and Psychopathy. The more expansive consideration of dark personality includes as many as 11 clinically defined personality disorders, including narcissistic, paranoid and antisocial personalities (American Psychiatric Association, 2000). A Special Issue of *Applied Psychology: An International Review* is devoted to the study of dark personality in the workplace (Schyns, 2015).

Boddy and his colleagues have been concerned with the presence of *corporate psychopaths* in organizations.[8] In a series of reports from a management sample in Australia they found: "greater levels of psychopathy at more senior levels of corporations than at more junior levels" (Boddy et al., 2010a, p. 121); "when corporate psychopaths are present in a work environment, the level of bullying is significantly greater than when they are not present ... [and] supervisors are strongly perceived as being unfair to employees" (Boddy, 2011, p. 367); and when such individuals are present within leadership positions in organizations employees are less likely to see the organization as socially responsible and as committed to employees (Boddy et al., 2010b).

A study in Great Britain concluded "psychopaths have large and significant impacts on conflict and bullying and employee affective wellbeing; these have large and significant impacts on counterproductive work behavior" (Boddy, 2014, p. 107). And in a small-*n* qualitative study in England, senior managers who worked with six corporate psychopaths saw them "as being organizational stars and as deserving of awards ... while they simultaneously subjected those below them to extreme behavior, including bullying, intimidation and coercion" (Boddy et al., 2015, p. 30).

8 They use the term "corporate psychopath" to differentiate these individuals from criminals.

And finally, Boddy (2011) presented a theoretical rationale about the role of senior financial corporate directors in the recent global financial crisis.

Note should be taken how, in this border area between moral philosophy and applied social science (i.e., virtue ethics), empirical evidence of the *descriptive* relevance of virtue theory—as represented by positive and negative personality attributes—(e.g., virtuousness leads to a number of favorable outcomes for the actor and/or others, and viciousness the opposite) seems to be taken by some as sufficient confirmation of its *normative* value. In some quarters that might be seen as an inappropriate conflation (recall the admonition against "concluding *ought* from *is*"); but, as discussed earlier, it is in keeping with the essential conception of what is generally meant by a virtue—"characteristics of a person that are morally praiseworthy." And it is consonant with the epigram offered at the start of the previous chapter: *an ethical judgment that is no good in practice must suffer from a theoretical defect as well, for the whole point of ethical judgments is to guide practice.*

Organizational Behavior

Virtue theory has even been extended from the level of individual attributes to apply to "the organizational level of virtue" (Chun, 2010, p. 55)—as from the field of positive psychology in particular to *positive organizational scholarship* (POS) (Dutton et al., 2006). Similarly, Moore (2008) argues that one can "think not just in terms of particular individuals and their exercise (or not) of the virtues at the institutional level … but also in terms of *institutional* level virtues (and vices), and hence of institutional *character*" (Moore, 2008, p. 499, emphases in the original). And the notion of "organizational virtue" has been extended even further to a notion of *organizational environmental virtuousness* (Sadler-Smith, 2013). Chun (2010) applies this perspective to a consideration of *corporate social responsibility*:

> Developing the ethical character of an organization is the core theme in virtue ethics theory. Virtue ethics theory denies that making moral decisions is a matter of calculation or principle-based duties … . Instead, it focuses on aspirational values through the ongoing development of ethical character. Despite the increasing popularity in the last decade of applying the virtue ethics perspective to business ethics, the managerial implications of organizational-level virtue have not been well transmitted, mainly because existing studies within virtue ethics have tended to focus on a person's moral character, not on the organization as a whole … . The strength of organizational virtue ethics is its focus on stakeholder emotion and satisfaction through the development of organizational ethical character, factors that are known to influence the satisfaction of both internal and external stakeholders. (p. 55)

A good place to conclude, therefore, is with the observation that recent empirical research lends some credence to these notions. In an organizational setting (non-academic employees of a university) leaders' wisdom, humanity and temperance were related to employee affective commitment, well-being, organizational citizenship behaviors and trust (Thun & Kelloway, 2011); as summarized by Peterson and Park (2006), a number of strengths of character have been found related to work satisfaction, better grades (after controlling for ability test scores), good health, long life, "freedom from accidents," and regarding one's work as a "calling" rather than just a way to make money.

Critique

There are quite a number of critical issues to consider, at least briefly, including some basic definitional ones:

1. There is some lack of consensus regarding what is a virtue and even more uncertainty regarding how many of them there might be. One might say that *moral virtues* are not clearly independent of the two traditional dimensions of morality: e.g., the virtues of honesty and integrity are reflected in the application of *justice principles,* and may be implicated in the dimension of *caring* or *beneficence* as well. Perhaps virtue does not demarcate a separate content domain of morality.

2. What legitimately and appropriately constitutes the expression of a virtue—e.g., kindness?. Suppose I learn before you do that you are not going to get the promotion for which you were hoping. Suppose I am also aware that you are a realist who generally prefers to know where you stand, even if it means facing bad news. What is the "kind" thing for me to do? Should I tell you what I believe you'd like to know (thereby, however, making you feel terribly disappointed), or not tell you, allowing you to continue mistakenly feeling optimistic and hopeful?[9]

3. There also are problems having to do with whether virtue ethics can stand on its own. In attempting to correct an overreliance on rules and reasoning, it has been faulted for going overboard in the opposite direction by eliminating the ethical principles that may be needed for guidance in order to know *what to do in order to be virtuous.* Critics would say that the virtue theorist ultimately has to rely on deontological rules or utilitarian considerations in order to take moral action. In the example above, I might base my choice on my anticipated discomfort at being the bearer of ill tidings—irrespective of any consideration of being kind. At least one scholar (Melé, 2009) believes in the viability and usefulness of an amalgam of moral principles and virtue ethics. He focuses on *the personalist principle* (a version of the golden rule or Kant's categorical imperative) and the *common good principle*—when each member of a community strives to create the

---

9 Note that the question of which option is the better expression of kindness is not the same as the (deontological) moral question of whether I have a duty or obligation to impart my knowledge. And it also does not incorporate any (consequentialist) concerns I may have regarding your reaction if/when you find out that I, your friend, was aware of this information and did not tell you.

conditions in which all members of the community may flourish. These are supposed to provide the guidance needed to make virtuous decisions.

4. Virtue ethics puts great emphasis on the importance of personal character so that it may underestimate the role of the interpersonal, psychological and cultural contexts in influencing moral behavior in general (Doris, 2002) and unethical behavior in organizations, in particular—such as the *ethical climate* of the organization (Andreoli & Lefkowitz, 2009; Lefkowitz, 2009b; cf. Chap. 7). In opposition, it has been noted that "A virtue is not merely a principle. The practice of an ethic of virtue requires that a person have perceptive insight concerning the context of each act. What is most right to do depends on the situation, including recognition of coercive pressures and intentions for acting" (Whetstone, 2001, p. 105).

5. Virtue ethics also shares with absolutist rule-deontology the problem of what to do when two or more virtues are in conflict. The example above might be interpreted as posing a conflict between my being kind versus honest. One solution to that problem, as has occurred (not entirely successfully) in the deontology camp, could be prioritizing moral character traits in order of degree of virtue—if such ranking could be agreed upon. First, we'd have to have agreement on the list of virtues to be ranked; and do we include very comprehensive virtues as well as more narrow domain-focused virtues? Second, could there be just one ranking that would pertain across all relevant situations? As we shall see in chapter 6, ethical challenges vary in *moral intensity*, which includes attributes such as the magnitude of the potential consequences (Jones, 1991). Third, how do we prioritize while remaining true to the aretaic perspective—i.e., without resorting to anticipated utilitarian consequences in order to do so?

6. Following Aristotle's original approach of giving primacy to character traits over moral acts, "virtue ethics tells us to do what a virtuous person would do in our situation" (Shafer-Landau, 2015). But there are many virtuous people, and they cannot all be expected to do the same thing in the same situation. Therefore, virtue ethics seems to violate the moral principle of *universalizability* (cf. Chap. 3; i.e., an ethical choice is one that ought to be made in a given situation regardless of who the actor is). But that may not be so problematic if we think of virtue ethics, along with deontology, as indicating which among many options are permissible versus impermissible, rather than as a consequentialist analysis indicating which option is required.[10]

7. As noted above, virtue ethics starts out with the notion of the virtuous or good person but does not provide a uniform definition of what that consists of,

---

10 Since the 1990s in the U.S. another popular solution to the quandary (i.e., that one should do what a virtuous person would do; but we don't have agreement on what that consists of), has become popular among Christian believers. The approach is taken from a novel *In His Steps* by Charles Sheldon (1896), in which the parishioners always ask "What would Jesus do?" (WWJD). However, I'm not aware of any studies investigating the degree of (in)consistency in the answers generated by that question.

although it is presumed to be a long and winding road to acquire such moral character. Moreover, as we know from moral psychology and personality development (cf. Chaps. 6 & 7) moral motivation and other character traits are formed rather early. Therefore, "difficult as it may be to teach ethics, especially to those who are no longer children, teaching virtue seems even more difficult since virtue demands not only right action but right motivation and emotion" (Sison et al., 2012, p. 209).[11]

8. All-in-all, then, the addition of virtue theory contributes to a more complete understanding of the nature of ethics or morality. But let us not make three mistakes that I believe characterize the views of some virtue proponents, especially those with a religious perspective: (i) the tendency to overestimate the consistency of behavior (i.e., one's general character) irrespective of the situation, with the corresponding tendency to underestimate social and contextual influences on behavior. For example, evidence regarding the stability of values over time is generally assessed at the group, not the individual, level of analysis—which merely illustrates the stability of group Means, such as for samples of managers, not the consistency of individual personality (Oliver, 1999); (ii) the inclusion of the "selfish virtues" in the conception of morality; and (iii) the promotion of a politically-tinged societal agenda that emphasizes the virtues of self-denial and obedience to authority (e.g., abstinence as the only "solution" to the "problem" of teenage sexuality, or strict rules accompanying rote learning of the "basics" as the only appropriate classroom strategy). These inclinations tend to result in a highly moralistic (and here I use the term pejoratively) outlook in which people are often characterized as uniformly and irretrievably good or bad, strong or weak.

Adding Further to the Framework for Ethical Decision Making

12. It was concluded previously (cf. Learning Point # 7) that the prudent option is to remain open to both deontological and consequentialist reasoning. Similarly, notwithstanding that there are both contributions from, as well as limitations to virtue ethics, that suggests we be prepared to accept aretaic views as well. Contrary to the "either/or" attitude of many scholars of business ethics, there are those like Melé (2009) who insist that the best approach is an integration of some broad-based ethical principles into virtue-based ethics. Similarly, "Moral reasons can include both the duty to act *and* the consequences expected from the act *as well as* the belief that so acting is characteristic of the kind of person one wants to be. One might refrain

---

11 In fairness to those authors it should be pointed out that they remain optimistic regarding such education and management training.

from cheating because this is the right way to act, *and* because so acting will create a better world, *and* because one is an honest person" (Whetstone, 2001, p. 102, emphases in the original). All well and good … . I would be remiss, however, to not point out the likely difficulties associated with situations in which the three perspectives do not agree on a preferred choice.

In this integrative vein it is also valuable to acknowledge "that there is a correspondence between many major virtue concepts and at least the majority of plausible moral principles that many writers in ethics have defended" (Audi, 2012, p. 283). For example, some "moral principles" have identical corresponding "virtues" (e.g., justice, fidelity, veracity, beneficence). In other cases where there is not a direct translation, some moral principles have close correspondences: e.g., the principle of non-maleficence links to virtues of gentleness, kindness, respectfulness, etc.

A compelling argument for considering virtues and vices is that from time to time characters come along whose actions are so odious, egregious and persistent that to describe them as merely behaving unethically seems inadequate. For example, think of the notorious Ponzi-schemer Bernard Madoff. I have elsewhere referred to such actions as *intentional misbehavior* (Lefkowitz, 2006) or as *corrupt* (Lefkowitz, 2009b), in order to distinguish them from "mere" unethical behavior (cf. Chap. 7). Conversely, thinking of someone like Mother Theresa as merely an ethical person also seems to not do justice to her virtuousness.

6

MORAL PSYCHOLOGY:
I. MORAL DEVELOPMENT

Philosophers tell us that there is an element of rational choice in human morality, psychologists say that there is a learning component, and anthropologists argue that there are few if any universal rules. The distinction between right and wrong is made by people on the basis of how they would like their society to function. It arises from interpersonal negotiation in a particular environment, and derives its sense of obligation and guilt from the internalization of these processes.

—Frans de Waal

The preceding four chapters have focused on some of the metatheoretical issues and normative theories constituting moral philosophy. The primary concerns of philosophers have been the specification of prescriptive (i.e., normative) models of moral action, the metatheoretical assumptions on which they rest, the logical adequacy of the criteria that define each model, and its inclusiveness—frequently in comparison with some competing model(s). The quotation from de Waal (1996) introduces us to a couple of additional things: (i) social science, as well as philosophy, has contributed a great deal to the understanding of moral behavior; and (ii) moral behavior is a complex phenomenon, not only with aspects to be illuminated by multiple fields of study but always expressed through the interpersonal intentions and agentic behavior of sentient social beings.[1]

Philosophers have also long been mindful of such important "realistic" topics as the association between making moral judgments and the motivation of moral behavior (cf. Adams, 1976; Stocker, 1976) and the applicability of their normative

---

1 That does not refer to only humans.

DOI: 10.4324/9781003212577-7

theories. However, those are empirical issues that have remained largely secondary in philosophers' interests. As summarized by Doris et al. (2010),

> The study of morality has historically been a special province of philosophy, while the study of mental processes has, for the past century or so, largely been the province of psychology and allied sciences. At the same time, recent philosophy has been largely speculative or theoretical ... while the methods of contemporary psychology have characteristically been empirical or experimental ... . The results have been uneven: philosophy has often been light on fact, and psychology has often been light on theory. (p. 1)

In contrast, a growing domain of *moral psychology* that consists of "attempts to analyze moral phenomena in terms of psychological concepts and processes" (Emler & Hogan, 1991, p. 72), has developed and grown enormously during the past few decades and has attracted the productive involvement of philosophers (Doris et al., 2010; Sinnott-Armstrong, 2008; Tiberius, 2015).[2] Although moral psychology has not reached the degree of institutional structure to be designated as a formal specialty area in psychology akin to experimental, clinical, social or I-O psychology, it has a rather clearly articulated domain of theory, research and even application (Alfano, 2016; Jensen, 2020; Killen & Smetana, 2014; Rest & Narvaez, 1994). In the same year that the first edition of this book was published (2003), a Moral Psychology Research Group was formed in the United States, consisting of 23 philosophers, psychologists, cognitive scientists and ethicists.

> Moral psychology—a field in which philosophers are at least as prominent as psychologists—is growing exponentially ... . Some would say it is blossoming, others that it is spreading like a weed, but even detractors must admit that, since it emerged 15–20 years ago, moral psychology has told us a great deal about what people consider to be wrong, the types of psychological and neurobiological mechanisms involved in making moral judgments, and where those mechanisms come from.
>
> *(Heyes, 2021, p. 4391)*

Contrasted with moral philosophy moral psychology obviously is a broader field of inquiry that has the following interrelated attributes:

1. **Multidisciplinary:** The field counts among its participants developmental, social, clinical, cognitive and neuropsychologists, behavioral economists,

---

2   Even more recently, the term *behavioral ethics* has gained much currency, especially in business schools (Banaji & Greenwald, 2013; Bazerman & Gino, 2012; De Cremer et al., 2010; Kluver et al., 2014). Although those who use the term refer to many of the same phenomena incorporated in *moral psychology*, they seem to focus almost exclusively on implications for ethical decision-making.

philosophers, as well as psychoanalysts, evolutionary biologists, bioethicists, sociologists and anthropologists.

2. **Process oriented:** Beyond studying the substantive content of "morality" there is a focus on the developmental, social and contextual antecedents that influence moral judgment processes as well as the determinants of whether and how such judgments lead to moral behavior, including its evolution in the human species.

3. **Empirical:** As with any facet of the behavioral and social sciences, the ultimate criteria for the evaluation of hypothetical explanations (e.g., hypothesized stages of moral development; evolutionary origins) are empirical research findings as well as theoretical and logical consistency. This includes work in the relatively new field of "experimental philosophy."

4. **Comprehensive and multidimensional:** As a consequence of its process and multidisciplinary orientations it includes the study of a wide array of relevant factors: the inborn capacities for moral behavior like empathy and other individual-difference variables; the maturational bases for the appearance of moral reasoning and altruistic feelings in children as well as the developmental sequences by which they unfold; the social influence processes by which cultural norms, values and standards are imparted; the interplay between motives to behave ethically and motives driven by competing values; and other situational and contextual influences affecting moral actions, including those that would pertain to employment in organizations.

5. **Theoretically driven:** The empirical study of moral behavior has been organized around fundamental theoretical issues: (a) the specification of what is meant by morality, moral behavior or moral judgment; (b) the extent to which moral behavior is unique to humans or is also reflected in the social lives of other species; (c) the relation between general cognitive and emotional development in humans and their moral development; (d) the extent to which moral behavior might be inherited and its development progress innately as a reflection primarily of maturational processes, as opposed to being socially constructed as a consequence of the transmission of cultural norms and values; (e) the bases for people's moral attributions regarding the blame or praise due others for specific actions; (f) whether moral development proceeds in an orderly sequential fashion and, if so, whether the sequence is hierarchical (i.e., cumulative), and if so whether it is characterized by discretely separable stages; (g) whether the fundamental features of moral development and moral behavior are invariant across cultures; and (h) specifying the multiplicity of antecedents of moral behavior, often in theoretical causal models—e.g., why are people (un)ethical?

I have organized a synthesis of the field into a developmental model of moral action (DMMA) that is presented as Fig. 6.1. Note that several theoretical

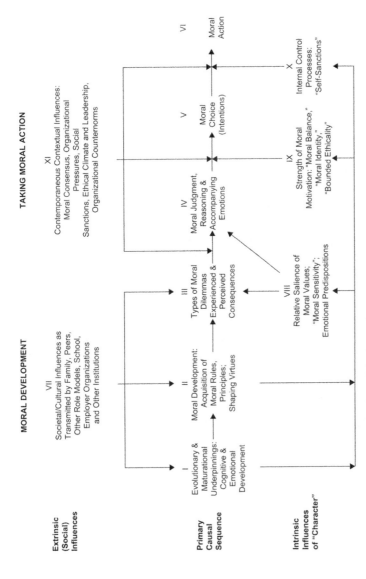

FIGURE 6.1   A developmental model of moral action

models of ethical reasoning and behavior have been presented previously in the literature.[3] Although I have drawn from them, the model presented in Fig. 6.1 is more general and abstract—e.g., it is comprised of classes of constructs rather than individual variables. It should be thought of primarily as providing an analytic framework to facilitate a comprehensive view of the field. It is presented for didactic convenience and is not testable empirically. The constructs and processes illustrated in the model are discussed in this chapter and the next. This chapter covers the developmental (longitudinal) processes that contribute to the formation of a moral sense, which (in part) accounts for the ethical challenges we encounter and how we experience them. They are represented as categories I, II, III, VII and VIII, in the left portion of Fig. 6.1. Chapter 7 essentially begins where chapter 6 leaves off, and concerns how the experience of and reactions to a particular challenge culminate in a response ("taking moral action")—represented by the right portion of the figure as categories IV, V, VI, VIII, IX, X and XI.

The first portions of the primary causal sequence (Categories I–III) are components of human development, encompassing a longitudinal life-span perspective, and they are influenced by societal and interpersonal influences (Category VII). *Moral action* refers to all the psychological and social processes involved from the time at which one is confronted by and apprehends an ethical problem, with its attendant emotional arousal, to the process of moral reasoning that culminates in a moral choice and some eventual behavioral response (which may or may not correspond to the moral choice), as well as the factors that moderate those hypothesized causal sequences. In Fig. 6.1 moral action is represented by the sequences that comprise all the causal relations following Category III and the relations among variables within each of those categories. They are discussed in chapter 7.

A Developmental Model of Moral Action (DMMA)

Based on the preceding chapters we can conclude that human social interactions can be segmented into three broad domains: (a) *egoistic behavior* (sometimes referred to as *personal* or *psychological*) that is dominated by self-interest, with little or no consideration of other people except as they impact the gratification or frustration of our needs and are the source of consequent emotional reactions; (b) *conventional behavior* (sometimes called *societal*) that constitutes much of our social interaction and heteronomously reflects society's consensual rules and customs, whether construed pessimistically as a necessary restraint on our

---

3 Those models are presented, elaborated, and investigated in the following sources: Bommer et al. (1987); Cole et al. (2000); Dubinsky and Loken (1989); Ford and Richardson (1994); Hunt and Vitell (1986); Jansen and Von Glinow (1985); Jones (1991); Jones and Kavanagh (1996); Loe et al. (2000); Near and Miceli (1995); Rest (1986b, 1994); Schminke (1998, 2010); Stitch et al. (2010); and Treviño (1986).

unbridled egoism (as per Hobbes' account) or optimistically as reflecting the worth of each individual (cf. Rawls). In this regard Prinz (2008) points out that "much in our life is governed by norms" (p. 368); and (c) *moral behavior* that reflects adherence to higher standards governing our interpersonal lives than mere social consensus and sanctions. As reviewed in the prior chapters, those standards are generally conceived alternatively as adherence to moral principles or duties ("doing right"), maximizing positive outcomes ("doing good"), or expressing exemplary character ("being virtuous"). Considerable attention has been paid in moral psychology trying to distinguish clearly between conventional social (non-moral) norms versus moral norms accompanied by emotional reactions that contribute to adherence to those norms (Prinz & Nichols, 2010). Prinz (2008) refers to the latter as "moral norms [which] are grounded in the moral emotions" (p. 368). Much individual behavior is, of course, motivated by a combination of influences from more than one of these three realms, and as discussed later there is some disagreement regarding whether they deserve to be thought of as separate domains.

Following a common theme in moral philosophy (Frankena, 1973) psychologists have generally viewed moral behavior as two-dimensional, consisting of: (a) *justice*, with its attendant criteria of fairness, impartiality and universalizability, in the deontological Kantian tradition of treating people with respect and dignity; and (b) *welfare*, or *care*, with its criteria of beneficence, avoiding harm, caring and altruism, that has been proposed as an important yet underappreciated qualification for effective management (Kracher & Wells, 1998). Based on the recent re-emergence of virtue ethics, its application to organizational life and potential applicability to research with human participants, I have added the dimension of (c) *moral virtue* or *character*, with its criteria of honesty, integrity, fidelity, trustworthiness and responsibility in one's dealings with others (Lefkowitz, 2003).[4] Although *justice* is most frequently construed as an abstract deontological principle, it can be defined in consequentialist terms, such as the equitable allocation of society's (or an organization's) rewards, or as virtuous attributes such as being fair-minded. Conversely, although *welfare* clearly implies a utilitarian focus on the consequences of social acts, it may entail generalized rule-based proscriptions against certain harmful actions, as well as virtues like compassion.

---

4   Audi and Murphy (2006) highlight the definitional ambiguities of terms such as *integrity*—especially as used in the world of business. It can be used holistically, meaning someone who acts in a consistently moral and ethical way (in which case it is arguably redundant with those terms). Or it can refer roughly to having a "morally sound character" comprised of "at least as many facets as there are moral virtues … . These facets cannot all be cited here … . But one way to identify them is to speak of *integrity as*—as honesty, as sincerity, as fairness, as adherence to high moral standards, as devotion to principle … ." (p. 14, italics in the original).

This compact three-component traditional view of the moral domain is reflected in many somewhat more detailed contemporary statements of ethical standards such as the APA's (2017) *Ethical Principles of Psychologists and Code of Conduct,* Smith's (2000) outline of the moral foundations of psychological research with human participants, and the *Canadian Code of Ethics for Psychologists* (Canadian Psychological Association, 2017).

The framework presented in Fig. 6.1 reflects the belief that to understand [un] ethical behavior one has to consider multiple determinants, including the actor's individual background and personality, the nature of precipitating situations, and situational/contextual influences (Kish-Gephart et al., 2010). The model begins with the maturational bases for the eventual expressions of moral behavior— behavior reflecting considerations of justice, welfare and moral character. The Roman numeral following each of the sections in the following discussion refers to the category of latent constructs in Fig. 6.1.

Evolutionary and Maturational Underpinnings: General Cognitive and Emotional Development (I)

The Evolution of Morality

Hare (2017) observed recently that "Darwin viewed the evolution of human intelligence and morality as the greatest challenge to his theory of evolution through natural selection" (p. 156). While there is considerable evidence suggesting that moral behavior and perhaps even thoughts and feelings about moral behavior (e.g., moral judgment; moral emotions and motives) have some innate bases, the issue remains contentious (cf. Prinz, 2008 versus Dwyer, 2008, and Tiberius, 2008). As noted earlier, in chapter 2, Prinz concluded that " … I think the evidence for moral nativism is incomplete, at best" (p. 403). Similarly, Jensen and Silk (2014) conclude "the evidence for anything resembling moral behavior in nonhuman animals is limited … . the emotional substrates of moral behavior are only weakly exhibited" (p. 488).

Succinctly, "it remains unclear whether, and in which sense, morality evolved" (Machery & Mallon, 2010). What those authors mean by "in which sense" is extremely thought-provoking. They propose that there are three interpretations of what might be meant by the evolution of morality. (I find it helpful to think of them as weak, moderate and strong versions of the evolution hypothesis, but that is not their characterization.) "The first interpretation asserts that specific components (e.g, emotions, dispositions, rule-based reasoning systems, or concepts) of moral psychology or specific behaviors typically *associated with* morality evolved" (p. 5, emphasis added). This "weak" characterization does not propose that a full-blown moral stance is innate (such as a justice motive), merely that the necessary components to develop such a motive are—e.g., the ability to make social comparisons.

The second interpretation is somewhat more demanding: "the claim that *normative cognition*—that is, the capacity to grasp norms and to make normative judgments—is a product of evolution" (p. 4, emphasis in the original). In other words, arguably we have evolved with the ability to readily learn what our society approves and disapproves of, and that includes the propensity to experience the corresponding emotions when we are compliant or violate those norms—pride versus shame or guilt, respectively.

The third, most ambitious, interpretation the authors discuss involves "drawing a distinction among different types of normative cognitions and … singling out one specific type of normative cognition … [called] 'morality'" (p. 20), which is presumably inherited. After reviewing a variety of forms of arguably relevant empirical evidence, Machery and Mallon (2010) conclude that, although there is some tenuous evidence in support of the first two interpretations, with respect to the more critical third version of the hypothesis,

> … we see little reason to believe that the grasp of distinctively moral norms and the capacity to make moral judgments … evolved at all … . We conjecture that in this respect, the capacity to grasp moral norms and the capacity to make moral judgments might be similar to chess or handwriting. The capacities to play chess and to write involve various evolved cognitive traits (e.g., visual recognition and memorization of rules for the former), but they did not evolve. Similarly, we conjecture that the capacity to grasp moral norms and the capacity to make moral judgments involve various evolved cognitive traits (including … a disposition to grasp norms in general), but they themselves did not evolve. In any case … none of the available evidence suggests that they did. (p. 23)

A great deal of empirical and conceptual work in moral psychology is focused on some aspect of the neurological underpinnings and putative inheritance of moral behavior (Ellemers & van Nunspeet, 2020). For example, one line of inferential research reveals similarities between human personality and character attributes with those of non-human primates—e.g., factor analyses of rated personality attributes of chimpanzees and bonobos map very closely onto the well-known five-factor model of personality (Weiss et al., 2015). And there are apparently a great many commonalities in the processes of social learning and aspects of culture between human and chimpanzee societies (Whiten, 2017). A similar line of research seeks to document aspects of adult morality in the very early life of infants that "do not appear to stem from socialization or morally specific experience" (Hamlin, 2013, p.191; also, Warneken, 2018). Some are investigating the role of genetic inheritance in attributes as disparate as work-related behaviors like social and aggressive interactions, job satisfaction and leadership (Arvey & Zhang, 2015) and marital infidelity (Zietsch et al., 2015). And others are embarked on physiologically mapping the neural mechanisms that appear to underlie moral cognition (Decety & Cowell, 2014).

Maturational changes

Even if not inherited directly, it seems clear to most developmental psychologists that minimum requisite levels of maturation must be reached to develop the protobehaviors that will eventually be recognized as expressions of morality. However, "recent research on infancy provides compelling demonstrations that the foundations of morality are present early in child development—in the infant's responsiveness to the feelings of others and the young child's appreciation of standards" (Gilligan & Wiggins, 1987, p. 280). Similarly, Thompson (2009) reviews what he considers to be

> convincing evidence that rather than confusing their own perceptions, feelings, and desires with those of another person because of egocentrism, infants and toddlers are aware of these differences early and, equally important, strive to understand the mental states in others that account for these differences. (p. 164)

There is less agreement on identifying these behaviors, the precise timing of their appearance, their degree of heritability and what, if any, are the necessary social circumstances for their emergence.

But much of the disagreements about those matters need not concern us here. It is sufficient for our purposes to start out with the knowledge that largely during the second through fifth years of life the capacities to engage in moral reasoning, to appreciate the benevolent and harmful consequences of events on others (including the effects of one's own actions), and to feel concern for others develop. These changes can be thought of as analogous to the cognitive and social growth that is a prerequisite for speech and the neural and psychomotor development necessary for locomotion (Kagan, 1987). The analogy between speech and morality is probably more apt because of the considerable cross-cultural variation in manifest content that characterizes each.

In general, some of the biopsychosocial changes (Bandura, 1991) that constitute the developmental trends associated with moral development are:

- a shift from concrete to more abstract forms of reasoning so that more sophisticated moral judgment becomes feasible;
- a broadening social reality that expands the relevant domain of moral concerns, moral choices, and the potential influence of social sanctions;
- a shift from external (heteronomous) regulation of behavior to increasing autonomy and self-regulation; and

- the adoption of standards reflecting the child's more sophisticated cognitive functioning and more complex social world in which he or she functions.

These trends are all influenced greatly by—and reciprocally influence the potential effectiveness of—familial and societal factors such as the nature of social sanctions used (e.g., threats, discipline and reasoning); the modeling of interpersonal behavior by parents, siblings, peers and teachers; cultural and subgroup values; and various indirect forms of cultural communication, such as television and social media.

Following are some of the most important emerging capacities that have been highlighted by empirical findings as providing the soil in which moral development ripens (they are not independent; several are overlapping):

1. The development of *fundamental ego processes* (abstractions of the psychological operations that mediate intrapsychic events and external behavior) is necessary for all complex behavior (Bredemeier & Shields, 1994): For example, the ability to concentrate on a moral dilemma so as to engage in the moral reasoning necessary to resolve it is dependent on the attention-focusing ego function of *selective awareness*.

2. The perceptual, cognitive, and affective process of *decentration* (Bernstein et al., 2015; Gibbs, 1991): To cope with more and more complex and difficult intellective problems and social situations, the young child must gradually move away from the limitation of being able to concentrate or center on only one or a few salient components of a situation (centration) to achieve a more comprehensive and balanced view of all the relevant issues (thus, decentration). Without a maturing of these abilities we could not hope to deal with complex moral dilemmas characterized by competing interests, potentially conflicting values of our own such as professional integrity and career advancement, multiple moral standards, and ethical guidelines of ambiguous applicability.

3. A cognitive grasp of oneself—a *self-concept*—as distinct from the rest of the world, including other people. When combined with a sense of *empathy*—the ability to respond effectively to someone else's situation—this enables a growing ability to demonstrate care for others (Hoffman, 1988). Even five-year-old children exhibit substantial helping behavior (Plötner et al., 2015), although there's a lot we still don't know about the prosocial behavior of children and how it develops (Martin & Olson, 2015). And the construct of empathy itself has been characterized as inadequately defined (Bloom, 2017; Zaki, 2017).

4. Even infants seem to understand human behavior in terms of people's intentions (Woodward, 2009). The capacity to reason about mental states and to use that reasoning accordingly has been called having a *theory of mind* (ToM; Wellman, 2014). Ding et al. (2015) have shown experimentally that

three-year-olds can learn to have a ToM, and that it enables social behavior (albeit in this case, learning to lie)—although, as with "empathy," there is some definitional confusion re ToM (Quesque & Rossetti, 2020; Schaafsma et al., 2015).

5. An altruistic responsiveness to the distress of others: De Waal (1996) pointed out the irony that the biological principle of natural selection, which functions through the process of competition, has given rise to enormous capacities for caring and sympathy (not restricted to *homo sapiens*) because they are so adaptive for the species. In this context it should come as no surprise that organizations and I-O psychologists have come to value the advantages of cooperative team performance (Ilgen et al., 2005) and prosocial and organizational citizenship behaviors (OCBs; Penner et al., 2005; Podsakoff & MacKenzie, 2000).

6. An *ethical sensitivity* based on awareness of the nature of our own actions, especially its effects on others (Rest, 1994): To develop this disposition even more basic capacities need to have been realized, such as a grasp of *means–ends relationships* or cause-and-effect in interpersonal affairs, and *role-taking skills*—that is, the ability to appreciate another person's perspective.[5]

Moral Development (II)

The topic of moral development has been for the past century one of the most frequently researched and debated topics in psychology. Virtually every major discipline and subdiscipline in the social and behavioral sciences (not to mention evolutionary biology, as noted earlier) has weighed in heavily on this topic: sociology, cultural and physical anthropology, psychoanalytic theory, and behavioral psychology—both traditional operant views as well as more contemporaneous social learning theory, cognitive psychology, and humanistic faith-based views (both religious and secular varieties). A comprehensive compendium of the field (Jensen, 2020a) notes that recent research emphasizes a "broad array of theories and research foci .... addressing moral development across the entire life course, rather than focusing on childhood," and attempts "to include research with diverse groups within and across nations" (Jensen, 2020b, pp. 3–4).

Notwithstanding that enormous diversity of recent input, there have essentially been two dominant paradigms in the social-scientific study of moral development: the *cultural transmission model* and one or another form of *cognitive stage theory*.

---

5 Although one recent model of moral action, discussed shortly, posits that *moral intuitions* emerge early and are responsible for moral judgments, not moral reasoning (Haidt, 2001).

Morality as Based on the Transmission of Cultural Standards

For most of its history, the developmental aspects of moral psychology have reflected the sociologist Emil Durkheim's (1858–1917) theory of functionalism (cf. the consideration of cultural relativism in Chap. 2). As applied to social behavior functionalism emphasizes the socialization processes by which we internalize society's norms, values, traditions and conventions, and it is represented most prominently in the work of psychologist Martin Hoffman (1977, 1988; discussed shortly) and remains an influential perspective (Dunn, 2014; Grusec et al., 2014). A contemporary restatement of the Durkheim approach defines

> the function of moral systems as an interlocking set of values, virtues, norms, practices, and identities that work together to suppress or regulate selfishness and to make cooperative social life possible. What seems clear is that regardless of the definition, a central focus of morality is the judgment of the rightness or wrongness of acts or behaviors that knowingly cause harm to people.
>
> *(Decety & Cowell, 2014, p. 526)*

Ironically, however, Durkheim (1898/1953, 1893/1956) was very concerned with establishing the legitimacy of sociological analyses and argued against the reductionist view that social phenomena were explicable at the level of individual psychology or biology. For him social phenomena are social facts that exist outside of and independent of the individual. The duties we feel in connection with our roles as spouse, parent, or employee; the legal obligations we accept because of our citizenship or as a consequence of being an employer; the good manners we exhibit to behave properly, all derive from external laws, norms, customs, and so on, that existed prior to our birth and are independent of our individual consciousness. Among these social facts are the moral standards and principles characteristic of our society in general as well as those that pertain to someone who occupies our particular role(s) in it. For Durkheim, society's rules, norms and values provide the social integration that is indispensable for the effective functioning of society and the individual. Contemporary scholarship in cognitive science views some distinctively human cognitive mechanisms that underlie the acquisition of moral reasoning as due in part to "cultural evolution (culture) [as] a third member of the design team, along with nature and nurture" (Heyes, 2020, p. 399)—in particular, "to the extent that moral development depends on learning from other agents, there is the potential for cultural selection of moral beliefs and values" (Heyes, 2021, p. 4391–4414).

In Durkheim's view, because the maintenance of social integration is so important for the perpetuation of society and for individual adjustment, it is not based solely on external controls like laws, customs, parental sanctions, teacher discipline, company regulations, and so forth. Through the psychological process of internalization those standards, including morality, become part of each one of us in the form of common sets of values, assumptions, and expectations. Because of these socialization mechanisms society is both an external social fact and present within all of us. And the process starts early: preschoolers are already sensitive to the violation of normative expectations by others, and even to whether the violations seem intentional (Thompson, 2009).

Virtually all psychological theories of moral development since Durkheim have shared the notion that we internalize the conventions, values, and standards of our society as they are taught to us directly by an ever-widening array of educators, from parents and siblings to peers, teachers, and colleagues, and indirectly via other mechanisms of socialization, such as television, film, social media and the internet. Among the first such theories was Freud's *psychoanalytic theory* which emphasizes the oedipal situation, parental controls and the child's introjection of parental prohibitions as the foundation of superego development (conscience). *Social learning theory* focuses on the generalization of aversive or positive emotional reactions to social reinforcers or the observation and imitation of models being reinforced for their actions—so-called observational learning.

In recent years more attention has been paid to the notion that the substance of moral socialization processes may be somewhat different in different cultures and that the predominant Western theories (Hoffman, Piaget and Kohlberg, following) may not be as universally applicable as we usually assume. For example, Miller et al. (2017) showed

> that Indians tend to treat helping family and friends as moral duties whereas Americans tend to treat them as matters for personal decision making [and in other research] Indians tended to categorize meeting the needs of family and friends as a moral obligation, whereas Americans tended to categorize meeting these needs as a matter of personal choice. (p. 868)

Hoffman's Empathy-Based Model of Internalization

Hoffman's (1977, 1983, 1988, 1991, 2000) model of moral development is a sophisticated version of socialization theory in that it emphasizes the individual's active participation in the internalization process (i.e., the child is not simply a passive recipient of society's mores in the process of making them his or her own). And it employs an integration of both cognitive and affective processes to understand the child's readiness for socialization, especially the capacity for empathy—which is a prime motivator of prosocial behavior.[6] The *human self-domestication hypothesis*

---

6   Although Cialdini et al. (1997) propose that at least some prosocial actions in adults are motivated not by empathy, but by an attempt to improve one's mood and reduce sadness.

"proposes that these early emerging social skills [cooperative-communicative abilities] evolved when natural selection favored increased in-group prosociality over aggression in late human evolution" (Hare, 2017, p. 155).

Accordingly, attention has been paid to how altruism could have evolved by natural group selection (Sober & Wilson, 1998). de Waal (2008) views empathy as a mechanism that evolved "in all animals in which reproduction relies on feeding, cleaning, and warming of the young" (p. 282) and that "evidence is accumulating that this mechanism is phylogenetically ancient, probably as old as mammals and birds … [and is likely] to underlie so-called directed altruism, i.e., altruism in response to another's pain, need, or distress" (p. 279). For example, Crocker et al. (2017) conclude that empirical research indicates that the "assumption that humans are fundamentally or primarily self-serving, self-centered, and self-interested … is wrong or at least overstated" (p. 300). They go on to study the nature of *otherishness* and document that "giving is an extremely common social behavior, even in individualistic cultures where the norm of self-interest reigns" (p. 301).[7] Some psychologists believe that empathy is a predictor of many later behaviors like kindness, cooperation, tolerance, forgiveness, helping, volunteering, charitable donation, and better relationships with strangers (Abramson, 2021).

Hoffman (1991) described his theory as essentially an information-processing approach, and it is comprised of three major components: (a) three ideal types of moral dilemma from which one may, subject to appropriate child-rearing practices, develop an internalized sense of morality, guilt and prosocial concern for others; (b) consideration of the nature and development of our capacity for empathy; and (c) the nature of the discipline procedures by which one acquires an appreciation for the effects of our behavior on others. It is worthwhile to consider, albeit briefly, each of Hoffman's three ideal types of moral problems because they can serve as a means of further structuring our understanding of the ethical challenges we are likely to encounter as adults.

Hoffman's first ideal type of moral problem, being an innocent bystander to someone else's pain or distress, engenders the motivation to help because of our capacity for empathy. Hoffman defined empathy as "a vicarious affective response that is more appropriate to someone else's situation than to one's own" (1988, p. 509) and believed that this capacity is inborn as a product of natural selection. That belief is supported by the knowledge that highly similar caring behavior occurs in infrahuman species (de Waal, 1996; Strum, 1987) and that cooperative behavior in humans is mediated by that part of the brain associated with experiencing pleasure (Billing et al., 2002). In I-O psychology it has been observed that employees may be angered when seeing a coworker undeservingly abused by a supervisor (Mitchell et al., 2015).

7 *Otherishness* (Def.): "Wanting or striving to benefit others because one cares about their well-being" (Crocker, et al., 2017, p. 301).

A note of caution was introduced recently by Decety and Cowell (2014), who review the case for concluding that "morality and empathy are two independent motives ... . Empathy has older evolutionary roots in parental care, affective communication, and social attachment; morality, on the other hand, is more recent and relies on both affective and cognitive processes (p. 526)."

Experimental and observational findings indicate that the expression of empathic behavior becomes more complex and sophisticated concomitant with the individual's social–cognitive maturation. Hoffman (1988) described the process as beginning with the generalized emotional contagion of a *global* empathy in which the very young child lacks sufficient sense of self to apprehend that the source of distress is someone else. As he or she develops a sense of self as distinct from others, the child is able to distinguish the distress as emanating from another. Nevertheless, it is an immature *egocentric* empathy in which he or she cannot yet appreciate that the other's affect may be different from his or her own emotional reactions. At this stage of development the child may begin to experience feelings of compassion or *sympathetic distress* for the victim, generating motives to help because of feeling sorry for the other person rather than just to ease his or her own empathic discomfort. That shift is enabled when the child acquires the cognitive capacity to make causal attributions for behavior—for example, that the other person's distress is not their own fault.

Empathy for another's feelings and empathy for another's life condition are the highest levels of empathy in Hoffman's scheme. These affective reactions depend on the child's becoming able to understand that other people's feelings, based on their needs, may be different from one's own and may be related to more generalized conditions than the immediate situation. But not only does one's perception of the world become more complex, so too does one's affective empathic reactions. For example, if a third party is to blame for someone's pain, sympathetic distress may also lead to *empathic anger* at the perpetrator. And if the victim is seen as undeserving of this treatment, what Hoffman referred to as a sense of *empathic injustice* may be engendered.

Hoffman's second ideal type of moral problem, being the cause (or potential cause) of harm to another, is the type of situation in which moral behavior is acquired as a function of the discipline procedures used frequently by our caregivers when we are children. For example, Minton et al. (1971) found that mothers of two-year-olds attempt to change the behavior of their children against their will an average of every 6 to 7 minutes.

Hoffman (1988, 1991, 2000) outlined three basic kinds of disciplinary techniques, and he concluded that they have different consequences with regard to the internalization of moral mechanisms (e.g., anxiety, guilt, altruistic feelings and justice principles). They include power-assertive discipline, consisting of physical or psychological punishment, commands, threats, or deprivations; and love-withdrawal techniques, which may be needed to get the child to stop what he or she is doing and pay attention to what the adult is communicating, but which by themselves are inimical to the internalization of moral standards. According to Hoffman (1988) the acquisition of a moral orientation consisting of internal motives to act morally irrespective of external sanctions is achieved via the use of *inductions,* which are "disciplinary techniques that point up the effects of the child's behavior on others, either directly ('if you keep pushing him, he'll fall down and cry') or indirectly ('don't yell at him, he was only trying to help')" (p. 524). These inductions serve to generate guilt feelings that, when repeated many times, may produce a moral motive, and they also provide the content within which those motives are embedded: for example, why certain things are right or wrong, what the values are that are being expressed, and so forth.

The essence of why Hoffman (1991) referred to his model as an information-processing theory is that in his view the child "semantically integrates the information contained in many inductions over time … this results in an increasingly complex structure of knowledge about the harmful effects that one's actions may have on others" (p. 107). Further, this knowledge structure is charged with the empathic and guilty feelings that were generated by the inductions and thus has motivational force. For that reason, and because the source of the induction (the parent or other caregiver) lacks salience and a connection to the knowledge structure and so is forgotten, the product of the information processing—a moral standard—is experienced as one's own (i.e., it is internalized).

Hoffman's third ideal type of moral problem, having to reconcile competing obligations to two or more persons, is a common adult dilemma encountered, for example, by parents who have more than one child or by managers who must make human resource decisions affecting several subordinates. In such instances Hoffman (1991) noted that empathy-based moral considerations alone may be insufficient. For example, the decision maker may have equal or equivalent empathic concerns and attachments to all those involved. Hoffman emphasized that "mature moral judgments in these situations may therefore require the application of moral principles that transcend empathy and contribute a note of impartiality" (p. 108). The moral psychologists who have most concerned themselves with such "impartial principles" have been the cognitive stage theorists to whom we now turn our attention.

Morality as Reflecting Cognitive Stages of Development

Piaget's Stages of Moral Development[8]

Jean Piaget's (1896–1980) work on moral development was an outgrowth of his work on cognitive development, which was his primary concern. He began his

---

8   Much of the discussion of Piaget's work on moral development is informed by Lickona's (1994) helpful and succinct review.

research in the 1920s when learning theory, in particular behaviorism, was the dominant view in American psychology. Intellectual growth and development was viewed largely as a quantitative phenomenon—an increase in associations and reinforcement connections. But Piaget was a European who had studied both philosophy and zoology as well as clinically oriented psychology with Carl Gustav Jung and Eugen Bleuler. Based on his experiences administering reading tests to Paris schoolchildren, he came to appreciate the cognitive development of children as representing qualitative changes.

In particular, he viewed such development as progressing through four qualitatively distinct stages, increasing in intellectual sophistication, and culminating in a stage of thinking that is akin to adult reasoning. They are: the *sensorimotor* stage during the first two years of life; the *preoperational* stage, from age 2 to 6 or 7, during which we learn to manipulate the world psychologically through words, images and thoughts; the *concrete operational* stage, from approximately age 7 to 11 or 12, marking the beginning of logic, classifying objects according to their differences and similarities, and developing abstract notions like number and time; and the *formal operations* stage, extending through adolescence into adulthood, during which an adult-like mastery of logical thought and the capacity to manipulate abstract notions and foresee the implications of ideas develops.

Piaget (1932/1965) carried over fundamental aspects of this model of cognitive development into his views on moral development: (a) development moves through sequential stages that are cumulative, each one necessary for the passage to the next; (b) passage from one stage to the next, although conceived as universal and innately based, is nevertheless constructed uniquely by each individual based on stimulating interactions with environmental objects; and (c) each stage is constituted of successively more mature cognitive operations, allowing for increased success with handling more complex situations and a more sophisticated and abstract conceptualization of the world. But most important of all is his assumption that moral development depends on, first and foremost, general intellectual growth—an assumption that has been largely supported by the subsequent empirical literature (see Lickona, 1994).

As shown in Table 6.1, Piaget's theoretical formulation of the stages of moral development consists of only two stages in contrast to his more refined four-stage model of cognitive development. The shift from the less mature to the more mature level of morality is accomplished for most healthy children during the preoperational (2–6 yrs.) or, at the latest, the concrete operational stage (7–11 yrs.) of cognitive development. The shift is conceived to be a gradual one, and there may be a considerable period in which both modes of thinking coexist until the more mature one comes to dominate due to its greater utility as a basis for shaping the child's social interactions. In fact, reviews of the available research suggest that the dimension changes outlined in Table 6.1 do not represent qualitative shifts in thought processes (Gelman & Baillargeon, 1983) but may best be viewed as "steady

TABLE 6.1 A Comparison of Piaget's Stages of Moral Development and Their Constituent Dimensions

Early Stage of Moral Development: The Morality of Constraint		Later Stage of Moral Development: The Morality of Cooperation
1. Absolutist or egocentric moral perspective. There is only one viewpoint on right and wrong, and it is held by everyone.	versus	1. Awareness that there may be alternative views of right and wrong and that people may differ in that regard.
2. Rules are permanent and unchangeable largely because they emanate from powerful adults.	versus	2. Rules are flexible and can be changed, and that is not the same as breaking the rule.
3. Belief in immanent justice that punishment for wrongdoing is automatic and inevitable.	versus	3. Punishment, like the misdeed itself, is a social phenomenon and so not necessarily inevitable.
4. Responsibility for behavior is judged objectively in terms of its consequences or effects on others.	versus	4. Responsibility for actions is judged subjectively based on the actor's motives or intentions (i.e., intentionality).
5. What is morally wrong is defined in terms of external sanctions of what is prohibited and/or punished.	versus	5. Moral wrongness is defined in terms of that which violates notions of fairness, trust, or cooperation.
6. Acceptance of arbitrary or expiatory punishment (e.g., spanking) that bears no intrinsic relation to the offense.	versus	6. Belief in restitution or reciprocity-based punishment, allowing the offender to suffer the adverse consequences of his or her actions.
7. Approval of punishment for peer-initiated aggression administered by an authority.	versus	7. Approval of direct retaliation to the culprit.
8. Acceptance of the arbitrary and unequal distribution of goods or rewards by an authority.	versus	8. Insistence on the equal distribution of goods or rewards.
9. Duty is conceived as obedience to authority	versus	9. Allegiance to the notion of equality, equal relations with peers, and concern for the welfare of peers.

Source: Note. —Based on Lickona (1994).

age increases under most circumstances, rather than as closely knit *stages* of moral thought" (Lickona, 1994, p. 331, italics added).

The early-stage *morality of constraint* (also referred to as *heteronomous morality* or *moral realism*) is largely shaped, according to Piaget, by the child's limited intellectual capacities and his or her unconditional subservience to adults. The gradual shift to a *morality of cooperation* entails a growing capacity to appreciate the separateness and worth of others as social equals to oneself. Later scientists stressed the role of both genetic and cultural evolution in the origins of human sociability and cooperation (Henrich & Muthukrishna, 2021).

Piaget hypothesized that shifts, especially in the first four dimensions of the moral stages (cf. Table 6.1), were the aspects of the child's moral system most dependent on cognitive development, and this has largely been supported by empirical research (Lickona, 1994). Cognitive development enables the child to acquire a set of moral beliefs based on the variety of social interactions with peers and adults that typifies middle childhood, and an absence or a distortion of reciprocal childhood social interactions can result in a retardation of moral development.

Overall, Piaget's theories of cognitive and moral development reveal a growth from externally controlled or heteronomous behavior to more autonomous functioning. In his morality of cooperation we see the influence of Kantian notions of respect for all individuals as our moral equals (cf. Dimensions 1, 5, 6, 7, 8, and 9), the conception of the moral person as one with good intentions (Dimension 4), and the reasoning capacity and freedom to acquire an independent sense of morality beyond mere obedience to external constraints and sanctions (Dimensions 1, 2, 4, 5, 6, and 9). In addition, we can see in Piaget's focus on cooperative social relations as the ultimate criterion of morality the influence of social contractarian ideas, especially Rawls' view (Dimensions 3, 5, 6, 7, 8, and 9).

Kohlberg's Cognitive Stage Model[9]

The dominant view of moral development among psychologists and other social and behavioral scientists long has been Lawrence Kohlberg's (1981, 1984) individualistic *cognitive stage theory*. To fully understand the development of Kohlberg's theory it should be appreciated as a reaction to the then-prevailing socialization models of moral development. Although Piaget's study of moral development was secondary to his involvement in exploring cognitive development in general, the outlines of his theoretical approach and the assumptions on which they rest accrued great significance because of their influence on Kohlberg's thinking. Kohlberg expanded on Piaget's work philosophically, psychologically and methodologically. The substance of his theory is informed by philosophical thought even more than Piaget's was (especially Kant, Hare's universal prescriptivism, Rawls, and Habermas). In fact, he even attempted a sort

---

9   This review of Kohlberg's theory was aided by comprehensive yet succinct summaries by Kagan (1987), Kegan (1993), and Rest (1994).

of reconciliation of the long-standing philosophical dispute between con-sequentialism and deontology, viewing them both as providing the basis for the highest level of moral judgment (although, as discussed later, he did not see them as equivalent). His psychological theory is much more elaborate than Piaget's; it is more complex—three broad levels of moral development are recognized, with at least two stages each (depending on which version of the theory is consulted). And from a methodological perspective much greater attention is paid to the development of a reliable measuring instrument by which to operationalize the constructs.

There are six basic aspects or assumptions underlying Kohlberg's theory and research, all of them with roots in Piaget's model: (a) in contrast with the dominant socialization view of moral development in the 1950s and 1960s when Kohlberg started his work, and the influence of behaviorism in American psy-chology prior to the so-called "cognitive revolution," Kohlberg's focus was on the cognitive processes by which individuals construct a system of moral rea-soning for themselves; (b) moral development proceeds invariantly through successive stages (six of them in the most widely cited version), without re-gression to an earlier stage or skipping a stage; (c) the stages are defined by the nature of the moral reasoning engaged in—i.e., as prevailing cognitive operations for the person, with each successive stage representing more complex judgment processes; (d) because of the focus on reasoning processes, as well as the inclusion of children as research participants, the empirical method of choice was the oral presentation of social dilemmas or conflicts with free, open-ended responses that could reveal those processes; and (e) as the child gets older, movement from one stage to the next is dependent on both the increasing capacity to engage in the more complicated cognitive reasoning required and on being confronted with more complex social situations for which the old reasoning is inadequate. Consequently, Kohlberg extended the domain of empirical research beyond Piaget's focus on early and middle childhood into adulthood; (f) the stages are conceived as universal across cultures and historical eras back as far as classical Greek civilization. This assumption is not based on a strong biological de-terminism but—as with Piaget—on the presumed logical sequence by which simpler reasoning processes must precede and form the foundation for more complex solutions to interpersonal problems.

An outline of Kohlberg's stage model is presented in Table 6.2. There have been several versions of the stages, with attendant theoretical revisions advanced over the years most notably by Kohlberg et al. (1983; but also see Sonnert & Commons, 1994). The most frequently-seen formulation is comprised of three levels of moral development, each in turn comprised of two stages, for a total of six. At various times, Kohlberg and his collaborators also utilized transitional stages between each of the six, as well as two substages within each one; toward the end of his life, Kohlberg was concerned with elaborating a somewhat me-taphysical seventh stage (cf. Kohlberg & Ryncarz, 1990, published after

TABLE 6.2 Kohlberg's Stages of Moral Development

Level and Stage	Normative Definition of What is Right	Motivation: The Reasons for Doing Right	Meta-Ethical Issue: Who Counts? (Social Perspective)	Example of Moral Reasoning
A. Preconventional Stage 1. Punishment and Obedience	Obedience to rules and authority for its own sake and avoiding doing physical harm to others and property.	Avoiding punishment and deference to the superior power of authorities.	Egocentrism. A person at this stage does not consider the interests of others or recognize they differ from one's own. Does not relate two points of view. Actions judged in terms of physical consequences, not psychological interests of others. Confusion of authority's perspective with one's own.	"I don't pad my expense account because they watch that like hawks."
Stage 2. Individual instrumental purpose and exchange	Following rules when it is in someone's interest. Acting to meet one's own interests and if necessary allowing others to do the same. Right is also what's a fair exchange, a deal, or an agreement.	Serving one's own needs or interests in a world where one must recognize that others have interests too. "You scratch my back, and I'll scratch yours."	Individualism (qualified egoism). A person at this stage separates own interests from others' and is aware that different persons' interests may conflict, so that right is a fair exchange, deal, and instrumental agreement.	"If you cover my shift this Friday, I'll work two shifts for you early next week."

B. Conventional **Stage 3. Mutual** **interpersonal** **expectations,** **relationships, and** **conformity**	Living up to what is expected of someone. Occupying one's social role(s) as child, sibling, friend, and so on. Being good is an important aim and means showing concern for others and maintaining their trust, loyalty, and respect.	Needing to be a good person in one's own eyes and others', caring for others, and respecting the Golden Rule. Being good by being nice.	Group perspective. A person at this stage is aware of shared feelings, agreements, and expectations, which take precedence over individual interests. Relationships based on a concrete use of the Golden Rule; generalized social systems not recognized.	"I'll stay late to help you with that problem because we're on the same team here, and I know you'd do the same for me."
Stage 4. Social system **and conscience** **maintenance**	Fulfilling the duties to which one has agreed and contributing to the group, an institution, or society. Laws to be upheld except in extreme cases when they conflict with other fixed social duties or rights.	Maintaining one's self-respect or conscience by meeting one's obligations or facing the consequences ("what if everyone did it?"). Also, wanting to keep the institution going as a whole.	Societal perspective. A person at this stage takes the viewpoint of the relevant social system, which defines law and order, roles, and rules. Interpersonal relationships are considered in terms of people's places in the system.	"I will work this weekend to finish the proposal—afterall, satisfying the client is what our business is all about."
B/C. Transition **Stage 4.5. Postconventional** **but not yet principled**	One's personal and subjective choices, because duty and right are arbitrary and relative.	Emotional reactions concerning maintaining one's sense of integrity as an individual irrespective of society's particular mores or norms.	An asocial perspective (subjectivist). A person at this stage stands outside his or her own society and makes decisions without any generalized commitment or contract with society. One can pick and choose obligations, but one has no principles on which to base it.	"I don't care if the company regulations say we should do that. I just don't feel like doing it."

(Continued)

TABLE 6.2 (*Continued*)

Level and Stage	Normative Definition of What is Right	Motivation: The Reasons for Doing Right	Meta-Ethical Issue: Who Counts? (Social Perspective)	Example of Moral Reasoning
C. Postconventional & Principled **Stage 5. Prior rights and social contract or utility**	Awareness that people hold a variety of values and opinions, that most values and rules are relative to one's group but should be upheld in the interests of fairness, impartiality, and because they are part of the social contract. Some nonrelative rights and values must be upheld regardless (e.g., life and liberty).	Feeling obligated to obey the law as an expression of one's participation in the social contract, which is for the benefit of all. Family, friends, and work obligations are also voluntary social contracts to be respected. Laws should be based on rational assessment of overall utility: the greatest good for the greatest number.	Prior-to-society perspective (universalism). A person at this stage has a rational awareness of values and rights prior to social attachments and contracts. The person integrates perspectives by formal agreements, objective impartiality, and due process. He or she recognizes that the moral and legal points of view may conflict and finds it difficult to integrate them.	"I'm really sorry that I can't go with you to the Knicks game this evening, but I promised that I'd finish the ABC company report today; they really need it."
Stage 6. Universal ethical principles	Abiding by those laws or social agreements that rest on universal ethical principles and refusing to obey those which violate them. Principles are universal principles of justice: equality of human rights and respect for the dignity of human beings as individuals.	Belief in the validity of universal moral principles and a sense of personal commitment to them, based on rational evaluation (i.e., exercising one's individual conscience).	A principled moral point of view on which social arrangements are grounded. It is self-chosen based on reason. A person at this stage recognizes the nature of morality—that persons are to be respected as ends in themselves, not means.	"I know my boss doesn't like her and I won't win any points for doing it, but she deserves an increase and I'm going to fight for it."

Kohlberg's death). Table 6.2 omits the substages, Stage 7, and all but one of the transitional stages (Stage 4½ has been the most frequently considered one).

A good way to approach Kohlberg's work is operationally, by understanding the methodology by which a person's current level of moral reasoning is assessed. Kohlberg presented his participants, frequently children who were reexamined and assessed every few years, with a series of moral problems (one at a time) and asked them to explain what they would do in the situation (this is the Moral Dilemmas Interview or Moral Judgment Interview) (MJI) (Colby & Kohlberg, 1987). The most widely known of these is the Heinz dilemma, a slightly abbreviated version of which is as follows: *Mr. Heinz's wife is dying from cancer and the only thing that can save her is a new drug that has recently been developed by a druggist, who is its only source. The druggist, however, is charging a great deal for the drug—more than Heinz has or could hope to raise. Should Heinz steal the drug in order to save his wife's life? Why, or why not?*

The essence of Kohlberg's theory is reflected in the fact that it does not matter what choice the respondent makes; it's the nature of the judgment processes by which the decision is reached that gets assessed, i.e., how the moral choice is justified. This is so because "the reasoning by which different people arrive at a moral conclusion can be structurally the same even though the specific issues attended to, the circumstances modifying the problem, and the concrete details may be different" (Snarey, 1985, p. 221). Over years of research the scoring system by which the open-ended responses are scored was revised and refined several times until it now consists of a quite elaborate set of guidelines and scoring examples that yield reliable results (Colby & Kohlberg, 1987).[10] In addition, Rest (1986a) developed a widely used self-administered, paper-and-pencil, multiple-choice inventory, the Defining Issues Test (DIT), which employs some of the same content as Kohlberg's dilemmas. Rest (1994) was noncommittal on the issue of whether the DIT measures the same constructs as the MJI procedure, but Eckensberger and Zimba (1997) indicated that it does not.

Children who are at the first (preconventional) level of moral reasoning can think only in subjective terms. They are incapable of taking another perspective, of putting themselves in someone else's shoes, so their reasoning entails consideration only of their own needs and feelings. At Stage 1 the young child's reply might be something like "Well, if the druggist is the only one in the store and he can't see you do it, I'd take the drug," or perhaps "You're sure to get caught stealing, so I wouldn't do it." A child in Stage 2 might reflect that "It depends on how nice his wife is; if she is really good to him then he should steal it." Older children who are at the second, or conventional, level of morality have grasped Piaget's cognitive principle of reversibility, so they are able to engage in

10 That's the good news—increased reliability. The bad news is that, as Snarey described (1985), it is extremely difficult to compare and integrate studies that were conducted over a period of years with different scoring criteria and algorithms.

reciprocal role-taking socially and understand the ongoing nature of social relationships. Consequently, at Stage 3—during which social morality is exclusively dyadic, involving only one's personal relationships—they may respond "If they are married then he must love her, so he should get the drug; it's not like stealing for himself." If they are in Stage 4—at which time their sociomoral meaning-making has led to a conception of social relations extending beyond merely one's personal contacts, and so requires a formal system of institutions and controls—the response might entail "Stealing is against the law, so he shouldn't do it. It's too bad for his wife, but we can't just let everyone go around stealing whatever they want." The transitional Stage 4½ represents an ambiguous period of cultural and ethical relativism in which the societal, conformist views of Stage 4 are seen as unjustifiably arbitrary, but a principled morality has not yet emerged to take its place. A person at this stage somewhat ambivalently reverts to a less social, more individualistic sensibility.

Young adults and older persons who have reached the principled morality of Level 3 have resolved the ambiguities of the transitional stage by the cognitive construction of objective universalizable principles that can be justified rationally. As Kagan (1987) interpreted:

> "Rightness" and "wrongness" are defined by reference to objective principles detached from the subjective feelings and perspective of either the self or the group. What is correct and virtuous is defined in terms of universalizable standards, reflectively constructed by the individual, of justice, natural rights, and humanistic respect for all persons … . For the post-conventional thinker, there are objective obligations that any rational person can come to discover and is bound to respect, that stand above the feelings of the self or the demands of others. (p. 5)

In the first segment of Level 3, Stage 5, those standards and obligations reflect notions of the social contract and utilitarian fairness that are owed deference by virtue of their value in promulgating a just society in which rules and norms are based on the greatest good for the greatest number. An adult in Stage 5 might respond to the Heinz dilemma:

> That's tough; I'm not sure what I'd do. The druggist has a right to his profit, and I don't condone stealing, but … I guess I'd try to arrange for installment payments … It might depend on whether he was gouging people: that's unfair. If that was the case, maybe I'd steal it.

Kohlberg's highest stage of moral reasoning, Stage 6, consists of having an inclusive moral system that, in the Kantian tradition, rests on a belief in the worth and dignity of all people and their equal entitlement to fair consideration. An adult at this stage might reply

I certainly respect the druggist's right to earn a living, but isn't someone's life more important? If I couldn't convince him of that or make some sort of deal, I'd have to steal the drug and just take the consequences.[11]

A fuller understanding of Kohlberg's theory can be facilitated by noting some of the criticisms that have been leveled at it.

Critique of Kohlberg

One indicator of how widely researched and influential Kohlberg's views have been is the depth and variety of criticisms to which it has been subjected. Poignantly, because his theory represents an attempt to integrate both psychological and philosophical thought, it has enticed criticism from both disciplines. The major charges are: (a) the model is an incomplete representation of moral behavior; (b) there is insufficient justification to characterize the transitions in reasoning processes as progressive invariant stages with no regression, rather than as continuous changes; (c) the theory contains an ideological philosophical bias; (d) the theory is culturally biased; and (e) it is also biased against women.

Incompleteness

The elements of Kohlberg's theory are comprised exclusively of modes of reasoning concerning social relations that are based on fundamental cognitive operations. Kohlberg's focus on reasoning or judgment processes was probably overdetermined by his reliance not only on Piaget, but on his attempt to embed his psychological model of morality in the historical philosophical tradition that, as shown in chapters 2, 3 and 4, focuses on moral reasoning. Consequently, if one is interested in understanding the processes by which people act morally (or fail to do so), it is clear that a great deal more is involved than the conscious rationales by which moral choices are reached. As noted earlier, it is one of the substantial differences between moral philosophy and moral psychology. Figure 6.1 suggests that there are many other social, emotional, motivational, and institutional factors that come into play in the relationship between moral judgment and moral action. Consequently, the correlations between moral judgment and real-life moral behaviors are generally reported as no more than .30 to .40 (Rest, 1994). This criticism of incompleteness has been raised frequently (Snell, 1996; Sullivan, 1994), and it was acknowledged early by Kohlberg (1973) himself who referred

---

11 Note that researchers, including Kohlberg, have always had difficulty in scoring Stage 6 and differentiating it from Stage 5. The incidence of people scored as at Stage 6 has been minuscule (Kagan, 1987); in the revised scoring manual for the MJI, Stage 6 is not scored (Colby & Kohlberg, 1987). Similarly, the DIT collapses Stages 5 and 6 to form a single composite *principled stage* (Rest, 1986a).

modestly to his theory as one of moral reasoning not of morality in general. One of the major areas of deficiency has been a failure to consider the critical directive role played by relatively stable personality attributes, such as the moral dimensions of one's character and values—thus the significance of a book title that includes both *Being Good* and *Doing Right* (Dobrin, 1993).

Not "Stages"

The reader may recall that it is generally conceded that Piaget's characterization of the changes that occur in the nature of moral reasoning are more justifiably thought of as "steady age increases" rather than discrete "stages" (Lickona, 1994). The same may be true for Kohlberg's stages as well. The available empirical research does not establish the levels of moral development as discrete stages characterized as structured wholes, that is, by consistent intra-stage uniformities and between-stage differences. Eckensberger and Zimba (1997) observed that "most cross-cultural Kohlbergian research provides very little information about the homogeneity of stages ... . Quite generally, it seems that inconsistencies are more frequently reported by researchers outside Kohlberg's group" (p. 312). That opinion was reached independently by other reviewers as well (Bandura, 1991; Krebs et al., 1991).

Complicating matters is the fact that the vast body of empirical research is based on several different operational measures that employ as few as 5 to as many as 13 stages, with varying degrees of psychometric reliability (Snarey, 1985). Where are the stage demarcations? Moreover, although the moral development score that characterizes each person's stage admittedly tends to show an upward progression with few regressions in both cross-sectional and longitudinal research, it is always an average score with considerable variation in the individual's many responses to the dilemmas. In fact, it is not unusual for participants to be categorized as at two or more stages simultaneously, and it is not known the extent to which this may reflect mere measurement (rater) error as opposed to a disconfirmation of the stage model.

In addition, the work of Turiel (1983) and his colleagues (Nucci & Turiel, 1978; Nucci & Weber, 1991; Turiel et al., 1987; Turiel et al., 1991) also challenges the sequencing of Kohlberg's stages from another perspective. They produced and reviewed a considerable amount of evidence in support of the theoretical view that conventional understanding, having to do with social customs and practices (equivalent to Kohlberg Stages 3 and 4), represents a "conceptually and developmentally distinct form of social knowledge" (Turiel et al., 1991, p. 319) that is independent of moral understandings having to do with issues of harm, welfare, fairness and justice. They are coexisting but separate social orientations. The moral orientation having to do with justice, fairness, rights, obligations, and others' welfare is based on intrinsic (i.e., context-independent) notions of rightness, wrongness, and harmfulness. The conventional orientation is based on elements of social organization, authority, and custom, which tend to be context-dependent. And their view is that the rationales underlying morality are cognitively more accessible to young children (the harmful consequences of transgressions, e.g., hitting a playmate) than those of social conventions (learning the rules of social behavior) so that "children's commitment to upholding moral rules consequently develops *earlier* than their commitment to conventional rules" (Edwards, 1993, p. 95, italics added). Therefore, conventional values and moral values are viewed as distinct domains; the former is not a stage on the way to the latter. In fact, according to these scholars, principled morality precedes conventionality.

Shweder et al.'s (1987) work tends to confirm the potential independence of the two domains but suggests that the distinction may exist only in certain cultures, including our own. Orthodox Hindus in India made no distinction between morality and convention. I believe that most Americans probably experience and conceive the two domains as independent: most of us have probably observed that the appropriateness of people's behavior may be very different in each. A business acquaintance's adherence to respectable business attire, proper etiquette, and norms of sociability is not likely to tell us much about whether they may be cheating customers, exploiting subordinates or cooking the books. By all accounts, several executives at Enron who deceived and swindled their employees and shareholders were well-liked and charitable pillars of their communities (Eichenwald, 2002b).

Philosophical bias

Is it justifiable for Kohlberg to have singled out a particular moral philosophy as the culmination of his entire stage sequence—that is, as the epitome of human moral development?[12] Is it defensible to assume as a result that consequentialism (utility theory) entails a less complex, less mature stage of moral reasoning (Stage 5) than does deontology (Kant & Rawls, Stage 6)? Philosophers (and others) who have attended to the issue generally think not (Puka, 1991; Thomas, 1993). As Sullivan (1994) put it, Kohlberg's "stage 6 becomes *'the* model of moral man' rather than *'a*

---

12 It is both interesting and ironic that Kohlberg seemed to have committed the obverse of the naturalistic fallacy (Moore, 1903). Recall, from chapter 2, that Hume's Law refers to the inappropriateness of justifying what ought to be (e.g., normative moral standards) merely based on what is (empirically prevalent patterns of behavior). Here, Kohlberg seemed to have defined what is—the empirical nature of moral behavior—largely as a reflection of his preferred normative standard, Rawls' and Kant's moral philosophies. As Simpson (1994) noted, "The distinction between normative philosophy and empirical psychology remains blurred, and normative thinking especially governs the description of what [Kohlberg] calls empirically derived categories of 'post-conventional' or principled reasoning" (p. 21).

model of moral man"' (p. 51, italics added). Puka (1991) was, nevertheless, sympathetic to Kohlberg's likely intent:

> When Kohlberg entered the field of research on "morals," he encountered a relatively simple-minded relativism. A credible source of nonrelativistic thinking was needed simply to distinguish moral norms among the diversity of norm systems. Kohlberg turned to moral philosophy to find sophisticated distinctions between the moral and nonmoral, along with well-justified criteria of adequacy in moral reasoning. (p. 374)

But, Puka speculated, Kohlberg could have simply extracted and synthesized the best and most relevant of what the diverse moral philosophies might contribute to psychology. Instead, he

> became a philosophical convert and partisan, to some extent ... . He decided that a particular philosophical tradition had defined the scope and adequacy of morality best. Then he set its view up as a somewhat a priori standard for moral psychology and development. (p. 375)

Thomas (1993) added, with respect to the implicit view that utilitarian thinking is less cognitively mature than deontological thinking, that "The very idea seems ludicrous when one considers the long line of distinguished thinkers who have embraced some form of utilitarianism: Jeremy Bentham, John Stuart Mill, and Henry Sidgwick" (p. 468).

Compounding this criticism are the empirical findings that, as noted previously, the incidence of research participants scoring at Stage 6 was so low, and the reliability of such scores so poor, that Stage 6 was eventually dropped from Kohlberg's scoring scheme, and Stage 5 and Stage 6 were condensed into a single category by Rest (1986a) in the DIT. Therefore, as measured operationally by the two primary measuring instruments in the field, Kohlberg's stage model consists of only a single stage of principled morality that is comprised of an amalgam of ethical relativism, Hobbesian social contractarianism, as well as the Rawlsian variety, utilitarianism (variant unspecified), Kantian notions of respect for people, and universalizability of moral principles, as well as elements of natural law theory in the form of universal rights!

Such a conglomeration of principles derived from multiple ethical theories is unlikely to be able to satisfy reasonable criteria for an internally consistent structural stage because several of these theories are philosophically incompatible. Nevertheless, that is not necessarily a grave problem for Kohlberg's theory—especially if one simply drops the strict stage assumptions that are not supported empirically in any event. One of the criticisms that has been leveled by philosophers doing what they do best—analyzing the logical consistency of a theory—is that, whereas the first four stages adhere more or less to Kohlberg's intent that they be defined by the nature of the reasoning processes by which moral judgments are achieved, Stages 5 and 6 do not. Content issues were smuggled into the definition of those stages. That is, they encompass particular moral values (e.g., the right to life and liberty) and personal attributes (e.g., the moral courage to stick to one's principles despite social disapproval; Thomas, 1993). Truncating the third level, principled morality, to a single stage corresponding to principled moral reasoning of whatever stripe (i.e., content neutral) may actually enhance the logical consistency of the theory. The composite Stage 5/6 would not be limited to any particular version of moral reasoning, as long as some rendering of morally right reasoning is the basis for moral choice.

Cultural bias

Kohlberg's theory has been charged with being culturally biased from both a conceptual as well as empirical point of view, thus challenging his claim that the stage progression model is universal. Clearly, the normative philosophical theories that inform and define the substance of principled morality are western philosophies (Kant, Rawls, Mill, Dewey, and Habermas). They are part of a tradition emanating from the classical Greeks that embodies substantive notions of social relations and morality (beliefs, attitudes, and values) not necessarily shared by the non-western world, that is, most of humanity (Simpson, 1994). For example, the ideals of life, liberty, and adherence to principle are defined within the western model of individualism and having the courage to "buck the crowd" (Sampson, 1977). But political philosophers point out that individual autonomy and liberty are not universal values (Gray, 2000). In contrast, eastern and Asian cultures emphasize communal contribution and fitting in. These two sets of values correspond to Stages 5 and 6 and to Stages 3 and 4, respectively.

Perhaps even more important in this regard are the findings of systematic differences in perceptual and cognitive style and reasoning processes between easterners and westerners. That is because the primary meta-concept on which Piaget's and Kohlberg's theories of moral development are based is that modes of cognition, including moral reasoning, are universal and thus provide a culture-free (i.e., content-free) means of evaluation.[13] Nisbett et al. (2001) produced and reviewed a great deal of evidence from a variety of psychological domains indicating that westerners tend to be analytic, "paying attention primarily to the object, categorizing it on the basis of its attributes, and attributing causality to the object based on rules about its category memberships," whereas "East Asians are held to perceive and reason holistically, attending to the field in which objects are embedded and attributing causality to interactions between the object and the

---

13 Although, as was just described, Kohlberg failed to adhere to that assumption with respect to Stages 5 and 6, which are defined by their normative philosophical content.

field" (Choi et al., 1999, p. 48). Consequently, westerners are more likely to attribute the causes of people's behavior to their dispositional attributes, whereas easterners are more likely to attribute the causes to features of the situation or context within which the person acts. Therefore, in that sense, the reasoning processes by which, according to Kohlberg, moral development is defined may not be content- or culture-free.[14] Because these tendencies extend to self-descriptions as well as to descriptions and attributions about others, they may be reflected in the judgment narratives offered in response to Kohlberg's moral dilemmas.

To what extent does the empirical research reflect the biases suggested by these cultural differences? One way of examining the question is an assessment of the extent to which Kohlberg's claim of universality holds up—that all stages will be found, at least to some degree, in all societies. To begin with, the reader should recall that Stage 6 was dropped from the Colby and Kohlberg (1987) scoring scheme, so is not even assessed. Snarey (1985) reviewed 45 studies of Kohlberg's theory in 27 different cultural areas and observed that, among the 25 studies conducted with participants who were at least 18 years old, nine studies reported having no one scoring as high as 4/5 or 5.[15] However, those nine studies were not all nonwestern societies; they were classified as tribal or village folk societies—western European, nonwestern and non-European. Snarey (1985) concluded that "the available data thus suggest that the significant difference lies between folk versus urban societies rather than between Western versus non-western societies" (p. 218). However, that conclusion may be premature as even the nonwestern European samples were categorized by Snarey (1985) as "Westernized, urban complex societies" (p. 217) (including Hong Kong, Israel, Japan, Puerto Rico and Taiwan).

Another question one could ask of the empirical research is whether Kohlberg's six (operationally, only five) stages are exhaustive. Are there other cultural variants of principled morality that do not seem to be recognized by the theory? After examining this question Snarey (1985) concluded:

> In sum, the evidence from the Israeli kibbutz, India, Taiwan, New Guinea, and Kenya suggests that some culturally unique moral judgments do not appear in the theory or scoring manual. Collective or communalistic principled reasoning, in particular, is missing or misunderstood. (p. 226)

---

14 Of further relevance is the position advanced by Nisbett et al. (2001) that it is simply not possible to clearly separate cognitive processes and cognitive content.

15 Similarly, Rest (1994) presented a summary of DIT P-scores (a continuous-scale measure of principled morality) from six countries, including western and nonwestern societies, in which the oldest participants, all college students at least 20 years old, averaged approximately only 46 on a scale with a theoretical range up to 95.

For example, in response to the Heinz dilemma, a village leader from New Guinea responded by placing blame on the community: "If nobody helped him [to save his dying wife] and so he [stole to save her], I would say *we* had caused that problem" (Snarey, p. 225).

Thus, the bias toward moral individualism as just discussed seems to infect the Kohlberg system, but it is not, as anticipated, reflected in a clear east–west dichotomy. Similarly, the cross-cultural studies reveal significant class differences in moral development scores within cultures: In virtually all cases, upper- and middle-class respondents scored higher than lower- and working-class participants. This is also associated with significant differences in educational level, and Snarey (1985) concluded that these differences suggest the "possibility of a bias in the scoring system" (p. 221). Similarly, Eckensberger and Zimba (1997) reviewed evidence indicating that moral stage development correlates with socioeconomic status, urbanization, religiosity, modernization, and educational level and/or intelligence, "but the psychological meaning of these sources of variance are usually difficult to interpret" (p. 317).

Sex bias

We have seen that restricting the definition of morality to western notions of justice principles and individual rights does not appear to be justified epistemologically (elevating a philosophical theory to an empirical psychological ideal), and its operationalizations may contain cultural and class biases. Gilligan (1982) and Noddings (1986) argued that Kohlberg's theory is also biased against women, even urban western women. The central argument they advanced is that an objective and rational approach to moral dilemmas, consisting of a dispassionate search for the operative principles of equity or justice or deliberations on the relative credence to be given to conflicting justice principles, is (a) a typically male orientation and (b) overlooks the orientation more typical of women, characterized as one of caring. That orientation involves attending to the contextual elements of a social dilemma, especially the needs, feelings, and interests of the people involved. Not only are such social concerns not likely to be scored any higher than Stage 3 on the MJI, but the brief bare bones presentations of the moral dilemmas do not include the rich contextual material in which real-life ethical problems are encountered—and which comprise the most salient aspects of the situation for women.

Gilligan and Wiggins (1987) agreed with Piaget and with developmental psychologists in general that the origins of morality depend on the differentiation of the self in relation to others. One element of that differentiation involves the young child's initial sense of helplessness, powerlessness, and dependence on others—one of inequality. Another simultaneous facet of differentiation is the child's growing attachment to caregivers. These two dynamics are seen as laying the groundwork for two social orientations or moral visions—justice and caring.

> Since everyone is vulnerable both to oppression and to abandonment, two stories about morality recur in human experience ... . Two moral injunctions—not to treat others unfairly and not to turn away from someone in need—define two lines of moral development, providing different standards for assessing moral judgments and moral behavior ... .
>
> *(Gilligan & Wiggins, 1987, p. 281)*

The hypothesis of sex bias in the measures of morality has generally not been demonstrated empirically. When proper controls are used for age, class and educational level neither Kohlberg's MJI nor Rest's DIT reveal statistically significant sex differences (Kohlberg, 1984; Snarey, 1985; L. Walker, 1984).[16] And the latest meta-analysis of sex differences in moral orientation reveals relatively small differences, albeit in the predicted directions: Males were higher in justice orientation and females higher in care orientation (Jaffee & Hyde, 2000). Although it might reasonably be concluded therefore that this critical feminist position has lost the battle over whether our measures of morality are biased, they have clearly won the war in that caring has been firmly established as a dimension of morality.

Moral psychologists have routinely accepted the duality of morality as including both justice concerns and caring (frequently labeled *welfare*). The latter is prominent, for example, in Hoffman's (1977, 1983, 1988) influential empathy-based socialization model. Moreover, the caring orientation may be an indication of healthy psychological adjustment. For example, it has been shown that degree of prosocial behavior, including instances of caring, among eight- and nine-year-old boys and girls is significantly predictive of their academic achievement and positive relations with peers five years later (Caprara et al., 2000).

It is also pertinent to take note of the application of an "ethics of care" perspective to organizations (Antoni et al., 2020). Interestingly, however, those authors focus on the potential problem of "care allocation" in which employees can experience a conflict between caring for coworkers and responsibility and caring for their work. There is more likely to be a conflict when substantial work demands require personal sacrifices that lead to caring for work as a strong priority with which caring for others would interfere. In any event there is at least some evidence that training can increase managers' emotional skills and compassion (Paakkanen et al., 2020).

---

16 The lack of significant differences may, in part, be artifactual. Recall that both the MJI and the DIT are restricted at the upper level of principled morality at which the putative sex differences are expected to be manifested. Stage 6 scoring has been abandoned in the measuring instruments, and the incidence of respondents at Stage 5 is very low. Thus, the measures do not appear capable of providing an adequate test of the sex-bias hypothesis.

Mere rationalization?

A recent and important reconceptualization of moral behavior suggests that it is caused primarily by innate, automatic, emotional and quickly-occurring intuitive reactions to situations, and much less frequently by moral reasoning such as contemplated and measured by Kohlberg (Haidt, 2001). Thus, the moral reasoning elicited by Kohlberg's stories is seen as largely after-the-fact rationalizing of an automatic intuitive judgment. Let us consider that view in more detail.

Morality as Based on Innate Intuitions: The Social Intuitionist Model

Jonathon Haidt (2001, 2008; Haidt & Joseph, 2004; Haidt & Kesebir, 2010) introduced a vigorous critique of the dominant rationalist approaches to understanding moral behavior (such as Piaget's and Kohlberg's) that he calls a *social intuitionist model* (SIM). Based on his review of "recent findings in social, cultural, evolutionary, and biological psychology, as well as in anthropology and primatology" (Haidt, 2001, p. 814), he believes that this model fits much better what psychology has uncovered about cognition and emotion over the past few decades. His presentation elicited a number of substantially critical commentaries such as those by Kennett and Fine (2009), Narvaez (2010), Pizarro and Bloom (2003), Saltzstein and Kaschkoff (2004), as well as others, prompting corresponding rebuttals (Haidt, 2003, 2004, 2010). The SIM has also been presented and considered widely by others in moral psychology (Blasi, 2009; Malle, 2021; Prinz & Nichols, 2010; Tiberius, 2015) and some recent evidence suggests that moral emotional reactions "may not be intuitive" and that further research is needed (Skitka, et al., 2018).

The SIM incorporates and accentuates the role of several ideas that have been presented in the past few chapters. Its major elements include: (a) a dual-process model of human cognition; (b) a nativist or evolutionary basis for morality; (c) the primary importance of moral emotions and intuitions; and (d) the emergence of moral virtues, as shaped by social and cultural influences. And, as noted above, it de-emphasizes the role of rational processes like the moral reasoning emphasized in earlier chapters, here.

Dual-processes

The SIM is an example of *dual-process models* that have permeated cognitive psychology for several decades, especially but not exclusively in judgment and decision-making (Kahneman, 2011). It is thought that they represent two different neurocognitive systems of brain function, sometimes referred to as the S-system and the C-system (Lieberman et al., 2002). Many I-O psychologists probably first encountered the genre in the form of *automatic* and *controlled processing* of skill acquisition (Ackerman, 1987).[17] Later on in this book we will consider another variant, in the domain of values, in which it is posited that people simultaneously possess a set of normative, rational values that are expressed in the form of espoused beliefs, as well as a set of "normal," experiential values that are less conscious and more affective and automatic (Epstein, 1989; cf. Chapter 8). In fact, the current *zeitgeist* in psychology seems to be that conscious, intentional control of behavior is much less prevalent than once thought, "so that most of moment-to-moment psychological life [such as judgments, emotions and a variety of behavior] must occur through nonconscious means ... . These various nonconscious mental systems perform the lion's share of the self-regulatory burden" (Bargh & Chartrand, 1999). Some scholars believe that the case is overstated (Vancouver & Scherbaum, 1999). And, as we shall note, the contentiousness of the issue has spilled over to the issue of moral behavior, as well.

Primacy of intuitions, not reasoning

The novel and controversial aspect of the SIM is its insistence on the indispensable and primary importance of automatic intuitive and emotional reactions to relevant situations as the causes of moral judgment, and the simultaneous diminution of the role of moral reasoning. Summarizing, Haidt (2001) argues that

> Rationalist models made sense in the 1960s and 1970s ... . Now we know (again) that most cognition occurs automatically and outside of consciousness ... and that people cannot tell us how they really reached a judgment ... . Now we know that the brain is a connectionist system that tunes up slowly but is then able to evaluate complex situations quickly ... . Now we know that emotions are not as irrational ... , that reasoning is not as reliable ... , and that animals are not as amoral ... as we thought in the 1970s. (p. 830)

Intuitions are defined as notions

> that pop into consciousness without our being aware of the mental processes that led to them ... . Moral intuitions are a subclass of intuitions, in which feelings of approval or disapproval pop into awareness as we see or hear about something someone did, or as we consider choices for ourselves.
> *(Haidt & Joseph, 2004, p. 56)*

---

17 However, a major distinction is that dual-process models in the cognitive-affective realms of personality, attitudes, values and morality are generally conceived as relatively independent, co-existing, parallel systems. In the field of learning or knowledge and skill acquisition it is customary to think of controlled processes as characterizing early-stage learning, especially of novel and/or difficult material. With experience and reinforced repetition, those efforts may be transformed into more habitual and automatic responses.

It is this automatic, intuitive nature of moral judgment that supposedly accounts for the phenomenon of perceiving, knowing, feeling or believing that something is wrong, shameful, disgusting or immoral—yet not immediately being able to explain why: called *dumbfounding*.

According to the SIM, whatever moral reasoning we engage in occurs primarily ex post facto, subsequent to the appearance of that immediate moral judgment—in the form of (a) rationalizing one's emotional reaction to oneself; or (b) attempting to justify one's judgment by trying to rationally persuade others—which, according to Haidt (2001), rarely works and if it does it's through "triggering new affectively valenced intuitions in the listener" (p. 819). He also posits a role for unintentional social influence processes on friends, acquaintances, colleagues, etc., from those who have made a moral judgment, but these do not necessarily involve any *reasoned* persuasion. He does not acknowledge much role, if any, for the way in which prior cognitive appraisals, including moral reasoning, can shape the nature of subsequent intuitive moral appraisals—what Pizarro and Bloom (2003) refer to as "educating the moral intuitions" (p. 194).

However, Haidt does acknowledge two (rare) occasions when moral reasoning may play a causal role: (a)

> people are capable of engaging in private moral reasoning … . particularly … philosophers, one of the few groups that has been found to reason well … . However, such reasoning is hypothesized to be rare, occurring primarily in cases in which the initial intuition is weak and processing capacity is high; (p. 819)

and (b)

> In the course of thinking about a situation … a person comes to see an issue or dilemma from more than one side and thereby experiences multiple competing intuitions. The final judgment may be determined either by going with the strongest intuition or by allowing reason to choose among the alternatives … . (p. 819)

From the perspective of this book, aimed largely at improving the quality of ethical behavior, these are important observations to which we will return.

Inherited moral modules

What are the origins and bases for the moral intuitions and emotions that are the core of the SIM? To explain them Haidt and Joseph (2004) rely on the notion of the *modularity* of mind.

An evolved cognitive module is a processing system that was designed to handle problems or opportunities that presented themselves for many generations in the ancestral environment of a species. Modules are little bits of input-output programming, ways of enabling fast and automatic responses to specific environmental triggers. (p. 60)

So, in this view, a moral intuition (or a closely related set of them) is the output of a module that evolved to meet a particular set of circumstances having to do with the approval/disapproval of people's behavior or character (or our own). The *proper domain* of a module refers to the actual situation it evolved to deal with. The *actual domain* of a module "is the set of all things in the world that now happen to trigger the module" (Haidt & Joseph, 2004, p. 60) (cf. Table 6.3).

It should be noted, however, that the notion of modularity in evolutionary psychology is the subject of considerable debate and is viewed by some as "ill-posed and confused" and constitutes the "primary grounds for skepticism of evolutionary psychology's claims about the mind" (Pietraszewski & Wertz, 2022, p. 465; also see Goldfinch, 2015).

Virtues

As noted earlier, the re-emergence of virtue ethics over the past 50 years or so can be attributed to dissatisfaction by some moral philosophers with both deontological and consequentialist perspectives—i.e., having limited the conceptualization of morality to reasoning or problem-solving, whether involving abstract principles or utilitarian quasi-metrics. By rejecting the analogous cognitive-rationalist models in developmental-moral psychology, the SIM proceeds in that renewed tradition. Recall from chapter 5 that a virtue is a commendable character trait that is morally praiseworthy; that it is grounded in corresponding motivations and emotions; and that it is culturally shaped. As Haidt and Joseph (2004) put it, "virtues are acquired inductively, that is, through the acquisition, mostly in childhood but also throughout the life course, of many examples of a virtue in practice" (p. 62). This sounds very reminiscent of Hoffman's empathy-based model discussed earlier in this chapter.

It is important to recognize that the SIM emphasizes that the acquisition of virtues is constrained by "the kinds of virtues that 'fit' with the human mind" (Haidt & Joseph, 2004, p. 62)—thus theoretically linking the innate moral modules, their intrinsically associated emotions and intuitions, and extended domains of expression, with the resultant substance of moral virtue. This is illustrated in Table 6.3.

TABLE 6.3 Five Intuitive Moral Modules and Their Associated Expression

Pattern of Innate Intuition	Suffering	Hierarchy	Reciprocity	Purity	Ingroup*
Proper Domain (original triggers)	Suffering and vulnerability of one's children	Physical size and strength, domination, and protection	Cheating versus cooperation in joint ventures, food sharing	People with diseases or parasites, waste products	A co-residing kin group
Actual domain (modern examples)	Baby seals, cartoon characters	Bosses, gods	Marital fidelity, broken vending machines	Taboo ideas (communism, racism)	Ethnic groups, teams, hobbyist gatherings
Characteristic Emotions	Compassion	Resentment versus respect/awe	Anger/guilt versus gratitude	Disgust	Trust, vigilance against betrayal
Relevant Virtues	Kindness, compassion	Obedience, deference, loyalty	Fairness, justice, trustworthiness	Cleanliness, purity, chastity	Loyalty, self-sacrifice

Source: Adapted from Haidt and Joseph (2004). Intuitive ethics: How innately prepared intuitions generate culturally variable virtues. *Daedalus*, Fall, 55–66. Used by permission. Note. —Table 1 in Haidt & Joseph presents only four modules. The Ingroup module is suggested in a footnote and presented more formally in Haidt and Joseph (2007) and Haidt and Kesebir (2010). A later work (Haidt, 2012) provisionally adds a sixth foundation, Liberty/Oppression.

Evaluation

Scholarship in this area has been hampered by the somewhat contentious, sometimes adversarial nature in which views have often been presented and rebutted. Some have phrased the issue as one of "deciding *versus* reacting" (Monin et al., 2007, emphasis added); and some have presented experimental evidence purporting to demonstrate that "deliberative decision making may actually increase unethical behaviors and reduce altruistic motives when it overshadows implicit, intuitive influences on moral judgments and decisions" (Zhong, 2011, p.1). In his seminal presentation Haidt (2001) "reviews evidence *against* rationalist models and proposes an *alternative*" (p. 814, emphases added). Although he does not deny a role for moral reasoning, he does relegate it to a secondary, nearly insignificant causal role in the appearance of moral judgments—to an extent that seems exaggerated and, to some scholars, ignores counterfactual evidence. Accordingly, his position is read by Saltstein and Kasachkoff (2004) as claiming "that nonrational evolutionary forces *rather than* rational processes motivate moral choices" (p. 274, emphasis added); similarly, Narvaez (2010) ponders "how do we sort out the *competing views* of intuitionism and rationalism?" (p. 164, emphasis added) and observes that "the intuitionist *challenge* to rationalism is formidable" (p. 165, emphasis added) and that "intuitionist theories have been effective in *capturing* the academic discourse about morality" (p. 163, emphasis added).

But, as we have described, although Haidt assigns a lesser role to moral reasoning (perhaps to an extreme), it does play some part in the SIM. Therefore, there seems to be more potential for agreement (for a "mixed-model") among these scholars than is sometimes acknowledged: "it is likely that the moral decision-making/judgmental process will be an iterative process whereby intuitive processes are intermixed with more rational, deliberative ones" (Saltstein & Kasachkoff, 2004, p. 281), to which Haidt (2004) replied "this is very similar to what I wrote ... . The difference is that I say the iteration of intuitive and reasoned processes happens when people talk about moral issues; it rarely happens in a single head" (p. 285). And some years later, perhaps wishing to encourage a rapprochement, Haidt and Kesebir (2010) present the relevant discussion under the title of "Intuitive Primacy (*But Not Dictatorship*)" (p. 801, emphasis added).

In a similar vein, while focusing on the specific issue of how we make causal attributions of blame or praise for other people's actions, but extending their concerns to the role of intuition in morality generally, Alicke et al. (2015) observe that it involves

> ... a conflation of automatic, intuitive, top-down with deliberate, evidence-driven, and bottom-up judgment processes. In particular, in assessing the evidence regarding an actor's causal role in a morally praiseworthy or blameworthy act (deliberate, bottom-up), the observer's

attitudinal or emotional reactions (automatic, top–down) to the event and its consequences influence causal judgments. (p. 806)

Haidt's point, that moral reasoning rarely occurs flying solo, is worth further reflection in the context of a book like this one, which aims (in part) to enhance the quality of ethical problem-solving. It is in that context that the nature of the SIM as a descriptive model of the hypothesized antecedents and nature of human morality should be noted. It is not, nor does it purport to be, a normative prescription of what our moral judgments should be or how they should be processed. As Haidt (2001) has acknowledged, the model concerns claims

> about how moral judgments are actually made. It is not a normative or prescriptive claim about how moral judgments ought to be made ... . people following their moral intuitions often bring about nonoptimal or even disastrous consequences ... . (p. 815)

This is an important distinction. For example, Haidt (2003) cites "the empirical research on reasoning, which shows that people rarely search on their own for evidence on both sides of an issue" (p. 197). However, that is exactly what the study of applied ethics is all about; that is precisely the intent of books such as this; the enterprise is premised on the belief that the incidence and quality of one's ethical reasoning and attendant actions can be improved via both reasoned internal dialogue that takes nonrational influences into account, as well as social discourse.

The prescriptive intent and the recommended model of individual moral decision-making presented in chapter 15 are not negated or necessarily even challenged by the descriptive SIM (or any other account of moral behavior) unless the recommended decision processes exceed realistic expectations of people's capabilities and inclinations. And I do not believe that to be the case—even if, as Haidt suggests, we are not all as talented at it as trained philosophers. Moreover, as Haidt acknowledges, SIM is a descriptive model and it "focuses on moral judgment and moral thinking rather than on moral behavior" (Haidt & Kesebir, 2010, p. 801), which is a limitation we are not able to avail ourselves of in the prescriptive domain of applied professional ethics in which we are generally required to *do* something in response to a dilemma.

More important, in addition to the role of moral reasoning in the form of discussions *between* people, the SIM does acknowledge two or three circumstances in which "private moral reasoning" may be anticipated,

> occurring primarily in cases in which the initial intuition is weak and processing capacity is high ... [and] ... in the course of thinking about a situation ... a person [may] come ... to see an issue or dilemma from more than one side and thereby experiences multiple competing intuitions.

Let's take a quick look at each of those conditions: *weak intuitions; competing intuitions;* and *high processing capacity.*

Most of the empirical evidence cited in support of the SIM involves presenting experimental participants with issues such as the following: "abortion, homosexuality, pornography, and incest ... . eating one's dead pet dog, cleaning one's toilet with the national flag, eating a chicken carcass one has just used for masturbation" (Haidt, 2001, p. 817); "showing a disgusting video clip ... mak[ing] moral judgments in the presence of a bad smelling 'fart spray' ... . abortion and gay marriage ... gun control and affirmative action" (Haidt & Kesebir, 2010); and "harmless cases of cannibalism" (Haidt & Joseph, 2004, p. 61). These experimental provocations are theoretically relevant to the questions under investigation—e.g., investigating the nature of disgust emotions as part of the purity intuition module. But they are likely to be very much more intense, emotionally arousing, and with a greater sense of immediacy than the ethical problems one is likely to encounter during more mundane life circumstances such as in the work setting (cf. Lowman, et al., 2006). Monin et al. (2007) observed that "authors presenting diverging models are considering quite different prototypical situations: those focusing on the resolution of complex dilemmas conclude that morality involves sophisticated reasoning, whereas those studying reactions to shocking moral violations find that morality involves quick, affect-laden processes" (p. 99). Consequently, it seems reasonable to believe that the ethical issues likely to be confronted by the I-O psychologist, while perhaps stressful and of some consequence, are likely to yield relatively "weak intuitions," thus permitting (granting the accuracy of the SIM) the initiation of individual moral reasoning processes.

Regarding the second of Haidt's exceptions, "competing intuitions," the reader may recall Hoffman's three ideal types of moral dilemma, discussed earlier in this chapter, from which an internalized sense of morality (e.g., intuitions of guilt) develops. They include contemplating intentionally causing harm to another out of self-interest, in which the dilemma is occasioned by competing empathic motives reflecting prosocial qualities; and facing competing, mutually exclusive, obligations or responsibilities to two or more persons. It is such "competing intuitions" that account for our characterization of such situations as an ethical *dilemma.*[18]

Haidt's (2001) characterization of one of the rare occasions when "people may at times reason their way to a judgment by sheer force of logic, overriding their initial intuition ... . [requires a situation] in which the initial intuition is weak and *processing capacity is high*" (p. 819, emphasis added). I have not been able to find any

18 I have added two additional types to Hoffman's three, both of which also entail competing intuitions—values conflict, and being pressured to violate one's ethical standards (cf. Table 6.4 and "Adding Further to the Framework for Ethical Decision Making" at the end of chapter 7).

explanation or examples in the literature of the SIM concerning what is meant by high processing capacity. I infer, however, that it is exemplified obliquely by Haidt's reference to "philosophers, one of the few groups that has been found to reason well" (p. 819).[19] In any event, as I concluded in chapter 1, this book (and others) represents an attempt to enhance the capacity of I-O psychologists to process ethically relevant information in the service of "rais[ing] the level of discourse … in moral reasoning and ethical problem-solving among I-O psychologists." It is, perhaps, worth noting in the present context that such education and training in ethical problem-solving may be effective (if and when it is) by developing what Narvaez (2010) refers to as relevant "experience-based, postreflective, well-educated intuition [that] comes about at the back end of experience (when conscious effort becomes automatized)" (p. 171), which is far different than the "naïve intuition" in the SIM. Perhaps the most telling criticism is the observation that it is simply not clear theoretically which of the four classes of moral judgments (evaluations; norm, wrongness, or blame judgments) moral intuitions refer to (Malle, 2021). The challenge to ethical reasoning is taken up again in chapter 15.

The Nature and Experience of a Moral Dilemma (III)

The results of moral development, regardless of which theory is used to conceptualize the process, are internalized sets of cognitive schemas with associated motivational and emotional components. These consist of generalized social orientations, personal values, behavioral norms, social expectations, conceptions of fairness and justice, prosocial motives, motives to avoid causing harm, as well as a variety of emotional reactions that may be associated with these. These schemas provide the bases by which one perceives, defines, and evaluates the sorts of social problems that we label moral or ethical. Much research in moral psychology is focused on determining what processes seem to be more or less universal and can be generalized across social classes and even cultures. Nevertheless, it seems evident that there exists considerable interindividual variation in those processes—e.g., in what ethical situations different people will experience as particularly upsetting. Much of that variation is undoubtedly attributable to differences in the socialization experiences among people—even among those in the same national, cultural, religious, and social class groupings.

The Problem Situation

But another group of potentially relevant variables has to do with the nature of the ethical issue itself with which one is confronted. Several factors are important.

---

19 Assuming his characterization is accurate it is not clear the extent to which the profession of philosophy selects individuals who reason well and/or trains candidates well in such abilities.

For example, a pertinent aspect of any such problem is its complexity. *Moral complexity* reflects the number of values and concerns elicited by the stimulus array and the relations among them. For example, Thiel et al. (2012) suggest that in the organizational context, "ethical misconduct may stem from the difficulties leaders have with accurately making sense of the dynamic business environment or other cognitive limitations" (pp. 49–50).

Of particular relevance, of course, are situations in which conflicting or incompatible values are evoked. An example encountered frequently in the moral philosophy literature illustrates the common conflict between interpersonal commitments (e.g., duty and responsibility) and personal ambition, needs, or objectives. It is called the *Gauguin dilemma,* representing the conflict between a self-actualizing motive—in this case, to go off to the South Seas to paint—and the responsibilities one has to one's family. Jean Paul Sartre raised the issue in terms of the young Frenchman during World War II who was torn between the desire to leave home and join the resistance to fight the Nazis and the duty to stay home to care for his elderly mother. What should he do?

Those are particularly vexatious dilemmas insofar as there may be little possibility for compromise. When we can compromise between competing ethical and social imperatives, we often do so; when we cannot, we may vacillate painfully. An example is provided in Stanley Milgram's (in)famous experiments in which research participants were instructed by the experimenter, under the guise of a learning experiment, to administer higher and higher levels of (fake) electric shock to experimental confederates when they made errors. Most (but not all) of the participants did so, even reaching levels of shock at which the confederates were apparently in considerable discomfort and pain. Turiel et al. (1991) noted that the research participants were confronted by "two separable contextual elements in conflict with each other. Embedded within the experimental situation is what [has been] referred to as a moral context and a social organizational context (p. 315)."[20] The moral dimension had to do with the issue of inflicting harm on others; the social organizational dimension had to do with the implicit rules and authority relations of the social system established by the experiment, including its scientific aims and legitimacy. To comply with the social influence meant violating the morality of care; to avoid inflicting harm meant denying the social dictates of the study. Most subjects, whichever choice they made, betrayed

20 Turiel et al. (1991) did not use the term *context* as it is customarily used and as I used it in Fig. 6.1 (cf. Category XI). What they referred to as the moral context and social organizational context of the situation refer to dimensions or facets of the ethical problem itself, not its surround.

considerable ambivalence and reluctance in doing so, as a reflection of the conflict and the attempt to arrive at a psychological compromise of sorts.[21]

Jones (1991) was among the first to point out that theories of moral reasoning such as Kohlberg's and models of ethical decision-making in organizations have uniformly omitted consideration of characteristics of the situation itself. In his theoretical exposition of an "issue-contingent model," he introduced the multidimensional construct *moral intensity* that "captures the extent of issue-related moral imperative in a situation" (p. 372). It is comprised of six characteristics of a moral issue:

1. **Magnitude of the consequences** of the decision, defined in accord with general utility theory as the sum of the harms (or benefits) done to potential victims (or beneficiaries).
2. The **social consensus** surrounding the ethical issue, defined as "the degree of social agreement that a proposed act is evil (or good)" (p. 375).
3. The **probability of effect** (or likelihood of the consequences) is an expectancy-like notion corresponding to the joint probability that the contemplated act will occur and will result in the consequences anticipated.
4. **Temporal immediacy** refers to the interval between taking moral action and the onset of its consequences.
5. By **proximity** is meant the degree of social, cultural, psychological or physical "nearness" that the actor feels for the potential victims or beneficiaries of the action. This seems to reflect the empathy-based considerations discussed earlier (Hoffman, 1988).
6. The **concentration of effect** of the ethical behavior is an inverse function of the number of people affected by the act (assuming the overall magnitude is constant). In other words, it is the average consequence per person affected. Thus, cheating an individual out of a given sum of money has a greater concentration of effect than cheating a corporation out of the same sum.

Jones (1991) proposed that dilemmas of high moral intensity are more likely to be recognized as moral issues, will elicit more sophisticated moral reasoning as well as a greater intent to act on a moral decision, and will thus more likely result in ethical behavior. The empirical results appear to generally support the importance of moral intensity, but they are limited primarily to the first three of the six components (Barnett, 2001; Chia & Mee, 2000; Frey, 2000; Harrington, 1997; Morris & McDonald, 1995; Paolillo & Vitell, 2002; Singer et al., 1998; Weber, 1996).

---

21 Could this be interpreted as a refutation of the SIM? That is, were those research participants struggling through an *internal* ethical reasoning process in their attempt to reconcile conflicting impulses?

In a similar fashion, Collins (1989) proposed that value judgments regarding potential ethical transgressions (defined in terms of harms) will be influenced by three factors. The first is the *nature of the harm,* in which Collins suggested—following distinctions made in jurisprudence—that physical harms are viewed as most severe, followed by economic harms and psychological or emotional harms—in that order. The second component is the *nature of the harmed,* in which it is postulated that harm to persons is viewed as more serious than harm to nonhuman entities, as is harm to many people than to few and to those with higher social status people than to those of lower social status. The third factor is the *stage of the resource transformation process* at which the harm occurs. Whereas the first two factors pertain to any consequentialist analysis, regardless of venue, the third refers specifically to transgressions within organizations in which, for example, ethical issues concerning hiring practices, promotion policies, and dismissal procedures correspond to the resource input, throughput and output stages of human resource management, respectively. Collins suggested that all else being equal, organizations are likely to be held more blameworthy for harms in the input and output stages because they are more visible to a greater number of observers. Certainly, the enormous focus on the fairness of employee selection testing and on the justification for repeated organizational downsizing of workers is consonant with that inference, although there does not seem to be many direct empirical tests of the hypotheses. However, as expected, Weber (1996) found that managers use successively higher stages of moral reasoning in dealing with dilemmas involving psychological, economic and physical harm.

Ethical dilemmas

The focus of this book emphasizes a conceptualization of unethical behavior as a consequence of the person's experiencing and failing to successfully resolve an *ethical dilemma.* This assumes at least some motivation on the part of the protagonist to do the right thing—if that can be determined and any obstacles, external pressures and/or competing motives and self-serving temptations can be overcome (Lefkowitz, 2011c, 2021; Lefkowitz & Watts, 2022). Within this definitional framework, then, unethical behavior is actually an indication of a person's failure (to resolve the ethical dilemma successfully).[22] Volitional transgression, whether characterized as intentional misbehavior, deviance, counterproductive behavior, corruption or research misconduct, is quite another thing. (I prefer the term *corruption* to cover all of them.) The distinction affects our assumptions regarding the causes of the actions in question, the character of the actor and the likely effectiveness of various organizational strategies and programs designed to

---

22 Which does not necessarily mean that the person is blameworthy. The failure might be due in large measure to circumstances.

encourage ethical compliance, such as a formal code of conduct (Lefkowitz, 2009b). Yet another type of misbehavior often conflated with unethical behavior is *incivility* or *rudeness*—violating social norms and expectations, not moral norms.

Building on Hoffman's three ideal types, Table 6.4 presents a useful taxonomy of five structural forms of ethical dilemmas, along with the two other

TABLE 6.4 Five Structural Forms of Ethical Dilemma and Other Misbehavior

Form	Definition
Ethical Dilemmas	
I. Opportunity to Prevent Harm	Awareness, anticipation or foreknowledge of someone or some entity (e.g., the organization) to be harmed or wronged by another or by circumstances.
II. Temptation	Contemplating (or taking) an action in accord with some self-serving motive, goal or ambition that would be deceitful, unjust or potentially harmful to another or to the organization; or would be knowingly inappropriate (such as not professionally competent, or in violation of accepted standards/rules).
III. Role Conflict	Having competing legitimate obligations or responsibilities (sometimes to two or more persons or other entities) such that fulfilling one entails failing to meet the other.[23]
IV. Values Conflict	Facing equally (or nearly equally) important but conflicting personal values that have been placed in opposition. Expressing one entails denying the other(s) expression.
V. Coercion	Being subject to external pressures to violate one's ethical or professional standards or legal requirements.
Incivility or Rude Behavior	Violation of conventional norms and expectations, resulting in some harm, disrespect or insult to others; but not violating moral principles.
Corruption	Intentional, voluntary acts of misbehavior, misrepresentation, deviant or counterproductive workplace behavior; not abiding by accepted norms or commitments made; or corruption directed against individuals or the organization for personal or organizational gain.

Source: Reproduced from Lefkowitz (2021). Forms of ethical dilemmas in industrial-organizational psychology. *Industrial-Organizational Psychology: Perspectives on Science and Practice, 14*(3), 297–319. Used by permission.

23 A special case of Role Conflict (which may also incorporate several other forms as well) is represented by the so-called "dirty hands" problem, in which the individual is obliged to do wrong or harm in order to be able to achieve a greater good (cf. Chap. 5).

types of misbehavior that are often mistakenly conflated with them. The forms are commensurate with the individual-level orientation of most treatises on personal or professional ethics. But it is worthwhile noting that in recent years attention has begun to be paid to the phenomenon of *collaborative dishonesty* (Leib et al., 2021).

Some people believe that "mere" rudeness doesn't deserve to be considered in the same context as more serious transgressions like unethical behavior and corruption. But there are several factors that contradict that position: (a) in practice, it is often difficult to differentiate between rude behavior that violates conventional social norms, and unethical behavior violating moral norms; (b) all three categories of misbehavior manifest on a continuum of severity or harmfulness—i.e., there are instances of mildly unethical or corrupt behavior as well as extremely offensive and hurtful rudeness; (c) rudeness or incivility has attracted considerable study in its own right by I-O psychologists (Cortina et al., 2017; Hülsheger et al., 2020; Lim & Cortina, 2005; Motro et al., 2020; Schilpzand et al., 2016; Yao et al., 2022), which seems justified by (d) employees will often have extreme and organizationally dysfunctional reactions to being treated rudely, especially by their supervisor. For example, in some anecdotal reports the high levels of voluntary terminations that occurred during the pandemic of 2021 (often referred to as "the great resignation" or "the big quit") often resulted from employees' reduced tolerance for inappropriate or insensitive behavior—i.e., no longer being willing to work for/ with jerks (Goldberg, 2022, B6; Holub, 2021). (Cf. "the dark triad" in Chap. 5.)[24]

In 2009 the Society for Industrial and Organizational Psychology (SIOP) sponsored an ethics survey of its members. They were asked to provide (among other information) one or two narrative descriptions of ethical incidents they had recently personally experienced. The critical incident narratives were coded according to the taxonomy presented in Table 6.4 and were reported in Lefkowitz (2021). Table 6.5 contains some illustrative verbatim responses to the survey.

Emotional arousal

Moral or ethical dilemmas are often, if not invariably, accompanied by emotional arousal, and a very active line of research in moral psychology focuses on the so-called *moral emotions* (cf. Chap. 7). An interesting way to introduce the topic is with some results obtained by applying the methods of cognitive neuroscience to the study of morality. Greene et al. (2001) were among the first to investigate

---

24 More than 50 years ago, shortly out of graduate school, I worked with an experienced I-O psychologist who used to tell managers with whom he consulted, "Your brains will get you hired and promoted; your personality will get you fired."

alternative explanations of a long-recognized puzzle among moral philosophers involving so-called trolley problems. These are "a class of scenarios that have been used so often in studies of ethical dilemmas that one might refer to them as the fruit flies of moral judgment" (Bennis et al., 2010, p. 189).

The moral dilemma posed by the trolley problem and the footbridge problem are alike, but people typically endorse very different actions in each.[25] Why do apparently similar situations engender opposite reactions? In the first situation, a runaway trolley is headed for five people who will be killed if it continues on that track. You can save them by switching the trolley to another track where it will kill one person. Should you throw the switch, turn the trolley, and save five people at the expense of one? In the second problem, as before, there is a trolley bearing down on five people. You are standing next to a large stranger on a footbridge spanning over the tracks between the trolley and the people. The only way to save the five people is to push the stranger off the bridge onto the tracks; he will die, but the trolley will be stopped. Should you do so? Most people respond yes to the first scenario and no to the second. Why? What's the difference?

While structurally similar, and apparently morally equivalent, the two dilemmas differ in that the first appears to be indirect or relatively impersonal whereas the second involves more direct and personal action. Greene et al. (2001) found that dilemmas characterized as personal in nature, like the footbridge problem, activated areas of the brain associated with emotion, whereas structurally similar impersonal moral dilemmas, like the trolley problem, activated areas associated with working memory during cognitive processing. The results suggest, therefore, that there are systematic differences in moral judgment associated with the degree of emotional arousal inherent in the dilemma, having little if anything to do with a rational assessment of the situation. More important, as the experimenters pointed out, the personal/impersonal distinction was merely "a useful 'first cut,' an important but preliminary step toward identifying the psychologically essential features of circumstances that engage, or fail to engage, our emotions and that ultimately shape our moral judgments" (p. 2107).

As it turns out, partly in response to a critique of their work, and partly based on additional experimentation, Greene (2009) believes that the personal/impersonal distinction is not necessarily a valid explanation of the findings—at least he agrees that it has not been demonstrated to be so. The more apt (albeit incomplete) explanation is a *dual-process theory of moral judgment* (Greene, 2007).[26] Automatic,

---

25 In recent work the "trolley problem" is sometimes referred to as the "switch problem."

26 A version of which is the SIM, just discussed. Dual-process theories in social and cognitive psychology generally refer to System (or Type) 1 and System (or Type 2) cognitive processes (Kahneman, 2011)—referring, respectively, to automatic, effortless and involuntary mental events versus conscious, effortful, reasoning activities. These are probably best thought of as classes of theories, with different versions more-or-less supported by the empirical evidence (Evans & Stanovich, 2013).

TABLE 6.5 Sample Responses Representing the Forms of Dilemma or Misbehavior

Form	Illustrative Descriptions

Ethical Dilemmas

I. Opportunity to Prevent Harm

1. *We discovered a computational error in an assessment report and were faced with whom to inform and how. After careful review, we decided to inform only those who were affected by a score that would place them in an incorrect "bracket" on their report—i.e., that would change their score from medium to high.*

2. *Two managers in a client company were engaged in a bitter longstanding feud. I was asked by the general manager to facilitate the resolution of the conflict. One of the managers would be fired if the situation was not resolved and I learned that the other manager knew this. I decided I needed to withdraw from the situation knowing that one of the managers had every incentive not to work through the issues.*

II. Temptation

3. *In the context of organization development a client wanted to revise their performance appraisal system and had fairly strong, but poor ideas (bad science and practice) about how to do it. My partner and I discussed at length what obligation we might have beyond just expressing our opinions on the ideas. How strongly should we argue against what the client wanted to do? Would the strength of our arguments be influenced by the likelihood of losing the client? And finally, if they decided to proceed should we insist on not being involved in the design and implementation of a system we thought was poor? After expressing our opinions, the client did decide they didn't need our services anymore, and frankly I was relieved.*

III. Role Conflict

4. *I often receive solicitations to participate in research surveys (some from I-O Psych. Grad students). Often the solicitation letter makes no mention of the research having been approved by an Institutional Review Board. If I do not know that the research has been reviewed and approved, should I participate or not?*

5. *A troubled female student who failed to complete her research project reported she felt "uncomfortable" with me, as her reason for this. To me, this is a vague allegation of sexual harassment.*

IV. Values Conflict

6. *The ongoing ethics concern I have as a consultant is the fact that we work with any type of organization regardless of their business or the way that they conduct business. There is no particular situation, just the ongoing concern I have when I consistently consult for businesses who violate human rights (some mining organizations), or animal rights (pharmaceutical, slaughterhouses, factory farms), or health care rights (insurance, pharmaceutical).*

V. Coercion	7. *While consulting in a large organization, I was asked to initiate several coaching and development assignments with two senior executives. Several discussions and meetings occurred with the senior executives, the CEO and the SrVP-HR to get agreement on the confidentiality ground rules for the engagements. After three months into both assignments the CEO pressured me to divulge assessment and coaching information that were clearly covered in our agreement as confidential to the participant. He implied that my future work in the company might be in jeopardy if I did not cooperate with his request. After some thought I chose not to share the information.*
Incivility or Rude Behavior	8. *In a practicum defense meeting, a female student was approached by a female committee member who commented on her outfit as "very professional, except for the 6" stiletto hooker high heels." A meeting between the director, student, and committee member was conducted addressing the details of the situation and a resolution which involved a formal apology by the committee member to the student as well as formal documentation of the incident was provided to the dean of the college according to the policies and procedures handbook. The issue was resolved, however the student still harbors ill-feelings toward the committee member.*
Corruption	9. *An I-O faculty member submitted a SIOP conference poster proposal with a brand new graduate student as the first author—to enable the faculty member to submit more than the limit of 3 submissions. The poster was accepted as an interactive poster. The student told the faculty member she did not feel qualified to present in the interactive session. The faculty member then dismissed the student as a research assistant and dropped the student as a thesis advisee. As director of our grad program, the student told me about this. I helped the student find a new thesis advisor. She graduated two years ago, but contacted me recently to ask if her picture and name could be removed from the faculty member's webpage identifying students working for the faculty member.*

Source: Reproduced from Lefkowitz (2021). Forms of ethical dilemmas in industrial–organizational psychology. *Industrial-Organizational Psychology: Perspectives on Science and Practice, 14*(3), 297–319. Used by permission.

negative emotional responses (e.g., disapproval or anticipated shame at the idea of intentionally killing one person even to save five others) entail characteristically deontological judgment processes; whereas controlled cognitive processes drive utilitarian reasoning that approves of killing one to save several others. He believes that the *footbridge* dilemma elicits a much stronger negative emotional reaction than does the *switch* dilemma, while acknowledging that we do not know for sure why that is so—although it could be, among other things, the personal/impersonal distinction. He notes, moreover, that "utilitarian judgments, as compared to characteristically deontological judgments, are associated with increased activity in … a brain region associated with cognitive control" (p. 582).[27] Another clue is provided by research revealing that people are more willing (hypothetically) to kill one person to save several when using a foreign language rather than their native language—perhaps because it "might stunt emotional processing, attenuating consideration of deontological rules, such as the prohibition against killing" (Hayakawa et al., 2017, p. 1387).

Yet a third interpretation (and there are more) is that the apparent contradiction is explained by *The Doctrine of Double Effect*, which is "a normative principle according to which in pursuing the good it is sometimes morally permissible to bring about some evil as a side-effect or merely foreseen consequence; the same evil would not be morally justified as an *intended means* or *end*" (Di Nucci, 2014, p. 80, emphasis added). One intends to push the bystander off the bridge only to save the others, not to intentionally harm him; harming him is a side-effect.[28]

However, it should also be kept in mind that such scenarios are invariably presented to participants under conditions of *closed-world assumptions* (CWAs) in which "the scenario is accepted as stated as complete and accurate with no other considerations or interpretations introduced. To satisfy closed-world assumptions, it is off limits to consider any alternative actions" (Bennis et al., 2010, p. 188), so that it's something of an open question as to the external validity of the findings. (Recall a similar issue raised regarding the moral dilemmas comprising Kohlberg's MJI.) And in fact, Shallow et al. (2011) show that changing the contextual conditions of the footbridge and switch scenarios changes people's judgments.

But just in case the reader was thinking that exercises like the trolley problem are rather meaningless because they are so unrealistic, we now have successful self-driving *autonomous vehicles* (AVs) not so very far away from commercial availability. Each AV will have to be preprogrammed with "moral algorithms" directing it to

> choose the lesser of two evils. For example, running over a pedestrian on the road or a passer-by on the side; or choosing whether to run over a group of pedestrians or to sacrifice the passenger by driving into a wall.
>
> *(Bonnefon et al., 2015, p. 1)*

27 The interested reader can refer to Bennis et al. (2010) for a summary of other potential explanations for the difference in reactions to the two scenarios.

28 Analyses get complicated. For example, an often proposed condition for applicability of the doctrine is that the two effects are independent; that the good effect cannot directly be achieved via the bad effect.

Who should make those choice(s)—the purchaser/driver? The manufacturer? Should different drivers of the same AV be able to activate a different algorithm? Should the decision(s) be government-regulated? Who will be legally responsible for traffic deaths and damage?

There will be more to say about moral emotions in chapter 7, as an aspect of our reactions to a moral challenge.

Societal and Cultural Influences on Moral Development (VII)

The astute reader of this chapter so far will not have missed the fact that it was impossible to discuss the developmental aspects of moral behavior without considerable reference to interpersonal transactions. Even the cognitive self-construction model of moral development does not require the view that children simply construct their moral standards endogenously:

> Rather they "reconstruct" or "re-create" culturally appropriate moral meaning systems. That is, with increasing age and experience, children apply progressively more complex and mobile logical schemas to cultural distinctions and categories; they transform what they are told and what they experience into their own self-organized realities. These realities are idiosyncratic to each individual child and yet bear witness to extensive cross-cultural commonalities in early moral reasoning.
>
> *(Edwards, 1987, p. 149)*

As Aronfreed (1994) summarized, moral judgment and conduct are best characterized "by the view that they evolve from continuities in the interaction between the child's cognitive capacity and his social experience" (p. 185). At the microlevel the earliest and most fundamental of these social experiences are parental inductions and modeling, as well as peer encounters reinforced by praise, rewards, punishment, withholding affection, scolding, reasoning, teasing, shaming, and so on. For adults who work in or for large organizations, later socialization processes continue somewhat more indirectly and subtly in the form of organizational roles, rules and regulations, performance objectives, norms, values, and other mechanisms of assuring behavioral consistency and predictability (Katz & Kahn, 1978). In the next chapters I discuss the values-shaping aspects of one's professional training and experiences.

One aspect of the socialization process is the production of a certain degree of fundamental commonality among members of the moral community, which enables a society to function in a relatively frictionless manner—such as the inculcation of a generalized trust in others (Van Lange, 2015). For example, it is generally taken for granted by people in the United States that moral concepts of fairness and justice are defined according to merit and the equity principle, rather than by equality. However, it is important to avoid an erroneous conception of the cultural environment as homogeneous and producing homogeneous social orientations (Turiel et al., 1991). These authors reviewed experimental and field research from several areas indicating that the contextual influences of any given social situation may be complex and that they vary as a function of the domain of social interaction—particularly with respect to the distinction between conventional and moral behavior. For example, even in the United States, although equity reigns in the employment sector (both private and public), equality is the norm in the legal arena.

Moreover, there is some evidence of social class differences in moral values and/or (un)ethical behavior, but it may depend on which aspects of class are investigated (e.g., wealth, income, job level, education, etc.) and how they are measured (Ariely & Mann, 2013; Trautman et al., 2013). Across multiple operationalizations of social class, using a variety of samples, Piff et al. (2012) consistently found that "upper-class individuals behave more unethically than lower-class individuals ... [and their] tendencies are accounted for, in part, by their more favorable attitudes toward greed" (p. 4086).

....

Additions to the framework for ethical decision-making are deferred until after the following chapter to integrate suggestions drawn from the consideration of both aspects of moral psychology—moral development and taking moral action.

7

MORAL PSYCHOLOGY:
II. TAKING MORAL ACTION

> Morality is not just about issues of harm and fairness … . Morality is also about
> binding groups together in ways that build cooperative moral communities,
> able to achieve goals that individuals cannot achieve on their own.
>
> —Jonathon Haidt and Selin Kesebir

Developmental Model of Moral Action (Continued)

Chapter 6 attempted to summarize a vast body of research and theory describing
how personality and moral development (categories I and II in Fig. 6.1), as shaped
in part by primary and secondary socialization experiences (category VII), contribute to the way in which one experiences moral and ethical dilemmas, as well as
some salient attributes of those situations (category III). These processes are represented longitudinally in the left portion of the figure. This chapter describes the
processes depicted in the right portion of the figure, representing a single incident,
by focusing on what happens then—i.e., the processes involved when we encounter and react to an ethical challenge at a given point in time. Haidt and Kesebir
(2010) remind us that such single ethical incidents cumulatively impact the quality
of our adaptive moral communities. This is akin to the point of view expressed in
chapter 1 regarding the inherent, expanding connections between our personal and
professional ethics, the morality of the institutions in/for which we work, and their
impact on society as viewed through a lens of social and economic justice.

Moral Reasoning and Emotions (IV), and Choices (V)

Much about moral reasoning has been presented in chapters 2–5. What seems to
have been relatively underappreciated by the moral philosophers whose work is

DOI: 10.4324/9781003212577-8

reviewed there is the relation of moral reasoning and choice to psychological realities and real-life behavioral outcomes.[1] As reflected in the content of this chapter, that is a major contribution from moral psychology (or *behavioral ethics*). A portion of that contribution also consists of attempts to delineate the influences had by other individual difference variables that have behavioral implications, such as moral sensitivity, moral motivation, moral identity and self-control, as well as additional contextual influences and limitations on moral reasoning, choice and behavior, as discussed later. Arguably, moral psychologists have focused more on moral judgments than on moral behavior (cf. Malle, 2021)—consisting of evaluations (good and bad), norm judgments (whether something is permissible, obligatory, forbidden), wrongness judgments (it's immoral) and blame judgments (usually as a composite consequence of the first three). Applied psychologists tend to be more concerned with behavioral outcomes.

The role of attitude and cognition in choice behavior has long been a major focus in social psychology. In Ajzen's (1988; Ajzen & Fishbein, 1980) model, a person's intention to perform a volitional action is the proximal determinant of behavior, just as moral choice influences moral action in Fig. 6.1. That is why intentions correlate more highly with behavior than do attitudes regarding the behavior. For example, I-O psychologists typically find that the intention to quit one's job is more highly related to subsequently leaving than is one's level of job (dis)satisfaction (Mobley et al., 1979).

Obviously, not all attitudes concern moral issues. An interesting research question is when does a person's attitude (e.g., regarding civil rights, abortion, political ideology) begin to reflect their moral convictions (Skitka et al., 2018, 2021).

The developmental model depicted in Fig. 6.1 differs from Ajzen and Fishbein's insofar as it assumes that *external control processes* such as organizational norms and ethical climate, and *internal control processes* like self-judgments moderate the relation between choice or intention, and action. (In Ajzen's model, they impact intention directly, so that intention is defined as the subjective probability of performing the action.) I believe that the moderation view is consistent with what we know about how prejudices, unconscious biases, heuristics and competing motives often result in our making choices or taking actions that are not at all reflective of our conscious intentions (Banaji & Greenwald, 2013; Bazerman & Tenbrunsel, 2011; Fischoff & Broomell, 2020; Kahneman, 2011; Kahneman et al., 1982; Kim et al., 2015; Sunnstein, 2005;

---

1 Perhaps that is a bit of an overstatement. For example, philosophers like Singer (1995), have expressed concern for the psychological realism of moral theorizing. And it has been observed a number of times (Krebs et al., 1991; Krebs et al., 2005) that the moral dilemmas utilized in Kohlberg's MJI are not sufficiently realistic and that the responses people make to real dilemmas are frequently not the same as those they make to the MJI dilemmas. And applied ethicists such as in medicine certainly focus on outcomes.

Tversky & Kahneman, 1974). Such decision-biases even characterize the cognitive processes of nonhuman primates (Santos & Rosati, 2015).

Among the two most dramatic recent contributions to the study of moral action has been the introduction of the dual-process model, consisting of both automatic (often referred to as the "X-system" or "system 1") and higher-order (the "C-system" or "system 2") conscious reasoning processes, as co-existing systems (cf. discussion of the social intuitionist model in chapter 6). These systems are not abstract or metaphorical; they refer to literal neurophysiological processes (Lieberman et al., 2002) and they have provided the components of integrated psychological models of moral behavior and ethical reasoning (Haidt, 2001; Haidt & Kesebir, 2010; Reynolds, 2006).

The other, even more recent development has been exploration in the use of formal modeling of moral decision-making—i.e., "specifying mathematical models that describe in a precise, quantitative way how features of a choice problem are transformed into a decision" (Crockett, 2016, p. 85). This area of scholarship seems tantalizing and promising, and is just beginning:

> No single model can provide a definitive and unifying mechanism for moral decision making. Nor can the parameters derived from a single study serve as the final word on the numerical weights that apply to various components of moral decisions … . It may be the case that a relatively small number of models can capture most aspects of moral judgment and decision making. Alternatively, the richness and complexity of human morality may be impossible to boil down into a manageable set of mathematical equations. But we won't find out unless we try, and we will undoubtedly learn a lot in the process.
>
> *(Crockett, 2016, p. 89)*

Moral Emotions

The widespread popularity of Piaget's and Kohlberg's work (despite the criticisms) perhaps led to an overemphasis on cognitive development. But "emotions are particularly influential in the growth of the moral self during the second year, especially the emergence of self-referential emotions like pride, guilt, shame, and embarrassment" (Thompson, 2009, p. 171). Similarly, Haidt (2001) criticized that since the cognitive revolution in psychology in the 1960s, the dominant conception guiding work done in the study of moral psychology has been limited to the rationalist model "in which moral judgement is thought to be caused by moral reasoning" (p. 814).

"In recent years, the field of emotion has grown enormously" (Ekman, 2016, p. 31). For our purposes, this includes potentially important work that emphasizes the primacy of affective reactions as antecedent to cognitive processes (Zajonc, 1980), including moral judgment processes (Haidt, 2001;

cf. Chap. 6). Haidt made a well-supported case for an intuitionist approach in which morally relevant situations unconsciously elicit immediate intuitions that are experienced as intrinsic, automatic, or self-evident moral judgments, such as the immediacy of most people's reaction to a story of incest in our culture. Those automatic reactions then, according to this model, may elicit moral-reasoning processes that are "engaged in after a moral judgment is made, in which a person searches for arguments that will support an already-made judgment" (p. 818). Note that Fig. 6.1 indicates that moral reasoning and judgment processes are *accompanied* by emotional reactions, admittedly begging the issue at this stage of our knowledge whether those reactions are truly antecedent to moral judgment. That seems to be a reasonable stance given that, although a recent "'emotions revolution' has taken place, particularly in the neuroscientific study of decision making, putting emotional processes on an equal footing with cognitive ones" (Volz & Hertwig, 2016, p. 101), those reviewers go on to conclude that "disappointingly little theoretical progress has been made" (p. 101). In some ethical decision-making models, the regulation or reappraisal of emotional reactions (such as anger) is called for in order to facilitate the process (Thiel et al., 2012).

Interestingly, Haidt (2001) acknowledged two instances in which the traditional rationalist model may be an accurate depiction. The first is that we use moral reasoning as an ex post facto process (after the emergence of our immediate moral judgments) to influence the intuitions and judgments of others. The second, relevant to our concern with ethical dilemmas, is when a situation elicits multiple competing intuitions. Under those circumstances, the expectation is that the several intuitions trigger contradictory judgments which then elicit the sort of reasoning processes being considered here, resulting in a comparative analysis of the alternative justifications. Thus, it may be that both the intuitionist and the more rationalist models predict similar psychological processes in response to the multifaceted situations that comprise professional ethical dilemmas.

In any event, it seems clear that it has taken the advent of moral psychology to advance the importance of emotions in the study of morality (Russel & Giner-Sorolla, 2013; Tangney et al., 2007). For example, as noted by Prinz and Nichols (2010),

> It is difficult to find a philosopher who does not think emotions are important to morality … . Despite this consensus, there is considerable disagreement about the exact role that emotions are supposed to play … . Indeed, it would be hard to exaggerate the extent to which philosophers … have neglected psychological research on the moral emotions. (p. 112)

What they mean by moral emotions are "those that promote behavior that accords with moral [as opposed to conventional] rules or those that play a causal … role in mentally representing such rules" (p. 120). The importance of the topic is due to the motivating properties of such emotional reactions in promoting moral behavior. A great deal of the empirical research in moral psychology has to do with elucidating why, how and under what circumstances this occurs—or fails to occur.

Obviously, one way in which moral emotions arise is as accompaniments to the experience of a moral challenge (Category III). Even more likely is their appearance during the process of moral reasoning leading to moral choices being made. In other words, "actual behavior is not necessary for the press of moral emotions to have effect. People can anticipate their likely emotional reaction (e.g., guilt versus pride/self-approval) as they consider behavioral alternatives" (Tangney et al., 2007, p. 347).

Previously discussed was Hoffman's work on the appearance of empathy and its role in the development of *prosocial* moral emotions such as altruistic feelings, loyalty, compassion and justice sentiments. Prinz and Nichols (2010), building on the work of others, suggest that there are two other basic categories of moral emotions: those of *self-blame* and *other-blame*.[2] The particular emotions elicited are a function of the particular moral norms being transgressed. We feel *contempt* for others when they violate communal norms (e.g., by being untrustworthy); we feel *disgust* when someone violates norms of purity; and *anger* arises when someone violates another's autonomy by causing them harm or unfairly depriving them of their rights. (Composites of two or even all three simultaneously are possible.)

The two primary emotions associated with self-blame are *guilt* and *shame*; also considered to a lesser extent is *embarrassment* (Tangney et al., 2007). The primary cause of guilt feelings is having harmed someone, especially a person one cares about or has some responsibility for. One's actual role in causing the harm may even be doubtful, as when victims of a tragedy feel "survivor guilt" or when an employee feels undeservedly over-compensated in comparison with peers. Prinz and Nichols (2010) proceed to point out four distinctions between guilt and shame: (i) guilt results from our causing harm whereas shame is the result of a transgression that doesn't necessarily involve others (e.g., cheating on an exam); (ii) guilt generally depends on our feeling that we have had some control over the situation (e.g., the power to have prevented the harm) whereas shame may occur even when one feels not in control (as with addictive behavior); (iii) one's re-actions to feelings of guilt are likely to entail attempts to apologize or make amends whereas shame more likely results in secrecy, withdrawal and avoiding social contact; and (iv) guilt is behavior-oriented—i.e., one feels guilty about one's actions or inaction—whereas shame is existentially oriented—one feels shame about who one is or what one has failed to become.[3]

---

2 Although it is true that the other- and self-blame emotions of anger and guilt, re-spectively, can also motivate prosocial behavior by leading us to make recompense for transgressions (others' or our own).
3 Other moral emotions that have been studied but are not considered here are the other-condemning emotions of *contempt*, *anger* and *disgust*, and the positive emotions of *gratitude*, *pride* and *elevation*.

Character: Moral Values and Sensitivity (VIII), Motivation (IX) and Internal Controls (X)

The primary preoccupation of moral psychology has been an adequate explanation of the biopsychosocial processes responsible for moral development. This is a point of view that, according to some critics, has paid inadequate attention to matters of virtue or *moral character* (cf. Chap. 5). That is a legitimate issue to be acknowledged, especially with respect to the Kohlbergian cognitive stage model perspective. The emphasis on cognitive processes has contributed to a sense that "there's no 'there' there" in the study of moral psychology. Where is the locus of morality, the person, in this psychological theory? As indicated in chapter 2, this is an Aristotelian criticism in that he construed morality not in terms of "what is the right thing to do?" but "what is the right sort of person to be?" The concern has been seen as critical in the selection of public sector administrators (Hart, 2001), and taken up in the business world with calls for greater attention to the "identification of those already predisposed to live according to high moral standards" (H. B. Jones, 1995, p. 867). And I-O psychologists interested in the origins of workplace deviance have implicated some "normal" personality attributes ("Big Five" traits of agreeableness and conscientiousness) as well as two of the "Dark Triad"—Machiavellianism and psychopathy (Ellen, III et al., 2021).

Character is one of those elusive terms that is more frequently used than defined and understood. Following Boyd's (1994) approach in a general way, I refer to relatively stable dispositional aspects of personality that account for relatively consistent attitudes and behavioral tendencies across a variety of circumstances. (As discussed in chapter 5, it is critically involved in defining what is meant by a virtue.) I would have no great quarrel with a reader who views character traits as having much in common with values and one's character as reflected in one's value system (see Chap. 8). Among the differences, however, is one of vantage point. One's "character" is invariably judged or inferred by others, whereas one's "values" are more frequently a matter of self-reflection and revelation. These dispositional tendencies are what allow us to "characterize" people in terms of particular trait descriptions because personality traits appear to be relatively stable in childhood through middle-age (Caspi et al., 2005). They are generally what we mean when we say that we know what someone is like.

Not all aspects of the character are moral in nature. *Moral* character refers to those dispositional tendencies that relate to some normative moral stance, most frequently reflecting aspects of one or more of the dimensions of moral behavior: justice/fairness, welfare/caring, and honesty/integrity. To describe your friend as very friendly, sociable, and outgoing does not have the same moral implication as describing them as very caring. But in some circumstances, it might. If your friend were going out of their way at a social event to be especially welcoming to someone who is a shy outsider that would be a positive reflection of their moral character because of its beneficent aim. Positive traits of moral character may sometimes be the same as those attributes commonly labeled as virtues—loyalty, courage, patience, and so on. I agree with Boyd (1994), however, that these attributes are best thought of as subordinate character traits that may be expressions of or derived from the primary traits of moral character: "That is, they can be considered *moral* character traits only insofar as they are put into context by the moral point of view framed by benevolence and justice" (p. 119). For example, "loyalty" to a dishonest employer, or having the "fortitude" to follow a company directive to fire someone unjustly, or being gratuitously hurtful to a colleague under the guise of being "honest," are neither virtuous acts nor indications of good moral character. This is in accord with philosophical conceptions of virtue as including good intentions and motives as well as virtuous actions.

Some of the relevant research in this area has focused on pathological attributes—the so-called "dark triad" of narcissism, Machiavellianism and psychopathy (Muris et al., 2017). The three attributes seem to be substantially interrelated and associated with a variety of negative psychosocial outcomes including unethical behavior (especially psychopathy). "Of course, this result hardly is surprising because the dark traits themselves are defined partly by malevolent and antisocial behaviors" (Muris et al., p. 196). From our perspective the most problematic situations are the existence of narcissistic leaders and the sort of organizational cultures they create (O'Reilly et al., 2021).

The bottom portion of Fig. 6.1 presents three sets of latent variables that have been studied by moral psychologists, which I construe to be aspects of moral character.

Moral Values, Moral Sensitivity, Moral Imagination and Emotional Predispositions

Moral values and *moral sensitivity* reflect those aspects of moral character that play a directing and defining role in determining whether one experiences a situation as morally challenging. "People's values and beliefs affect what information they seek and how they interpret what they see and hear" (Bandura, 1991, p. 94), and individual differences in values have generally been acknowledged as an important element in managerial ethics and organizational conflict (Gortner, 2001). The personal values of managers have been shown to be related to their stage of moral reasoning (Weber, 1993) and to their ethical judgments (Douglas et al., 2001)—although the influence of personal values on their ethical decision-making may be suppressed if the managers are accountable to a higher authority whose preferences are known (Brief et al., 1991). That is an important contextual/organizational effect to keep in mind (discussed later). Managers can be expected to differ in values that result in different ethical concerns and outcomes. And the pattern of value differences that accounts for the different outcomes may be contingent on the nature of the ethical dilemma (Fritzsche, 1995).

Just as important as one's individual values is the relation among a person's several values—their value *system*. Not only do interindividual differences in values contribute to what often seem to be irreconcilable differences among people, but the multiplicity of values we each possess is a potential source of intrapersonal conflict. Fortunately, their relative ordering in importance is a mechanism by which such conflicts can be resolved. "Intraindividual conflict can be traced in part to the clarity with which values are crystallized and prioritized. A critical first step in the decision-making process is to reduce this source of uncertainty" (Brown & Crace, 1996, p. 212). But it is probably best for us to anticipate that the complexity and ambiguity of professional decisions will engage multiple motives, reflecting our diverse values and goals (DiNorcia & Tigner, 2000).

Suppose the organization for which you work decided to "restructure" its operations and in so doing terminated the most experienced older (i.e., middle-aged) employees and after a short period of time replaced many of them with younger, part-time and supposedly more "vital" workers who "coincidentally" were able to be hired at much lower salaries with few benefits.[4] Whether you perceive this as a possible moral transgression by the company and how suspicious you may be of management's motives, or conversely your readiness to concede them some benefit of the doubt, will depend on, among other things, your values and opinions regarding management prerogatives, obligations and motives, employee rights, principles of justice and fairness, and the relation among them. (As well as your prior experiences with this organization, of course.)

Perhaps your values are such that viewing the company as a transgressor is tenable, but you simply "failed to put two and two together" regarding the dismissals and subsequent acquisitions of younger replacements. That lack of perceptiveness might reflect your low level of *moral awareness* or *moral sensitivity*, an attribute that has been viewed as a salient component of professional ethics. Moral sensitivity is probably better understood from a phenomenological perspective as

> the awareness of how our actions affect other people. It involves being aware of different possible lines of action and how each line of action could affect the parties concerned. It involves … knowing cause—consequence chains of events in the real world; it involves empathy and role-taking skills.
>
> *(Rest, 1994, p. 23)*

---

4   "Restructuring" is frequently a euphemism for the less-palatable "downsizing," which may be aimed at "enhancing our profit margin," by "selecting out" people—which are of course additional euphemisms for the act of dismissing people from their jobs (Bandura, 1991). Euphemisms are used frequently by organizations to provide a "language of nonresponsibility" (Gambino, 1973, p. 7) in which ethically questionable behavior is described in the passive form, with no agent (akin to "stuff happens"), to seem that no people are responsible (Bolinger, 1982).

Given the haphazard nature of moral development and ethical training, it is likely that people's degree of moral sensitivity is not uniform across domains of potential transgression. For example, an I-O psychology college professor might be more sensitive with respect to the ethical implications of their behavior toward employees in an organization for which they consult than toward students in their classes. Research also suggests that sensitivity can be shaped by either a consequentialist's recognition of harms or a deontologist's recognition of norm-violation (Reynolds, 2006).

Figure 6.1 construes moral sensitivity as influencing the nature of our experience of moral dilemmas as well as our reactions to them. Empirical research has confirmed that moral sensitivity influences the recognition of moral issues; both, in turn, influence moral evaluation processes (May & Pauli, 2002). The conception of moral sensitivity as a dispositional variable is supported indirectly by the finding that it was unrelated to industry and organizational environment among a sample of accountants (Patterson, 2001). However, it can be conceived of as an acquired, developmental ability (Pederson, 2009), and it apparently can be successfully taught (Bebeau, 1994; Duckett & Ryden, 1994). Similarly, Frey (2015) outlines an approach to teaching *moral responsibility*, which is defined as "moral responsiveness to essential moral relevance" (p. 317).

Moral sensitivity is probably reflected in one's *moral imagination* (Carroll, 1987; Werhane, 1999). Moral imagination refers to one's ability to think beyond the situational particulars and moral guidelines that may define a dilemma and it probably depends in part on one's powers of empathy (Hoffman, 1991). Werhane (1999) views it as an inherent aspect of business and economic relations and has applied the notion to organizations:

> In managerial decision-making, moral imagination entails perceiving norms, social roles, and relationships entwined in any situation. Developing moral imagination involves heightened awareness of contextual moral dilemmas and their mental models, the ability to envision and evaluate new mental models that create new possibilities, and the capability to reframe the dilemma and create new solutions in ways that are novel, economically viable, and morally justifiable. (p. 93)

And, indeed, it has been found that MBA students who scored high on a measure of moral imagination were more likely to develop a mutually beneficial solution to problems (Godwin, 2015).

Because moral sensitivity, identity and imagination are intrinsically involved with one's moral values, they are seen as precursors to moral emotions. We have already discussed how these emotions often are experienced as an aspect of a moral dilemma, and how they may play an anticipatory motivating role in the ensuing decision/judgment processes. At this point we note their existence (to varying degrees) in the form of the individual's *predispositions* to experience morally-based self-blame (shame, guilt, embarrassment), other-condemning emotions (contempt, anger, disgust) and morally relevant positive emotions (gratitude, pride, elevation) (Tangney, Stuewig & Mashek, 2007).[5]

Moral Motivation, Balance and Identity

Once a situation is encountered in which our values and moral sensitivity (and innate intuitions?) lead us to recognize as morally relevant our moral cognitive schemata are engaged, consisting of moral reasoning and accompanying emotional reactions. Hopefully, this results in some solution or choice (or set of alternative choices needing further resolution), which then leads to action. Relatively little research has been performed regarding the processes whereby values are translated into ethical action (Weber, 1993). In Fig. 6.1 motivational issues are implicated in moderating the relation between moral judgment processes and the choice: The option chosen is not necessarily what one has reasoned to be the most ethically defensible action. For example, in response to a scenario in which they imagined taking an important qualifying exam unsupervised, 80% of a sample of third-year university students maintained that it would be wrong to cheat, but 50% indicated that they would nevertheless decide to do so (Nisan, 1991). Motivational (control) processes are also implicated regarding the relation between the choice and actual behavior. What impels implementation of the choice or failure to act in accord with it? These control processes are discussed in the following section.

Some philosophers have acknowledged that most moral theories deal only with reasons, values and justifications, and that "they fail to examine motives and the motivational structures and constraints of ethical life. They not only fail to do this, they fail as ethical theories by not doing this" (Stocker, 1976, p. 453). Similarly, another philosopher observed:

> Many philosophical views of morality show little or no concern for any psychological substratum that explains how a human being does, or can come to, live in accordance with morality ... . If rational argument can demonstrate a certain view of morality to be compelling, that is all the philosophical grounding it needs. Some conceptions, for example Kant's, make the further assumption that such rational acceptance is sufficient to motivate conformity to the morality. But it must be admitted that many philosophical views take no stance either way on this point, assuming tacitly that philosophical acceptability has no connection to psychological reality.
>
> (Blum, 1987, p. 307)

---

5 Not all pridefulness is morally related—e.g., pride in personal achievement. *Elevation* "is the positive emotion elicited when observing others behaving in a particularly virtuous, commendable, or superhuman way" (Tangney et al., 2007, p. 362, attributing it originally to Johnathan Haidt).

Not to be outdone, psychologists have also been as critical of psychological theories on similar grounds:

> A theory of morality must explain both the motivators for cognitive change in moral principles and the motivators for acting morally. Stage theorists address the motivation for cognitive change but largely ignore the motivation for pursuing moral courses of action ... .
>
> *(Bandura, 1991, p. 61)*

One potential (albeit partial) answer might involve the extent of *moral conviction* with which an attitude is imbued (Skitka et al., 2021).

Reviews of a substantial amount of empirical research indicate that there is a significant relation between people's scores on measures of moral judgment (the MJI and DIT) and relevant behavioral outcomes concerning delinquency, honesty, altruism, and so on (Blasi, 1980; Thoma & Rest, 1986). In the nomenclature of Fig. 6.1 those are correlations between variable Categories IV and VI. As Thoma (1994) pointed out, the relations are modest—at best 10% to 15% variance in common—and "the nature of the typical study rarely ... helps us understand the processes that actually describe how judgments inform actions" (p. 202). He suggested that such understanding will be advanced, and statistical effect sizes increased, by a consideration of other relevant individual difference variables of the sort Rest (1984) incorporated into a Four Component Model and which I subsumed under the rubric of moral character in Fig. 6.1 (Categories VIII, IX and X). The model presented here, moreover, explicitly includes consideration of social, situational, and contextual influences (Categories VII and XI), which are at best only implied in the Four Component Model.

Moral Balance

One of the most interesting motivational constructs relevant to the connection between moral judgment and choice is Nisan's (1990, 1991) concept of *moral balance*. He presented evidence in support of his model which specifies that one of the important determinants of moral choice-making is the maintenance of a sort of implicit moral balance sheet for oneself, based on a review of all of one's comparatively recent morally relevant actions. He was quite explicit in indicating that for many of us moral choices are not merely a reflection of moral judgments focused on each individual situation in isolation, but they reflect a "limited morality" in which we allow ourselves some deviations from the ethically ideal choice—as long as the transgressions do not fall below some personal standard of minimal acceptability.

The moral balance model is in opposition to two other motivational models, the *ideal* or *maximization model* of moral action and the *slippery slope model*. The maximization model is generally implied by most moral theories: i.e., the assumption that we always strive to ascertain and do the morally best thing, as determined by the finest moral reasoning of which we are capable. The slippery slope model posits that individuals tend to avoid even minor transgressions because of the fear that they will lead inevitably to greater and greater breaches. That is, it suggests that one violation of moral standards will lead to self-deprecation and lower self-expectations, predisposing to further violations. In contrast, the maintenance of the moral balance model posits that it is more likely for us to indulge ourselves in a limited moral transgression following a period in which we have been relatively good, whereas a recent history of ethically wrongful behavior is more likely to be followed by righteousness. Although Nisan found more empirical support for the moral balance model than for the other two, he acknowledged that there may be individual differences among people in their characteristic modes of acting. His surmise is supported by Cornellisen et al. (2013), who found that "individuals' ethical mind-set (i.e., outcome-based versus rule-based) moderates the impact of an initial ethical or unethical act on the likelihood of behaving ethically on a subsequent occasion" (p. 482). Some recent research has given more credence to the slippery slope model and suggested that the process is aided by a dissonance-reducing strategy of *moral disengagement* that serves to attenuate one's inhibitions and facilitate unethical behavior (Detert et al., 2008; Moore et al., 2012; Welsh et al., 2014; cf. section on Internal Control Processes, following).

Conversely, in a recent review, Mullen and Monin (2016) report on a considerable amount of surprising evidence supporting the so-called *licensing effect*—when "acting in one direction enables [i.e., licenses] actors to later do just the opposite" (p. 364)—akin to moral balance without the homeostatic allusion. They consider it surprising because of the long history in psychology of observing behavioral consistency—e.g., when "past moral behavior leads people to do more of the same" (p. 363). For example, Lin et al. (2016) found that among supervisors "displays of ethical behavior were positively associated with increases in abusive behavior the following day" (p. 815). Mullen and Monin concluded that there are substantial moderator effects influencing which pattern holds:

> individuals are more likely to exhibit consistency when they focus abstractly on the connection between their initial behavior and their values, whereas they are more likely to exhibit licensing when they think concretely about what they have accomplished with their initial behavior. (p. 363)

And Wang et al. (2017) observed that level of moral identity moderated the effect (those who were low in moral identity were more likely to behave unethically following ego depletion).

Just to make things even more complicated, some empirical findings indicated that people were *less* likely to engage in corruption (experimentally) when they had previously engaged in minor corruption (i.e., they were presumably on a slippery slope), than if they were abruptly given an opportunity to engage in it—"sometimes the route to corruption leads over a steep cliff rather than a slippery slope" (Köbis et al., 2017).

We can expect circumstances to also play a role: when a potential transgression is so severe that it represents an intolerable deviation/threat to one's moral identity, we are more likely to see the inhibitions of the slippery slope in action. Or when individuals in an organization are held publicly accountable for their actions to those who have the power to reward or sanction, their behavior is more likely to conform to the expectations of the audience (Beu & Buckley, 2001; Tetlock, 1992). Indirect evidence for the operation of moral balance dynamics comes from a study indicating the existence of contrast effects in ethical judgments. Boyle et al. (1998) found that students rating the ethically ambiguous behavior of a salesperson tended to rate the target as more ethical if they had previously been exposed to an unethical scenario and as less ethical if they had been primed with an ethical scenario. This suggests that organizations should provide behavioral examples of ethical and unethical behavior to serve as anchors for their policy statements to avoid this unacceptable type of moral relativism.

A more recent version of a balance model was developed by Mazar et al. (2008), who presented a *Theory of Self-Concept Maintenance*. In some ways it is diametrically in opposition to slippery slope notions. The theory starts with the premise that most people typically value honesty, believe themselves to be moral, and are motivated to maintain that self-concept. Nevertheless, people are often tempted, and cheating, dishonesty, and unethical and rude behavior are not unknown. The theory concerns the mechanisms by which this apparent conundrum can be explained:

> people who think highly of themselves in terms of honesty make use of various mechanisms that allow them to engage in a limited amount of dishonesty while retaining positive views of themselves. In other words, there is a band of acceptable dishonesty that is limited by internal reward considerations. (p. 642)

Shalvi et al. (2015) add evidence that "self-serving justifications emerging before and after people engage in intentional ethical violations mitigate the threat to the moral self, enabling them to do wrong while feeling moral" (p. 125).

Slippery slope arguments are sometimes invoked at the societal level as justifications against some proposed or anticipated social reform (Shafer-Landau, 2015), prognosticating ever-increasing, inevitable dire consequences over time if the proposed policy is allowed to happen. Shafer-Landau illustrates the phenomenon with several interesting fearful expectations: (a) allowing voluntary active euthanasia will eventually yield to the moral corruption of doctors (and others) intentionally killing people who want to live; (b) any small relaxation of the Hollywood production code that prohibited any profanity in movies up through the 1960s would ultimately lead to rampant profanity, scenes of brutal torture, full nudity and even simulated sex; (c) any lifting of Jim Crow segregationist laws in the southern United States that prevented African Americans from voting, attending whites-only public schools and other public and private facilities would lead to the ruination of society—maybe even to the acceptance of "mixed-race" marriage.

Shafer-Landau points out that

> it is sometimes easy to determine when a prediction of disaster is unreasonable. The slippery slope defenses of Jim Crow laws, for example, were based on unwarranted fears, long-standing prejudice, and deep-seated ignorance. But sometimes it's quite difficult to know whether a prediction at the heart of a slippery slope argument is plausible. (p. 136)

In other words, what is the factual accuracy of the prognostication(s)? Allowing Blacks to order a sandwich and a coke at a Woolworth's lunch counter actually did contribute to their also being allowed to vote and attend the better public schools in town. But will requiring more effective psychiatric screening prior to purchasing a firearm lead to repeal of the 2nd Amendment to the U.S. Constitution? Perhaps the reader can think of some examples relevant to organizational life. Some managers anticipate dire consequences from a proposal that, in the interests of fairness, transparency and preventing discrimination, all salaries should be public.

Moral Identity, "Bounded Awareness" and "Bounded Ethicality"

Whereas moral philosophies and even psychological theories like Kohlberg's focus exclusively on moral judgments, Nisan's (1990, 1991) model, like much of what we have been reviewing here, includes consideration of the actor's personal characteristics, current circumstances and past behaviors. A person's deviation from an ethical ideal should not necessarily be interpreted as stemming from insufficient willpower, disaffection with moral standards, character flaws or other inferred moral failings. They may be motivated by an attempt to reconcile conflicts between various components of one's personal identity, of which *moral identity* is just one. Moral identity is generally conceptualized as a particular dimension of social cognitive identity, which in turn is embedded within general social identity theory (Aquino & Reed, 2002; Bandura, 1986, 1991, 2001; Deaux et al., 1995).

From a psychodynamic perspective, moral identity has been defined as the "use of moral principles to define the self" or the "level of integration between self-identity and moral concerns" and viewed as "the key source of moral commitment throughout life" (Damon, 1999, pp. 76, 78). "The motivational driver between moral identity and behavior is the likelihood that a person views certain moral traits as being essential to his or her self-concept" (Aquino & Reed, 2002, p. 1,425). For example, in an organizational setting, the level of moral identity moderated (i.e., attenuated) the relationship between supervisor injustice and retaliatory reactions against others (Skarlicki et al., 2016). Similarly, the accessibility of moral identity within the working self-concept (experimentally situationally manipulated) affected the participants' intentions to behave prosocially (Aquino et al., 2009).

From a content perspective, moral identity has been defined as a "commitment consistent with one's sense of self to lines of action that promote or protect the welfare of others" (Hart et al., 1998, p. 515). The notion is extremely compatible with the recent attention to virtue theory: being a virtuous person is to have a strong, salient moral identity that is central to one's self-concept (Weaver, 2006).

We know that people are subject to a variety of logical judgment errors and cultural prejudices (Banaji & Greenwald, 2013; Bazerman & Tenbrunsel, 2011; Kahneman, 2011; Kahneman et al., 1982; Kim et al., 2015; Tversky & Kahneman, 1974), and show individual differences in decision-making competence (Fischoff & Broomel, 2020). Some of the cognitive heuristics (mental short-cuts) we rely on have their analogues as *moral heuristics* (Sunstein, 2005). The significance of this for us is the realization that there are quite a few empirically documented reasons why people's reactions to an ethical dilemma may not live up to the ideals of their moral identity. This may be due to our *bounded awareness* and *bounded ethicality* (Bazerman & Tenbrunsel, 2011; Kim et al., 2015) and constitutes what has been called the "radical behavioral challenge (RBC)" to moral decision-making (Kim et al., 2015, p. 341). The "challenge" is that we might simply be incapable of living up to our espoused moral principles and value ideals, irrespective of our good intentions: "RBC challenges moral guidance with respect to the values of fairness and justice in business organizations" (Kim et al., p. 346).[6]

Kim et al. (2015) present an extended discussion of the relevance of RBC to business ethics education. (This will come up again in chapter 15.) Probably the most important "take-away" from their treatment is the realization that in virtually all the psychological experiments illustrating the various manifestations of bounded ethicality …

> … many subjects act wrongly, succumbing to influences representing bounded ethicality, but other subjects do not. This suggests that the impact of bounded ethicality is fixed not by the laws of human nature but by human choice … . There are individuals who, even under stressful conditions, can stop and do what seems most commendable … . If these [experiments] confirm the phenomenon of bounded ethicality, demonstrating that psychological influences can cause people to act wrongly, they also demonstrate that people can find ways to avoid or limit the effects of these influences. (p. 349)

6   Some of the challenges have been listed briefly by Kim et al.: "ordinary prejudice," "in-group favoritism," "self-serving bias," "illusion of control," "(overly) discounting future consequences," and "motivated blindness."

In short, the human attributes and limitations that give rise to our "bounded awareness" and "bounded ethicality" are not inevitable and do not provide a ready justification for not doing the right thing. In fact, Bandura (2016) describes several mechanisms we use to psychologically achieve *moral disengagement* to live with ourselves after doing harm: moral justification, displacement or diffusion of responsibility, distorting consequences, externalizing blame, et al.

Internal Control Processes

Moral balance and moral identity may be viewed in the larger context of the self-regulation of behavior. However, whereas those conative aspects of the moral action sequences seem most relevant as moderators of the link between moral reasoning and moral choice (IV → V in Fig. 6.1), the influences of self-regulation pertain more to the processes by which moral choices are or are not reflected in moral behavior (V → VI). A succinct definition of *self-control* is offered by Duckworth et al. (2016), as "effortful, in-the-moment self-mastery in the face of pressing temptation" (p. 36). Virtually every theory of moral behavior, both secular and models embedded in religious teachings, incorporates notions of inhibition, self-regulation or self-control. These notions are indicated popularly by terms such as *conscience, superego, duty, denial, sin* and *willpower,* and in the literature of cognitive psychology by *executive function, executive control, agency* and *delay of gratification.* Such resistance to temptation, however labeled, reflects what some people mistakenly think of as the entirety of moral character. Implicit in several of those views is the assumption that human beings are in some fundamental or essentialist way driven primarily by egoistic motives unless otherwise deflected from that path. My theoretical preferences in this regard are the explanations of cognitive social learning theory (Bandura, 1986, 1991, 1999; Mischel, 2014) which do not entail that assumption.

In social cognitive theory the expression of ethical behavior is controlled by two anticipatory regulatory mechanisms—*social sanctions* and *internalized self-sanctions.* In this section I discuss only the self-regulatory mechanisms. And they consist of three components: self-monitoring, self-judgments and self-reactions. (Although more complex and comprehensive models of self-control in general have been presented—cf. Kotabe & Hofmann, 2015). There is considerable evidence that it is a learned skill (Mischel, 2014).

Once a tentative choice or a few alternative potential ethical choices have been arrived at, they are subject to a process of self-scrutiny and evaluation in light of one's moral identity and the current level of one's moral balance in relation to the specific contextual situation. According to Bandura (1991), however, the most important elements in the process are the resultant "affective self-reactions [that] provide the mechanism by which standards regulate conduct. The anticipatory self-respect and self-censure for actions that correspond with, or violate personal standards serve as the regulatory influences" (p. 69). (Note the similarity to the Theory of Self-Concept Maintenance.) In other words, the primary internal regulators are the anticipated self-satisfaction and self-respect associated with the confirmation of our moral ideals and the contemplated sense of self-condemnation or self-contempt should we transgress. These feelings are the result of repeated and eventually internalized inductions during one's childhood, which form the basis for Hoffman's (1991) empathy-based model of moral development.

Bandura (1991) also made an important point concerning the influence of more fundamental personality attributes on these moral self-sanctions:

> Effective self-regulation of conduct requires not only self-regulatory skills but also strong belief in one's capabilities to achieve personal control ... . The stronger the perceived self-regulatory efficacy, the more perseverant people are in their self-controlling efforts and the greater is their success in resisting social pressures to behave in ways that violate their standards. (p. 69)

He went on to highlight that, unlike internalization theories that emphasize constantly vigilant control mechanisms like conscience, self-reactive influences do not operate unless we engage them. Selectively activating and disengaging internal controls allows for our engaging in different behaviors even under the same moral standards—a situation akin to what Nisan (1990, 1991) described as the limited morality enabled by maintaining one's moral balance. More recently, Duckworth et al. (2016) have pointed out the effectiveness of "situational self-control strategies—which can nip a tempting impulse in the bud" (p. 35). For example, if I am concerned about possibly driving after drinking too much at a party, I might leave the car keys at home that night.

Moreover, as noted earlier, Bandura (1999, 2016) has also been concerned with how we justify our bad behavior during and/or after the fact of what he refers to as "detrimental conduct." The process is referred to as *moral disengagement*:

> Regulatory self-sanctions can be selectively disengaged from detrimental conduct by converting harmful acts to moral ones through linkage to worthy purposes, obscuring personal causal agency by diffusion and displacement of responsibility, misrepresenting or disregarding the injurious effects inflicted on others, and vilifying the recipients of maltreatment by blaming and dehumanizing them.
>
> *(Bandura, et al., 1986, p. 364)*

Applying this perspective to organizations, Huang et al. (2017) found that employees' experience of job insecurity led to organizational deviance and intention to leave, mediated by the mechanism of moral disengagement. Moral disengagement has also been found to mediate employee reactions to a leader's unethical behavior (Fehr et al., 2020). Those high in moral disengagement propensity are more likely to support the unethical leader.

A related line of research has to do with what happens when a person exercises self-control over their behavior. It proposes a "strength model" (a muscle analogy) in which such effortful control causes *ego fatigue* or *ego depletion*, which leads to the conservation of energy—hence subsequent enhanced self-control (Baumeister et al., 2007, 2018). However, in applying this perspective to I-O psychology, organizational studies have found that "ego depletion leads to a high level of unethical behavior" (Wang et al., 2017, p. 188) and that "individuals depleted of self-control resources were more likely to behave dishonestly … [and] … resisting unethical behavior both requires and depletes self-control resources" (Gino et al., 2011). In other words, the anticipated "enhanced self-control" was not observed.

A somewhat different perspective is suggested by moral psychologists who have resurrected interest in the moral emotions, such as *empathy* and *sympathy* (Davis, 1994; Eisenberg & Miller, 1987); *guilt* and *shame* (Baumeister et al., 1994) and *embarrassment* (Tangney et al., 2007); and feelings of *moral obligation* (Gorusch & Ortberg, 1983), *forgiveness* (Kurzynski, 1998), and *gratitude* (Alzola, 2015; McCullough et al., 2001). Such moral affects or the anticipation of such are important both as potential motivators of moral behavior or as reactions to others' behavior. In addition, the appropriate expressions of these affects can serve to reinforce the people who are the objects of the emotional responses, thus encouraging further moral behavior (i.e., beneficent actions). For example, a student's expressions of gratitude at being allowed to hand in a paper late with no penalty make it more likely that I will repeat that action in the future with other students.

Some moral psychologists also tend to view these matters of self-control or self-sanctions from an evolutionary perspective:

> Humanity's ancestors have been living in groups with at least occasional violent intergroup hostility for most or all of the last seven million years … . Human beings therefore can be expected to have many ancient 'inside the head' mechanisms (such as for coalitions, tribalism, and territoriality …) that co-evolved in more recent times with 'outside the head' cultural creations (such as law, religion, and political institutions), to serve the function of suppressing selfishness and increasing group cohesion, trust, and coordinated action.
>
> *(Haidt & Kesebir, 2010, p. 815)*

So, let's now consider some of those "outside the head" cultural creations.

The Situational-Organizational Context of Moral Action (XI)

Even within the limited perspective of behaviorist learning theory it was understood that the same stimulus conditions do not always lead to the same responses, because of the social context in which the stimuli appear (Gewirtz, 1972). And of course, in social psychology the effects of situational variations on perceptual judgment, bystander intervention, conformity with instructions from an authority, and many other processes, have long been the very focus of investigations. Consequently, it should come as no surprise to learn that contextual influences on ethical behavior have been of some interest to moral psychologists. For example, ethical judgments have been shown to be biased as a function of contrast effects dependent on whether one has just previously observed an instance of ethical or unethical behavior (Boyle et al., 1998) and whether one is primed to identify with the perpetrator or the victim of a moral transgression (Kronzon & Darley, 1999). One of the more dramatic illustrations of situational effects comes from Milgram's (1963, 1974) "shocking" experiment mentioned earlier. Under experimental conditions in which some contextual elements were manipulated, such as the distance of the participant from the experimenter or from the "victim," participants showed greater resistance to compliance with the authority figure. A more recent example, in an organizational context, are findings that although employees can tire of, or feel drained from engaging in prosocial organizational citizenship behaviors (OCBs), the effect can be ameliorated by organizational support (Bolino et al., 2015; Trougakos et al., 2015)—which calls attention to the value of promoting an *ethical climate* in the organization (see below).

A proactive use of situational arrangements to influence positive ethical behavior is the REVISE framework (*reminding, visibility* and *self-engagement*) offered by Ayal et al. (2015), which focuses on the individual. It is built on the assumption that people generally care about being moral (Aquino & Reed, 2002) and that they can be helped to fulfill that aim by: (a) providing cues in the environment that remind them of their own moral standards; (b) "designing visible environments to enhance social monitoring" (p. 739); and (c) engaging their moral selves by "establishing a direct relationship between people's [potential] concrete transgressions and their general perceptions of their morality" (p. 740).

The variety of contextual influences on moral action is conceived as having moderating effects (as in the above two citations, and as per Treviño, 1986)—rather than affecting the dependent variables directly. For example, the positive relation between individual trust and social cooperation is enhanced when there is a greater rather than smaller degree of conflict (Balliet & Van Lange, 2013; also Barnett & Vaicys, 2000). The contextual variables moderate three causal relationships: (a) the nature of the moral judgment processes that are invoked and emotional reactions elicited in response to a perceived ethical dilemma (causal path III→IV in Fig. 6.1), (b) the ethical choices and behavioral intentions that are arrived at as a consequence of the moral reasoning and emotional processes (causal path IV→V), and (c) the connection between moral choice/intention and behavior (causal path V→VI).

Organizational Influences

In recent years I-O psychologists and other organizational scholars, perhaps motivated by the appalling incidence of well-publicized corporate corruption, have demonstrated mushrooming interest in the systemic organizational, social and interpersonal antecedents of (un)ethical behavior in organizations (Andreoli & Lefkowitz, 2009; Burke & Cooper, 2009; Darley et al., 2001; Greenberg, 2010; Kish-Gephardt et al., 2010; Lefkowitz, 2004, 2009; Mitchell et al., 2020; Treviño et al., 2014). The ethicality of employees' behavior in organizations is subject to the same situational influences that impact other role-related and extra-role behaviors, including one's position and status in the organization, its *ethical culture* and *ethical climate*—as communicated by top management and reinforced by the normative expectations, social sanctions and reward structure of the company—and how one is treated. For example, in writing about honesty in the workplace, Murphy (1993) noted that "to understand honesty in the workplace, we must examine the norms, customs, and assumptions of members of the organization, as well as the messages conveyed by the organization about the range and limits of acceptable behavior" (p. 6). Moreover, underlying even those proximal situational influences are the morally relevant social, political and economic macro-level assumptions and values that provide the context within which the organization, especially corporations, function. Those meta-issues are taken up in chapter 8 regarding matters of social justice; in chapters 9, 10 and 12 concerning the rights and responsibilities of those in the professions in general and in psychology and I-O psychology in particular; as well as in chapter 11 pertaining to alternative models of political economy such as *laissez-faire* profit maximization versus *corporate social responsibility* (CSR).

But before focusing on relevant organizational antecedents of (un)ethical behavior some basic conceptual and methodological difficulties that have characterized this field of study should be noted.

Some Definitional, Theoretical and Methodological Problems

In reviewing the literature regarding misconduct in organizations Lefkowitz (2009b) raised some problematic meta-issues that warranted consideration. Others writing at about the same time also expressed a variety of such concerns and suggested guidelines for the field of study (Ashforth et al., 2008; Robertson, 1993; Spector & Fox, 2005). Probably the most important question is the definitional one concerning "what is the focal construct" (i.e., unethical behavior)? Also noted by Lefkowitz were measurement issues in operationalizing the construct(s), the nature of the general explanatory system, interpretive errors due to levels issues (lack of correspondence among the level of theory, level of measurement and level of data analysis) and issues of causal inference. Space here precludes consideration of all but the primary definitional issue.

Robertson (1993) observed that "empirical research must state its assumptions about what constitutes ethical and unethical behavior based on normative theory" and that empirical studies "sometimes purport to measure what is ethical without ever defining it" (p. 586, 594). Mitchell et al. (2020) agree: "Though it is a well-known issue in the field … the study of behavioral ethics continues to struggle with the definition of its central term, (un)ethical behavior" (p. 12). My own review suggested the existence in the literature of at least six conceptualizations of misconduct in organizations: unethical behavior (as generally applied to the study of business ethics); incivility, or rude behavior; organizational deviance (in the sociological tradition); organizational corruption; organizational misbehavior; and deviant or counterproductive workplace behavior. A summary of observations from that review is presented in Table 7.1.

Our understanding of this domain is impeded by a number of difficulties: (a) "each of these conceptualizations is represented by its own rather separate body of theoretical and empirical scholarship" (Lefkowitz, 2009b, p. 60); similarly, Kish-Gephardt et al. (2010) "found little intersection between the antecedents studied by

TABLE 7.1 Overlapping Constructs Representing Misconduct in Organizations

Construct	Definitional Criteria	Motivational Assumptions	Target & Outcomes
Unethical behavior	Violation of moral principles	Unintentional failure to meet one's own standards; or intentional self-serving breach of trust	Harm or wrongdoing to others
Incivility or rude behavior	Violation of conventional social norms	Unintentional or intentional actions	Minor harm, disrespect or insult to others
Organizational deviance	Violation of organizational norms	Unintentional, intentional or accidental events	Harm to others or to the organization
Corruption	Violation of public norms or trust	Intentional breach of trust for personal or collective gain	Harm to others or to the organization
Organizational misbehavior	Violation of organizational (and/or public) norms	Intentional violations on behalf of one's self or the organization	Substantial or minor harm or benefit to others or to the organization, depending on the norms violated
Counterproductive work behavior	Violation of organizational and public norms	Intentional self-serving actions	Substantial or minor harm to others or to the organization

Source: Reproduced from Lefkowitz (2009b). Individual and organizational antecedents of misconduct in organizations: What do we [believe that we] know and on what bases do we [believe that we] know it? chapter 2 in C. Cooper & R. Burke (Eds.), Pp. 60–91. *Research companion to crime and corruption in organizations.* Cheltenham: UK, Northampton, MA: Edward Elgar. Used by permission.

behavioral ethics and deviance investigators" (p. 22); (b) there are multiple sub-categories of misconduct within several of them, usually based on who or what is the target or aim of the behavior—e.g., individual corruption versus collusion by two or more people in an organization (Pinto et al., 2008); unethical behavior undertaken for the organization's benefit (Umphress et al., 2010; Vardi & Weitz, 2016); nevertheless (c) reviews of research frequently pool data across a wide variety of exemplars within each conceptualization; and (d) there is little in the way of theoretically-driven construct validation research aimed at justifying either "a single integrative view of the entire domain" (Lefkowitz, p. 65)—yielding what Ashforth et al. (2008) refer to as "a deep-structure understanding of the phenomenon" (p. 677)—or justifying the current disaggregation into six or more domains.

On a more positive note, attention has been paid recently to more carefully defining what might be meant by ethical behavior in the world of work, in terms of job performance dimensions (Russell et al., 2017; see Box 7.1), and more clearly differentiating unethical behavior from mere rudeness or incivility (Cortina, 2017; Schilpzand, 2016). As noted earlier (Chap. 6), the notion of an *ethical dilemma* is central to this book's approach to understanding the etiology of [un]ethical be-havior and in distinguishing it from incivility and corruption (cf. Table 6.4).

Technology

Anyone even casually familiar with the business world cannot help but be im-pressed by the pace of technological change in recent decades and its impact on the nature of work and organizations (Cascio & Montealegre, 2016). Some of those technologies have been characterized as potentially *disruptive* rather than *sustaining* (Christenson, 1997), such as excessive surveillance and monitoring systems implemented in the name of performance management. (Amazon's use of *time-off-task* surveillance monitoring as a means of punishing fulfillment center employees is described in Chap. 12.) These sorts of changes frequently have substantial effects on an organization's employee relations policies, climate, and may engender new ethical problems (cf. Box 1.2). In that regard it is valuable to keep in mind that even though such changes may impact

> the ways in which moral problems are *manifested* ... [it is nevertheless true that] the paradigmatic forms taken by these problems, the character traits and motives needed to recognize them as such, the ethical reasoning used to address them, as well as the substance of the ethical principles on which such reasoning is based are all essentially unaffected and still pertain.
>
> *(Lefkowitz, 2006, p. 245, emphasis in original)*

Probably no other area of technological advance has prompted such excitement, awe, hopeful expectations and hyperbolic claims of utility—as well as fear, an-xiety, distrust, criticism and hyperbolic claims of disaster as has the field of *big data*

BOX 7.1 DEFINITIONS OF ETHICAL JOB PERFORMANCE DIMENSIONS

1. **Truthfulness.** Does not knowingly mislead others when offering advice or consultation regarding such things as product/service quality data, use of financial resources, effort levels, and performance outcomes.
2. **Conflict of Interest.** Avoids or acknowledges potential conflicts of interest—i.e., situations that involve personal gain versus achieving organizational, professional, or public goals. A person must be aware of the conflict and its ethical or legal implications.
3. **Intellectual Property.** Does not violate the intellectual property rights of others, including plagiarism, taking credit for others' work, or stealing ideas, plans, etc.
4. **Confidentiality.** Maintains appropriate confidentiality regarding client, customer, coworker or organizational information, as specified by the organization's ethical code or contractual obligations, or by law.
5. **Unfair Treatment.** Does not provide an unfair advantage to self or others via nepotism, insider information or granting special favors that disadvantage others, regarding remuneration, performance evaluation or job advancement.
6. **Defamation of Others.** Does not maliciously/intentionally harm the reputation, work or performance of others.
7. **Workplace Bullying.** Does not subject others to physical or psychological harassment—based on gender, nationality, ethnicity, religion, sexual preference/identification, or other reasons.
8. **Whistle-Blowing.** Reports maliciousness, harmful or unlawful behavior to the appropriate authority.
9. **Abuse of Power.** Does not use his/her own position power to coerce others into unethical or unlawful behavior, or retaliate against whistle-blowers.
10. **Rule-Abiding.** Does not violate federal, state or local laws, or legitimate policies and contractual arrangements.

Source: Adapted from Russell, et al. (2017). Situating ethical behavior in the nomological network of job performance. *Journal of Business and Psychology*, *32*, 253–271. Used by permission.

(BD), *artificial intelligence* (AI), *machine learning* (ML) and *robotics*. Much of that material concerns ethical issues (privacy, confidentiality, construct validity, bias) and it is too voluminous to do anything more here than to characterize and highlight some of the issues. Relevant publications (in the present context) tend to focus on one or another of these overlapping themes:

Introductory/Educative. Some articles aim to familiarize I-O psychology with uses for this new field such as in employee selection and interviewing—albeit generally also including an exploration of pros and cons (Gonzalez et al., 2022; Guzzo et al., 2015—with accompanying "commentaries"; Jackson et al., 2020; Langer et al., 2021; Poeppelman et al., 2013; Sajjadiani et al., 2019; Tavallali et al., 2018).

Generally Concerned. Many publications are almost wholly devoted to serious scientific, ethical and legal concerns about the field, sometimes perceiving it as an existential threat to I-O psychology (Landers, 2019), and often with vigorous "calls to action" (Martin, 2015; Murphy & Aguinis, 2019; Tippins et al., 2021).

Unfair/Biased Algorithms. A subset of the "generally concerned" are those who warn about the unthinking development of predictive algorithms from big sets of empirical data that serve to reify biases residing in the original data—a concern for *algorithmic justice* (Goldstone, 2022; Kearns & Roth, 2020; Kim & Routledge, 2022; Maurer, 2021; Mittelstadt et al., 2016; Yankov et al., 2020). Moser et al. (2022) are concerned that we may replace human *judgment* with the mere *reckoning* of which present-day computers are capable (including "rule-driven rationality"). "Decisions are 'better' when they are, or can be, justified and accounted for on the basis of some appropriate substantive value orientation …; that is, decision-making and morality are related" (Moser et al., p. 142). (Cf. Learning Point #1 in Chap. 2).

Adverse User Reactions. As another subset of the "generally concerned," some have emphasized the apparently common negative reactions of jobseekers to AI selection (Gonzalez et al., 2019; Tomprou & Lee, 2021; Wesche & Sondregger, 2021).

Positional Status and Power

Organizational scholars have long recognized that the nature of the scientific, economic and market environments within which a firm operates serve to shape its structure and function—at least for successful adaptive organizations (Lawrence & Lorsch, 1969). These in turn influence the concerns, beliefs and attitudes of managers in different segments of the organizational structure, so that structure influences individual values (Hinings et al., 1996). Thus, one's position in the organization may be expected to influence the problems and dilemmas one is most likely to encounter, both technical and ethical. In fact, Victor and Cullen (1988) found that the several dimensions of ethical climates in organizations varied within organizations as a function of position, tenure and workgroup membership.

Among a sample of almost 1,500 American supervisory, middle, and executive managers, it was found that judgments that their organizations were administered ethically were related positively to job level. Whether the managers sometimes had to compromise their personal principles to conform to organizational expectations was related inversely to job level (Posner & Schmidt, 1987). That is, high-level managers, who are more involved in policy-setting activities and in determining and implementing strategic decisions are more likely to see their organizations as ethical and less likely to experience pressure to conform or compromise personal principles than lower-level managers and supervisors. A similar explanation is advanced in a more recent series of studies by Pitesa and Thau (2013), who found that those in positions of power were able to focus more on their own values and preferences and thus were more likely to disregard the normative social compliance pressures of an ethical culture. Unfortunately, that is likely to include managers with dysfunctional dispositions who treat their employees poorly, thus engendering distrust and misconduct (Hogan & Hogan, 2001). Abusive behaviors are more likely from power holders who are of low status themselves (Anderson & Brion, 2014).

But we are reminded by Anderson and Brion (2014) that the acquisition, maintenance and implementation of power in organizations are not due to only positional status, but to individual competencies, demographics and personality attributes. Other "dark side" personality traits (e.g., narcissism, lack of integrity) have also been found to be associated with unethical behavior (Grijalva & Newman, 2015; Hong et al., 2012). Moreover, it has been observed that those high in *Machiavellianism* may be adept at "displays of ethical leader behavior [that] may not always be an authentic expression of an internalized moral identity or true ethical traits" (Den Hartog, 2015, p. 424).

Organizational Ethical Culture and the Climate for Ethical Behavior[7]

Personality and social psychologists characterize social situations as relatively "strong" or "weak," reflecting the extent to which they include salient cues as to

---

7   The constructs of ethical culture and ethical climate have not been well differentiated in the literature. Sometimes they have been used interchangeably (Ford & Richardson, 1994; Loe et al., 2000). I follow traditional social science custom (cf. Schneider et al., 2013) by using the term *ethical culture* to refer to a shared commonality of values, goals and norms regarding the ethical behavior to be expected from the members of a social system, such as a workgroup or an entire organization. *Ethical climate* refers to the individual perceptions of members of the system with respect to their personal experience of the ethicality of organizational practices, which may include their perceptions of the system's ethical culture. The distinction between the two is often blurred operationally because aspects of [organizational] culture (e.g., normative expectations) are frequently measured via [individual] perceptions. Moreover, those individual-level perceptions are often taken inappropriately to be measures of culture without demonstrating that they represent a shared commonality of views.

how one should behave (such as a publicized code of ethics), and this has been applied to an understanding of the expression of honesty and dishonesty in the workplace (Murphy, 1993). In settings as disparate as sports and international accounting firms, such influences have been referred to as constituting the *moral atmosphere* (Bredemeier & Shields, 1994) or *organizational ethical culture* (Douglas et al., 2001). For example, one well-documented finding with implications for I-O psychologists is that a competitive environment tends to lower one's sensitivity to the concerns of others and focuses attention on one's own needs and goals (or that of one's team, work unit or company as a whole), resulting in less prosocial and more aggressive behavior (Bredemeier & Shields, 1994). Similarly, situations that enhance the salience of one's moral identity are more likely to result in expressions of ethical behavior (Aquino et al., 2009).

A major contextual component of the way in which we experience an ethical dilemma and how that experience structures our moral reasoning and intentions has to do with the relative salience of moral standards in the pertinent social environment. This is the potential advantage of having a clearly explicated corporate code of ethics, conducting ethical instruction, and otherwise engaging in activities that promote the awareness of a moral perspective and encourage ethical behavior (Fudge & Schlacter, 1999; also cf. Ariely et al., 2015)—i.e., developing an organizational ethical culture. Unfortunately, not much has been delineated clearly beyond very general statements (and a focus on ethical leadership) regarding what an ethical culture consists of. Ardichvili et al. (2009), based on extensive interviews with senior executives and some academic business ethics scholars, proposed that it consists of five clusters: Mission- and Value-Driven, Stakeholder Balance, Leadership Effectiveness, Process Integrity, and Long-Term Perspective.

A key component of the value-driven cluster is generally thought to be having a corporate code of ethics (CCE). However, after reviewing reports of approximately 120 primary studies concerning the effectiveness of CCEs, Lefkowitz (2009b) concluded that fewer than half reported clearly positive findings regarding code effectiveness. "Moreover, it appears that a large majority of the studies used extremely varied, sometimes rather equivocal, and occasionally unspecified definitions of 'effectiveness' (p. 76)." Additional studies reviewed suggested that the effectiveness of an ethics code may be contingent on

> the organization having a formal ethics training program …, managers' degree of familiarity with code content …, the nature of the enforcement provisions provided …, whether those who observe code violations report them …, and the extent to which it is seen as being administered fairly … . (p. 77)

It may be that the process by which a code is developed and implemented in the organization (as a bottom-up, collaborative activity) is also of critical importance (Hill & Rapp, 2014), as is the existence of senior managers who value ethics and act and communicate accordingly (Stevens, 2008; Weaver et al., 1999) (see the following section).

Only recently has much attention been paid generally and systematically to the potential role of incentives (such as a CCE) on ethics. A comprehensive review of the literature confirms that the effects of incentives on [un]ethical behavior are rather equivocal (depending on the definition of key variables, such as ethical behavior, as noted above) and varied—as a function of type of incentive and professional domain (Park et al., 2022).

A review of the literature several years ago (Lefkowitz, 2009b), found that (a) "both individual and situational-organizational antecedents are implicated in the appearance of organizational misconduct" (p. 86); and this generally also was observed by Kish-Gephardt, et al. (2010), Newman et al. (2017) and Treviño et al. (2014); (b) demographic attributes were not consistently associated with outcome measures of organizational deviance; but that (c) perceptions of organizational ethical climate were related to misconduct—with the relationship often mediated by affective constructs such as job satisfaction or organizational commitment. Hsieh and Wang (2016) also found job satisfaction to mediate the relationship between perceived ethical climate and organizational deviance. Andreoli and Lefkowitz (2009) found that "formal organizational compliance practices and ethical climate were independent predictors of misconduct" (p. 309).

We should not forget that these matters pertain equally to other types of organizations and institutions, such as universities, and similar findings have been reported with respect to research misconduct by published scientists and graduate students in academe. There is some inferential evidence that "publish or perish" pressures in academia may increase biased views (Fanelli, 2010), but not necessarily overt scientific misconduct (Fanelli et al., 2015). And the more positive the perceptions of the ethical climate for research among almost 3,000 biomedical and social science research faculty, the greater the likelihood of (self-reported) desirable research practices (Crain et al., 2013); similar findings were also reported for graduate students in biological, health and social sciences (Langlais & Bent, 2014). Fanelli et al. (2015) found evidence indicating that

> scientific misconduct is more likely in countries that lack research integrity policies, in countries where individual publication performance is rewarded with cash, in cultures and situations were [sic] mutual criticism is hampered, and in the earliest phases of a researcher's career. (p. 1)

Victor and Cullen (1988) developed a well-known multidimensional conception and measure of nine types of ethical work climate. Subsequent research demonstrated that at least some of those climate types were associated with different forms of organizational governance (Shepard, & Markham, 1997a; Wimbush et al., 1997a;), although there may be some questions regarding the nine-factor structure of the scale (Wyld & Jones, 1997). Several dimensions have been found to be related significantly to ethical intentions or organizational misbehavior (Vardi, 2001; Vardi & Weitz, 2016; Wimbush et al., 1997b) or to moderate the relation between ethical judgment and behavioral intentions (the IV→V causal path in Fig. 6.1; Barnett & Vaicys, 2000). Others have similarly documented the relation between the organization's ethical climate and responses to ethical problems (Bartels et al., 1998; Falkenberg & Herremans, 1995; Sims & Keon, 1999). Meta- and path-analyses support the significant role of ethical climate dimensions in impacting psychological well-being and dysfunctional behavior, mediated by organizational commitment and job satisfaction (Martin & Cullen, 2006). In that context it is rewarding to find evidence that "Two years after a single training session, we find sustained, positive effects on indicators of an ethical organizational culture" (Warren et al., 2014, p. 85).

Other measures of ethical climate have been created (cf. Newman et al., 2017) including one regarding scientific research in university settings, whose scales appear related to perceptions of organizational justice (Martinson et al., 2013). And Kuenzi et al. (2020) showed that the organizational ethical climate was based on six factors such as employee perceptions of their training, the organization's reward system, accountability policies, and ethics codes.

A review of the climate literature focused on traditional organizational outcomes and found that egoistic (i.e., purely instrumental) climates

> are the least preferred type of climate, as they have been linked with a variety of negative and undesirable organizational outcomes. Conversely, it appears that benevolent and principled climates are much to be desired, as they have been linked with so many different positive and desirable organizational outcomes.
>
> *(Simha & Cullen, 2012)*

And reflecting the interactionist perspective discussed in chapter 5 (*The disposition versus context issue*), an individual's overall identification with the organization is significantly related to their job involvement, job satisfaction, commitment, role- and extra-role performance (Lee et al., 2015); and having a salient moral identity is associated with attraction to a socially responsible organization, lower unethical behavior and lower turnover intentions (May et al., 2015)—what the authors refer to as *moral identification*. And in that vein, some of the voluminous work being done on corporate social responsibility (cf. Chap. 11) indicates that an organization's actions in that regard have positive effects on employees' attitudes and behaviors (Greenwood & Freeman, 2011; Wang et al., 2020).

Leadership and Other Interpersonal Influences

Leadership processes have been for many years, and probably continue to be by far, the most frequently investigated antecedent of ethical culture/climate and

[un]ethical organizational behavior. (In Oct. 2021 a Google search on "leadership and unethical behavior," limited to just scholarly articles yielded approximately 96,000 results.) It has become a truism that organizational leaders, especially founders, have a profound effect on the culture and climate of their organizations (Schein, 2010; Schneider et al., 2013), and it is pretty well established that organizational members "are more likely to be ethical when they are led by ethical leaders at multiple levels, feel supported by ethical colleagues, and are fairly treated" (Treviño et al., 2014, p. 645; also cf. Fehr et al., 2020); Freeman et al., 2009). Top management's commitment to ethics influences the nature of the organization's control systems with respect to ethical behavior (Weaver et al., 1999) and can produce a cascading effect of positive ethical culture across organizational levels to lower-level followers (Schaubroeck et al., 2012). Unfortunately, the opposite is also true. For example, narcissistic leaders tend to "prefer and lead organizational cultures that are less collaborative and place less emphasis on integrity... . and ... employees follow the culture in determining their own level of collaboration and integrity" (O'Reilly III, et al., 2021, p. 419). Similarly, supervisors with a strong bottom-line mentality (BLM) can influence subordinates to engage in so-called pro-organizational unethical behavior (Zhang et al., 2020), although BLM can also have a positive effect for the organization via focusing attention on work goals (Babalola et al., 2020).

Excellent reviews of this area are available (Den Hartog, 2015; Newman et al., 2017) and research has begun to bore-in on the processes by which the positive influence of ethical leadership occurs. The positive effects of ethical leadership are thought to come about in at least two ways (Hunter, 2012): (a) via role-modeling, in which "an ethical leader provides indications as to which behaviors are appropriate or inappropriate in a given organization" (p. 80); and (b) as a motivational influence, in which ethical leader behavior inspires employee engagement and initiative, and contributes to psychological well-being, and job satisfaction. For example, ethical leadership is associated with followers' moral identity and moral attentiveness (akin to what I referred to earlier as moral sensitivity) (Zhu et al., 2016); it's also been shown to generalize to employees' feelings toward the organization (e.g., prideful v. scornful) which in turn are associated with constructive or dysfunctional behaviors (Ng et al., 2020). Also implicated have been moderators having to do with dispositional attributes of the leader such as moral character, values, perceived authenticity and type of leadership orientation (Den Hartog & Belschak, 2012; Fehr et al., 2015; O'Reilly, III, 2021; Pless et al., 2012; Van Zant & Moore, 2015), and attributes of followers such as their degree of trust in the leader, motivational orientation, and moral identity (Gan et al., 2020; Neubert et al.; Ng & Feldman, 2015; Roberts, 2013; Wang et al., 2021).

Ahmad et al. (2021) have provided a reverse take on the topic by investigating the effects of followers' behavior on leaders' ethicality. Their interesting findings seem counterintuitive and warrant further investigation: "These studies provide evidence that good behavior [organizational citizenship behaviors] on the part of followers may psychologically free leaders to engage in subsequent unethical behavior" (p. 1374).

Acting on behalf of the organization is no guarantee against unethical or illegal behavior; the organization itself might be the beneficiary of corruption (Pinto et al., 2008, Zhang et al., 2020). (Also, see the discussion of groupthink that follows and chapter 11 regarding the excesses of profit-maximizing values). In fact, there are instances in which employees intentionally behave unethically to benefit or protect their organization—deemed *unethical pro-organizational behavior* (Umphress & Bingham, 2011). It has been observed that those with a traditional business orientation (belief that the only legitimate managerial objective is maximizing shareholder value) are more likely than nontraditionalists to view ethically questionable actions as justifiable—as long as the conduct is aimed at benefitting the organization rather than being self-serving (Mason & Mudrack, 1997).

Schminke and Wells (1999) demonstrated that the ethical predispositions of college students were enhanced by their participation in a four-month interacting group strategic-management simulation, although they offered no explanation of why that should be so or how it might have occurred. Of particular interest, however, are the findings that the degree of group cohesiveness was predictive of the increase in utilitarian perspective but not of the increase in formalism (i.e., a rule-based or deontological approach); a structuring leadership style by group leaders was predictive of changes in formalism but not in utilitarianism. In other words, interpersonal processes may affect ethical behavior differently as a function of the ethical orientation of the actor, as well as the nature of the ethical problem or other aspects of the situation. For example, the risk of being excluded from one's social group, or being ostracized from one's work group can lead to (in the first instance) unethical behaviors that benefit the group, or (in the second instance) self-serving unethical behavior (Thau et al., 2015; and Kouchaki & Wareham, 2015, respectively).

It has been recognized for quite some time that group processes can have maladaptive consequences as well as positive effects. In fact, Mitchell et al. (2020) have recently called attention to the paucity of research on organizational ethics at the team level or higher; similarly, little attention has been paid to the extensive literature on the effects of social norms (cf. Legros & Cislaghi, 2020, for an overview). Therefore, a welcome addition is a systematic consideration of "How groups encourage misbehavior" (Murphy, 2021). One of the best-known example(s) of the influence of group dynamics on decision-making concern the deleterious effect of what Janis (1982) termed *groupthink*—a collective pattern in cohesive decision-making groups of defensively avoiding contradictory information, suppressing alternative arguments, reinforcing the dominant group perspective, and otherwise pressing for uniformity of opinion, thus leading to ineffective outcomes. Peterson (2001) listed 21 high-profile documented cases of groupthink-induced disasters, and Sims (1992) extended the application of the phenomenon as a precursor to unethical as well as merely inept actions. He observed that the likelihood of groupthink occurring is enhanced by three factors:

(a) when decisions are made under stressful circumstances (e.g., financial or time pressures), (b) when the group is characterized by a degree of arrogance, and (c) group members are loyal to one another. Of course, these are circumstances not infrequently found in large business enterprises. To avoid the disastrous consequences of groupthink Sims recommended that groups intentionally program conflict into the decision-making process by having someone (on a rotating basis) play the role of devil's advocate to promote legitimate dissent.

Bandura (1991, 2001, 2016) and colleagues (Bandura et al., 1996) sounded a similarly cautionary note. *Social sanctions* exist as a regulatory mechanism parallel to internalized self-sanctions. Just as a positive climate for ethical behavior can encourage it, they noted that there are innumerable contextual factors that may serve to facilitate our engaging in questionable behaviors that we would ordinarily repudiate. The (in)famous Stanford Prison Experiment (Haney et al., 1973; Zimbardo et al., 1973) comes to mind as a "classic, dramatic demonstration of the potentially destructive dynamics that can be created when one group of people is given nearly total power over a group of derogated others" (Zimbardo & Haney, 2020).

Institutions or organizations may provide a moral justification for reprehensible behavior, allowing the person to cognitively reconstrue its moral qualities. Thus, killing is admirable in wartime and manufacturing cigarettes is respectable because it is legal and provides employment to lots of people. Other institutional mechanisms include (a) the use of euphemisms as part of the "language of nonresponsibility" to mask ethically questionable activities; (b) displacing responsibility for one's actions onto an authority figure; (c) diffusing responsibility entirely to others as a function of the division of labor (e.g., contributing to the success of a cigarette manufacturer is fine—"I'm only in Human Resources, I don't manufacture or sell the product"); and (d) diffusing responsibility to a collective group decision in which no one is individually accountable ("mistakes were made").

Organizational Norms, Policies and Procedures

An important and underappreciated point was raised by Jansen and Von Glinow (1985) regarding ethical ambivalence. As already reviewed, we know that social sanctions play a critical role in shaping ethical climate and behavior, as do the nature of organizational reward structures (Loe et al., 2000). One way that behavior change is facilitated is by changing the salient relevant norms (Miller & Prentice, 2016).

Moreover, based on earlier theoretical writings by the sociologist Robert Merton, Jansen and Von Glinow illustrated how organizational reward systems may shape behaviors in directions opposed to the prevailing norms such as those promoting ethical conduct, thus establishing *counternorms*. Dominant norms generally express positively valued standards of conduct ("abide by the rules"), whereas counternorms may express implicit, largely unacknowledged expectations that conflict with the norms ("do whatever it takes to get the job done on time"), thus leading to ethical ambivalence. Counternorms may be related to the financial reward system of an organization, as with individual incentive pay when the organization ostensibly promotes team effort and responsibility. The resulting ethical ambivalence can be personally upsetting and induce actions that are dysfunctional for the organization. Remedying the situation may be extremely difficult if key policymakers are not prepared to acknowledge the problem and redesign those portions of the organizational reward systems that are at variance with the ostensibly desired culture of the organization.

For example, Wal-Mart was indicted for requiring employees to work overtime for no pay (Greenhouse, 2002). Despite official policies to abide by wage and hour regulations, the company also pressured store managers to keep payroll costs down and provided substantial bonuses for them based on the profit of their stores. According to some managers, payroll and staffing levels were set so low that it was nearly impossible to run the stores adequately unless they illegally forced off-the-clock overtime work.

Another example was at Wells Fargo. Senior managers at the bank were presumably unaware that some employees were trying to meet high sales objectives by creating sham bank accounts and credit cards in the names of customers without their permission or knowledge—resulting in substantial financial harm and distress for many of those people (e.g., adverse credit ratings; inability to obtain a mortgage) (Corkery, 2016). It was estimated that as many as 1.5 million bank accounts and up to 565,000 credit cards were opened (Lieber, 2016). Former employees described the organization as having an "aggressive sales culture, which was nurtured and honed over decades at the bank's highest levels" (Corkery & Cowley, 2016). This culture apparently was maintained despite overt pronouncements and training programs denouncing the practice.

How were such counternorms brought about and maintained in the face of a public posture to the contrary? Newspaper reports indicated that high-level sales goals were set and maintained; meeting the stringent goals was factored into yearly bonuses; employees were chastised for not keeping up; some tellers were threatened with discharge for not meeting the objectives; and a particular branch with a high level of new accounts was held up as a model for the rest of the bank. Thousands of low-level employees eventually were fired for engaging in these practices; the bank paid $185 million in fines; and no senior managers were held accountable or even acknowledged for creating or participating in the promulgation of the sales goals driving the behavior.

Adding Further to The Framework for Ethical Decision Making

13. The psychological capacities that may develop into a mature moral perspective (e.g., empathic sensitivity, innate moral intuitions, an appreciation for standards of conduct and the consequences of one's

actions) appear very early in life in virtually all cultures, suggesting that ethical behavior is a critically important and indispensable feature of human existence. This implies that ethical considerations should be afforded considerable deference and not conceived of as a discretionary afterthought.

14. **The three general types of moral problems studied by** Hoffman (1988) **provided the beginning of a useful taxonomy of ethical challenges (including situations that may entail combinations of two or more of them) which was gradually expanded to five** (Lefkowitz, 2003, 2006, 2011c; Lefkowitz & Lowman, 2010/2016) (See Table 6.4). The final five *forms of ethical dilemmas* have proven to be a useful and accurate means of understanding real-life ethical problems self-reported by I-O psychologists (Lefkowitz, 2021; Lefkowitz & Watts, 2021). The forms are structural in nature—essentially "content-free"—so they can be used generically in other domains.

   a. **Paradigm I. The opportunity to prevent harm: Awareness, anticipation or foreknowledge of someone or some entity (e.g., the organization or profession) to be harmed or wronged by another or by circumstances.** Having a personal relationship with either the transgressor(s) or the victim(s) makes this type of situation more salient emotionally. Having a formal relationship with the transgressor(s), (e.g., being employed in the same organization) may invoke one's own ethical sensibilities ("Is this really the kind of company I want to be working for?").

   b. **Paradigm II. Temptation: Contemplating (or taking) an action in accord with some self-serving motive, goal or ambition that would be unjust, deceitful or potentially harmful to another person or entity; or would be knowingly inappropriate (such as not professionally competent, or in violation of accepted standards/rules).** The classic example of this dilemma in modern moral philosophy is the Gauguin problem noted earlier. Of particular relevance for organization members are situations in which the contemplated action is self-serving by proxy—i.e., your behavior serves the objectives of the organization. This might be in response to the external pressures of organizational policies or directives—for example, being instructed by your manager to do something that you consider ethically wrong (cf. Paradigm V).

   c. **Paradigm III. Role conflict: Having competing legitimate obligations or responsibilities (sometimes to two or more persons or entities) such that fulfilling one means failing to meet the other(s).** This type of dilemma is complicated in accordance with the nature of the personal relationships between the actor and the other(s). It may be especially painful for the actor when they are involved personally with the competing beneficiaries of the obligations. A personal relationship or identification with only some of the potential beneficiaries invites unfair bias.

d. **Paradigm IV. Values Conflict: Facing equally (or nearly equally) important but conflicting personal values that have been placed in opposition. Expressing one entails denying the other(s) expression. Or being pressured to comply with values contradictory to one's own.** There are several examples that might strike a chord with the reader: (i) In designing an employee selection testing program it may be that the organization's (and your) goal of maximizing economic utility seems at odds with its (and your) objective of also decreasing adverse impact on minority applicants (De Corte et al., 2007); (ii) Perhaps you are energized by a research proposal that you feel has the potential to make a substantial contribution to knowledge in an important area, but the design of the study requires deceiving the research participants in a manner that could be harmful. But it may be that compromises are feasible and acceptable. (Also see Box 1.1.)

e. **Paradigm V. Coercion: Being subject to external pressures to violate one's ethical or professional standards or legal requirements.** Managers are often, if not continually, subject to pressures to achieve productivity, efficiency, speed and profitability that can at times be at odds with ethical standards (Wahn, 1993). And some of these managers may be the client or superior of an I-O psychologist, who is pressured in-turn. It is not uncommon to find that much unethical behavior in organizations is the result of downward pressures on lower-level employees to deviate from their moral standards, and that such compromises may be associated with managerial success (Den Hartog, 2015; Jackall, 1988; Posner & Schmidt, 1987).

15. **Empirical evidence suggests that many cultures are characterized by moral principles and standards other than the individualistic rights-based notions of fairness and justice that characterize western morality**. In portions of Africa, the Middle East, Southeast Asia, and the Far East (especially in non-urban areas) communitarian group-based concerns are more salient. Westerners need to be mindful of this when interacting with and/or judging the behavior of nonwesterners.

16. **The study of moral psychology reveals that ethical behavior is like other complex, intentional, interpersonal and patterned action sequences.** That is, (a) it has perceptual, cognitive, motivational and dispositional components on which people may be expected to vary; (b) it involves schema-based reasoning processes informed by the acquisition of prior knowledge and principles; and (c) despite the human tendency toward some consistency of character and maintenance of one's moral identity, it is subject to intra-individual variability due to competing values and intentions, past reactions to ethical

challenges, unrecognized differences in the nature of the dilemmas such as their personal or impersonal nature, and a variety of contemporaneous contextual influences including organizational determinants that may include countervailing pressures for both ethical behavior and misbehavior. It is also subject to (d) a variety of cognitive errors and affective biases that give rise to a notion of our having a "bounded ethicality." Consequently, there is no good reason to anticipate that consistently behaving ethically is necessarily very easy to do or can be taken for granted.

SECTION II
Values

8

THE GUIDING ROLE OF VALUES IN ETHICAL DECISION MAKING AND SOCIAL POLICY

> The concepts of value and value system are among the very few social psychological concepts that have been successfully employed across all social science disciplines. Anthropologists, sociologists, political scientists, and organizational and individual psychologists are all accustomed to speak meaningfully about values and values systems at different levels—cultural values, societal and institutional values, organizational and corporate values, and individual values ….
>
> —Milton Rokeach and Sandra Ball-Rokeach

Individual Values

Values is a singularly core construct in the conception of morals and ethics presented in this book. And there is, arguably, no one who has contributed more over many years to its study, and in establishing its widespread utility, than the Rokeaches quoted above from 1989 (cf. Rokeach, 1973). But I believe the best way to introduce the topic is anecdotally … ."

Suppose that, as an organizational consultant, you receive a request from a manufacturing company to conduct a climate survey for the company. Knowing something about the dynamics and pitfalls of organizational consultation, you spend considerable time up front talking with key managers and other potential stakeholders so that you can consider their expectations for the survey in designing its implementation. The senior managers reveal nothing particularly surprising: They seem to have a genuine concern for employee relations and would like help in identifying the company's strengths and weaknesses so they can build on the strengths and, to the extent possible, correct or improve the weaknesses. Sounds fine.

DOI: 10.4324/9781003212577-10

Further suppose, however, that the management of this company has privately learned—without revealing it to you or acknowledging it publicly—that in the coming year a national labor union will try to organize the company's hourly employees, and that the covert purpose of the survey is to identify the company's points of "vulnerability" to lessen the likely success of the potential union certification election. What's your reaction?

When I have posed this scenario to classes of I-O psychology students, some immediately take umbrage at being deceived. Surprisingly (to me), there are often students who do not take offense at being treated in this fashion. They seem to have no problem, at least at this point in the discussion, with being manipulated for an ulterior purpose and view it as a reasonable management prerogative for the company executives to maintain the secrecy of their "war plans," even to the extent of such deceit. Eventually I steer the discussion around to what else might have been withheld by these managers, what other deceits might be going on, and what kind of company this might be to have as a client or employer.

At that point, probably influenced by my "nudge," one or more of the students who didn't mind very much being lied to sometimes change their minds about the situation and become more skeptical about this consulting assignment. Alternatively, sometimes an offended student, upon reflection, voices an opinion like "Oh, what the heck … I don't like being lied to, but a job's a job." At this point, there is frequently a cloud of uncertainty in the room—a stage in group processes that the venerable Kurt Lewin referred to as "unfreezing." As a consequence, the students sometime begin to reflect on such issues as (a) the relative importance of money in our lives and what we are willing and not willing to do for it; (b) the distinction between being a full-time consultant dependent on this client and being a salaried professor with a part-time consultancy; (c) whether our views would be any different if we were an employee of this company serving as an internal, rather than external, consultant; and (d) the possibility of accomplishing positive change in this organization despite the circumstances. These are all relevant and interesting points, and consideration of them is invariably instructive. But those matters, including even the issue of being deceived, are not the reason I introduce the example.

"Now, what if," I say at this point, "the managers had been completely honest with you and told you upfront that you are being enlisted in a confidential corporate effort to keep out the union," what then? After a brief pause, and with an almost palpable feeling of relief from some at not having to compromise one's self-respect to work with clients who have treated them dishonestly, some students affirm their willingness to proceed with the project. They see nothing wrong with management's perfectly legal objective or with their contributing to its accomplishment. In contrast, I would be very opposed to continuing. What is the nature of that difference, and what accounts for it?

In part—but probably only in small part—the answer lies in my foreseeing some difficulties with this client and some problems with the way in which this company relates to its employees, which the less experienced students have not had the opportunity to think through. The students are generally of the opinion that, irrespective of the actual objectives of management, there is positive value in implementing a project that is ostensibly aimed at benefitting employees ("Hey, if management is going to respond positively to employee complaints and end up improving things, what does it matter if there's an ulterior motive?"). At first blush that may seem reasonable, but the more one thinks about it the more one might be disturbed by some nagging questions. Why has this management apparently not shown such concern for employee well-being until threatened by unionization? Why do they require an external survey to find out this information? Even if they implement positive changes as a consequence of our survey, what is the likelihood that the changes will be maintained—especially if the union subsequently fails to win certification? And should we not be concerned about management's deceitfulness to its employees who, after all, will be our survey respondents? If we are questioned by employees concerning the purpose of the survey, are we expected to lie, too? How would that square with adherence to our ethics code (APA, 2017)?[1]

Much more important is the difference between some of the students and me in our assumptions, attitudes and expectations regarding labor unions and labor–management relations. During my formative years in the 1950s and '60s, when my father was a union member, I learned about the history of the labor movement in the preceding decades as one of workers working under terrible conditions and struggling against exploitation and violence on the part of politically influential and sometimes ruthless employers. The formative years of the students in my classes were a generation or more later, by which time those early labor struggles had become ancient history, widespread worker benefits achieved by unions and their political allies are taken for granted, and union membership has declined drastically in the United States so that unions are not a particularly salient force. Moreover, somewhat ironically, the refusal by corporations in the past several decades to share with employees the increased profits from productivity gains (Mishel, 2021a; Mishel et al., 2012), coupled with the ineffectualness of unions to prevent that from happening, has apparently resulted in much displaced hostility toward unions on the part of potential constituents.[2]

1   In particular, Principle A: Psychologists strive to benefit those with whom they work and take care to do no harm; Principle B: psychologists establish relationships of trust with those with whom they work; Principle C: Psychologists seek to promote accuracy, honesty, and truthfulness in the science, teaching, and practice of psychology; Principle E: Psychologists respect the dignity and worth of all people, and the rights of individuals to privacy, confidentiality, and self-determination; Standard 3.10: obtaining informed consent of participants when providing consulting services; Standard 3.11: providing information to participants beforehand regarding the nature and objectives of services delivered to or through organizations.
2   I believe that a similar dynamic at least partially accounts for the hostility toward public-sector unionized employees (who have been able to retain many of their benefits) on the part of those same employees who have been powerless because of the demise of unions in the private sector.

Contrary to the belief of many, studies indicate that the presence of unions is generally associated with higher productivity, although organized firms tend to have lower rates of profit than nonunion firms because they are frequently unable to pass on the entire cost of higher wages to customers or consumers; when unionization is associated with lower productivity, it is usually in the context of poor labor-relations (Belman, 1992). And, in his review of the data, Pfeffer (1994) concluded that the commonplace suppositions that unions have (a) raised wages to noncompetitive levels and thus compromised the position of U.S. firms in the world economy and (b) in an effort to protect the jobs of their members, retarded the introduction of technology that would enhance U.S. organizations' competitiveness are both incorrect. Just as important, moreover, should be the recognition that freedom of association in the form of the right of workers to organize a union "is a hypernorm, instrumental to fully realizing basic human rights ... . respect for labor rights is a non-substitutable requisite of corporate citizenship" (Dawkins, 2012, p. 473). If one is concerned with ethics and justice issues one ought not ignore the too-frequent unacceptable anti-union activities of many corporations (Lafer & Loustanau, 2020; McNicholas et al., 2019).

Consequently, I would be unlikely to accept this consulting assignment without some written safeguards and reassurances from the management. For example, employees surveyed should be informed of the context in which the survey is being conducted; and no attempts should be made to use the survey for purposes of identifying individual employees and their views regarding unionization. Of course, my conditions are likely to be moot as I suspect that at this point my chances of being retained by this company are not great. The broader issue, however, is that family background, socioeconomic status and early socialization experiences influence one's personal and work-related values and behavior (Hofstede, 2001; Kinnane & Bannon, 1964; Kish-Gephart & Campbell, 2015, p. 1628; Paine et al., 1967).

The critical issue to be appreciated is that whether one even experiences a situation as ethically challenging—as well as how one defines, analyzes and responds to it—depends greatly on one's values concerning issues relevant to the situation.[3] Our value systems define the nature of potential ethical dilemmas we will experience in life. If we have different values we will likely not experience all the same ethical challenges. For example, broad-based political value systems can play a salient role in determining which groups we perceive as threatening (Brandt et al., 2014).

In the DMMA presented in chapter 6 moral values were presented briefly as one of the characterological determinants that play a primary role in defining and shaping the ethical conflicts with which we are confronted. It's time to pay more attention to what is meant by values in general.

---

3   My choice of this illustration was not accidental. As Pfeffer (1994) indicated euphemistically, "the subject of unions and collective bargaining is, in my experience, one that causes otherwise sensible people to lose their objectivity" (p. 160).

The Definition of Values

The reader may recall the discussion in chapter 2 of subjectivist meta-ethical theories, such as Stevenson's (1944) emotivism and Hare's (1981, 1993) universal prescriptivism, in which I explored the various meanings of a hypothetical difference between the reader and myself regarding our views of affirmative action programs. The hypothetical difference is one of values: That is, I hold such programs to be morally right, and I see them, despite some drawbacks, as effective and beneficial for society and thus to be promoted; you perhaps maintain opposing views. As suggested by the example, virtually every philosophical and psychological definition of values is rooted in the notion of *evaluative preferences* (Rokeach, 1973), although philosophers have sometimes used the term *interests* instead (Perry, 1963). Values define and shape the process of moral reasoning, they are just one among many determinants of moral reasoning, intentions and behavior. Also common to virtually all definitions of values is the assumption that they are implicitly ranked approximately according to their importance in the psychological economy of the person so that we may speak of the person's value profile, pattern, or *value system* (Roe & Ester, 1999).

But even when considered as just a component in the process of moral behavior, preference by itself is an unsatisfactory defining construct because of its ambiguity. It is both too inclusive a term by which to define values and too narrow. It is too inclusive because it fails to distinguish values from interests and attitudes, which also entail preferences. In a concise and informative review of the area Dawis (1991) differentiated values from attitudes in that the former are "more ingrained, permanent, and stable, more general and less tied to any specific referent, and provide a perceptual framework that shapes and influences behavior" (p. 838). Values differ from interests in that their affective quality pertains to the quality of relative importance rather than degree of liking. The distinction harkens back to the earliest scholarly treatments of the concept of values, in which Dewey (1939) and Kluckhohn (1951) contrasted what is merely desired or preferred with what is desirable or preferable, the latter including beliefs about what *ought* to be. For example, one thinks in terms of how *important* the values truth, justice or caring are to the individual, not how much they are *liked*. In addition, we need to restrict the term's referents to things that are truly important to the person—even if we remain somewhat flexible in how we define importance. Thus, Rokeach (1973) viewed values as central aspects of one's self concept—relatively stable but not permanent—and in the model of moral action presented earlier I have similarly placed them among the characterological components of personality. Schwartz (1996) defined them succinctly as "guiding principles in people's lives" (p. 2) that shape our perceptions and evaluations.

There are several reasons why preferences is also too narrow a definition. Although values generally refer to preferences regarding desired objectives or end-states, we think of them as having a broader referent than is frequently connoted by the term *goal* which also refers to a desired end-state. Values refer to *generalized* end-states or *classes of objectives* that invest specific circumstances and goals with positive or negative valence. Your general reactions to the scenario presented at the outset of this chapter were determined in great measure by your values concerning worker representation, labor unions, management prerogatives, and so on. But values do not only pertain to end-states; they may also refer to generalized behavioral tendencies or modes of conduct (e.g., respect for research participants)—what Rokeach (1973) referred to as *instrumental values,* in contrast with *terminal values* that pertain to end-states. The generality of values is another way in which they can be distinguished from *attitudes* as well: Attitudes refer to evaluative beliefs about specific goals, situations or behaviors, whereas values refer to evaluative beliefs about generalized end states or modes of conduct.

What psychologists have emphasized in the understanding of values is the recognition of their cognitive, affective and behavioral components. For example, Feather's (1992) definition of values is typical in that he "treats values not only as generalized beliefs about what is or is not desirable, but also as motives … that influence people's actions" (p. 111). All in all, values may be defined as *relatively stable cognitive representations of what the person believes are desirable standards of conduct or generalized end states. They have affective and evaluative components in that they are experienced in terms of their relative importance in the person's ideal self-concept; they have a motivational component in that they serve to initiate and guide people's evaluations, choices and actions.*

Normative and Normal Values: Dual Systems?

"Dual-process models" of cognition were considered in chapter 6, in connection with the social intuitionist model of moral judgment. Some years prior to the development of the SIM, Epstein (1989) suggested that we have two relatively independent value systems. The first is a *rational* conceptual system in which our values are expressed as conscious beliefs about the relative desirability of outcomes, along with associated attitudes. The beliefs tend to be relatively rational, analytic and motivated by a need for empirical and logical confirmation. Thus, we tend to experience them as under volitional control. Reese and Fremouw (1984) referred to these as *normative* or *prescriptive values*—what one believes ought to be—and Argyris and Schon (1978) referred to them similarly as *espoused values.* The second set of processes is an *experiential* conceptual system which is tied more closely to preconscious, emotional, and affective processes. Consequently, these are experienced as more automatic and are more action-oriented. These have been characterized as *normal values* (Reese & Fremouw, 1984) or as *values in use* (Argyris & Schon, 1978).

Most of these scholars view the two value sets as overlapping, not discrete. That is, some rational, espoused, normative values may also be expressed in normal or customary behavior. Nevertheless, the distinction between the two components is important both theoretically and because of its measurement implications. The typical survey inquiry or standardized inventory assessing people's values depends on verbal report; hence, it reflects mostly the first system. The second system is more likely to be reflected in people's behavior and may not be readily accessible for self-report—hence the development of the Implicit Association Test (Banaji & Greenwald, 2013). The fact that the two systems are relatively independent (having different determinants and reflecting different psychological processes) means that discrepancies between the two—for example, behaving in ways inconsistent with the values one professes—does not necessarily imply that one is hypocritical. It also does not necessarily mean that the measurement operations lack construct (i.e., convergent) validity.

A Definitional Taxonomy of Values

There are two (nonorthogonal) dimensions on which a taxonomy of specific values can be based. The first has to do with the issue of generality or domain specificity in which we can distinguish between *general values* or *life values* of broad relevance versus narrower domain-relevant attributes such as *work values*. The second dimension has to do with the level of analysis at which a value or value system is considered—that is, who or what is it that reflects the values? This book so far has considered only the individual level of analysis, including values from an individual-differences perspective. But it is also common to speak of values at a more macro-level (e.g., business values, the values of a particular organization or political party, or Judeo-Christian values) in which the values characterize a societal institution or other social entity. And it is not uncommon for social scientists to study the values of even larger social units such as the *cultural values* of an entire country or ethnic group (Hofstede, 2001, 2004; Hofstede et al., 2010), or of even larger historical–cultural units as when we speak of *western values* of individualism in comparison with *eastern values,* which are more collectivist (Triandis, 1995).

The Varying Generality of Values

General or Life Values

General values or *life values* are usually segmented into the two categories of *personal values* and *social values,* referring to self-centered or interpersonal concerns, respectively. Personal values refer to important attributes of the person's own self (preferred modes of action and classes of objectives). As such, they correspond closely to what has long been studied in personality theory as the *ideal self* (Wojciszke, 1989). Social values refer to one's preferred broad objectives and modes of accomplishing them that are interpersonal, and society centered. Among the more frequently studied social values are those involving power (e.g., social status and prestige, and dominance over others), universalism (e.g., social justice, equality and protecting the environment), benevolence, tradition, conformity (e.g., politeness and obedience) and security (e.g, safety and stability of society and social order; cf. Ros et al., 1999).

Because general values have frequently not been differentiated clearly from beliefs, attitudes, interests, preferences and other personality attributes, the number of values that have been considered in the literature is vast. A review of the topic is not possible here, but concise summaries that focus on definitional problems are available (Dawis, 1991; Elizur & Sagie, 1999; Musser & Orke, 1992; Roe & Ester, 1999). One approach to developing a more manageable number of values is the rational construction of a conceptual typology such as Rokeach's (1973) dichotomy of 18 *instrumental values* such as ambitious, broadminded, helpful, and honest, and 18 *terminal values* like a comfortable life, a world at peace, and inner harmony. Rokeach also categorized the 36 values as either personal or social. A similar typology is Elizur and Sagie's (1999) three-modality classification of *material values* (having to do with physical and economic conditions), *affective values* (concerning interpersonal relationships), and *cognitive values* (e.g., achievement, independence, freedom, and curiosity). Another example is Schwartz's (1999) seven values categories: harmony, egalitarianism, intellectual autonomy, affective autonomy, mastery, hierarchy, and conservatism. A prevalent procedure is the use of mathematical techniques such as factor analysis or smallest space analysis to derive an empirically based taxonomy. These procedures have been performed frequently on data from samples obtained from several nations in the hopes of identifying a modest set of basic values with great cross-cultural generality. Overall, the results have been relatively disappointing, resulting in the "theoretically unsatisfactory situation of having a multitude of 'basic dimensions' that are difficult to compare and to combine" (Roe & Ester, 1999, p. 7).

One of the perennial concerns in the study of values has been the frequently observed discrepancy between a person's espoused values and actions. As noted earlier, this can sometimes be explained by a model of two simultaneously held value systems--dual processes. But we have, of course, also considered a similar issue previously with respect to a potential disconnect between moral reasoning and moral behavior. In fact, if we understand moral values to be the internalization of moral principles, it is essentially the same issue. Recall that Epstein's (1989) understanding of values is that:

> Values exist at two levels, a conscious, verbal level and a preconscious, experiential level. The values at the two levels can differ in content and degree, as they are embedded within different conceptual systems that not only differ in content but also operate by different rules. This does not mean that the two systems never correspond; they often do, but it is important to note that they need not correspond, and, when they do not, self-reported values are often poor predictors of emotions and behavior. (p. 13)

Although Epstein went on to explore the way in which values from each system may be assessed (verbal report vs. actions); he did not offer us much help regarding the issue of which system will be activated at any particular time, other than indicating that the experiential system is more closely linked to emotional arousal. This is an important question with respect to the relation between ethical deliberations or moral reasoning and eventual ethical behavior. Because our moral values serve a directing and shaping function in our perception and definition of ethical dilemmas, it is obviously critical to know when the experiential system, which is the one presumably more apt to affect behavior, is likely to be activated.

Two Definitions of Social Values

Mueller and Wornhoff (1990) called attention to a frequently unnoticed ambiguity in the definition, measurement and interpretation of "social values." Social values have traditionally been defined as referring to interpersonal behavior, as with honesty, friendship or justice (in comparison with self-centered personal values like achievement or independence). The ambiguity derives from a second possible meaning that pertains to the valuation of goals and activities at the *societal level*. In other words, values may also be defined according to who is the referent—that is, according to whom the value is being applied—to oneself, or to others, even if the value is not inherently interpersonal in nature (i.e., even if it is not a social value according to the first definition). As an example, consider the value independence—it is not a social value according to the first definition, but it can be, according to the second. How important independence is to you, personally, is not the same question as generally, how important you think it should be for young people growing up nowadays to be independent. And contrary to what one might expect, Mueller and Wornhoff observed only a modest correlation between scales measuring these conceptualizations with the two different referents ($r = .39$).

Many of the social issues that have roiled our country for the past generation or more (affirmative action, sex-based discrimination, pro-choice v. pro-life views, capital punishment, privatization of public education) all involve social values as per the second definition, in the form of competing norms. What makes the issues contentious is that each of us is certain that we know how society ought to function, and our social values get expressed as social policy. We would be wise, when considering the topic of social values, to be clear about which of the two types is being referred to, the relatively benign one concerning interpersonal relations, or politically tinged societal norms.

Social values (defined as per the first, traditional conceptualization) are frequently an object of study by social scientists interested in the relation between individual personality attributes and meaningful outcomes that have real-world moral significance. Whereas "attitude theory ... suggests that global attitudes are poor predictors of specific behaviors ... values are important because of their measurable impact on behavior, despite the generality" (Karp, 1996, p. 115).

A prominent example is the work of Felicia Pratto and her colleagues (Pratto & Shih, 2000; Pratto et al., 1994; Pratto et al., 1997; Sidanius et al., 1996) on *social dominance orientation,* defined as one's desire to have one's own in-group dominate and be superior to other groups. It has been found related to sex (men score higher), a belief in ideologies that enhance hierarchical group differences (anti Black racism and nationalism), political conservatism, and career aspirations for occupations that preserve existing social hierarchies (e.g., business), rather than for hierarchy-attenuating roles (e.g., counseling). Other related examples include a significant relationship between commitment to democratic values and tolerance for the unpopular political views of others (Sullivan & Transue, 1999) and the finding that readiness for social contact with an out-group member is related positively to having universalist values (concern for the welfare of all people) and negatively to a strong tradition, security and conformity values (Sagiv & Schwartz, 1995). Similarly, possessing prosocial or universalist values has been found to be related positively to pro-environmental behavior, whereas pro-self and self-enhancement values were related negatively to such environmental concerns (Cameron et al., 1998; Karp, 1996).

Domain-Relevant Values

I refer to *domain-relevant* rather than "domain-specific" values because many work values, family values or scientific values are not limited to one domain, although their specific content and expression may vary among each. Not surprisingly, the domain of values that has most interested I-O psychologists is that of work values.

Work Values

A detailed treatment of this topic is not germane to the purposes of this text, but it should be noted that work in this area is characterized by considerable concern for definitional clarity. The questions addressed most frequently are "What are work values?" and "What is their relation to general values?" (Carter et al., 1984; Gushue & Weitzman, 1994; Dawis, 1991; Elizur, 1984; Elizur & Sagie, 1999; Pryor, 1979, 1982; Roe & Ester, 1999; Ros et al., 1999; Sagie et al., 1996). Most scholars working in this area have adopted a position like that of Ros et al. (1999) to the effect that general values are seen as "desirable, trans-situational goals that vary in importance as guiding principles in people's lives" (p. 51) and that work values "are specific expressions of general values in the work setting" (p. 54).

However, the conceptualization of work values as expressions of general life values fails to specify whether work values are *merely* the expressions of personal values in the work setting. Take the general value of honesty, for example. Are my professed values regarding honesty the same with respect to the domain of work as in my social life? Is my actual behavior, when this value is challenged, similar at work and on the tennis court? Is the relative importance to me of honesty at work equivalent to its relative importance at home with my family? Is my conception of what I even mean by honesty the same for all these circumstances? In fact, Elizur and Sagie (1999) found that "the comparability between life and work values was observed mainly in their structure rather than in the relative importance of individual values. The differences that were found between the rank orders of certain life and work values indicate that the importance of a personal value is not context-free. Rather, it depends on the environment in which the value is considered" (p. 85).

Nowadays, a person's work values are often used, along with other attributes such as skills and interests, in the process of vocational counseling or choosing an occupational objective, in the belief that a work role that corresponds to one's personal attributes is more satisfying. For example, the U.S. government's Occupational Information Network (O★Net) provides a self-administered *Interest Profiler* and *Work Importance Locator* to be used in occupational exploration. Six broad interest areas are combined with six domains of importance (i.e., work values: achievement, independence, recognition, relationships, support and working conditions) to yield 36 categories of relevant occupational groups. Similarly, in the private sector, Monster.com, the global online employment site, facilitates career exploration by providing a Work Values Checklist of 15 intrinsic values, 15 extrinsic values and 15 lifestyle values.

Focusing on the values of individuals can be thought of as a "bottom-up" approach; some I-O psychologists have also taken a "top-down" approach by focusing first on *occupational values* (Dierdorff & Morgeson, 2013). Occupational values are conceived of by these scholars as inherent "occupational reinforcer patterns" (p. 689) that are "indicative of the preexisting conditions under which an individual's work occurs" (p.690). These serve to gratify corresponding individual employee needs through their influence on the elements of work design or job characteristics.

Moral or Ethical Values

Earlier sections of this book concluded that human social interactions can be segmented conveniently into three domains: (a) egoistic behavior dominated by self-interest; (b) conventional, sometimes even automatic, behavior reflecting society's consensual rules and customs; and (c) moral behavior reflecting higher-level rules, principles, values and/or (more controversially) intuitions. It was further observed in chapters 6 and 7 that moral psychologists, following a long tradition in moral philosophy, have generally conceived the last category, moral behavior, as consisting of two dimensions: (a) justice issues, which are intimately bound up with the notions of fairness, rights and duties, for which we owe much to the work of Piaget (1932/1965) and Kohlberg (1981, 1984); and (b) *welfare* or *caring,* involving issues of beneficence and harm or wrongdoing, which owes much to Hoffman's (1977, 1983, 1988) work on empathy and to Gilligan (1982; Gilligan & Wiggings, 1987). Those two dimensions are sometimes construed as corresponding to the two main categories of normative ethical theories, deontology, and consequentialism, respectively. However, modifications and elaborations of both normative positions have rendered them more similar to each other than their idealized versions (e.g., the development of act-deontological and rule-utilitarian views). Moreover, principles of justice are often defined in consequentialist terms of reward allocation, and welfare may entail rule-based proscriptions against certain wrong actions. Consequently, it is an oversimplification to entirely equate the dimensions of justice and caring with deontology and consequentialism, respectively.

And it is also the case that matters of justice and caring may both be expressed in terms of a third normative category—moral virtue or character--emphasizing the characterological attributes of the people whose deeds and words reflect such. In fact, with its emphasis more on "who do I want to be?" than simply "what should I do?" it could be argued that virtue ethics provides a better theoretical fit for understanding moral values.

Dealing with Interpersonal Values Conflict: Resolution or Rationalization?

An especially intriguing aspect of values is the ego defensive role they may play in maintaining self-esteem. Rokeach (1973) indicated that values:

> ... tell us how to rationalize in the psychoanalytic sense, beliefs, attitudes, and actions that would otherwise be personally and socially unacceptable so that we will end up with personal feelings of morality and competence, both indispensable ingredients for the maintenance and enhancement of self-esteem. An unkind remark made to a friend, for example, may be rationalized as an honest communication. (p. 13)

Social psychologists have extended Rokeach's (1973) suggestion to a formal *value justification hypothesis* concerning attitudes toward social issues and interpersonal relations (Eiser, 1987). The notion is that people who hold different attitudes about a social issue such as economic globalization or toward a targeted group such as Latinx or labor unions employ different values to justify or account for their attitudes (Kristiansen & Zanna, 1988). Elsewhere, those authors explain:

> Although attitudes may originally stem from the relative importance that people ascribe to various values, once formed, attitudes may well produce self-serving biases that affect both the values that people deem relevant to an issue and the complexity or open-mindedness of their reasoning about an issue. In addition, just as people may appeal to values to justify their attitudes toward social issues such as nuclear weaponry or abortion, data suggest that people may exaggerate perceptions of intergroup value differences in an effort to rationalize prejudicial intergroup attitudes and justify discrimination.
>
> *(Kristiansen & Zanna, 1994, p. 47)*

Kristiansen and Zanna (1994) reviewed several studies indicating that "values play a stronger role as defensive justifications of already established attitudes rather than as guides to the development of people's attitudes and related behaviors" (p. 61). This is one of the reasons that conflicts regarding social issues are so difficult to resolve: People on different sides resort to different, frequently incompatible values to support their attitudes and beliefs. And Yong et al. (2021) have emphasized that "rationalization processes (e.g., cognitive dissonance reduction, *post hoc justification of choices, confabulation of reasons for moral positions*) are aimed at creating the fictions we prefer to believe and maintaining the impression that we are psychologically coherent and rational" (p. 781, emphases added).

Tetlock and Mitchell (1993) emphasized the extent to which researchers' sociopolitical values, affect the conduct of supposedly neutral psychological research, especially research concerning public policy. Similarly, Lefkowitz (1990, 2009a, 2011b, 2012a, 2013a, 2016)has long argued that the economic/business value system that has dominated I-O psychology has had unacknowledged adverse effects on our science and practice.

Without subjecting our ethical judgments to the standards of right reason and the scrutiny of others who are less (or differently-) opinionated on the issue at hand, even the most apparently principled ethical stance can be a mere post-hoc rationalization of self-serving goals and objectives (Banaji & Greenwald, 2013) or automatic intuitions (Haidt & Joseph, 2004). Habermas (1990) emphasized that the resolution of interpersonal values conflicts depends on people understanding the cultural influences that underlie the differences and engaging in the necessary moral discussion to resolve them. This is commensurate with the first point raised in the Framework for Ethical Decision Making in chapter 2, emphasizing the critical importance of ethical reasoning.

Values at The Macro Level[4]

When the unit of analysis for a consideration of values is larger than the single individual, the concept of culture is inevitably engaged. This includes groups identified by a common social identity (e.g., their ethnicity or nationality), common social role (e.g., work groups) or a composite of both (e.g., members of the same organization or occupation). In all, values are incorporated within a multilevel conceptualization of culture in which they represent the more deeply embedded core, which influences the overt patterns of behavior and their artifacts at the periphery (Cooke & Rousseau, 1988; Rousseau, 1990; Schein, 1990, 2010). Rousseau and Schein distinguished between values, by which they meant the espoused or normative values that are readily articulated, versus the more deeply held

---

4   I mean the term to include groups and organizations (i.e., meso level) as well as larger societal and national entities.

assumptions of the social group or organization. The latter corresponds to what Epstein (1989) referred to as *experiential values* or what Argyris and Schon (1978) called *values in use*. In their review of research on business values, Agle and Caldwell (1999)emphasized the importance of the multiple levels of analysis at which values may be studied. They articulated five levels as well as relations among levels. Individual values represent the bulk of empirical research, and there are four levels of macro or group values: organizational, institutional, societal (i.e., national), and global (i.e., universal). In addition, sub-organizational units of analysis are important to consider (e.g., work-group or team-level goals and values), as well as units of analysis based on biosocial and social identity (e.g., chapter 12 discusses the values of I-O psychology).

A Structural-Functional Perspective

An interesting issue is the relation between values (or culture in general) and social structure. For example, with respect to organizations, Hinings et al. (1996) discussed several theoretical possibilities concerning the relation between the two: (a) the values of senior managers shape structural arrangements to reflect their personal values (e.g., how tall or flat is the management hierarchy?); (b) social position and status influence the attitudes and values of individuals by virtue of their different perspectives, experiences and concerns (cf. Lawrence & Lorsch, 1969) (e.g., people in production have different priorities than those in sales); (c) external societal values produce organizational forms that must adapt accordingly (cf. Katz & Kahn, 1978) (e.g., the growth of an EEO function in HR following passage of the civil rights act in the U.S.); and (d) that "organizational arrangements develop from the ideas, values, and beliefs that underpin them" (Hinings et al., 1996, p. 890). The same general approach may be applied with respect to collectivities of individuals who share a social, but not necessarily organizational, identity. Those who occupy a similar location in the larger social structure (sharing a common social identity) by virtue of their age, ethnicity, sex, occupation or other personal attributes often develop common values as a consequence of their shared experiences and cultural identity.

These perspectives are essentially functionalist in nature, reminiscent of the sociologist Emil Durkheim's view of social norms, rules and values serving to provide the integrative glue by which society holds together and functions effectively. (Rubber bands might be a more apt metaphor than glue.) This functionalist approach has been elaborated in social science into the view that all human societies provide implicit answers to a few meta-problems such as: What is the character of innate human nature? What is the basis for human relationships? The answers reflect value orientations; and because there are presumably only a limited number of potential answers to each question, there are likely to be substantial values commonalities across cultures. This has given rise to a universalist perspective in which it is believed by some that all cultures and societies can be described adequately on the same set of universal values. Among organizational scholars probably the best-known work conducted in this tradition is that of Hofstede (2004, 2010; cf. also Gelfand et al., 2007; and Oyserman, 2002), and the contemporary conceptualization that aims at achieving the most widespread generality is that of Schwartz (1992, 1994, 1999; Schwartz & Bilsky, 1987, 1990; cf. also Karp, 1996; Stem et al., 1998).

At the meso level, the functionalist approach leads to "a view of organizational values as those things that are important to the organization's accomplishing its purpose—those things that help the organization to survive and flourish" (Scott, 2002). The perspective can be extended to the macro level of social institutions within society, as depicted in Table 8.1. Because it is based on an analysis of the societal functions performed by the fundamental categories of social structure, or institutions of society it is a structural—functional analysis. The values—both those that are espoused and/or values in use—are inferred from the functions. In other words, each institution generates values supportive of its objectives. "A social institution embodies individual values when, in the normal course of its operation, the institution offers people roles that encourage behavior expressing those values and fosters conditions for their further expression" (Schwartz, 1990, p. 7). Although the different institutions can be reasonably clearly demarcated, there is overlap in some functions and values among them. This helps facilitate the integration of society. For example, much of the primary socialization of children that occurs within the nuclear family enables the secondary socialization that begins with early school experiences which, in turn, facilitates the still later accommodation to the role- and extra-role requirements of employment (occupational and organizational socialization).

A couple of observations should be made regarding the economic institution comprised of free-enterprise capitalist businesses shown in Table 8.1. First, although business contributes a great deal to the material and social well-being of society in many ways beyond the mere production of resources, goods and services, I have implied (by their absence) that those social factors find relatively little representation in the value system of business. Thus, we see the overwhelming dominance of the profit motive in the value systems of business to the detraction of potential social contributions. In other words, for the time being I am assuming the dominance of the classical laissez-faire free-market model of business activity in which the sole responsibility of business is to make a profit. But this is a somewhat contentious issue that will be considered explicitly in chapter 11. Second, note that in the classical model there is just one overriding terminal business value—profitability. Productivity and efficiency are instrumental values that support it. Frederick (1995) referred to this entire value cluster as *economizing*.

In addition, whereas I think it is legitimate to infer the espoused value of competition for the economic institution at that macro level, it should be clear that, beyond mere lip service, competition is not generally a prized value of the specific business organizations that comprise the institution or of the individual leaders of those organizations. Even Adam Smith (1976/1776) noted that if left to

TABLE 8.1 A Structural—Functional Analysis of the Values of Major American Institutions

Societal Institution	Functions Served	Espoused Values and/or Values In Use
Family	Assure physical survival. Foster emotional well-being. Accomplish primary socialization, including the capacity for moral development.	Interpersonal trust. Empathy and love. Loyalty and responsibility.
Schools	Create an educated citizenry. Accomplish secondary socialization, including the capacity to adhere to social norms and conventions.	Excellence (knowledge, competence, achievement, and creativity). Conformity to legitimate authority.
Government (political)	Maintain domestic order and peace. Represent those governed. Advance the commonweal by raising and spending monies. Advance the nation's international goals and relations.	Fairness and justice (equality or need). Egalitarianism. National pride.
Government (military)	Provide national security and defense. Advance and enforce international goals and relations.	Patriotism. Honor, valor, and self-sacrifice. Obedience to legitimate authority.
Economic– Business	Foster physical survival. Advance material, psychological and social well-being. Provide profit for owners.	Profitability (productivity and efficiency). Accumulation of wealth. Competition. Merit.
Religion	Provide transcendent meaning to life. Advance moral and ethical standards of conduct.	Subordination to an unknowable higher authority. Belief in a unifying metaphysical explanation of all. Moral treatment of others.
Science and its applications	Produce knowledge and expertise. Enhance physical survival, health, and well-being. Provide transcendent meaning to the natural world.	Belief in the utility and heuristic value of scientific methods and explanatory systems.
Aesthetic—Cultural	Provide expressive and transcendent meaning to life.	Self-expression and artistic creativity.

their own devices businesses would always form *anti*competitive monopolies. This perspective is in keeping with that of Donaldson and Walsh (2015) who point out the fallacy of confusing "what counts as value for a single firm … [with] what counts as value for business in general" (p. 181).

Empirical Research

A great deal of empirical research on values consists of group comparisons among those who differ in social identity and/or roles. The comparisons are generally of three sorts. In the first type of study the entire human population is segmented into just two groups that are sampled and compared—men and women. For example, a meta-analysis of 20,000 student respondents indicated that women are more likely than men to perceive specific business practices as unethical (Franke et al., 1995). However, the effect size is rather small, and the difference virtually disappears with samples of men and women who have greater work experience (suggesting the effects of secondary socialization experiences).

The second large body of empirical research consists of cross-cultural or cross-national comparisons (cf. Earley & Gibson, 1998; Gelfand et al., 2007; Hofstede, 1980, 2001, 2004; Hofstede et al., 2004, 2010; Singelis et al., 1995; Triandis, 1995). For example, "Out of the long list of cultural values, individualism-collectivism and power distance may be considered the most prominent values that distinguish the East from the West, as they are at the core of how people view/deal with their relationship with others" (Barkema et al., 2015, p.463).

The third area of research pertains to the study of occupations. Although some of these studies treat individual-level values as an independent variable that influences occupational choice (Duff & Cotgrove, 1982; Feather, 1982; Rosenberg, 1957; Wooler, 1985), most focus on post-hoc characterizations of occupational groups or on comparisons of two or more groups. Consideration of the substance of that research would take us too far afield from the focus of this book on ethical issues and moral values.[5] What is of special concern for this section, however, is the representation of ethical and moral issues at the societal level. That is the issue of *social justice*.

---

5 Among the occupational groups whose values have been assessed are psychological counselors (Carter, 1991; Chapman, 1981; Kelly, 1995); military personnel (Clymer, 1999; Guimond, 1995) and police officers (Hazer & Alvares, 1981); physicians (Blackburn & Fox, 1983); organization development practitioners (Church et al., 1994); and, of course, managers, both as an individual description (England, 1967; Sikula, 1973) as well as in comparison with other groups such as labor union leaders (Giacobbe-Miller, 1995), public administrators (DeLeon, 1994; Posner & Schmidt, 1996), entrepreneurs (Kecharananta & Baker, 1999), and organization development practitioners (Goodstein, 1983), or as within-group comparisons across functional areas (Posner et al., 1987), and as cross-national comparisons (England & Lee, 1974; Hofstede, 2001; Ralston et al., 1992).

Social Justice

This chapter takes the value(s) of social justice as a pertinent and important topic to be studied and understood, as well as a legitimate ethical concern to be promoted. In chapter 10 the issue of the relationship between values and science, or the role of values in science as a contentious issue—i.e., the ideal of "value-free science"—is taken up.

The relevance of *justice* to the study of ethics is exemplified by the distinction between injustice and misfortune. Misfortune is the result of external, frequently unavoidable natural events, whereas injustice refers to socially mediated, often intentional human acts (Shklar, 1990). Singer (2000) pointed out that the notion of justice has always been accorded a pivotal status in normative theories of ethics. For example, it was considered "the sum of all virtues" by Aristotle; in Kantian terms it involves a rational balance between people's rights and duties. In psychology, the *belief in a just world* has been posited as a core attribute of most people "in the sense that their underlying need to believe in a just world motivates them to behave as if they believed that the world is a just place and as if they wanted to preserve this belief" (Hafer & Bègue, 2005). Business ethicists have observed that "Justice includes treating others as they *should* or *deserve* to be treated by adhering to standards of right and wrong. In other words, justice is in part a judgment about the morality of an outcome, process or interpersonal negotiation. It is concerned with what people view as ethically appropriate" (Cropanzano et al., 2003, emphasis in the original). And *social justice* has been defined in psychology "as the goal to decrease human suffering and to promote human values of equality and justice" (Vasquez, 2012, p. 337).

The concept has generally been studied within the context of the second of Mueller and Wornhoff's (1990) two definitions of social values. That is, social justice pertains to the fairness or morality of meso- or macro-level social systems such as a work team, an organization, a national culture or even as reflected in international relations. It includes the principles by which the system determines the distribution of rewards and resources (e.g., power, status or financial remuneration), how those distributions are implemented, as well as its avowed standards of right and wrong.

There are four aspects of social justice that are of particular relevance for I-O psychology: (a) the role of large business organizations in society (to be discussed in chapter 11); (b) organizational justice; (c) economic justice, including pay equity; and (d) changes in the nature and terms of employment (to be covered in chapter 12). These are primarily matters of *distributive justice* (DJ)—pertaining to "rules that reflect appropriateness in decision outcomes" (Colquitt & Zipay, 2015, p. 76). At the organizational level justice is determined by human resources policies, supervisory actions, and administrative programs such as those for determining compensation. And those policies and programs are shaped largely by the nature of the political and economic systems of the nation and its culture

(Schäfer et al., 2015). In other words, the values of the economic system (in the case of the United States, free-market capitalism) determine the form that the value of justice takes throughout much of society (in our case, *equity*) and, by extension, within individual organizations (*merit*). Although equity pertains in the private/economic sector; by comparison, the normative criterion of justice in the public domain, the legal system, is *equality* of treatment and representation.[6]

There are two main scholarly traditions in the study of justice: a largely empirical one from psychology—represented by a meso-level focus on *organizational justice* (OJ), and the macro-level normative modeling of a just society from political and moral philosophy.[7]

Organizational Justice (OJ)

Social and I-O psychologists have been studying matters of justice and the decision heuristics people use to satisfy particular criteria of justice such as equality or equity, for quite some time—and across the globe (Adams, 1965; Cropanzano, 1993; Cropanzano & Ambrose, 2015; Cropanzano et al., 2001; Gilliland et al., 2001; Harris, 1993; Lind & Tyler, 1988; Messick, 1993; Schäfer et al., 2015; Shao et al., 2013). (Cropanzano & Stein, 2009, provide a succinct review.) Several years ago, however, I noted that there are several reasons why much of that work is not fully responsive to a moral concern for fairness and justice in organizations and to the potential for improving organizations in that regard (Lefkowitz, 2009a). There are three features to the critique.

Measuring Only The Perception of Justice

It is, of course, not particularly surprising that a construct in psychology is defined and measured as a psychological variable—in this instance, *perceived* justice. For example: "Justice reflects the perceived adherence to rules that represent appropriateness in decision contexts" (Colquitt & Zipay, 2015).[8] Such perceptions

---

6   But in Finland equity functions in at least part of the legal system as well. There is progressive (i.e., equitable, not equal) punishment for speeding infractions, which are calculated according to the speeder's income. A millionaire business person was recently fined about $58,000 for driving 64 m.p.h. in a 50-m.p.h. zone (Daley, 2015). Presumably, the objective is to have an *equivalent* deterrent effect on all speeders.

7   By characterizing the study of OJ as largely empirical I do not mean to suggest that it is atheoretical. In fact, at least eight different theories have been used to explain its findings (Colquitt & Zipay, 2015).

8   There is some conceptual confusion regarding the distinction, if any, between justice and fairness. Colquitt and Zipay (2015) distinguish between the two: justice is "the perceived adherence to rules that reflect appropriateness in decision contexts" and fairness is "a global perception of appropriateness—a perception that tends to lie theoretically downstream of justice" (p. 76). Goldman and Cropanzano (2015) make a similar distinction.

and reactions are also understood to include evaluative and emotional components so that we speak of feelings of injustice in terms of relative deprivation (Cropanzano & Randall, 1993). But the Nobel laureate Armatya Sen (2009) warns that we "need to go beyond our *sense* of justice and injustice .... We must have a theory of justice. To understand the world is never a matter of simply recording our immediate perceptions. Understanding inescapably involves reasoning" (p. viii, emphasis added).

In I-O psychology whether institutional procedures are fair or just is inferred ex post facto from people's reactions to their experiences with them—perhaps based on just a single experience such as a corporate layoff or an anticipated promotion not received. The convenience of this psychological/perceptual approach is that it does not require an a priori objective definition of justice. This is similar to the way in which *preference utilitarianism* finesses the issue of having to define the components of aggregate utility by allowing each person's preferences into the definition of what is utile (cf. Chap. 4). Perceived justice is similarly a phenomenological construct—it's in the eye of the beholder. However,

> ... mental representations, like DJ, concern beliefs about external events or conditions that may be verifiable. Although it is of psychological interest, some importance, and arguably useful to study people's *perceptions* of DJ, what if they are wrong? Or some of them are wrong? Or there is great variability among all those in the same position? Or they have no knowledge of the actual distributive rules and outcomes?
>
> *(Lefkowitz, 2009a, p. 223, emphasis in the original)*

Moreover, recent work suggests that employee perceptions of supervisor fairness depend not only on the extent to which the supervisors' actions are seen as just but also on attributions of the supervisors' motives—why they acted in that manner (Muir [Zapapta], Sharf & Liu, 2022). For example, Chesher (2000) discusses "the ethics of employment" from a free-market perspective, through the parable of the vineyard owner in need of workers, from the Gospel according to Matthew:

> The owner strikes a bargain with some men early in the day and makes the identical bargain several times later with other men, as the day progresses. At the end of the day, all of the workers discover that they have been paid the same sum, to which they had initially agreed, regardless of the hours worked. Those who worked the least were paid the same as those who labored for the entire day. Those hired earliest complained of unjust treatment, to which the vineyard owner replied, Friend, I do thee no wrong; dids't not thou agree with me for a penny? ... Is it not lawful for me to do what I will with mine own?
> No doubt in contemporary American society the aggrieved workers would cry exploitation and take the owner to court. But from a moral point of view, the complaint is groundless. (p. 21)

No, it is not groundless. It certainly is exploitation (i.e., unjust): "the complaint can be viewed as morally 'groundless' only if one ignores the unfairness of the employment contract as a consequence of the workers' apparent ignorance of going wage rates and/or their lack of bargaining power, and if no credence is given to the moral relevance and importance of equity considerations involving social relations" (Lefkowitz, 2012b, p.118).[9] Moreover, most would agree that the vineyard owner was acting more out of self-interest, than any attempt to be just.

Perhaps even more important from a moral perspective, the psychological approach to OJ does not entail having an objective a priori definition of justice:

> In order to take a normative or moral position, one must move beyond mere description and putatively scientific "value-free" perspectives. One has to take a stand and assert what interpersonal, organizational, political, or societal positions ought to exist—and defend that position in moral terms. And that—as a profession—we avoid like the plague ... .

> To study and draw conclusions regarding distributive justice, one needs to articulate a *normative* view of what distributions are right, fair, or just to use as evaluative standards. That entails a willingness to state what is *not* right, and is *unfair* or *unjust* about our organizations ... . We sidestep entirely the normative questions and arguments—unlike other branches of study ... which often encompass debates about normative positions.
>
> *(Lefkowitz, 2008, p. 446, emphases in the original)*

Similarly, Thomas Piketty (2014) admonishes: "social scientists ... cannot be content to invoke grand but abstract principles such as justice, democracy, and world peace. *They must make choices and take stands in regard to specific institutions and policies* (p. 574, emphasis added). In other words, in I-O psychology we really do not focus on nor measure (in)justice as it is widely understood.

In political and moral philosophy the focus is on the conditions necessary to arrive at a fair system in accordance with the assumptions of a particular model of justice (Barry, 1989; Mappes & Zembaty, 1997). Those conditions include the assumed motives of the parties determining the system (e.g., senior management of a company) and the contextual circumstances under which an agreement is reached (e.g., the terms of employment); any arrangement that is developed under the appropriate conditions is presumed to be just, and there may be many different ones that qualify.[10]

---

9 The laborers' ignorance, inferior status, and lack of bargaining power relative to that of the vineyard owner is what Rawls (2001) condemns as incapable of leading to a just social contract, and which he replaces by circumstances of "the original position." (Discussed later, this chapter.)

10 Obviously, it is not so cut and dried. The requisite conditions may be only partially met, resulting in *relatively* fair or unjust decision rules and/or procedures.

In distinguishing between justice and fairness, Goldman and Cropanzano (2015) come close to grappling with the issue: "Justice describes normative standards and how these are implemented; fairness describes reactions to those standards" (p. 315); and "Distinguishing just workplaces from fair ones provides *independent standards* of good conduct" (p. 317, emphasis added). From the previous pages, it should be apparent that I agree with them that it is important to distinguish between the rules or standards versus reactions to them. However, for these scholars, the normative standards, no less than the fairness reactions, refer to employee perceptions of those standards or rules. By not focusing on and assessing independently the actual system of justice in the organization I-O psychology overlooks much. For example, we ignore the moral implications and consequences of the fact that the terms of social exchange are usually established under conditions in which one party (a corporation) has infinitely greater power than the other (individual job applicants or employees)—if they are even party to a real "agreement" at all.

Cugueró-Escofet and Fortin (2014) have built on the distinction that they recognize, between social scientists' "subjective fairness perceptions" of organizational justice versus "justice as a normative requirement in societal relationships" as used by philosophers and ethicists. They have proposed "a 'reconciliation' model, as a third way of considering justice in the workplace, taking into account normative and psychological issues pertaining to justice ... . Our model also implies that justice researchers can and should be concerned with the moral implications of their own subject of research" (p. 435).

On a different tack, emphasizing person-variables that they feel have been overlooked in the study of OJ, Cropanzano and Stein (2009) propose that the study of OJ should pay attention to people's internalized moral convictions and standards, their moral identity, and to individual differences in that regard.

Emphasizing Procedural Justice (PJ) and Interactional Justice (IJ), not Distributive Justice (DJ)[11]

The past several decades have been marked by a horrendous set of circumstances for working people: companies closing operations in the United States and moving them to foreign countries with abysmal standards of living and cheap labor; job loss; double-digit unemployment; full-time jobs with benefits being replaced by the "gig economy" and part-time jobs without benefits; stagnant minimum wages (in constant dollars); skyrocketing medical and health insurance costs--no longer employer-provided; virtually all corporate profits going to upper management and shareholders, not to workers; lack of pay transparency in

---

11 Interactional justice is often disaggregated into *interpersonal* justice (IPJ) and *informational* justice (IFJ) (cf. Colquitt & Zipay, 2015).

organizations; the 2008 financial crisis and recession; loss of home ownership; and to top it off, the economic and emotional ravages of the Covid-19 pandemic.

These are extremely adverse outcomes, not "processes" (albeit some are viewed appropriately as misfortune, not injustice). One might anticipate, therefore, that the study of OJ would be characterized prominently by shining a spotlight on distributive, especially economic, outcomes. But during this time, the study of DJ (the perceived fairness of societal benefits and actual allocations such as pay) has greatly diminished in favor of a focus on procedural and interactional justice (PJ and IJ) (Gilliland & Hale, 2005; Schminke et al., 1997). These reflect the perceived fairness of the procedural rules and actions by which allocations have been administered (Cropanzano et al., 2001)—"and include voice, consistency, accuracy, bias suppression, and correctability" (Colquitt & Zipay, 2015, p. 76).[12]

Almost all the studies considered in a meta-analysis of OJ research (187 of 190) investigated PJ and/or IJ, but only 54% of them included distributive justice (Cohen-Charash & Spector, 2001). A more recent and much larger meta-analysis of 493 independent research samples revealed even more diminution in the study of DJ (Colquitt et al., 2013). The authors examined the relationships between perceptions of OJ and eight outcomes: organizational citizenship behavior, task performance, counterproductive work behavior, trust in supervisor, trust in organization, organizational commitment, perceived organizational support and leader-member exchange. I compared the number of studies that investigated DJ in comparison with the number that looked at procedural and/or interpersonal and/or informational justice (i.e., the sum of all three). The results are rather consistent across the eight outcome categories: the proportion of investigations that included DJ are 28% (36 of 128), 36% (45 of 124), 33% (24 of 73), 35% (26 of 74), 37% (20 of 54), 35% (77 of 221), 28% (17 of 60), and 38% (16 of 42), respectively.[13] That's a weighted average of merely one-third.

Granted, the focus on procedural and interactional (interpersonal and informational) justice is accommodated nicely by the study of employee perceptions: a reasonable way to measure how fairly employees believe they are treated is to ask them. But what if one is concerned about the fairness of organizational policies and practices in terms of their distributive *outcomes*, such as for pay? That ordinarily requires (a) having some notion(s) about what the outcomes should be, according to some articulated criteria of distributive justice such as pay equity, (b) measuring the actual outcomes in relation to those criteria, and (c) all concerned having access to that information (i.e., *pay transparency*).

---

12 It should be acknowledged that John Rawls's political model of justice-as-fairness is a model of procedural, not distributive, justice. But with a big difference: it specifies the requisite circumstances that should be met so that procedural fairness will result in distributive justice.

13 Calculated from data presented in Tables 2–6 in Colquitt et al. (2013).

Perhaps the study of DJ has diminished because PJ is a more salient issue in organizations (Folger & Lewis, 1993; Landy et al., 1978; Viswesvaran & Ones, 2002). For example, police officers who believe that they are in a procedurally fair department are "more likely to trust and feel obligated to obey their supervisors, less likely to be psychologically and emotionally distressed, and less likely to be cynical and mistrustful about the world in general and the communities they police in particular" (Trinker et al., 2016, p. 158). The apparent greater salience of PJ might indicate merely that most employees simply take for granted the culturally dominant values of DJ which, in the United States, is the principle of equity or merit–which they assume to be implemented accurately. (Even though, given the customary absence of pay transparency, they usually have no way of knowing that to be the case.) But it might also reflect problems in justice research, leading to invalid conclusions. One critic charged that DJ studies often "conflate differences in mere outcome level with distributive injustice. Moreover, DJ is often assessed in experimental participants who have no way of actually judging it" (Lefkowitz, 2009a, p. 222).

Constrained Practice Recommendations

The foregoing criticisms (lack of a normative position for guidance; reliance exclusively on perceptual measures; focus mostly on procedural, interpersonal and informational justice to the diminishment of concern for distributive justice) are not merely "academic;" they have serious consequences. It is not surprising to learn that a leading I-O psychology scholar and justice proponent has voiced concern over how little we do to "help promote justice in organizations" (Greenberg, 2009, p. 181). Recommendations for improvement are generally restricted to attempts at enhancing the fairness and considerateness by which the distribution rules are implemented procedurally, as opposed to challenging the fundamental distributive assumptions of the rules themselves. For example, the "practical implications" of the massively impressive meta-analysis noted above advise forlornly that "more attention should be paid to fostering justice as a component of a supervisor's leadership style" (Colquitt et al., 2013, p. 220).

Moreover, it seems important to acknowledge the potential dangers of PJ being used deceptively: "Low power groups can be fooled into believing that there will be distributive gains when they are given voice. This has been shown to occur at the macro, meso, and micro levels of analysis" (Druckman & Wagner, 2016). At the meso level, "an organization might introduce task-assignment procedures that appeared to allow workers voice prior to the allocation of task assignments when in fact the voiced preferences and values are never really considered" (Lind & Tyler, 1988, p. 201). This is reminiscent of Greenberg's (2009) observation, "These findings make a compelling case that adverse reactions to distributive injustice are mitigated by interactionally fair treatment. This suggests that managers may have at their disposal a useful tool for buffering the adverse effects of an undesirable organizational policy" (p. 185). To which I replied at the time, "is that all we stand for? Might that suggestion reasonably be construed as facilitating injustice? What about challenging the appropriateness of the undesirable organizational policies?" (Lefkowitz, 2009a, p. 223).

Another effect of the way we study OJ, is an important "levels issue" to consider. Regarding matters of social justice, we are concerned about the [actual distributive] justice of organizations as major social systems, not simply individual employee perceptions. As noted earlier, by focusing on perceived justice at the individual level,

> … we misconstrue a system-level construct at the individual level of theory and analysis. It's not that perceptions are unimportant. Indeed, we would be foolish to consider enhancing the actual fairness of a system without assuring that the work was noted and understood by all stakeholders. But the "levels" error contributes to an avoidance of the normative issues.
>
> *(Lefkowitz, 2009a, p. 224)*

Accordingly, scholars have recently attended to "studying justice perceptions at the collective level, generally referred to as justice climate" (Shminke et al., 2015, p. 727; Whitman et al., 2012). However, even when the theoretical focus is on larger organizational units, the operational measurements are still at the micro level of individuals' beliefs and attitudes, albeit aggregated to provide a social index of how the unit of focus is perceived by the group. In contrast, it is possible to study the actual conditions of justice that give rise to justice perceptions and climate, analogous to the way in which anthropologists study cultural artifacts (Colquitt et al., 2005; Harrison et al., 2006; Stone-Romero & Stone, 2005).

Modeling Justice[14]

Moral and political philosophers and their intellectually related colleagues in economics, political science and social theory are more likely to be using a combination of moral philosophy and mathematical decision theory and game theory to model what a just system (including organization) would look like. Potentially, at least, this can provide the bases for modifying the existing system (s). Moreover, in the tradition of *social contract theory* (see chapter 3) their focus is on modeling the process whereby the parties affected by the distribution of power, status or money (or their representatives) engage in an agreement-reaching process stipulating the terms of the contract. Their approach may be

14 This section illustrates the approach taken to the study of justice in political and moral philosophy—generally at the macro/societal level. However, some scholars have made noteworthy attempts to extrapolate some of that--the very influential work of John Rawls (2001) and Amartya Sen (2009) --down to the level of individual organizations and OJ. The interested reader is referred to Lindblom (2011) and Shrivastava et al. (2016), respectively.

criticized as overly theoretical–paying insufficient attention to the messy empirical realities that have to be contended with to implement a justice model, especially insofar as the prerequisite conditions for justice may not exist in a particular situation. On the other hand, those idealized models of justice enable us to focus more clearly on the underlying moral assumptions of practices that we take for granted and on ways in which our real-world social systems may be deficient in that regard, needing improvement.

Brian Barry's (1989) illuminating *A Treatise on Social Justice: Vol. 1. Theories of Justice* points out that the real-world issue of justice arises when it is recognized that social, political and economic inequalities are largely the consequence of human conventions so that we feel the need for some justification of them. If we reject metaphysical justifications such as "God intends it to be that way" and so-called "natural" justifications like Social Darwinism, virtually the only type of justifications left are rational and reasonable agreements that are therefore acceptable to those involved. The question of justice arises when two or more parties (individuals, work groups, organizations or nations) have a conflict of interest over resources; and Barry proposed that:

> Whether we are dealing with individual acts or whole social institutions, justice is concerned with the way in which benefits and burdens are distributed. The subject of justice is the distribution of rights and privileges, powers and opportunities, and the command over material resources … And if we ask what we are saying about an action or an institution when we say it is unjust, the general answer is, I suggest, this. *We are claiming that it cannot be defended publicly—that the principles of distribution it instantiates could reasonably be rejected by those who do badly under it.*
>
> *(p. 292, emphasis added)*

Even though one party to an agreement may be unhappy with it, feel deprived and want more, the situation is not unfair unless they can rationally and reasonably justify a claim for more. In other words, injustice must be shown as violating terms of the agreement (as per which model is being used), not merely as "perceived injustice."[15]

Most institutions in society are not directly concerned with issues of justice, so social justice is not the primary criterion by which they are judged. Primary criteria relate to the essential objectives of the institution. For example, corporations are in business primarily to provide goods and services to society at a profit for the owners; schools exist to educate our children to become knowledgeable, happy and effective citizens. Thus, productivity and profitability in the

---

15 Of course, actual injustice may also be perceived as such. And this approach gives rise to careful consideration of what is or is not "reasonable." A great deal has been written about that.

first instance and quality of education delivered and student well-being in the second are the primary criteria. But institutions and organizations may also be evaluated morally from the standpoint of their contribution to or detraction from the overall quality of the society of which they are a part. Regarding corporations, e.g., procedures by which employment opportunities are allocated and the extent and equity of income differentials are pertinent. Regarding our schools, e.g., the determinants of disparate educational preparation for further academic advancement or desirable occupational choices is a relevant justice issue. This contrasts with the point of view that business corporations if they obey the law and adhere to minimal standards of ethical conduct, should not be held to any evaluative criteria other than making profits for their owners.

Barry (1989) developed a taxonomy of eight models (actually, eight families of models) of justice based primarily on two alternative assumptions regarding (a) the motives people have to reach an agreement and (b) two different structural assumptions.[16] The assumed motivational alternatives are (i) people are motivated primarily, if not exclusively, by the pursuit of self-interest so that the primary motivation to be just is that it is to one's own long-term advantage—because others are also motivated that way; or (ii) people are motivated to a considerable degree by the attempt to be fair, without considering morally irrelevant bargaining strengths and weaknesses such as position power or social status. These alternative assumptions stem from the enlightened egoist and universalist meta-ethical traditions, respectively, in moral philosophy, and both are within the tradition of normative social contract theory.

The structural distinction is between (i) two-stage models in which there is an explicit or implied existing starting baseline from which to compare the advantageousness of the eventual agreement and (ii) baseline-free "original position" models that eliminate existing differences in bargaining power. Table 8.2 outlines and compares the bare-bones features of three of the eight models. Actually, there are four models represented because Model III summarizes two versions.

Model I: Bargaining or Gaming

This is the embodiment of classical social contract theory as developed by Hobbes and Hume. It is the quintessential representation of a family of two-stage models in which it is assumed that the parties to a potential agreement start out in a pre-agreement stage of independent self-striving or direct competition (the non-agreement baseline). The parties achieve an agreement (a metaphorical contract) because they each anticipate some advantage to themselves from the bargain. "Justice consists in playing one's part in mutually advantageous cooperative

---

16 Several other attributes are used as well to develop the classifications. These two are the most important for understanding his work.

TABLE 8.2 Three Models of Social Justice

Model	Structure of the Model	Predicate Conditions	Motives of the Participants	Nature of "Justice"
I Bargaining or Gaming (Thomas Hobbes, David Hume)	"Two-Stage Model"	"The Circumstances of Justice": • Moderate Scarcity • Moderate Selfishness • Relative Equality of Power	Egoism: Maximizing Self-Interest, in the Context of Others Attempting to do the Same	Justice as Mutual Advantage: Compliance With Cooperative Agreements Based on Long-Term Mutual Advantage
II Decision-Making Under Uncertainty (John Rawls)	"Original Position" (baseline independent)	The Three "Circumstances of Justice": • Moderate Scarcity • Moderate Selfishness • Relative Equality of Power + Quasi-Impartiality (see below)	Egoism: Maximizing Self-Interest, Constrained by Ignorance of Personal Circumstances ("Veil of Ignorance")	Justice as Mutual Advantage: Compliance with Cooperative Agreements Based on Long-Term Mutual Advantage
III Persuasive Debate (David Hume, John Rawls)	"Original Position" (baseline independent)	"The Circumstances of Impartiality": • Comparable Organization and Resources • Comparable Political Representation • Common "Fellow-feeling" • Politics as Genuine Debate	Universalism: Achieving Terms that None Can Reasonably Reject (The "Justice Motive"). Either With Full Knowledge or Under a "Veil of Ignorance"	Justice as Impartiality: Compliance With Cooperative Agreements Based on Their Impartiality (fairness & reasonableness) to All With no Consideration of Personal Advantage.

Source: Based on *A Treatise on Social Justice: Vol. 1. Theories of Justice* (Barry, 1989). The dotted lines indicate aspects of different models that are the same or similar.

arrangements, where the standard of comparison is some state of affairs defined by absence of cooperation" (Barry, 1989, p. 361).

Taking his lead from Hume, Barry pointed out that it is the *circumstances of justice* (see Col. 3 of the table) that enable the operation of this state of affairs. Some level of "scarcity" of benefits must pertain; if there were complete abundance notions of justice would be moot. The second critical component is that the nature of the self-interest that motivates the participants needs to be more in line with what is referred to in this book as *enlightened self-interest,* and what Barry called *intelligent self-interest.* This simply means that people give a higher priority to their personal security (which entails constraints on one's selfishness and aggressiveness) than to the ability to aggress freely (because that would leave one susceptible to the same from others). And the third critical component of predicate conditions is the relative equality of power among the participants. Because one party is not so much more powerful than any other, reaching an agreement is the only way (under this model) to achieve a mutually advantageous outcome. Given the strength of self-interest motivation, if one party were so powerful as to be able to impose their will on the other(s), justice would not be likely. An agreement might be coerced, but the disadvantaged party would not accept it as reasonable/just. Hume, in fact, used the behavior of Europeans toward Native Americans in the 18th century as an illustration of that situation.

But any agreement reached under the circumstances of justice is to be abided. And, following the Hobbesian tradition, abiding by such covenants is taken as the definition of justice. It is a content-free definition because there is no a priori definition of what constitutes a fair agreement.

The reader may recall that in critiquing Hobbes' social contract theory in chapter 3 the issue was raised of whether such a scheme, based on constrained self-interest could reasonably be considered a moral theory of justice at all. Barry (1989), and many others, make a similar point by noting what seems to be a fatal flaw in this model: it excludes from consideration situations in which there is a great imbalance of power among the parties. When there is such a power imbalance that one party can arbitrarily impose its will, the circumstances of justice are not met and the resulting agreement likely will not be accepted as reasonable/just by all affected. But it is precisely under those circumstances that one needs a serviceable concept of justice! So, another model is necessary.

Model II: Making Decisions Under Rawls's Veil of Ignorance[17]

John Rawls' (1958, 1971, 1999, 2001) *justice as fairness* is probably the best-known contemporary model of justice from political philosophy—although it has its detractors (e.g., Arneson, 1999), as well as strident defenders (Lindblom,

---

17 This section owes much to an excellent review by Lindblom (2011).

2018). It seeks to establish conditions for a "society as a fair system of social cooperation over time from one generation to the next" (Rawls, 2001, p. 5).[18] It is based on two principles that should characterize the processes of the institutions comprising a just society of free and equal citizens. A society meeting these two notions will provide *fair and equal opportunity* (FEO) for all, which is the definition of justice. The First principle, which provides the *basic structure of society*, is that all share fully a set of basic liberties. They are (1) The rights and liberties provided by the rule of law, (2) Those provided by virtue of our physical and psychological integrity, (3) Freedom of association, (4) Political freedom, (5) Liberty of conscience (i.e., religious freedom), and (6) Freedom of thought.

Rawls' well-known second principle has to do with when social and economic inequalities are justified. It has two parts. To be just, the inequalities: (i) must be associated with positions open to all under conditions of *fair equality of opportunity*—so it doesn't come into play unless principle 1 (the six freedoms) is satisfied; and (ii) "are to be to the benefit of the least-advantaged members of society" (Rawls, 2001, p. 43)—so it doesn't come into play unless the institutions in question meet principle 1, as well as the first part of principle 2—which Rawls famously refers to as the *difference principle*.[19] Sometimes it is called the *maximin* rule. It is the mechanism for achieving distributive justice. The difference principle says, in effect, that inequities in societal goods are acceptable if everyone benefits, and the least well-off do better than they would under any other distribution.

Although Rawls's principles pertain primarily to what he called *the basic structure* of the large institutions of society (which are the domains of international *global justice* and national *domestic justice*, he did offer suggestions applicable to operations within organizations—what he referred to as *local justice*. Lindblom (2011) has done a careful job of extrapolating from the "basic structure" to organizations and the level of individual employment relationships.

Rawls objected to the assumption of a strategic self-serving baseline condition (as per Barry's Model I), that operates as the starting point for the establishment of fairness. He substitutes the concept of the *original position* in which the parties are free to bargain under the circumstances of justice of the two-stage model, but the circumstances are modified so that no party garners an advantage by virtue of superior power or bargaining strength. The implicit moral view is that an outcome should not simply reflect the relative strength of people's strategic positions to begin with. Therefore, those factors are removed from the situation by a metaphorical *veil of ignorance* under which all bargaining occurs. The so-called veil

---

18 He contrasts "the idea of society as a fair system of social cooperation between citizens regarded as free and equal… [versus] … the idea of society as a social system organized so as to produce the most good summed over all its members" (2001, p. 95).

19 The difference principle is a dynamic not a static criterion. It is not met if we improve the lot of the least fortunate by having them rise above another group—who would then become the least advantaged.

of ignorance hypothetically conceals from the parties all information regarding who they are, their social position, and the time and place in which they live—in short, all the potential determinants of an agreement that are morally irrelevant. Thus, no real bargaining is necessary: because everyone in the original position is unaware of their situation in life, they will all agree to a fair and just arrangement—as defined by the two principles.

It is unlikely that you (or Rawls) believe that the veil of ignorance is a realistic or even feasible device. But it is also not so unrealistic or metaphorical as might first appear. Rawls pointed out that we may accept as fair agreements reached under circumstances in which it is *as if* all parties were in the same position.[20]

Under the constraints of the veil of ignorance, which forces impartiality, virtually any criterion of distributive justice may be arrived at: maximizing overall utility, equity, equality or need-based allocations. Under these conditions, according to Rawls, the parties would agree on the two fundamental principles of justice: equal civil and political rights for all, with a fair opportunity for all those qualified to obtain positions with varying social and economic rewards; and the economic inequalities resulting from those positions are organized so that the least advantaged group (e.g., the bottom quintile in annual income) could not do any better under an alternative arrangement. In other words, although Rawls is sometimes misinterpreted as advocating the elimination of differential rewards, income and wealth, he clearly indicates that "The basic structure is arranged so that when everyone follows the publicly recognized rules of cooperation, and honors the claims the rules specify, the particular distributions of goods that result are acceptable as just (or at least as not unjust) whatever these distributions turn out to be" (2001, p.50).

Model III: Persuasion

This differs from the first two models by virtue of introducing a different assumption about human motivation. As originated by Hume and developed further by Rawls, in this model self-interest is replaced by the *justice motive* as the operative force. This is akin to a progression from Stage 4 or 5 of Kohlberg's moral reasoning to Stage 6 and is consonant with the universalist tradition in moral philosophy. The essence of moral justice becomes *impartiality*, the ability to defend a single decision or distributional system from the standpoint of its fairness and reasonableness to all those with different vested interests. I.e., an agreement is reached that no one can reasonably reject. This is enabled not only by the justice motive but also by the circumstances of impartiality, which include the assumption that the parties enjoy comparable resources and political representation

---

20 Analogous to the defense of Thomas Hobbes (see Chap. 3) to the criticism that our social lives don't generally involve making actual "social contracts": it can be understood *as if* we had such contracts.

so that all sides may be represented adequately in the persuasive debate, and the existence of a common fellow-feeling among all parties. In other words, people must be willing to be convinced by the positions of others even if it runs against their self-interest. This model can operate either under the veil of ignorance or with full knowledge of one's position. If the assumptions of the justice motive are met (desire for fairness, reasonableness and impartiality), the veil is unnecessary.

Yet Another Take: Sennian Justice

20 years after Barry published his analysis of justice models, Armatya Sen (2009) published *The Idea of Justice*, building on earlier work of his. I have already mentioned previously in criticizing the study of OJ in I-O psychology, his view that the study of justice requires a theoretical approach that goes beyond perceiving, feeling or sensing injustice. He highlights what I referred to in chapter 2 as "right-reasoning" as necessary to understand justice. He illustrates by showing how it takes reason to understand that an apparent calamity like a raging famine is actually a case of injustice "if it could have been prevented, and particularly if those who could have undertaken preventive action had failed to try" (Sen, 2009, p. 4). And he emphasizes, from the two classical Sanskrit words for justice, that it requires considering both *niti* and *nyaya*—formal correctness/institutional propriety, as well as an overall assessment of the real-life outcomes and experiences of people.

He criticizes not only those who (like many I-O psychologists) are stuck entirely at the level of perceptions and attitudes (e.g., utilitarians focused on net satisfaction); he also criticizes the models of justice proposed by the political and moral philosophers we have just considered (including John Rawls) as unrealistically focused on trying to characterize "perfectly just societies."[21] It is a mistake, he argues, to accept that Rawls' two principles are the only reasonable definition of justice; "we could have a strong sense of injustice on many different grounds" (Sen, 2009, p. 2). His theory is essentially explanatory, showing us what we should really be attending to in making evaluations regarding human flourishing. And flourishing entails more than just economic/financial success; it includes justice (as he defines it; see below), well-being and personal development.

Most I-O psychologists would probably sympathize with the meta-objectives of his theory, which are pragmatic, not theoretical or idealistic. "Its aim is to clarify how we can proceed to address questions of enhancing justice and removing injustice, rather than to offer resolutions of questions about the nature of perfect justice" (Sen, 2009, p. ix). And, indeed, an attempt has been made to demonstrate the applicability of his work to I-O psychology (Gloss et al., 2017). In the tradition of social choice theory, Sen focuses on arriving at "an agreement, based on public reasoning, on rankings of alternatives that can be realized" (p. 17); the outcomes are called *realizations*. And critically, he argues that a

---

21 Although his book is dedicated in memory of John Rawls.

complete understanding of people's realizations or potential realizations (what he calls the "comprehensive outcome") includes the combination of both the "culminating outcome" as well as all the institutional and social procedures by which it came about. In other words, justice is defined in terms of the inseparable integration of both procedural and distributional justice.

Sen describes his theory as an informational approach in that it directs our attention to what information ought to be considered in assessing [in]justice. It is our *capabilities*, which reflect the opportunity aspect of freedom, i.e., what people are actually able to do and to be. They can then choose which options/capabilities to pursue.

> In contrast with the utility-based or resource-based lines of thinking, individual advantage is judged in the capability approach by a person's capability to do things he or she has reason to value. A person's advantage in terms of opportunities is judged to be lower than that of another if she has less capability—less real opportunity—to achieve those things that she has reason to value.
>
> *(Sen, 2009, p. 231)*

Justice means being able to achieve, i.e., to be and to do, what one reasonably values. This means one must also consider the appropriateness and fairness of all of the historical, social-psychological, institutional and societal factors such as normative expectations that influence one's set of capabilities. What we direct our capabilities to—what we want to be and do—Sen calls *functionings*.

He also emphasizes that the capability approach does not require instituting social policies designed to equate everyone's capabilities, regardless of the consequences of such a change. It doesn't propose specific solutions; its major contributions have been in indicating what information we should be looking at (people's capabilities) in informing such policy decisions, and in providing the basis for extending that metric to many areas of society. It has contributed in recent years to the focus on non-financial and non-economic indices of well-being such as in the *Human Development Reports* of the United Nations (also see Nussbaum & Sen, 1993).

The early theory has been elaborated by others (e.g., Robeyns, 2005)—most notably by Nussbaum's (2000, 2003) special focus on gender issues, and her emphasis on capabilities as providing the essence of human dignity, which is "being able to develop and exercise one's human powers" (Nussbaum, 2000, p. 21).[22] Shrivastava et al. (2016) have applied the theory to the study of OJ; Bertland (2008) to virtue ethics in business; and Giovanola (2009) to an anthropological approach to business (cf. Westermann-Behaylo, 2016, for a review

---

22 Such *conditional dignity* is over-and-above the *unconditional dignity* we owe each other merely by virtue of always treating others as ends in themselves, not only as means (cf. Kant, chap. 3).

of multiple business applications, especially multiple stakeholder theory). And of course, it has generated much criticism (e.g., Robeyns, 2016) and debate (e.g., Claasen, 2011) in a variety of fields to which it has been applied.

Economic Justice

First, a Mea Culpa

It may be surprising to some that this book has almost nothing to say directly about racial prejudice, discrimination and racism—even in a chapter concerned with social and economic [in]justice. It's just too big; the topic necessitates book-length treatment of its own.[23] Its absence certainly does not reflect a wider neglect in psychology generally, or in I-O psychology. Since Gordon Allport (1954) first tried to help us understand *The Nature of Prejudice* almost ¾ of a century ago, we have been at work on that enterprise—some would say, unfortunately to little avail. Nevertheless, we have learned much. A contemporary and controversial conceptualization of the issues is *critical race theory* (CRT):

> The critical race theory (CRT) movement is a collection of activists and scholars interested in studying and transforming the relationship among race, racism, and power. The movement considers many of the same issues that conventional civil rights and ethnic studies discourses take up, but places them in a broader perspective that includes economics, history, context, group- and self-interest, and even feelings and the unconscious. Unlike traditional civil rights, which embraces incrementalism and step-by-step progress, critical race theory questions the very foundations of the liberal order, including equality theory, legal reasoning, Enlightenment rationalism, and neutral principles of constitutional law.
>
> *(Delgado & Stefancic, 2001, Pp. 2–3)*

We have some idea of the several social, psychological and cognitive "factors known or theorized to motivate racism as it plays out in the American cultural context" (Roberts & Rizzo, 2021). One of them is *passivism*, consisting of an apathetic attitude toward racist systems, or denial that they exist. The denial corresponds to what is sometimes characterized as "color-blind racial ideology" (Neville et al., 2013), which can be thought of "as an ultramodern or contemporary form of racism and a legitimizing ideology used to justify the racial status quo" (p. 455). It is probably an instance of what Hertwig and Engel (2016) have called *deliberate ignorance*. For example,

---

23 Although a great deal of what follows concerning the nature, causes and consequences of income and wealth inequities implicitly pertains to racial gaps.

... for centuries, Americans of color were forced into free or cheap labor and denied the right to own businesses and properties, vote in political elections, and receive an education or fair employment. These realities, many of which persist today, continue to exert their effect ... . To maintain such racism, individuals and institutions need only do nothing about it."

(Roberts & Rizzo, 2021, p.483)

Very recently, academic research psychologists have begun to acknowledge racial inequalities in the conduct of psychological research (Roberts et al., 2020) and to present "examples of how epistemic oppression exists within psychological science, including in how science is conducted, reported, reviewed, and disseminated" (Buchanan et al., 2021, p. 1097).

Applied psychologists, too, have focused on better understanding and documenting workplace discrimination (Dhanani et al., 2018; Ruggs et al., 2012), improving our measurement of the phenomenon (Blanton et al., 2015), and on reducing discrimination and enhancing diversity, equity and inclusion in work organizations (Grice et al., 2021; Hebl et al., 2019; Marcy & Bayati, 2020; Preston & De Graaf, 2019).

Political Economy and Distributive Principles

How should the wealth, rewards, and benefits of society be distributed to achieve an economically just society (or organization)? Wolff (2005) notes that economic justice entails balancing efficiency with justice concerns: "If we are concerned with both efficiency and justice, we must determine how far we can depart from capitalist forms of the free market, in the name of justice, without losing 'too much' of its efficiency advantages" (p. 433). (The approach sounds like a reasonable compromise, except that the implicit assumption that the free market is always efficient, and the conditions of justice are not, is unwarranted.)

In general, cultural norms are highly related to a country's economic system, and both determine the prevailing criterion of distributive justice (cf. James, 1993, for a brief review). For example, individualistic cultures with free-enterprise economic systems value people for their perceived contribution to the productivity of the society (frequently by means of contributing to the effectiveness of an organization) and so reward people in accord with their economic utility (i.e., "equitably"). In the United States. the answer taken for granted is that income and wealth should be based on what one has achieved or contributed—that is, what one has "earned." This is viewed as morally right and proper. But social scientists have listed as many as five (Mappes & Zembaty, 1997), seven (Bar-Hillel & Yaari, 1993) or even 11 (Deutsch, 1975) possible distributive principles. They are usually condensed into the following three. The economic benefits and burdens of society could accrue to individuals (a) equally, (b) according to need, or (c) according to merit or equity. Following the publication of *A Theory of Justice* (Rawls, 1971, 2001), another has been considered frequently, emphasizing that (d) benefits should accrue to those who are the least well off.[24] However, in the realm of public policy and government programs that by law must be made available to all citizens (e.g., education programs), this often leads to widening the gap between the disadvantaged and others (Ceci & Papierno, 2005).

Mappes and Zembaty (1997) pointed out that at the societal level judgments about these four alternatives involve values concerning the ideals of liberty and equality and the proper role of government as a reflection of the society's political values (also see Wolff, 2005). We will unavoidably return to these issues in chapter 11 when considering the moral values and role of business organizations in a democratic society and, by extension, those of I-O psychology which serves those organizations. Mappes and Zembaty suggested that three primary sociopolitical conceptions of justice can be articulated, as follows.

The Libertarian View of Justice

Libertarianism can be understood as a political representation of the egoist tradition in moral philosophy. It holds that each person has the moral right to life, liberty and property, and the only legitimate function of government is to protect these (cf. section on John Locke and Natural Rights in chapter 3). All else is a matter of individual responsibility and achievement. Thus, libertarianism is most compatible with the merit or equity principle of distributive justice. It is the contemporary label for the 18th-century liberal tradition in western political thought, referred to as classical liberalism, or as "conservative" in contemporary U.S. politics.[25] People (or their representation in the form of the state) do not have the right to interfere in the affairs of the individual—unless of course, the person is threatening someone else's life, liberty or property.

The minimalist conception of the state, restricted to preventing harm, arguably gives rise to a serious limitation to the morality of classical liberalism. As we have covered previously, avoiding harm and wrongdoing (nonmaleficence) is only one aspect of moral action. It disregards the positive or affirmative side of the coin, so to speak, having to do with empathic caring and beneficence. It also disregards Kantian notions of duty, or in more common terms, obligations (other than to oneself). It is important to recognize that liberty is not synonymous with

---

24 Rawls calls this the *difference principle*, sometimes referred to as *maximin utility*, and it is frequently misunderstood or misrepresented. Maximizing the benefits received by the least well-off will invariably require increasing benefits to those better off as well. It does not entail elevating the least advantaged to a position superordinate to others, as those others would then become the least advantaged. Or, looked at another way, "inequalities in income and wealth are permitted providing that they make the worst-off group as well off as possible" (Wolff, 2005, p. 438).

25 Although Kymlicka (2002) explains how most contemporary "right wing" positions are not based on Libertarian principles.

freedom; liberty pertains to the absence of coercion or intentional restraint, especially as might emanate from the government (such as being required to contribute to social security, to wear a helmet when riding one's motorcycle, to obtain a license in order to practice medicine, or to be vaccinated and wear a face mask in the midst of a deadly pandemic).[26]

But libertarians tend to be not much concerned with other manifestations of freedom or the constraints thereon. They seem unconcerned about the possibility of some people being unjustly denied the opportunity for many freedoms. That fits with some empirical evidence that those who favor Libertarian positions are predominantly white males and are characterized by self-interest (Lizotte & Warren, 2021). That is in contrast with the Nobel Laureate Armatya Sen's position that "assessments of justice must entail assessments of whether people are genuinely free to be or do whatever it is that they value" (cited by Shrivastava et al., 2016, p. 99). For example, a libertarian presumably would be sanguine about your "freedom" to obtain any job you desire, notwithstanding that through no fault of your own, you were born and raised in circumstances with numerous social, economic and educational constraints such that many of the most rewarding and prestigious jobs are now beyond your reach. As Anatole France (1894/1930) said, "In its majestic equality, the law forbids rich and poor alike to sleep under bridges, beg in the streets and steal loaves of bread" (chapter 7). For approximately 50 years the role of the government of the United States has been under attack by adherents of this point of view (marked by slogans such as "starve the beast"), and in the opinion of some it has weakened the government sufficiently as to cause the United States to slide down the international rankings of indicators of social progress--e.g., public health, education, early childhood education, et al. (Hacker & Pierson, 2016).

The Socialist View of Justice

Socialism may be interpreted to some degree as the political equivalent of the universalist Kantian tradition in moral philosophy in that there is a commitment to the ideal of equality, both pragmatically and morally. The moral dimension refers to what is called "equality of interests" (see Chap. 2). The pragmatic aspect envisions a genuine equality of opportunity for everyone, to the extent that it can be enabled by social conditions. If achieving that equality requires some restrictions on individual liberty, so be it. The socialist tends to view the liberty advocated by libertarians/conservatives as meaningless or cynical under conditions in which some people have inadequate food, shelter, health care, and

---

26 Note that many such "infringements" on one's liberty serve one's own interests as well as one's community and the wider society. A faithful Libertarian ought to recognize that their right to refuse pandemic safety measures does not extend to violating others' right to avoid being infected.

inferior educational and job opportunities. Such disparities are considered ethically unjustifiable as we are all moral equals, equally entitled to dignity—especially if those disadvantages are attributable in some significant measure to systemic socio-political factors (see CRT, previous).

Some forms of socialism hold that equality can be achieved only under an economic system in which there is public (i.e., government) ownership of the means of production, but there are other varieties in which that is not so, most notably the Social Democrat parties of western Europe. An interesting variation on this theme has been referred to as "Socialism, American-Style," a form with appeal to both contemporary liberals and conservatives (Alperovitz & Hanna, 2015). It consists of state ownership of productive enterprises (e.g., the Tennessee Valley Authority; the Alaska Permanent Fund) in which the profits go toward reducing taxes or are distributed directly to citizens.

The Contemporary Liberal View of Justice

The liberal tradition has been important in Western moral and political thought since its classical manifestation during the Enlightenment. That libertarian point of view, and the revisionist liberal perspective that we now call *Liberal* in the United States (Danley, 1994), join in viewing some freedoms ("civil liberties") as important—freedom of speech, assembly, privacy, and so on (Mappes & Zembaty, 1997). But the contemporary liberal outlook also tends to agree with the socialist view that the social and economic constraints that de facto confine certain freedoms to the privileged are not morally justifiable so society does have an obligation to aid those less well off. To the extent that freedom, especially in the economic sphere, is likely to lead to disparities in income and wealth, it will conflict with egalitarian principles and so require compromises.

In an extension of Rawls' (1971, 2001) views Barry (1989) pointed out that we cannot fail to acknowledge the role of economic incentives in motivating individual performance and probably maximizing overall financial utility for society as a whole. However, most liberals want also to attend to the *distribution* of benefits in society, not just aggregate utility, and will be concerned that a free market also increases income disparities. They hold that a system of justice in which the gains accrue virtually entirely to those already best-off is not morally justifiable—especially when the structure of the social system favors those people to begin with. Thus, in comparison with an ideal of equality, even though economic incentives may be necessary to promote overall utility, the resulting large disparities in income and wealth are viewed as not entirely justified morally and should be attenuated.

The conviction is held by many that the proper role of societal institutions is the attempt to increase aggregate utility or well-being by promoting both individual freedoms *and* assuring at least a minimal level of need gratification for all. This has been seen in contemporary western society as a prescription for the simultaneous functioning of a relatively free-market system for the generation of wealth, along with a governmental system for the partial redistribution of wealth to provide a safety net for those who need it, or to approximate the moral ideal of equality more closely. (Of course, there are those who view any redistributive policies as immoral).

The economic manifestation of the universalist moral tradition and egalitarian political tradition rests on a belief to which I have alluded previously but have not stated explicitly. It is radical because it is seemingly at odds with the dominant American (and I-O psychology) value of meritocracy, although various declarations of the position can be found in moral and political philosophy (Barry, 1989; Rawls, 2001; Singer, 2011). The argument has been most thoroughly developed recently by the political philosopher Michael J. Sandel (2020). The belief is that *income and wealth disparities based on merit or equity reflecting differences between people in occupational achievement are not morally justifiable.*

Consider the source of income and wealth disparities based on merit. To simplify a bit, it is possible to say that individual achievement is due to three broad sets of factors: (a) one's social class of origin; (b) one's native endowments and the opportunities to develop these as a function of social class origin; and (c) one's good or bad luck over the course of life (Rawls, 2001, p. 55). Determinants (a) and/or (c) are sometimes referred to as the *social lottery*. Winning the lottery might include such disparate things as: being in the right place at the right time when a good job becomes available; being part of an age cohort that first enters the labor force during an expanding economy; being born into a family of high socioeconomic status and wealth, in a good neighborhood, with all the associated advantages; having a wise and nurturing boss early in one's career, etc. Obviously, the beneficiary of the goods stemming from those factors has done little, if anything, to "merit" them. That there is no great moral justification for advantages based on such good fortune would seem uncontroversial, although it is only relatively recently that much attention has been paid to "research on the effects of the 'birth lottery' on economic fortunes" (Sharkey, 2019, p. 15).

What about (b), one's "natural talents and abilities" (Rawls, 1971, p. 72)—the *natural lottery*--as these are nourished or stunted by the first set of factors? But basic abilities have high heritability components for which one obviously can't claim the credit. For example, is it an indication of merit or some other things that at the macro-level "the fit between individuals' actual personality and the personality demands of their jobs is a predictor of income" (Dennisen, et al., 2018, p. 3)?

As startling as the moral contention regarding the meritlessness of merit-based disparities may sound, *it reflects commonly accepted notions in I-O psychology and human resources administration.* Two examples will illustrate this. The first concerns the perennial issue in I-O psychology of *the criterion problem* (Austin & Villanova, 1992), i.e., the attempt to develop fair and valid measures of individual employee performance, reflecting merit. A measure is biased *(criterion contamination)* if the assessments it generates are influenced to an appreciable degree by determinants that do not reflect performance elements under the employees' control. Those extraneous sources of variance do not really indicate how well or poorly the employee is performing, so the measure is biased. The classic illustration is the case of two factory workers each producing (metaphorical) widgets, one on an old piece of widget-manufacturing machinery with a maximum capacity of 200 widgets per hour (wph) and the other on a more efficient state-of-the-art widget machine with a capacity of 235 wph. Other things being equal, we would hold a simple numerical output criterion to be a biased representation of these two workers' productive contribution to the organization. The second example stems from the use of personal history information ("biodata") as predictors in employee selection. The issue pertains to the *controllability* of the item content, which is "the extent to which the item addresses events that were under the direct control of the respondent (e.g., their prior behaviors), as opposed to events over which the respondent had little or no control (e.g., their demographic attributes)" (Stokes et al., 1994, p. 4). It is generally conceded that it would be improper (unfair, biased or unethical, and in some instances illegal) to premise employment decisions on such factors (Lefkowitz et al., 1999; Mael, 1991).

In both examples, the operative principle is that it is inappropriate (i.e., unethical or unjust) to premise performance-based rewards or societal benefits like obtaining a job, on attributes of the individual over which they had no control. As Rawls noted, we normally ascribe occupational achievement to people's *intelligence and talents* as these have been nourished in *stimulating and supportive home environments* and reinforced with *effective educational and social experiences*, as well as to their *affective and motivational traits* such as perseverance, interpersonal skills, and the like, similarly conditioned by the nature of *the social environment* in which they were nurtured. None of those highlighted determinants of individuals' capacities or performance are or were entirely under their control—certainly not the social and economic circumstances into which the person is born, nor the quality of the neighborhood school in which they get enrolled, or the person's hereditary endowment (the primary determinant of individual differences in intelligence).

Some who deny the moral legitimacy of ability-based allocation systems are more sympathetic to an allocation system reflective of people's differential efforts (e.g., Singer, 1993). But effort largely reflects one's motivation, conscientiousness and perseverance—which also depend considerably on those innate and socially reinforced disparities that we are dealt and over which we have had relatively little or no control. Prilleltensky (1997) asserted that "Under conditions of equality of opportunity, the principle of merit may apply, but an argument can be made that in conditions of inequality, need is the more appropriate criterion" (p. 522).[27] But the more vexing moral issues are how we define equality of opportunity and the extent to which it exists.

---

27 Cf. the section on Rawls regarding "fairness as equal opportunity" (FEO).

Moreover, beyond those moral questions,

> those who celebrate the meritocratic ideal and make it the center of their
> political project … . also ignore something more politically potent: the
> morally unattractive attitudes the meritocratic ethic promotes, among the
> winners and also among the losers. Among the winners, it generates hubris;
> among the losers, humiliation and resentment. These moral sentiments are
> at the heart of the populist uprising against elites. More than a protest
> against immigrants and outsourcing, the populist complaint is about the
> tyranny of merit. And the complaint is justified.
>
> *(Sandel, 2020, p. 25)*

Economists concerned with social ethics have noted that whereas people may
indeed be held responsible for their own choices, it is not reasonable to hold the
least skilled accountable for the impoverished set of opportunities from which
they must choose (Schokkaert & Sweeney, 1999).

A third example that should be of interest to I-O psychologists, given our
longstanding endorsement of merit pay policies, is the extraordinary and growing
disparity between the income of CEOs and senior financial executives versus
everyone else, and *the lack of association between their pay and the performance of their
firms.* (Cf. section following, this chapter.)

Despite all the above, this is not an argument for abandoning merit policies.
Too much good results from rewarding achievement, both material rewards as
well as the psychic gratification derived from recognized accomplishment. As
even Sandel (2020), the great critic of meritocracy, put it: "If I need a plumber to
fix my toilet or a dentist to repair my tooth, I try to find the best person for the
job" (p. 33).[28] Nor is the moral point negated by the fact that most people try to
be conscientious and do work hard, so that successful people generally feel that
they have earned their success. (Although many economically not-successful
people also work very hard.) It is a plea for the attenuation of extreme disparities
when they are not justifiable, for some humility on the part of those who have
benefitted from the lottery system, and empathy for those who, through no fault
of their own, were not advantageously situated. It is a plea for greater appreciation of the benefits to be had from advancing the common good.

In this vein of social justice theory, it has been asserted that "material incentives should not be necessary in a society whose members are committed to
justice" (Barry, 1989, p. 393). However, as psychologists we know that self-
interest is a salient (if not necessarily always the most important) motive and that
people do expend effort for the attainment of productive goals and personal

---

28 He goes on to describe "how the tyranny of merit undermines the dignity of work"
(p. 155), which will be considered in chapter 12.

rewards (Jenkins et al., 1998). That is, the incentive-based free-enterprise system (when supported by broad-based education and a democratic political and legal system) does, in fact, appear to have been the most effective economic arrangement for maximizing aggregate material benefit for society as a whole. And that is partly because it does provide many people the freedom to maximize their accomplishments in the expectation of personal gain. In the words of the business ethicist Patricia Werhane (1999): "I believe that free enterprise is the least worst economic system, given the alternatives" (p. 237).[29] But it would be a mistake to believe that financial incentives are all that drive company performance (Pfeffer & Sutton, 2006); it also fails to address the moral challenge of unjustified distributional inequities.

Pragmatically, the best society potentially available to us is probably one in which material incentives exist as a means of maximizing the production of overall income and wealth, but the means of attenuating potentially egregious economic and social disparities are institutionalized and supported. Two related ways of doing this are: by implementing compensation policies that limit the dispersion of pay distributions within organizations—preferably as part of a program of reducing hierarchical status differences in general; and by basing performance incentives on work group, team or even organization-wide accomplishment rather than on individual productivity (Pfeffer, 1994). Pfeffer (1998) pointed out that it is the contingent nature of the reward that has a motivating effect, not the level at which it is applied (individual, group or organizational). He reviewed the evidence that group- or organizational-level rewards are at least as effective as individual incentives and present fewer associated problems, although Rynes et al. (2005) concluded that "both individual- and group-based pay plans have potential limitations" (p. 586) and that group-based incentives work best with smaller groups and when jobs are interdependent.

Attenuating extreme income disparities is certainly not a particularly radical notion as it represents a reasonable description of the dominant sociopolitical philosophy of the United States since the passage of the 16th amendment to the U.S. constitution in 1913, which re-introduced a progressive tax on income.[30] Moreover, sophisticated analyses have demonstrated that progressive taxes do decrease income inequality and increase self-reported happiness among poorer

---

29 There are critics, however, who believe that this too readily concedes to free-market capitalism results that may be due to a mix of factors (Donaldson, 1982). For example, the most successful capitalist countries (the United States, Western Europe and Japan) had relatively high levels of education and technology even before the emergence of capitalism; also, they are all political democracies. Others point to the likely effectiveness of cultural factors having to do with work habits, religion and primary socialization experiences. And governmental policies that encourage capital investment may also play a part.

30 The first income taxes were introduced during the American civil war, in 1861, 1862 and 1864, and were rescinded in 1872. Progressive taxes entail a higher rate of taxation for higher income brackets.

Americans (the bottom 40%)—with no significant diminution of happiness among the richest 20% (Oishi et al., 2018).

The macrolevel social contract that has characterized the western industrial democracies since the end of World War II has entailed a de facto division of responsibilities between the private sector generating wealth and maximizing profits, and the public or governmental sector concerned with issues of social justice, human rights and the equitable sharing of wealth (Cragg, 2000). What is new, and perhaps more socially challenging, are: (a) the explosive growth in the magnitude of the income disparities between the extremes of the distribution in the United States and between the have and have-not nations of the world; and (b) questions regarding the allocation of responsibility for attenuating these disparities in the name of decency and social justice. Should responsibility be left entirely to the government in the form of redistributions, or should the institutions that generate the wealth themselves have a hand to begin with? This last point refers not only to alternative compensation systems, as Pfeffer suggested, but also to the growing concern for socially responsible business (to be discussed in chapter 11).

Income and Wealth Inequity: The Data[31]

Income

Psychologists have studied the psychological and societal aspects (antecedents, cor-relates and consequences) of inequality, poverty, unemployment, underemployment, the lack of decent work and living wages, etc. However, they are mostly vocational, counseling or developmental psychologists, few industrial-organizational psycholo-gists, and for the most part the work does not appear in I-O journals (cf. Adler et al., 1994; Leong et al., 2017; Blustein et al., 2019; Bullock & Quinn, 2019; Kirsch et al., 2019; McWhirter & McWha-Hermann, 2021; Oishi et al., 2018; Searle & McWha-Hermann, 2020; Thompson & Dahling, 2019). Amis et al. (2021) and Tsui and Enderle (2018) are exceptions in focusing on the role of organizations in the creation and potential amelioration of economic inequality, as are Reburn et al. (2018) and Stuart Carr and his colleagues with respect to poverty reduction and living wages (Carr, 2007; Carr et al., 2017). The notion of a basic (unconditional) income has also received some attention (Hüffmeier and Zacher, 2021).

The founder of the World Economic Forum observed that:

> Despite all the gains of globalization, there's a widening gap between the haves and have-nots. This simply is not sustainable. So it's in the self-interest of the

---

31 This section might have been entitled neutrally as referring to mere " ...*disparity.*" Alternatively, use of the more common " ...*inequality*" might or might not convey a moral judgment. In the context of I-O psychology, my use of " ...*inequity*" connotes injustice, as intended.

> privileged to make sure that the gap is closed. All this may sound idealistic, but it's not idealistic, it's pragmatic. In our interdependent world, you can't afford to let people lose out in pursuit of a decent life. Everyone must be a winner.
>
> *(Schwab, 2000, p. 82)*

The economic disparities among nations have been widening for about 200 years (United Nations Development Programme, 2015). Guillen (2001) similarly concluded "The evidence unambiguously indicates that there is today more inequality across countries than ten, twenty, fifty or even one hundred years ago" (p. 247). It should also be recognized that a modern conception of poverty goes beyond mere "monetary poverty." A measure of "Multidimensional poverty" includes ten indices of health, education and standard of living, emphasizing poverty's broad impact (United Nations Development Programme, 2021). And in most poor countries the incidence of multidimensional poverty is greater than monetary poverty.

Similarly, wage disparities *within* countries have also grown in most advanced countries, especially the United States. The last quarter of the 20th century saw an explosion in family income disparities in the United States. between the top of the income distribution and everybody else, but especially in comparison with those at the bottom, including the so-called *working poor*. In 2011, 28% of workers in the United States were earning "poverty level wages" or less ($11.06/hr. for a family of four) (Mishel et al., 2012). This is largely because the federal minimum wage (currently $7.25/hour) has not been increased since 1968. And our within-nation disparities are more extreme than in most of the rest of the industrialized world (Chetty et al., 2014a, 2014b; Gottschalk, 1993; Mishel et al., 2012; Proctor, 2016.).

> The United States has the most unequal income distribution and one of the highest poverty rates among all the advanced economies in the world. The U.S. tax and benefit system is also one of the least effective in reducing poverty … . Contrary to widely held perceptions, the United States offers less economic mobility than other rich countries.
>
> *(Mishel et al., 2001, pp. 11–12; also see Mishel et al., 2012)*

The United States has greater income inequality (as measured by the Gini Coefficient) than almost all the countries of Western Europe, as well as Canada, Australia and Japan.[32] The situation was exacerbated by the 2017 Tax Cuts and Jobs Act which, by reducing corporate taxes, was supposed to dramatically increase investment, hence employment and income levels. But "investment has

---

32 The Gini Coefficient is a measure of dispersion in which zero = perfect equality (everyone has the same income) and 1.00 is maximum inequality (one person receives all the income). The 2021 value for the U.S. is .48, up from .41 in 1990, indicating a substantial increase in inequality. South Africa has the highest index, .63. Source: https://worldpopulationreview.com/country-rankings/gini-coefficient-by-country.

not boomed since the TCJA's passage" (Economic Policy Institute, 2019)—even prior to the Covid-19 pandemic.

On a more optimistic, but likely temporary note, during the full pandemic year of 2021—which turned out to be one of economic recovery—the labor market tightened and average wages of the bottom 25% of the labor force actually increased at a faster rate than those of the top 75% (Rattner, 2021).

An interesting revelation is the extent to which inequality and lack of mobility is geographic. "Labor market opportunities, social networks, environmental hazards, and institutions like schools, governments, banks, and police departments vary dramatically depending on where one lives, creating a rigid geography of opportunity ... . our life chances are becoming even more closely tied to our geographic origins than in the past" (Sharkey, 2019, p. 16). And, given the degree of racial segregation in housing in the United States, it is not surprising to find that "The immense disparity in wealth between White and Black households has reached its highest level since 1989" (Price, 2017, p. 13) (also see Rothstein, 2018).

One side of the coin of income disparity is *wage stagnation*. From around the end of World War II through the 1970s the percentage increase in hourly compensation of nonsupervisory production workers matched the increase in productivity. From 1979 to 2019 net productivity in the United States rose 60% while the typical worker's compensation increased by 16% (Mishel 2021). (See Figure 8.1.) In other words, the fruits of increased productivity largely went elsewhere—to shareholders and executives.

The other side of the coin of disparity is the fantastic income growth of those at the top of the distribution, most notably the managerial elite, which even a former chief executive officer (CEO) more than 20 years ago referred to as "obscene" (Lear, 2000). Figure 8.2 shows the enormously disproportionate growth of the top 1%. Moreover, the earnings growth of that top 1% is accounted for primarily by people in the finance sector (including executives) and nonfinancial-sector executives (Bakija et al., 2010, 2012). "The income growth of executives is the largest factor that led top 0.1% and top 1.0% incomes to greatly increase over the last four decades" (Mishel & Kandra, 2021, p. 15).

The disparity with respect to CEOs is most egregious. Since 1978 CEO compensation has increased 1,322% (Mishel & Kandra, 2021). Much of the growth has come in the form of incentive pay via stock options, and more recently, outright stock awards, which tend to induce greater risk-taking by executives focusing on short-term gains, and which "promote a lack of caution in CEOs that manifests in a higher incidence of product safety problems" (Wowak et al., 2015, p. 1082).[33] Even during the pandemic recession of 2020 the pay of CEOs at the top 350 firms grew by almost 18.9% (average $24.2 million) while

---

33 Such as General Motors ignition switches, Takata airbags, the Massey Energy coal mine collapse and Volkswagen emissions cheating, among others.

The gap between productivity and a typical worker's compensation has increased dramatically since 1979

Productivity growth and hourly compensation growth, 1948–2019

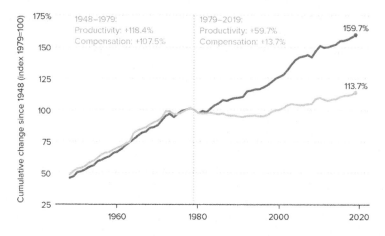

Notes: Data are for compensation (wages and benefits) of production/nonsupervisory workers in the private sector and net productivity of the total economy. "Net productivity" is the growth of output of goods and services less depreciation per hour worked.

Source: EPI analysis of unpublished Total Economy Productivity data from Bureau of Labor Statistics (BLS) Labor Productivity and Costs program, wage data from the BLS Current Employment Statistics, BLS Employment Cost Trends, BLS Consumer Price Index, and Bureau of Economic Analysis National Income and Product Accounts

Updated from Figure A in *Raising America's Pay: Why It's Our Central Economic Policy Challenge* (Bivens et al. 2014)

Economic Policy Institute

FIGURE 8.1   The gap between productivity and a typical worker's compensation has increased dramatically since 1979. Productivity growth and hourly compensation growth, 1948–2019

Source: Fig. A in Mishel (2021). Source: EPI analysis of unpublished Total Economy Productivity data from Bureau of Labor Statistics (BLS) Labor Productivity and Costs Program, wage data from the BLS Current Employment Statistics, BLS Employment Cost Trends, BLS Consumer Price Index, and Bureau of Economic Analysis National Income and Product Accounts. Used by permission.

worker compensation grew 3.9% (Mishel & Kandra, 2021). The ratio of CEO compensation to that of the median employee at their companies grew from 245:1 to 274:1 during that year (Eavis, 2021). Especially important from the perspective of an I-O psychologist is the contention that "the distance has grown between individuals in leadership positions and the majority of people within and around their organizations" giving rise to the "dehumanization of leadership" (Petriglieri & Petriglieri, 2015, p. 628).

The long-term enormous disparity in compensation between the top of the corporate hierarchy and everyone else has been found worrisome for some time now, even by those who embrace the principles of equity, merit and individual

Cumulative percent change in real annual wages, by wage group, 1979–2019

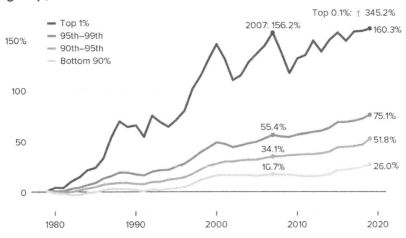

Source: EPI analysis of Kopczuk, Saez, and Song (2007, Table A3) and Social Security Administration wage statistics

Economic Policy Institute

FIGURE 8.2 Cumulative percent change in real annual wages, by wage group, 1979–2019

Source: Fig. A in Mishel and Kandra (2020). Economic Policy Institute. Source: EPI analysis and update of Kopczuk et al. (2010), *Quarterly Journal of Economics*, Feb. and Social Security Administration wage statistics. Used by permission.

recognition. As reviewed in Barron's, while corporate profits grew 116% from 1990 to 1999, and average worker pay failed to keep pace at 32%, CEO pay rose 535% (all unadjusted for inflation; Blumenthal, 2000; cf. also Anderson et al., 2000). Those sources reported that in 1980 the CEO-to-worker pay ratio was 42:1 and by 2000 it had risen to 475:1. More recently, Mishel and Kandra (2021) reported that the CEO-to-worker compensation ratio rose from 21:1 in 1965, peaking at 366:1 in 2000, to 351:1 in 2020.

Years ago, it was believed, and some people still believe, that a significant factor accounting for this trend in CEO pay is the composition of Boards of Directors' compensation committees—specifically, that most committees were dominated by company insiders (e.g., present and former employees). But many committees are now independent and still approving deals just as generous as those authorized by insider committees (Lavelle, 2000). Of course, many of those committee and board members are themselves chief executives of other firms, and most board members are in effect appointed by the CEO who approves their perks and whose compensation they will ultimately be asked to approve (Nichols & Subramaniam, 2001). Studies have often concluded that these managers have "considerable power to shape their own pay arrangements" (Bebchuk et al., 2002, p. 1). Calls have been made for increasing the leverage of compensation committees and of shareholders in general over CEO compensation packages (Walters et al., 1995). In fact, it's been more than 10 years since the Dodd-Frank law required companies to let shareholders vote, in an advisory capacity only, on executive compensation. But it's made no difference (Morgenson, 2015b).

There are two typical justifications for the very high levels of CEO compensation, both having to do with equity and merit. First is the notion of equitable "pay for performance." That is, that CEOs, because of their great impact on corporate performance, deserve to be compensated grandly. Moreover, a sharply increasing proportion of executive compensation has taken the form of stock options, vested stock awards and bonuses, and/or long-term incentive pay, presumably to align managers' interests with those of shareholders (Ozanian, 2000; Mishel & Kandra, 2021). A leading executive compensation consulting firm reported that at 100 large U.S. firms surveyed 59% of CEO pay was in the form of such options and an additional 32% was based on performance incentives (Pearl Meyer & Partners, 2000). It would seem reasonable that when the company (or, more specifically, the company's stock price) does well, the CEO deserves to be rewarded accordingly (Weinberg, 2000). So, for the 1st edition of this book, based on the *Business Week* 2000 executive compensation survey (Executive Compensation Scoreboard, 2000) of the top two executives (generally the CEO and the COO) of 364 companies, I noted which companies had actually produced a *negative* return on equity for the preceding period from 1997 to 1999. There were 146 of them—not an easy task to have accomplished in the booming stock market of the late 1990s. Of the 279 chief executives of those companies for which compensation data could be obtained, 210 (75.3%) of them received *increases* in their salary plus bonus packages in 1999. It should be borne in mind, moreover, that salaries and bonuses amounted to only about 23% of chief executives' realized compensation (Ozanian, 2000). Not even *The Wall Street Journal* believes that executive compensation is based on merit: "Pay for performance? Forget it. These days, CEOs are assured of getting rich—however the company does" (Lublin, 1999, p. R1).

But perhaps, especially considering the recession that began in 2008, the situation got better recently? So, in preparing the 2nd edition of this book, I used data collected by Equilar (2015) and made available publicly (Gelles, 2015; Morgenson, 2015), regarding the 2014 compensation of 200 chief executives of public companies with capitalization of at least $1 billion, and the performance of their companies during the prior year. The results of the analyses are shown in Table 8.3.[34] To summarize the few most important features: (a) average total

---

34 Many thanks to Manuel Gonzalez for performing the data analyses; the responsibility for their accuracy is entirely mine.

TABLE 8.3 2013-to-2014 Company Performance and 2014 C.E.O. Compensation

MEASURES	Arithmetic Mean (Range)	Correlations with Change in Revenue	Correlations with Change in Stock
CEO Cash Bonuses	$4.5 million (0–$25 m)	−.03, *ns*	−.02, *ns*
CEO Total Stock and Options	$15.7 million (0–$145.1 m)	.09, *ns*	−.09, *ns*
CEO Total Compensation	$22.6 million ($12.6 m–$156.1 m)	.08, *ns*	−.11, *ns*
Change in Compensation From 2013	934% (−68%–126,993%)	.01, *ns*	−.07, *ns*
Company Revenue— Change from 2013	15%(−52%–224%)	—	—
Company Stock Return—Change from 2013	17% (−47%–92%)	—	—

Source: Based on data from Equilar (2015).
Note: ns = not statistically significant.

CEO compensation was $22.6 million, approximately 69% of which comprised stock and options; (b) their average increase in compensation over the prior year was almost ten times (934% increase)—in comparison with their company's increase in performance of approximately 16%; (c) none of the correlations between the four aspects of CEO pay and the two indices of company performance were statistically significant—confirming the judgments noted above that CEO pay simply continues to rise astronomically, bearing no relationship to company performance.

But some business analysts believe that revenue and stock performance, the two indices used in Table 8.3, are less important for evaluating a CEO's worth to the company than is *return on capital* (the prior two may over-emphasize short-term performance). But additional analyses of the same data set of 200 companies, calculated each company's return on capital for the prior 5 years—in relation to all other companies in the same industry, yielding a measure of *relative return on capital.* That was compared with analogous relative CEO compensation. "The study concluded that 74 [of 200 companies] overpaid their chief executives in 2015 based on 5 years of underperformance in return on capital. The total overpayment ... was $835 million" (Morgenson, 2016b). So much for the first justification, equitable pay-for-performance.

The second justification is a free-market argument that CEOs merit such rewards simply because that is commensurate with the increases that virtually all high-wage earners have been enjoying (Kaplan, 2012). In other words, there is a highly competitive market and high demand for the considerable skills and talents of CEOs. But analyses have shown that the pay gains have had very much to do with the power of CEOs to extract concessions from their companies (Bivens & Mishel, 2013), as described above. Moreover, CEO compensation has outstripped even the fantastic growth in earnings of the top 0.1% of the population (Mishel & Kandra, 2020) suggesting that it's not merely due to a competitive market for talent.

Regardless of the rate of growth of executive pay or whether one views it as obscene, the question can nevertheless be asked, is it right—or even permissible?

> Moral theorists of all stripes have a stake in the debate. Egalitarians should be concerned by the size of the disparity between CEO and worker pay. Libertarians should wonder whether owners freely agree to pay their CEOs $8 million per year ....[35] What is needed ... is an ethical framework for thinking about justice in pay. After elaborating this framework, I will argue that CEOs get paid too much.
>
> *(Moriarty, 2005, p. 257)*

Why should we care about those growing inequalities and the greed manifested by notorious chief executives? There are both moral reasons having to do with justice and fairness and pragmatic reasons (the two are not mutually exclusive). Elsewhere, Moriarty (2009) goes on to

> focus on the duties [that] *executives themselves* have with respect to *their own* compensation ... . CEO's fiduciary duties place a moral limit on how much compensation they can accept, and hence seek in negotiation, from their firms. Accepting excessive compensation leaves the beneficiaries of their duties (e.g., shareholders) worse off, and thus is inconsistent with observing those duties.
>
> *(p. 235, emphases in the original)*

Cropanzano et al. (2001) also note that

> sometimes what we *do not* say about human behavior is as important as what we *do* say. If organizational justice (OJ) theorists include only economic and social considerations, and exclude morality and ethics, then it is a short step to inferring that the former are important and the latter are not .... It is important to recognize that human beings are sometimes motivated by moral principle and beliefs, as well as by economic and social concerns. (p. 199)

---

35 Note that the $8 million figure was an apt example almost 20 years ago.

In addition, as Meara (2001) pointed out, "an important prior question to discussing organizational justice (OJ) is what kind of person or organization we want to make the fairness decisions that affect us or those close to us" (p. 230). From a more practical perspective there is evidence that individualized (as opposed to standardized) pay-for-performance deals negatively affect the performance levels of peers not included (Abdulsalam et al., 2021).

I-O psychologists ought to be embarrassed by the scandal of executive compensation because of the roles we play in developing and implementing performance appraisal (PA) systems. PAs are used to assess the "merit" of those *below* the level of senior executives for purposes of compensation, advancement and even job retention—notwithstanding regular reports of companies such as GE, Adobe, Netflix, Accenture and others abandoning them (Wilkie, 2015). The situation is exacerbated by the observation that "Given the importance of pay and performance to employers and employees as well as the potential for well-designed [pay for performance] systems to improve performance, one would think that research examining [pay for performance] would be plentiful in psychology. However, this has not been the case, particularly in recent years" (Rynes et al., 2005, p. 572). But the situation has changed.

Some years later Shaw (2014) provided a very careful review of the literature on pay dispersion and its effects on employee performance, turnover and attitudes--at organizational, team and individual levels. This is an important matter because it has been advanced that a degree of wage compression can lead to overall efficiency gains, and that, in contrast, extreme "vertical pay dispersion sends a signal that the lower-paid, lower-level people matter comparatively less. This may be fine in some technologies and under some strategies, but it is quite inconsistent with attempting to achieve high levels of commitment and output from *all* employees" (Pfeffer, 1994, p. 52). It would seem to be destructive of the sense of community, empowerment, common fate, and personal reinforcement that most I-O psychologists would agree contribute to organizational success. But Shaw (2014) concluded that "When evaluating the findings from the literature in toto, it is clear that there is not a well-defined conceptual or observed empirical relationship between the overall dispersion of pay … and the performance of organizations, teams, or individuals" (p. 534). Although, when it has been possible to eliminate or partial out the effects of illegitimate sources of pay variance, leaving only sources such as incentives, seniority, tenure, education, or the employees' historical performance, the remaining variance has been related to performance. There is evidence that pay-for-performance systems affect organizational productivity via differential quit rates of good- and poor-performers (Shaw, 2015), but that "management bonuses may strain the employment relationship by negatively impacting how managers treat their employees" (Pohler & Schmidt, 2016, p. 23). Moreover, a meta-analysis by Garbers and Konradt (2014) yielded more optimistic findings of substantial effect sizes of individual and team-based financial incentives on performance (larger for the team-based)—and larger effects for equitably distributed rewards than for those distributed equally.

Wealth

As disturbing as are those findings regarding pay inequity, income inequality in the United States is exceeded by the degree of inequality in the distribution of wealth, and has been throughout the 20th century (Keister, 2000; Mishel et al., 2001; Wolff, 1995)—and it manifests in an enormous and growing black–white racial disparity (Price, 2017; Rothstein, 2018; Taylor et al., 2011). In 2010 the wealthiest 1% of households controlled about 35% of national wealth—considerably more than the entire bottom 90% (who controlled about 23%) (Mishel, et al., 2012). "In the past, Americans smugly assumed that European societies were more stratified than their own, but it now appears that the United States has surpassed all industrial societies in the extent of its family wealth inequality" (Keister, 2000, p. 4). Keister went on to explain that the reason this is important is that, despite the general focus on income and income disparities (largely because income is relatively easy to measure), "wealth comes closer both theoretically and empirically to our general understanding of well-being .... Wealth implies a more permanent notion of security and an ability to secure advantages in both the short and long terms. It is this latter concept that likely fits our shared conception of well-being" (p. 11).

Piketty (2014) observed that

> when the rate of return on capital exceeds the rate of growth of output and income ... capitalism automatically generates arbitrary and unsustainable inequalities that radically undermine the meritocratic values on which democratic societies are based.
>
> *(2014, p.1)*

Moreover,

> the history of the distribution of wealth has always been deeply political, and it cannot be reduced to purely economic mechanisms .... The resurgence of inequality after 1980 is due largely to the political shifts of the past several decades, especially in regard to taxation and finance .... Furthermore, there is no natural, spontaneous process to prevent destabilizing, inegalitarian forces from prevailing permanently (p. 20, 21).

The political forces over the past 40 years or so that Piketty alludes to have generally been characterized as *Neoliberalism* (Harvey, 2005), which is discussed in chapter 11.

Because, surprisingly, wealth and income are not very highly correlated, looking at wealth yields a different picture of economic advantages and disadvantages. For example, pronouncements about the emergence of an African-American middle class, with an attendant narrowing of the racial disparity with White Americans, are based on average income figures, not wealth (Holmes,

1996), and generally ignore the expansion of a chronic African-American underclass (Wilson, 1996). Considering family wealth rather than income suggests no such narrowing (Oliver & Shapiro, 1995). In fact, "persistent and profound racial and ethnic disparities in wealth … are far greater than racial and ethnic disparities in wages and incomes" (Mishel et al., 2012, p. 385). And "unfortunately, there is little indication that the tide is turning for the positive" (Price, 2017, p. 13)

The relevance of income and wealth disparities to a consideration of social justice is illuminated by two factors. First is their widespread adverse consequences for the well-being of individuals and society, and perhaps specifically for organizations (Bapuji, 2015). Second is an appreciation that these conditions don't just "happen"; they are not entirely "natural" phenomena as the Social Darwinists proposed more than a century ago; they are caused in part by systemic neoliberal social and political policies. Referring to a distinction made earlier, they are more a reflection of injustice than misfortune (Shklar, 1990). The first factor makes the case for why we should be concerned; the second suggests what might be done about it. But there is space for only a cursory enumeration of these matters.

Consequences of Inequity

A considerable body of evidence is accumulating regarding the adverse societal effects of the unequal distribution of income. Wilkinson and Pickett (2009a, 2009b) present cross-country data indicating that

> Population health tends to be better in societies where income is more equally distributed. Recent evidence suggests that many other social problems, including mental illness, violence, imprisonment, lack of trust, teenage births, obesity, drug abuse, and poor education performance of schoolchildren, are also more common in more unequal societies. [These] differences … seem to be large and to *extend to the vast majority of the population* *(Wilkinson & Pickett, 2009b, p. 493, emphasis added).*

The highlighted portion of the quotation indicates that the adverse effects of greater income dispersion are not restricted to only the poor; they affect people at all levels of society. These are some indicators of the affects *within* the United States:

1. The gap in life spans between rich and poor has grown, despite advances in medicine, even since 2001, and this is exacerbated by where one happens to live (Irwin & Bui, 2016; Tavernise, 2016).
2. Because the rich live longer, they collect more social security benefits, thus reducing the progressive character of a program originally instituted for the working class (Irwin, 2016). Economic factors largely determine housing patterns and result in *distressed communities* that have deleterious

effects on people's "lifetime chances of achieving economic stability or success" (Economic Innovation Group, 2016, p. 4; cf. also Chetty, et al., 2014a; Rothstein, 2018). "Many of those affected will feel alienated from society and behave accordingly" (Freeman, 1996, p. 119).

3. "Family economic status, family structure, parents' educational levels, and ethnic group are not only correlated in the population; they are also causally interrelated in the sense that they affect one another"; and "children growing up in poverty are at a disadvantage in almost every domain of development" (Huston & Bentley, 2010, pp. 414, 417; cf. also Sleek, 2015).

4. The dramatic decline in real earnings has directly affected health and the absence of adequate medical care for many (Association for Psychological Science [APS], 1996a, 1996b; Goode, 1999; New York Academy of Sciences, 1999), with particular effects on infant mortality in the U.S. and around the world (Gladstone, 2015; Porter, 2015, p. 8).

5. Because the working poor are more likely to experience extended periods of unemployment, they experience "lower psychological and physical well-being than ... their employed counterparts" (Mckee-Ryan et al., 2005).

6. At the societal level, high-income inequality may explain why even when there is economic growth, it fails to lead to increases in life satisfaction (the *Easterlin Paradox*) (Oishi & Kesebir, 2015).

7. I-O psychologists should be especially concerned that "excessive CEO pay matters for inequality, not only because it means a large amount of money is going to a very small group of individuals, but also because it affects pay structures throughout the corporation and the economy as a whole" (Baker et al., 2019, p. 2).

In general, from the standpoints of political democracy, the common good and a shared sense of community, "Too great a gap between rich and poor undermines the solidarity that democratic citizenship requires .... As inequality deepens, rich and poor live increasingly separate lives .... The affluent secede from public places and services, leaving them to those who can't afford anything else" (Sandel, 2009, p. 266). There are, of course, numerous other distressing circumstances that could be mentioned. Mishel et al. (2012) summarize:

As income and wealth become more concentrated in American society, so do access to higher education, to political power, to good neighborhoods with good schools, to decent health care, and ultimately to opportunity itself. This reality undermines a core American principle: fair opportunity for all. The indicators and trends investigated ... warrant action. If market forces are failing to provide fair opportunities—and there is ample evidence to support this claim—then policy intervention is necessary. (p. 168)

Some Pertinent Causes

From a societal perspective extreme disparities in income and wealth do not just happen "naturally" because of exogenous economic processes; nor do they merely reflect individual and group differences in effort and ability. "It is not inevitable that market economies generate chronically rising inequality …. The American economy delivered extraordinarily equal, and much more rapid, growth in family incomes between 1947 and 1979 than between 1979 and 2007" (Mishell, et al., 2012, p. 26). To a considerable degree, they reflect the unequal distribution of political power and intentional governmental policies (cf. Rothstein, 2018). "Inequality is a choice" (Stiglitz, 2013). For example, a chart like Figure 8.2 depicting *after*-tax income would show even more, not less, disparity. "Between 1979 and 2007, the inequality-reducing effect of taxes and transfers actually *declined* across most measures of inequality (Mishel et al., 2012, p. 26, emphasis in the original), and the trend was aided still further by the 2017 Tax Cuts and Jobs Act favoring the wealthy.

Several factors appear to be implicated in much of the income disparity:

1. **Decline in the number and bargaining power of unionized workers.** In 1979 the share of workers covered by collective bargaining was 27.0%; in 2019 it was 11.6% (Hirsch & Macpherson, 2020). Not only do unionized workers earn more than comparable nonunion workers, but they are also more likely to have health insurance, pension coverage and paid leave (Mishel et al., 2012). Importantly, the decline of organized labor explains about a third of the growth in income inequality (Mishel, 2021c; Western & Rosenfeld, 2011). Examining data spanning 100 years (1917–2017) Farber et al. (2021) also found "consistent evidence that unions reduce inequality" (p. 1326). Not only has "declining unionization widened inequality between high-wage earners and middle-wage earners (Mishel, 2021b), many will be surprised to learn that unionization positively affects *management* compensation—via the union's uplifting effect on workers' base pay and the companies' attempts to maintain pay equity (Colvin et al., 2001). Accordingly, unionized organizations had more egalitarian (i.e., lower) manager-to-worker pay ratios. The prevalence of union membership historically has improved wages even for nonunionized workers and reduced income disparities (Economic Policy Institute, 2021). "Despite its great wealth, for decades the United States has had greater income inequality than all other developed economies" (Tsui & Enderle, 2018, p. 156). Figure 8.3 shows the remarkable inverse relationship between union membership and the share of income that goes to the top 10%. And because much of the top 10% is comprised of senior managers, it "suggests that corporations may be a major cause of income inequality and, as such, may be a major solution" (Tsui & Enderle, p. 2018).

9

As union membership declines, income inequality increases

Union membership and share of income going to the top 10%, 1917–2017

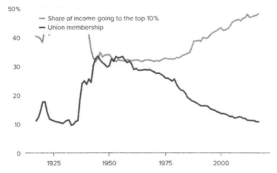

Source: Reproduced from Figure A in Heidi Shierholz, *Working People Have Been Thwarted in Their Efforts to Bargain for Better Wages by Attacks on Unions*. Economic Policy Institute, August 2019.

FIGURE 8.3 As union membership declines, income inequality increases. Union membership and share of income going to the top 10%, 1917–2017

Source: Reproduced from Figure A in Heidi Schierholz, working people have been thwarted in their efforts to bargain for better wages by attacks on unions. Economic Policy Institute, August 2019. Used by permission.

Anti-union activities by companies include actions that would ordinarily be considered unethical in other contexts and sometimes even illegal (Calacci, 2021; Lafer & Loustaunau, 2020; McClendon, 2006; McNicholas et al., 2021) (e.g., threatening pro-union workers; aggressively interfering with union elections). And in the opinion of some, the nearly-century-old National Labor Relations Act (1935) is inadequate to deal with contemporary anti-union corporate activities (Greenhouse, 2019; Loomis, 2021).

One might infer the sorry state of working conditions and pay for hourly workers in the United States—i.e., the rise in the amount of *precarious work* (Kalleberg, 2009)—from the dramatic shortage of available labor in the Fall and Winter of 2021 (while I am writing this chapter) despite the incipient "opening-up" of the economy after almost 2 years of the pandemic. The labor force has shrunk by 8 million people during that time: there are five million fewer employed and 3 million fewer even looking for work (Casselman, 2021); there were 10.9 million open jobs at the end of July 2021 (Cook, 2021). The phenomenon is being referred to as "the great resignation," or "the big quit."

Some people attribute it all to a disincentive effect of government subsidies and unemployment benefits, but studies have shown those to have a very small impact. In fact, states in the United States that chose to not cut federal pandemic unemployment insurance had, on average, greater job growth than the 26 states that cut benefits to unemployed workers (Hickey & Cooper, 2021); resignation rates are highest among mid-career employees and in the tech and health care industries (Cook, 2021); and many people are not returning to work even months after the subsidies have ended (Delaney & Golshan, 2021). They seem to be reluctant to return to unattractive jobs, for low pay and few benefits (Rosenberg, 2021)—conditions resulting from many years of anti-union and anti-worker political action funded by contributions from the right-wing American elite (Greenhouse, 2019).

Workers seem to have acquired greater leverage (Irwin, 2021; Scheiber, 2021a); as one economist put it, "It's like the whole country is in some kind of union renegotiation" (Stevenson, 2021). For example, as I write this (Spring 2022) there are major strikes at John Deere, Frito-Lay, Kaiser Permanente, and other companies that have been very profitable during the pandemic; Kellogg workers had a successful strike outcome (Scheiber, 2021c); workers at more than 175 Starbucks stores in 25 states have filed for union elections and 16 have already voted for union representation (Eavis, 2022; Scheiber, 2022). In recent years even professionals such as architects and graduate students who are university employees have sought to join unions (Scheiber, 2021b), and some recently went on strike and won improved wages and health benefits at New York University, Columbia University and Harvard University (Goldberg, 2021; Wong, 2021).

But with union membership in the private sector down to 10.3% in 2021, unions have a long way to go. As one of the largest, and most anti-union employers, Amazon presents a dynamic and fascinating case study. Warehouse employees in Alabama apparently rejected unionization decisively (Weise & Scheiber, 2021)—although, as reported by the Society for Human Resource Management (SHRM), the National Labor Relations Board (NLRB) has ordered another election because of Amazon's intimidation of its workers (Smith, 2021). And that election is now in dispute. Meanwhile workers at the largest Amazon fulfillment center in New York just voted to be represented by an independent union (Weise & Scheiber, 2022).

2. **Decline in the real value of the federal minimum wage and lack of overtime pay.** Table 8.4 shows that more than 40 years ago, the value of the federal minimum wage (FMW) of $3.10 was substantially greater than the current $7.25. At that time, it amounted to 45.3% of the average nonsupervisory production worker's wages. In 2020 it was only

TABLE 8.4 Value of the U.S. Federal Minimum Wage (FMW), 1980-2020

Year	Nominal amount	In 2018 dollars	Average workers' wage*	FMW as % of Aver. Workers'
2020	$7.25	$7.25	$24.67	29.4%
2015	$7.25	$7.92	$22.98	34.5%
2010	$7.25	$8.63	$22.65	38.1%
2000	$5.15	$7.76	$21.12	36.8%
1990	$3.80	$7.32	$19.65	37.3%
1980	$3.10	$9.30	$20.51	45.3%

Source: Based on data contained in Economic Policy Institute (2019). State of Working America Data Library. Minimum Wage, 2019 (updated Sept. 2021). Retrieved from https://www.epi.org/data/ on Oct. 14, 2021. Used by permission. Adapted from Economic Policy Institute (2019). State of Working America Data Library. Minimum Wage (Updated Sept. 2021).

Notes
* Production and nonsupervisory workers.

29.4% of the average worker's wages. If the current FMW were set at the 1980 level of 45.3% of the average worker pay it would now be $11.18.[36] If the Raise the Wage Act of 2021 passes congress it will phase in a $15 minimum wage by 2025. That would raise the earnings of 21% of the workforce—32 million workers (Cooper et al., 2021). Contrary to the widespread belief that the minimum wage primarily pertains to teenagers and minority workers, among those who would benefit from an increase in the minimum wage from $7.25 are: full-time workers (54.1%), whites (56.1%), women (54.5%), those age 20 and above (87.9%), and single or married parents (28%) (Mishel et al., 2012, Table 4.40). A rise in the FMW to $15 would not only help low-wage workers, it would also reduce greatly government expenditures for public assistance programs, increase revenue from FICA, and reduce the number of families in poverty (Zipperer et al., 2021).

Salaried workers who make more than $23,600 p.a. do not automatically qualify for time-and-a-half overtime pay (a policy implemented by the Fair Labor Standards Act in 1938 for those in jobs that didn't have union protection; and not updated for inflation since 1975). In current dollars that threshold would have been equivalent to $69,000 in 1975 (Hanauer & Reich, 2016).

3. **Absence of pay transparency.** Lack of within-job level transparency ("pay secrecy") contributes to worker exploitation in general, and may play an especially significant role in pay discrimination by sex—and it

36 Moreover, bear in mind that workers' wages have not nearly kept up with the rise in Productivity (see Figure 8.1), so there is an even greater inequity than is shown by these numbers. The figure should be substantially higher.

is illegal (Kissinger, 2016).[37] But enhancing transparency might not enhance the relative pay of women, depending on their propensity to actively negotiate their pay (Rosenfeld, 2016).

4. **Public subsidization of the private sector.** The first three factors, in combination with government safety net transfers (food stamps, Medicaid, etc.) enable some companies, in effect, to include substandard pay as an integral part of their business model—along with a substantial budget for lobbying the U.S. congress for supportive legislation. More than half of the growth in family incomes over the past 30 years or so has come from government transfers. This enables companies like McDonald's and Walmart, most banks, many colleges and universities, private child- and home-care agencies, and others, to pay their fast-food workers, service and sales employees, bank tellers and adjunct faculty less than it takes to make ends meet, requiring those workers to turn to the federal and state governments for supplements (Allegretto et al., 2014; Americans for Tax Fairness, 2014; Jacobs et al., 2015). Just between 2009 and 2011 the federal government spent $127.8 billion annually and the states spent $25 billion (in 2013 dollars) annually for *working families*. In other words, U.S. taxpayers spent over $150 billion/year indirectly subsidizing private enterprise (in this fashion—not counting more direct means such as with tax policy).

5. **Managerial decisions.** The past 30 years or more have been marked by: (a) downsizing of higher wage manufacturing jobs and corresponding growth in lower paying service sector jobs; (b) effects of "globalization," as U.S. manufacturers moved abroad and/or outsourced some operations, with a concomitant increase in immigration of unskilled workers; and (c) growth in temporary and part-time jobs (eventually morphing into a "gig economy") whose incumbents typically earn less and receive few if any benefits—to the point that they may start to organize (Scheiber, 2016).

6. **Greatly increased import competition.** "Since the early 1990s, expanding global trade, propelled by China's spectacular growth, is playing a much larger role in the U.S. labor market" (Autor & Hanson, 2014). It has contributed to job displacement and chronic economic hardship—especially concentrated in particular geographic regions (Autor et al., 2013).

7. **Technological displacement.** The past 150 years have witnessed advancing "workplace technologies [that] are designed to save labor" (Autor, 2015). They include agricultural machinery and methods, construction equipment, computers, information technology, robotically-produced

---

37 Pay secrecy is sometimes justified in the name of protecting privacy. Notably, however, such arguments are generally advanced by employers, not the recipients of the pay, who are kept in the dark about the rate system.

automobiles, artificial intelligence, et al., affecting both production and white-collar workers. Acceleration in the power of computers has created a resurgence of the "automation anxiety" that characterized the 1950s and '60s (Akst, 2013).

But economists have disagreed since then over whether the overall effect has been a decrease or increase in jobs or no net change. Acemoglu and Restrepo (2018, 2019) start out by defining automation as "the development and adoption of new technologies that enable capital to be substituted for labor in a range of tasks" (2019, p. 3) and go on to describe three simultaneous processes. "*Displacement effects*—as capital takes over tasks previously performed by labor …. [But] automation also increases productivity … which we call the *productivity effect* [which] contributes to the demand for labor in non-automated tasks" (2019, p. 4). Moreover, technologies sometimes also create new tasks/jobs in which people have a comparative advantage over machines—a *reinstatement effect*. It is clear that displacement effects in the United States have substantially outweighed productivity and reinstatement effects, especially with respect to the effects of industrial robots on employment levels and wages (Acemoglu & Restrepo, 2020). Moreover, the adverse effects on labor are exacerbated by the bias of the U.S. business tax code in favor of capital expenditures over those for labor (Acemoglu et al., 2020). This also leads to the introduction of "marginal automated tasks [that] do not bring much productivity gains but displace workers, reducing employment below its socially optimal level" (p. 231). This marginal automation has been referred to as "so-so technologies" (Lohr, 2022c), such as self-checkout machines at the supermarket.

The "technology shocks" caused by automation, unlike the effects of import competition, tend to be spread throughout the United States (Autor, et al., 2013). A consensus is building, however, that even though automation enhances efficiency, it does not greatly reduce aggregate unemployment (Autor, 2015), although "automation makes us better off collectively by making some of us worse off" (Akst, 2013, p. 12). In fact, Akst goes on, "physical jobs are disappearing into the second economy, and I believe this effect is dwarfing the much more publicized effect of jobs disappearing to places like India and China" (p. 6).[38]

---

38 Arthur (2011) coined the term *second economy* and described it as follows: "all across economies in the developed world, processes in the physical economy are being entered into the digital economy, where they are 'speaking to' other processes in the digital economy, in a constant conversation among multiple servers and multiple semi-intelligent nodes that are updating things, querying things, checking things off, re-adjusting things, and eventually connecting back with processes and humans in the physical economy" (p. 3).

Therefore, "the main challenge of the economy is shifting from *producing* prosperity to *distributing* prosperity …. Perhaps we will have to subsidize job creation. Perhaps the very idea of a job and of being productive will change over the next two or three decades" (Arthur, 2011, p. 7, emphasis in the original).

8. **Demographic risk factors.** The above factors impact people differentially. Data from a large scale, ongoing longitudinal study begun in 1968, as well as U.S. census data, "have shown that certain characteristics tend to increase the likelihood of experiencing poverty …. Those with less education, not married, nonwhite, and who are younger tend to be at a higher risk of poverty" (Rank & Hirschl, 2014). The Covid-19 pandemic has accelerated those patterns. And seemingly mundane factors such as living in communities or neighborhoods not well-served by mass transit, making commuting to a job difficult, exacerbate the situation further (Bouchard, 2015).

9. **Government Policies in support of the wealthy.** The United States has experienced three previous gilded ages, in the 1790s, 1880s and 1920s; in each instance--just like our current era since the 1980s--they were promoted by power elites (including the founding fathers) advancing their own "familiar conservative economic and demographic patterns of preferment" (Phillips, 1990, p. xx). Phillips further pointed out, "Since the American Revolution the distribution of American wealth has depended significantly on who controlled the federal government, for what policies, and in behalf of which constituencies" (p. xix) (cf. also Stiglitz, 2015). (Cf. Chap. 11 concerning *neoliberalism*.) A good example of the role of government policy in this regard is the long-term refusal by congress to raise the FMW. As noted above, it has declined considerably in purchasing power since 1968. A full-time job would bring the worker annual gross earnings of $13,195).[39] The economic metaphor of a rising tide lifting all boats becomes a cynical caricature when a very few are luxuriating in comfortable yachts (as likely to have been inherited as earned) whereas many others are working longer and longer hours each week to acquire vessels that are barely seaworthy. Other examples of government policies having regressive effects are significant lowering of the maximum marginal income tax rate, the deregulation of the financial sector of the economy (while maintaining the financial guarantees for those institutions), the much lower tax rates for investment income than for wage income, and numerous tax loopholes for corporate and investment

---

39 FT = 35 hrs./week. In 2021 the official federal poverty line for a family of four is $26,500, and except for inflation adjustments the criteria have not changed much since they were created by President Lyndon Johnson as part of the war on poverty in the 1960s.

income (Cohen, 2015a). Consequently, a government study found that "the dispersion of market income grew by about one-quarter between 1979 and 2007, while the dispersion of after-tax income grew by about one-third" (Congressional Budget Office, 2011, p. xii).

Do You Care?

Although there are instances of pushback (cf. Lohr, 2022c), including some attention in I-O psychology to achieving "living wages" (Huffmeier & Zacher, 2021; Searle & McWha-Herman, 2020) it is obvious that in general there has not been a great deal of motivation and political will to address these inequities in the United States. Why might that be? It is at least conceivable that a portion of the explanation involves the under-studied phenomenon of *deliberate ignorance*—"defined as the conscious individual or collective choice not to seek or use information or knowledge" (Hertwig & Engel, 2016). Among the nine likely functions of deliberate ignorance proposed by these authors is the strategic device of eschewing responsibility, including moral responsibility, to avoid cognitive dissonance. Quoting Abraham Maslow, they note that "often it is better not to know because if you *did* know, then you would *have* to act and stick your neck out" (p. 362).

Potentially dovetailing with deliberate ignorance is the proposed workings of *system justification*—described as "a general ideological motive to justify the existing social order … at least partially responsible for the internalization of inferiority among members of disadvantaged groups [and] it is observed most readily at an implicit, nonconscious level of awareness" (Jost et al., 2004, p. 881). According to this view, people tend to have a lot invested in maintaining the status quo.

With the foregoing as context, some empirical findings are very suggestive. First et al. (2016) found that: (a) cross-culturally, the higher the level of income mobility in a country, the more tolerant were its citizens of income inequalities;[40] (b) a country's level of immobility was an even better predictor of dissatisfaction with inequality than the actual level of inequality; (c) within the U.S., those at higher levels of income (above approximately $65,000) "were more satisfied with the level of social mobility …, more tolerant with current levels of income inequality …" (p. 377), and more likely to see "their station as the product of their own efforts" (p. 379); and (d) all participants, across income levels, "expected significant upward mobility for themselves … and their children" (p. 378). And the last piece of the puzzle is supplied by Davidai and Gilovich (2015) and Kraus and Tan (2015) who confirmed that Americans substantially overestimate social class mobility in the United States.

---

40 "Income mobility" is a calculation of "the intergenerational income elasticity between a father's and his son's income" (p. 374).

To the extent that we are even cognizant of these inequities, we are likely to perceive them as justifiably reflecting individual effort; and to view wealth as considerably more attainable for ourselves than is likely.

Adding Further to The Framework for Ethical Decision Making

17. Values refer to relatively stable cognitions concerning the importance of generalized end-states or standards of conduct. They have salient affective, evaluative and motivational components and guide the formation of more specific beliefs and attitudes and consequent behaviors. Therefore, it is at the level of one's values that we must look to understand principled conflicts, including ethical dilemmas.

18. Not all values are self-evident or readily amenable to assessment. Consciously espoused (normative or prescriptive) values may coexist with an experiential set of normal values-in-use that are preconscious yet more closely linked to action. Because the two value systems are not identical people may sometimes behave in ways that reflect values that are inconsistent with their espoused principles. This is not necessarily an indication of hypocrisy.

19. Ethical or moral values are those that have to do with issues of fairness and justice, duties and responsibilities, beneficence and caring, or moral virtue (character).

20. In addition to the proactive guiding role that values serve in the formation of beliefs and attitudes, they may also serve—especially moral values—a somewhat insidious role of providing post-hoc rationalizations or justifications for attitudes whose less savory origins are elsewhere. For example, prejudicial attitudes toward some disliked social groups are frequently justified by exaggerating perceptions of values differences between them and ourselves as a means of rationalizing those attitudes and justifying discriminatory policies and actions. We don't always recognize their ego-defensive function as rhetorical devices for rationalization.

21. A structural–functional perspective on values formation suggests that the particulars of our upbringing, social status and identity, occupation, organizational position, and so on, result in individual differences in values, attitudes and beliefs, including notions of what is just. Hence, people are likely to differ in their perceptions of potential ethical dilemmas and what is right or fair. That is why devices such as ethical codes and casebooks may be helpful despite their limitations; they promote uniform standards of evaluation.

22. A convincing moral argument can be made for the superiority of the distributive justice criteria of equality or need over merit or equity. Conversely, from a historic and empirical perspective, one cannot fail to recognize the aggregate economic utility of reward systems based on merit.

The latter is consonant with our cultural norms, the character of our economic system, and with much of human motivation. However, it also seems clear that merit is frequently used as a justification for the maintenance and promotion of morally questionable social inequities and extreme disparities in income and wealth, irrespective of their source. Reasonable compromises may entail the acceptance of material incentives to produce income and wealth, while also promoting both government and corporate programs and policies that attenuate the resulting extreme disparities. This could entail enhancing the capabilities of "have-nots" to contribute meaningfully to society, to access its opportunities and share in the rewards, as well as providing necessary safety nets.

23. **I-O psychology should broaden its narrow conceptualization of social justice from simply the perceived fairness of organizational processes. It should include objective real-world criteria, including meso- and macro-economic indications of injustice, as judged by normative standards.** The social, economic, political and international forces that account for inequities in income, wealth and well-being, are mediated in great measure by the organizations in/for which we work. Consequently, like it or not, we are already involved; and our silence on these matters is unseemly.

24. **The functioning of most institutions of society as well as individual organizations can be evaluated from an ethical standpoint with respect to their promotion of or detraction from social justice, irrespective of their primary functions.** This is especially true of large corporations—if for no other reason than because of their extraordinary power and dominance in our society. As professionals who contribute to the maintenance and effectiveness of those organizations, these ethical considerations are legitimate matters of concern regarding our personal decision to participate in particular organizations, and in what manner. Moreover, it is extremely inconsistent and of dubious moral standing, to be concerned with individual- and organizational-level values and ethics while apparently remaining unconcerned about many indications of the extreme economic and social injustice of American society.

9
VALUES AND VALUE CONFLICTS IN THE PROFESSIONS

> Why is it that experts primarily teach techniques to young professionals, while ignoring the values that have sustained the quests of so many creative geniuses?
>
> —Gardner, Csikszentmihalyi and Damon

The tendentious question from Gardner et al. (2001), above, succinctly expresses the critical role played by values in shaping professional practice, research and ethics, as depicted throughout this volume. This chapter and the remainder of Part II deal with professional values, values conflicts and role conflicts that are attributable to the complex nature of any profession and the settings in which it is performed. Some reflect strains within the field of psychology and the sciences in general; some characterize the interface between the values of psychology and those of business, which is, of course, the meeting ground on which I-O psychology is practiced.

The professions used to be an active subject of research in organizational psychology but no longer seem to be. Moreover, it was primarily the classic white-collar professions that were studied (e.g., medicine, law, accountancy), not blue-collar professions. It remains a more active focus in sociology, in which journals such as *Work and Occupations* and *The Sociology of Occupations* remain vibrant.

It is obvious that the particular ethical issues and dilemmas that arise in the practices of medicine, law, psychology, anthropology, policing, accountancy and engineering are very different. The knowledge bases of the fields, as well as the nature of the services provided and their setting, the degree of autonomy enjoyed by the practitioners as sanctioned by society, and the norms and values characterizing each are all distinctly different. Consequently, the ethical guidelines adopted by members of these occupations are different. Accordingly, there are

DOI: 10.4324/9781003212577-11

some scholars who believe that a consideration of professional ethics must be particular to each profession—or occupation aspiring to the status and privileges of a profession. Supporting that view is research indicating that the values of those in different professions, even at the beginning of their careers, at the time of their graduate training, are different (Edwards et al., 1981) and that different professional groups within the same employing organization may experience values conflicts (Davidson, 1985; DeLeon, 1994).

But there are some scholars who emphasize that there is a common underlying set of norms and values by which all professional practice may be linked. This view holds that professional ethics are built on a core of common or personal morality that transcends occupational distinctions. The moral perspective most compatible with this approach is virtue theory, which emphasizes the centrality of moral character and motivation, not specific principles (cf. Chapter 5). For example, Brien (1998) focused on trust as the essential ingredient in all professional relationships. And "While formal codes of conduct can sometimes be a useful guide, developing those traits of character that are particularly suited to the lawyer's role is at the core of what we ought to mean by professional ethics" (Wilkins, 1996, p. 250). Consistent with this cross-disciplinary view, Wilkins went on to describe the development of a single ethics course for both law students and medical students at Harvard that was being expanded to include students of business and government as well. Note that the relatively "content-free" five paradigmatic forms of ethical dilemmas facilitate cross-discipline applicability and study (cf. Table 6.4).

Although it is not necessary for us to take a stand on this issue, it does implicitly raise a point that is of some value to consider. If there is anything at all to be said for the conceptualization of a generic approach to professional ethics—or more accurately, in my opinion, professional values—one should at least be able to specify more or less unambiguously what are the professions that rest on this common moral bedrock. But arriving at a definition of what characterizes a profession is not as simple as it would seem (Crompton, 1991). Some social theorists (e.g., Wilkins) are of the opinion that it is impossible to generate a set of ahistorical criteria for designating some occupations as professions and not others. A great deal of work of that sort has been conducted by sociologists who study the occupational structure and professions. For example, *professionalism* has been conceived essentially as "a strategy for coordinating work where incumbents to an occupation enjoy the privilege to organize tasks themselves" (Seron, 2002). This contrasts with areas in which the market (consumers) have a primary determining influence or bureaucracy/managerialism in which managers determine the structure of what gets done (Freidson, 2001). In fact, many critics decry the distortion of professions by market and/or bureaucratic forces.

I assume that the reader agrees with me that psychology, including I-O psychology, is in fact a profession, so it is important to explore what that means—including what values inure to the field by virtue of that status.

What Is a Profession?

The origin of the word *profession* is theological. In the Middle Ages it denoted a "declaration, promise or vow made by one entering a religious order" (Kimball, 1992, p. 19). Gradually, it came to stand for the group of people who made the vow, that is, a particular order of monks, nuns or other professed people. By the 15th and 16th centuries the term had expanded to include the learned professions—not only theology but also law, medicine and education. By far the most esteemed among the four was theology; education sort of snuck in the back door by virtue of the medieval universities being a site of scholarship regarding the first three. That is pretty much how things stood until the colonization of the new world. In the 17th century and early 18th century in the colonies, ministers were most esteemed, and it is they who imparted special dignity to the notion of a profession as referring to a "particular calling" with an "ethic of selfless service" (Kimball, 1992, p. 302). By the late 18th century in America politics and the law became the preeminent professions. However, it was an idealized politics having to do with the noble enterprise of developing a legal and political system by which to order society (think of the greatly esteemed founding fathers: Washington, Jefferson, Madison, Adams, Franklin, et al.).

From the late 19th century and into the early years of the 20th century law and politics declined in status (perhaps as a consequence of the civil war), education greatly increased in status (being a professor was a very highly esteemed occupation), and science entered the picture—the natural sciences, not social science. The university as the nidus of scientific scholarship and activity served to re-inforce the status of education and to merge the identification of science and learning. Medicine also increased greatly in status, as an integral aspect of biological science. In fact, the continued supremacy of medicine resulted in its being held as a model of "the true professional ideal" in America during the 20th century (Kimball, 1992, p. 308). Professions are often characterized (or idealized?) as more concerned with altruistically doing good work as opposed to self-interest and economic reward (Freidson, 2001; Zelizer, 1983).

Throughout the 20th century, scholars flirted with the idea of whether business had become a profession. Louis Brandeis (1914/1971) thought that it already had, and sociologists such as R. H. Tawney (1920) and Talcott Parsons (1937) thought that it had not yet but ought to become so—to attenuate its acquisitiveness and self-interest with the altruistic service character of the professions. But whether an occupation is a profession is not simply a matter of its being anointed as such; if it were, attention would certainly shift to who had the authority to perform the ritual. After considering the attributes that characterize professions, we will be in a better position to consider the extent to which business satisfies those criteria and the role that the so-called professionalization of management plays concerning the putative social responsibilities of business.

The last half of the 20th century witnessed a rapid increase in the number of occupations claiming the mantle of the profession, as well as an expansion in scholarship devoted to the topic. It was during this time that the notion of a "true professional ideal" developed denoting "a dignified vocation practiced by 'professionals' who professed selfless and contractual service, membership in a strong association, and functional expertise modeled on the natural sciences" (Kimball, 1992, p. 303). The fruits of that scholarship, conducted mostly by sociologists—I-O psychologists curiously having been nearly absent—will help us understand better what is meant by a profession.

But it should also be noted that the positive—some would say idealized—view of professions characterized by *the professional ideal, the professional model* or *the service model* is offset by a negative, perhaps cynical—although some would say realistic—view. In this power-oriented conception, professions are simply economically successful monopolies that have managed to persuade society to honor their claims for special privileges (Brien, 1998; Newton, 1982). They are *market shelters* serving to shield the members of the profession from outside competition and government interference (Freidson, 2001; Timmermans, 2008). In other words, whatever altruistic public service may exist is simply a byproduct of the primary motivation which is self-interest. It seems to me that one can accept the ubiquitous existence of a certain amount of self-interest (a modified *psychological* or *rational egoism*) without having to adopt such a one-sided unflattering portrait. We can take mixed motives as the expected basis for most complex human behavior. Crompton (1990) observes that

> commentaries on 'the professions' have long reflected a tension between two, apparently conflicting, perspectives. On the one hand, professions are viewed as uniquely ethical occupations; on the other, as powerful groups who have masked their pursuit of self-interest behind essentially spurious ethical codes. (p. 147)

Attributes of Professions[1]

The historical evolution of what Kimball (1992, p. 303) referred to as "the true professional ideal" is more frequently characterized less grandiloquently by sociologists as "the professional model" (e.g., Hall, 1975, p. 72). The ideal is a set of characteristics by which occupations that are professions may presumably be distinguished from those that are not (Freidson, 1986; Haber, 1991). It is important to recognize, however, that it is indeed a model—i.e., it is a prototypic representation that may not be fulfilled in all respects by every profession.

---

1   This discussion draws substantially on the classic work of Hall (1975), Lynn (1965), Etzioni (1969), Elliott (1972), and Goode (1960, 1969). It is also consonant with Macrina's (2014) understanding of scientific professions.

And the attributes are not "all-or none": Professions will vary in the extent to which they meet each of the components. "There is no absolute difference between professional and other kinds of occupational behavior, but only relative differences with respect to certain attributes common to all occupational behavior" (Barber, 1965, p. 17). Some of the components are structural in nature, referring to the social organization of a profession and/or its position in society; some are functional, referring to the nature of professional activities; and some refer to the characteristics or attitudes of the profession's members. Almost all can be viewed from a value perspective, reflecting the profession's generalized preferences concerning goals and objectives as well as the means of achieving them.

Point 1: Professions Are Organized around a Systematic Theoretical Body of Knowledge

The nature of the theories may be either "pure," as with scientific inquiry or pragmatic, as with the application of knowledge. Some professional occupations are primarily research-oriented; some are largely practice-oriented; and some are comprised of significant components of both, like medicine and psychology. The relative balance doesn't matter with respect to the designation as a profession. "If some occupations become professions by developing an intellectual interest, others do it by becoming more practical" (Hughes, 1965, p. 6). Within those professions that have significant pure and applied components, some members may be involved in both sets of activities, but most adherents tend to be involved primarily in one or the other. For example, practitioners tend not to do research; one study found that only about 10% of the published research in I-O psychology is authored by organizationally based practitioners (Sackett et al., 1986). More than 20 years later a survey of the membership of the Society for Industrial-Organizational Psychology (SIOP) confirmed that only 10% were "nonpractitioners" (Cober et al., 2009).[2]

Point 2: Society Confers Legitimate Authority to the Profession over the Interpretation and Application of Knowledge in Its Domain in Providing Services to Clients

A major implication of a profession's being organized around a specialized body of knowledge is the presumption that clients are at best incompletely and inadequately informed about the best course of action in the profession's domain, and so they depend on the professional's judgment. Another important aspect of this attribute is that the profession becomes accepted as the arbiter of any disputes over theoretical or technical matters within its domain. And in some views, it wins that right in competition with other similar professions (Evans, 2021).

2   That was 99 of 1,005 respondents. But the overall response rate was only 36% of the SIOP membership.

Thus, for example, the AERA, APA, and NCME (2014) *Standards for Educational and Psychological Testing* and SIOP's (2018) *Principles for the Validation and Use of Personnel Selection Procedures* are afforded great deference in legal deliberations concerning alleged discrimination involving employment testing. An important aspect of this attribute is that the professional implicitly asks to be trusted by those whom they serve (Hughes, 1965). In contrast to the marketplace in which the prevailing ethos might be *caveat emptor* ("buyer beware"), within the sphere of professional practice it is *credat emptor* ("buyer have faith"). Although, based on the vulnerability of the public the government also requires professionals to be licensed to practice. (E.g., the state of New York licenses approximately 130 occupations, including psychologist.) Evans (2021) illustrated how members of a profession also "mobilized their accounts about the morality of their work to integrate the moral definitions of their work within their boundaries of expert authority. The outcome of their actions was the development of a form of moral authority" (p. 991).

Point 3: Society also Confers Considerable Formal and Informal Sanction Power to the Profession

This is reflected in the substantial role that professions play in determining the educational and training requirements necessary to enter the profession, including providing input into the standards for licensing and accreditation. Hall (1975) also pointed out that, to the extent professional–client communications are privileged, it not only protects the right of the client but also asserts the authority of the professional. The extent to which some form of accreditation is seen as desirable is indicated by the fact that more than 1,000 fields have professional certifications (McKillip & Owens, 2000).

Point 4: Professions Generally Have Some Form of Ethical Code as a Guide to Appropriate Action Regarding Clients, Colleagues and the Public at Large

Evans (2021) has described how professions often set the technical boundaries of their field in conflict with other professions. Some of that has appeared in I-O psychology—e.g., to the extent that practitioners in other (related) disciplines have been referred to as representing a confluence of "anti-industrial-organizational psychology" factors (Rotolo et al., 2018). But Evans (2021) also notes that professions "manage moral challenges by reconfiguring their conventional domain of expert authority to include moral as well as technical expertise" (p. 989). Part of that reconfiguration involves development of a formal code of ethics.

Often concomitant with a code is a set of administrative regulations by which the code is enforced—for example, through the agency of a professional association, such as the APA. However, there is considerable disagreement among scholars and social critics, practitioners of the professions, and public advocates concerning the extent to which professions may be relied on to sanction the behavior of their members. Hall (1975) suggested that the norm of professional self-regulation does not work all that well because of the absence of observability of much professional work, by which he meant observation by those who can judge its appropriateness. In any event, the development of an ethical code is one of the clearest specific indications of an occupation or subfield of specialization aspiring to the status of profession.

Those who maintain the more cynical attitude alluded to earlier regarding professions have similar beliefs regarding codes of ethics, which they see as primarily helping to construct "a carefully polished image to win elite support, designed for public relations and justification for the status and prestige" of a profession (Newton, 1982, p. 34). As explained by Kouchaki (2015), the codes and sense of superiority of professionals may even lead paradoxically to an increased likelihood of engaging in unethical behavior (cf. the motivational constructs of *moral licensing* or *moral balance* in Chapter 7).

Point 5: Professions Have Their Own Culture of Values, Norms and Professional Opinion

These serve to present a relatively uniform face to the public regarding such matters as standards for training and admission to the profession, as well as structuring the nature of client–professional relationships. The culture is generally represented by a formal association such as the APA, APS, SIOP, SHRM, et al. In fact, the presence of such a professional association may be taken as an indicator that an occupation has reached the status of a profession (Lounsbury, 2002). In culling a variety of documents having to do with *research integrity*, Macrina (2014, p. 37) annotated a list of nine core values for scientists: honesty; trust (and trustworthiness); fairness; openness (to the scientific community and the public); accountability; stewardship (of resources and research participants); objectivity; accuracy and reliability; impartiality and independence (especially re conflicts of interest).

One interesting aspect of professional culture has to do with the relative degree of specialized knowledge and terminology that characterizes the field. Such specialization serves to mark the distinctiveness of a profession from the rest of society, thus enhancing its status, while accentuating its separation. Professionals sometimes exacerbate the social consequences of that separation by adopting an attitude of superiority. Elliott (1972) pointed out that professionals tend to justify their activities as not merely useful but "right." The authority conferred on a profession combined with that sense of separation and superiority may set up a professional group as a potential object of public hostility—especially if its members are particularly well paid. Think, for example, of the many hostile lawyer jokes.

One recent experimental investigation (which happened to have been carried out with I-O psychologists as the participants) suggests that if there is a perceived mismatch between one's own political values/orientation and that of one's occupation (liberal—conservative) it could result in lowered levels of occupational identification (Zacher & Rudolph, 2022).

Point 6: Professionals Have a Professional Attitude toward Their Work

We ordinarily think of a professional as one who is intrinsically motivated by the inherent nature of the work, with a high degree of personal involvement in their activities and a sense of commitment and obligation to those served. MacIntyre (2007) has written about the pursuit of excellence in what he refers to as a *practice* (which can extend to even non-professional activities). A professional attitude also involves a sense of identification with one's colleagues through membership in professional organizations and personal interaction. This serves to solidify a degree of cohesion to the field, as reflected in a common culture, as already noted.

But a note of caution is introduced by Kouchaki (2015), who reviews literature suggesting that "professionals are expected not only to be competent, knowledgeable, objective, and highly rational ... but also to be cool, distant, impersonal, and unemotional .... Professionalism dampens compassion and empathy as people perceive expressing emotions as unprofessional" (p. 379). She even maintains that this contributes to a professional schema that values amoral, self-interested and unethical behavior. Obviously, this seems to be an issue that warrants continued empirical investigation.

Point 7: The Service Provided by the Profession Is Deemed Important by Society

This attribute is implied by several of those preceding. It underlies the authority and power conferred on the profession by virtue of its unique capabilities. The essentially monopolistic control over a particular domain of knowledge and its application would not mean much if they were not considered to be important.

Point 8: Professionals Typically Undergo a Longer Period of Socialization than Is Associated with Other Occupations

The specialized education and training that is required to master the knowledge domain and its applications mean a longer period of time in professional, graduate, or technical school, as well as in some form of internship or apprenticeship. Moreover, professional knowledge acquisition does not end with graduate education: It is a lifelong process. An often-overlooked aspect of these educational experiences is the process of occupational socialization. Such socialization develops not just through exposure to the profession's formal curriculum, but through the important "informal curriculum," and even more important "hidden curriculum" (Hafferty, 1998). Hafferty explains that the former is the "unscripted, predominantly ad hoc, and highly interpersonal form of teaching and learning that takes place among and between faculty and students," and the latter is "a set of influences that function at the level of organizational structure and culture" (p. 404). "These are the two modes, I believe, in which many of our students are implicitly socialized into I-O's corporatist value system" (Lefkowitz, 2014a, p. 41).

The common socialization experiences contribute to a substantial degree of commonality of attitude and outlook among professionals in the same field, perpetuating the profession's culture. Elliott (1972) emphasized that "through socialization, students acquire built-in regulatory mechanisms. These can be measured as the norms, values and attitudes they hold" (p. 89). These homogenizing forces can be overstated, however: individuals' outlooks may differ in many ways. Moreover, the degree of subspecialization that marks many ostensibly uniform professions (e.g., the APA has 54 divisions) as well as the differing role requirements and values associated with the "theoretical" versus the "practice" dimensions of a field assure some heterogeneity of outlook.[3] Values differences have even been explored, between "scientists" and "practitioners," within the field of I-O psychology (Brooks et al., 2003).

Point 9: The Power and Responsibility of a Profession Extend beyond Its Direct Clients to Society at Large

This is a consequence of the public's relative ignorance regarding the technical expertise nearly monopolized by the profession (cf. Point 2), the profession's power to control its own standards and discipline its own members (Points 3 and 4), the attitude of professional responsibility assumed to be characteristic of its members (Point 6) and the importance of the service provided in the eyes of society (Point 7). This extension of power is reflected, for example, in the influence wielded by a profession over the shaping of legislation concerning the profession itself. Hughes (1965) described the attribute well:

> Physicians consider it their prerogative to define the nature of disease and of health, and to determine how medical services ought to be distributed and

---

3 The ever-finer gradations by which professions have become subspecialized raise the interesting question as to what the boundaries of a particular profession are. For example, the salient knowledge domain as well as the norms, values, attitudes and ethical concerns of an emergency room doctor in a public hospital and a celebrity dermatologist on Park Avenue (New York City) who does not accept medical insurance vary considerably. The same may be said regarding the many subspecializations in psychology. Whether there is (or should be) a common core curriculum in psychology has long been a matter of some dispute (Benjamin, 2001, 2002).

paid for. Social workers are not content to develop a technique of case work; they concern themselves with social legislation. Every profession considers itself the proper body to set the terms in which some aspect of society, life or nature is to be thought of and to define the general lines, or even the details, of public policy concerning it. The mandate to do so is granted more fully to some professions than to others; in time of crisis it may be questioned even with regard to the respected and powerful professions. (p. 3)

Point 10: A Profession Is Typically a Lifelong Commitment for Its Members

The length of training and preparation as well as the socialization and identification with the field that takes place usually makes a profession the terminal occupation for members. The fact that professionals are generally well-paid probably also contributes to occupational longevity. Hall (1975) made the point that these factors tend to render the professional incapable of changing occupations because of relatively fixed skills and attitudes. A major (partial) exception to this observation—especially germane to I-O psychology—pertains to professionals who are employed in large organizations and who advance hierarchically by becoming administrators or managers and largely abandoning their professional functions. That suggests the next important topic.

Professional Work Settings

Professionals work in four primary settings: (a) as individual practitioners, (b) as members of autonomous professional organizations, (c) in heteronomous professional organizations, or (d) in professional departments in larger organizations (Hall, 1975). The individual practitioner, as exemplified by a one-person law practice, an independent psychotherapist, your neighborhood dentist, or an I-O psychology consultant, is the prototypic professional. However, not much is known empirically about the nature of this work arrangement across the professions in comparison with the other three. That is probably because most professionals are employed in organizational settings (Freidson, 1986). For our purposes, probably the most striking fact about being an independent private practitioner is one's potential isolation when faced with values conflicts and potential ethical dilemmas. On those occasions, the wise solo practitioner will attempt to make full use of informal personal consultation with colleagues—friends and other resources available through the appropriate professional associations. For example, the Ethics Committee of the APA welcomes proactive letters of inquiry seeking advice. Mentors and former professors are often good sources.

Autonomous professional organizations, such as an I-O psychology consulting firm, are settings in which professionals establish the organizations' structure, norms, policies, and so on—presumably in accord with the culture of the profession and the expectations of the members. Thus, the goals of the organization are those of the professionals employed. It may be impossible to generalize much about these work settings, which might include a pair of consulting I-O psychologists, a private medical clinic comprised of ten doctors, a firm of 50 consulting engineers with 100 draftspersons, or a Wall Street law firm of more than one thousand attorneys, paralegals and other support staff. Hypothetically, at least, in comparison with the single practitioner these arrangements permit professional collaboration and consultation, the advantage of performance standards being set by fellow professionals, and greater observability of potential ethical transgressions. However, Hall (1975) reported conflicting findings from studies of law firms and medical clinics regarding the effectiveness of the self-regulation systems. Another matter that is frequently a salient issue for the principals of such consulting firms is the pressure for revenue flow due to having established a considerable level of overhead commitment. I am not aware of any extensive or systematic published material in I-O psychology regarding the potential impact of these pressures on professional concerns, such as choice of clients or projects, methodologies employed, substance of findings, or integrity of evaluations reported to clients. Anecdotal evidence suggests that the pressure for billable hours frequently conflicts with professional ideals and is especially discomforting to young practitioner–consultants.

Heteronomous organizations, in which professional employees are subordinated to an overall administrative structure and granted little autonomy, represent a structure typified by teachers in secondary schools, social workers in welfare agencies, or librarians in libraries. It is a form of organizational work setting that is not (to my knowledge) represented in the field of I-O psychology.

In contrast, many I-O psychologists are employed in professional (human resources) departments in large private-sector organizations or governmental agencies, as are chemists in pharmaceutical companies, librarians in law firms, engineers in manufacturing companies, and economists in brokerage houses—to name a few other examples. This is an arrangement that has considerable potential for conflict related to the disjunction between professional and organizational norms and values—even to the point of potentially precipitating organizationally deviant (i.e., maladaptive) behavior by the professional (Raelin, 1984, 1989, 1994).[4] Consequently, it has been the object of study by organizational scholars and social theorists for quite some time (cf. Parsons, 1954).

Professional-Organizational Conflict

The predominant view of the nature of the relation between professionals and the large business organizations in which they often are employed has been one

---

4   A related issue that has interested some scholars is the potential conflict among different professional subgroups within the same organization (Davidson, 1985; DeLeon, 1994). That topic is not considered here.

of inevitable conflict, as illustrated by Kornhauser's (1962) well-known research documenting the adverse effects on scientists of working in an industrial setting. Typical of this line of thought, Etzioni (1969) and Hughes (1965) emphasized the contrast between a professional's need for autonomy and freedom to innovate or take risks without undue fear of failure and the hierarchical administrative authority structure of most organizations. A contrary, and what appears to be a minority opinion, is offered by Lipartito and Miranti (1998) to the effect that, rather than serving to corrupt professional values, corporations have actually enhanced the development and status of many occupations. I return to this view shortly.

Values Issues

Kornhauser (1962) found that there are four areas of values conflict that may be expected between industrial scientists and engineers and the large organizations that employ them, and I believe they are potentially relevant for I-O psychologists as well. First is the conflict between the scientists' adherence to professional and scientific objectives and standards and the organization's continuous demands for productivity and profitable developments. For example, the organization's standards for evaluating the effectiveness of a popular pilot project (e.g., initiation of a "flex-time" work schedule) might be very different from those of a conscientious I-O psychologist. Kornhauser outlined the quandary for the professional:

> Opposition to professional expertise is illustrated by the client's impatience with the niceties of professional procedure. The consequence is pressure to evade that procedure in order to get immediate results or operational ease rather than technical perfection. Professional autonomy clashes with the client's desire to exercise control over actions that vitally affect his [sic] interests. *When the client is also the employer, the conflict often is severe … .*
>
> If professions seek to accommodate internal strivings and external pressures by lowering standards, they dilute their values. If, on the other hand, professions respond merely by conforming to their standards without finding ways of taking client and member interests into account, they run the risk of losing their effectiveness. (p. 2, emphasis added)

This potential strain between corporate and professional standards was brought to my attention by a former student of mine shortly after he began work for a very large multinational corporation. He was asked to continue the development of a *competency model* that had been initiated prior to his arrival on the job. Following some discussion with him of the situation, I was prompted to write the hypothetical discussion case presented in Box 9.1, which describes the situation. I offer it here, in the context of values conflict, without further comment.

BOX 9.1 ORGANIZATIONAL VERSUS PROFESSIONAL STANDARDS

You have been retained, at a very attractive salary, by a large multinational corporation with headquarters in the United States to develop and implement a worldwide talent management program for executive development. It is based on a model of corporate leadership that was developed before you were hired. You shortly learn that this "model" consists merely of: (a) rather abstract, undefined or poorly defined platitudes—e.g., "does what it takes," "dynamic people-manager;" (b) positive stereotypes—e.g., "smarts," "trustworthy," "passion to win," "fires up people;" and (c) undefined outcome indicators, with no hint of how those outcomes ought to be achieved—e.g., "does what it takes," "world-class business manager."

You learn that this model was developed entirely from interviews with approximately 20 very senior executives and essentially fails to meet much of what you have learned about doing good applied organizational research—e.g., no behavioral representation of what is meant by these attributes was developed, nor how they may be achieved; no representative sampling was conducted nor any investigation of possible differences in requisite attributes as a function of level or functional area in the organization; no exploration was undertaken of possible national or cultural differences in effective leadership behavior across countries, or other possible context effects; there has been no confirmation that these attributes in fact are related empirically to effective leadership; and there is an emphasis on dispositional attributes unlikely to be amenable to the ostensible goal of the program, which is the *development* of mid-level and senior managers.

Upon reflection it appears that the only positive contribution that might be made by this project is the relatively minor one of providing a common vocabulary for managers to use in describing or evaluating other managers irrespective of whether that vocabulary stands for anything useful. Yet, an enormous investment in resources is planned for this development program. You realize the fallaciousness of the enterprise, based as it is on unsophisticated and unprofessional HR research, and you feel that you ought to say something to your superiors—after all, what did they hire you for if not for your expertise? But you're new to the job, the salary and perks are all you dreamed of, senior management seems committed to this program, and who are you to rock the boat? On the other hand, you have considerable misgivings about participating in the implementation of a very expensive program based on such shoddy organizational research. You have said to yourself, wouldn't the company save a lot of wasted money and effort and derive much positive benefit if you could get them to do it correctly? What will you do?

Control Issues

The second area of potential conflict concerns the nature of control over the scientists' work. "Control over work performance is of course the basic prize over which occupation and administration contend in particular work settings" (Freidson, 1973, p. 33). In many organizations the work is arranged based on rational principles of hierarchical administration that may not be the most effective for facilitating scientific creativity. Supervision may be a significant problem. The reliance on formal organizational authority, as opposed to technical expertise and professional autonomy, represents a major clash of normative expectations (Bledstein, 1976). In general, "professionals feel that only members of one's profession are capable of judging one's work" (Edwards et al., 1981, p. 126). For example, many I-O psychologists in corporations, who are engaged in sophisticated technical applications (e.g., test validation, the evaluation of training programs, theory-based work reorganization, and other organization development interventions) report to managers of human resources who are not psychologists. These administrators usually have no training in research methodology, and all too frequently have even had careers outside the sphere of human resources. Achieving an appropriate understanding and evaluation of the professional I-O psychologist's performance may be a daunting task under those circumstances. However, the opinion expressed by Edwards et al. may be only partially correct—truer with respect to process than outcome. A patient may not be able to judge the skillfulness of a surgeon's technique, but frequently they will have some postoperative indications of whether the surgery has been successful. Similarly, neither the human resources nor the line managers of a manufacturing company may be able to judge the quality of the selection test validation study or team-building intervention implemented by an I-O psychologist, but they will probably be able to evaluate in the first instance whether there has been an improvement in the quality, productivity or longevity of new hires and whether, in the second instance there has been a decline in intergroup conflict (assuming those were the objectives).

This view of the large, nonprofessional employing organization as constraining the professional's expected autonomy, leading to interpersonal and organizational conflict, has been the dominant model guiding research in the area. The research has tended to confirm that professionals working in highly formal or bureaucratic organizations are indeed less likely to perceive themselves as autonomous and more likely to experience role conflict (e.g., Engel, 1970; Organ & Greene, 1981). However, research has also indicated that the organizational structure variables are not the only significant antecedents; the outcomes also depend on the nature of the professionals' psychological identifications. Those who, in fact, have a high bureaucratic (i.e., organizational) orientation, irrespective of whether they may also have a high professional orientation, are likely to be high in job satisfaction (Sorenson & Sorenson, 1974) and experience less role conflict and alienation than those who identify strongly with their profession (Greene, 1978).[5] Greene also found that the two factors interact: The most dysfunctional reactions were experienced by those who identified with their profession (senior scientists and engineers) and were in more formalized organizational settings.

Motivation

The third area of likely conflict identified by Kornhauser (1962) relates to differences in the incentive systems between the scientific community and the organization. Professional recognition for scientific accomplishment is achieved in the world or national community of one's disciplinary colleagues, whereas organizational recognition is achieved locally by advancement within it.

> The organization expects its members to be local in orientation, with loyalty to the organization and its purposes, but the scientist is cosmopolitan in that his [sic] rewards and references are in the wider scientific community. For the cosmopolitan, advancement in the local organization may not be an attractive incentive.
>
> *(Hall, 1975, p. 104)*

Confirming this aspect of the scientist versus practitioner split, I-O psychology practitioners tend to feel that the research published in our journals has little impact on what they do in their organizations, and they are not rewarded for publishing research and so don't do it much (Campion et al., 1986; Sackett, 1986; Sackett et al., 1986). The issue of knowledge transfer between academe and professional practice has been a perennial problem (Rynes et al., 2001).

Decision-Making

The fourth source of potential tension stems from the decision-making authority residing in the organizational hierarchy, including dominion over the scientists' activities. Organizational criteria (e.g., rapidity, marketability, productivity) are the controlling factors, not scientific standards (e.g., statistical effect sizes and internal validity of a program's effects or their generalizability). In a very real sense, higher-level managers determine the meaningfulness of the professional's work to the organization; the professional may have very little influence in that regard. It is true that in many instances the scientist can acquire such influence by

5   Professional and organizational identification have been found to be orthogonal (i.e., independent) orientations. Respondents are typically categorized as having a professional identification (high on professional but low on organizational identification), an organizational identification (high on organizational and low on professional identification), a mixed orientation (high on both), or as being indifferent (low on both).

advancement up the managerial hierarchy, but that may be at the cost of relinquishing the role of scientist and technical competence as the basis for authority. And not all professionals have the motivations to express power and influence and the needs for dominance and upward mobility that tend to distinguish those who aspire to management positions (Mael et al., 2001). Moreover, the ultimate scope of managerial responsibility may be limited to the administration of the professional department. The professional may lack sufficient knowledge and experience of the organization's core business to achieve significant policy-making responsibilities beyond that restricted domain.

Intellective Orientation

Hughes (1965) added a fifth source of tension that is compatible with Kornhauser's (1962) analysis. He spoke of the professional's relative detachment from the specifics of a particular case in the sense of having much greater interest in understanding all such cases. It is this interest and curiosity that leads to greater comprehension. In contrast, the organization is generally much more focused on specific actionable instances. "Great corporations, too, although they may seek men [sic] who know the science of management, want an executive's curiosity about and love of the universal aspects of human organization tempered with a certain loyalty and commitment to his employer" (Hughes, 1965, p. 6). This tension, and ultimate equilibrium, between the universal and the particular in a profession is an aspect of the relation between scientific theory and practice, as just noted, that characterizes almost all professions. Hughes observed that "many learned societies show strain between the intellectuals and the professionalizers" (p. 7)—which is largely what led to the formation of the Association for Psychological Science (APS) in reaction to the perceived "guild orientation" of the clinical practitioners who dominate the APA (cf. Hakel, 1988; Rosen, 1987). I return to this issue in Chapter 10, in a consideration of the paradigm of postmodernism in which, for epistemological reasons, little distinction is made between research and practice.

Responsibilities

I add a sixth source of tension and potential ethical dilemmas for the professional in organizations, one that is sometimes signified by the question "who is the client?" I refer to the dual ethical responsibilities professionals like I-O psychologists experience with respect to the individual employees of a client or employer organization who are the voluntary participants, respondents or "subject-matter experts" on which we rely, as distinct from the organization as a whole. The point to emphasize is that issues of professional ethics are frequently more complicated for us than personal ethics in that there are additional interests represented besides those of the actors and those immediately affected—in particular, the organization and those with whom it interacts, the profession, colleagues, and so on.

The Case of I-O Psychology

Kornhauser (1962) emphasized that these strains and conflicting values did not always lead to actual conflict between professional scientists and their employers: Accommodations are made on both sides. He devoted a chapter (albeit a short one) in his book to "adaptations of professions and organizations." The most salient adaptation to the strain between professional autonomy and bureaucratic control entails the creation of new roles for research administration. The organization develops higher-level positions for managers and directors of research who control general administrative policies (e.g., employee selection, compensation decisions and budget recommendations), whereas technical matters are decided closer to the level of the actual work, by the professionals themselves and lower-level research supervisors. This creates two or more career paths for scientists in the organization. However, there is not a great deal of overlap between scientific and managerial competencies, so the administrative path may not be viable or attractive for everyone. As already noted, commitment to a profession is generally intensive and lifelong. Moreover, organizations vary considerably in the extent to which they are willing to make structural accommodations such as this.

In contrast to Kornhauser's (1962) main thesis, a more optimistic note was sounded by Wallace (1995) who disputed the assumption of an inherently conflictual relation between professionals and large bureaucratic employing organizations. Wallace observed lawyers

> working under conditions in which they have retained control over the objectives of their work and participate in policy making and thus in helping direct their employing organization by making explicit their professional system of norms and values and by maintaining collegial and supportive ties .... [These] professionals in nonprofessional organizations have preserved autonomy and discretion over their work. (p. 247)

Not considered by Wallace, however, was the extent to which these findings may be uniquely characteristic of lawyers—who are interpreting the boundaries of legal business practice for their organizations—and not reflective of the job attributes of engineers, scientists or I-O psychologists.

But there is a more interesting observation to be made in this regard. It is my opinion (admittedly unencumbered by consideration of empirical data) that I-O psychologists in industry experience less strain and conflict of the types noted by Kornhauser and Hughes than do most other professionals similarly employed. There are several reasons why that is to be expected. First, as human resource professionals I-O psychologists generally work for HR managers who are likely to be sensitive to the potential conflicts and other HR issues under consideration here. Notwithstanding that many HR managers have not trained professionally for their current assignments, they are probably more attuned to these matters than is true for managers of other professional groups in engineering, finance, legal, information systems, or scientific research and development departments.

Second, as I-O psychologists, the substance of our education and training includes the very organizational, structural, managerial and leadership concerns at issue. Therefore, we are probably better informed and ready to deal with these matters than most other professional and scientific groups. Third, the explicit adoption and salience of the scientist–practitioner model in I-O psychology (Latham, 2001) may account for a reduced sense of antagonism between cosmopolitan versus local professional orientations.

Fourth, I-O psychologists are directly *useful* to organizations—and perceived by management to be so (Feinberg & Lefkowitz, 1962; Ronen, 1980; Tiffin, 1956)—because the professional practice that constitutes our work activities are largely defined by the needs of the organization. Much of what we do in organizations concerns the necessary nuts-and-bolts activities of employee selection and managerial assessment, performance appraisal, training and development, job analysis and competency modeling, and so on (Campion et al., 1986; Rassenfos, & Kraut, 1988). Even professional practice in the "O" side of the field (e.g., in organization analysis, design and development) is aimed at the pragmatic objective of enhancing organizational effectiveness. This additional dimension of professional practice has historically been a major distinction between I-O psychology and those of our sister social scientists in sociology and anthropology, who study organizations but who are less frequently employed in organizations. Even more important and commensurate with our career choices and participation in organizations, it is likely that I-O psychologists have a strong organizational orientation and identification, which has been found to attenuate potential professional—organizational conflict (Greene, 1978; Sorenson & Sorenson, 1974).

But perhaps even more important, it may be that I-O psychology is one of those professions that, according to Lipartito and Miranti (1998), have flourished by virtue of their integration into modern business systems:

> Some historical models equate the rise of professionalization with the middle class's desire to escape corporate control of its labor. Historically, professions offered an enticing middle ground between independent proprietor and corporate employee. Here the conflict between business and profession is explicit. Professionals seek to avoid corporate supervision and to preserve their autonomy in socializing their expertise ... .

> [But] many occupations, in fact, have risen in status precisely because of their function in the modern business system. These include the older professions of law, engineering, and accountancy, and such newer professions as advertising, public relations, and management. (p. 302)

Those professions, consequently, may be expected to exhibit fewer and less extreme values conflicts with business organizations than others do. This is commensurate with Bell's (1985) views:

> Where organization and profession share similar values, as with physicians in hospitals or social workers in welfare agencies, conflicts probably affect the direction of organizational policy only marginally. The effects on policy are more important where professional values diverge sharply from organizational purposes .... From the standpoint of professional autonomy, all organizational hierarchies that attempt to routinize work are similarly threatening. But the threat to substantive professional values ... is less radical where organizational purposes and professional values are closely related. (p. 22)

I believe that I-O psychology generally fits the model of professions that Lipartito and Miranti and Bell have in mind. It is also my opinion that individual I-O psychologists who have opted to pursue an organizational career commonly share the perspectives and values that characterize organizations and their managerial hierarchies. This is probably less true, for example, of the biologists, chemists, and physicists who work in industry. (Obviously, to the extent that these reflections have any veracity at all, they are generalizations that cannot be expected to characterize every individual.) Nevertheless, interviews with particularly successful organizational I-O practitioners—those with high earnings—revealed them to have more of a business than scientific orientation, to be socially compatible with successful businesspeople, and to be unconflicted about the acquisition of wealth as a legitimate objective (Greller, 1984). In fact, it was "not uncommon for a high earner to say, 'I used to be an I-O psychologist,'" reflecting greater identification with the enterprise than with the profession" (p. 56). I-O psychologists, especially those in administrative positions, consistently remain the highest-paid psychology specialization (APA, 2000, 2010b, 2017c).

Succinctly, then, I-O psychologists employed in large organizations probably experience less strain and fewer conflicts than many other types of professionals in organizations because we tend to have personal values that are more congruent with those of the corporation and its managers, and our domain of expertise encompasses important aspects of organizational policies, systems, and procedures. This compatibility is a consequence of the long-standing integration of the field into the modern business world (the psychologist Walter Dill Scott wrote *The Psychology of Advertising* in 1902) and has in no small measure contributed to the success of I-O psychology as an occupation and career choice. However, as suggested in Chapter 12, there is a negative aspect of this integration. I believe that the embrace of business objectives and corporate values has not been without cost: much of our ethical and humanistic heritage from psychology has been abandoned. However, this characterization may not be unique to I-O psychology:

In addition to the traditional categories of professions, modern corporate life creates new ones. The systems analyst, the marketing specialist, the labor negotiator, the management theorist, and the public relations expert are necessary ingredients in the modern corporate success formula. These new professionals possess most of the traditional characteristics associated with professions: they rely on a theoretical store of knowledge, are graduated from research-oriented institutions, apply their knowledge to practical problems, and subject their work to review and criticism from colleagues.

Many of the new "technocratic" professions, however, lack a key characteristic associated with traditional professions. With the professions of medicine, law, or teaching, we associate a spirit of altruism or service; but the new technocratic professions often lack this characteristic and thus raise special problems of moral responsibility. We associate the goal of healing with the physician, and of knowledge with the professor (no matter how mercenary doctors or professors may be in fact), yet there are no corresponding goals for the marketing specialist, the public relations manager, or the advertising expert. The standards of the new professional do not explicitly include moral standards, in part because his or her profession does not recognize an altruistic element in its overall goals. The old professions have frequently failed to apply the moral standards articulated in statements of their professional goals; but the new professions fail, it seems, because they do not even attempt to articulate moral standards.

(Donaldson, 1982, p. 113)

So, we should challenge ourselves with the following question: Is I-O psychology more akin to the minimally moral new "technocratic professions" referred to by Donaldson than to the traditional professions in which responsibility and service to society at large are major value components? The question will be taken up in Chapter 12, but before doing so two faults in Donaldson's presentation should be noted. First, the failure to articulate an explicit morality should not be equated with an amoral posture. Most individuals, for example, try to lead an essentially moral existence without necessarily having articulated an ethical code for guidance. Second, his assertion contrasts the moral professions against the newer professions that serve corporate objectives, as if corporations were entirely or essentially amoral enterprises. Thus, a most relevant question becomes, what is the moral status of business—especially large and enormously powerful corporations? What, if any, is their moral justification? That is the underlying theme of Chapter 11. But a preliminary issue to be dealt with concerns the extent and nature of values in the profession and science of psychology, which is considered in Chapter 10.

Adding Further to the Framework for Ethical Decision Making

25. It can reasonably be inferred that a number of social and ethical obligations accrue to I-O psychologists by virtue of the status of our field as a profession. Professional status means that, in many respects, society views what we do as important, defers to our expertise in appropriate areas, and gives us considerable latitude with respect to determining the qualifications to enter the profession and regulate its practice. In return, we are expected to behave as professionals—responsibly and with integrity—and to utilize our expertise for the benefit of the entire society, not only our direct clients. (This does not imply that the two aims are necessarily incompatible, although at times they may be.)

26. Some I-O psychologists work in settings in which they may not have regular contact with professional colleagues (e.g., as solo practitioners or in relatively small organizations) and so may feel relatively isolated when faced with an ethical difficulty. The worst thing to do under those circumstances is to remain isolated. The advice of professional friends and colleagues, mentors, or former professors should be sought. The ethics committee of the APA also welcomes advisory inquiries.

27. The sociological study of the professions has revealed several areas of potential conflict between professionals employed in large hierarchical organizations and structural or administrative features of those organizations. I have speculated that there are several reasons why that is less likely to be the case for I-O psychologists than for other professional groups. Chief among those reasons is that I-O psychology historically has been functionally integrated into the administration of the business and that I-O psychologists tend to "self-select" from a population that has an organizational orientation marked by values compatible with those of the corporate enterprise. A warning note is sounded, however, insofar as those values may not always be compatible with the broader obligations owed by professionals to the society that supports their professional status. The way in which these potential conflicts are resolved or averted may give rise to other values conflicts and attendant ethical issues that, as suggested in Chapter 12, are not well recognized in our field.

10

THE CONTENTIOUS ROLE OF VALUES IN PSYCHOLOGY

> The commitment of professionals to the values central to their professions is what leads society to grant them—individually and collectively—the authority and resources to pursue those values in the service of others … . it is the profession's core values that both anchor and trigger the virtues and duties expected of its members … . The very essence, then, of being a professional, and not just acting as one, is understanding and committing to the spirit as well as to the letter of the profession's values and ethical prescriptions.
>
> —Gellerman, Frankel and Ladenson

It is worth noting that Gellerman et al. (1990) are organizational psychologists.

At the same time as the organizational psychologists Gellerman et al. (1990) were alerting their colleagues to the critical nature of professional values (as expressed in the epigram above), I was attempting for the first time to deliver a similar message regarding the faults and deficiencies of I-O psychology's professional values model (Lefkowitz, 1990; cf. Chap. 12). As was done in chapter 8, I believe the most effective way of introducing the topic of this chapter is also anecdotally… …

In 1951 a young African-American social psychologist at the City College of New York, Kenneth B. Clark, was asked by the National Association for the Advancement of Colored People's (NAACP) Legal Defense and Education Fund (LDEF) to chair a committee of social scientists who would write a legal brief in support of the NAACP–LDEF's lawsuit against the Topeka, Kansas, Board of Education. The social science statement they prepared, *The Effects of Segregation and the Consequences of Desegregation,* played an instrumental role in the Supreme Court's unanimous decision on May 17, 1954, favoring the plaintiffs in *Brown v. Board of Education of Topeka* (347 U.S. 483), which (eventually) led to the desegregation of

DOI: 10.4324/9781003212577-12

public schools in the United States (Jackson, 1998).[1] The content of the statement consisted of a review of the social science literature which led to their conclusions that (a) there were no differences between the races in the ability to learn; (b) legally segregated education caused psychological damage to African-American children; and (c) desegregation could be implemented relatively smoothly, even in the South.

The account of the committee's work is replete with descriptions of how they tried "to maintain the persona of objective scientific expert while writing for the ultimate adversarial forum—a Supreme Court hearing" (Jackson, 1998, p. 150). The final version of the statement begins:

> The problem of the segregation of racial and ethnic groups constitutes one of the major problems facing the American people today. It seems desirable, therefore, to summarize the contributions which contemporary social science can make toward its resolution. *There are, of course, moral and legal issues involved with respect to which the signers of the present statement cannot speak with any special authority* and which must be taken into account in the solution of the problem. *There are, however, also factual issues involved with respect to which certain conclusions seem to be justified on the basis of the available scientific evidence. It is with these issues only that this paper is concerned.*
>
> *(Cited in Jackson, p. 151, emphases added)*

The italicized portions of the preceding quotation express the concern of these psychologists over the extent to which their views would be perceived as related as much to their personal and social values as to their appraisal of objective scientific evidence.

The view that there is a clear division between values and scientific facts is both an assumption regarding the nature of science (its subject matter, aims, conduct and products) as well as an implicit value statement regarding that nature—that is, that science *ought* to be distinct from values issues. A considered statement of this traditional perspective was offered recently by Ferguson (2015), in the context of psychology's public image (cf. Chap. 14):

> Perhaps one of the bigger challenges for academic psychology is the dual role that psychology often finds for itself in advocating for human welfare while at the same time attempting to find objective scientific facts. This duality is not surprising given that many of the subjects open to scientific psychology touch upon concerns related to psychological wellness, social justice, and public policy…. I propose that mixing science with advocacy almost inevitably ends in damage to the objectivity of the former. (p. 532–533)

---

1 One may feel compelled to pause and reflect on the current state of public education in the U.S., and that the supreme court decision was almost 70 years ago.

But that view is no longer unanimous among philosophers of science or among natural and social scientists, including psychologists. And the general issue has a rather long history—beyond even Max Weber's founding of the German Society for Sociology in 1909 based on *wertfreie wissenschaft*, value-free science (cf. Winston, 2011 for a historical review). Also, the reader may recall Hume's Law (Chap. 2; mid–18th century), indicating that facts (i.e., science) cannot tell us anything about morality (i.e., values); we cannot deduce *ought* from *is*.

Moreover, the issue is not as simple as refraining from social advocacy. One's personal and social values don't need to be voiced openly as opinions to be expressed and to shape one's work. They come out in more subtle, implicit and sometimes biasing ways. (This perspective is developed further in chapter 12, re I-O psychology.) Knowing that, the issue becomes one of striving for truth and transparency. That is why I started off by acknowledging in chapter 1 that my own values "have influenced the content of this book—in choice of topics, opinions expressed, what I have criticized, what I have lauded, and how they impact my ethical analyses. But I have tried to make those values explicit ... and thereby subject to scrutiny."[2]

The issue is an integral component of a much larger and more complex controversy. For the sake of exposition, I have segmented the controversy into three facets, but they are highly interrelated; only with some difficulty have I been able to discuss them separately. The first, as just illustrated, is the issue of the relation between science and values. The second facet consists of whether the "inquiry paradigm" (Guba & Lincoln, 1994) of *logical positivism*, which served natural science so well that it was adopted wholeheartedly by psychology, is adequate for achieving a meaningful understanding of human beings or should be replaced by (or supplemented with) the *postmodern* paradigm.[3] Third is the matter of the relation between research and practice within the profession of psychology.

2   Interestingly, the same issue has bedeviled journalism and journalists since the 1920s, when the attempt to make journalism "scientific" was introduced (Smith, 2021). In contrast, some realized that "excessive fealty to its own traditional notions of balance and objectivity" had actually distorted the reality being reported (Berger, 1979, p. B4).

3   The term *paradigm* was introduced by Thomas Kuhn (1996) in the first edition of his book *The Structure of Scientific Revolutions*. He defined the term narrowly as a concrete model of the fundamentals of a scientific field, consisting of a set of "rules and standards for scientific practice" (p. 11) that account for the shared consensus and commitment of those in the field. In the third edition, he discussed definitional problems of the earlier editions and referred to those matters as a "disciplinary matrix." I use paradigm in its somewhat looser and more popular version in which it is defined as a set of basic beliefs that deals with the nature of the world (Guba & Lincoln, 1994). Similarly, Stricker (1997) summarized: "Thus, a paradigm ... encompasses the whole disciplinary matrix that surrounds a theory, including an epistemological framework, a corpus of knowledge, a means of generating and understanding that information, a set of values, and possibly even a worldview" (p. 443).

It is sometimes the case that those who declaim against the inappropriate intrusion of what appear to them to be social values into what ought to be objective and value-free scientific inquiry are simply objecting to the expression of values different from their own. That happens because sometimes we fail to recognize or acknowledge the value assumptions implicit in our own thinking, research and practice. An interesting example of this dynamic is the disparaging comments made by Henry E. Garrett, chair of the Psychology Department at Columbia University in the 1940s and 1950s, about Kenneth Clark and the other social scientists whose work was relied on by the Supreme Court in *Brown v. Board of Education*. Not so coincidentally, Garrett was a strong advocate of segregationist beliefs and helped organize an international group of scholars dedicated to "preventing race mixing, preserving segregation, and promoting the principles of early 20th century eugenics and 'race hygiene'" (Benjamin & Crouse, 2002, p. 45, quoting historian A. Winston).

Science and Values

The Positivist Paradigm

The science of psychology was modeled after the natural sciences of the 17th to 19th centuries in the tradition of *logical positivism* and empiricism as the only fruitful way to uncover reality, truth or the facts. The natural science model is predicated on the objective, unbiased and dispassionate ("tough-minded") search for truth, which is defined in terms of impartial scientific facts. "The essential position of positivism is that humans can, with the help of the tools of science, gain true knowledge of a reality that exists outside of human thought. Implied in the belief that formal procedures of science will produce a progressively accurate picture of reality are the notions that other modes of reasoning are inadequate for generating valid knowledge" (Hoshmand & Polkinghorne, 1992, p. 56). Raw data are to be collected in an objective manner so that it is of no consequence which scientist collects them (assuming all are equally competent), and it is assumed that the process of data collection does not appreciably alter the phenomena under study. Moreover, the only determinants of the problems to be studied and the means of studying them are theoretical relevance and methodological rigor, respectively. Thus, science is conceived to be "value-free." This traditional "value-free ideal" (Douglas, 2009) is argued on behalf of psychology by Kendler (1993, 1999) who referred to the "unbridgeable chasm between facts and values" (1999, p. 829) and who asserted "science's incapacity to identify what is good or bad" (1999, p. 832).

But rarely specified are the ethical implications of strict adherence to this model when applied to the study of human beings—e.g., the consequences of treating research participants essentially as a physical scientist treats inanimate objects. The participants have no voice in deciding what is to be investigated, in what manner, or how the results are to be interpreted, disseminated or used. A more nuanced view, especially pertinent here, is voiced by Kurtines et al. (1990): "although debate over values is an integral part of all scientific discourse, it plays a more explicit role in fields within the human sciences (e.g., anthropology, psychology, sociology, etc.) that touch on moral phenomena" (p. 283).

A complicating feature of psychology is that it has been comprised, almost from its inception, of two aspects: scientific research and the application of psychological knowledge and techniques for the betterment of humanity. The preamble of the APA's (2017) *Ethical Principles of Psychologists and Code of* Conduct indicates that psychologists' "goal is to broaden knowledge of behavior and where appropriate, to apply it pragmatically to improve the condition of both the individual and society." The latter objective is exemplified by the subfields of clinical, counseling, educational, and I-O psychology, among many other applications as well (Deutsch, 1969; Mays, 2000; Miller, 1969; Tyler, 1973). "From the beginning, the American expression of psychology has contained a strong utilitarian component. More than our European counterparts, we have asked what uses can be made of knowledge about human function" (Peterson, 1991, p. 422). There continues to be a general acceptance that part of the profession of psychology includes applying our knowledge to complex societal problems to further social justice (Vasquez, 2012). Consequently, "despite the positive outcomes derived from political activism, many psychologists have struggled with how to advocate for social justice while maintaining their professional responsibilities and ethical boundaries" (Nadal, 2017, p. 935).

These two facets of psychology correspond to two conflicting views of education—knowledge for its own sake and learning in order to produce good citizens and a good society—that have been traced back to Socrates and the Sophists, respectively (Furedy & Furedy, 1982). William James (1907) labeled these as "tough-minded" versus "tender-minded" outlooks, and Luria (1976), who viewed them as ethical principles, referred to them as "the ethic of knowledge" and the "ethic of innocence" (p. 332). Leona Tyler (1973) observed that disparaging characterizations like "do-gooder" have often been applied to those "who were mainly interested in what psychology could do to help people and improve the human condition" (p. 1021).

Constructive proponents of the traditional view believe that only by adhering to the separation of science and humanistic values can the former serve to promote the latter. That is because it is only the value-neutral, unbiased and objectively determined facts that can putatively be used legitimately and justified publicly as bases for informed social policy (Kendler, 1993). In other words, a two-step process is called for: the production of relevant but impartial empirical data and a separate exploration of its implications for society. Otherwise, what passes for scientific knowledge may easily be dismissed as mere personal, social or political preferences of the particular scientist–advocates involved. It is in this context that we understand the difficulties faced by Kenneth Clark and the social science committee members who prepared the NAACP–LDEF brief in the early 1950s. In the subsequent opinion of some psychologists (cf. Gerard, 1983), the failure of de jure school desegregation to have increased the educational success of minority children in the United States to the extent anticipated is due to the inadequacy of our knowledge regarding the complicated issues that constitute the problem and how to solve it. Gerard suggested that, in their interpretation of the available research evidence and the attendant optimistic predictions for de-segregation, the committee members were overly influenced by their personal values and well-meaning intentions.

That may or may not be true; we can't know; it's a very inferential conclusion. But the argument overlooks a related important issue. Is Gerard, and similar-minded critics, saying that the scientist, even (or perhaps especially) the social scientist can't also be an advocate for social policy? Advocacy is "any activity which communicates work in a way that expresses a judgment about what social effects the research might have, and especially if it is communicated to non-scientists … . There is the danger that scientists with political ties will interpret data in ways that independent scientists would not. One proposed solution is to make science autonomous" (Brister, 2014, p. 23, 24). She goes on, however, to observe that that solution is impossible because "science is interdependent with the public sector in numerous ways" (p. 24). She espouses the view, also adopted here, that "although bias is of concern, normativity also plays an important and inevitable role in science … . [and that] since scientists are citizens, too, it would be an unfair burden that they withdraw from forms of civic life" (p. 24, 25).

The traditional positivist argument against the representation of humanistic or social values in the scientific enterprise ideally entails the exclusion of *all* values from the domain of scientific enquiry. But that classical empiricist tradition from the natural sciences, in particular the fact–value dichotomy, has been under siege for a long time. Almost 100 years ago, the great American pragmatist John Dewey pointed out that data are infused with implied values: we don't just passively, disinterestedly, discover neutral facts; they are actively chosen for purposes of "affording signs or evidence to define and locate a problem, and thus give a clew [sic] to its resolution" (Dewey, 1929, p. 178).

More recent critics have charged that the positivist view represents an over-simplified erroneous view of the nature of scientific knowledge and process; regardless of its worth as a model (i.e., whether it might be a worthy ideal for which to strive), it does not—never has—accurately characterized actual scientific research. Values do affect people's research (Elliott, 2014). "Developments in philosophy of science … have challenged the assumption of the value neutrality of science. The result has been a growing consensus that science is not and cannot be value free" (Kurtines, et al., 1990, p. 283). Some go so far as to suggest that "the naive positivist position of the sixteenth through the nineteenth centuries is no longer held by anyone even casually acquainted with these problems [i.e., the critiques noted over the past several decades]" (Guba & Lincoln, 1994, p. 116).

The Role of Values in Science

For quite some time now, a persuasive case has been made for the relatively unacknowledged reality that all scientific research is value-laden (Feyerabend, 1975;
Kuhn, 1977; Schwartz, 1990; Szasz, 1970; Toulmin, 1973) to the extent that many
scholars believe that "the controversy is no longer about *whether* values influence
scientific practice, but rather about *how* values are embedded in and shape scientific
practice" (Howard, 1985, p. 255; also Kurtines, et al., 1990). This view is commensurate with those of philosophers of science such as Rorty (1979) and Popper
(1972). Although Popper's aim is not essentially antipositivist, he pointed out that
reality, truth or "objective knowledge" (the title of his book) does not reside in the
physical world of so-called "facts," as is maintained by "the commonsense theory of
knowledge" (p. 63) advanced by the positivists and empiricists. Instead, it "consists
of the logical content of our theories, conjectures, [and] guesses" (p. 73). And all
knowledge, including even the "subjective knowledge" of our conscious experiences such as the "knowledge of self" depends on these theoretical formulations.
According to Popper this world of our theories, although a human construction,
nevertheless is real, as demonstrated by their effects on the physical world (e.g., the
manifestations or applications of atomic theory, economic theory, reinforcement
theory or goal-setting theory, et al.).[4]

Science, therefore, does not consist in the accumulation of facts but in the
"invention of ever new theories, and the indefatigable examination of their
power to throw light on experience" (Popper, 1972, p. 361). This "examination"
consists in the definition of a problem situation, the formulation of a tentative
theoretical interpretation, a critical investigation that leads to the elimination of
mistaken notions, and the reformulation of the problem; and the process of
"conjecture and refutation" is repeated. Thus, theories are never proven true or
even confirmed in any absolute or even probabilistic sense by research; they can
only be disconfirmed. The search for truth is "the critical search for what is false
in our various competing theories" (p. 319).

In addition, the observations we make to test our possible explanations—by
means of the process of conjecture and refutation—are always (as Dewey pointed out
many years earlier) *selective,* that is, determined by our definition of the problem and
tentative theoretical explanations. Thus, one of the implications of Popper's work is
the realization that knowledge or truth does not lie in "objective facts": empirical
data are not independent of the theoretical perspective(s) within which they are
generated. As revealed by the physicist Fritjof Capra (cited in Howard, 1985):

> Human consciousness plays a crucial role in the process of observation, and
> in atomic physics *determines to a large extent the properties of the observed*

4 See the "Comment" in the American *Psychologist* by Champion (1985) for a succinct
review of the relevance of Popper's work to psychology.

phenomena … . The crucial feature of quantum theory is that the observer is not only necessary to observe the properties of the atomic phenomenon, but is necessary even to bring about these properties. *My conscious decision about how to observe, say, an electron will determine the electron's properties to some extent. If I ask a particle question, it will give me a particle answer; if I ask it a wave question, it will give me a wave answer.*

(p. 259, emphases added)

Moreover, as Bronowski (1960) noted,

What we have really seen happen is the breakdown of the plain model of a world outside ourselves where we simply look on and observe … . For relativity derives essentially from the philosophic analysis which insists that there is not a fact and an observer but a joining of the two in an observation. This is the fundamental unit of physics: The actual observation. And this is what the principle of uncertainty showed in atomic physics: That *event and observer are not separable.*

(pp. 83–84, emphasis added)

In addition to the interdependence of observer, theories and data (i.e., "facts"), a related implication of Popper's position is "the underdetermination of theory" (Guba & Lincoln, 1994): "Not only are facts determined by the theory window through which one looks for them, but different theory windows might be equally well supported by the same set of 'facts.' Although it may be possible, given a coherent theory, to derive by deduction what facts ought to exist, it is never possible, given a coherent set of facts, to arrive by induction at a single, ineluctable theory" (p. 107). In other words, contrary to the traditional positivist view, facts do not "speak for themselves."

Therefore, to summarize, not only do scientists choose problem situations and tentative explanations of them based on personal considerations (interest, curiosity, fashion, the likelihood of success, etc.); but the facts observed have no knowable state of privileged existence apart from the process of human observation, which is theory directed; and scientists also choose among competing alternative theories on bases other than merely the data. This latter decision process is generally conducted (at least in part—hopefully in great measure) based on criteria that reflect scientific values (Spence, 1985).

Scientific Values

Scientific values are also referred to as *epistemic values* (Howard, 1985) or *cognitive values* (Laudan, 1984) and it must be acknowledged that the scientific process is laden with these value judgments. Howard discussed five widely agreed-upon value criteria by which scientific theories are evaluated and suggested the possible inclusion of at least five more. These include the degree of *predictive accuracy* enabled by the theory; its *internal coherence;* its *external consistency* or the degree to which it fits with better-established theories; its *unifying power,* i.e., the theory's capability of integrating disparate knowledge; *fertility* or heuristic value in extending our base of knowledge; *simplicity* or parsimony; *testability; potential falsifiability;* the *reproducibility of experiments;* and *measurement accuracy.*

Thus, even in the physical and natural sciences subjectivity is extensive. Not only are data ("facts") dependent on theory and the observer, and theories underdetermined by data, but the choice of theory is based on subjective normative evaluations of epistemic values. And there may be considerable differences among scientists in the relative weighting and application of these criteria, and others—e.g., what standards of evidence are sufficient to accept a hypothesis, and on which to base a policy decision; what level of risks are acceptable (as in biomedical research) (Pelley, 2014). It follows, therefore, that the very bases by which we endow scientific knowledge with a privileged status—these epistemic values—rest on subjective value judgments. "The objectivity of sciences must be understood as emanating from a nexus of judgmental presuppositions, and the efficacy of the entire enterprise is a function of the adequacy of those fundamental assumptive stances" (Howard, 1985, p. 258). In *The Sociology of Science* Merton (1973) articulated four scientific norms that give institutional and public expression to these epistemic values: *universalism,* judging scientific endeavors by impersonal criteria, regardless of the personal attributes of the scientist; *communalism,* the sharing of scientific data; *disinterestedness,* disregarding one's personal opinions and values; and *organized* skepticism, subjecting all scientific findings to the strict scrutiny of replication, peer review, and so on.

The Practice of Scientific Research

Merton's (1973) norms exist not just in the scientific community. Supporting the value-free conceptualization of science has been the stereotypic image of scientists as dispassionate and neutral observers of natural phenomena that have little if any emotional meaning to them. As a corollary, the public image of the impassioned, driven researcher is likely to be associated with that of the "mad scientist" a la Drs. Jekyll and Frankenstein. However, Mahoney (1976) contrasted the prevalent "storybook image of the scientist" with the actuality of "the biased and passionate … impetuous truth spinner" (p. 6). The stereotype of the neutral observer/scientist has actually been debunked for quite some time. Platt (1964) pointed out that personal attachment to one's hypotheses affects one's research and leads to interpersonal conflicts among scientists rather than to a search for truth. Bevan (1980), for example, noted "Doing science is like running a race, and one's colleagues in the field can therefore only be viewed as strong competitors" (p. 780). If that characterization sounds overly dramatic, one need only recall the recent spectacle of peevish insults, charges, and countercharges traded by the two competing teams of genetic researchers racing to be the first to decode the human genome (Wade, 2001a, 2001b), confirming earlier conclusions that egocentric attributes color scientific research (Mahoney, 1976; Mitroff, 1974). Sociologists have also noted that personal norms and values influence the work of physical scientists at virtually all stages of the enterprise (Hagstrom, 1965; Merton, 1973). Mitroff went so far as to assert "There are very sound psychological reasons why [a scientific] inquirer *should* hold onto his convictions even though his colleagues believe the evidence is against him" (p. xi). The point has even been made that it has been those biases, rather than adherence to the empiricist ideal, that have accounted for the greatest scientific advances in the past (Feyerabend, 1963). Kessel (1969) put it this way:

> Persistence in the face of both contradictory facts and the disapproval of those committed to the prevailing paradigm, the intuitive apprehension of a reality as yet undiscovered, the altering of fundamental presuppositions by the creative act—these are all crucial elements in the progress of science, elements for which the classical conception has little, if any, room. (p. 1004)

Psychological research seems even more vulnerable than the natural sciences to the same sorts of personality quirks, belief systems and other subjective biases of the researcher (MacCoun, 1998; Suedfeld & Tetlock, 1991; Unger, 1983). Krasner and Houts (1984), Kimble (1984), and Lipsey (1974) documented that psychologists can be differentiated with respect to whether they identify primarily with the experimental, scientific and objective, i.e., "tough-minded" positivist or "postpositivist" (Guba & Lincoln, 1994) value position, or with the humanist position that is focused more on social concern and relevance to the solution of social problems.[5]

More important, however, is the realization that one's objectives, values and interests can surreptitiously (unconsciously) influence the scientific enterprise. For example, forensic psychologists can be biased according to which side of a court case retained them (Murrie et al., 2013); the findings of biomedical researchers can be influenced by whether their studies were industry-funded (Bekelman, et al., 2003; Lesser, et al., 2007); and, of special interest for us, among a sample of 138 criterion-related employee selection validation studies, those "concerned with EEO compliance and augmenting existing selection systems yielded significantly higher validities in comparison with those who simply wished to obtain a high validity" (Russell et al., 1994, p. 167).

---

5 *Postpositivism* or *neopositivism*, in contrast with the positivism of prior centuries, is not value-free insofar as epistemic values are acknowledged as intrinsic to the scientific enterprise. It retains the reliance on empirical methods as the accepted path to an understanding of external reality, but it concedes that the understanding will not be perfect and will be probabilistic not certain; theories and their hypotheses cannot be verified, only falsified.

Nonscientific Values

It seems rather clear that the bulk of respected scholarly thought in the natural and social sciences and the philosophy of science has eradicated any reasonable belief in the scientific enterprise as intrinsically objective and totally value-free. However, many of those who criticize the conflation of values and psychological science have in mind only the inappropriate intrusion of personal, social, political and moral values (as these *non-epistemic values* are expressed in the promotion of particular goals and social policies), not the epistemic values by which the adequacy of scientific research and theory are evaluated. The pragmatic question is whether such "intrusions" are preventable. For example, in the context of considering research on justice, Tetlock and Mitchell (1993) believe that "it is difficult, perhaps impossible, to avoid political and moral issues ... . The difficulty is especially great, in part, because of the passions evoked in the investigators ..." (p. 246). However, the paradigmatic question that should take precedence is whether such intrusions *should* be avoided. Or expressed another way, are they really intrusive? "Current debates revolve primarily around the question of whether nonepistemic values also have a legitimate role to play in activities at the very heart of scientific reasoning, such as the evaluation and justification of scientific claims" (Elliott, 2011, p. 304).

In any event, it seems reasonably clear that personal values and prejudices have always affected the way in which questions have been posed and data interpreted in social and behavioral science (Gould, 1981). In an underappreciated contribution to I-O psychology, McCall and Bobko (1990) observed "Although objective scientific method is meant to offset human subjectivity, there are many examples of objectivity actually abetting subjectivity. Rather than pretend that such value structures aren't there, they ought to be made more explicit, perhaps as part of the methodology itself" (p. 396). For example, more than 70 years ago Pastore (1949) showed that among scientists who were prominent in the nature–nurture controversy regarding the source of racial differences in tested IQ, advocacy of *either* a hereditarian or an environmentalist position was associated with one's general political attitudes, conservative or liberal, respectively. The scientists' opinions on the specific scientific question were reflective of their general world views.

Contemporary *neopositivist* or *postpositivist* psychologists might accept that nonepistemic values and other biasing factors are an unfortunate and unwanted fact of scientific life, but they are to be guarded against, uncovered and gradually weeded out of the scientific enterprise so that only the more legitimate epistemic values are left as determinants of our scientific progress. Some make a distinction between nonepistemic values that are acceptable when they serve only an indirect role in influencing standards of evidence, versus inappropriately influencing directly the scientific enterprise–i.e., when they serve as "reasons in themselves to accept a claim" (Douglas, 2009, p.96). For example, in this view it is perfectly acceptable for me to want to investigate the causes and consequences of injustice or inequity, but inappropriate for me to accept a set of putative causes because they fit my preconceived notions—unless I can describe the results objectively, and they are testable and replicable (D'Andrade, 1995).

MacCoun's (1998) excellent review discusses several prototypes of biased interpretation of scientific evidence, aside from fraud (the conscious intentional effort to fabricate, conceal or distort evidence).[6] These include *cold bias,* which is the unintentional and unconscious bias that may result from a variety of strategic and other cognitive factors, and *hot bias,* which is directionally motivated albeit unintentional and maybe even an unconscious reflection of a preferred outcome. For example, research on these sources of bias has produced a great deal of evidence indicating a *biased assimilation* effect—one's supposedly objective evaluation of scientific methodology and results is influenced strongly by one's initial views (e.g., evidence supporting a view contrary to one's own is evaluated more stringently). Which, if any, of these biases might be contributing to the fact that I-O psychologists employed in industry and concerned with complying with equal employment opportunity laws tend to produce higher selection test validities than their colleagues whose primary employment is in academia (Russell et al., 1994)? And what might be the mediating behaviors by which the motivational differences operate? "Does this suggest that, if two hypothetical investigators were asked to examine the same predictor–criterion relationship, they would conduct their research so differently that dissimilar criterion validities will result? Possibly" (Russell et al., 1994, p. 169).

Social Advocacy

Recall that the second of psychology's professional goals is "to improve the condition of individuals, organizations, and society" (APA, 2017). The process of attempting to accomplish that, as eloquently stated by Abraham Maslow (1969), unabashedly involves social advocacy in the service of those objectives and values that comprise such "improvements":

> It is now quite clear that the actualization of the highest human potentials is possible—on a mass basis—only under "good conditions." Or more directly, good human beings will generally need a good society in which to grow. Contrariwise, I think it should be clear that a normative philosophy of biology would involve the theory of the good society, defined in terms of "that society is good which fosters the fullest development of human potentials, of the fullest degree of humanness." (p. 726)

6 MacCoun's analysis is not concerned with the related topic of bias in the conduct of research, including such issues as research design, choice of study populations, statistical analyses, and the effects of experimenter sex or expectancies.

MacCoun (1998) included *advocacy,* "the selective use and emphasis of evidence to promote a hypothesis, without outright concealment or fabrication" (p. 268), as one of the prototypes of biased evidence processing in psychology. However, he concluded that "advocacy is normatively defensible provided that it occurs within an explicitly advocacy-based organization, or an explicitly adversarial system of disputing. Trouble arises when there is no shared agreement that such adversarial normative system is in effect" (p. 268). He went on to acknowledge that the widespread acceptance of the traditional public norms for scientists (Merton, 1973) "… surely doesn't preclude advocacy activities on the part of scientists, but it does mean that we must be quite explicit about which hat we are wearing when we speak out, and whether we are asserting our facts … or asserting our values …" (p. 280). Similarly, "policy-relevant scientific debates would be more productive and transparent if scientists disclosed their presumptions upfront, disclosed conflicts of interest, and clarified the pros and cons of multiple interpretations of the science" (Pelley, 2014, p. A192; also Kelman, 2021; Nadal, 2017).

Some may feel that Maslow's (1969) criterion of "the fullest development of human potentials" (p. 726) is an inadequate definition of the *good society* and that we lack direction on how to implement the humanitarian goal articulated by the APA. For example, "Although discussions about the role of values in psychology have become frequent in recent years, … there is still confusion about the moral obligations of psychologists" (Prilleltensky, 1997, p. 517). Prilleltensky suggested that the process of clarification will entail psychologists first articulating their individual and collective vision of the good life and the good society, and second, formulating ways of translating these visions into action. He articulated several values, assumptions and questions about professional practices as a moral framework for assessing different psychological approaches or paradigms. He advanced five values that should be promoted by psychology to live up to its moral obligations: (a) care and compassion for the physical and emotional wellbeing of others; (b) the ability of people to pursue their own goals (self-determination) while considering other people's needs; (c) respect and appreciation for diverse social groups; (d) citizens having meaningful input into decisions that affect their lives (collaboration and participation); and (e) fair and equitable allocation of bargaining powers, resources and obligations in society (distributive justice).

Similarly, Koocher and Keith-Spiegel (1998) synthesized from a number of sources a set of nine values or "core ethical principles that we believe should guide the behavior of psychologists" (p. 4): (a) non-maleficence (avoiding doing harm); (b) respecting autonomy; (c) beneficence (benefitting others); (d) being just, fair, and equitable; (e) being loyal and truthful; (f) according others dignity and respect; (g) treating others with caring and compassion; (h) maintaining professional competence and pursuing excellence; and (i) accepting accountability and responsibility for one's actions. Not surprising is the overlap between the two lists and their similarity to the three-dimensional structure of moral values based on the long history of moral philosophy and the short history of moral psychology: justice issues, welfare or caring, and moral virtue or character. They also incorporate core principles introduced earlier in the Framework for Ethical Decision Making: universalizability of judgments, universality of concern for all people, and enhancement of the quality of life, especially for those most in need. All these accounts of the moral domain coalesce nicely with the values reflected in the APA's (2017) ethical code. The five "general principles," which are meant to be aspirational goals "to guide and inspire psychologists toward the very highest ethical ideals of the profession," (p. 1062) are: beneficence and non-maleficence, fidelity and responsibility, integrity, justice, and respect for people's rights and dignity.

Prilleltensky (1997) emphasized that a moral system must treat the values he suggested as a complementary set, thus potential conflicts among them may force uncomfortable decisions concerning their relative precedence. Those decisions can only be made in light of the details of the particular situation—an act-based rather than rule-based ethical position. Scholars have noted frequently that difficult ethical dilemmas are those that entail having to choose between two or more right alternatives (Kidder, 1995). Many who have given the matter some thought follow the spirit of the Hippocratic Oath ("First, do no harm") and give considerable primacy to the principle of nonmaleficence: avoiding harm or wrongdoing is more important than doing an equivalent amount of good. Thus, with respect to an I-O psychologist's obligations to job applicants (as opposed to our traditional obligation solely to the employing organization), inappropriately rejecting a candidate who would have succeeded if hired (a false-negative prediction) ought to be more momentous than inappropriately hiring a candidate who fails (a false-positive).[7] The dilemma for the I-O psychologist, however, is that we have obligations to both the individual applicants and to the organization. And that, under customary conditions, reducing false positives necessarily is accompanied by a proportionally larger increase in the number of false negatives (Lefkowitz, 2011c; Lefkowitz & Lowman, 2017).

It seems likely that fulfilling the first of Prilleltensky's (1997) criteria, articulating principles for the good society, is easier than meeting the second, translating this vision into action. People, including psychologists, are more likely to agree on what is good than on the best ways to achieve it. Nevertheless, agreement is possible among diverse groups of psychologists regarding the ways in which psychology can contribute to the formulation of national policy for the betterment of all citizens (APS, 1992, 1993a, 1993b, 1996a, 1996b).

---

7   This does not deny or ignore the likely negative effects on the failing and disappointed employee who was hired and perhaps discharged.

Political bias? An important issue is raised by Redding's (2001) criticism of social advocacy in psychology, as represented by policy positions advanced by the APA. Echoing a characterization made a decade earlier by Suedfeld and Tetlock (1991), he made a convincing case that most psychologists have politically liberal rather than conservative world views. And more recently Duarte et al. (2015) and Haidt and Jussim (2016) make that same case, especially regarding social psychologists, and make a plea for greater political diversity. The reason this is important is because

> Science frequently is interpreted in a manner consistent with the values and beliefs of the scientists doing the research ... As studies have shown, sociopolitical biases influence the question asked, the research methods selected, the interpretation of research results, the peer review process, judgments about research quality, and decisions about whether to use research in policy advocacy ... .
>
> *(Redding, 2001, p. 206)*

This would account, therefore, for his finding that a content analysis of 31 *American Psychologist* articles dealing with social issues during the 1990s indicated that 97% of the articles advanced liberal themes or policies, and only one article reflected more conservative views. This view is confirmed by later research indicating that "prejudice derives from perceived similarities and dissimilarities in political ideologies (the value-conflict hypothesis)" (Chambers et al., 2012, p. 140) rather than attitudinal prejudice per se.

Based on the quotation above, Redding (2001) apparently does not dispute the salient role played by personal and social values throughout the scientific enterprise, and he does not advance a case (e.g., as does Kendler, 1999) for value-free science; his concern is with *which* values will be expressed, supported and promoted. I assume he would not object on principle to the role traditionally played by professionals in shaping public policy in areas germane to their profession's expertise (Hughes, 1965). His is a plea for political diversity and sociopolitical pluralism in psychology, which at first blush seems reasonable and fair. In fact, the same plea has been repeated (Duarte, et al., 2015; Haidt & Jussim, 2016)—including the application to organizations (Swigart et al., 2020), although those authors concluded that "Much remains unknown about how and when political ideology influences organizational life" (p. 1083).

But some important issues go unrecognized in Redding's arguments—perhaps because he fails to ask "why" there might be this political difference, thus potentially confusing cause and effect. Duarte, et al., on the other hand do consider why social psychologists seem to be mostly liberal. Although they admit of some self-selection (both liberalism and academic careers are associated with the Big-5 trait of openness to experience), they attribute the primary causes to a hostile climate and discrimination against conservative social scientists. Similarly, Haidt and Jussim believe that "the underrepresentation of nonliberals in social psychology is most likely due to a combination of self-selection, hostile climate, and discrimination" (p. 5). There is insufficient space to pursue that line (in recent years a great deal has been written about the putative "liberal bias" in the social sciences), but we should take a brief look at the nature of Redding's (2001) "data." In my opinion he fails to recognize the biased nature of the evidentiary criteria used.

He had coders judge whether an article concerning APA policy contained conservative or liberal views, i.e.,:

> whether the articles recognized traditional/status quo versus progressive/ change-oriented themes or positions on social issues; ... advanced either anti- or pro-government involvement in, and spending on, welfare and social programs; were elitest/meritocracy-oriented versus egalitarian/social justice-oriented in their values; or favored capitalist/self-reliance versus socialist/communitarian values. (p. 206)

It seems logical (i.e., consistent) that people who endorse the capitalist, elitist, status quo society and who are against spending public monies on social programs are not well-represented in a profession that avowedly is concerned in part with addressing social problems. Endorsement of the status quo and the views associated with it suggests that one would not likely perceive the consequences of employment discrimination, inferior schooling and other manifestations of racism, as well as sex discrimination, the number of working poor and homeless amid enormous wealth for a few, and so on, as necessarily representing *problems*. After all, those conditions *are* the status quo. Moreover, if one believes—as conservatives do--that these conditions (not "problems") reflect primarily the intellectual, social or moral inadequacies of those affected (i.e., their lack of merit and personal failure to succeed in the free-enterprise system), and if one has an egocentric view of society (i.e., self-reliance is the preeminent moral stance so that one has scant interest in social justice), then it's understandable that one would have little if anything to be concerned about. If one believes that systemic sociopolitical and socioeconomic factors play little or no role in producing these outcomes, then there is little need to be concerned with systemic ameliorative actions (i.e., progressive social policies)—especially those to be undertaken at public expense. So, there is a straightforward explanation, involving occupational attraction and "fit," without having to speculate about discrimination, as to why psychologists trend liberal.

It is undoubtedly true, however, that we are just beginning to explore the complexities of behavior at the intersection of personal values, social issues, political beliefs, morality and ethical decision-making. Who could imagine, for example, that people have physical bodily reactions (*subjective somatosensory experiences*) to scenarios involving moral violations—and that "body patterns corresponding to different moral violations are felt in different regions of the body depending on whether individuals are classified as liberals or conservatives" (Atari et al., 2020)!

While serving as president of the APA, George Miller (1969) was not optimistic about the likely effectiveness of organizations such as APA addressing social problems *qua* organizations. He nevertheless counseled that APA should not tacitly endorse a system "that presides over the inequitable distribution of health, wealth, and wisdom in our society" (p. 1065). Although he saw little formal role for the APA in this regard, this is nevertheless the famous speech in which Miller advocated "giving psychology away" to the public by each psychologist's individual contribution to the advancement of psychology as a means of promoting human welfare.

Classes of Scientific Inquiry and the Scientific Study of Morality

D'Andrade (1986) has posited and Kurtines et al. (1990) have elaborated an overall perspective of science as comprised of three classes (one is tempted to use the term "levels," although they do not—perhaps because of the considerable evaluative baggage attached to the term in the philosophy of science). There are the physical sciences, natural sciences and *semiotic* sciences.[8] The bases for the distinctions are the nature of the phenomena studied in each and the associated kinds of scientific generalizations thus possible in each. They are not the same. "The phenomena of focal concern for the human sciences differ in fundamental ways from the phenomena of concern for the physical and natural sciences" (Kurtines, et al., 1990, p. 287). The physical sciences (e.g., physics, chemistry) can achieve universal generalizations (albeit sometimes probabilistic) because of the invariant nature of what is studied. In the natural sciences (including biology and much of economics and psychology such as neuropsychology) the generalizations tend to be more limited because the natural phenomena studied are generally contingent. In the semiotic sciences (e.g., some psychology and sociology, anthropology) the aim is to understand the *meaning* of phenomena that are "constructed" or "imposed" by language, culture, history, etc., they are not physical or natural. The key point, from our standpoint, is that the scientific study of morality is largely semiotic.

8 Semiotics, or semiology, is the study of signs and symbols (visual, aural, written, spoken, symbolic, etc.) and what they signify, i.e., their meaning. The meaning is not necessarily inherent in the sign; it may be socially constructed. In fact, semioticians are much focused on the processes by which meaning is created. The assumption is that signs very much shape our perception of life and reality.

The Inquiry Paradigm of Postmodernism[9]

To whatever extent some of us may hold tenaciously to a positivist or post-positivist conception of value-free natural science, it seems less tenable when applied to the social sciences, including much of psychology:

> The way in which a social scientist selects problems to work on, the factors cited to explain behavior, and the evidence sought to substantiate these explanations all reflect the significance and meaning the social scientist attaches to them. To focus on a particular problem is to evaluate it as more important than others, and importance is based on evaluation in the light of human values … .
>
> *A social science that sought to efface the moral dimension from its descriptions and explanations would simply serve the interests of some other moral conception.* It would reflect values foreign to those that animate our conception of ourselves.
>
> *(Rosenberg, 1995, p. 205, emphasis added)*

The view in social science characterized as *postmodern* (or as *social constructionist*), as distinct from positivistic natural science, involves much more than simply the values choices Rosenberg (1995) noted. It extends beyond realizing that the intrinsic interdependence of theory, data and interpretation means that total scientific objectivity is illusory. It is a perspective that emphasizes that human beings as objects of study are very different in very important ways from the objects studied in the natural sciences and that—most important—those human attributes cannot be understood adequately by the traditional objectivist positivist paradigm, but require a different mode of scientific inquiry. Howard (1985) put it simply: "if humans possess characteristics that are unlike the characteristics of subject matters studied by other sciences, then an appropriate science of human behavior might need to be somewhat different from other extant sciences" (pp. 259–260).[10]

This chapter does not attempt to do more than present a brief description of this broad humanistic approach as it has been applied to psychology; more extensive summaries are available (Gergen, 1985, 1992, 1994, 2001; Guba & Lincoln, 1994;

---

9 *Postmodernism* is the name of one of several variations of the point of view summarized here. The description is a synthesis of some (not all) of them, and I have chosen this label because it seems to be the most widely recognized, although *social constructionism* comes close. Rosenberg (1995) and Guba and Lincoln (1994) discuss the various versions.

10 Some scholars in this area, notably Kuhn (1970, 2000) for one, believe that the interpretive paradigm discussed in this section is no less true for the natural sciences as for the social sciences. As an amusing aside, Kuhn (2000) who, in the first edition of *The Structure of Scientific Revolutions* many years ago, introduced the importance of scientific paradigms plaintively observed "I seldom use that term these days, having totally lost control of it …" (p. 221).

Rosenau, 1992; Rosenberg, 1995), including as applied particularly to the study of morality (D'Andrade, 1995; Kurtines et al., 1990). The essential idea is that although the aim of social science is the same as that of physical and natural science—to achieve a greater understanding of the phenomena under study—the nature of the subject matter dictates that a different sort of "understanding" is necessary. In the physical and natural sciences, understanding is characterized as explanation that consists in formulating universal laws that are testable and falsifiable (Popper, 1972).[11] The ultimate expression or confirmation of these laws is the successful prediction and control of the phenomena under study.

In contrast, the postmodernist conceptualization of understanding has much in common with that of the humanities (e.g., history or literary criticism) insofar as it consists of achieving meaning, which necessarily is interpretive in character. *Hermeneutics* is the name given to this process of interpretation. To the extent that meaningfulness may be expressed in the form of certain regularities in the character or occurrence of psychological entities or processes, they are more like rules than universal laws or generalizations.[12] The meaning of human action is provided by the motives, beliefs and intentions that reflect the rules that govern our actions. "Human action is thus a matter of following rules, and the aim of social science is to uncover these rules" (Rosenberg, 1995, p. 93). The rules may be precise or vague, obvious or esoteric, conscious or unconscious, but they are all communal in nature in that they are shared among a relevant community of people to whom they apply. Some rules (comprised of beliefs, normative expectations, intentions, etc.) may be "constructed" and shared only by some groups within a culture or by the entire culture; in some instances, they may be shared by several cultures. The primary distinction between a rule and a scientific law or generalization is that the rule can be violated without invalidating it. The rule retains its explanatory power, whereas frequent exceptions to a scientific law result in its being rejected as a causal explanation.

Whereas the extreme postmodernist would hold that virtually all of social science must be a hermeneutic enterprise, Kuhn (2000) had no problem with accepting a mixture of traditional and social constructionist approaches. Similarly, Gergen (2001) pointed out that although postmodern critiques are highly critical of the dominant empirical hypothesis-testing research tradition on both conceptual and ideological grounds, "there is nothing within the postmodern critiques that is lethal to this tradition ... the postmodern critiques are

---

11 Although even in natural science sought-after generalizations may be contingent and ephemeral. Have you ever tried to interpret (much less replicate) a 4-way, or even 3-way ANOVA interaction effect?
12 Popper (1972) was of the opinion that "Labouring the difference between science and the humanities has long been a fashion, and has become a bore" (p. 185) because the nature of "understanding" is the same for each: i.e., the method of "conjecture and refutation."

themselves without foundations: they constitute important voices but not final voices" (p. 808).

Some Specific Tenets

Several specific differences between psychology as conceptualized and practiced for most of the first century of its existence in the tradition of positivistic natural science, and the postmodernist movement of the past couple of generations or so have been emphasized. A few of the most important ones are discussed next.

The Significance of Human Actions as the Object of Study

Psychology and the other social sciences face issues that do not exist in the natural sciences or even in most of biological science. Largely through the utility of symbolic language human beings plan and monitor their own actions. Contrary to the backward-looking focus of behaviorism or psychoanalytic theory (in which the major determinants of behavior are one's reinforcement history or family history, respectively), humans anticipate and try to shape their futures (Kelly, 1962; Smith & Vetter, 1982). Unlike the chemist's solutions, the physicist's particles, the astronomer's galaxies, or even the biologist's organ systems, we study "objects" that are the active agents of their own behavior (Manicas & Secord, 1983). Evidence suggests that even infants understand behavior in terms of motives (Woodward, 2009). There are several implications of this fact, such as the role of *reflexivity* in human action (Howard, 1985).

Human beings are *reflexive,* that is, we are generally aware of what we are doing and what is happening to us; we make attributions regarding the determinants of our actions. One implication of this is that, as objects of psychological research, people are not unaware of the research procedures that they experience. Contrary to the assumptions of the classical scientific paradigm, the psychological researcher cannot fail to intervene in the activity of the objects studied. As researchers, we try to deal with this fact methodologically, usually with mixed success, by developing unobtrusive measures, by ethically questionable means like failing to fully inform our research participants of the purpose of the research, or even by deceiving them about its purpose. The postmodernist would say that more frequently we simply ignore the issue, as if it did not exist as a serious threat to our conception of "knowledge." But the full extent of the problem goes beyond merely the way in which people's actions are altered because they are being studied. Everyday behavior is affected by public knowledge of the results of other research. For example, it appears that the standardized test performance of women, African Americans, and other minorities is affected adversely by knowledge concerning the prior performance of members of their social group and the stereotypic interpretations it is given (APA, 2006; Aronson et al., 1998; Shih et al., 1999; Spencer et al., 1999; Steele, 1997, 1999; Steele & Aronson, 1995).[13]

A Phenomenological and Contextualized Perspective

In the postmodern perspective the reflexive and planful nature of human activity means that it can only be understood or interpreted adequately from the internal perspective of the person. This point of view has a long history in social science, as illustrated by the phenomenological perspective in psychology, the emic (insider) view in anthropology (as distinct from the outsider's etic view), the early laboratory studies in psychophysics that attempted to systematically relate the external physical and internal psychological worlds, as well as the more recent cognitive revolution that reintroduced the internal perspective to scientific psychology after more than a generation of behaviorist hegemony.

The most important consequence of the phenomenological perspective is the need to contextualize human action which, in turn, implies (a) abandonment of reliance exclusively on the ideal of controlled experimental methodology and quantification of variables and (b) an emphasis on the cultural context in adequately interpreting human behavior. In this view, the classic experimental procedures "that focus on selected subsets of variables necessarily 'strip' from consideration, through appropriate controls or randomization, other variables that exist in the context that might, if allowed to exert their effects, greatly alter findings. Further, such exclusionary designs, while increasing the theoretical rigor of a study, detract from its *relevance,* that is its applicability or generalizability" (Guba & Lincoln, 1994, p. 106). Moreover, the greater understanding to be achieved by the inclusion of a more fully contextualized study of human actors will therefore also require the use of qualitative data to assess the meanings and purposes of people's actions.

Postmodern social scientists take culture quite seriously—as permeating all human action—and not merely as either moderators of more general or universal laws of behavior or simply as a means of testing the cross-cultural generalizability of those laws (Gergen et al., 1996). Culture represents the "local context" in which behavior must be understood.

Psychologists as a group are unaware of how small and unrepresentative of human variability is the range of behavior that constitutes American

13 In the opinion of some, however, modern advances in neuroscience are threatening our understanding of human cognition, intention, social behavior, morality, religion and associated mores because of the extent to which behavior can be accounted for in terms of brain processes; they "all result from physical mechanisms" (Farah, 2012, p. 588). It remains to be seen whether such reductionist explanations are sufficiently meaningful.

culture ... . Because psychologists' ethnocentric understanding of 'the environment' is implicitly limited to the United States today, they have a truncated view of environmental influences on behavior that confirms their bias toward biologized explanations.

(Fish, 2000, pp. 555–556)

An interesting example of this approach is Greenfield's (1997) explanation of the way cultural differences in the social conventions having to do with values and with ways of knowing and communicating may invalidate the apparent findings of cognitive ability tests when applied outside their culture of origin.

The Centrality of Language and Rejection of Representationalism

To a postmodern social scientist, the most important rules that govern human action are those having to do with language because language shapes our conception of reality. And it does not do so by merely being a neutral representation of an assumed objective external reality, but by creating that reality. This *social constructionist* point of view denies the traditional *representationalism* assumption that there is an inherent relation between our words and the world (Gergen, 1985, 1992), and it is finding voice in the study of organizations (Hancock & Tyler, 2001). For example:

> Although in much of the existing work on organizations and management researchers treat language as a tool of description, constructivists would have us consider that the world we live in and experience is a product of language.
>
> Not only does language describe but it also creates the very world in the description. Indeed, some would argue that it is not possible to experience the world independent of language and that it is impossible to have organizations or their management independent of language. Language, then, is both context and content.
>
> If we view language as context, what happens to our understanding of organizations and their management? What if we consider organizations not as mechanical or political, or even organic, but as linguistic? What would culture be if an organization were a discursive system engaging in multiple discourses? How would we construct management if what got managed was linguistic rather than material (e.g., resources) or organic (e.g., people)? How would we talk about motivation and leadership, and other traditional organization and management topics, if organizations *were* linguistic systems in which there was only language?
>
> *(Ford, 2001, pp. 328–329)*

Thus, according to postmodernism, the traditional positivist view of science and the search for objective knowledge (most especially in the social sciences) is just one among many possible linguistic constructions of reality that positivists justify tautologically "by relying on methods that embody these same constructions" (Gergen, 1994, p. 413). Whereas, in the opinion of the postmodernist, the positivist denigrates all other views as unscientific or value biased, the postmodernist does not seek to dominate discourse but to encourage multiple ways of understanding. Thus, "there is nothing about postmodern thought that argues against continuing research ... However, what postmodern thought does discourage is the reification of the languages used by the communities of scientists conducting such research. It militates against the dissemination of this language as 'true' beyond the communities that speak in these particular ways." (Gergen, 1994, p. 414)

Socially Constructed, Value-Laden Truths

The description I have provided so far of a social scientific understanding of human behavior (postmodern version) emphasizes the contextualized interpretation of the interpersonal cultural rules that people use implicitly to shape their reality. The rules consist of semantic conceptions shared among a community defined by that sharing, and there may be as many conceptions of a given construct as there are cultural communities in which it exists.[14] Questions regarding the extent to which these conceptions accurately represent external reality or which among several alternative conceptions is correct are moot; they are simply outside the paradigm. The notion of correctness as a representation of objective truth is an illusory positivist issue. Although postmodernism claims to have placed the traditional empiricist standards of validity in doubt (at least as applied in social science), even Gergen (1985) acknowledged "constructionism offers no alternative truth criteria" (p. 272). Conversely, some constructions may be more informed, inclusive, and/or sophisticated than others. And in the realm of science, they still must satisfy the normative expectations of the community of concerned scholars. Moreover, of special relevance for I-O psychology, the "proof of the pudding" for postmodernists comes in the effective *application* of their interpretations.

Once the philosophical problems inherent in maintaining the dualism between subject and object are recognized (Rorty, 1979), knowledge becomes the social practices constructed by our shared language, not an attribute or veridical representation of an external object. And because cultural meanings

---

14 Positivists believe that this problem is evaded by clearly operationalizing a construct and, if appropriate, translating its exemplars and/or method of measurement into a foreign language. In that way, the cross-cultural generality of the construct can be investigated. The postmodernist would argue that the initial operationalization is probably invested with culture-specific content that invalidates the process.

reflect social values (including political values, postmodernists emphasize), virtually all meaning is value-laden, including scientific meanings. Thus, social constructionist analyses have been applied to such broad psychological topics as person, self, child, gender, aggression, mind, emotion, morality, and so on (cf. Gergen, 1985), the meanings of which are seen as imbued with social and political values that are bounded by cultural and historical contexts.

Perhaps the most radical aspect of the postmodernist perspective is the application of the social constructionist view to the institutions of society. In the same way that rules govern individual action, sets of rules combine to form social roles in society (e.g., manager or professor), and the roles combine with others to form organizations and institutions (Rosenberg, 1995). And just as uncovering the rules that guide an individual's behavior explains the meaning and significance of his or her actions, explicating the rules and roles that constitute institutions can explain their social and cultural meaning.[15] Therefore, the institutions of society are understood as social constructions, not as inevitable "givens." That is a radical notion because it suggests that, as constructions, institutions can be altered. Rosenberg put it well:

> To say that social institutions are "constructed" means roughly that they do not exist independent of people's actions, beliefs, and desires—their reasons for acting. On one interpretation, this claim may not be controversial, for all will grant that without people there is no society thus no social roles to be filled by people. The claim becomes controversial when we add in the idea that people can do otherwise than what they in fact have done hitherto. They can violate the rules that constrain their actions, and they can construct new rules. That makes social institutions we may have thought were natural and unavoidable look artificial and revisable. (pp. 101–102)

In this sense, postmodernism can be seen as constituting a radical challenge to much of the status quo human enterprise, from literary criticism to social and behavioral science, to the very institutional structure of society itself. That it has met with stiff resistance from many quarters is not surprising. For example, an attempt to promote the postmodern perspective in psychology (Gergen, 2001) drew nine unsolicited published commentaries, some rather vociferous, that characterize it as "untested speculation" (Kruger, 2002,

---

15 And an anthropologist would tell us that institutional meanings might not be known consciously by the individual participants in a cultural institution. Explanations may have to be discovered at the societal level. Thus, societies have hidden or deep meanings. The two prominent examples of social science theories that constitute explanations of the hidden meanings of society and its institutions are Freudian psychoanalysis and Marxism (Rosenberg, 1995).

p. 456), "historically frozen" (Krueger, 2002, p. 461), "of little value for the advancement of psychology as a science" (Hofmann, 2002, p. 462), "the dead end of philosophy" (Locke, 2002, p. 458), and "inevitably foster[ing] nihilism" (Friedman, 2002, p. 463).

Professional Roles: Research and Practice in Psychology

As noted earlier, a long-avowed goal of the profession of psychology is the betterment of the human condition (APA, 2017). That this has been an accepted aspect of the role definition of the past generations of psychologists is reflected in surveys of psychology faculty and students who overwhelmingly viewed the relevance of psychology to social problems and the real world as the most important issue facing the field (Lipsey, 1974). It has also been presented as a moral obligation: "… psychologists, as well as members of other scientific disciplines, have a collective obligation to develop knowledge that at least in the long run will contribute to the solutions of the critical problems of the society that literally and figuratively supports their research and themselves" (Spence, 1985, p. 1286). It is not uncommon, however, for leaders in the field to decry the extent to which we have failed to live up to those obligations and expectations:

> As the twentieth century wore on, psychological knowledge increased enormously, and psychologists assumed respected and influential positions. But somehow the hopes for continuous improvement in the condition of mankind through psychology declined. It became almost naive to assume that what was discovered through research could have much effect on man's nature or institutions.
>
> *(Tyler, 1973, p. 1021)*

Similar negative evaluations of the amount and/or effectiveness of our applications and professional practice have been voiced for many years, especially in comparison with the progress and wonders achieved in the physical sciences (Fishman, 1999; Miller, 1969). For example, after decades of social psychological study of intergroup relations, we still are plagued with racial hostility and conflict; after studying learning and the educational process for the better part of a century we still have mostly disastrous public educational systems and high rates of adult illiteracy; despite the generally acknowledged utility of I-O psychology's contributions to organizations, after many years of both basic and applied research, a considerable gap still remains between organizational research findings and management practices (Rynes et al., 2001); and the utility of our best employee selection procedures for predicting job performance (cognitive ability tests), while described as having "high validity," barely account hypothetically for about 30% of the variance in job performance criteria (Ones et al., 2010, p. 262; Schmidt & Hunter, 1998). Perhaps the public's skepticism about psychology (Lilienfeld, 2012) is not surprising.

The Postmodern Challenge to the Distinction Between Science and Practice

The typical reactions to psychology's alleged failures one is likely to hear from psychologists are: (a) "Yes, that's true, but we are a young field and will produce much useful knowledge in the future"; or a variant of that, (b) "Yes, while that may be true, it's due to the fact that social problems and human behavior are much more complicated and difficult to understand and change than phenomena in the physical world"; or (c) "That's not entirely correct: We have produced a lot of potentially useful knowledge but for a variety of reasons have not been effective in getting it translated into policy applications or used by practitioners." A case can probably be made for each of these three explanations. But convincing arguments refuting each of them are also readily available. Be that as it may, the point I make here is that a very different explanation has been offered by the postmodernist social constructionist school of thought.

Popper (1972) set the groundwork for this view by making the point that the theoretical aim of explanation and the practical aim of technical application "are, in a way, two different aspects of one and the same activity" (p. 348). Indeed, "Perhaps where human beings are concerned, that which is most practical is of most theoretical interest" (Howard, 1985, p. 263). In recent years, more and more of psychology, regardless of specialty area, has shown "our commitment to real-world phenomena" (Conner, 2001, p. 9) and the "commensurability" of science and practice in psychology has been reasserted forcefully (Stricker, 1997).[16] Moreover, there even have been recent signs of a developing rapprochement between natural and social science approaches to the study of human functioning (Damasio et al., 2001).

These trends may, in part, represent reactions to the postmodernist charge that it is the unnecessary and artificial positivist distinction between pure science and basic research on the one hand and applied research and professional practice on the other that is responsible for the relatively limited accomplishments of social science in the real world. In that unidirectional ideal model, adopted from the physical sciences, we discover basic knowledge that consists of the general principles uncovered by our controlled laboratory experimentation, which are then transformed into technologies to be applied to real-world problems and clients; professional practice is always assigned a secondary role as the application of knowledge (Hoshmand & Polkinghorne, 1992; Peterson, 1991). The separation of the two realms is an intrinsic component of the positivist conception of the former as entirely free of the values issues with which the latter is imbued. One unfortunate fallout from this

16 A cautionary note is sounded by Peterson (1991) who argued that, because of emphases on traditional scientific research, typical doctoral training in psychology does not equip psychologists for sophisticated professional practice. That is a complaint not unheard of among those who hire young I-O psychology practitioners as well.

paradigm, however, is that psychologists in many academic specialty areas have tended to bury themselves in the data from laboratory situations and have lost track of the broader questions that may even have stimulated the research (Spence, 1985; Tversky, cited in Conner, 2001). The fundamental impediment is that the basic theoretical principles uncovered in artificially decontextualized, controlled experiments, in which one or only a few variables are investigated, and the reflexivity of research participants is not accounted for, yields limited truth at most, biased by the particular theoretical (and other unacknowledged) values of the researcher. No wonder the application of this knowledge to the messy real world has been disappointing and that some I-O psychologists are concerned with reducing the gap between organizational research and practice by encouraging more field research in organizations (Rynes & McNatt, 2001). In a similar vein, Campbell (1990) chided that we rarely "inquire as to whether the 'role of theory' has anything to do with the problem(s) of concern" (p. 67).

In contrast with the traditional approach adopted from the physical sciences, postmodern psychological researchers begin with a client (individual, group, organization, community or country) with a problem that needs solving. The problem assessment in terms of the client's objectives, the research and/or interventions as well as their evaluation all take place *in situ* (Peterson, 1991). "In this interpretation of science, the test of knowledge is not whether it corresponds exactly to reality, as it is impossible to ascertain whether there is such a direct correspondence. Instead, *the test for knowledge is whether it serves to guide human action to attain goals.* In other words, the test is pragmatic … not logical" (Hoshmand & Polkinghorne, 1992, p. 58, emphasis added).

It is interesting to reflect on the extent to which I-O psychology, despite its generally neopositivist orientation, may have much in common with the postmodern view. Postmodern perspectives have been less in evidence in academic psychology than in the other social sciences—probably because of psychology's strong identification with the natural sciences (Gergen, 2001) and the recent preeminence of biopsychology (Farah, 2012). And—with a few exceptions (e.g., Ford, 2001; Hancock & Tyler, 2001; Weick, 1995)—they have been even less in evidence in I-O psychology. But our field has from its inception taken real-world organizational problems as both the intellectual and emotional stimulation for systematic inquiry (Boehm, 1980; Campbell et al., 1982) and has emphasized the reciprocity between research (basic or applied) and professional practice (Cooper & Locke, 2000; Hakel et al., 1982; Latham, 2000, 2001; Lawler et al., 1985). Nevertheless, the extent to which knowledge created in one of these two realms infuses the other is still perceived as extremely problematic (Gioia, 2021; Rynes et al., 2001). Conversely, the postmodernist critique that such knowledge transfer is invariably and inappropriately assumed to be unidirectional (research always informs practice) is probably less true of I-O psychology than for other areas of application.

Fishman (1999) contrasted the postmodern technological model of what he called "pragmatic psychology" with the traditional model. His intent is compatible with Nogami's (1982) concerns for the difference between often-ineffective applied research and what she called "applicable research." Although Fishman's problem-driven, uncontrolled research model emphasizes a variety of methodologies not well represented in I-O psychology, including qualitative methods and case studies (cf. Coghlan & Brannick, 2000; Gummeson, 1999, for some exceptions), his description of postmodern pragmatism sounds a great deal like a model of organizationally driven research in the practice of I-O psychology:

> While natural science emphasizes academic freedom of the individual researcher, technology is guided by goals and objectives that are established by the society. While natural science ideally takes place in the laboratory, technology is conducted "in the field," within the actual situation in which a problem presents itself. While basic research focuses on testing hypotheses derived from academic theories, technology focuses on directly altering conditions in the real world. While natural science focuses upon the parameters in its laboratory experiments, technology develops systematic pictures of psychological and social phenomena in the outside world, using standardized measures and large-scale norms … . Finally, while the goal of natural science is theory development and "truth," the goal of technology is to guide practical action by suggesting effective solutions to presenting problems within the constraints of a particular body of knowledge, a given set of skills, and available resources. (p. xxii)

Fishman suggested that his approach represents a middle way between the positivist who attacks the case study as too context-specific from which to generalize and the social constructionist who attacks the positivist for trying to achieve generalization by ignoring individual contexts and oversimplifying complex phenomena. He did so by advocating the accumulation of multiple cases organized into computer-accessible databases that would eventually permit some generalizations without the loss of important contextual factors. This appears to be responsive to Hulin's (2001) observation "… we will never learn about the few underlying general constructs that account for many manifest behaviors and attitudes if we study problems and behaviors one at a time" (p. 230). Similarly, Rynes et al. (2001) presented a taxonomy of means by which tacit and explicit forms of organizational knowledge may be transferred between academics and practitioners, including the use of protocol analyses, ethnographies and action research—all emanating from the practitioner domain.

Potential Value Conflicts and Ethical Dilemmas: Considering Consequences

I anticipate that most I-O psychologists will concur with the orientation of Fishman's pragmatic psychology that real-world (organizational) settings should be recognized as both necessary sites for achieving psychology's goal of bettering the human condition through professional practice, as well as methodologically appropriate sites for conducting meaningful research on fundamental psychological phenomena. But because Fishman's focus is on community psychology, educational reform and psychotherapy—all exclusively concerned with providing human services—he failed to consider an attendant problem that is extremely relevant for I-O psychologists. It has to do with the values, goals and objectives of the clients served. His position is that the pragmatic paradigm "supports our democratic ideals by requiring collaboration with program stakeholders in program goal setting" and that "goal and other value questions are to be resolved by open, democratic dialogue among relevant stakeholders" (p. 290). Or, as Peterson (1991) succinctly stated, "The practitioner does not choose the issue to examine, the client does" (p. 426).

That is all well and good when the meta-objectives of the institutions to be served (e.g., schools and mental health clinics) are entirely commensurate with the humanitarian objectives that comprise the practitioner's value system; no additional ethical issues are raised. However, when those served are business organizations governed largely by a value system of profit-making for just one stakeholder group, actions on their behalf may sometimes conflict with our objective "to improve the condition of individuals, organizations, and society" (APA, 2017). This important matter will be explored further later. For now, it is sufficient to simply make the point that, to whatever extent one might attempt to advance the case for a value-free conception of scientific psychology and basic psychological research, it clearly does not characterize applied research, much less the practice of applied psychology in business organizations. Those institutions have their own value systems and demands that largely define the role and objectives of the applied psychologist in service to that client. For example, employee selection and its major components such as test validation are not, as many I-O psychologists claim, value-free because they represent solutions to organizational requirements that are defined by and reflect the values and objectives of the organization. In so doing, they determine the nature and scope of the problem and the range of acceptable solutions, generally without reference to the benefits or harms received by other stakeholders and institutions. I believe it's an example of what McCall and Bobko (1990) characterized as "objectivity actually abetting subjectivity." For example, one would not expect to see cooperative hiring procedures among several companies to minimize the overall amount of unemployment in a community.

The postmodernist emphasis on applied research inevitably invites consideration of "the sociocultural ramifications of both the research and the manner in which it is framed" (Gergen, 1994). In other words, unlike the niceties of strictly controlled laboratory research procedures, one cannot investigate and manipulate real-world situations unmindful of the effects of such orchestrations.

This is a reprise of an issue discussed in chapter 3 regarding ethical responsibility for the foreseeable consequences of one's professional actions, even if those consequences are not the intended purpose of the intervention. Referring to the humanitarian pursuits he called "the ethic of innocence," Luria (1976) admonished that: "Morality does not exist in a vacuum. Human pursuits should always be judged in terms of what their consequences are for other human beings" (p. 333). And finally, Gergen (1985) explained:

> To the extent that psychological theory (and related practices) enter into the life of the culture, sustaining certain patterns of conduct and destroying others, such work must be evaluated in terms of good and ill. The practitioner can no longer justify any socially reprehensible conclusion on the grounds of being a "victim of the facts"; he or she must confront the pragmatic implication of such conclusions within society more generally. (p. 273)

There is both a macrolevel and microlevel challenge implicit in Gergen's statement. The first suggests that one cannot ethically be engaged in furthering the fortunes of powerful institutions in our society while turning a blind eye toward their possible adverse social actions, and our potential complicity in them—what has been referred to as "the conundrum of industrial-organizational psychology" (Lefkowitz, 2019). Similarly, as scientist—practitioners, if we take that hyphenation seriously: we cannot ethically hide behind a narrow technological or scientific definition of competent professional practice without considering all of the consequences of that practice. The first challenge comprises much of the substance of chapter 11, and the second is taken up in chapter 12.

Adding Further to the Framework for Ethical Decision Making

28. The role played by values in the scientific enterprise is a topic marked by considerable controversy. The question of what role they ought to play is even more controversial. The question is important, as values entail choices to be made in the conduct of human affairs; hence, the possibility arises of values conflicts and ethical dilemmas. The consensus of current scholarly opinion appears to be (a) even in the physical sciences, arguably the hallmark of the positivist empiricist value-free tradition, epistemic values are intrinsic to scientific inquiry, and personal values of scientists unavoidably play a part in their work; (b) the social and behavioral sciences are even more susceptible to such influences because human beings, who exist in social relationships, are the objects of study by other interested human beings; and (c) social norms, beliefs, and values are clearly suffused throughout applied social science research and professional practice because the clients served generally provide the goals and objectives that define the nature of that research and practice. *Therefore, it is self-deluding of I-O psychologists to deny that social and political values are inherent in much of our work on behalf of corporations and other organizations.* It seems preferable for each of us as individuals as well as for the profession to articulate, and if necessary, debate the extrinsic values that in part shape our work.

29. Whether one accepts all the epistemological, ontological and methodological critiques by postmodernists, the social–constructionist viewpoint seems to be a potentially fruitful approach to understanding the nature of much of what we study as organizational scientists. Moreover, it should be acknowledged that mainstream psychology has gradually been adopting on its own much of the postmodernist platform without necessarily accepting the overall paradigm. For example: (a) in planning and executing research, moral issues (i.e., research ethics—see chapter 13) are considered along with the scientific questions (APA, 2017); (b) the use of multivariate statistical techniques, including causal modeling, as well as the continued use of field experiments, quasi-experimental designs, and action research (Coghlan & Brannick, 2000), along with systematic questioning of the generalizability of laboratory research findings (Locke, 1986), all represent modes of achieving greater contextualization of meaning; (c) growth in the acceptability of qualitative procedures and methods of analysis (case studies, ethnography, discourse analysis, etc.; Gummeson, 1999) as well as the use of insider perspectives (Oyserman & Swim, 2001) reflect more interpretive phenomenological approaches; (d) the cognitive revolution in psychological theory and research begun in the 1960s has given greater recognition to the intentionality and reflexivity of people as objects of study, which was begun as long ago as the Hawthorne studies (Roethlisberger & Dixon, 1939); (e) this was given prominence by Orne's (1962) illumination of the distinction between experimentation in the natural and behavioral sciences, with research participants in the latter subject to the *demand characteristics* of the experimental situation; and (f) I-O psychologists in particular, like postmodern social scientists, have long viewed professional practice both as an inspiration and source of knowledge, as well as a venue for its application. Nevertheless, it is probably still true that "industrial and organizational psychologists tend to use only a limited number of the many available research strategies and tactics" (Sackett & Larson, 1990, p. 419) and that "Ideally, the field would find a better balance between the quantitative and qualitative and show a greater tolerance for and appreciation of all approaches" (McCall & Bobko, 1990, p. 412).

30. I-O psychologists should recognize that the avowed goal of psychology to use knowledge "to improve the condition of individuals, organizations, and society" (APA, 2017) potentially may conflict with the goals and objectives of the organizations for which we work. One could argue, conversely, that the enormous economic and social benefits contributed by business organizations to society indicate that such putative conflicts are exaggerated. It seems to me, however, that the latter position can be maintained only by disregarding the essentially capitalist nature of the corporate enterprise that frequently leads to excesses of concern for shareholder profits, as well as the frequently self-serving features of managerial actions, to the detriment of other employees, stakeholders, and segments of society. The perspective advanced here is that our moral obligation as I-O psychologists is to work toward attenuating those excesses and consequent injustices.

11

BUSINESS VALUES

The normative bill of particulars brought against American corporate business is lengthy, shocking, and saddening. From many quarters and over long stretches of time, a clamorous chorus has sounded out a damning indictment of specific business practices and, in some cases, a condemnation of the institution itself. Greed, selfishness, ego-centeredness, disregard of the needs and well-being of others, a narrow or nonexistent social vision, an ethnocentric managerial creed imposed on nonindustrial cultures, a reckless use of dangerous technologies, an undermining of countervailing institutions such as trade unions, a virtual political takeover of some pluralist government agencies, and a system of self-reward that few either inside or outside business have cared to defend as fair or moral—all of these attributes have been credited to the business account.

—William C. Frederick

Frederick's forthright assessment is rather poignant because he is a supporter and proponent of business, not primarily a critic. The bill of particulars he enumerated does not even mention the serious accusations brought by those who see contemporary business organizations as all-powerful corrupters of political democracy (e.g., Korten, 1995, 1999; Luttwak, 1999; Mokhiber & Weissman, 1999; Soros, 2000). Nor does it even reference recent scandals such as those concerning General Motors ignition switches (Ivory et al., 2015), Takata airbags (Ivory & Tabuchi, 2016; Tabuchi, 2016a), systemic Volkswagen emissions control cheating (Ewing & Tabuchi, 2016; Hakim & Tabuchi, 2015; Mouawad & Jensen, 2015; Sanger-Katz & Schwartz, 2015), and outrageous drug company profiteering (Creswell et al., 2015; Goldstein, 2016; Pollack & Goldstein, 2016; Thomas & Pollack, 2016).

DOI: 10.4324/9781003212577-13

But one would have to be in serious psychological denial to fail to appreciate the enormous positive contributions made by modern business institutions. The widespread material well-being afforded by the resources, products and services provided by businesses are just the beginning. Also to be acknowledged are the economic benefits of employment—viewed from both an individual and societal perspective, the social and psychological gratification experienced by people performing meaningful work activities (when jobs are structured in that fashion) as well as the emotional security and sense of self-worth attendant upon one's long-term enactment of a career, the philanthropic and community activities supported by businesses, and the potential accumulation of widespread personal wealth made possible through the mechanism of public corporate ownership. What, then, is to be made of the disparity between these two divergent re-presentations of corporate America? How can we best understand this corporate rendering of the Jekyll and Hyde metaphor? What are its moral implications? And most important for our purposes, what is the appropriate ethical stance for I-O psychologists, who sustain, support and contribute to corporate goals and objectives, and so might be characterized as playing an instrumental role in both scenarios?

Agle and Caldwell (1999), DeGeorge (1987) and Danley (1994) noted that the study of business values and ethics necessitates recognizing several levels of analysis, notwithstanding that the overwhelming bulk of research and theory is at the individual level and to a lesser degree the organizational level, and they focus on the relations between the two. A major weakness in the study of business ethics (no less true of professional ethics in I-O) is the

> focus primarily upon individual cases while ignoring the larger institutional frameworks … . This obscures the extent to which our intuitions about individualistic ethical judgments are shaped by our views about broader issues of economics, social theory, law, and political philosophy.
>
> *(Danley, 1994, p. 20)*

This chapter and Chapter 8 are especially responsive to that criticism.

A relevant illustration of the independence of levels of social analysis was mentioned briefly in the commentary on Table 8.1 concerning the institutional business value of "competition." It should be appreciated that competition, as an instrumental (not terminal) business value, is a cherished attribute of the classical free-market economic creed (Adam Smith, 1776/1976), that is, of the institution of business. But not necessarily cherished by individual business organizations and managers. Competition is generally forced on companies as a necessary fact of life because there are other companies in the same business. Business activity is aimed at winning, not competing—even to the point of eliminating the competition. That's why the enactment of antitrust legislation was necessary. Although competition is romanticized as part of the American ethos and business creed, businesses whenever possible opt for anti-competitive strategies. Thus, we see the monopolies, oligopolies and trusts of yesteryear and the mergers and acquisitions of recent years.

Adam Smith, the father of modern economics, predicted these patterns more than 200 years ago, and salient empirical evidence goes back at least as far as to J. P. Morgan, who reorganized the entire railroad industry after the panic of 1873 caused by the failure of one railroad and the bank that financed it. He reorganized the industry by consolidating the railroads in a monopolistic process that became known as *Morganizing*. The lesson was learned well by the "robber barons" who followed, such as John D. Rockefeller who monopolized the oil industry. The adverse effects of these anti-competitive practices led to the Sherman and Clayton Antitrust Acts and the creation of the Federal Trade Commission, all by 1914. These laws were strengthened by the Antitrust Improvements Act of 1976 in response to the growing number of mergers and acquisitions.

What might be the source of the dismaying bill of particulars brought by Frederick (1995) (and many others since then) against American corporations? I suggest that the exercise of power, especially in the service of the single-minded pursuit of short-term profits and increased stock price, is an extremely salient value of business institutions that is determinative. I argue later that this expression of power, although related to the business values of productivity and efficiency—or what Frederick (1995) called *economizing*—is relatively independent and autonomous. The adverse consequences of the power motive, especially in the single-minded pursuit of profit maximization, may be seen directly in the well-documented excesses of exploitative, unethical and illegal corporate actions. What I find more interesting, however, is the way it may be seen indirectly in attempts to extend the power/profit-motive value to societal institutions outside the business domain with the effect of undermining the inherent values that characterize those institutions and jeopardizing the fulfillment of their objectives. But I'm getting a little ahead of myself.

As noted in Chapter 1, "the ethics of what we do are not reasonably separable from the moral standing of the institutions and organizations in which we do it." In other words, understanding normative ethical positions requires some appreciation of the social, political and economic context in which it all takes place. That means delving a little into *political philosophy* and *political economy*. Political philosophy concerns normative judgments about how social and political power ought to function—especially as pertains to what makes for a just, free or good society (Kymlicka, 2002)—as introduced in Chapter 8. Those matters are closely intertwined with the subject matter of political economy, having to do with the interrelationships of individuals, business, society and government in the conduct of economic activity, especially matters of public policy. The general normative focus is on the moral justification of an economic system (such as communism or capitalism), involving the relationships among individuals, society, business and government. Four primary theories or models are the classical liberal model of free-enterprise capitalism, the revisionist classical Keynesian model, the multiple-stakeholder model of corporate social responsibility, and the hyper-free-enterprise model known as neoliberalism.

The Classical Liberal Model of Free-Enterprise Capitalism[1]

The classical free-enterprise model of economic activity, based primarily on the economics of Adam Smith (1776/1976) and the political philosophy of John Locke (1689/1988), dominated Western thinking, especially in North America, from the industrial revolution through the 1920s. Following the depression of the 1930s and World War II in the 1940s, two modified conceptions of free enterprise—emphasizing social responsibility, multiple stakeholders, an affirmative role for government, and the role of the manager as a professional—held sway for about a generation. They have been followed by a hyper-resurgence of the classical model starting around 1970 and marked in the United States by President Reagan's "cowboy economy" (Cavanagh, 1984). Many believe that spurred in large measure by the excesses and inequities associated with the globalization of the capitalist system, as well as by public and governmental reactions to corporate scandals, we are now in a period in which all may be in contention. Or, as Danley (1994) argued, they may have become inadequate because

> As markets transcend national boundaries, individual nation states have little ability to deal alone with transnational corporations or international markets. At the world level, there are no mechanisms for coping with market externalities or market failures, or for providing for the needs of the 'losers.' There are virtually no international safety nets … . (p. 286)[2]

Adam Smith

Adam Smith's (1723–1790) revolutionary recasting of the nature of economics was done in the context of 18th-century classical liberalism based on John Locke's conceptions of inalienable rights not to be abridged by government, Jeremy Bentham's hedonistic utilitarianism and Thomas Hobbes' and Jean Jacques

1 The balance of this section owes much to the work of Cavanagh (2009), Danley (1994), Donaldson (1982), Frederick (1995), and Post et al. (1996).
2 *Market externalities* (more commonly, *negative externalities*), also referred to as *neighborhood effects* or *market failures,* are social costs of economic activities that are not paid for by those who purchase the goods and services produced, nor are they borne by the producer. For example, the degradation, property damage, depreciation and medical costs caused by industrial pollution and the costs of environmental cleanup are not factored into the sales prices of the output of which they are the byproducts. They are often paid for by individual citizens who are adversely affected or by us all through our taxes, which finance remedial projects and programs.

Rousseau's notions of the social contract. Smith's brilliance was in literally re-defining the nature of wealth as constituting the goods and services produced by a society and elucidating its origins as due to the use of capital under conditions of organizational specialization or the division of labor. Wealth is produced by the efficient utilization of capital and labor in merely following one's own self-interest, and it results in the aggregation of maximum benefits for the entire society. In other words, under ideal free-market conditions the egoistic pursuit of one's own concerns will result in maximizing overall utility. The presumed inevitability of this result from the interplay of free markets suggested to Smith the operation of an "invisible hand." But for the system to work, the market must truly be free—that is, protected from the monopolistic tendencies of businesspeople themselves and from the putative inefficiencies introduced by government involvement—notwithstanding the ironic contradiction that the latter is the only effective means of accomplishing the former.

Smith is sometimes interpreted unfairly as having proposed an amoral model of economic activity. But he was more sophisticated and empathic than that. He was quite clear on the necessity for trust, honest dealings and a sense of fairness as an underpinning for the effective operation of the market. He would be appalled at the contemporary practices of insider trading, hiding costs and inflating revenues to mislead shareholders, as well as the egregious enrichment of top executives at the expense of shareholders, employees and consumers. In addition to the moral virtues of honesty, fairness and trust, he emphasized the significance of beneficence as more important than self-interest at the personal level. As pointed out by Gonin (2015), "Smith defines the business enterprise primarily as the endeavor of an individual who remains fully embedded in the broader society and subject to its moral demands" (p. 129).

Smith presaged Hegel, Marx and 20th-century psychologists such as Abraham Maslow, Charles R. Walker, and Frederick Herzberg, in anticipating the stultifying social and psychological effects on workers of extreme job specialization and routinization. He was sympathetic to that condition and advocated increased educational opportunities for laborers—even though it entailed government activity in the world of commerce. Perhaps most important, Smith's justification of the profit motive was essentially a moral one (utilitarian) in that the competition for profits spurs greater efficiencies and productivity, thus raising the overall economic status of the entire society. He believed—presaging Rawlsian conceptions of justice and/or "trickle-down theory" by 200 years—that, although capitalism might produce disparities in wealth, the poor are better off in its sway than they would otherwise be.

Critique of the Classical Free-Enterprise Model

Broadly speaking, the classical model embodies two fundamental issues of political and social economy. The first has to do with the relation between business and government, with a focus on the extent of government regulation of the economy and business organizations, versus a laissez-faire approach and free markets. The second focuses on the relation between business and the rest of society, especially regarding whether businesses have any social responsibilities that might attenuate a strategy of exclusive profit maximization. It might seem that only the second issue is relevant to our focus on the moral implications of business values; however, the two issues are intertwined (in the belief of some, for example, that businesses should have the unrestricted and unregulated freedom to pursue profit maximization and should otherwise display moral disinterest). Nevertheless, the two concerns are not coterminous, and each is supported by different rationales, so critiques of the model tend to focus on one or the other issue.

With regard to the first, many Americans believe that government regulation invariably detracts from productivity, so the question for them becomes what is the minimum necessary or justifiable amount of regulation for which we are willing to accept some inefficiencies.[3] The answer, of course, largely reflects the relative salience of one's values regarding economic productivity and many other societal goods such as social justice, fairness, social responsibility and protection of the public. Adam Smith structured the issue as a matter of degree of regulation rather than an "either–or" choice between free versus regulated markets when he acknowledged the need to protect against the inevitable collusive tendencies of business owners. Voicing a more constructive, empirical (and optimistic) point of view, Thomas L. Friedman (2002) wrote that what distinguishes the U.S. version of capitalism from others in the world, and why it is envied, is "our system's ability to consistently expose, punish, regulate and ultimately reform" the "greedy excesses" of capitalism by means of "an uncorrupted bureaucracy to manage the regulatory agencies, licensing offices, property laws and commercial courts" (p. 13). But the zeitgeist has begun to question over the past years whether those government agencies might, in fact, be co-opted by those they are meant to oversee (cf. *Neoliberalism*).

Scholars have suggested that there are several primary flaws in the classical model.

The Weaknesses of Natural Rights Theory

The free-enterprise model rests a great deal on Locke's classical liberal (i.e., libertarian) political theory of a minimalist state not harming or interfering with our inalienable rights. As noted in Chapter 2, the basic philosophic problems with

---

3 Even that may be conceding too much too readily to the extreme free marketers. Businesses that dominate their markets (e.g., local utilities) have been known to operate inefficiently and restrict productivity to keep consumer demand and prices high. Conversely, not all government regulation is inefficient or results in a net cost to society—e.g., fraud prevention.

natural rights theory are the lack of any clear, nontheological basis for such rights, whatever they may be, and the justifiability of Locke's short list of rights versus someone else's longer list. (For example, is there a moral "right" to not be vaccinated during a global pandemic, thus endangering others; and if so, what is its justification?) In addition, defining the moral dimension of the state as merely refraining from doing harm seems deficient in its disregard for the moral principles of beneficence and fairness, as well as the broader perspective of virtue. For example, Danley (1994) portrayed minimalist natural rights theorists as "fanatical in denying the moral relevance of anything except not harming another. This view excludes, not only consideration of social good, but any other goods as well" (p. 51). It eliminates from consideration a great deal of what many think of as the essence of morality: positive duties, obligations and responsibilities that we accrue as intrinsic to human relationships. Locke's minimalist state is justified by an implicit social contract entered into by people to form that sort of society from the imaginary anarchic "state of nature" (see Chapter 3). To which Danley responded, in effect, "so what?" He holds that such hypothetical agreements among hypothetical people are certainly no basis on which to ignore or deny moral legitimacy to real individuals who may have acted altruistically to create a more beneficent state.

The Limits of Property Rights

The particular right that provides one of the most basic underpinnings of the free-enterprise, profit-maximization model is the notion of private property rights. For example, shareholders own the corporation and no one, especially not the government, has the right to require them to do anything that detracts from their attempts to maximize their financial returns—so long as the actions of the company stay within the bounds of law and acceptable moral behavior. The justification of property rights under capitalism is generally traced to John Locke's (1988/1689) philosophy of natural rights that, as noted, provides a somewhat shaky foundation. Be that as it may, it is noteworthy that Locke did not view property rights as anywhere near absolute or unrelated to moral issues. According to Locke, one acquires previously unappropriated property such as land by dint of one's labor, by working it—but under the following two conditions: (a) one is modest in one's appropriations, not acquiring an excess that will spoil; and (b) with the proviso that there is enough comparable property left over for others. Even in Locke's day, the second condition was considered unrealistic (England was getting crowded), and he responded to such criticisms by noting the availability of much land in the New World.[4] Nozick (1974) updated Locke's second

---

4   Defenders of the classical free-enterprise model might criticize this conception of limited property rights as "unrealistic." But realism as a criterion would not seem to be a fruitful approach given the generally acknowledged assessment that an entirely free-market system does not exist and probably never did.

qualification to the more manageable condition that the acquisition and use of the property should not worsen the position of others, or if so, compensation should be made. (This sounds very much like a version of Rawls's "difference principle"—cf. Chapter 8.)

Obviously, therefore, Locke's and Nozick's "right" to use one's property is not independent of a consideration of the consequences on others. And, as Donaldson (1982) pointed out, there is considerable debate among philosophers and political scientists as to when a person's position is worsened in a given instance and whether, therefore, an exclusive profit-maximization strategy can always be justified by the property rights argument. (For example, think of the negative externality of environmental pollution.) Contemporary scholarship reinforces the notion that, because property rights cannot properly be separated from other human rights, the right of ownership is not unrestricted (Munzer, 1992; Pejovich, 1990). As a practical matter, our laws are generally based on the assumption that rights are accompanied by obligations—at least to the extent of placing some limits on the rights. Corporations are not free, for instance, to maximize profits by disregarding federal wage-and-hour regulations. Admittedly, however, the question of just what *nonlegal* obligations the corporation might have remains to be answered, as does whether any of those entail a proactive beneficence over and above merely refraining from doing harm.

Limitations of the Fundamental Utilitarian Justification

The primary ethical foundation of the classic laissez-faire free-market model rests on the empirical accuracy of utility maximization under those conditions. If any other system produces equal or greater net utility for society, the alleged moral superiority of free markets is undercut. As Danley (1994) pointed out, even the frequent argument that market freedom is indispensable to political freedom ultimately rests on the same justification. No other intrinsic defense of political freedom is offered other than it is valued because freedom supposedly "produces the greatest net goodness" for all affected parties (Danley, 1994, p. 88).

Almost everyone except the most doctrinaire free marketer recognizes, however, that there are no large-scale economic systems constituted of perfect free markets; there probably never have been. It is an ideal that could not exist for many reasons. For example, a perfect free market would require the following conditions (and others): (i) consumers have complete knowledge of all relevant product and pricing information so that they can immediately change their buying behavior when an entrepreneur offers a better and/or cheaper product. But in fact, the three men awarded the 2001 Nobel Memorial Prize in Economic Science—Joseph E. Stiglitz, George A. Akerlof, and A. Michael Spence—won it for their work in explicating the necessary strong role of government in a market system as a consequence of the reality of "imperfect information"; (ii) all economic behaviors such as consumer purchase decisions and employer personnel decisions are entirely rational (e.g., there would be no such things as consumer brand loyalty, industrial purchases influenced by personal friendships among manufacturers' sales representatives and company purchasing agents, advertising and marketing that create irrational wants such as cyclical changes in clothing fashion, or any social identity-based discrimination in hiring and promotion); (iii) sufficient capital is readily available to all those with an acceptable business plan; (iv) sellers always follow competitive pricing policies rather than, say, taking advantage of a price rise by a competitor to raise one's own prices; (v) employees and their families are geographically mobile to follow the vicissitudes of employment opportunities; (vi) citizens decline to empower their government with any interventionist or regulatory powers over the markets—even on behalf of their own health and safety or for emergencies. For example, the $15 billion in grants and loan guarantees by the federal government to the airlines following the September 11, 2001, World Trade Center catastrophe would be prohibited, as would be the government relief provided to businesses and individuals in the 2008 recession and 2020–2021 covid-19 pandemic.

It is generally acknowledged that a perfect free market does not exist. The empirical question then becomes, under existing world conditions of mixed welfare and market economies that bear varying degrees of resemblance to the classical free market or socialist ideals, can it be demonstrated that a system that more closely resembles the free-market ideal produces a greater net good than those that resemble it less? There are several difficulties that must be overcome successfully to make such a demonstration.

First, actual empirical cross-national economic comparisons are tricky. Although it seems clear that the western mostly free-market economies have produced greater aggregate wealth than the rest of the world, concluding from such case comparisons that there is a direct cause–effect relation between those two sets of variables is uncertain—much less being able to estimate the magnitude of effect. To what extent might the success be attributable in part to western-style political democracy as well as to the market system? Dalton (1974) suggested that cultural factors play a key role in economic development irrespective of the system, and the view that historical, political and cultural factors such as values are crucial determinants of economic systems and success has become more prevalent (Harrison & Huntington, 2000). For example, it might have been critical that England and the United States both had relatively high levels of education and technology before the rise of capitalism. Also, the United States and Western Europe have divergent values regarding the acceptability of government involvement (i.e., what many in the United States see as "interference") in the capitalist free-market system. What role was played by mere historical accident? Europe already had relatively strong central governments before the promulgation of Adam Smith's minimalist state; the United States did not.

Second, relying exclusively on a consequentialist definition of morality means that one must be comfortable with the consequentialist rebuttals to the criticisms leveled against utilitarianism. For example, consequentialism omits vital aspects of morality having to do with fulfilling one's duties, meeting one's obligations, and acting in accord with the moral virtues. As noted in Chapter 4, the rebuttal entails the adoption of *preference utilitarianism*, in which such aims can be incorporated in the utilitarian algorithm as representing one's preferences (or *welfare utilitarianism*, which focuses on one's welfare or what is in one's best interests). In other words, those moral goods—one's preferences or interests—may be included in the definition of utility or what is valued. But if that is the case, then shouldn't the preferences of many among us for a more just and equitable distribution of economic rewards throughout society, as well as other nonmonetary social concerns, also be incorporated into the calculation of net utility?

Third, even if one is content to remain exclusively in the consequentialist camp, one is unlikely to surmount on such a large scale the "ethimetric" difficulties of act-utilitarianism (cf. Chapter 4). It is highly problematic that we could measure quantitatively the relevant attributes of all consequences of all economic activity under competing systems so that comparisons of their net utility could be made. Similarly, many will find the aggregate utility justification ethically flawed in those instances in which the greatest overall good is to be accomplished by committing what would otherwise be viewed as harmful or immoral acts, such as cheating or product misrepresentation (not unknown occurrences under the pressures of profit maximization). The consequentialist response to both criticisms entails using the more generalizable consequentialist theory, *rule-utilitarianism*, as is done by most economists.[5]

Therefore, assessing the moral justification of the capitalist free-market system is distilled to rule-based preference utilitarianism. But that still leaves two key issues to be considered. The first, discussed in Chapter 8, concerns the inattention to distributional inequities within the exclusive focus on aggregate or net utility. The other point, just alluded to, concerns the metatheoretical issue of how utility or well-being is defined in the process of putatively demonstrating the superiority of the free-market system in producing goods. For example, recall Sen's (2009) emphasis on opportunity capabilities rather than traditional financial indicators, in Chapter 8.

Disregarding for the time being the theoretical issue of defining utility, Table 11.1 presents the hypothetical economic results of four alternative social policies. The results pertain to four hypothetical (equal-sized) population groups such as those comprising different socioeconomic status (SES) groups. To simplify comparisons, it assumes that the same definition of utility provides a relevant criterion for each policy alternative and that all persons are equally morally deserving of the outcomes.

---

5   The reader may recall that rule-utilitarianism substitutes culturally based guidelines concerning the generally beneficial or harmful consequences of classes of actions, rather than a specific analysis of the consequences of the act in each instance.

TABLE 11.1 Anticipated Outcomes of Four Alternative Economic Policies in Which a Minimum Outcome of 21 *Benefit Units* (BUs) Is Necessary to Maintain an Adequate Level of Well-being

Population	Policy I (BUs)	Policy II (BUs)	Policy III (BUs)	Policy IV (BUs)
Pop. Group A	90	54	33	24
Pop. Group B	12	16	30	22
Pop. Group C	6	10	13	22
Pop. Group D	−8	20	14	22
Aggregate Utility	**100**	**100**	**90**	**90**

Source: Based on Danley (1994). Used by permission.

Because utility theory defines morality entirely in terms of aggregate effects, it provides no basis for choosing between Policy I and Policy II, both with aggregate utilities of 100, even though 75% of the total population is better off under Policy II—at no meaningful cost to the remaining 25%. (In fact, that group, Pop. Group A, does far better than all the other groups and is still well above the point needed to maintain an adequate level of well-being—i.e., minimally acceptable levels of shelter, sustenance, medical care, etc.).

Similarly, there is no basis to choose between Policies III and IV, both with aggregate utilities of 90. Yet Policy IV has the advantage of much less diverse outcomes overall (remember, all people are equally deserving), as well as the fact that the entire population is above the requisite level for minimal well-being. Moreover, under an exclusive net utility definition of morality we must choose Policies I or II over Policies III or IV even though 75% of the population is worse off under the former than the latter. It is this disregard for differential allocation effects in general and for the distributive criteria of "need" or "equality" that lead many to question the utilitarian justification of the free market.

Note that no consideration has been given to the reasons for the distributional disparities, which also will impact people's moral reasoning. (Recall from Chapter 8 Sen's [2009] theory in which procedural and distributive justice are integrated.) For example, one's views might change if the distributional advantages of Group A in Table 11.1 are primarily the result of hard work and individual initiative as opposed to inherited wealth. However, it may be that the overall distributional effects for the entire population are in fact determined in large measure by Group A, because they already have greater access to the educational, economic and social resources of the society, greater inherited wealth, and superior political power such that they exert considerable influence over the politicians charged with making these policy decisions. If so, then one must consider the inadequacy of the utilitarian justification from the perspective of social justice. For the pragmatist, the question boils down to the joint consideration of (a) whether the insufficiencies under some policies suffered by Groups B and, especially, C and D are more than offset by their supposedly better position under the free-market system than under any other system (as per Rawls and Nozick) and, if so, (b) the extent to which such relative deprivation is the inevitable consequence of the policies needed to achieve the overall result or represent epiphenomenal injustices. Those considerations provide a segue into the final issue to consider.

The most important critique of the utilitarian justification of the free-market system has to do with its limited definition of utility in terms of the aggregate satisfaction of our preferences regarding the acquisition of resources, products and services. Restricting human goods to that materialistic definition of wealth is simply a myopic vision of human concerns. This, of course, is not an original criticism. Recall from Chapter 4 that John Stuart Mill and G. W. F. Hegel each expanded Jeremy Bentham's hedonistic utilitarian "doctrine worthy only of swine" to include a wider representation of human pleasures, including the exercise of personal freedom and autonomy, aesthetic and intellectual gratification, self-realization and self-expression through meaningful employment, as well as social recognition and the assurance of a social identity. And that tradition is extended further by Armatya Sen's focus on comprehensive outcomes, or people's realizations, and their capabilities to actually attain them, whatever they are. In fact, this broader conceptualization is in keeping with the notion of fulfillment represented by Aristotle's eudaimonia and is experienced, according to Hegel, in the context of a coherent life focus such as might be provided by a commitment to one's work, family or community. Philosophers commonly refer to these concerns as comprising one's *interests* (cf. Danley, 1994; Feinberg, 1984; Perry, 1963), whereas social scientists, including psychologists, generally refer to them as *values*.

The importance of all this is the extent to which the classical free-market definition of utility corresponds to our conceptions of human value and well-being. Even if free markets provide the most efficient source of wealth in terms of the production of goods and services, if such wealth does not adequately capture what we intuitively or explicitly understand to be the components of human welfare, then so what? "It is not unreasonable to believe that even if [the] ideal Classical Liberal state would maximize actual preference satisfaction, there may be alternatives which promote greater wellbeing in the broader sense" (Danley, 1994, p. 129). Implicit recognition of this point of view is indicated by the growing use of the Human Development Index (HDI) as an alternative to gross national product (GNP) as a means of assessing human welfare at the national level (United Nations Development Programme, 1999, 2015, 2020). It is based on four indicators of life expectancy, education, and income per capita.[6]

---

6   The United States ranked third in the world in its HDI in 1999; in 2015 we ranked eighth.

Individual- and Organization-Level Business Values

One of the most interesting and unusual scholarly considerations of the values that characterize individual businesspersons and organizations is Frederick's (1995, 1999) controversial theory. It is especially noteworthy because it attempts to explain the frequent misbehavior by businesses in our society as due to fundamental intrinsic values conflicts. I focus on those portions of the theory that seem most useful and appropriate here without embracing the overall model, which has received intense critical commentary (cf. Danley, 2000). For example, one of Frederick's major concerns is to anchor business values in a naturalist biological and physical justification, as a manifestation of basic evolutionary processes for which we have been culturally reinforced because of their antientropic qualities. This justification is of considerable concern for Frederick because of his presentation of the theory as a normative or prescriptive as well as a descriptive model. If we focus on only its descriptive usefulness, the naturalist justification becomes less important.

Frederick's model is comprised of four multifaceted values clusters, the first of which, *economizing values*, comprises the values that virtually define distinctively what is meant by business.[7] The second set, *power-aggrandizing values*, are "neither the distinctive property of business firms nor determinative of business's unique function in society" (Frederick, 1995, p. 26). (In other words, lots of people seek power.) From some perspectives (e.g., critical theory) "power is not just one possible topic among many but rather provides an epistemic frame through which the dynamics of organizational life can be understood" (Mumby, 2019, p. 430). These two value clusters are conceived as "master values sets [which] dominate business institutions and business practice" (Frederick, 1999, p. 207). The third and fourth values sets, *ecologizing* and *technological values*, are contextual in nature, extending both within and beyond the organization's boundaries, and are of less concern for us, here.

Economizing Values

This value set is comprised of the three original values of business: *economizing, growth,* and *systemic integrity*. Their cumulative meaning is consistent with what I referred to in Chapter 8 as the instrumental values of productivity and efficiency. The nature of economizing has to do with all the intentional actions of individuals, groups, work teams or organizations that are designed to produce net positive outputs or benefits from a given set of resources, and it may be conceived of as an antientropic energy-transformation process. The forces of growth represent a continuation of the economizing process that is sustained by the repeated reinvestment of resources. Systemic integrity or unit wholeness refers to the integrative processes

---

7   There is, in addition, a fifth set of "X-factor values" that reflect the idiosyncratic and personal values of the people who populate any given organization and that, therefore, account for much of the interorganizational differences in values among firms.

that characterize any (biological or social–organizational) unit that allows economizing and growth to occur. As I-O psychologists we have long focused on integrating organizational mechanisms—including structural ones like work-flow design, bureaucratic ones like company policies, as well as social–psychological ones such as corporate culture, socialization, loyalty, work- and job-involvement, group cohesiveness and organizational commitment.

Power-Aggrandizing Values

According to Frederick there are four values that comprise this cluster: *hierarchical organization, managerial decision power, power-system equilibrium,* and *power aggrandizement.* Although they are not unique to the business enterprise, when viewed in tandem with the economizing values they present a familiar characterization of corporate America. Perhaps the most ubiquitous and traditionally accepted aspect of corporate organization is that authority and associated power are arranged hierarchically. Hierarchy is experienced as the legitimate structure within which work gets organized and accomplished, decisions are made, social relations are shaped, and social status is determined. The perceived legitimacy of status-based power differentials is reflected in the fact that the authority structure is generally maintained in equilibrium, notwithstanding trends advocating "flatter" rather than "taller" hierarchies in some circumstances. In other words, the first three values components of the power cluster may be viewed as instrumental values in the service of adaptive economizing.

Power Aggrandizement

The power aggrandizement value occupies a special place in Frederick's model because its expression conflicts frequently with the manifestations of both economizing and ecological values. These conflicts yield organizational and societal tensions that may be maladaptive for the organization and destructive for society. That is in keeping with the scholarship of organizational psychologists who remind us that the acquisition and use of power has as much to do with individual-difference factors as with position in the organization structure (Anderson & Brion, 2014). Economizing or power-aggrandizing tensions may be seen most dramatically in hostile corporate takeovers. These are often undertaken primarily for the purpose of expanding the power and wealth of the corporate raiders even though few economizing gains may be expected—notwithstanding their promulgation of an economizing rationale. The frequent result of these mergers and acquisitions is massive employee layoffs due to the need to raise cash to service the debt acquired (Cascio, 1993; Rousseau, 1995), not due to the cost or redundancy of labor. But such tensions are probably most frequently observed within the organization in the form of labor–management conflict, middle-management "turf battles," or power struggles among senior executives:

> Whether occurring inside the company, between companies, or between companies and their various external constituencies, these power contests always tend not only to erode the firm's economizing base, diverting it from the economic mission that justifies its societal existence, but also to weaken and damage the life-support activities of many corporate stakeholders. Neither business nor society gains much, if anything, of positive value from these warlike struggles.
>
> *(Frederick, 1995, p. 11)*

But, with respect to our focus here, the most important ramification of individual and managerial power is the extent to which it is associated with a great deal of discretionary authority (Mitchell et al., 1998) and contributes to the abuse of lower-level employees (Vredenburgh & Brender, 1998), as well as to other unethical and even illegal activities (Dunkelberg & Jessup, 2001). Most models of moral behavior assume that among the significant components of ethical decision-making is a rational element culminating in a conscious choice or behavioral intention preceding the action (Ajzen, 1988; Ajzen & Fishbein, 1980; see Figure 6.1). The intention that underlies dramatic instances of abusive, unethical or illegal actions is frequently the pursuit of additional power, recognition, personal enrichment, or corporate profits (Dunkelberg & Jessup, 2001).

Profit

One of the points at which my views depart from Frederick's is the secondary and derivative role he ascribes to profit as a value and motive because he could not attribute it to the natural evolutionary processes by which he normatively justified economizing and power aggrandizing. I agree with his observations that profit is a sign that economizing has occurred successfully, and that an individual business can exist without turning a profit; but conversely, profits can be produced by businesses that seem to contribute little of much meaning to society, thus not fitting the evolutionarily adaptive economizing principle. Therefore, we might agree that both economizing (e.g., productivity and growth) and profit-making are potentially separable objectives, as is the case with not-for-profit organizations that strive to be efficient. My own view is that at the level of the individual values of businesspeople profit-making represents a powerful terminal value that is implemented by economizing values that are instrumental to it, and it is reinforced by socially powerful external sanctions. In fact, a careful reading of Frederick's (1995) book indicates that his position is not very different from my own: "In all cases, profit rests on a base of economizing ... " (p. 53).

Frederick attributed much of the shocking "bill of particulars" against business (quoted at the outset of this chapter) to power aggrandizement. But because he did not view profits as one of the essential values of the business he failed to view profit maximizing as a culpable component—as if the only motives for the exercise of power were intrinsic gratifications devoid of the extrinsic and symbolic rewards that also are accrued. In contrast, Donaldson (1982) acknowledged "although the profit motive may … work to aid society in the sense of sharpening efficiency and motivation, it has often been appealed to as an excuse to fix prices, sell dangerous products, and exploit employees" (p. 167). For example, the deaths of at least 14 people and injuries to more than 100 from defective airbags have been attributed to the attempt by auto manufacturers to save just a few dollars on the cost of a new car (Tabuchi, 2016b).

Because CEO compensation has consisted mostly of stock options and financial performance incentives, the form that malfeasance has taken often involves fraudulent financial reporting. "A system that lavishly rewards executives for success tempts those executives, who control much of the information available to outsiders, to fabricate the appearance of success. Aggressive accounting, fictitious transactions that inflate sales, whatever it takes" (Krugman, 2002, p. 19).[8] This seems to be an extreme example of the more mundane "earnings management" that financial analysts have always known corporations practiced to meet predicted earnings figures (Berenson, 2002). Frederick (1995) seems insufficiently sensitive to the potentially corrupting influences of the synergistic alliance of greed and power aggrandizement in the service of profit-maximizing (and vice versa): "An antipathy for business that is rooted in a disdain for or a rejection of profit misses the mark and is closely equivalent to a rejection of the nature-based economizing process that sustains all life" (p. 54).

Yet, as alluded to earlier, one of the most interesting and potentially insidious manifestations of American business power and influence is the inappropriate extension of business values—especially profit-seeking—to social, educational, religious, and other organizations that are designed to serve the commonweal, not to produce profits.

Commercialization and Privatization

It has been more than 50 years since one of my mentors, the late Frederick Herzberg (1966), observed that

> The business organization has given its coloration, methods, skills, objectives and values to all the other institutions that serve Western societies … .

8   Those of us old enough may be reminded sadly of an aspect of the Viet Nam War, in which the number of enemy dead, reported on the evening news each day, was used as an indication of how well we were doing. (In a guerilla war, the traditional indicator, amount of territory controlled, is unreliable as it changes from day to night.) Military commanders in the field simply inflated the "body counts," as they were known, to present a more favorable picture, just as executives at Enron inflated the company's earnings to profit from the resulting stock increases.

> Not only have the systems of the businessman [sic] given their complexion to the nonbusiness institution but they have also, in fact, taken over many of its functions, as all dominant institutions eventually do. (pp. 1, 8)

Herzberg did not make the comment in the spirit of condemnation. He was open-minded regarding whether this state of affairs would turn out to be a good or a bad thing. He was concerned with whether business, as the dominant institution, would take a leadership role in enhancing the human condition in the many areas it influences. The question was raised in a very similar manner 30 years later by Post et al. (1996):

> Most questions of corporate power concern how business uses its influence, not whether it should have power in the first place. Most people want to know if business power is being used to affirm the broad public-purpose goals, values, and principles considered to be important to the nation as a whole. (p. 276)

Many critics have responded essentially, "No, it is not!" (Derber, 1998; Fraser, 2001; Korten, 1995, 1999; Luttwak, 1999; Mokhiber & Weissman, 1999; Rayman, 2001), but that is too large a topic to explore here.

More to the point for us, is the narrower but still very important issue raised by Herzberg concerning the extension and application of business values to nonbusiness institutions and organizations. Schwartz (1990) decried a growing "economic imperialism"—the transformation of a noneconomic activity, organization or institution by the pursuit of external economic objectives like profit-making. The potential danger is that this pursuit pushes the institution in directions it otherwise would not take and that may, in fact, be contrary to its traditional societal function and its values, goals and objectives.

That danger is part of the broader issue of the "commodification" or "commercialization" of society (Hirsch, 1976; Sandel, 2012; Schwartz, 1990; Tittenbrun, 2014). As noted more recently by Sandel (2012), "We live at a time when almost everything can be bought and sold. Over the past three decades, markets—and market values—have come to govern our lives as never before" (p. 5). Markets have been promoted during the past several decades by the political-economic movement of *neoliberalism*, which

> values market exchange as an ethic in itself, capable of acting as a guide to all human action, and substituting for all previously held ethical beliefs … . It seeks to bring all human action into the domain of the market … . [and it views] strong individual property rights, the rule of law, and the institutions of freely functioning markets and free trade [as] essential to guarantee individual freedoms.
>
> *(Harvey, 2005, pp. 3, 64)*

For example, in many ways education has ceased to be viewed as the means to creating a well-informed, sophisticated, sensitive and enlightened citizenry; it is seen as merely a means to job entry and a source of job training, and its cost is therefore an "investment" from which one expects to profit in the future. At the extreme, institutions of higher learning now have to be sensitive to "market demand" to remain in business, and teachers and professors must restrict their curricula to what is immediately "useful" or "relevant" occupationally or risk the displeasure of students and disapproval of administrators. Many educators are concerned about the adverse consequences on academe (Bok, 2009; Murray, 2000), and the problem is exacerbated by the increased role of research universities in commercial ventures (see Conflicts of Interest in Chapter 14).

Viewed in this context the *privatization* of goods and services is one facet of the commercialization of society. It may be defined descriptively, and benignly, as "the act of reducing governmental involvement, or increasing private-sector involvement, in an activity or in the ownership of assets" (Savas, 1987, p. 270). Savas presented a concise, albeit one-sided positive summary of the nature and presumptive advantages of privatization. There are two supporting and inter-connected rationales. First, the pragmatic perspective views it instrumentally as a strategic approach to improving the productivity of government functions. The second point of view is more ideological and stems from the minimalist government political philosophy of John Locke and the free-market economics of neoliberalism; it is simply aimed at reducing the role of government. Savas made the interesting point that many critics of the business sector who vigorously oppose the monopolistic tendencies of companies in the private sector are silent about de facto government monopolies in many areas of public service. (The reason may be that, for those people, the risks of government inefficiency in the cause of furthering the commonweal are less onerous than the greedy excesses of monopolistic profiteering.) He also presented a useful taxonomy of four types of goods and services and an analysis of how each is affected by five different versions of privatization (e.g., government contracting with or awarding franchises to private organizations, or government issuing vouchers to eligible citizens who then choose the supplier).

To Savas,

> the real issue is monopoly versus competition rather than public versus private, as it is so often posed for rhetorical purposes ... . The reason why privatization works so well is ... because privatization offers choice, and choice fosters competition, which leads to more cost-effective performance. (pp. 279, 280)

I disagree—both factually and regarding what is important. Although cost-effectiveness ought not to be ignored, I think the "real issue" is whether the infusion of business values such as a press for profits jeopardizes the public good represented by the societal objectives of the institution under consideration. (As well as the unsettled empirical matter of whether privatization really does "work so well.")

Savas' (1987) analysis itemizes ten characteristics by which to evaluate the different versions of privatization in comparison with government agency. Not surprisingly, viewed from a free-market perspective, they all appear to have positive advantages (e.g., the extent to which each arrangement promotes competition, achieves economies of scale, relates costs to benefits, and limits the number of government employees). But we can achieve economies of scale in schools by increasing the student-to-teacher ratios, or in prisons by meting out egregiously long sentences to nonviolent offenders, leading to overcrowding. Are those really goods? Is that really what we want? And although competition may stimulate cost efficiencies, it may also have deleterious effects by pushing people to extremes. For example, the educational needs of a community served by a privatized school don't always fare very well in the face of shareholder or owner pressures for profits.

As I argued earlier, competition is not a value usually sought by individual businesses or managers. Their aim is not to compete, but to take business away from their competitors—in the extreme, to put the competitor(s) out of business. Is that a relevant institutional value for a school or a community health center? What happens to those who live in the areas serviced by the schools and medical facilities that have been "bankrupted"? News reports are filled with instances in which people are offended by the inappropriate extension of business values and principles: by police officers issuing traffic citations to fill assigned quotas; maltreatment and malnourishment of youthful prisoners in an effort to cut costs at a juvenile prison run by a for-profit corporation; the threat to independent academic research posed by corporate sponsorship and ownership of the products of the research (Press & Washburn, 2000); and for-profit colleges incentivizing their recruiters to admit large numbers of even marginally qualified students whose billions of dollars in tuition is paid to those colleges by federal aid to the students, and/or private bank loans. Those schools have very high failure-to-graduate rates, leaving students uneducated, jobless and considerably in debt, while the schools and their backers profit handsomely (Cohen, 2015b; Rich, 2016; Saul, 2015a, 2015b). If the school goes out of business (not a rare occurrence) the students are still left with their debt.[9] When reviewed recently, one such large for-profit educational company with 138 campuses in 39 states of the U.S., had 191,225 student-borrowers, carrying $4.6 billion in debt (Morgenson, 2016a), which

---

9   The government does offer a potential "false certification discharge" of student debt, if it can be shown that it was obtained by false representations made by the school.

may ultimately be "forgiven" with taxpayer money (Carey, 2016). So much for "privatization"!

Since the 2008 financial crisis private equity firms (which are pretty good at making money; not so good at providing emergency public services) have taken over municipal emergency medical services and fire brigades. Results have included slower ambulance response times leading to deaths, the cessation of ambulance availability, and a homeowner being served with a $15,000 bill by the local fire department despite having failed to show up soon enough to save his house (Ivory et al., 2016).

In the summer of 2016, the U.S. Justice Department began the process of ending the practice of contracting with private prison companies to house federal inmates "to ensure that inmates are in the safest facilities and receiving the best rehabilitative services—services that increase their chances of becoming contributing members of their communities when they return from prison" (Yates, 2016, para. 3). This follows years of repeated documentation of poor medical care and dozens of questionable deaths in privatized federal prisons (Flannery, 2018; Porter, 2017; Weiss, 2015; Wessler, 2016).

What is missing from most pleas for privatization is a consideration of its relation to each of the separable twin business values of economizing, and power aggrandizement or profit making. Any organization seeking to economize or to make effective use of human resource business practices is to be lauded. Schools may buy supplies more cheaply in bulk, and nearby medical facilities may in some instances be able to share expensive diagnostic equipment. Large public bureaucracies might even be managed better by experienced businesspeople such as two prior Chancellors of New York City's school system, both noneducators. And the deceased Cardinal Edward M. Egan, former head of the New York Archdiocese, had been known within and outside the Catholic hierarchy for his success in addressing the staffing problems of the church in America with effective recruiting and training of priests. Even private healthcare practitioners such as our clinical psychology colleagues are advised to follow good business practices (Clay, 2000; Yenney & APA Practice Directorate, 1994).

The danger does not stem from mere economizing; it originates from a press for profits that goads the practitioner, organization or institution to policies and practices that jeopardize its primary societal function and supporting values. That is what accounted for the fiasco of Health Maintenance Organizations (HMOs) in the United States some years ago. An investigation of quality-of-care data for over 400 HMOs indicated that investor-owned plans had significantly lower scores on all 14 quality-of-care indicators than did the not-for-profit plans (Himmelstein et al., 1999). In addition, physicians whose practices were primarily in managed care plans were found to be considerably less likely to provide charity care and spend fewer hours providing charity care than other physicians (Cunningham et al., 1999). HMO financial rewards, contrary to the primary function of a health care system and the fundamental values of the medical profession, incentivized the *denial* of medical treatment to patients.[10]

To summarize, it seems clear that privatization does not always lead to more effective organizational functioning, and that the profit motive can incentivize policies that are detrimental to the avowed goals and values of the institution. Oliver Hart and Bengt Holmstrom won the 2016 Nobel Prize in economics for showing how privatized contracts can have dysfunctional effects. If we take as a point of reference Savas' two rationales for privatization, the *pragmatic* perspective is not supported clearly by the empirical evidence, so that one is tempted to conclude that the zeal of privatization proponents is based more on a neoliberal *ideological faith* in the invariable superiority of free markets.

The Revisionist Free-Enterprise Mixed Model

The discussion of the classical free-enterprise model was introduced by noting that it embodied two primary dimensions of political and social economy, one having to do with the role of government vis-à-vis business and the economy, the other concerning the relation between business (especially corporations because of their power) and the rest of society. In the classical model the first dimension is marked by the normative ideals of laissez-faire and free markets that stem from the classical liberal (i.e., Libertarian) political tradition; the second is characterized by prescriptions for exclusive profit maximization and minimal moral interest. The revisionist ideology that followed, beginning in the 1930s, also can be re-presented by these two issues. But first, a note is in order regarding the set of circumstances that is generally conceded to have prompted the revisionist views: recognition of the growing power of the corporation during the first half of the 20th century, and the so-called "managerial revolution."

Antecedents of the Revisionist Model: Corporate Power and the Rise of Managerialism

From the waning decades of the 19th century through the first half of the 20th century a significant concern of economists, social critics, and interestingly, many

---

10 In a dramatic "about face" consequent to the unrelenting criticism of the industry, two HMOs implemented incentive pay systems for their doctors based on patient satisfaction and other indicators of quality care (Freudenheim, 2001), rather than cost cutting. Wicks (1995) argued that the ethics of medicine and of business are not incompatible, but he did so by setting up and knocking over a "straw-person argument" to the effect that medicine is (not really) all altruistic, and business is (not really) all selfishness and greed, so that an integration is possible. He did not reflect on whether the fundamental values of each may be contradictory; he did not acknowledge the excesses that all too frequently result from the drive for profits and increasing shareholder value.

business leaders themselves was the growing economic and political power and anticompetitive monopolistic tendencies of American corporations, in contrast with the competitive ideal of the classical model. Corporations were envisioned not merely as business enterprises, but as major social institutions whose activities had widespread effects on the commonweal.

The formidable growth of American corporations in the late 19th and early 20th centuries that prompted the enactment of antitrust legislation also prompted the beginning of what was eventually called a *managerial revolution* (Berle & Means, 1932). The growth of corporations in size and the attendant diffusion of stock ownership as more and more capitalization was obtained diminished the role of the original few owners, separated shareholders from the actual running of the firms, and gave prominence to largely autonomous managers. The role of management is thought to have acquired, during this time, both greater power and discretionary latitude in which to exercise it. This was reinforced by the division of labor requiring technical expertise in a range of areas, as well as by the geographic dispersal of the companies. All of this, it was argued, gave rise to the professionalization of management by recognizing the responsibilities that ethically accrue to such discretionary powers. The interested reader should consult Kaufman et al. (1995) for a history of the struggle between managers and owners in U.S. corporations.

Some of the ten attributes of a profession described earlier (Chapter 9) include the confluence of technical expertise, power to control its own standards and means of occupational entry, sense of responsibility, and the acknowledged importance of the societal functions provided—all of which contribute to a profession's duty not just to the clients served, but to society at large. In hopes of inculcating this value into the world of business, famous opinion makers like Brandeis (1914/1971), Parsons (1937) and Tawney (1920) promoted and hailed the increased "professionalization" of managers. They believed that the aims and values of managers had changed from an exclusive concern for shareholder value to one of enlightened concern for the best interests of society, thus laying the foundation for the corporate social responsibility (CSR) model, some years ahead. This putative transformation in the values, goals and objectives of U.S. corporations and their managers was characterized as "the big change" (Allen, 1952), "the great leap" (Brooks, 1966), or "a new era" (Lilienthal, 1953). "The really great corporate managements have reached a position for the first time in their history in which they must consciously take account of philosophical questions. They must consider the kind of community in which they have faith, and which they will serve, and which they will help to construct and maintain" (Berle, 1954, p. 64).

These antecedent conditions are seen as having given rise to a tapestry of revisionist free-market capitalism, woven of the two complementary strands of interventionist political economy, and the normative CSR model, each of which is considered next.

Keynsian Interventionism

If the formation of monopolies and oligopolies and generally rapacious activities of the "robber barons" during the late 19th and early 20th centuries were not enough to warrant a wholesale challenge to the model of business-government relations characterized as laissez-faire, the onset of the great depression in 1929 and the ensuing years of economic and social misery certainly did. They ignited a political explosion known as the "New Deal" which encompassed a different economic model of the proper relationship between government and business in promoting the general welfare. Among the things that crashed in October 1929 along with the stock market was any residual belief in the self-regulating and self-correcting nature of free markets. Even the massive unemployment of the 1930s was not sufficient to bid down the price of labor enough to increase hiring and stimulate production and demand, as predicted by the free-market model.

The two enormously influential books of John Maynard Keynes (1883–1946), *A Treatise on Money,* and *The General Theory of Employment, Interest and Money,* were written during the great depression, in 1930 and 1936 respectively. They reflect his, and others', observations that the classical model had not predicted the cataclysm, nor was equilibrium being restored by so-called natural business cycles. No rectifying effects of "the invisible hand" were to be seen. In fact, the effects of the recession (low employment, low wages, low productivity, low investment, low sales, high despair and pessimism) seemed to be self-perpetuating. And there were no public policies available—or even admissible—to address the situation. Keynes' revolutionary idea was that

> ... aggregate demand—measured as the sum of spending by households, businesses, and the government—is the most important driving force in an economy [and] free markets have no self-balancing mechanisms that lead to full employment. Keynesian economists justify government intervention through public policies that aim to achieve full employment and price stability.
>
> *(Sarwat et al., 2014, p. 1)*

In other words, consumers had little confidence or money to spend, resulting in little business investment, hence low business output and sales. The solution is government purchases and expenditures in the market to increase demand, hence employment.

Moreover, starting even prior to the great depression, it became accepted that the government had to intercede to restrain monopolies *in defense* of the competitive marketplace to encourage business growth, productivity and investment by means of fiscal, monetary and trade policies, to limit the inequities of negative externalities and other market failures, and even (during the depression) to become a major employer. In other words, the view developed that government is needed to promote competition and guide economic activity using incentives and disincentives to businesses and consumers in the service of legitimate public objectives (e.g., environmental protection, anti-discrimination, or encouraging investment by lowering interest rates). This is the antithesis of the classical liberal model.

It reflects not only a different explicit economic model—involving constructive government intervention and regulation in service of the public good—it also reflects a different political philosophy regarding the proper relation between the state and its citizens. In the face of enormous and widespread corporate power and the devastation of the depression, the concept of the minimalist government whose only legitimate aim is classical liberalism's prevention of harm seemed extremely inadequate. Danley (1994) made the point that classical liberalism (contemporaneous libertarianism or economic conservatism) had lost sight of the original metamessage of liberalism, which was an underlying commitment to assure people's well-being:

> Revisionist Liberals recognize that human well-being requires more than merely leaving individuals alone to compete in the market, and that interference in economic freedom for the sake of improving the conditions of general welfare is a trade-off that is sometimes defensible. (p. 269)

Similarly, economist Paul Krugman (2001) admonished

> I believe that markets are very good things indeed. But the great economic lesson of the 20th century was that to work, a market system needs a little help from the government: regulation to prevent abuses, active monetary policy to fight recessions. (p. A27)

For example, with the failure of Congress to pass an economic stimulus package in the last quarter of 2001, it was anticipated that the recession at that time would worsen. But an uncoordinated and fortuitous rise in government spending (along with that of consumers) was seen by the first quarter of 2002 as responsible for limiting both the severity and length of the recession (Uchitelle, 2002b). And the next and even more severe recession of 2008, sparked by the subprime mortgage crisis, led to much more intentional government stimulus spending (The Emergency Economic Stabilization Act of 2008) creating the $700 billion Troubled Assets Relief Program (TARP) which seems to have ameliorated the crisis and high unemployment. Nevertheless, some were concerned that it set an inappropriate "precedent of preferential treatment for some [businesses] and not others" (Peirce, 2012, p. 1).

Given that a pure free market does not exist, and that government involvement in business could detract from efficiency by imposing some regulatory burdens on individual organizations, the question becomes one of whether potential inefficiencies and added costs are outweighed by the overall public good. And that question, as the reader of this book probably gathers by now, cannot be answered by a straightforward empirical assessment because the outcomes are shaped by and reflect individual values and preferences.

Corporate Social Responsibility (CSR) and the Multiple Stakeholder Model

The rise of corporate power and "managerialism" in the mid-20th century gave rise to questions such as "What responsibilities to society may businessmen [sic] reasonably be expected to assume?" (Bowen, 1953, p. xi), and many responses such as...

> ... to achieve a complete moral picture of a corporations' existence, we must consider not just its capacity to produce wealth, but rather the full range of its effects upon society: its tendencies to pollute or to harm workers, or, alternatively, its tendencies to help employees by providing jobs and other benefits for society.
>
> *(Donaldson, 1982, p. 38)*

And still, a generation later, "Businesses are facing a host of new, epochal challenges, such as the need to uphold justice and human rights in global value chains spreading across national borders" (Reinecke et al, 2016, p. xiv). This perspective is known, in general, as advocating *corporate social responsibility* (CSR). The assumption was that the managerial revolution had increased the power and discretion of managers to pursue objectives beyond the narrow constraints of profit maximization on behalf of owners. By the third quarter of the 20th century, this view had blossomed into a substantial field of scholarship and practice under the rubric of *business and society* (Preston, 1975), dominated by three descriptive and normative models: the *social control of business* (SCB), *corporate social performance* (CSP), and *stakeholder theory* (Jones, 1995). Social Issues in Management had already been founded in 1971 as a division of the Academy of Management devoted to "foster[ing] corporate capitalism that is accountable, ethical, and humane" (Epstein, 1999, p. 253).

Corporate Social Responsibility

The area has become one of the most intensively studied and theorized about in business and management scholarship. Husted (2014) reviewed the practice of CSR from the 19th century through World War I in the U.S., U.K., Japan, India and Germany. One of the foremost contributors to the field, Archie Carroll (1999) presented a concise history of the CSR movement over the prior 50 years in the United States, and then extended the history through the next 20 years (Carrol, 2021). Additional reviews are available from Aguinis and Glavin (2012) and Barney and Harrison (2020). Special issues of journals have been devoted to the subject(s), such as *Academy of Management Journal* (Wang et al., 2016); *Business & Society* (Barney & Harrison, 2020; de Bakker et al., 2020; Griffin & Prakash, 2014), *Business Ethics Quarterly* (Cragg et al., 2012) and even *Personnel Psychology* (Morgeson et al., 2013).

The substantive domain has expanded to include *political corporate social responsibility* (PCSR), *corporate philanthropy* (CP), *corporate community programs* (CCPs), *embedded* CSR versus *peripheral* CSR, *corporate social irresponsibility* (CSiR), "business and peace," "human rights and business" and "organizational environmental virtuousness," as well as a focus on how CSR plays out globally for multinational corporations (Aguinis & Glavas, 2013; Cragg et al., 2012; Doh et al., 2016; Endrikat et al., 2021; Ford, 2015; Hadani & Coombes, 2015; Kim et al, 2022; Kolk, 2015; Rehbein & Schuler, 2015; Rhee et al., 2021; Sadler-Smith, 2013; Tsutsui & Lim, 2015; Westermann-Behaylo et al., 2015). In the opinion of some, however, these constructs "which are focused on redefining the role of corporations in global governance processes, have made waves in academic journals but are unheard of in practice" (Baumann-Pauly, 2016).

Additional developments have included, on one (micro) hand—focusing specifically on the "orientations that leaders may use to demonstrate responsibility and implement corporate social responsibility" (Pless et al., 2012), the effects of employees' perceptions of CSR (Wang et al., 2019), CSR's effect on individual stakeholders (Chen et al., 2020) and the practice of human resource management (Greenwood & Freeman, 2011). On the other (macro) hand some have emphasized the social context in which an organization's CSR occurs (Athanasopoulou & Selsky, 2015). Some have begun to study whether the compositions of Boards of Directors play a role in its adoption—with inconsistent and/or complicated findings (Endrikat et al., 2021). Interestingly, Kim et al. (2022) found that executives who migrated to other companies over a 14-year period "assimilate[d] elements of their old firms' CSR profiles into their new firms … and this is true for both CSR and … CSiR" (p.155). Moreover, it seemed "that CSiR is more responsive to managerial discretion, compared with CSR" (p. 183).

Most studies that have explored an organization's CSR as an independent variable have considered its external effects such as on the company's reputation. However, looking within the firm, Zaman et al. (2022) reviewed many studies concerning the relationship between CSR and corporate governance. And Lu et al. (2022) found that "firms with better CSR performance are more likely to adopt integrated risk management strategies" (p. 496).[11]

Yet with all of that scholarship, in the opinion of some "there is still no universally agreed upon definition or boundaries for the concept" (Rhee et al., 2021,

---

11 Different business units within a company have traditionally set their own risk management strategies independently. More recently a strategy of *enterprise risk management* (ERM), integrated across the enterprise, has gained favor.

p. 584). In the context of our concerns this chapter can only skim the surface of this voluminous body of work.

The general justification for the normative models can be represented by Cavanagh's (2009) view that the great power of companies should be accompanied by a commensurate corporate conscience. And the perspective is most often fleshed out within the framework of the social contract (Carroll, 2021; Donaldson, 1982; Jones, 1995; Post et al., 1996). Just as classical liberalism extended the model of the social contract from political philosophy to business, as a justification for laissez-faire relations and the voluntary association of shareholders to further their own financial interests through agreement with management, it is extended still further by the managerialist model. It is the mechanism by which the very existence of the corporation is justified morally, and the relation between the corporation and the rest of society is to be understood. It consists of two intertwined normative positions: Business corporations, because of their power, size and impact on many spheres of public life, have (a) an obligation to help solve social problems and (b) a responsibility to consider and balance the interests of the many constituencies who are impacted by its actions and may be said to be parties to implicit social contracts. The social obligations position has led to a focus on the relation between business and society, and the ways in which corporations might function as socially responsible citizens (i.e., their social performance).

A popular classification scheme for conceptualizing CSR and CSP is Carroll's (1991, 2021) itemization of the four general obligations of organizations to (a) maximize profits (i.e., meet economic responsibilities), (b) obey the law (legal responsibilities), (c) act within prevailing societal norms (ethical responsibilities) and (d) promote society's welfare in a variety of ways (discretionary responsibilities). Moreover, "business should not fulfill these responsibilities in sequential fashion ... each is to be fulfilled at all times ... the CSR firm should strive to make a profit, obey the law, be ethical, and be a good corporate citizen" (Carroll, 1999, p. 289). However, "if companies want to be successful, their economic role must be regarded as foundational" (Carroll, 2021, p. 1263).

The Multiple Stakeholder Model

The balance-of-interests position led to the development of what has probably been the most prominent model of business and society over the past generation or so, *stakeholder theory,* the study of which has mushroomed following Freeman's (1984) seminal work. Descriptively, the basic notion of stakeholder theory is that "an organization's success is dependent on how well it manages the relationships with key groups such as customers, employees, suppliers, communities, financiers, and others that can affect the realization of its purpose" (Freeman & Phillips, 2002, p. 333). Acknowledging the corporation's multiple stakeholders serves as a means of focusing attention on those who are affected by the organization's ethically relevant social actions. That is, stakeholders have legitimate interests that may be furthered or harmed by corporate conduct. In fact, that potential to be affected by corporate acts constitutes the most frequently used definition of who is a stakeholder (Donaldson & Preston, 1995; Freeman, 1984).

Moreover, a stakeholder's perceived utility may be determined by more than just their dyadic relationship with the organization; it may be influenced by their perceptions of how the business treats other stakeholders—positively or negatively (Lange et al., 2022).

> For example, it may detract from one group of employees' utility to learn that another group of employees … is receiving superior income relative to the perceived level of contributions made by each group … . As another example, shareholders in the past have responded positively to Walmart's relatively stingy treatment of its employees. (p. 10)

Stakeholders may also, singly or jointly, have power that influences and constrains the corporation's freedom of action (e.g., social activist groups or competitors) (Rhee et al., 2021). In fact, recent research has shown that CEOs' positive public responses to "direct pressure received from … focal social activists confronting the firm" may be perceived paradoxically as greater "attractiveness of the firm's corporate opportunity structure for social activism" (Neville, 2022). In other words, it may invite further pressure.

Some stakeholders are directly and formally engaged with the business activities of the corporation and are thus referred to as *primary stakeholders* for whom the organization has some direct obligations; they are mostly employees and consumers, but also stockholders, suppliers, and creditors. Indirect obligations may be owed to *secondary stakeholders* with whom the organization maintains indirect relations (not necessarily intentionally), such as its competitors, the local communities in which it is located—including foreign countries, municipal, state, federal, and foreign governments—special interest groups, social activist groups, the general public, and the media.[12] The nature of the "stake" or interests each constituency has in the organization may be different and stem from different bases (Donaldson & Preston, 1995). For example, the stake of long-term productive employees is based on their effort, commitment and loyalty to the enterprise; that of customers is based on the explicit and implied promises made to them regarding the effectiveness and safety of the product or service purchased.

12 Some business scholars characterize competitors as among the organization's primary stakeholders (e.g., Post et al., 1996). Others place competitors, along with the media, in a separate category of influencers—those who may exert some influence on the firm but have no stake in its success (Donaldson & Preston, 1995). Conversely, there may be some stakeholders (e.g., job applicants) who wield very little or no influence. The definition of stakeholder is generally confined to human beings, although a case has been made for considering the natural environment (i.e., "nonhuman nature") as a stakeholder (Stank, 1995).

Not surprisingly, different stakeholder groups (and even those occupying different roles within a particular stakeholder group) may have different *corporate social orientations,* defined in terms of the extent to which they emphasize each of the various economic, ethical, legal and discretionary responsibilities of the organization (Smith et al., 2001).

In its normative, rather than descriptive version, the stakeholder model has been used as a framework in which to criticize the adverse long-term effects on employees and other stakeholder groups of the preeminence of short-term "shareholder value" as the sole guiding principle of corporations (Kennedy, 2000).

Under normal circumstances the broad outlines of the corporation's business and ethical obligations with respect to its primary stakeholders tend to be relatively stable and well-articulated, although not necessarily in all particulars. For example, regarding consumers the enduring obligations are to produce the best quality product or provide the best quality service consistent with an optimum pricing strategy and to do it within the bounds of the law and generally accepted ethical standards. In contrast, the "revolutionary" character of the doctrine of CSR is the assertion of moral and social obligations to secondary stakeholders with whom the organization maintains only indirect and/or unintentional relations (most notably, the public). There is the expectation of new implied social contracts with segments of society beyond the dual obligations of providing affordable quality products or services for consumers and meaningful jobs and fair treatment for employees. In other words, the normative stakeholder model explicitly includes as part of legitimate corporate obligations the harmful "externalities" that would be ignored within the profit-maximization model.

Thus, a full consideration of ethical issues by those who work or conduct research within an organizational environment ought to incorporate the much broader issues of social justice considered in Chapter 8.[13] In that chapter Sen's and Nussbaum's theory of justice, with its emphasis on human dignity in terms of people's *capabilities* was presented. It has been elaborated and applied to the stakeholder perspective by Westermann-Behaylo et al. (2016). They discuss...

> ... the normative bases for firms to engage in stakeholder capability enhancement—the ways in which firms enhance the capabilities of their stakeholders to achieve the kind of lives people have reason to value. We also develop a model of how businesses can have positive impact on the development of capabilities, and therefore the dignity, of their stakeholders, to achieve cooperative advantage. (p. 530)

13 Although stakeholder theory is generally considered to be a liberal point of view (in contemporary nomenclature), Freeman and Phillips (2002) made a case for construing it as a libertarian perspective.

Their focus seems entirely compatible with the broad scope of the original statement of the principles of stakeholder management, presented in Box 11.1.

BOX 11.1   PRINCIPLES OF STAKEHOLDER MANAGEMENT

Principle	Clarkson Principles of Stakeholder Management
1	Managers should acknowledge and actively monitor the concerns of all legitimate stakeholders, and should take their interests appropriately into account in decision-making and operations.
2	Managers should listen to and openly communicate with stakeholders about their respective concerns and contributions, and about the risks that they assume because of their involvement with the corporation.
3	Managers should adopt processes and modes of behavior that are sensitive to the concerns and capabilities of each stakeholder constituency.
4	Managers should recognize the interdependence of efforts and rewards among stakeholders, and should attempt to achieve a fair distribution of the benefits and burdens of corporate activity amongst them, taking into account their respective risks and vulnerabilities.
5	Managers should work cooperatively with other entities, both public and private, to ensure that risks and harms arising from corporate activities are minimized and, where they cannot be avoided, appropriately compensated.
6	Managers should avoid altogether activities that might jeopardize inalienable human rights (e.g., the right to life) or give rise to risks that, if clearly understood, would be patently unacceptable to relevant stakeholders.
7	Managers should acknowledge the potential conflicts between (a) their own role as corporate stakeholders, and (b) their legal and moral responsibilities for the interests of stakeholders, and should address such conflicts through open communication, appropriate reporting and incentive systems and, where necessary, third party review.

Source: From *Principles of Stakeholder Management: The Clarkson Principles* (p. 4), by the Clarkson Centre for Business Ethics (now David & Sharon Johnston Centre for Corporate Governance), Joseph L. Rotman School of Management, University of Toronto, 1999, Toronto: Author. Copyright © 1999 by University of Toronto. Reprinted with permission.

Implicit in the social responsibility multiple stakeholder model is the recognition that the interests of the many stakeholder groups vary in content and scope and are even frequently in conflict with one another. Hess (2001) presented a concise list of the issues of concern to seven major stakeholder groups. In addition, the various groups differ widely in the degree and kind of social power they can bring to bear in the attempt to achieve their objectives. There may be very broadly focused and powerful stakeholders such as the federal government, as represented by its various specific and cross-industry regulatory bodies, employment and antitrust laws, taxing authority, and so on; there may be loose coalitions of stakeholders who come together around a specific issue, such as reducing global warming by restricting industrial emissions; and there are stakeholders, such as the media, who may be characterized as simply having an open agenda of potential concerns. Management's objective is to strategically take account of, or "balance," the various stakeholder interests despite their multiplicity, diversity and even incompatibility. This is made more difficult by the fact that salient social issues change over time, so a great premium is placed on skillful managerial maneuvering—especially when one considers that managers are themselves vitally concerned stakeholders with their own special interests. A continuum of strategies of corporate social responsiveness has been described, from inaction and resistance, to reactive, proactive, and interactive strategies (Post et al., 1996). An interactive strategy entails merging and/or balancing corporate and public goals through ongoing dialogue with all relevant stakeholders and is often referred to as a *strategic stakeholder approach to management*.

Critique of the Social Responsibility Model

Regarding the Antecedent Conditions

There seems to be little dispute regarding the phenomenal growth in the power and productivity of corporations beginning in the last decades of the 19th century. What may be questioned, however, is the presumed concomitant increase in the social conscience of management. One can argue, based on the sort of data summarized in Frederick's (1995) "bill of particulars" against business, that this putative values shift was not widely institutionalized and that any increase in managerial discretion was used by many executives in the service of self-aggrandizement and other expressions of power, such as multiple business acquisitions. In fact, during the 1920s—the beginning years of managerialism—managers were primarily concerned with reasserting control over workers, following the end of World War I (cf. Chapter 12). Danley (1994) found little empirical evidence of an enhanced corporate conscience, such as increased philanthropy, that would indicate that the actions of corporate managers became more socially responsible. Thus, he gave little credence to "the big change" (Allen, 1952) as a descriptive thesis of changes in the values, goals and objectives of American corporations and their managers. Conversely, Donaldson and Preston (1995) reviewed several studies indicating that a substantial number of firms and a great many individual managers reported adhering to the notion that their role is to satisfy a wider set of stakeholders than only shareholders.

Regarding the Political and Economic Theory

There are no pure free markets. Perhaps the people who best recognize this are the executives who, on the one hand, must contend with a degree of government oversight and regulation of their businesses, but who, on the other hand, have recognized the political dimension of economic policy and have used it so effectively through expansive political campaign contributions, effective lobbying, and otherwise achieving considerable influence over the regulatory agencies (cf. next section on Neoliberalism).[14]

Nevertheless, there is considerable contentiousness about prescriptive or normative advocacy. For example, political battles are fought repeatedly over whether there should be more regulation or deregulation, higher or lower tariffs, quotas or other trade barriers, and whether (or to what extent) private free-market conditions should be extended to other domains as diverse as the delivery of health care and primary education services, the custodial care of prisoners, or the "safety net" provided workers by the federal Social Security fund.

Yet from the standpoint of our consideration of the ideals of corporate profit maximization and social responsibility, the economic arguments are probably moot. Even if one advocates in most respects a more- rather than less-regulated mixed-economy, it holds no necessary imperative for businesses to do anything other than profit maximize within those constraints, as they define social responsibility minimally as simply following the law. The moral issue is not one of economic and political policy per se; it is a question of whether there are sufficient or at least acceptable ethical arguments to be made in support of the CSR approach.

Regarding CSR and Stakeholder Theory

Donaldson and Preston (1995) argued that "the underlying epistemological issue in the stakeholder literature is the problem of justification: Why should the stakeholder theory be accepted or preferred over alternative conceptions?" (p. 73). They observed that there are three versions of stakeholder theory—the descriptive/empirical, instrumental, and normative—each corresponding to a different usage and requiring different types of evidence and appraisals (i.e., they require different sorts of justifications).

---

14 See Kaufman et al. (1995) for a balanced analysis of the financial impact of corporate political action committees.

In comparison with the instrumental and normative aspects of CSR and stakeholder theory, the *descriptive* version is relatively uncontroversial. The descriptive/empirical justifications have to do with whether and to what extent the stakeholder model is an accurate description of managerial values, beliefs and behaviors, as well as corporate actions. That is, to what extent do managers actually employ stakeholder thinking in their strategic decisions? (The most basic descriptive questions, e.g., "Do corporations have multiple stakeholders?" are merely definitional.) Nevertheless, Donaldson and Preston (1995) were positive in their assessment of the extent to which managers are sensitive to stakeholder issues, whereas Danley (1994) was skeptical. The first authors illustrate the salience of the stakeholder model descriptively with an example that is familiar to most I-O psychologists—Title VII (of the 1964 Civil Rights Act) employment discrimination litigation. That is, the force of law affirms the legitimate stakeholder status of even those whose relation to the corporation is limited to the position of job applicant. In other words, stakeholder status may be defined more by one's legitimate interest in the organization than by the company's interest in the person(s). At the descriptive level, stakeholder theory has even been cast in a developmental model, suggesting that stakeholders are differentially important to the organization as a function of the organization's life cycle stage (Jawahar & McLaughlin, 2001). Danley cautioned, however, that even if CSR is descriptively correct its proponents frequently conflate that empirical accuracy with a moral justification—a violation of Hume's Law concerning the inability to infer "ought" from "is."

The *instrumental* version of the theory (does it "work"?) has to do with the extent to which there are empirically demonstrable connections between CSR-driven management and the achievement of traditional corporate objectives and accomplishments. Early proponents argued that promoting ethical behavior in the corporation contributes to productivity (Dunfee, 1987), i.e., that "good ethics pays" (Lynn, 2021). The rationale is as follows:

> There are many reasons to believe that adoption of a "stakeholder" approach to management will contribute to the long-term survival and success of a firm. Positive and mutually supportive stakeholder relationships encourage trust, and stimulate collaborative efforts that lead to "relational wealth," i.e., organizational assets arising from familiarity and teamwork … . In addition, more and more executives are recognizing that a reputation for ethical and socially responsible behavior can be the basis for a "competitive edge" in both market and public policy relationships.
>
> *(Clarkson Centre for Business Ethics, 1999, p. 2)*

For much of the early years of CSR research a review of the literature could conclude that "the simple hypothesis that corporations whose managers adopt stakeholder principles and practices will perform better financially than those that do not … has never been tested directly, and its testing involves some formidable challenges" (Donaldson & Preston, 1995, p. 77). However, this is an area of considerable research productivity and if we are willing to expand the definition of the independent variable to include a variety of measures of CSR in general rather than just stakeholder indicators in particular, then the results appear more positive (Griffin & Mahon, 1997; Heinze et al., 1999; Kim et al., 2018; McMillan, 1996; Orlitzky et al., 2003; Pava and Krausz, 1996; Roman et al., 1999; Simpson & Kohers, 2002; Stanwick & Stanwick, 1998). The measures of financial performance used included stock prices, return on equity, various measures of financial accounting returns, and so on. Sun and Ding (2021) observed long-term negative effects of corporate social *ir*responsibility, especially for firms in competitive markets. Nevertheless, skeptics remain unconvinced. Most recently, Lynn (2021) concludes that inquiry into "the question of how social responsibilities and ethical behavior intersect with the profit-seeking and more economic functions of business … . has been plagued with flaws, inconsistencies, and sloppy application, leaving much of it simply inconclusive" (p. 512).

Most of the studies failed to analyze whether the generally positive associations found between CSR/CSP and CFP indicated that (a) social responsiveness pays off economically, (b) financially successful firms are more likely to engage in socially responsible actions or (c) successful management is likely to include both effective economic performance and social responsiveness. But Orlitzky et al. (2003) were able to conclude from their meta-analysis of 52 studies, that CSR affects CFP—although the particular operational measure of each moderates the relationship. In an earlier study of 469 firms using time-lagged correlations over three years, Waddock and Graves (1997) confirmed that the relation between CSP and financial performance (return on assets, return on equity, and return on sales) was bidirectional, supporting the existence of a "virtuous circle."

Perhaps the key point to take away from these findings is the modest conclusion that at the level of management practice there may be no inherent conflict between the aims of corporate profit maximization (at least long-term) and social responsiveness.

Much attention has been focused on "*strategic* corporate social responsibility" or the strategy of "shared value" (Porter & Kramer, 2011; Wilburn & Wilburn, 2014), analogous to the notion of strategic human resource management (Okhuysen et al., 2013)—in which the socially responsible actions or the employee policies, respectively, are instituted only in so far as they contribute to the economic goals and competitiveness of the organization. "Instead of the traditional notion of CSR as a punitive cost … , when done well, strategic CSR expands the totality of economic and social value in the creation of shared value" (Rhee et al., 2021, p. 587). This is in keeping with Carroll's admonition that a company's "economic role must be regarded as foundational"—as long as we also reflect the belief that "the economic responsibility is laced with an ethical dimension" (Carroll, 2021, p. 1263).

Nevertheless, one can at least ponder the relevance of the instrumental arguments and justification to the moral issue. To the extent that the primary reason for supporting CSR is long-term profit maximization, its moral status as a normatively justified policy arguably is undercut, and CSR is just another profit-oriented strategy, albeit of a strategically beneficent sort.

Business scholars and interested philosophers are generally in agreement that the most important issue regarding a potential supporting rationale for CSR in general or stakeholder theory in particular concerns its normative or moral justification. But it is a claim about which there is some contention. (cf. next section on Neoliberalism.) Danley (1994) argued forcefully that proponents of the CSR/managerialist position offer little in the way of normative justification beyond mere assertions of its "correctness." (In fairness, Danley also found little adequate moral justification for the classic profit-maximization model.) Fieser (1996) argued that businesses have no obligation to be moral beyond merely what the law requires because (a) any moral obligations beyond explicit legal requirements are optional, and it is simply unreasonable to expect business people to assume such volitional obligations; and (b) in any event, there is no uniformly agreed-upon useful set of moral principles or duties in our society by which to structure obligations beyond those that are incorporated in law.

But there are rebuttals to both arguments. The first implies either that businesspeople are uniquely outside what philosophers call the *moral community* of persons in society or that managerial role requirements are both amoral and more important than all other determinants of moral action. In both cases, managers—in the conduct of their jobs, which is presumably independent of their personal behavior—are thereby to be exempted from the rules of morality that we generally accept as intrinsic to the human condition. But at the individual level morality is indeed optional, and there is no basis for such a managerial exemption. The second point simply ignores more than 3,000 years of moral thought that provides guidance as we make our way past life's ethical challenges, and it is logically flawed. As should be clear to the reader at this point, moral philosophy and moral psychological theories are indeed pluralistic and, to some extent, conflicting. But the fact that a single universally endorsed set of moral standards does not exist does not mean that *no* applicable supralegal standards are applicable. To conclude so betrays a fundamental misunderstanding of the values-based nature of moral reasoning and action. The fact that we may not always agree in our ethical judgments does not mean that we should abandon making them and struggling to justify them by "right reasoning."

The CSR/Stakeholder model is sometimes justified normatively by virtue of the failure of the classical profit-maximization model to withstand critique (Donaldson & Preston, 1995). But that is inadequate: Even if one held free-market profit maximization to be morally bankrupt, it would not imply the ethical superiority of any particular alternative. However, the CSR/Stakeholder model is essentially consistent with a number of meta-ethical positions and normative ethical theories that can serve as affirmative moral justifications even though the fit is not flawless. In general, CSR appears to reflect and be consistent with all three of the broad facets representing the domain of moral values and behavior that I proposed: justice or fairness, virtue (i.e., honesty and integrity) and caring—both in terms of nonmaleficence as well as beneficence (Burton & Dunn, 1966; Wicks et al., 1994). The notions of universalism, the social contract and Kant's deontology seem especially apropos.

The meta-ethical principle of universalism is a central defining tenet of most normative ethical theories. It refers to the premise that no person's or group's interests have a priori moral precedence over those of any other person's or group's. Given that stakeholders are defined by their interests in the organization, the application of this moral principle seems relatively straightforward. Note, however, the qualifier *a priori* in the statement of the universalist principle. It suggests that the precept does not require that everyone be treated equally, but that there be a justifiable reason for not doing so that does not depend on a view of some folks (or, in the case of egoist positions, oneself) as inherently more morally worthy than others. Thus, there may be acceptable justifications for giving precedence to the concerns of some stakeholders over others when they conflict (e.g., legal obligations to primary stakeholders may consistently be given priority over supralegal obligations to secondary stakeholders; some stakeholders may at times be more important than others based on legitimate needs of the organization).

Stakeholder theory is most frequently justified within the conceptual framework of the social contract (Post et al., 1996), which is extended to include many secondary stakeholder groups beyond the primary groups of employees and customers. Social contract theory would seem to be ideally suited to provide a normative justification for the stakeholder model, irrespective of whether one is more comfortable with the Hobbesian or Rawlsian versions. The essence of the social contract for Hobbes involves the reciprocal relinquishing of some personal rights to achieve the greater goods of security and social harmony. The implied "contract" consists of the mutual expectations of the corporation and its stakeholders regarding their respective rights and obligations, which presumably works to their mutual advantage. The assertion of one's rights entails the need to recognize the rights of others.

But the Hobbesian version of contract theory has two major normative weaknesses as a potential moral justification for the stakeholder view. One stems from its extremely egoistic assumptions regarding human nature, which lead to the necessity of positing a "sovereign" to oversee and enforce society's "contracts." Therefore, Hobbesian theory provides no hypothetical justification for stakeholder rights beyond those that are codified and enforceable by law or other comparable authority. Thus, his philosophy does not afford much moral justification beyond simply the obligation to be law-abiding as per the classical model. The second normative weakness has to do with Hobbes' inattention to the power differentials between "contractors," irrespective of their origins; one's "bargaining power" is accepted as part of the status quo. Hobbesian social contracts are not necessarily what most would consider as fair ones; the terms may reflect vast differences in the bargaining power of the parties. One might acknowledge that this has the virtue of veridicality under capitalist free enterprise, but it fails as a prescriptive moral model of "voluntary contracting" with the corporation (Hessen, 1979; Kelley, 1983).

These flaws are theoretically overcome by the Rawlsian versions of social contracting that emphasize the importance of fairness or justice and fairness as reciprocity (Rawls, 1958, 1971, 2001). Rawls' normative contracts are made either (a) under the hypothetical "veil of ignorance" that assures impartiality among those who are self-interested; that is, it precludes bargaining based on one's competitive advantage, or (b) under the assumption of "the justice motive" rather than self-interest, meaning that (hypothetically) the standard of impartiality or fairness is internalized by those contracting. Especially under the latter circumstances, Rawls envisioned justice evolving ideally from agreements made voluntarily by autonomous and mutually respected parties who are willing to be convinced of the fairness of a position irrespective of their self-interests. Thus, the stakeholder model is rooted in the Rawlsian conception of justice. And Rawls' views, in turn, are based in part on Kantian assumptions.

Stakeholder theory has been justified normatively as providing the basis for "Kantian capitalism" (Gibson, 2000). The elements of Kant's morality include (a) the paramount importance of one's moral motivation (good intentions), (b) those, in turn, reflect our standing as autonomous and rational beings, (c) that rationality and those good intentions lead us inevitably to recognize our moral duty despite inclinations to the contrary, (d) the ultimate moral law is the generalized duty to act only on those maxims (principled motives) that are universalizable as a basis for everyone's behavior, and (e) human beings have absolute value (one's value is not contingent on any instrumentalities), and so people are always to be treated with respect and dignity as ends in themselves.

So in a nutshell, the Kantian justification of CSR/Stakeholder theory is that the legitimate interests of corporate stakeholders are to be respected and given credence just as if they were one's own, to the extent, of course, that they do not infringe on the legitimate interests of others. Stakeholders are not to be viewed simply in terms of their utility for accomplishing business objectives. The qualifier regarding lack of infringement emphasizes the "strategic balancing" of multiple stakeholder interests inherent in the stakeholder approach. The question naturally arises, however, concerning the foundation on which the legitimacy of interests rests. What is the basis for such a claim? As mentioned earlier, it usually rests on the capacity to be benefitted or be harmed by corporate actions, which raises two issues. First, the determination of "benefit" and especially "harm" may be more ambiguous than ordinarily acknowledged, especially as pertains to the public as a stakeholder. Second, it illustrates the interconnectedness of the normative (moral) and the instrumental justifications of social or business policy.

The major difficulty for the justification of the social responsibility model in general and stakeholder theory in particular is at the operational level (Ullman, 1985). "Evaluation of these theses, whether interpreted descriptively or pre-scriptively, is extremely difficult given the vagueness of the notion of social responsibility or professionalism" (Danley, 1994, p. 170). To which "social re-sponsibilities" should (any particular) organization attend? What manner of con-tribution is called for? What levels of involvement are sufficient? What are the standards by which CSP should be measured and evaluated? How are the interests of various stakeholder groups to be determined and assessed? How is the relative im-portance of those goals and objectives to be determined to achieve a balance among them? Despite considerable attention to the problem of measuring corporate social performance by means of social audits (cf. Bauer & Fee, 1972; Hess, 2001; Kok et al., 2001; Sethi, 1973) most of the empirical research in this area relies on gross re-putational indices such as Fortune magazine's annual survey of corporate reputations.

Even if one is sanguine about the moral justification for CSR, an overriding practical issue remains regarding the implementation of such corporate actions. Why should executives want to make those sorts of decisions, and why would they? This is, of course, a variant of the same question that we have considered at the individual level—"why be moral?"—that is, the correspondence between ethical reasoning (knowing what is right) and moral action (doing so). That is why so much attention is paid to the empirical relation between CSR and CFP: in the business world it is assumed that if it pays, it will be done. Martin (2002) recently helped illuminate the issues by pointing out the ways in which some manifestations of CSR are not only compatible with but even enhance share-holder value (he refers to these as *instrumental.*). Some are mandated by law (e.g., health benefits extended to employees' dependents), and some are volitional but are customary and normatively expected (e.g., corporate philanthropy). Corporations tend to get little credit for those, which Martin referred to as the *civil foundation* of socially responsible corporate practices. One of the most in-teresting aspects of Martin's analysis is his conceptualization of the "frontier" of socially responsible practices, in which the motivation for the practice is intrinsic (because it is the right thing to do) and its value to shareholders is not apparent at the present time or may even be negative (albeit of considerable value to society). The trick is to find ways to encourage corporations to take socially responsible actions of the latter sort. It may come from consumer agitation, the en-couragement of peers who have already tried and succeeded, publicity received by those successes, lobbying by nongovernmental organizations, or from gov-ernmental mandate (e.g., mandatory airbags in cars).

I will give the last (downright pessimistic, if not fully cynical) word on this topic to the *Business & Society* scholar Bobby Banerjee (2021):

> One thing is clear based on decades of research that has examined how corporations address negative social and environmental impacts of their

activities: self-regulation through voluntary initiatives like corporate social responsibility (CSR), codes of conduct, and multistakeholder initiatives do not work. These measures give the appearance that firms and suppliers are working to address problems with little evidence of outcomes. Naming and shaming companies and pressure from customers are unlikely to force companies to act either: There are plenty of shameless companies around that deploy CSR strategically to manage their reputation and the ethical consumer is a myth, apart from a small group of activist consumers and niche products. (p. 416)

Neoliberalism

Bettache and Chiu (2019) have observed that "neoliberalism, originally an economic theory, has evolved into a sociopolitical ideology and extended its hegemonic influence to all areas of life, including the production of psychological knowledge in academia and *the practice of psychology in various domains*" (p. 8), emphasis added).

In 1947 the Austrian political philosopher Friedrich von Hayek assembled a small group that called themselves the Mont Perelin Society (still active today), and which included the American economist Milton Friedman, to respond to perceived challenges emanating from socialism, social democracy and other such trends that they saw as threatening the central values of civilization: human dignity, freedom, the primacy of the individual and the voluntary group, freedom of thought and expression, denial of absolute moral standards; as well as questioning the rule of law, a belief in private property and the competitive market. These were all deemed essential to have a free society—especially free markets (Harvey, 2005; Smith 2021).

Thus was born the origins of modern *neoliberalism*—

> a theory of political economic practices that proposes that human well-being can best be advanced by liberating individual entrepreneurial freedoms and skills within an institutional framework characterized by strong private property rights, free markets and free trade. The role of the state is to create and preserve an institutional framework appropriate to such practices.
>
> *(Harvey, 2005, p. 2)*

The movement has been remarkably successful since the governments of Ronald Reagan in the U.S. and Margaret Thatcher in the U.K., in opposing government involvement in promoting the commonweal, and in furthering the interests of wealthy corporate elites in the name of market freedom. And its success is commonly viewed as having resulted in greatly increased income and wealth inequities, as described in Chapter 8 on social and economic justice. There may be, however, some strengthening of social forces willing to oppose the cause of these excesses (Lohr, 2022c).

Thus, neoliberalism is antagonistic to the role government plays under Keynesianism—mitigating the excesses of free-market failures—as well as to the nascent role played by managers in putatively diverting resources from profit-making to social concerns for the greater good. What Harvey (2005) refers to as "the neoliberal state" becomes preoccupied with furthering the freedom and authority of private enterprises as the only legitimate means of economic and social improvement including reducing poverty through "trickle down" effects from the top. So, for example, government regulatory agencies, designed to ensure legal and appropriate private sector action on behalf of the public get co-opted to serve the interests of the firms they are supposed to regulate. As Danley (1994) cynically put it,

> By the 1970s, the scholarly debate was not whether [regulatory] agencies primarily reflected the interests and needs of the large corporations in industries which were purportedly to be regulated for the public interest. The debate hinged on whether the regulatory agencies originally acted in the public interest and were then captured, or whether in their very inception they represented the influence of corporations seeking to control markets through the facade of the government. (p. 232)

For example, in a short period of time in 2021 on at least 35 occasions lawyers for large accounting firms in the U.S. left to join the U.S. treasury department's tax policy office in which many of them granted tax breaks to their former firms' clients and stalled efforts to clamp down on loopholes used by their firms. Upon then returning to their firms almost half of them were promoted to partner (Drucker, 2022).

For our purposes it is important to note Mumby's (2019) observations concerning the conception of work and the nature of jobs within neoliberalism (to be taken up further in Chapter 12):

> At the center of this privileging of the market is the sovereign individual, defined as an entrepreneur of him/herself … . From a worker/employee perspective, this means that the ontological security once provided by the social contract between workers and employers and its accompanying lifetime employment has largely disappeared, and has been replaced by rules of the game that are constantly shifting. Career events such as promotions and dismissals are no longer grounded in clear and stable hierarchies … . Each social actor is viewed as human capital … . That is, we each possess a set of skills, knowledge, and abilities that we are responsible for maintaining and improving so that we accumulate more capital (and hence accrue more market value). (p. 436)

This has resulted in the dramatic growth of *precarious work* during the hegemony of neoliberalism—jobs that are uncertain and unpredictable, hence insecure (Kalleberg, 2009). (During the week in which I am working on this chapter Vishal Garg, the chief executive of a company called Better.com, fired more than 900 employees all at once on a recorded Zoom call [Goldberg, 2021].) It is interesting that while one still occasionally hears concerns about the monopolistic tendencies of powerful corporations to impose high prices on consumers, very rarely are voices raised about its twin, *monopsony*. That is the term for the hegemony of corporations over some labor markets, allowing them, in the absence of local geographic competition for labor, to underpay their workers (Marinescu & Rathelot, 2018). An increase in the concentration of any labor market (i.e., fewer employers) leads to decreases in employment and hourly wages (Marinescu et al., 2021).

It is only a bit more than 20 years since Kevin Bales (1999) wrote the seminal book *Disposable People*, ushering in a consideration of what has begun to be called *modern slavery*. (Unfortunately, only a very modest level of "consideration.") It has been defined as "situations of exploitation that a person cannot refuse or leave because of threats, violence, coercion, deception, and/or abuse of power" (International Labor Organization, 2017, p. 9). It has begun to be studied by management scholars (Caruana et al., 2021)—mostly up to now with respect to corporations attempting to manage (or not) the workers comprising their supply chains. Bannerjee (2021) is no less pessimistic about banishing these conditions than he is concerning the genuineness of CSR (see above):

> The real problem of modern slavery [is] the relentless pursuit of low-cost manufacturing to maximize profits and the pressure on suppliers to deliver their products as cheaply as possible. If modern slavery has to be eradicated, that business model has to be changed. But I for one will not be holding my breath. (p. 418)

The most influential modern spokesperson for the unattenuated free-enterprise model has undoubtedly been the economist, Milton Friedman. Notwithstanding the prominence of the profit motive and individual self-interest in Adam Smith's writings, there is relatively little therein that invites Friedman's vociferous condemnation of "social responsibilities" for business or what Donaldson (1982) charged was an attitude of "moral disinterest."

Milton Friedman

Friedman's (1970, 1982) forceful defense of the classical free-market, anti-regulatory model of corporate action was first presented in the early 1960s as a defense against the growing influence of the "social responsibility" model. From a broader perspective it can be seen as a reflection of the anti-socialist aims of the

Mont Perelin Society. To appreciate Friedman's position, one needs to get past his sometimes overly combative tone. For example, he stated that "Businessmen [sic] who talk [about the social responsibilities of business in a free-enterprise system] are unwilling puppets of the intellectual forces that have been undermining the basis of a free society these past decades" (Friedman, 1970, p. 33). His vehemence reflects his passionate neoliberal belief that the economic freedom of the corporation to exclusively pursue the maximization of profits is an essential component of political freedom. In his view limiting the former necessitates restricting the latter.[15]

If one deconstructs and condenses Friedman's general position, it can be outlined by four main points:

1. The freedom of corporations to pursue single-mindedly the maximization of profits is an expression of inalienable *rights* in a free society; in particular, rights of association of shareholders to freely come together for that purpose and their property rights to use their corporation in that fashion. Friedman acknowledged that those rights are not unlimited: companies, through the actions of their managers, may be expected to obey the law and to adhere to the basic ethical customs of the society such as refraining from fraud. It is not clear whether Friedman meant, by basic ethical customs, anything beyond simply obeying the law.[16]

2. A free-market economy in which everyone has the right to buy and sell freely is necessary to maintain political freedoms such as freedom of speech. Thus, the influence of government should be kept to the bare minimum, based on the principle of protecting the public from harm. There is some grudging justification for antitrust regulations, a criminal justice system—including enforcement of the law of contracts and of property rights, regulation of the money supply, some limited "safety net" provision for citizens who cannot be responsible for themselves (i.e., children and the mentally impaired), and some minimal regulation of "neighborhood effects" if they are sufficiently serious, and not much else. This represents Friedman's notion of the "ideal state" in support of a "perfect free market." He recognized, however, that in the real

---

15 Friedman restricted his focus to corporations, which are publicly owned. The right of an individual proprietor or owners of a closely held corporation to spend their money any way they wish—even on supposedly unjustifiable things like supporting local literacy programs or training unskilled former welfare recipients for a productive life of employment—is not denied. But from a normative standpoint he was clear in his belief that they *ought* not reduce their profits by doing so, and those who fail to disdain such practices are actually "approaching fraud" (Friedman, 1970, p. 124).

16 Defenders of the "anything goes" school of thought frequently exaggerate Friedman's position by omitting his acknowledgment of the necessity to adhere to basic ethical tenets. In all fairness, however, Friedman was not clear whether any ethical practices are necessary beyond those enshrined in law.

world we have neither. One wonders what he might say about neighborhood effects today in light of almost 50 more years of industrial pollution and consequent global warming effects.

3.   Because what businesses do best is conduct their business, the most effective way they can contribute to society is by efficiently producing the goods and services they provide. In other words, as indicated by the title of Friedman's classic (1970) statement, "the social responsibility of business is to increase its profits." The assumption is that by responding to the pressures of free competition, businesses become more and more efficient and productive so that society as a whole benefits.

4.   Corporate executives and managers are agents for the owners and thus have no right to spend the corporation's profits in any ways not in the financial interests of those owners, such as making "expenditures on reducing pollution beyond the amount that is in the best interest of the corporation or that is required by law … " (Friedman, 1970, p. 33). Managers who do so are behaving unethically by violating their social contract with shareholders. Moreover, those managers are in effect inappropriately performing the governmental functions of imposing taxes and determining how they will be disbursed—powers they have neither been elected to possess nor trained to implement.

Critique

The Moral Objections to Markets

The objections to neoliberalism are not a priori nor absolute, but they are profound. They pertain to (i) market excesses and (ii) their extension to virtually all of life. A tragic example of the first issue is happening as I write this. The reader may recall the serious supply chain problems that bedeviled manufacturers and consumers in late 2021 as the pandemic economy was picking up—especially the extreme scarcity of computer chips, leading to intense competition among the multitude of companies whose products depend on them, such as automobiles. The companies that produce life-saving medical devices "can't keep up with customer demand as the shortage of computer chips puts [them] in competition with bigger companies with more clout" (Goodman, 2021, B1). One CEO of a company that makes ICU ventilators and similar machines observed, "Do we need one more cell phone? One more electric car? One more cloud-connected refrigerator? Or do we need one more ventilator that gives the gift of breath to somebody?" (p. B5). At least during the Covid-19 pandemic, I think a moral case could be made for temporary crisis intervention in the market.

The person who has been clearest about the second issue is the political philosopher Michael Sandel (2012): "Why worry that we are moving toward a society in which everything is up for sale? For two reasons: one is about inequality; the other is about corruption" (p.8). (Note— many of the indicators of reason #1, unfairness or injustice, were covered in Chapter 8.) Sandel goes on to note that

> In a society where everything is for sale, life is harder for those of modest means. The more money can buy, the more affluence (or the lack of it) matters ... . If the only advantage of affluence were the ability to buy yachts, sports cars, and fancy vacations, inequalities of income and wealth would not matter very much. But as money comes to buy more and more—political influence, good medical care, a home in a safe neighborhood rather than a crime-ridden one, access to elite schools rather than failing ones—the distribution of income and wealth looms larger and larger. Where all good things are bought and sold, having money makes all the difference in the world. (p. 8)

In other words, when virtually all options beyond the most minimal levels of basic rights (e.g., to a healthy, productive and satisfying life) have been commodified, inequalities become injustices. Free-marketers and libertarians love markets because they are supposedly free (people are free to buy, sell, or not). But we all know that such choices are often coerced, or made from desperation, or for lack of bargaining power or other options. Having a market economy is one thing, being a *market society* is quite something else.

Moreover, from the standpoint of the kind of society we want,

> commercialism erodes commonality. The more things money can buy, the fewer the occasions when people from different walks of life encounter one another ... . Democracy does not require perfect equality, but it does require that citizens share in a common life.
>
> *(Sandel, 2012, pp. 202, 203)*

Presaging Sandel's reason #2, corruption, recall from earlier in this chapter the observation made by the I-O psychologist Frederick Herzberg more than 50 years ago that the success of business had led to the inculcation of business values into other types of institutions and organizations. I made the point that the issue of concern was that "the profit motive can incentivize policies that are detrimental to the avowed goals and values of the institution." Sandel similarly warns about...

> ... the corrosive power of markets ... . Sometimes, market values crowd out nonmarket values worth caring about ... . So to decide what money should—and should not—be able to buy, we have to decide what values should govern the various domains of social and civil life ... . When we decide that certain goods may be bought and sold, we decide, at least

implicitly, that it is appropriate to treat them as commodities, as instruments of profit and use. But not all goods are properly valued in this way ... . Some of the good things in life are corrupted or degraded if turned into commodities ... . We have to decide how to value the goods in question— health, education, family life, nature, art, civic duties, and so on. (pp. 9, 10)

Sandel goes on to describe many examples of how commercialization, e.g., use of financial incentive systems in situations where they had been absent, resulted in surprisingly (to non-psychologists) counterproductive reactions. Social and organizational psychologists have long been familiar with the apparently paradoxical effects of extrinsic rewards on intrinsic motives (Deci & Ryan, 1991; Deci et al., 1999).

Managers Are Not (Only) Representatives of Shareholder Interests

Friedman (1982) believed that for corporate managers to engage in activities other than profit maximization on behalf of stockholders' interests, such as meeting alleged social responsibilities regarding environmental protection, is "fundamentally subversive" (p. 125)—that it is tantamount to an "explicitly collectivist doctrine" (p. 125). That is because money spent on those social objectives would otherwise go to shareholders as profits, to employees as increased wages, or to consumers in the form of reduced prices. By directing the money elsewhere, the executive "is in effect imposing taxes, on the one hand, and deciding how the tax proceeds shall be spent, on the other" (Friedman, 1970, pp. 33, 122). But that seems to be an overstatement. Taxes are mandatory, not volitional; one cannot voluntarily choose to ignore them without expecting legal consequences. Shareholders, however, invest in corporations voluntarily and are free to withdraw their holdings at any time they disagree with the way in which the company is being managed; they may even attempt to replace those managers. And, as indicated earlier, Adam Smith himself probably would not have agreed with Friedman. (In fact, as reviewed in Chapter 8, and to be discussed later, executive decisions about what to do with the increased profits of the past generation certainly did not involve raising employee pay or lowering prices.)

Beyond that, however, Friedman (1970) viewed such socially responsible actions as personal transgressions because

a corporate executive is an employee of the owners of the business [who] has direct responsibility to his employers. That responsibility is to conduct the business in accordance with their desires, which generally will be to make as much money as possible ... in his capacity as a corporate executive, the manager is the agent of the individuals who own the corporation ... . (p. 33)

But that argument was empirically and normatively refuted almost as soon as it was made (Stone, 1975). The nature of this alleged "responsibility" to shareholders is rather tenuous. As an empirical matter, management rarely if ever explicitly promises to maximize profits. To make such assertions to shareholders regarding future earnings could be construed as fraud or deceit if they are not realized. Also, short-term profit-maximization is not always the best business strategy. And if managers are defined as agents at all, they are by law agents of the corporation, which has an independent legal identity, not agents of stockholders. In any event, the precise nature of the relationship between shareholders as principals, and managers as agents, and what obligations and proscriptions accrue because of that agency remain very complicated and disputatious questions (Mejia, 2019).

Perhaps more important, from a normative perspective, even if promises had been made to shareholders and/or agency established, it does not follow ethically that there are no justifiable exceptions to be made. Other moral duties and obligations (e.g., avoiding doing gratuitous harm to innocent persons) can override a duty to keep one's promise so that not every choice need result in furthering the financial interests of owners. Therefore, to the extent that managers are in fact strongly motivated to pursue profits, we must look beyond just legal mandates and moral imperatives for the justification. Extrinsic influences like competitive pressures and organizational norms as well as intrinsic sources like the exercise of personal power and self-aggrandizement are not unlikely sources.

Moreover, this argument errs in assuming that the interests of shareholders are exclusively financial. On what basis can Friedman assume that? I own stock in corporations, yet I am in favor of those companies acting in socially responsible ways even if it means foregoing some profits. Many of us are shareholders; but we are also citizens and members of the community. And the same is true of business executives. In fact, not so long ago it was estimated by the Council on Economic Priorities that approximately $600 billion of investments are socially screened, including those made by more than 500 institutional investors (Pava & Krausz, 1996). In the ensuing recent years socially responsible investing (SRI) has grown (Escrig-Olmedo et al., 2013; Nath, 2021; Smith & Smith, 2016; Statman, 2007). In addition, corporations themselves value other business goals than short-term profits and share value: e.g., enhancing liquidity or market share, furthering technological advances, and expanding or diversifying the business via growth or acquisition. Even more importantly,

> While companies continue to make strides towards becoming better stewards of the environment, stronger governors of their companies, and consistent contributors within their communities, investment managers are also making their own strides by incorporating more refined screening criteria to identify these very companies for their portfolio strategies.
>
> *(Mahn, 2016)*

Gelles (2016), Stanley (2015) and Solomon (2015) describe the growth of investors who seek to consider environmental, social and governance (ESG) factors in their investments. More and more companies are seeking approval to become *certified B Corps*: "The B Corp Best for the World List recognizes those companies creating the most impact for a better world" (B Corporation, 2015).

Some have recognized the consolidation of enormous power in the hands of fewer and fewer corporations and called attention to what Tsusui and Lim (2015) refer to as *governance gaps*: "Such gaps arise when states are unable or unwilling to enforce citizens' basic rights against corporations" (Baumann-Pauly, 2016, p. 137). Yet, an optimistic perspective is offered by Kolk (2016) and Tsutsui and Lim (2015). They describe how the notion of CSR has spread in recent years among responsible multinational corporations (MNCs)—notwithstanding that it may have been initiated by pressure from external non-governmental organizations (NGOs) such as the UN Millennium Development Goals and Sustainable Development Goals, and promulgation of wellbeing indices by the OECD, and others.

Adding Further to the Framework for Ethical Decision Making

31. Ethical deliberations in the world of business cannot reasonably ignore the foundational moral justification of the business enterprise itself, which means appreciating the extent to which moral philosophy is enmeshed with issues of political philosophy and political economy. One's macro-level values, beliefs, and assumptions regarding the appropriate role of business in society provide a salient context for one's micro-level ethical deliberations.

32. Contrary to popular belief, scholars have for more than 200 years viewed business from a societal perspective as a moral enterprise— among other things. Even Adam Smith's classic laissez-faire free-market model is embedded in the moral philosophy of the enlightenment (e.g., natural rights theory), and he assumed that a precondition for effective economic transactions was virtuous interpersonal dealings. More fundamentally, however, the justification for free markets and the self-interested pursuit of profits has always been and continues to be the belief that everyone will benefit therefrom.

33. Notwithstanding those good intentions and its effectiveness in producing wealth, many contemporary business scholars and social theorists from many academic disciplines view the classical free-enterprise economic model as morally deficient and its relatively unrestrained implementation as the cause of a considerable degree of economic injustice. It is viewed as deficient because of its limited conception of what is good, its failure to deal adequately with the extreme and morally questionable inequities it creates, and the antisocial, unethical, and illegal consequences that an excessive pursuit of power and profits frequently produces.

34. The general perspective of CSR and the multiple stakeholder theory in particular present an alternative conception of the proper role of the corporation in society—judged by an ethical evaluation of all its effects on society, not simply its effectiveness in producing shareholder value. It is thought by many contemporary business scholars to be a more adequately justified moral position. However, the multiplicity of stakeholders and their differing—often conflicting—interests can serve to increase considerably the difficulty of ethical deliberations by corporate decision-makers. This difficulty is exacerbated by our natural partiality and sense of obligation toward those closest to us.

35. If the recent trends of economic globalization continue (and I have encountered no knowledgeable source who believes they will not) expanded individual moral sensitivity and ethical leadership from the top of MNCs will become more and more important as determinants of ethical action, commensurate with the likely continued diminution of external governmental and other regulatory controls on corporate behavior.

12

THE VALUES AND ETHICS OF INDUSTRIAL-ORGANIZATIONAL PSYCHOLOGY

Changes in the workplace have tended to significantly increase the demands placed on employees, often to the detriment of their health and personal life. As organizations have expected more from their workforce and have provided little in return other than simply a job or employability, it is perhaps not surprising that employee cynicism and mistrust have increased.

—Cartwright and Holmes

… the field of I-O psychology is not likely to become more visible or more relevant to society at large or to achieve the lofty goals it has set for itself unless researchers, practitioners, universities, and professional organizations implement significant changes.

—Cascio and Aguinis

That double-epigraph sets the tone for the essence of this chapter. The business scholars Cartwright and Holmes (2006) highlight the onerous and deleterious changes meted out to workers by corporations over the past (now) 40-plus years (cf. Chapter 11); and the I-O psychologists Cascio and Aguinis (2008)—although not in direct response—implicitly chide the field for its inaction on behalf of workers and the wider society.

This chapter offers a critique and an expanded vision of I-O psychology that attempts to go beyond the limited letter of our de facto values to include a better representation of its spirit. Not all the ideas put forth are original; some reflect criticisms of the field and of applied social science that were made earlier by I-O colleagues and predecessors, as well as by external critics. And evidence of some of the advocated changes can already be seen in the research and practice of some

DOI: 10.4324/9781003212577-14

among us. But the appeal here is to elevate those trends to the level of institutional attributes that will more nearly typify the field rather than represent the contributions of a relative few.

This expanded view is comprised of four interrelated facets. It's a disaggregation of a holistic (albeit generally unacknowledged) I-O value system, so writing about each facet separately inevitably entails some overlap. The four aspects of this proposed vision are (a) adoption of a broader model of values or value system than has long characterized the field; (b) the inclusion of an avowedly normative (i.e., moral) perspective to the field, along with the dominant scientific (i.e., descriptive and predictive) and instrumental (focus on productivity and organizational effectiveness) perspectives; this facet is the broadest, and to some degree might be considered inclusive of the other three; (c) a greater interest in and concern for individual employees, along with our predominant concern for organizational needs, goals and perspectives; (d) an expanded criterion of effectiveness beyond the narrow standard of technical competence, acknowledging the broader organizational and societal context and consequences of our work.

Because the substance of this critique was initially presented in the first edition of this book, published 20 years ago, it seems reasonable for the reader to expect some comments about how my current assessment compares with the one made then. The question seems relatively simple and straightforward; the answer is complicated; and 20 years is not all that long in the life of a profession. Nevertheless, I believe there are discernable trends worth noting—of the "good news/bad news" variety. First, there clearly have been positive—even inspiring—changes in I-O psychology during these years, along lines I might have hoped for. For example, in just ten years we went from a mind-set in which "ethical issues" was not even listed as an invited topic for submissions to SIOP's annual conference, to the Society's sponsorship of an edited volume on *Using Industrial-Organizational Psychology for the Greater Good* (Olson-Buchanan et al., 2013), establishing a standing committee for the advancement of professional ethics (CAPE), as well as sponsoring separate awards for work in humanitarian, as well as humanistic I-O psychology; and members of *The Global Organization for Humanitarian Work Psychology* have become a notable presence at those same annual conferences.

On the other hand, it has been pointed out to me (often inadvertently) in the writings of others, that some of the attributes of I-O I criticized have had even more widespread adverse effects than I had been sensitive to originally—so, unfortunately, the same criticisms remain salient. And lastly, it seems that the zeitgeist of the corporate world has become even more difficult, oppressive and antagonistic to employee security and wellbeing (cf. *neoliberalism* in Chapter 11)—perhaps not surprising following the financial crisis and recession of 2008, in which many people remain mired. Indicators of these trends will be noted throughout the following material, as appropriate.

Facets of I-O Psychology: I. The Values Model

In the middle of the last century industrial psychology—as it was then known, prior to our hyphenated or slashed social identity—was subjected to considerable criticism both from within the field and from concerned outsiders. Perhaps the harshest, certainly the best-known outsider was the social historian Loren Baritz (1960) who, in *The Servants of Power*, wrote:

> Throughout their professional history, industrial social scientists, without prodding from anyone, have accepted the norms of America's managers. If this attitude had not tended to influence their work, it would deserve merely passing mention. But this commitment to management's goals, as opposed to the goals of other groups and classes in American society, did color their research and recommendations. These men [sic] have been committed to aims other than those of their professional but nonindustrial colleagues. Though the generalization has weaknesses, it seems that making a contribution to knowledge has been the essential purpose of only a few industrial social scientists. Reducing the pressure of unionism while increasing the productivity of the labor force and thereby lowering costs have been among their most cherished goals, because these have been the goals which management has set for them. (pp. 197–198)

Baritz's criticism is two-pronged, comprised of one charge that essentially characterized the field as unscientific (relatively unconcerned with "making a contribution to knowledge"), and the other lamenting our supposed embrace of the goals, values and norms of business, including an anti-labor orientation, as opposed to other normative perspectives that could have been adopted. I explore each in turn.

I-O Psychology as Unscientific

At the time, Baritz's criticisms of the atheoretical and "unscientific" nature of the field were pretty much on the mark. Moreover, to our credit, such critiques were not unknown among members of the profession itself:

> Industrial psychology as management technique is well known and highly successful ... . In the main this has meant work on immediate, more or less technical problems ... . Meanwhile, industrial psychology as *social science* remains a puny infant—if not, indeed, still in embryo. The problem is serious.
>
> *(Kornhauser, 1947, p. 224)*

But by the time of Baritz's critique industrial psychology, along with the field of psychology in general, was already in the throes of major changes. The so-called "cognitive revolution" in academic psychology in the 1960s, which supplanted the hegemony that behaviorism had enjoyed for more than a generation, was beginning to make inroads into industrial psychology—most notably, at first, in conceptions of managerial decision-making, and evaluative processes such as performance appraisals. More important, the recently evolved field of organizational psychology started to blossom, as indicated by such markers as the first editions of Edgar Schein's (1980) *Organizational Psychology* in 1965, and Katz and Kahn's (1978) *The Social Psychology of Organizations* in 1966. These were, first and foremost, *theoretical* advances that emphasized the system characteristics of organizations and were as much or more concerned with explaining the behavior of groups, subsystems and the entire organization as of individuals. As Schein (1980) expressed it, "The traditional industrial psychologist either would not have considered questions such as these or could not have dealt with them scientifically because the necessary theoretical and research tools were lacking" (p. 7).

These trends culminated in the development of the field of *organizational behavior* or *organizational theory* defined as "the study of the structure and functioning of organizations and the behavior of groups and individuals within them" (Pugh, 1966, p. 235; 1969, p. 345). It is a multidisciplinary field, and it was intended from the outset to be distinct from "traditional industrial psychology" by virtue of being "a theoretical research oriented activity" aimed at "understand [ing] the behaviour of men [sic] in organizations, regarding organizational activity as an object of study in its own right, rather than as a setting in which to apply accepted psychological knowledge" (Pugh, 1969, p. 345).

The gravitational pull of the new multidisciplinary and integrative field, coupled with the popularity of organizational psychology, had a profound effect on the nature of industrial psychology itself. By 1970 it had expanded into "industrial *and organizational* psychology," with a substantial theoretical and scientific component even in traditional service areas like job analysis, employee selection, training and performance evaluation. Even twenty-plus years ago, a casual perusal (if such is possible) of the 3,000+ pages of the *Handbook of Industrial and Organizational Psychology* (Dunnette & Hough, 1990, 1991, 1992; Triandis et al., 1994) would have revealed that a theoretical and scientific research orientation predominates in virtually every chapter. The first section of the four-volume set, comprised of five chapters of more than 300 pages, consists entirely of theory and a consideration of metatheoretical issues. And I think it is a fair assessment to characterize even our empirical journals as reflecting research that is, for the most part, if not actually theory-driven, at least concerned with theoretical implications. Nevertheless, Marvin Dunnette (1984) still felt moved to observe that too many I-O psychologists are technicians rather than scientists or scientist–practitioners. Unfortunately, the prevailing view of the field by colleagues in other psychology specialties remains predominantly "applied industrial psychology—[an] exile from the university—[which] aims to secure optimal performances from employees" (Gardner, 2002, p. B8).

But it seems clear that I-O psychology can no longer reasonably be characterized as unscientific in the sense of being atheoretical. The changes in the field that have been wrought over the past 50 years or so in that regard have been profound: " … the world's understanding of such subjects as aptitudes, interests, motivation, fatigue, stress, group dynamics, leadership, ethnic and gender differences, and decision making, among others, would be impoverished were it not for the work of industrial and organizational psychologists" (Katzell, 1994, p. 72).

It seems extremely ironic that many of our practitioner colleagues are wont nowadays to complain about the *overly* theoretical—meaning not readily applicable—nature of our academic writings and research. One such critic recently blamed the preponderance of such "abstract and theory-oriented" research, along with the abysmally low level of our competence with modern technology (meaning "computer science, data science, and human-computer interaction") as possibly "caus[ing] I-O to become obsolete" (Landers, 2019). And it is doubly ironic in that he attributes the over-emphasis on abstract theory-building to I-O's mimicking and adopting the values and practices of Business School faculty.

But what about Baritz's other criticism, regarding our goals and values (a criticism also embedded in Gardner's more recent characterization of the field)?

I-O Psychology and Labor

Baritz's second critique was viewed as exaggerated by some I-O psychologists (Ferguson, 1962–1965; Meltzer & Stagner, 1980; Stagner, 1981a). For example, as early as 1920 Walter Dill Scott's consulting company was strongly advocating labor–management cooperation in the interests of industrial peace so that the schism that developed between industrial psychology and labor unions was not inevitable. But it seems clear that most industrial psychologists were sanguine about the purely technocratic character of the field and simply pleased that "industry is now accepting and paying for industrial psychology" (Tiffin, 1956, p. 372), although it seems as if practitioners needed continuing reassurance (Feinberg & Lefkowitz, 1962; Ronen, 1980). In any event, one searches pretty much in vain for studies of organized labor in the I-O psychology literature akin to what appears in related fields (e.g., Rosenfeld, 2019). For example, *The Guidelines for Education and Training in Industrial-Organizational Psychology* (SIOP, 2016) showcase four work areas for I-O psychologists: academe, consulting, industry and government. It would be valuable if labor unions and non-profit NGOs were included. And that is a shame because:

> A consideration of union views on topics of interest to I-O psychologists (e.g., selection, training, organizational commitment, organizational citizenship behavior, counterproductive work behavior, seniority) would yield very different perspectives and might even involve reconceptualizations of some constructs.
>
> *(Highhouse & Schmitt, 2012, p. 5)*

Although Stagner (1981a) believed that Baritz had distorted the activities of industrial psychologists, he acknowledged that "the tendency of industrial psychologists to ignore labor unions has been remarkable" (p. 321), and he even felt compelled to concede that there was "some justification" that "psychologists have been persuaded to use their selection skills to exclude from employment applicants with prounion sympathies" (1981b, p. 504). This has more recently been documented extensively (Zickar, 2001). Reviews of the history of the relation between psychology in general and I-O psychology with working people in general and organized labor in particular reveal considerable disinterest, distrust and antipathy on both sides (Baritz, 1960; Gordon & Burt, 1981; Huszczo et al., 1984; Shostak, 1964; Zickar, 2001). Gordon and Burt summarized these reactions as reflecting two major sources: (a) the association of I-O psychologists with U.S. companies who by-and-large have maintained an adversarial relation to unions (cf. Dawkins, 2012), along with the conduct of research and human resources practices, such as attitude surveys and personality testing, which have been used for "union busting" (Hamner & Smith, 1978; Schriesheim, 1978; Zickar, 2001); and (b) the eagerness of I-O psychologists to satisfy the strong management demand for psychological research and services. To these, Rosen and Stagner (1980) added (c) the typical secrecy and distrust of outsiders characteristic of many unions as following years of playing a reactive and adversarial role, and (d) the ignorance of most I-O psychologists about unions and the absence of any consideration of them in our training, along with the middle-class backgrounds typical of most of us.

But there have been more fundamental determinants of the schism and antipathy between organized labor and I-O psychology, underlying all the factors reviewed by Gordon and Burt and by Rosen and Stagner. And those are the prevailing zeitgeist of the first third of the 20th century and the extent to which the values and attitudes of industrial psychologists reflected the upper-middle-class and managerial perspective of the time (and, to a considerable degree, continue to do so). As noted by Clayton Alderfer (personal communication, July 2002), I-O psychologists are generally not educated to be self-reflective about their social identity or group memberships. Similarly, Walter Nord (1982) was perhaps the first I-O psychologist to point out that our field tends to be rather ahistorical in orientation and, as a result,

> Our ahistorical proclivities have contributed to important distortions in our view of the evolution of organizational forms and the influence of historical processes on the development of I-O psychology ... .
>
> The evolution of organizational forms, especially those aspects related to the management of people, is also heavily influenced by social, economic, moral, ideological, and political processes ... .
>
> Consider, for example, the period in U.S. history between 1880–1920—a critical era of great social turmoil, which influenced the development of

American work organizations and their environments … and witnessed the beginnings of modern management theory and applied social science … .

Although our I-O psychology field took root in this era, we have given little attention to the social context of these formative years … . In fact, historians who have extensively examined this period differ from I-O psychologists in their picture of the evolution of organizations. In particular, the doctrine of efficiency and the development of social and political institutions, which contributed to the development and viability of modern corporations, were much less the result of technical considerations and more a response to historical conditions than I-O psychologists assumed. (p. 943)

He went on to review historical analyses that have emphasized the critical role of worker exploitation and the attendant violent strikes of the 1890s in contributing to the social unrest that marked this time. And he observed that "although predictions such as the inevitable death of bureaucracy, the satisfaction of lower-level needs, self-actualization at work, and increased participation in management by lower-level participants may ultimately come true, for most people life along these dimensions has barely improved … things for many people have gotten considerably worse" (Nord, 1982, p. 942). I believe an honest appraisal today, 40 years later, would differ little.

O'Connor (1999) presented a similar but much more elaborated social analysis of the years following World War I up through the incredibly influential activities of Elton Mayo in helping establish the Harvard Business School and the Human Relations School during the 1920s and 1930s and in the conduct of the famous Hawthorne studies. In 1919 the western world was recovering from World War I, fearful of socialist and/or communist influences and was enduring the great influenza epidemic, inflation and intense industrial conflict. In Boston, the entire police force went on strike which led to three days of looting. Employers were pushing the government to rescind working conditions that had been improved for workers during the war and were buttressing their aims with what amounted to private armies; labor leaders were responding adamantly; and managers were beginning to assert their "professional expertise" in the control of the corporate enterprise, including control over workers. That is the social prism through which the introduction of Frederick Taylor's (1911) mechanistic and reductionist approach to job design, working conditions, employee motivation and financial compensation was viewed by labor. Unfortunately, Taylorism remains to this day a primary representation of I-O psychology to much of the public—including workers and their representatives.

Although there are signs that I-O psychology is becoming somewhat more self-conscious of its historical roots than it has generally been (Highhouse & Schmitt, 2012; Katzell & Austin, 1992; Koppes, 2002), one review served to confirm that "most I–O psychologists were (and continue to be) managerially oriented ... even the studies of worker attitudes were generally motivated more by the interests of management than by concern for employees" (Katzell & Austin, p. 810). Unfortunately, that is not in keeping with an understanding that "labor rights such as freedom of association—the right of workers to organize a union—are fundamental human rights" (Dawkins, 2012, p.473). Nor is it in keeping with adherence to our own ethical commitments to "respect the dignity and worth of all people, and the rights of individuals to privacy, confidentiality, and *self-determination*" (APA, 2017, **Principle E**, emphasis added), and to "take precautions to ensure that [our] potential biases ... do not lead to or condone unjust practices" (APA, 2017, **Principle D**).

Elton Mayo and the Hawthorne Studies

It is impossible to overestimate the role played by Elton Mayo in crystallizing the elitist managerial perspective that came to represent the application of social science in industry and provided the core of a professional identity that still characterizes I-O psychology. Although Mayo joined the Hawthorne Studies in 1928, after they had been in process for several years, he had already been a recognized social theorist for almost a decade. An abstract of his social, psychological, and anti-labor political views that he took with him into Western Electric's Hawthorne plant is terrifying (O'Connor, 1999):[1]

- A major flaw in democracy is that it has an "individualistic bias" that allows it to take advantage of the emotions and the irrationality of voters. "Reasoning ... is deliberately discouraged under the conditions of democratic government" (p. 125).
- Democracy is a "decivilizing force" (p. 125) because it exaggerates the irrationality in people and is therefore antisocial.
- Correspondingly, democratic influences in industry are to be deplored because they would "place the final power in the hands of the least skilled workers ... . The effect would be to determine problems requiring the highest skill by placing the decisions in the hands of those who were unable even to understand the problem" (pp. 125–126).
- The motives of the great majority of people "are largely determined by feeling and irrationality" (p. 126). This is what he meant by "the human factor," which is ignored by the reasoning and logic of economics.
- "Industrial unrest is not caused by mere dissatisfaction with wages and working conditions, but by the fact that a conscious dissatisfaction serves to 'light up,' as it were, the hidden fires of mental uncontrol. Passionate

---

1   The material in quotation marks is from Mayo's writings, cited by O'Connor (1999). The page references are to the O'Connor article, which contains the original sources.

emotions run wildly through the industrial group; tales of capitalistic conspiracy are eagerly accepted, and dispassionate logic is contemptuously spurned" (p. 126).

- The agitator "is usually a genuine neurotic" who "reads his own mental disintegration ... into the social world about him; and to him, in consequence, society is the scene of conspiracies and exploitations by reason of which he and his comrades suffer" (p. 126). Labor unrest, therefore, is a symptom of mental disorganization.

- "To any working psychologist, it is at once evident that the general theories of Socialism, Guild Socialism, Anarchism and the like are very largely the phantasy construction of the neurotic ... " (p. 127).

- "The worker, dimly aware of his loss of authority and prestige [as a consequence of the industrial revolution and scientific advance], has been encouraged to expect that this loss would be more than compensated by his political enfranchisement ... . The general effect has been the exacerbation of class feeling." Thus, democracy is responsible for having "divided society into two hostile camps—an achievement which is the first step downwards to social disintegration" (p. 127).

- "The worker has as little notion of the real ill he suffers as an individual afflicted with melancholia or nervous breakdown" (p. 128). The real ill is a disintegration of personality stemming from a lack of ability to adapt to the conditions of industrial life. Therefore, labor unrest should be studied by psychologists.

In the context of Mayo's antidemocratic and patronizing beliefs, which also generally characterized those of managers and the upper class, it is not surprising that the major conclusions and generalizations of the Hawthorne studies (Roethlisberger & Dixon, 1939) were that (a) interpersonal relations and emotional nonrational factors play a dominant role in the behavior and motivation of workers; (b) psychological techniques could be effective means of curing the dissatisfied workers' distorted perceptions of employment conditions, thus aiding their adjustment to the demands of working life and increasing their efficiency; (c) similarly, effective and enlightened management could satisfy the social and emotional needs of workers, ending the irrational manifestations of hostility in the workplace and obviate the need for workers to organize; and (d) in the absence of worker maladjustment and irrational fantasies, and under skillful and sophisticated management, the workplace could function as it should, conflict free, as a big happy family.

Bramel and Friend (1981) presented an analysis of original findings from the study suggesting that these conclusions were reached by virtue of interpretive errors. They found that for very rational reasons "worker resistance to management was commonplace at Hawthorne (despite absence of a union), yet tended to be covered up in the popular writing of Mayo and Roethlisberger"

(p. 874). They pointed out that the elitist biases of interpretation have been perpetuated in general psychology textbooks, social psychology and I-O psychology books, and research methodology texts because professional psychologists simply share the same values as Mayo and the other Hawthorne researchers and are therefore comfortable with the implicit social views.

Similarly, Gillespie (1988) illustrated "the political character of scientific experimentation" by means of comparing the "standard account" of the Hawthorne experiments with a close account of the archival records:

> The extension of the laboratory into the factory and the resulting experimentation constituted an essentially political process, for the science and politics of work are inseparable. Industrial managers and researchers believed that scientific experimentation on the organization of work and industrial relations would provide a body of objective knowledge that could be applied impartially in the workplace, thereby reducing conflict between labor and capital. However, ... the experimenters accepted in large measure the workplace relations of industrial capitalism and repeatedly rejected the viewpoint of workers. In so doing, they unconsciously reified management ideology so that it became scientific knowledge. The scientific findings of the Hawthorne experiments thus reflected the political values of the experimenters and the employers and provided techniques and a scientific ideology for an intensification of production and supervision. (pp. 115–116)

Ironically, the human relations movement spawned by these studies reflected a sociopolitical position but posited an apolitical view of workplace problems as due to workers' emotional maladjustment rather than genuine conflicts of interest (O'Connor, 1999).

It is possible to conclude that we have come a long way in our conception of and concern for employees' work adjustment (cf. Dawis & Lofquist, 1984; Keita & Sauter, 1992; Korman, 1994; Lowman, 1993a; the growth of *Occupational Health Psychology*, with a dedicated journal since 1996 and a professional association).[2] Nevertheless, the foregoing portrayal of the tenuous and antagonistic relation between I-O psychology and organized labor does not seem to have changed much over the years. There were early attempts sponsored jointly by the Industrial Relations Research Association, the Industrial and Business Division of the American Psychological Association, and the Society for the Psychological Study of Social Issues to forge an active role for psychology in improving labor–management relations (Kornhauser, 1949). During the 1980s, further attempts were made to

---

2 Information concerning the Society for Occupational Health Psychology (SOHP) is available at <http://www.sohp-online.org/index.html>

stimulate our involvement with unions (Huszczo et al., 1984; Meltzer & Stagner, 1980; Rosen & Stagner, 1980; Stagner, 1981a, 1981b). But the fact that these efforts have had little apparent effect reinforces the inference that antagonistic social, cultural, and political forces are at work, including the expression of basic values. The *Handbook of Industrial and Organizational Psychology*, for example, contains no chapter on unions among the 57 chapters comprising the four volumes. The topic is not even covered in chapters devoted to group influences and conflict and negotiation processes in organizations. A review of every article published in *Journal of Applied Psychology* and *Personnel Psychology* from 1963 to 2007 (5,780 articles) uncovered just 95 having to do with industrial relations issues or unions (Cascio & Aguinis, 2008). And others have called attention to our professional neglect of individual workers (Bergman & Jean, 2016; Ruggs et al., 2013; Weiss & Rupp, 2011).

Yet, the most significant professional and ethical questions arise for us if our mere disinterest in organized labor and worker representation is elevated to an active collaboration in the attempt to defeat legal worker attempts to organize, or otherwise engage in antiunion actions. At the least, such partisan activities have the potential to limit greatly our usefulness to the organization and all its members. In addition, it places us in the problematic position of working against people's right to attempt to advance their own wellbeing within acceptable ethical constraints.[3] Such actions are not legitimate functions for any psychologist, and, as noted earlier, they are contrary to "**Principle E. Respect for People's Rights and Dignity**" of our ethics code. Moreover, and more specifically, SIOP is a signatory to the United Nations *Global Compact* on human rights, for companies and other entities, Principle 3 of which reads "Businesses should uphold the freedom of association and the effective recognition of the right to collective bargaining" (Scott et al., 2013, p. 66).

The Humanist Tradition and the Scientist-Practitioner Model in Psychology

Approximately 75 years ago an eminent industrial psychologist, Arthur Kornhauser (1947) raised a cry for "industrial psychology as social science." He challenged us with the question "Do we work on the problems of the private businessman [sic], or on the problems of society?" (p. 224). One could quarrel

---

3   A position one frequently hears in this regard is that many unions are corrupt, are wasteful, do not care about the organization or other (nonunion) employees, and so on, so should be resisted by those whose sympathies lie with the success of the entire enterprise. This seems to imply that managements are never self-serving, corrupt or inefficient. If either is true, these might be reasons to oppose a particular union (or management) on a particular occasion. However, they more frequently represent rationalizations or post hoc *value justifications* of ideological bias (see Chapters 8 and 11).

with the juxtaposition of those as necessarily antagonistic enterprises—given the fundamental moral (utilitarian) justification for business activity (cf. Chapter 11). Nevertheless, in comparison with most short-term applied research aimed at solving immediate bottom-line problems,

> The emphasis of what we are calling industrial psychology as social science is on the broad, long-run, socially significant problems … . For example: what are the strains and the long-run effects which specialized machine processes and assembly lines impose on factory workers? What do unemployment and job insecurity mean in the personal development of working people and their children … . What are the possibilities and the limitations of democratic social participation within industrial units whose structure remains essentially autocratic? … Do men [sic] in top positions of power in industry genuinely believe in democratic participation by working people? What influences, positive and negative, are exerted by labor unions on the personal development and adjustment of working people? (p. 225)

The good news is that some of those issues have, in fact, been the focus of I-O psychology research and practice in the ensuing decades (e.g., Korman, 1994). Ray Katzell (1994; Katzell & Austin, 1992) pointed to a stream of research focusing on nontraditional outcomes (stress, strain and burnout; health and fitness; the personal consequences of work on people; career development; and the relation between work and leisure, family and other aspects of life) that are not related directly to the bottom line. The bad news is that, as even Katzell (1994) acknowledged, that stream of work is "still small relative to that comprising economic outcomes" (p. 51). I am not aware of any recent comparative data, but based on indicators such as the expressed concerns of SIOP for issues like work-life balance, inclusive diversity and ameliorating work demands (Fritz & Ellis, 2015; King & Gilrane, 2015; Rife & Hall, 2015) and other changes reflected in the existence of organizations such as SOHP, I am cautiously optimistic that changes have been taking place that have modestly tipped the balance of concern—at least in our research foci, if not necessarily in our professional practice. Recent analyses are still rather pessimistic concerning the degree of impact of I-O research on I-O practice (Cascio & Aguinis, 2008).

In Chapter 10, under the rubric of *social advocacy,* the goal of psychology "to improve the condition of individuals, organizations, and society" (APA, 2017) was discussed, especially the difficulty in specifying the values that inform professional and moral obligations, along with their implied actions (Prilleltensky, 1997). The important point, however, is to recognize the long-standing nature of this humanist tradition and commitment to social justice as one of "psychology's two cultures," along with the scientific tradition (Kimble, 1984; Vasquez, 2012). Starting in the 1960s, when I-O psychology began to overcome the stigma of being merely a technocratic service profession to business by becoming more theoretically oriented and scientific (Pugh, 1966, 1969), it adopted the scientist–practitioner (S–P) model to articulate and reinforce that change in character. But this did not address the values issue concerning the lack of representation of the humanist tradition from general psychology (Stagner, 1982). The reason for that relates in part to the difference between I-O psychology and clinical psychology, in which field the S–P model was developed. Some background is illuminating.

Still Needed: A Scientist-Practitioner-Humanist (SPH) Model for I-O Psychology

Following World War II, the federal government, mindful of problems that had occurred in the treatment of veterans of the previous war, was concerned with the wide variation in training and practice of clinical psychologists and the coordination among Veteran's Administration hospitals, mental health centers, and university departments of psychology (Baker & Benjamin, 2000; Benjamin, 2001). So, in 1949 the U.S. Public Health Service, enlisting the collaboration of the APA, organized and funded a conference to address the standardization of doctoral training in clinical psychology. Seventy-three prominent academicians and practitioners were invited to the University of Colorado at Boulder for a two-week conference that produced a detailed plan, *Training in Clinical Psychology* (Raimy, 1950). The major result of the Boulder conference was a clear professional consensus that the clinical psychologist should be both a researcher and practitioner (Baker & Benjamin, 2000). Within five years, similar conferences were held to formalize training in counseling psychology and school psychology; but no such structured process preceded the "adoption" of the S–P model by I-O psychology.

Notwithstanding the relatively explicit written guidelines for the S–P model in clinical psychology, over several decades there has been considerable disagreement and conflict regarding the nature of the relation that joins the two sets of professional activities, what their relationship ought to be, and their relative importance (Albee, 2000; Belar, 2000; Benjamin, 2001; Hoshmand & Polkinghorne, 1992; Stricker, 1997, 2000). In addition, there are both optimistic reports of the extent to which the model is followed in clinical training (O'Sullivan & Quevillon, 1992), as well as pessimistic assessments of the extent to which clinical research has failed to influence clinical practice (Nathan, 2000; Wiltsey & Beidas, 2020). It is certainly not surprising, therefore, that in I-O psychology—which never articulated a formal statement of its conception of the S–P model—similar disagreements and controversies exist regarding the articulation of basic and applied research with professional practice (Dunnette, 1990, 2001; Hulin, 2001; Kanfer, 2001; Latham, 2001; Olenick et al., 2018; Rotolo et al., 2018; Saari, 2001; Sackett & Larson, 1990).

Achieving effective articulations between the two components of the profession is undoubtedly an important and, for some, a critical and worrisome issue. But not often acknowledged is an important point that the notion of the scientist-practitioner represents "an incomplete model of values" for I-O psychology (Lefkowitz, 1990, p. 48) whereas that is not the case for clinical psychology. It is reasonable to equate clinical practice—an explicitly helping profession—with the ethical dimension of beneficence and the values of humanism: "Most [clinical] psychologists enter the profession with a desire to promote human welfare and, directly or indirectly, to serve others" (Koocher & Keith-Spiegel, 1998, p. 3). Although it would be unfair and misleading to suggest that I-O psychologists are not also motivated by an ideal of helping people (cf. Church & Burke, 1992), it is probably inaccurate to broadly equate I-O practice with the values of humanism. In the case of I-O psychology the practitioner portion of the S–P model has not been driven primarily by the beneficent concerns that are part of the heritage of psychology and part of our professional and ethical obligations. Thus, for I-O psychology the S–P model is incomplete.

It seems readily apparent that the values represented by the practitioner portion of the S–P model in I-O psychology have long been dominated by the economizing and productivity values of an idealized free-market capitalism. That observation should not be (mis)construed as uniformly critical. It is obvious that enormous social benefit flows from economic productivity (cf. Chapter 11), and the fact that our professional and ethical obligations extend beyond the employees with whom we work directly to the effective functioning of the entire organization is a constructive good. In fact, some among us have argued recently that we don't pay *enough* attention to the economic effectiveness of the organization as a whole (Schneider & Pulakos, 2022). But, as has been mentioned by many I-O psychologists, that duality of obligation is also a source of potential ethical conflict (e.g., "who is the client?"). And, as noted in Chapter 10, when the meta-objectives of the institution served are commensurate with the humanistic objectives that comprise one of psychology's two value systems, no ethical issues are raised. However, when those served are business organizations dominated by a value system of continuous short-term profit-making for shareholders, actions on their behalf may sometimes conflict with our avowed professional objective "to improve the condition of individuals, organizations, and society" (APA, 2017). The likely values conflict requires making explicit and salient our obligation under the professional service ideal to advance the welfare of all stakeholders.

Thus, the expanded vision of I-O psychology for which I have been advocating for a while now includes extending the S–P model to a scientist-practitioner–humanist (SPH) model (e.g., Lefkowitz, 1990, 2005, 2008, 2010a, 2011b, 2012b, 2013b, 2023). Neglecting the humanist component and conceiving of the professional and ethical difficulties that we encounter as representing a dialectic of only S–P tensions underestimates their complexity. It also ignores the economic and corporate social values of the current model.

Parenthetically, it is gratifying to learn of a similar *Scientist-Practitioner-Advocate* (SPA) model being proposed for all of psychology to demonstrate "how all psychologists can and do bring their work to bear to benefit society" (Miles & Fassinger, 2021). And paralleling all this in the world of business, considerable work has been done by Pirson and his colleagues in furthering the idea of *humanistic management* (Pirson, 2015b, 2017; Pirson et al., 2016; 2017), based on the human aspiration of wellbeing as the ultimate objective of human nature, and a dignity threshold indicating a balanced fulfillment of basic drives.

All this is not meant to suggest, of course, that the practice of I-O psychology has been devoid of the expression of humanistic values. To cite just a few examples, I-O psychologists have studied and worked to improve the human condition in areas like worker safety (Griffin & Kabanoff, 2001), the propriety of using psychological expertise in commercial advertising to children (Kanner & Kasser, 2000), the relation between work and family life (May, 1998), adaptation to shift work (Hartel, 1998) and other work stressors and dysfunctions (Lowman, 1993a; Spector, 2002), the emotional impact of potential and actual downsizing (Waldo, 2001), as well as enhancing the reemployment of displaced workers (London, 1996); some of us even contribute professional services pro bono to worthy causes (Klein, 2001; Ryan, 1999). And more recently many members of SIOP have demonstrated their concern for *Using I-O Psychology for the Greater Good* (Olson-Buchanan et al., 2013).

But my concern has been that the personal motives of individual I-O psychologists like these were conditioned only little, if at all, by their education, training and socialization as I-O psychologists. Values issues should be made an explicit part of graduate training in I-O (Lefkowitz, 2014a), as it has begun in management education (Bachani et al., 2018; Hancock, 2019; Pirson et al., 2017). Which is not to minimize the difficulties and complexities of such an endeavor:

> … many operational and ethical questions are bound to arise. For example, how are values issues best covered in graduate programs? How do we respectfully manage conflicting values positions among faculty? Should the existing values of graduate school applicants be considered in the admissions process? These, and other questions that are bound to appear, are difficult and perhaps contentious, but the transparency of considering them openly will be more advantageous in the long run than continuing to pretend that for us values don't exist.
>
> *(Lefkowitz, 2014b, p. 43)*

Facets of I-O Psychology: II. Absence of a Normative Perspective

As described in the previous section, we have essentially obviated the criticism of I-O psychology as an unscientific and atheoretical technology. But a profession is marked not only by its scientific and theoretical underpinnings and the effectiveness of its instrumental practice but also by its moral or normative stance regarding human well-being and its contribution to societal goods (Evans, 2021). It seems past time for a second "course correction" in this journey, one that more clearly acknowledges the normative component of ethical professional practice—incorporating the humanistic values that are part of psychology's professional heritage, examines the implicit values by which we have navigated to this point, and explicitly contemplates whether we might not be on the right heading in this regard. The position I advocate is in keeping with the recent pleas by Gardner et al. (2001) to understand that meaningful work—what they referred to as "good work"—entails both expertise and making a social contribution (i.e., it is "good" in two senses).

In Chapter 9 I offered a tentative analysis that took the form of the classic "good news–bad news" sort. On the positive side, I asserted (without much evidence) that I-O psychologists probably experience fewer and less intense conflicts in corporations than have been described for other professionals in such settings, such as physical scientists. And I further speculated that the reasons had to do with, at least in part, (a) the considerable contribution that our field has made to the effective functioning of such organizations, which is appreciated by those in positions of power; (b) the likelihood that I-O psychologists self-select from among those with strong business orientations and the propensity to develop managerial and organizational identifications (recall the successful practitioner who commented "I used to be an I-O psychologist"); and (c) that I-O psychology is among those professions, like accountancy, advertising, systems analysis, engineering and others, that have developed and risen in status because of their integration in the modern corporate enterprise.

The other side of that coin, however, is that these are "technocratic professions" that depart in significant ways from the professional model (Donaldson, 1982). Although they are based on a systematic theoretical body of knowledge that requires extensive education, and they enjoy a considerable degree of professional authority and status, they are—in the parlance of a contemporary euphemism—morally challenged. That is,

> The standards of the new professional do not explicitly include moral standards, in part because his or her profession does not recognize an altruistic element in its overall goals … the new professions fail, it seems, because they do not even attempt to articulate moral standards.
>
> *(Donaldson, 1982, p. 113)*

Instead, Bell (1985) argued, those professions are characterized more by values of the business organization than by professional norms, values and ethical standards. This appears to be confirmed by a survey of I-O psychologists indicating that their highest-rated ideals for the profession were business objectives: to increase efficiency, enhance productivity and promote quality (Church & Burke, 1992). I concluded Chapter 9 by posing the question, "Is I-O psychology more akin to the minimally moral new 'technocratic professions' ... than to the traditional professions in which responsibility and service to society at large is a major value component?"

There would have been little doubt about the answer to that question if it were posed when our field began, 100 years ago or so. I-O psychology was established within the prevailing positivistic science of the times, in which even *applied* psychology was considered separate and distinct from ethical, values-related and moral considerations. The person often referred to as "the father of I-O psychology" put it this way:

> Economic psychotechnics may serve certain ends of commerce and industry, but whether these ends are the best ones is not a care with which the psychologist has to be burdened. For instance, the end may be the selection of the most efficient laborers for particular industries. The psychologist may develop methods in his [sic] laboratory by which this purpose can be fulfilled. But if some mills prefer another goal—for instance, to have not the most efficient, but the cheapest possible laborers—entirely different means for the selection are necessary. The psychologist is, therefore, not entangled in the economic discussions of the day ... . He is confined to the statement: If you wish this end, then you must proceed in this way; but it is left to you to express your preference among the ends.
>
> *(Munsterberg, 1913, p. 19)*

I believe that such deference continues to characterize much I-O psychology practice.

At its inception around the beginning of the last century I-O psychology in the United States developed within business and industry by virtue of its demonstrable effectiveness in solving organizational problems. Its justification was essentially instrumental and empirical. The first well-known industrial psychologists (Hugo Munsterberg, Walter Dill Scott, Walter Van Dyke Bingham and Louis Leon Thurstone) were able to apply psychological knowledge to produce effective advertising, make accurate assessments of intelligence, and train employees in "scientific salesmanship" or efficient work methods. The facts of our origins appear consistent, whether illuminated positively from within by a member of the profession and participant in those activities (Ferguson, 1962–1965) or outlined in the harsh glare of the scathing critique of our professional integrity as social scientists by Baritz (1960). In Baritz's view, I-O psychology, by emulating the natural science positivist ideal of "value-free" practice, exemplified the moral predicament about which Rosenberg (1995) warned many years later: "A social science that sought to efface the moral dimension from its descriptions and explanations would simply serve the interests of some other moral conception" (p. 205).

Accordingly, in the opinion of some, I-O psychology came to be "regarded as an appendage of the business community" (Wolf & Ozehosky, 1978, p. 181). Wolf and Ozehosky were mistaken, however, in believing that the field simply needed to become a more objective and "autonomous scientific discipline"; the issue was—and is—one of morality and values, not science.[4] Twenty years later, a leading contemporary organizational psychologist declared

> I am concerned that we are allowing the economic and political forces of the times to reduce our capacity for theoretically based self-reflection. *We thus lose the ability to address the ethical dilemmas of this era inside the profession* with data and concepts developed by people who know the work from their own experience.
>
> *(Alderfer, 1998, p. 74, emphasis added)*

What Are Our Ethics and Values?

It can be assumed that Baritz's (1960) harsh perspective as a social critic and cultural historian (quoted at the beginning of this chapter) does not correspond with the professional self-image held by most contemporary I-O psychologists, which is probably reflected better in Campion's (1996) expression of professional pride. But how might one attempt to answer the question today? What are the normative values beyond simply the vaguely articulated S–P model that guide I-O psychology and underlie our ethical ideals? What are those ethical standards that presumably reflect the moral nature of our professional activities? The concerned I-O psychologist might acknowledge the relevance of such questions but dismiss them as moot—after all, we have an ethical code (APA, 2017) and a casebook (Lowman et al. 2006) for guidance. But the APA ethical code is a generic document meant to apply to all domains of psychology and varieties of psychological practice; moreover, in the opinion of many, it is weighted too heavily by issues associated with the provision of health services. Its overly general nature is suggested by the felt need for supplementary explications (Bersoff, 2008; Canter et al., 1994). And our casebook, like many such collections, is an inductive compilation of critical incidents (albeit helpfully referenced to principles from the APA code). In comparison, numerous texts exist that define the principles of ethical behavior for other professions—especially business managers (e.g., Castro, 1996; Deckop, 2006; Donaldson, 1982, 1989; Maclagan, 1998; Petrick & Quinn, 1997; Schminke, 1998, 2010; White, 1993)—and/or that grapple with the normative role of business in society and how the relation is affected by and determines much social policy (e.g., Post et al., 1996; Sethi & Falbe, 1987; Sethi & Swanson, 1981; cf. also Chapter 11).

---

4   Although, in all fairness, theirs was not such an errant interpretation 45 years ago.

SIOP (n.d.) does now at least have a *Strategic Plan* that encompasses statements of its vision, mission, values and objectives, and which includes the express concern for inspiring "individual and organizational health, well-being, and effectiveness" (p. 5). The issue is the extent to which those goals and sentiments exist beyond the printed page. In surveys of the SIOP membership concerning their level of interest in several dozen content areas ethics fares no better than the middle of the pack (Schneider & Smith, 1999; Waclawski & Church, 2000). Although integrity and ethics emerge as competencies for I-O psychologists in a job analysis, they are viewed by only 2% and 7% of the sample as among the most difficult or most critical ones, respectively (Blakeney et al., 2002). Historically, neither the values of the field nor the ethics of its practitioners appear to ever have been a major topic in I-O psychology (Cascio & Aguinis, 2008; Katzell & Austin, 1992). And in the "Call for Proposals" for the annual SIOP conferences up through 2002, ethics was not even listed among the more than 40 content categories for submissions. (Upon request, it was added as of the 2003 conference.)

Based on those indicators, if one were to hypothesize that the values and ethics on which our field rests lack salience or are inadequately articulated, what additional evidence might one bring to bear? One way to address the issue is by means of a content analysis of I-O psychology textbooks. Surely, if our moral underpinnings were a significant facet of the profession they would be expressed clearly and prominently in the texts by which we represent ourselves to the world and begin to train and socialize new entrants to the field. Accordingly, for the first edition of this book I searched the subject indexes of a convenience sample of 29 I-O psychology textbooks.[5] The topic of *ethics* was listed in just six of the books—referring mostly to a passing mention of the existence of the APA code and occasionally as a paragraph or so acknowledging a particular issue such as deception in research or the obligation for responsible use of tests in assessment. The term *morals* or *morality* (generally used as a synonym for *ethics)* was not mentioned at all. Mentioned in 11 of the texts, *values* fared better but, in all but two instances, it referred to external objects of study (e.g., work values as a component of organizational culture, or bureaucratic values). In only two instances were values discussed, even briefly, in the context of professional values that inform and shape the research, theory and practice of I-O psychology. Both of those instances have to do with the value system that putatively underlies

---

5   This was truly a convenience sample comprised of all those books I owned and those in my college library. I excluded special topics books (e.g., motivation and personnel staffing) as probably providing an inadequate test of the hypothesis and books of readings because they generally have poor indexes or none at all. If multiple editions of a text were available, I used only the latest one. The sample consisted of four texts from the 1960s, three from the 1970s, 14 from the 1980s, and nine from the 1990s. I invite the reader to examine more recent I-O texts.

the work of OD practitioners—and in one of the instances the values are characterized negatively, as a difficulty to be overcome:

> Humanistic values represent a problem for the field of organizational psychology because these features can conflict with the objectivity required of a science and because they can dilute a strong concern for performance effectiveness and productivity. This matter is particularly relevant to our discussion of organization development, because its practitioners have often been influenced by strong humanistic values.
>
> *(Miner, 1992, p. 293)*

Obviously, it is not my belief that humanistic values are something we need to shy away from. Also, it is not my intent to single out Miner's sentiments for criticism. In fact, as implied in the previous section and in Chapter 10, his position is probably representative of many I-O psychologists who adhere to a traditional logical positivist or neopositivist epistemology in which values, other than scientific or epistemic values, are assumed to be outside the domain of all science. It is nevertheless disturbing to hear colleagues' beliefs that "performance effectiveness and productivity" are incompatible with humanistic values.[6] It also should not be necessary to point out that "a strong concern for performance effectiveness and productivity" is also a value position. As noted earlier, there are no chapters concerned with professional ethics or values in the entire *Handbook of Industrial and Organizational Psychology*.

What does it mean to advocate that I-O psychology should incorporate more of a normative or moral perspective? That is, what would such an I-O psychology be like? In what ways might it differ from the traditional conception of the field? The answers will be informed by an incorporation into our self-image of: (a) the three foundations of individual ethics and morality (a concern for the principles of fairness and justice, the promotion of welfare and wellbeing, and personal integrity or virtue); (b) a professional model that elevates those foundations to the occupational level, emphasizing responsibility to the society at large, not merely to one's direct clients or employer (especially if the client or employer itself disavows any particular ethical or social responsibilities); and (c) the tradition of human betterment that is an integral part of the values of psychology in general (APA, 2017). A prominent example is offered by the changing circumstances of work over the past generation.

The Disappearance of Employer Loyalty, Job Security and Careers as We Knew Them

Two related themes have run powerfully through the American economy in recent decades: (1) the disappearance of corporate loyalty and good jobs

---

6   I can't resist the temptation to note that, as of 2019, SIOP, through its non-profit foundation, offers an "Early Career Award for Humanistic I-O Psychology."

(Wartzman, 2017); and relatedly (2) the decline of the labor movement which, alongside American business, "played a huge role in building the world's largest, richest middle class" (Greenhouse, 2019, p. xii).

As most Americans are aware, since the 1980s millions of employees have been summarily dismissed from their jobs following a merger, acquisition, downsizing, outsourcing, relocation or restructuring by their company. This has continued well into the 21st century (cf. Chapter 8)—more than 30 million layoffs from 1994–2010, and another 4 million in just the next 2 ½ years according to the Bureau of Labor Statistics.[7] (These are long-term trends predating the Covid-19 pandemic.) Less dramatically, but also occurring during approximately the same period (probably not coincidentally) has been a growing change in the nature of "careers:"

> Traditionally, careers were typically defined in terms of an individual's relationship to an employing organization. These linear careers were described as taking place within the context of stable, organizational structures … with individuals progressing up the firm's hierarchy seeking to obtain greater extrinsic rewards … . The employer-employee relationship was characterized by an exchange of worker loyalty for the firm's implicit promise of job security.
>
> *(Sullivan & Baruch, 2009, p. 1542)*

The traditional career, described above, has been replaced in great measure by the *protean career, boundaryless career, hybrid career* and/or *kaleidoscope career*, etc. (Burke, 2015; Hall, 2004; Sullivan & Baruch, 2009; Waters et al., 2015). Burke (2015) notes

> Career success was measured by objective criteria such as pay, perks, status and power. Today a career is more likely to be defined as a lifelong series of work experiences, with job movements being upward, lateral and in some cases downward.
>
> *(Burke, 2015, p. 13)*

And I would emphasize that this has often occurred contrary to employee intentions or aspirations. Moreover, many such jobs consist of what has been called insecure and *precarious work* (Kalleberg, 2009)—temporary, agency or contracting work; "on-call" or seasonal work; home- or part-time work—generally lacking in decent pay, working conditions or job security.

Ostensibly, careers have become more internally values-driven, self-directed and self-managed—at the cost of "decreased stability and increased uncertainty in

---

7   Retrieved from https://www.bls.gov/news.release/mmls.t01.htm# on Jan. 11, 2022. No data are available beyond mid-2013.

the work environment as well as changes in employment relationships, including reduced job security" (Sullivan & Baruch, 2009, p. 1549). Elsewhere, however, Baruch (2006) cautions us not to exaggerate:

> Much of the traditional notion of careers and their management is valid and exist in practice … . The organization role in shaping future careers should not be underestimated … . An interesting issue is to identify how many people actually have (and/or wish to have) a protean career or boundaryless career. (p. 135)

There has been no dearth of descriptive and analytic accounts by social scientists and business scholars reporting on the changed nature of jobs, organizations, terms of employment, careers and the "psychological contracts" between employees and employers (Gowing et al., 1998; Hall, 2004; Hall & Associates, 1996; Howard, 1995; Kalleberg, 2000; London, 1995; Rousseau, 1995; Rousseau & Schalk, 2000; Smith, 1997; Sullivan & Baruch, 2009). And concerned psychologists have focused on how employees can be motivated to maintain and even enhance their productivity in these changed circumstances (APS, 1993a).

I have no doubt these authors are well-intentioned:

> We need individual employees at all levels to have a strong internal 'compass' in an ethically challenged business climate. And to empower individuals to be able to act on their values, we need people to have the resources and capability for taking charge of their careers, when the employer doesn't help.
>
> *(Hall, 2004, p. 3)*

Accordingly, counseling programs have been developed to aid employees in achieving such empowerment (Verbruggen & Sels, 2008), as an addition to traditional professional career counseling programs (Niles & Harris-Bowlsbey, 2013); scholarly books to aid people in personally flourishing in these conditions (Burke et al., 2015), as well as practical self-help books (Alidina et al., n.d.) are widely available.

Sullivan and Baruch (2009) have candidly indicated the following problematic or troubling issues: (a) "the traditional linear career is still being enacted by some workers and is more prevalent in some organizations, industries, and countries than in others"; (b) some "career patterns [are] characterized by voluntary and involuntary multiple movements cycling in and out of the workforce"; (c) some employees have "obstacles to physical mobility (e.g., geographical immobility due to being a member of a dual-career couple or eldercare responsibilities)"; (d) scholarship in this area has "tended to emphasize the positive aspects with little mention of potential negative outcomes"; (e) "instead of enjoying increased job success and satisfaction, some workers have found themselves lost, shaken by the changing rules of the workplace, and unable to regain their footing"; (f) individual personality attributes "may be an obstacle to an individual's ability to reenvision career options"; (g) "some individuals may find themselves outside of the permanent, full-time workforce through job loss"; (h) "organizations may not consider it worth the time and money to investigate complaints from workers who will be employed by the firm for a relatively short time period [and] temporary and project workers, fearful that filing a complaint will earn them a negative reputation may fail to report problems … "; and not least, (i) the career changes have been in response to extrinsic factors such as "increased globalization, rapid technological advancements, increased workforce diversity, and the expanding use of outsourcing and part-time and temporary employees."

In other words, there are moral issues being ignored. The career changes are largely non-volitional—imposed on many people involuntarily by organizational policy changes that may or may not be justifiable. For example, a U.S. Federal District Judge found that there was "simply no basis" to Uber's claim "that some innumerable legion of drivers prefer to remain independent contractors rather than become employees" (Isaac, 2015, B1); and following a ruling by the British Supreme Court, Uber reclassified 70,000 drivers in Britain as qualifying for a minimum wage, vacations, and access to a pension plan (Satariano, 2021).[8] The number of "involuntary part time" workers in the U.S. grew from 3.2 million in 2000 to 8.6 million in 2011 (Mishel et al., 2012, p. 350). Overall, the percentage of workers in alternative work arrangements, "defined as temporary help agency workers, on-call workers, contract workers, and independent contractors or freelancers" was 10.1% in early 2005 and 15.8% in late 2015 (Katz & Krueger, 2016, p. 1). Moreover, these workers are notable among the groups not studied much by I-O psychologists (Lefkowitz, 2013a).

Invariably, these jobs entail employment with little or no job security, no health insurance or paid medical leave, no workman's compensation insurance, no unemployment insurance benefits and no retirement contributions. The irregular and unpredictable work schedules that are also typical have many adverse effects (Golden, 2015). There are normative questions that could be raised: Are people really better off with these kinds of careers? And how many workers are (in)capable of adapting to the new demands because they don't have a high "protean career orientation" (Waters et al., 2015, p. 235)? (I don't believe that I-O psychology has shown much concern for the adverse effects of these changed circumstances on the employees affected.) At the very least, it seems to illustrate the accuracy of Baritz's (1960) second criticism of the field—our unquestioning "embrace of the goals, values, and norms of business." It's not as if one could easily maintain ignorance about the unjust work conditions of part-time, temporary, contingent and contract

---

8   The court ruling was based on U.K. labor rules so may not foreshadow additional changes elsewhere.

workers of the *gig economy* in the face of regular disturbing reports in the popular press (Greenhouse, 2014; Irwin, 2016; Isaac, 2015; Scheiber, 2015, 2016; Scheiber & Isaac, 2016; Silver-Greenberg & Corkery, 2016). U.S. Senator Elizabeth Warren called for a new social contract in which "all workers—no matter when they work, where they work, who they work for, whether they pick tomatoes or build rocket ships—should have some basic protections and be able to build some economic security for themselves and their families" (cited in Schmitt, 2016, p. A23). It may be that the situation has begun to change (cf. Chapter 8 regarding "the great resignation"). An IBM Senior Vice President was quoted: "But it turns out, you actually do need to develop your own workers and can't just depend on hiring" (Irwin, 2021, p. 10).

In comparison to our relative quiescence regarding the moral consequences of these alternative work arrangements, more critical voices were raised questioning whether the wholesale downsizing begun in the 1980s is just, or when and in what ways it might be justified (Van Buren, 2000). The following findings were uncovered and should be read in the context of the material presented in Chapter 8 concerning economic and social justice.

- The initial round of organizational downsizing in the early 1980s was largely in response to business pressures, but subsequent occasions were mostly instances of executives simply imitating their competitors and peers (Rousseau, 1995).
- Similarly, companies did not downsize because they were losing money. Fully 81% of companies that downsized were profitable in that year (Cascio, 1995).
- Downsizing is not a reaction to the cost of labor per se; it is most frequently an attempt to raise the cash needed to service enormous debt burdens acquired through mergers and acquisitions (Cascio, 1993; Rousseau, 1995). It was justified in the 1980s as a response to difficult economic times and international competition, but it continued through the boom times of the 1990s as well.[9]
- Among 311 companies that downsized employees by more than 3% in any year during the 1980s, the amount of downsizing was not related to their pre-downsizing financial performance, and the level of downsizing did not affect post-downsizing financial performance or long-term stock price (Cascio, 1998; Cascio et al., 1997). Cascio (2002) later reported: "no significant, consistent evidence that employment downsizing led to improved

---

9   Pfeffer (1998) argued that reducing (labor) costs is never the primary objective in any event. Costs are reduced in the belief, more frequently the hope, that it will lead to greater efficiency, productivity, and profits. But it generally doesn't happen. Moreover, labor costs are usually not the major cost component in manufacturing; they are, however, frequently the easiest to reduce.

financial performance" (p.81) was found for 6,418 instances of changes in employment for S & P 500 companies from 1982 through 2000. The evidence suggests that it does not even effectively reduce costs (Pfeffer, 1998). Similarly, in comparison with the effects of voluntary turnover and individual dismissals, reduction-in-force turnover (downsizing) has been found to have a significantly greater negative impact on the productive efficiency of work units (McElroy et al., 2001).

- Fewer than half of mergers and acquisitions result in the benefits that were expected by the principals (Cartwright & Cooper, 1997).
- The chief executives who are responsible for the decisions to downsize generally benefit greatly from it financially through increases in the value of stock options that become more valuable because of immediate increases in stock prices (Van Buren, 2000).
- Laid-off workers who return to the job market are downwardly mobile and generally take huge pay cuts—frequently working at part-time, short-term, or temporary jobs (Cascio, 1995; Kalleberg, 2000). These jobs, reinforced by outsourcing many technical functions and relocating jobs to cheaper labor markets, tend to produce a bottom-tier workforce of employees who receive no health insurance, pensions, or other fringe benefits (Greenhouse, 1998; Kalleberg, 2000; Uchitelle, 2001).
- The spectacular growth of part-time, short-term and temporary jobs (reflected in the explosion of temporary help agencies and the gig economy) since the 1970s has been unilaterally employer-driven, resulting in the growth of involuntary part-time workers (i.e., those who would prefer full-time work; Kalleberg, 2000). Data suggest that the argument that employees do not really want long-term attachments to their organizations anymore "is largely untrue—even if believing these myths comforts the managers who daily test the bounds of employee loyalty and commitment" (Pfeffer, 1998, p. 167).

For the most part, I-O psychology has passively accepted the economic rationales (or rationalizations) that have justified the changed social contract between employers and employees. As was pointed out previously, we have generally deferred uncritically to corporate values and objectives as well as to the policies and actions they inspire. In this instance, it entails accepting that "downsizing and other forms of organizational change involving layoffs ... will continue as production and overhead costs remain noncompetitive ... and thus render job insecurity a lasting characteristic of working life" (Sverke & Hellgren, 2002, p. 36).

Perhaps we have been too ready to institutionalize and reify the notion that "downsizing is effective" (McKinley et al., 2000, p. 227) despite the cautionary message that it is detrimental to organizational learning (Fisher & White, 2000) and while ignoring the data presented above in the bullet-list of findings by some of our colleagues.[10] Our concerns have been restricted largely to determining the conditions conducive to employees *perceiving* that the procedures by which it is determined who gets dismissed *appear* "fair" (Brockner et al., 1994; Skarlicki et al., 1998). For example, we know that downsizing is more likely to be perceived as fair if it is justified by external reasons, such as a substantial loss of market share to a more efficient competitor (Rousseau, 1995); it is seen as less fair by people who believe that organizations play a social as well as an economic role in society (Watson et al., 1999); and seen as less ethical by both casualties and survivors of the process than by those higher up who were involved in formulating, implementing, and/or communicating the downsizing decisions (Hopkins & Hopkins, 1999). It should be noted that these perceptions are independent of normative judgments regarding the possible injustice of the actions.

In contrast, an explicitly ethical stance has been taken by those business scholars who have voiced a need for a resurgence of "employee relations ethics" (Sikula & Sikula, 2001) in the face of what has been described as "abusive organizations" (Powell, 1998). It is, perhaps, not coincidental that the study of trust in organizations became a popular topic (Kramer, 1999).However, it has been left largely to social critics to question the moral legitimacy of the corporate world of worker stress, insecurity, overwork, wage stagnation and alienation that has been created largely in the service of enhancing shareholder value and executive compensation (Fraser, 2001; Kennedy, 2000; Mokhiber & Weissman, 1999; cf. neoliberalism, Chapter 11). For example, the long-term trend of replacing full-time with part-time workers has been viewed as reflecting…

> … seismic changes in corporate political authority, rather than competitive adjustment in labor-market strategy. The public needs to understand that corporations are changing the nature of jobs to reduce the power of unions and workers, not simply to compete better; in fact, temporary and contract jobs may hurt productivity and competition in the long run. Ultimately, what's at stake here are the basic rights of workers, not whether they can be retrained or assured of benefits. Contingent labor is a political rather than an economic strategy, and requires a political solution: corporate accountability to workers.
>
> *(Derber, 1998, p. 199)*

Relatively few of us within I-O psychology have apparently thought to question the moral standing of this changed social contract, even though the changes have been imposed unilaterally by one extremely powerful party on the other(s). A more typical response to the growing problem of job insecurity

---

10 Perhaps this is an example of "deliberate ignorance" in service of avoiding moral concern, as noted in Chapter 8 (Hertwig & Engel, 2016).

is the (nevertheless commendable) attempt "to understand how the negative consequences of job insecurity for employee well-being and work attitudes can be buffered by various moderating variables" (Sverke & Hellgren, 2002, p. 36). But downsizing to achieve an increase in stock price for shareholders, or as a desperate attempt to redress a foolish, costly and aggrandizing corporate acquisition, is not morally equivalent to downsizing in response to genuine competition, technological challenges and cost pressures. How much credence should be given to putative economic threats when chief executives of poorly performing "right sizing" organizations simultaneously maintain annual compensation at seven-, eight-, or even nine-digit levels?

Some organizations, however, have resorted to downsizing only as a last resort and in conjunction with "responsible restructuring" (Cascio, 2002). Also affecting one's moral reasoning should be whether the organization has tried alternative cost-cutting measures prior to the wholesale elimination of jobs. Cascio (1998, 2002) found that, although downsizing did not lead to expected financial gains, restructuring to use employee talents more effectively without making cutbacks was effective, as were high-performance human resource practices (Guzzo et al., 1985; Huselid, 1995; Pfeffer, 1994, 1998).

Similarly, contrary to tenets of the "protean career," Tsui et al. (1997), in a sample of almost 1,000 employees in 85 different jobs in ten companies, found that "employees seem to respond favorably in terms of both performance and attitudes when employers are willing to commit to fairly long-term relationships with them" (p. 1117). Even Baruch (2006) has noted "There is a certain level of stability, as well as a strong need for security among people, which has to find different ways to be fulfilled" (p. 135). But the share of workers in long-term jobs (at least ten years tenure) dropped from 41% in 1979 to 35% in 1996; the median time that a 35 to 44-year-old male worker has held his job fell from 7.6 years in 1963 to 6.1 years in 1996 (Mishel et al., 1999).

Some among us have recognized that the mergers, acquisitions, delayering and downsizing "invariably have a negative impact on employees in terms of job losses, job uncertainty, ambiguity and heightened anxiety, which is not necessarily offset by any organizational benefits such as increased productivity and financial profits" (Cartwright & Holmes, 2006). It is not surprising, therefore, that some I-O psychologists have not only undertaken, from a scientific perspective, to understand the nature of "the new organizational reality" but, from instrumental and caring perspectives, have also recognized that

> the stress associated with job loss, relocation, and adjustment to the new, fast-paced environment will require attention to ways to help individuals, groups, and organizations maintain their health and well-being as they work their way through this period of transition on the way to the future.
>
> *(Gowing et al., 1998, p. xvii)*

Unfortunately, the most prevalent of those ways of helping has been attempting to have employees adjust to the reality that their companies no longer accept any responsibility for their career development, beyond providing the opportunity to work hard and succeed along with one's (remaining) coworkers. Therefore, they should not look to their companies to define their career; "they must shoulder the burden of ensuring their own employment security" (London, 1995, p. xv). As Hall (1996) observed, "what seems to be more important now is the internal career, the person's perceptions and self-constructions of career phenomena" (p. 1). Accordingly, popular books offering career management advice reveal "secrets" like "taking control," "market[ing] yourself," and "go [ing] it alone" (Boyes, 2010).

This is in keeping with the prevailing wisdom as trumpeted by management gurus such as Tom Peters: "corporate loyalty is rubbish … . If I can provide you with exciting new challenges, and if you respond accordingly, well, then I hope we do indeed grow old together—one project at a time" (cited in Wooldridge, 2000, p. 83).

> The 'psychological contract' between the employee and the organization has shrunk to what Jack Welch, [former] CEO of General Electric, has called a one-day contract, in which all that counts is the current value that each party contributes to the relationship.
>
> *(Hall, 1996, p. 5)*[11]

Yet managers still expect employees to be loyal and committed to the organization, and to perform accordingly. And I-O psychologists support the irony with a considerable amount of effort aimed at selecting employees who are *conscientious,* finding ways to enhance their *organizational citizenship behaviors, organizational commitment,* and more recently their *engagement* (Eisenberger et al., 2016), and *work passion* (Smith et al., 2022), as well as *coaching* them to "adjust" to the situation.[12] Is it overly harsh to believe that we have been too accepting of the inevitability of one particular form of an employer-determined, employee–organization relation? Tsui et al (1997) referred to this sort of relationship as *unbalanced underinvestment,* in which "the employee is expected to undertake broad and open-ended obligations, while the employer reciprocates with short-term and specified monetary rewards, with no commitment to a long-term relationship or investment in the employee's training or career" (p. 1093). In fact, however, they found that

11 Jack Welch was CEO of General Electric for 20 years, crowned "Manager of the Century" by Fortune magazine, and in the opinion of many "redefined what it meant to be a boss, personifying an aggressive, materialistic style of management that endures to this day" (Gelles, 2022, p. 8).

12 These, of course, represent major areas of recent and contemporary I-O research and professional practice.

employees working in such relationships manifested about the worst levels of performance, citizenship behaviors, attitudes, attendance, perceived fairness of organizational policies, and trust in coworkers compared with other forms of relations.[13] One might reasonably question the *moral sensitivity* (Rest, 1994) of a profession whose major preoccupations include enhancing worker loyalty to employers who are simultaneously in the process of consigning the notions of career, job security and fringe benefits to the dustbin of quaint historic relics.

Although it seems clear that those I-O psychologists focused on helping people adapt to the changed industrial circumstances are genuine in their concern for employees, there is nevertheless something disquieting about a position that propounds that "The key is to *discourage long-term career planning* and instead to facilitate managers and employees in self-assessment, empowering them to take advantage of opportunities for psychological success as they arise" (Hall & Richter, 1990, p. 7, emphasis added). That is likely to contribute to "a lack of meaning in the workplace" (Cartwright & Holmes, 2006, p. 202), with attendant adverse effects. The positions taken by career development specialists seem to afford no moral importance to the fact that (a) employees are generally put in this situation involuntarily by unilateral actions on the part of sometimes-abusive employers whose senior executives may be enriching themselves personally, (b) the business justifications for the changed social contract are in many instances spurious, (c) the financial benefits to the organization are frequently ephemeral, and (d) we know very well that not all employees are prepared emotionally to sustain an economic high-wire act.

Alderfer (1998) made the astute observation that organizational psychology practitioners have not reflected self-consciously on the changed nature of ethical practice since economic and political changes ushered in the era of downsizing:

> Prior to that time, our profession had primarily been called upon to assist in projects explicitly aimed toward such goals as human development and intergroup cooperation ... . After the political and economic changes of 1980, however ... a primary goal of ethically motivated practitioners became reducing harm rather than promoting development. (p. 73)

Security and stability comprise a primary "career anchor" for a substantial number of people (Schein, 1996). The moral issue of whether "rightsizing" corporations ought to behave in this fashion does not appear to arise in the literature on the "new career." Similarly, these writings are replete with references to meaningful

---

13 The only form of employee–organization relation that was consistently worse was the *quasi spot contract* relation, which resembles a pure economic exchange: "The employer offers short-term, purely economic inducements in exchange for well-specified contributions by the employee" (Tsui et al., 1997, p. 1091), such as the relations between a brokerage firm and a stockbroker.

jobs with challenging work assignments and learning opportunities, along with rewarding collegial relations—all of which are meant to replace "the old sense of security achieved through educational and career attainments and long-term organizational memberships" (Hall, 1996, p. 4). But I-O psychologists have been promoting and working to implement enriching, challenging and rewarding jobs for generations (cf. Hackman & Oldham, 1980; Herzberg, 1966; Herzberg et al., 1959; Walker & Guest, 1952)—even during the era of "long-term organizational memberships." It smacks of rationalization to suggest that these are newly developed quid pro quos for abandoning the hope of having a measure of emotional and job security and being treated respectfully by the organization rather than as a temporary and fungible cost. And why must it be *"either* (job security and respect)-*or-* (meaningful work)"? London (1996) sounded a more optimistic note as he considered some of these issues:

> Training and development are important to organizational growth. Employee development can be directed to business expansion and, in the process, increase career opportunities within the organization. Organizational restructuring and outplacement can be carried out in ways that create new ventures and job opportunities. Displaced workers can be retrained in needed skills and knowledge and simultaneously learn to demonstrate value and create job opportunities for themselves. Organizations should also consider ways to retain, motivate, and develop older workers rather than displace them. (p. 77)

This sort of optimism can also be found in the work of some collaborative public-private partnerships, started initially as a research demonstration project under the federal Social Innovation Fund (under the Corporation for National and Community Service). It is an evidence-based, apparently successful training program, running in four cities (New York, Tulsa, Cleveland and Youngstown), "designed to help low-income adults prepare for, enter, and succeed in quality jobs, in high-demand fields with opportunities for career growth" (Tessler, 2013). Similarly, small business entrepreneurs and private foundations have begun training programs for former coal miners in Appalachia (Stolberg, 2016).

Unacknowledged Value Positions

Explicitly incorporating a moral perspective into the field means accepting that the positivistic assumption of the separation of facts and values is at best an unrealized ideal, may have always been an illusion and, in the opinion of many scholars, would be inadvisable in any event (cf. Chapter 10). Social values and moral positions are implicit in much social science research, more so in *applied* research, and even more so in *professional practice* —including I-O psychology, in which the organizations served generally establish the goals and objectives to be accomplished. Rosenberg (1995) pointed out that whereas the natural sciences aim, for the most part, at technological progress, the social sciences aim at improving the human condition—which entails making moral choices that the natural sciences are not so regularly called on to make (e.g., what qualifies as an "improvement"). That is the condition that largely accounts for the importance of his admonition, which bears repeating: "A social science that sought to efface the moral dimension from its descriptions and explanations would simply serve the interests of some other moral conception. It would reflect values foreign to those that animate our conception of ourselves" (p. 205). Since its inception, that is what I-O psychology in great measure has done. For example, in considering the issue of employees who are wrongfully discharged from their jobs, I-O psychologists have counseled organizations against such "troublesome practices" —because they may lead to costly litigation against the company, not because they are disrespectful of employee rights, unethical or simply wrong (Dunford & Devine, 1998).

But also note that there have always been voices of moral dissent from within the field. Responding in the first volume of the *Journal of Applied Psychology* to Munsterberg's deferential views in *Psychology and Industrial Efficiency* (cf. quote from Munsterberg, 1913, p. 19, cited earlier), a first-generation American industrial psychologist and Yiddish scholar, Abraham-Aaron Roback (1917) wrote (in the same year in which he received his Ph.D):

> Surely the applied psychologist must have a broader outlook on life. He [sic] ought to be able to distinguish between what is *desired* and what is *desirable,* between the professional and the moral issues.
>
> No connivance on the part of a consulting psychologist can be justified on the ground that applied psychology is an *instrumental science* and is, therefore, not concerned with ends. If we choose to accept this professional view, we shall be involved in no end of difficulties. As no purpose is ultimate, or absolute, there will be a tendency to rule out all ends and to ignore every consideration but what is expedient. (pp. 233, 234, 241)

Incorporating a normative perspective into the field will frequently mean taking an advocacy position concerning the rectitude of professional activities or corporate aims and actions based on moral values and criteria (e.g., is it the right thing to do?) as distinct from traditional scientific criteria (e.g., is it valid?) or instrumental criteria (e.g., is it cost-effective?). Obviously, there is considerable room for disagreement about what is the appropriate moral position on many issues, and the moral, scientific and instrumental perspectives may conflict. But it is far better to articulate and clarify the moral values and ethical reasoning implicit in our professional practice than to abdicate any responsibility for them or, worse yet, to act as if there are none.

The opinions of I-O psychologists who, in their research or professional practice, claim to take no moral position on issues such as downsizing or affirmative action—expounding a putatively objective/scientific, instrumental or values-neutral stance—generally reflect a normative view representing the organization's economic goals and values. In the words of Roback (1917), perhaps the first I-O iconoclast, they consistently defer to expediency. Holding views entirely in accord with one's colleagues and social network, as well as with the dominant culture of one's profession and employer, can create the illusion that those beliefs and attitudes are "neutral" and render the values underlying them invisible or nonexistent. Our values often become apparent to us, and subject to (re)consideration, only when they clash with contrasting ones.[14] That is one of the values of diversity in education and organizations. Although the promotion of many organizational goals and values may be an economically defensible position, it is certainly not objective, neutral or value-free. Moreover, to the extent that the actions in question conflict with more widely accepted moral principles or with our professional ethical objective of human betterment they are morally dubious, as Rosenberg (1995) warned.

But what about questionable corporate actions of which we have had no part in the planning or implementation? Must we accept some ethical responsibility? After all, I-O psychologists—according to our own complaints—are rarely involved in significant policy decisions having to do with a corporation's core business, as opposed to its human resource practices. Even when true, however, that seems an equivocal position. One can adopt advocacy positions regarding the adverse social consequences wrought by dubious corporate actions. Our responsibilities can be indirect in that sense. For example, Wiley (1998) noted several intra-organizational roles that we might adopt with respect to ethical issues. And they include such things as "protecting employees from managerial reprisals," and "challenging the ethical aspects of managers' decisions." She emphasized that the professional loyalties and ethical commitments of human resource professionals, as well as an altruistic norm of service "may place them in direct conflict with their organization's business goals" (p. 147). Nevertheless, a national survey of HR professionals revealed that they maintained a position of ethical leadership and guidance in their organizations, in which senior managers often sought their advice about ethical issues. A set of potential roles to be played by HR professionals in their organizations was derived from qualitative survey responses and is presented as Box 12.1. Similarly, Cowan and Fox (2015) discuss the roles that HR professionals can take with respect to bullying situations in their organizations.

It is unfortunate, however, that HR departments and professionals are often viewed with suspicion and distrust by employees (Walker, 2015). I suspect that this is

---

14 This phenomenon was seen by many I-O practitioners a generation ago among White male managers who decried the inappropriate introduction of "cultural issues" into the organization with the employment of large numbers of women, African Americans and Latinos. Prior to that, according to these managers, "there was no culture in the organization!"

BOX 12.1 POTENTIAL ROLES AVAILABLE TO THE I-O PSYCHOLOGIST AND OTHER HUMAN RESOURCE MANAGERS WITH RESPECT TO ETHICAL PROBLEMS

Roles	Description
Advisory	Advising organizational members on ethical standards and policies
Monitoring	Monitoring actions/behaviors for compliance with laws, policies, and ethical standards
Educator	Instructing or distributing information regarding ethical principles and organizational policies
Advocate	Acting on behalf of individual employees or other organizational stakeholders, and protecting employees from managerial reprisals
Investigative	Investigating apparent or alleged unethical situations or complaints
Questioning	Questioning or challenging the ethical aspects of managers' decisions
Organizational	Explaining or justifying the organization's actions when confronted by agents external to the organization
Model	Modeling ethical practices to contribute to an organizational norm and climate of ethical behavior

Source: Based on Wiley (1998). Reexamining perceived ethics issues and ethics roles among employment managers. *Journal of Business Ethics, 17*(2), 147–161. Used by permission, Kluwer Academic Publishers.

---

due to the preeminence of *strategic human resource management*, which is "the pattern of planned human resource deployments and activities intended to enable the firm to achieve its goals" (Wright & McMahan, 1992), and which "seeks to understand how the management of work and workers may contribute to the competitiveness of organizations" (Okhuysen et al., 2013). In other words, HR decisions, no less than those of any other corporate unit, should be based on financial business objectives. But

> Might there be a potential dark side to this recently acquired respect and sense of relevance for HR professionals? Can the strategic perspective be taken too far? Are employees and their well-being to be valued only to the extent that their contributions to the bottom-line are demonstrable?
>
> *(Lefkowitz, 2006, p. 258)*

For example, it has long been a truism in education that learning is generally (but not uniformly) facilitated by the amount of time and attention the student pays to the material. This is known as the Time-on-Task (ToT) hypothesis (Godwin et al., 2021). It took the perverse creativity of an HR executive at Amazon to institute a performance management program based on the obverse—Time *off* task, for which employees are monitored precisely and punished, even fired, if they had a bad day (Cramer, 2021). The HR manager apparently missed the introductory psychology lesson regarding the efficacy of positive reward (for correct behavior) over punishment (for incorrect responses).[15] Based on a review of the literature, we also know that (a) attitudes toward performance monitoring "will be more positive when organizations monitor their employees within supportive organizational cultures"; (b) imposing such control will "reduce autonomy and increase perceived job demands—both factors that contribute to burnout"; and (c) "when electronic monitoring is seen as control-based rather than developmental, employees are likely to experience more negative outcomes" (Cascio & Montealegre, 2016, pp. 357–358.)

At times moral choices will entail advocating positions on issues that conflict with the perceived economic well-being and stated positions of our employers or clients, and thus our own economic self-interest. That's an ethical dilemma! Some may repress or choose to ignore it. Some may rationalize their behavior. My intention is to increase the salience of a moral perspective on such matters and to provide the tools for one's own ethical analysis and a discussion among ourselves.

Facets of I-O Psychology: III. Demise of Concern for the Individual Employee

Earlier in this chapter I noted the positive transformation of industrial psychology that took place in the 1960s by virtue of the theoretical advances that marked the development of organizational psychology and organizational theory—fields as much or more concerned with explaining the behavior of groups, subsystems and entire organizations as of individuals, which had always been the dominant perspective of industrial psychology. Notwithstanding its theoretical focus, this transformation dovetailed with the economizing values of the corporation emphasizing the macrolevel objectives of productivity and profitability. In reviewing the history of the field, Katzell and Austin (1992) confirmed the predominant emphasis since the mid-1980s on productivity enhancement as the primary focus

---

15 Perhaps worse still, there was apparently some indication that the program was not instituted out of ignorance but was part of an intentional aim to have a high rate of turnover and new-hires so as to not have an entrenched work force that would be more prone to unionize. (Reportedly, annual turnover was approximately 150% at this warehouse.)

of our techniques and interventions. And Werhane (1999) observed that even "the language of employment" reflects a model of economic objects or collectives, not individual human beings:

> Employees are talked about as 'human resources,' much like natural resources or manufacturing resources ... . We often tend [to] think of employees as a statistical phenomenon and we measure them that way. So when we downsize, we downsize groups of employees, not individuals. (p. 242)

What seems to have been largely sloughed off during I-O psychology's metamorphosis was our traditional individualist perspective and concern for individually defined personal goals and objectives (Weiss & Rupp, 2011). Interests and activities that once characterized I-O psychology but are now part of other professional domains and/or are encapsulated subspecialties in which most I-O psychologists claim little, or no expertise include individual employee counseling, vocational guidance and development, human factors engineering, employee assistance programs and occupational health and safety. For example, Highhouse (1999) related the history of personnel counseling and its preeminence in I-O psychology during the 1940s and 1950s and its subsequent demise, and Savickas (2001) noted that

> The focus on individuals differentiates vocational psychology from the fields of I-O psychology, organizational behavior, and occupational sociology. Of course, vocational psychologists work in organizations, yet when they do they concentrate on individual workers and their careers rather than on the organization and its leadership. (p. 168)[16]

The organizational perspective of our work as social scientists further reinforces professional practice in which we are invariably working as representatives of the organization implementing company-sponsored human resource policies and practices. Consequently, to the extent that some of

---

16 Conversely, although the value of this individualist perspective was extolled, do not lose sight of the avowedly political objectives of employee counseling during its origins in Elton Mayo's work in the Hawthorne studies: It was developed as a method of "counteract[ing] the increasing tendency for a worker's complaint to be elevated to the status of a union grievance" (Highhouse, 1999, p. 324). Moreover, some contemporary vocational psychologists also decry the absence of a "study of vocations in a broader understanding of social issues, with a focus on how interventions can help empower clients and change inequitable systems" (Blustein, 2001, p. 174). That broader understanding would have to include the organizational point of view that is so well represented in I-O psychology (Russell, 2001). Both perspectives are important.

those human resource activities may be experienced by employees as violative of their rights and/or as otherwise invasive or unfair—including instances in which their concern extends to the initiation of formal complaints or lawsuits against the organization—we may automatically be cast in the role of justifying those activities and defending the organization. Thus, regardless of the individual I-O psychologist's personal values or predilections, there is a social-structural determinant that predisposes the profession to one side of most employee–management disputes.

For example, among a sample of 100 I-O psychology experts in employee selection testing, of whom 70% had been involved in employment discrimination litigation, almost 2/3 of those had worked primarily as an expert on behalf of defendants (employers). Only 9% had worked primarily on behalf of plaintiffs (Lefkowitz & Gebbia, 1997). It is not difficult to think of other instances in which I-O psychologists maintain a partisan if not adversarial stance on behalf of employer interests or perspectives. In an article entitled "Invasion of Privacy: A Rising Concern for Personnel Psychologists," written by an I-O psychologist (Arnold, 1990) to alert colleagues to a growing problem, the major thrust of the "concern" referred to is not the invasion of workers' privacy by their employers. What is presumed to be the major source of distress for I-O psychologists are legislative initiatives *in support of* employee privacy. What is further decried is that highly publicized employee complaints "create an awareness among job applicants, making subsequent efforts to resist and seek redress for similar [intrusive] inquiries by potential employers more likely" (Arnold, 1990, p. 38).

Similarly, in an article also aimed at serving an educative function for I-O psychologists concerned with employee discharge and the common law doctrine of employment-at-will (Dunford & Devine, 1998), the employee's recovery of damages as a result of winning a lawsuit for wrongful discharge is lamented as one of the "negative outcomes" of discharge-related lawsuits (p. 904). Another negative outcome of such litigation lamented by the authors is "lowered morale on the part of [the remaining] workers." From a perspective that values the interests of employees, questions naturally arise: Why isn't the recovery of damages by a worker who has been wrongfully discharged a good thing? Why is the resulting litigation viewed as the cause of lowered morale rather than the wrongful discharge itself? From a normative frame of reference, wrongful discharge and other similarly motivated actions should be denounced and discouraged not only for instrumental reasons—that they are costly to the organization, or the resulting low morale will affect performance adversely—but because they fail to abide by ethical principles of fairness and justice and are violative of an employee's rights to be treated with dignity and respect; that is, they are simply wrong. The point is not that these authors are necessarily or atypically antagonistic to workers. Their views represent what is probably still a majority opinion among I-O psychologists, conditioned by our work on behalf of and identification with the organization and its managerial values system. And this perspective is not new to the field. Even during the great depression of the 1930s I-O psychology paid virtually no attention to the unemployed (Katzell & Austin, 1992).

Employee Selection

Employee selection is also conceptualized and conducted from the organization's perspective. Harking back to the multiple stakeholder approach (Chapter 11), the process could look somewhat different if the perspective of individual employees or, in this case, applicants were afforded consideration (Lefkowitz & Lowman, 2017). Simplifying a bit, selection is comprised of two major components, a valid means of assessing job candidates and a set of decision rules by which those assessments are turned into hiring decisions (sometimes called the *referral system*). Arguably, there is no inherent contradiction between the individual and organizational perspectives regarding the validity component. Organizations have an obvious economizing interest in selecting the most capable employees to minimize training time and/or maximize employee longevity, productivity and profitability. That can be accomplished by using valid selection measures. And it may reasonably be assumed that capable and qualified applicants are similarly interested in having their talents recognized and being hired. And it is neither unreasonable nor unfair to accept that candidates truly unqualified for a job ought not to be hired and so be spared the disappointment and frustration of failing at it and being dismissed. A hypothetically perfectly valid predictor or set of predictors would identify correctly all applicants as either successful or unsuccessful on the job if they were hired, i.e., they could be assessed as acceptable and hired or unacceptable and not hired.[17]

However, even the best selection measures (e.g., tests of general mental ability, integrity tests, scored biographical information, situational judgment tests and structured employment interviews) contain measurement error and are nowhere near perfectly valid. Operationally, they can account for approximately 40% of the variation in the level of job performance among employees (Schmidt, 2016; Schmidt & Hunter, 1998). And the job candidate's predicted performance score is merely a point estimate; it is made (a) within a range of error and (b) at a specified level of probability. "Most researchers

---

17 As any personnel psychologist will recognize, that is an oversimplification. Predictions or estimates are made of the candidates' scores on a particular criterion measure or set of criteria. Even for a perfectly valid predictor (unknown in actual practice) the extent to which those predictions of criterion performance presage success on the job depends on the relevance and comprehensiveness of the criterion as an indicator of overall job performance and on the location of the (sometimes arbitrary) dividing line between successful and unsuccessful performance on the distribution of criterion scores.

know both things, but in their statistical zeal, they tend to forget them" (Guion, 1998, p. 337). It is this imperfect level of prediction, along with the nature of the statistical regression procedure by which validity is demonstrated empirically, that causes a divergence of interests between the organization and (some) individual applicants. It occurs with respect to the referral system—the hiring decisions that are based on predictor performance (or estimated job performance). To say that prediction is imperfect is to acknowledge that some applicants are misclassified by our predictor measures. Some are misidentified as acceptable and so hired, but subsequently fail to perform successfully on the job ("false hires" or "false positives"); others are misidentified as unacceptable, hence not hired, but would have succeeded on the job had they been hired ("false rejects" or "false negatives").

The Dilemma of False Rejects

A problem arises because these two groups are not proportionally equivalent: there are invariably many more false rejects than false hires.[18] The organization's economizing interests are in minimizing still further the number of false positives, which it can do by raising the minimum qualifying score on the predictor measure(s) (decreasing the selection ratio) so that although fewer applicants are hired, proportionally more of them are identified correctly as true positives. In fact, with a highly valid predictor it may be possible to hire so few applicants (only the very highest scorers on the predictors) that all of them are successful on the job. But as one might expect, the smaller selection ratio serves to increase still further the size of the false rejects group—the candidates who would have succeeded but have been denied employment due in part to the fallibility of our selection technology. Typically, most organizations afford no consideration to the interests of these candidates (they are not considered to be legitimate stakeholders), and no substantial acknowledgment is made by I-O psychologists of what can arguably be viewed as an ethical issue in which we are intimately involved.

To the extent that I-O psychologists, as true professionals, should be concerned about the welfare of both the organization and of those incorrectly rejected for employment, we may think of this as an ethical dilemma (cf. Table 6.4). But acknowledging a dilemma is frequently easier than resolving it.

18 The relative proportion of false rejects to false hires when introducing a valid predictor is, in part, a function of the proportion of employees who are deemed to be acceptable or successful on the job. The greater the proportion who perform acceptably (as on a relatively "easy" job), the greater will be the proportion of false rejects to false hires. It seems reasonable to assume that on most jobs the proportion of acceptable or successful workers far exceeds those who are unacceptable. (It is hard to conceive of a functioning organization in which most employees are performing unacceptably.) Thus, in most situations, false rejects substantially exceed false hires.

Our most well-intentioned motives will be limited by the inability to differentiate a priori (i.e., at the applicant stage) between those who will be false rejects and true rejects. I surmise that most I-O psychologists would respond (accurately) to the effect that we are already engaged in the enterprise of attempting to solve this problem in the best way possible for all concerned: striving to maximize the validity of our selection procedures, thus reducing the proportion of mis-classifications of both types. But given our current awareness of the harm done those rejected incorrectly, the present imperfect state of our technology and the low level of improvement in prediction efficiency likely in the foreseeable future, that seems an ethically deficient response.

The possibility of retesting

In acknowledgment of this problem organizations and I-O psychologists have been admonished to allow failing candidates additional opportunities to qualify, such as by retesting, using alternative assessments, or by providing an opportunity for probationary job training (AERA, APA, & NCME, 2014; Equal Employment Opportunity Commission et al., 1978; London & Bray, 1980). Although "Retesting is intended to decrease the probability that a person will be incorrectly classified as not meeting some standard" (AERA et al., 2014, p. 115), those authoritative testing standards consider an applicant's opportunity for retesting to be merely a "privilege" (Standard 9.18). Unfortunately, not much is known about the effects of such retesting, and it is my impression that these practices are rather rarely instituted. Optimistically, some data exist indicating that "retesting does not negatively affect criterion-related validity and may even enhance it" (Schleicher & Campion, 2011, p, 941).

The possibility of alternative standards

In the context of enhancing the fairness of employee selection systems for potential "false rejects" critical attention is being paid to the necessity of requiring applicants to have a college degree for most decent-paying jobs, notwithstanding that more than 68% of U.S. workers do not have a four-year degree (Gould, 2018). It has been known for quite some time that there is a large differential in the job level, earnings and accumulated wealth of college graduates compared to those without degrees ("the college wage premium"), and the difference is especially marked for Blacks, LatinX, veteran and rural workers, and women (Gould, 2016). (Although evidence indicates that the college wage premium reflects social class-based advantages—an enormous gap between those in the top 5% of the wage distribution and everyone else, even within the college-educated group [Gould, 2019; Rothstein, 2020].)

Only since 2017 has the bachelor's degree as a minimum qualification (MQ) begun to be questioned by some employers (Lohr, 2022b; Opportunity@Work

& Accenture, 2020; Opportunity@Work, 2022). And there has been a marked decrease in the number of companies requiring that MQ with a corresponding increase in skills-based hiring, with supportive training programs (Fuller et al., 2022). The focus has shifted to looking for applicants who are or can become STARS (skilled through alternative routes)—such as Associate Degrees; technical schools; previous work experience, including in the military; company or union internships, apprenticeships, and other training/development programs. A recent large-scale study identified 71 million such workers currently active in the workforce, all of whom "have suitable skillsets to succeed in work that is more highly valued and therefore better paid than the work they do now" (Opportunity@Work & Accenture, 2020, p. 4). This implies being able to assess job requirements and to make quality assessments of relevant applicant attributes—i.e., their knowledge, skills and abilities—which has long been among the core strengths of I-O psychology (Brannick & Levine, 2002; Guion, 1991, 1998; Harvey, 1991; Lubinski & Dawis, 1992).

Organizations also should be encouraged whenever possible to increase their selection ratios (by relaxing the predictor cut-off scores), thereby hiring more of those who would otherwise be false rejects. This is especially feasible in large-scale or continuous hiring situations in which those people will not displace applicants with higher predictor scores. Although the average level of the job performance of the resulting group of hires will be lower than would be the case if a more restrictive cut-off score were used, it is likely to be well within tolerable limits in many situations—especially for lower-level jobs in which the economic utility of valid predictors is more modest than for higher level jobs. After all, we also know that the standard score difference in actual job performance between low- and high-scoring applicants is generally smaller than the difference between them on the predictors (Hartigan & Wigdor, 1989; Wagner, 1997). As long as the cut-off score remains near the upper levels of the score distribution of a valid predictor the number of previous false rejects now hired and successful will exceed the number of additional false positives.

Of course, the dilemma is caused in part by an a priori and unqualified acceptance of the economizing business value system that brooks no diminution of the effort to maximize productivity and profitability for the individual firm. Within that value system the only permissible standard for employee selection is the applicants' potential contribution to productivity (at least to the extent that such productivity is well reflected in the criterion measure used). But the expression of other goals and objectives is at least conceivable, leading to the consideration of other selection values. That is so only if we broaden our perspective to include (a) the welfare of all individuals as well as organizations; (b) other valued outcomes in addition to productivity; and/or (c) maximizing utility for the entire local community (or by extension, society), not simply for each organization considered independently and competitively. For example, instead of hiring only the highest test scorers, some consideration could also be given to selecting (a) those most in need; (b) those who are least likely to obtain other employment, thus putting their families at risk and becoming a drain on public resources; or (c) those most likely to contribute to organizational objectives other than productivity, such as enhancing its public image. Increasing ethnic, racial, age or sexual diversity in particular segments of the organization or for the organization as a whole can also be considered.

Employment could even be reconceptualized in large measure as a *placement* issue for the society as a whole or for a geographic region, in which our objective is to productively employ everyone seeking work, rather than entirely as a *selection* issue for each individual organization in competition with one another for employees. There are not enough "superior" people to go around (nor does every position require such, in any event): By definition, only 5% of any population is above the 95th percentile! Moreover, as Wagner (1997) noted, it is paradoxically true that the greater the number of organizations that use ability tests for selection, the lower will be the overall utility for the society as a whole, approaching the average of the population, thus putting more of a premium on training and on differential job placement.

The point is not that the values reflected in these alternative objectives are necessarily "better" than the economizing values, but that they all, including profitability, represent potential value choices that could be considered, discussed, analyzed and possibly integrated. As noted some time ago in considering the problem of imperfect prediction "the personal and societal costs must be considered in addition to the monetary costs, and it is the psychologist's duty to bring these costs to the employer's attention" (London & Bray, 1980, p. 898). Because the field lacks a salient normative point of view, we tend at best to be reactive rather than proactive in these sorts of matters. For example, I-O psychology's awakened concern in the U.S. in the 1960s for the fairness of our employee assessment methods derived not from a moral or even scholarly perspective of our own, but from sociopolitical ones—as a reaction to the civil rights movement and resulting legislation and jurisprudence (Katzell & Austin, 1992).

Employment-At-Will (EAW)

As noted earlier, millions of Americans experienced involuntary permanent loss of a job (or several) even before the recession of 2008 and the pandemic of 2020–2022. The reason that occurred so readily is that the bulk of employees in the United States work under the condition of EAW, meaning that, barring some limitations noted shortly, people

> must be left, without interference to buy and sell where they please, and to discharge or retain employees at will for good cause or for no cause, or even for bad cause without thereby being guilty of an unlawful act *per se*. It

is a right which an employee may exercise in the same way, to the same extent, for the same cause or want of cause as the employer.

(text of a famous 1884 judicial decision, cited by R. Edwards, 1993, p. 14; cf. Dunford & Devine, 1998, and Werhane and Radin, 1996, for concise reviews of EAW)[19]

EAW is a common law doctrine inherited from England, where—like most of the rest of the world's industrialized nations—it is no longer the dominant basis for employment as it is in the United States. Business ethicists have frequently decried EAW as incompatible with the development of mutual trust, loyalty and respect that ought to characterize the workplace (Werhane, 1999). Some organizational scholars have made the case that it is similarly incompatible with the sorts of modern "high performance" and employee-centered human resource practices that build employee commitment and contribute to effective organizational functioning (Dessler, 1999; Huselid, 1995; Pfeffer, 1994, 1998; Pfeffer & Veiga, 1999). In contrast, I-O psychologists have largely ignored the topic or have supported the prevailing corporate perspective by suggesting ways of "protecting at-will organizations from liability associated with discharging employees" (Dunford & Devine, 1998, p. 928).

For the first several decades of the 20th century EAW was virtually the only governing principle of employment relations, and it led to legal interpretations in which employees had virtually no rights. The courts uniformly reasoned that whatever rights might be claimed by an employee against an employer (in the absence of a legal individual contract) could simply and legally be refuted by firing the worker; thus, they were moot. During the middle of the century there was a substantial increase in federal statutory protections for workers in general (e.g., the Fair Labor Standards Act of 1938 and many subsequent amendments, or the Employee Retirement Income Security Act of 1974), accompanying regulatory bodies (e.g., the Occupational Safety and Health Administration, 1971), as well as civil rights legislation targeted at specific groups of employees (e.g., Equal Pay Act of 1963, Civil Rights Act of 1964, and Americans With Disabilities Act of 1990). Many states also passed similar laws, and "given the small number of relevant federal laws and their highly specific nature, state law tends to be much more important in discharge-related lawsuits" (Dunford & Devine, 1998, p. 907).[20]

---

19 This discussion of EAW pertains to private sector employees only. In the public sector, employees of federal, state or local governments have many more guaranteed rights. That is because of the political philosophy reflected in the fact that the U.S. constitution was written to protect individual citizens from the state, which includes its role as an employer. It does not pertain to relations among private people (even "quasipeople" like corporations).

20 In an Appendix R. Edwards (1993) noted 41 states in which a state court has recognized an implied contract and six states in which the existence of an implied contract has been specifically rejected.

Almost as important during those years was the growth of labor unions, which were given explicit legal recognition, so that a major source of worker rights and protections emanated from collective-bargaining agreements that would be enforced by the courts. Concomitant with the decline in labor unions and the protections they provided, state courts have partially filled that void by becoming somewhat more "pro-employee" in enforcing what might reasonably be interpreted as implied contracts between employer and employee (e.g., based on statements made in the organization's employee handbook). For reasons of public policy, the courts have also afforded workers protection against being fired for behaving ethically and responsibly, such as by alerting appropriate parties to wrongdoing by the organization (whistle-blowing).

Some of the most important limitations on EAW are the institutional enterprise rights of due-process or just-cause for dismissal.[21] Werhane and Radin (1996) distinguished between *procedural due process,* as "the right to a hearing, trial, grievance procedure, or appeal" in which the grounds for dismissal can be ascertained and challenged by an employee, and *substantive due process,* which is "the demand for rationality and fairness: for good reasons for decisions" (p. 420). Organizations may be characterized as either at-will (a majority in the United States) or those in which some form of just-cause policy for dismissal has been granted to employees as an enterprise right. Unfortunately, as noted in Chapter 3, there has been a trend for employers to institute due-process procedures contingent on employees signing away their rights to redress in the courts.

The major organizational justification for EAW is the traditional economizing one of promoting efficiency and productivity. Aside from specific legislative limitations, in a nonunionized, at-will company any employees deemed unproductive, uncooperative or no longer needed can be terminated expeditiously without the time-consuming and potentially costly procedures of due process. The justification has seemed even more pertinent in recent years as companies have striven to become more "lean and mean" in response to global competition. Long-term commitments to employees have become obsolete, and short-term flexibility in controlling labor costs are more important. "The result is more jobs with lower wages, reduced benefits, more part-time work and temporary workers, more subcontracting, and intensified work schedules" (R. Edwards, 1993, p. 15).

However, the empirical evidence regarding the extent to which these EAW-based practices have proven to increase productivity is rather mixed (Pfeffer, 1994, 1998; Pfeffer & Veiga, 1999; Tsui et al., 1997; Werhane, 1999b), and it is by no means clear that at-will companies are more productive than just-cause companies

---

21 *Institutional rights* stem from an institutional source (e.g., an employer, or the state) and justify decisions by the institution. *Enterprise rights* are afforded, explicitly or implicitly, by employers unilaterally (e.g., the right to know how one's performance will be evaluated, or the right to a formal grievance system). Those only implied by company practices may not be enforceable legally.

or that employees who feel respected, trusted, and protected from capricious personnel actions are not in fact more committed, productive, innovative and efficient than those who feel vulnerable (Dessler, 1999). Employees are at risk because labor costs are simply easier to reduce than others like capital costs.

From a moral perspective, however, unlike other costs, labor is inseparable from the individual human beings who provide it. The abstract economic objective of "reducing labor costs" can be accomplished largely by the dismissal of employees—who are, in this context, conceived of entirely in terms of money saved, not as individual human beings.[22] Although it may be tempting to conclude that this is an unfortunate but nevertheless necessary aspect of a successful free-enterprise economic system, another view—based on the writings of none other than Adam Smith—is possible (Werhane, 1999b). As noted earlier, Smith conditioned his views of laissez faire free enterprise within the context of principles of fairness and justice. He was primarily focused on a system of political economy—fusing both political and economic concerns—not simply on economic utility for the firm.

> Early on, then, Smith linked politics and economics, rights and utility ... . Smith's proviso is that system will be successful only when each operates under the constraints of respect for human rights, justice, and fair play, and early on he recognized that poor treatment of employees is both unfair as well as economically questionable on utilitarian grounds.
>
> *(Werhane, 1999b, pp. 243–244)*

This perspective has found a voice, at least in organizational scholarship if not necessarily in practice, in attempts to create "caring and compassionate organizations" (Rynes et al., 2012). That scholarship aims to "humanize people working inside organizations as people who suffer, people who care, and people who individually and collectively may respond to pain" (p. 505), and to promote "theories that reflect the accumulating evidence that other-centeredness and interconnectedness are central aspects of humanity" (p. 508). I believe it is worth noting that this enterprise is engendered primarily by management scholars in a scholarly management journal, not by I-O psychologists.

Facets of I-O Psychology: IV. Both Scientific/Technical Competence and Societal Consequences

The formal mission of the American Psychological Association is "to advance the creation, communication and application of psychological knowledge to benefit

---

22 An alternative of reducing the rates of pay of current employees is unlikely. More likely is reducing the hours they work—in effect, partial-dismissals. Ceasing hiring is, of course, possible, as is reducing the pay rates for new hires, but that doesn't reduce current costs.

society and improve people's lives" (APA, 2008). Benefitting society is an intrinsic objective of the scientific enterprise. Accordingly, the APA recently published a special issue of the *American Psychologist* concerning "Public Psychology: Cultivating Socially Engaged Science for the 21st Century" (Eaton et al., 2021). Similarly, SIOP's mission "is to enhance human well-being and performance in organizational and work settings … " (SIOP, nd). In other words, judging actions morally requires consideration of their societal consequences. This is reflected in the moral dimension of care or well-being and harm-avoidance, and it is true not only within a utilitarian framework. "Morality does not exist in a vacuum. Human pursuits should always be judged in terms of what their consequences are for other human beings" (Luria, 1976, p. 333). Evans (2021) generalizes that

> While professional occupations emerged with an avowed moral commitment to serving societal needs, professionals have since then largely restricted their authoritative claims to abstract technical expertise and excluded moral questions from their area of authority. In doing so, they have relinquished the capacity to control the moral debates related to their professional activities. (p. 991)

As indicated previously, I believe that I-O psychology has mostly steered clear of the moral implications of our work—in the mistaken belief that it is a necessary precondition for maintaining our scientific bonafides. But nowadays, even employees are pressuring their company's executives to speak up about contentious social and political issues in the U.S. (Kaye, 2021).

It is thought-provoking to compare this theme in our history with the views of a rare woman industrial psychologist in the U.K. 100 years ago, who believed that we could and should be playing an important role in developing autonomous and responsible citizens:

> Is it psychologically possible to have docile, externally controlled workers in industry, who are yet free, intelligent and responsible members of a democracy outside it? … . It is for us more than any other science to lend our knowledge for the re-creation, not only of industry, but of human society.
>
> *(Susan Brierly, 1920)*

Many ethicists like Rest (1986b), have virtually defined what is meant by an ethical situation or dilemma as one in which the consequences of a person's action affects the interests, welfare or expectations of others. The issue is particularly pertinent for I-O psychology because the business institutions in which or for which we practice set the agenda for that practice in accordance with their own values and objectives; those, in turn, define the organizational problems that we address and largely determine the range of potential applications (hence, consequences) of our work. As noted earlier, a version of this perspective has been promoted recently by Gardner et al. (2001), who suggested that satisfaction in "good work" entails developing one's expertise as well as helping society.

Any aspect of the professional practice of I-O psychology can be viewed from a perspective beyond that of the organization in which it is taking place. So much of what we do, developing and implementing human resources procedures and other organizational policies, has meaningful consequences for the financial, psychological and social well-being of the employees affected as well as their families and communities, and by extension the broader society (Aguinis & Kraiger, 2009). That is, in part, what accounts for the relevance to I-O psychology of the social justice issues considered in Chapter 8 (in addition to our mere membership in the moral community of responsible citizens). Moreover, it would be illogical and ethically remiss to believe that we can justifiably ignore the moral behavior of our clients and employers. But a review of 45 years of I-O research concluded that even with respect to human-capital issues of direct relevance to organizations (e.g., work-life programs, diversity, globalization, ethics and ethical leadership), our concerns have been modest and indirect (Cascio & Aguinis, 2008). Although organizations sometimes do terrible things, "how often have you heard an I-O psychologist assert that business organizations are sometimes (perhaps often) unhealthy, ego-dystonic places in which to work?" (Lefkowitz, 2019, p. 476). And that presents I-O psychology with a conundrum.

> If we (justifiably) take credit for our contributions to the societal goods attributed to these corporations, should we not also own up to some complicity in the harms they commit? In some instances, we are more actively culpable (regarding certain HR policies and decisions). More important, we should assume the role of actively challenging those decisions by engaging the system. (p.476–477) (cf. Box 12.1)

A good example, in the domain of organizational justice, is the issue of *forced arbitration*.

> Arbitration is a commonly used form of alternative dispute resolution (ADR). While voluntary agreements to arbitration have been used in commercial disputes for many years, today's employers are utilizing a different form of arbitration known as forced arbitration. Forced arbitration occurs when an employer conditions initial employment, continued employment, or important employment benefits on the employee's agreement to arbitrate any future claims against the employer.
>
> *(Workplace Fairness, 2016)*

Forced arbitration denies employees access to the public and transparent court system and, since a 2001 U.S. Supreme Court decision, is in most cases legal.[23]

Not so long ago the Allstate Insurance Company instituted a unilateral decision to convert its entire sales force of more than 15,000 from regular employees with pensions and health care benefits to independent contractors (Treaster, 2001). To keep their reorganized jobs the sales agents had to sign a waiver, or release, that they would not sue Allstate. Unfortunately, a spokesperson for the company was correct when she stated, "Releases are used routinely in the American workplace in connection with business re-organizations and have been consistently upheld in court (p. C4)." Also upheld in courts have been companies insisting that contracts contain private (forced) arbitration clauses that preempt any possibility of the organization being held accountable by a lawsuit for wrongdoing or wrongful discharge. Dramatically, these are not only used in employment contracts but "arbitration clauses have proliferated over the last ten years as companies have added them to tens of millions of contracts for things as diverse as cellphone service, credit cards and student loans" (Corkery & Silver-Greenberg, 2016, p. B5). Such clauses are even used by nursing home operators to shield themselves from charges of elder abuse, neglect and wrongful death. Are these actions we support as conducive to creating a healthy workplace (Clay, 2016)? Do they not run counter to SIOP's "mission [which] is to enhance human well-being and performance in organizational and work settings" (SIOP, 2021)?

In contrast with our traditional silence on such matters it is heartening to note SIOP taking social advocacy positions regarding the health of workers returning to work post-pandemic, dealing with the impact on the workforce of new technologies, veterans transitioning to civilian work, worker development and training, and even policing reform (SIOP, 2022). Similarly, the European Association of Work and Organizational Psychology (EAWOP) has recently promulgated a *Manifesto* for the future of the field emphasizing (among other things) our responsibilities toward individuals at work and their wellbeing, and towards society, as well as reducing inequality (Balhttp et al., 2019). And back on this side of the Atlantic, a studied big-picture view of the field by "prominent I-O scholars" yielded "a perceived need for more attention to the meaning of work in people's lives … [and] an increase in attention to worker welfare" (Highhouse & Schmitt, 2013, p. 3).

23 The workplace laws affected include the Civil rights Acts of 1964 and 1991; Age Discrimination in Employment Act; American with Disabilities Act, and its Amendments; Family and Medical Leave Act; Fair Labor Standards Act; Equal pay Act; Uniformed Services Employment and Reemployment Rights Act; National Labor Relations Act; and Lilly Ledbetter Fair Pay Act of 2009 (National Employment Lawyers Association, 2016).

The Past, Present, and Future Prospects

Some Consequences of the Longstanding I-O Psychology Value System

To summarize, I have argued that notwithstanding some notable and recent exceptions, the value system characterizing I-O psychology has been comprised of several problematic components: (i) a managerialist bias, with an accompanying disinterest in or even antagonism toward organized labor; (ii) a disavowal of humanist concerns and moral values because of a mistaken belief that normative judgements are incompatible with the appropriate conduct of both research and professional practice; while nevertheless (iii) adopting an economic corporatist value system; (iv) a near-exclusive focus on and concern for the organization, with correspondingly little concern for individual employees and other stakeholders; and (v) a failure to look beyond criteria of technical competence and economic utility for the firm, to acknowledge the importance of the societal consequences of what we do (or should be doing).

There would have been little purpose in offering up the foregoing criticisms if I did not believe that they have had adverse effects on the field (albeit also having contributed to the growth and success of the profession). It has been my hope that highlighting some of the negative consequences may serve to make them more salient, leading to even more positive change than has already been occurring (Lefkowitz, 2008). Some of these effects have been identified in recent years by other I-O psychologists, and those insights have been constructive for the field. But in my opinion those authors have generally misattributed the cause(s) of those effects solely to "technical" matters—deficiencies in the conduct of our science, research methodology, competencies or professional training and the like, rather than to the implicit values system that drives it all. Here is a sampling of some of those observations:[24]

A Self-Declared Identity Crisis

I-O psychology seems to have a *Chicken Little* problem. A substantial number of I-O psychologists have perceived existential threats to our field intermittently for more than 50 years (e.g., Aguinis et al., 2014; Byrne et al., 2014; Gasser et al., 2004; Kożusznik & Glaser, 2021; Lawler et al., 1971; Llwellyn et al., 2016; Rotolo et al., 2018; Ryan, 2003; Ryan & Ford, 2010; Steiner & Yancey, 2013). Such insecurities might explain why a relatively young and ostensibly successful profession has already been known by at least 11 names: *industrial psychology,*

---

24 It is possible that I have not done justice to the views of these colleagues in my attempt to briefly shape their observations to the current purpose. I have tried to not distort them. I apologize to any who believe that I have failed in those attempts.

organizational psychology, industrial-organizational psychology, work psychology, work and organizational psychology, organizational behavior, organization development, occupational psychology, occupational/organizational psychology, vocational psychology, and humanitarian work psychology. In the U.S., the field underwent a formal name change in 1970 (from I to I-O); but further proposed name changes in 2003 and 2009 resulted in failed referenda due to lack of consensus. One of the problems with this state of affairs is that genuine, realistic concerns potentially are lost in the ongoing hue and cry.

Much of the angst seems to be because we believe that we are not seen as differentiated from our competitors in the marketplace—or not "seen" at all; nor appreciated sufficiently for our unique talents. Some of us view those competitors as having become (perhaps unscrupulously) "the driving force behind the [talent management] movement in theory and practice ... . We are calling this confluence of factors in the workplace today *anti-industrial-organizational psychology*" (Rotolo et al., 2018, p. 178, emphasis in the original).

Most of the solutions proposed by the collection of authors noted above involve promoting our putatively superior education and training. For example, "our field needs to leverage what we do best (which serendipitously, is also what sets us apart from other fields)—namely, our ability to develop and apply evidence-based approaches to solve organizational issues" (Rotolo et al., 2018, p. 205). I agree; that is true. But I believe there is more to be considered.

Taking a historical perspective reveals that I-O has experienced recurring identity threats over the years:

> In the 1960s, our professional identity was threatened by the newly-emergent field of organizational psychology or organizational behavior. The threat was resolved both by compartmentalization—of OB to Business Schools—and by introjection—the transformation of industrial psychology into I/O psychology. We defended the perceived 1970s identity challenge from organization development (OD) and the values-based process consultation model by disparaging its scientific status so that it, too, became compartmentalized—in separate professional schools and free-standing institutes such as NTL. In the 1980s and '90 s we were aroused by incipient incursions into our corporate domain by clinical psychology colleagues—to which we responded adaptively, co-opting much of their potential contribution by becoming "executive coaches."
>
> *(Lefkowitz, 2005, p. 18)*

Perhaps the reader is familiar with the psychoanalytic perspective in which it may be

> expected that individuals would experience chronic feelings of threat to the extent that they were recipients of rigid and harsh treatment during their

formative years. As a result of the growing feelings of hostility and inadequacy that were produced by such experiences, people might display defensive derogation of devalued social groups.

(Branscombe et al., 1999)

In the 2005 article cited above I speculated quite inferentially, "An individual with an inadequately developed sense of self is likely to also be lacking a clear conception of an ideal self and to experience a high level of ego threat. Perhaps the same is true for a profession" (p.18). If so, I wonder what "rigid and harsh treatment" I-O was the recipient of in the early 20th century. (Box 12.2 is a tongue-in-cheek caricature).

BOX 12.2 IDENTITY CRISIS—A FABLE

One day, a well-dressed, mature gentleman—one might be tempted to describe him as elderly, except he appears extremely vital and alert—walks into a psychotherapist's office for a first visit. After just a few brief exchanges the therapist gets the impression that the gentleman is a socially adept, financially successful, educated professional, well-respected member of the community. But all is not as it seems on the surface. This new patient "presents" with lingering complaints of vague malaise; and despite his apparent success, he reports having experienced long-term intermittent bouts of anxiety and fear stemming from threats that the therapist can't be sure are real or imagined: various people seem regularly aiming to put him out of business; family relatives are always disrespectful and demeaning. Moreover, there's an existential quality to his anxiety: as a younger, middle-aged man, just becoming successful, he even changed his name legally because he felt it better suited his identity. In fact, he came close to changing his name twice again in recent years but could not make up his mind what to change it to; nothing seemed to "fit" well enough. The therapist got the impression, however, that the patient was more concerned with the impression his name would make on others, than with any genuine expression of his nature; and he seemed relatively unconcerned with maintaining his nominal family identity. It struck the therapist that his patient's insecurities were just not in keeping with his accomplishments in life. In fact, for an educated professional, the patient seemed to lack much insight into his own character and values.

Source: From Lefkowitz, J. (2017). The role of values in professional licensing: The resistance to regulation. *Industrial and Organizational Psychology, 10*(2), 223–233. Used by permission.

In my opinion our sense of unease has to do in part with our failure to specify a morally-embedded core *professional identity* as alluded to in this chapter, which I define as "our beliefs, goals, and meta-objectives concerning what it is [we] intend to accomplish in the organizations with which [we] work and how [we] prefer to go about accomplishing them" (Lefkowitz, 2010a, p. 294).

Others have voiced similar views. For example, a "declaration of identity" emphasizes I-O psychology's "responsibility as a profession to support difficult decisions at the societal, organizational, and group level so as to always ensure that workers and work-eligible people are reaping benefits rather than harmed by their work" (Kożusznik & Glaser, 2021, p. 1).

Some Other Exemplars

- Greenberg (2009) notes that even though we study organizational justice, and know a lot about it, we don't attempt many interventions to actually enhance OJ—primarily because such interventions are difficult to implement, and managers are ignorant of the issues. However, as discussed extensively in Chapter 8, I believe that the reasons we don't do much are because we study only *perceived* OJ (primarily the procedural and interactional aspects), rather than actual distributional inequities, because that would require adopting an explicit normative position regarding what an overtly *just* organization would be for its employees (Lefkowitz, 2009a).
- Weiss and Rupp (2011) justifiably decry the absence of an individualistic (person-centric) perspective in I-O research, and call for a "full and focused appreciation of the individual at work" (cf. Facet III of I-O psychology, previous). Although they acknowledge the limitation that "we are a science that takes its problems from organizational needs" they nevertheless see the issue as "conceptual," not "political." It should come as no surprise that I disagree. "The espoused descriptive person–centric view is not readily separable from a normative- or morally-driven empathic and humanistic approach to individual workers and their circumstances" (Lefkowitz, 2011b, p. 113). It would be at least inconsistent, and perhaps hypocritical, to maintain an individualistic employee-centric research perspective in organizations without *advocating* for employees—which the profession believes would be "unscientific"—so we don't.
- Byrne et al. (2014) believe that the graduate training of I-O psychologists should be improved to enhance our employability, guided by which "aspects of graduate training are sought out by employers." The authors assert that it is our cognitive, affective and interpersonal competencies that "differentiate I-O psychologists from other graduates" (p. 7). True enough, as far as it goes.

But "the education and training of I-O psychologists also includes being normatively socialized by means of *informal* and *hidden curricula*" (Lefkowitz, 2014a, p. 42, emphases in the original). Those curricula contain the societal norms and values, beliefs, goals and expectations that form the vital moral component of any profession including our own, by which it socializes its entrants.

- Ruggs et al. (2013) point out that our research samples are skewed by the virtual absence of seven marginalized and/or stigmatized groups. Similarly, Bergman and Jean (2016) note the over-representation of management and under-representation of lower-level employees in our work. The authors view these skews as primarily reflecting methodological issues that can be corrected with increasing replications and better sampling strategies.[25] However, to support the notion that something more basic is operating, Lefkowitz (2013) showed that five other worker groups or organizations are similarly absent from the literature and that these skews are in accord with attributes of our particular value system (Lefkowitz, 2016). Cascio and Aguinis (2008) also document our inattention to societal issues.

- Scherbaum et al. (2012) noted that despite our focus on *intelligence*, I-O psychology has contributed relatively little to the study and understanding of the construct, limiting ourselves to the narrow concern of predicting job performance for purposes of employee selection. They view this as primarily due to our having embraced a psychometric approach, and a "mission accomplished" mentality. Lefkowitz (2012a), however, suggested at least 11 other psychological constructs relevant to the field of I-O psychology about which the same observation could be made, in order to substantiate an inference that there is a broader (values) issue at work. In particular, "Corporate goals and objectives are not only preeminent in defining the nature, content, and criteria of professional practice in I-O psychology, they also influence greatly our scientific research agenda, partially to the detriment of the field" (p. 22).

The unacknowledged role of personal, social and professional values in influencing the perceived propriety of what we do (and don't do) is the proverbial "800-pound gorilla in the room" (Lefkowitz, 2011c). More specifically,

> At the individual level, it is one's personal values that shape one's moral sensitivities and ethical behavior. It is a *profession's* values that determine its

---

25 Although, in accord with the views expressed here, Bergman and Jean (2016) also include the possibility of *researcher bias*: "researchers might believe that managers are more critical to organizational functioning than their sheer numbers suggest ... . Further, highly educated researchers—like those in I-O psychology ... might not recognize that the experiences of workers could be different from the experiences of managers, professionals, and executives" (p. 104).

goals and self-construed duties, responsibilities, and ethical standards, its response to sociopolitical events that affect it (e.g., civil rights legislation; rampant downsizing), and the choices made by its members concerning where they work, what they study, and the criteria by which they evaluate that work.

(Lefkowitz, 2008, p. 440)

The Future [of] I-O Psychology: A More Optimistic View

The content of much of this chapter has, unfortunately, still had to be rather critical and negative in tone. Yet, I have also taken pains to acknowledge several encouraging changes. It is something of a relief to be able to conclude with a note of optimism. I foresee a future I-O psychology that is more positive and prosocial than the foregoing critique might suggest. There are three (related) themes worth noting: (i) the growth of a more humanistic outlook, especially among younger I-O psychologists; (ii) renewed attention to the potential meaningfulness of work, as well as endorsement of a "living wage" for most people; and (iii) occupational prospects for the profession itself.

A More Humanistic, Prosocial Future?

Approximately one-third of a century ago I observed that:

> Industrial-Organizational Psychology has contributed relatively little to the understanding and amelioration of important individual and social-psychological problems, even though many of these problems impact organizational effectiveness ... .

> Even less have we as a profession contributed systematically to national debates regarding ethical and social policy issues which, although arguably not within the domain of I/O Psychology, are at least indirectly related to it by virtue of their implications for employee and/or organizational functioning ... .

> This is not to say, of course, that the practice of I/O Psychology is devoid of humanistic values. My point is not that *no* I/O Psychologists have contributed to the study of social problems such as are mentioned at the beginning of this article, or to efforts at their solution—that is demonstrably untrue—but that *their endeavors are conditioned little by virtue of their being I/O Psychologists* ... . [They are] not likely to have acquired such values through a process of socialization while occupying a corporate "internship" (and perhaps not during his or her graduate education, either).

> *(Lefkowitz, 1990, p. 49, emphases in the original)*

But the past is prologue

The beginning of I-O psychology in the U.S. is often seen as marked by the publication of Hugo Munsterberg's *Psychology and Industrial Efficiency* in 1913. It took about 50 years for the transformative scientific and theoretical changes to develop that were marked by Edgar Schein's *Organizational Psychology* and Katz and Kahn's *The Social Psychology of Organizations* in 1965 and 1966. Now, after another 50-plus years, we seem to be in the throes of additional changes of a moral, ethical and socially conscious nature. These changes, too, are marked by potentially transformative volumes: *Using Industrial-Organizational Psychology for the Common Good: Helping Those Who Help Others* (Olson-Buchanan et al., 2013), sponsored by SIOP; *Humanitarian Work Psychology* (Carr et al., 2012); *Humanitarian Work psychology and the Global Development Agenda* (McWha-Herman et al., 2016), sponsored by the Global Organization for Humanitarian Work Psychology (GOHWP); *Humanitarian work Psychology: Concepts to contributions* (Carr et al., 2013); and *Industrial and Organizational Psychology help the vulnerable: Serving the underserved* (Reichman, 2014).[26]

In addition to the three editors of the SIOP-sponsored book, it has 43 I-O contributors. This is sufficiently large to encourage hope that a normative perspective is becoming institutionalized and representative of the field. In that regard, the inspiration that led Julie Olson-Buchanan, Lara Koppes Bryan and Lori Foster Thompson to the creation of the SIOP volume is illuminating. For each of them it entailed individual, personally rewarding experiences earlier in life, of voluntary charitable work in which they perceived the potential relevance of their I-O talents to the nonprofit organizations which they were aiding (Pp. xviii–xxii). (Perhaps the same is true for many of the other contributors, as well.)

In the second edition of this book, writing in 2016, I was cautiously optimistic: "It is not unreasonable to hope that the 100+ contributors to these new volumes represent the vanguard of a transitional and international generation of I-O psychologists who will be transforming the field and influencing subsequent members (cf. Sorenson et al., 2015)" (p. 390). The past few years have encouraged that (cautious) optimism. The recently updated SIOP (2021) Vision, Mission and Values Statements emphasizes a focus on both "individual and organizational health, well-being, and effectiveness." Similarly, the *Guidelines for Education and Training in Industrial-Organizational Psychology* (SIOP, 2016) include, in the description of competencies, "Just as both science and practice are inherent in each competency, we also feel that an appreciation of diversity and well-being can be applied to each area.[27] Graduate training in I-O psychology should take

---

26 GOHWP can be found at <http://gohwp.org/>.
27 The *Guidelines* takes a competency-based approach and enumerates 24 recommended areas of competence plus two "related areas."

every opportunity to emphasize working with all types of people, developing both an appreciation of diverse views and the well-being of others" (p. 4).

Renewed Focus on the Meaningfulness of Work and Consideration of a "Living Wage"

Many years ago a major aspect of I-O psychology was a consideration of the important role played by meaningful jobs in the emotional and physical well-being of workers (cf. Hackman & Oldham, 1980; Herzberg, 1966; Walker & Guest, 1952). For a variety of reasons, many of which have been chronicled earlier in this chapter as well as in Chapters 8 and 11, over the past 40–50 years those concerns retreated in the face of an onslaught of corporatist neoliberal ideology, declining union representation, stagnant wages and the gig economy. The result has been a realization that, as expressed even in the popular press, "Our Relationship to Work is Broken" (Malesic, 2021).

Renewed interest in the importance of meaningful work, in the "dignity" of work, has come from a variety of perspectives and disciplines: e.g., organizational psychology (Dik et al., 2013); the labor movement (Greenhouse, 2019); management scholarship (Carton, 2018; Frega, 2020); political philosophy (Sandel, 2020); those concerned with occupational health and worker wellbeing, including in I-O psychology (Kalleberg, 2008; Kaplan et al., 2017; Keita & Sauter, 1992; Kensbock et al., 2022; Ogbannaya et al., 2017); traditional Catholic social teaching, which views the "right to work" as based on material need, and consisting of both the right to decent work and working conditions, as well as "the duty to contribute to the common good through work" (Sison et al., 2016, p. 518); and even those who see adaptation to the need for protean careers (i.e., developing a *protean career orientation*) as contributing to well-being (Burke et al., 2015). Interestingly, in one recent review of the six general determinants of "what makes life meaningful" (e.g., social connections; religion and world views), no mention is made of work (King & Hicks, 2021).

Attention has begun to focus on "living wages" because statutory minimum wages in the U.S. (federal minimum of $7.25, since 2009) are so inadequate, because they don't even apply to those in the "informal economy," and because of the intractable nature of unemployment, underemployment and poverty (Carr, 2007; Carr et al., 2017; Gloss et al., 2017; Reburn et al., 2018; Searle & McWha-Herman, 2021; Thompson & Dahling, 2019; also cf. Chapter 8).

Huffmeier and Zacher (2021) have exposed I-O psychologists to an even more radical notion—the unconditional *basic income* (BI). The rationale behind the BI is that it would enhance autonomy and meaningful work by providing increased job choice for workers to reject or change jobs and allow them to better integrate their work and private lives by alternating periods of paid work. Huffmeier and Zacher discuss the history of the concept, what has driven the idea, arguments pro and con, as well as some reasons why it has not been a topic in I-O psychology.

The synergistic combination of a focus on meaningful work *and* living wages, in a framework of social and economic justice, comprises the current social movement for *decent work* (Blustein et al., 2019; McWhirter & McWha-Herman, 2021).

The Occupation of I-O Psychology

As a related matter, the future *of* I-O psychology, as a profession, seems secure. Just a decade or so ago, I-O ranked #1 among the 20 fastest-growing occupations in the United States, with a projected growth rate of 53% from 2012 to 2022, in comparison with a rate of 11% for all other psychologists and all other occupations (U.S. Bureau of Labor Statistics, 2014). Moreover, we had the third-highest 2012 median annual pay among the 20. (The two highest-paid occupations on the list ranked 13th and 16th in projected growth.)[28] In addition, indicators such as membership in our professional association, SIOP, has been on a steady rise for more than 40 years (approaching 10,000 members in 2022) as has been the number of attendees at our annual conference (until the Covid years of 2020 and 2021) and the number of doctoral programs in I-O psychology (Aguinis et al., 2014; Silzer & Parson, 2013; Vosburgh et al., 2021). These positive indicators contradict an earlier observation of a "long-term ongoing thread of self-doubt, worry, and perceived crisis among many I-O psychologists in our reflections on the status of the field" (Lefkowitz, 2014b, p. 316).

There are three interacting trends or sets of societal forces that seem to be converging and propelling a prosocial, moral perspective for I-O. They originate from within the field itself; from the world of business in which we practice, as well as management scholarship; and from global movements represented by the United Nations compacts, in which SIOP has participated.

Within I-O psychology

The five recent volumes noted above point the way (Carr et al., 2012, 2013; Olson-Buchanan et al., 2013; McWha-Herman et al., 2016; Reichman, 2014). I-O psychologists are newly morally engaged in three ways: (i) practicing "I-O psychology in new venues" (Lefkowitz, 2013b, p. 34) by "contributing to the work of humanitarian organizations" (Lefkowitz, 2015, p. 202) with our traditional competencies (e.g., employee selection, training); (ii) "assisting philanthropic contributions" in which we put our talents to use in facilitating the socially-responsive actions of others, whether they are in nongovernmental organizations (NGOs) created expressly for those purposes, or the companies with which we work

---

28 I have not been able to locate actual employment data in 2022. Unfortunately, projections for 2020–2030 are flat: 8% growth for all psychologists (equal to the average rate for all occupations), one-fourth of which is I-O (Bureau of Labor Statistics, 2022).

regularly, expressing CSR aims to benefit an array of stakeholders; (iii) practicing "as an inherently humanistic profession" (Lefkowitz, 2012b, p.108) in which *all* of our work, in whatever venue it takes place—including our traditional corporate clients and employers—is suffused with the normative, humanistic values promoted in these pages. I believe the last of those three to be the most important and, unfortunately, the least developed—with the exception of a great deal of recent attention paid to combatting workplace bias and discrimination—the very active field of *Diversity, Equity and Inclusion* (DEI), including SIOP-sponsored attention (Adler, 2022; King & Gilrane, 2015; Pappas, 2022; Shih et al., 2013; Stark, 2021; Woo et al., 2021)

At the institutional level, SIOP now has a standing educational *Committee for the Advancement of Professional Ethics* (CAPE) and has sponsored two substantial surveys of ethical issues faced by members (Lefkowitz, 2021; Lefkowitz & Watts, 2022).

Business, and management scholarship

It is possible that the changes within I-O are partly responsive to a more welcoming reception from the business community and its scholars: (a) *Corporate Social Responsibility* and *Corporate Social Performance* (CSR/CSP) are taken as commonplace and even instrumental to achieving business objectives (Cragg et al., 2012; Griffin & Prakash, 2014; Morgeson et al., 2013; Wang et al., 2016); (b) "The time is [seen as] right" for the notion of understanding and developing *caring and compassionate organizations* (Rynes et al., 2012); accordingly (c) a *humanistic management* perspective has been growing, with an international association of members and a dedicated journal that "focuses on the *protection of human dignity* and the *promotion of human well-being* within the context of organizations. It connects disparate fields including business ethics, sustainability and management studies via a humanistic research paradigm";[29] and (d) *social entrepreneurship* is becoming a popular topic in business schools. "Social entrepreneurship is used as an umbrella term for people and organizations that aim to solve a societal problem using entrepreneurial means … . In contrast to traditional entrepreneurs social entrepreneurs are guided by compassion to solve societal problems where the market or the government has failed so far" (Pirson, 2015a, p. 1; 2015b).

Worldwide focus: The United Nations impetus

In 2000 (just around the time all these transformations within I-O psychology and the business world were developing) the U.N. orchestrated a global anti-poverty mobilization, called the *Millennium Development Goals* (United Nations, 2015).

---

29 http://www.humanetwork.org/. http://www.springer.com/social+sciences/applied +ethics/journal/41463.

It was defined in eight broad goals (e.g., MDG1: Eradicate extreme poverty and hunger; MDG8: Develop a global partnership for development) and 18 more specific objectives. The case studies in McWha-Herman et al. (2016) are

> a compendium of HWP projects with two dozen authors focusing (collectively) on advancing every one of the ambitious Millennium Development Goals (MDGs) in countries as diverse and dispersed as Brazil, Egypt, Ghana, Hong Kong, India, Kenya, Nigeria, Sierra Leone, South Africa and Uganda!
>
> *(Lefkowitz, 2015, p. 200)*

They impressively demonstrate HWP in action.

Simultaneously, the U.N. also launched the business-focused *Global Compact*, which is "a strategic policy initiative that provides a framework for companies that endorse sustainability and responsible business practices" (Scott et al., 2013, p. 65); in particular, it is "aimed at aligning businesses and other organizations with ten accepted principles in the areas of human rights, labor, the environment, and anticorruption" (Mallory et al., 2015, p. 135). SIOP has become a signatory of the compact (Scott et al., 2013), as can individual academic I-O programs (Mallory et al., 2015).

The latest applicable U.N. initiative is a set of 17 *Sustainable Development Goals* (SDGs), adopted in 2015, that superseded the MDGs in January 2016.[30] The MDGs had focused on reducing world poverty and improving health; the SDGs also include environmental issues, climate change, human rights, gender equality and more. The MDGs had been drafted by a small group of technical experts at UN headquarters and were targets for poor countries to achieve with financing from rich countries. The SDGs were drafted over a few years by representatives from 70 countries to apply worldwide to all countries. Gloss et al. (2015) have presented an enthusiastic and thoughtful challenge to the field of I-O psychology to consider how our work—enhancing the health, welfare and performance of workers and organizations—can be used to further the SDGs. Doing so would entail expressions of the four facets of I-O psychology discussed in this chapter: an avowedly moral perspective, manifested in a composite Scientist-Practitioner-Humanist (S-P-H) model; and a focus on the welfare of both individual employees and the broader society along with that of organizations.

Conclusion

Nearly 20 years ago I posed a question from a values perspective, regarding I-O psychology—"Who are we?" (Lefkowitz, 2005). Notwithstanding the critical

30 http://www.undp.org/content/undp/en/home/sdgoverview/post-2015-development-agenda.html.

commentary that followed, I never really answered the question at that time. I have attempted to do so a few times since; the latest version of an aspirational values statement is as follows:

> *Along with improving the effective functioning of organizations, A fundamental objective of research and practice in industrial-organizational psychology should be to assure that organizations are safe, just, healthy, challenging and fulfilling places in which to work. There is no inherent conflict between those objectives and improving organizational effectiveness. In fact, the two are often related and interdependent. However, when it is anticipated that actions undertaken to improve organizational effectiveness will adversely impact the well-being of employees or other organizational stakeholders, the appropriate role of the I-O psychologist is to challenge the morality, wisdom and necessity of those actions and, if necessary, to attenuate their adverse consequences to the extent feasible.*
>
> *(Lefkowitz, 2016, p. 143)*

Adding Further to the Framework for Ethical Decision Making

35. **Virtually from its inception, I-O psychology was reproached by social critics outside the field and by some I-Os among us as merely a technocratic profession serving the economic objectives of corporations. One facet of those criticisms—that the field is unscientific, atheoretical, and fails to contribute to the advancement of knowledge in psychology—has not been true for some time. A second facet is more problematic. Many contemporary instances can be cited that support the view that we have not outgrown the organizational–managerial values biases which accounted for our early accomplishments and continued success in serving organizations, even when those organizations stand in opposition to employee rights and do little to advance their well-being.** I have argued that this bias largely goes unrecognized by I-O psychologists because our values are congruent with those of the economic system and corporations within which we function. Consequently, we misperceive and mischaracterize our activities as entirely scientific, objective and "value-free," and sometimes view those who propound other values positions (e.g., that corporations have broad social responsibilities; workers have a right to organize) as themselves biased, naive, unscientific or otherwise misguided. The perspective taken throughout this book is that values positions permeate virtually all scientific and moral enterprises, and that our ethical standing will be well served by attempts to articulate and examine the implicit values assumptions that guide our moral reasoning.

36. **Although it is obvious to anyone who cares to look that there are many generous and caring I-O psychologists whose professional goals include human betterment, there is room for improving the extent to**

which the profession *qua* profession reflects that sensitivity. The expanded vision of the field projected in this chapter attempts to do that. It
aspires to do so by advocating (a) the adoption of a broader model of values or
value system than currently characterizes the field—for example, by adding a
humanist dimension to the S–P model; (b) a greater interest in and concern for
the well-being of the individual employee that is on a par with our predominant
concern for organizational needs, goals and perspectives; (c) an expanded criterion by which we gauge the effectiveness of our own work beyond the narrow
standard of technical competence to include a consideration of its broader societal
consequences as well; and overall (d) the incorporation of an avowedly *normative*
(i.e., moral) perspective to the field, along with the *scientific* (i.e., descriptive and
predictive) and *instrumental* (i.e., focus on productivity and organizational effectiveness) perspectives that predominate.

37. In 2003, in the first edition of this book, it was opined that "the
difficulties in implementing the moral agenda proposed in this chapter
can hardly be overestimated" (p. 327). I also believed then that "those
who attempt to do so will find allies in the management scholars,
business ethicists and progressive business leaders who are already engaged in the process." What has clearly changed since then, and which
justifies more optimism, has been the increase in I-O psychology colleagues who take seriously psychology's ethical mandate to apply our
knowledge of behavior pragmatically to improve the condition of individuals, employees and society as well as organizations.

SECTION III

The Responsible Conduct of Research

13

RESEARCH ETHICS: INFORMED CONSENT, CONFIDENTIALITY AND THE USE OF DECEPTION

> Trust lies at the heart of virtually every decision that must be made by the researcher, and all human participants in the research process depend on the trust of others at all levels. Research subjects trust the researcher to treat them with dignity and respect, to protect their well-being, and to safeguard them from potential dangers or risks of harm. Researchers trust their subjects to maintain honesty in their responding, to respect the seriousness of the research enterprise, and to maintain their promises not to reveal certain aspects of a study to future participants. Society lends its trust to researchers to pursue worthwhile research questions which stand to benefit humanity, to protect participants from research abuses, and to maintain honesty and objectivity throughout the research process.
>
> —Alan J. Kimmel

While Kimmel (2007)—and this chapter—focus on the implicit trust necessary among all stakeholders involved in the research enterprise, it warrants emphasizing how central trust is to all that we do. Chapter 1 of this book begins

> As psychologists we study human behavior. To do so, we depend on the goodwill and trust of the persons who cooperate with us voluntarily, sometimes revealing their private selves to us, enabling us to do our applied work and research. As industrial and organizational (I-O) psychologists, we further depend on the goodwill of organizational decision makers who trust us when we say that we can improve the effectiveness of their enterprises.

The *responsible conduct of research* (RCR) refers to "conducting research in ways that fulfill the professional responsibilities of researchers, as defined by their

DOI: 10.4324/9781003212577-16

professional organizations, the institutions for which they work and, when relevant, the government and public" (Steneck, 2006, p. 55). It is a large domain of knowledge, comprising four broad areas (Macrina, 2014), only two of which are included in this book. First, *research ethics* has to do with the proper treatment and protection of research participants (for our purposes, limited to humans) and is the subject of this chapter. Second, *scientific integrity* has to do with protecting the scientific/research enterprise and is covered in the next chapter.[1]

In biomedical fields of professional practice and research with human participants utilizing procedures like randomized drug trials or experimental surgery techniques, the core ethical issue is generally the consequentialist one of possible serious harm to the participants from the procedures administered, in relation to their potential benefits. That is sometimes also the case for research and practice in clinical psychology or for research with vulnerable groups such as children, the elderly or the impaired. But the safety of research participants is not often a salient issue for the social and behavioral sciences in general, and it is even less frequently the case in I-O psychology (except perhaps for threats to confidentiality). However, as Mann (1994) noted, "psychology subjects may have their self-esteem manipulated, their mood changed, or their abilities questioned" (p. 140). And applied I-O research with employees in organizations can be experienced by some as coercive. This chapter and the next one cannot hope to explore the entirety of RCR, about which many books have been written. In addition to the APA's (2017) ethical code, excellent, readable treatments are available from Chastain and Landrum (1999), Greenberg and Folger (1988), Israel and Hay (2006), Kimmel (1988, 2007), Macrina (2014), the National Research Council (2003), Rosenthal and Rosnow (1991), Sales and Folkman (2000), Shamoo and Resnik (2009) and Sieber (1992).

The Social Nature of the Research Enterprise

Notwithstanding some high-profile examples of questionable research procedures involving the deception of research participants, the overriding issue that ought to influence our ethical deliberations is the realization that our research is not usually aimed at benefitting directly the people who participate in it as subjects. This is the case whether they are college students in a subject pool or company employees. Of course, the results of some organizational research have direct positive consequences for employee–participants, and employees may benefit from the research indirectly through systemic organizational improvements prompted by the findings. But the research is most frequently driven by organizational objectives or problems defined by those relatively high in the organization's authority structure, and the primary benefits of the research may not be

---

1   *Research ethics* and *research integrity* pertain to two (related and overlapping) content domains. Steneck (2006) defines them as constituting two different perspectives or ways of looking at RCR: moral principles, and professional standards, respectively.

experienced by the current participating employees—as with the validation sample in personnel selection research, for example.

In addition, much I-O psychology research is conducted with employee participants and college students in which the aim is to achieve generalizable knowledge of constructs and the relations among them (e.g., organizational commitment, procedural justice, rater bias), with no expectation that the investigations will necessarily yield immediately useful applications in the organization(s) providing the research sites, much less direct benefits to the research participants themselves. In fact, the participants may be a *convenience sample* whose members and organization(s) have no special relevance to the topic or aims of the research. Box 13.1 describes categories of research performed by I-O psychologists based on who are the intended primary beneficiaries of the research. The question of "who benefits?" has implications for the professional and ethical issues of informed consent, the obligation to participate in the study, confidentiality of data and deception. This sort of analysis is like one made in clinical psychology or biomedical research, in which a distinction is drawn between therapeutic and nontherapeutic research. Participants in the former, but not the latter, can expect to derive some benefit from having participated.

There are three things to note about the categories of I-O research described in Box 13.1. First, of course, is that they are oversimplifications of the complexity of research forms actually carried out. For example, the basic theoretical issues under investigation in Category I-type research—for example, investigating the construct validity of alternative types of individual assessments or the nature of cognitive information-retrieval processes—may have been inspired by applied organizational questions concerning the utility of assessment centers and the accuracy of performance appraisals, respectively. Secondly, the categorization is more a set of prototypes than a realistic taxonomy within which all empirical studies can be neatly classified. For example, it is very common for I-O psychologists to "piggyback" assessment instruments pertinent to their own Category I or II research interests on to those administered by the organization as part of its own Category III-type enterprise.

Third, and most important, is that Box 13.1 serves to emphasize the fact that the extent to which our research is intended to benefit those whom we depend on to carry it out varies considerably. The five prototypic categories form a continuum from Type I, in which there is no intent to provide any benefits for the participants and in which they are unlikely to perceive any advantage for themselves by participating, to Category V, in which the research is focused on serving the interests of the participants. For research categories of Types I, II, III and sometimes IV, there is no direct value evident to the prospective research subject in participating in the proposed study. Thus, the issue of obtaining subject participation, and the various inducements to participate that may be made, assume considerable ethical importance.

BOX 13.1 A CATEGORIZATION OF RESEARCH IN I-O PSYCHOLOGY BASED ON ITS INTENDED BENEFICIARIES

I Basic Psychological Research in Which Neither the Study Participants Nor the Setting Are of Particular Relevance to the Topic

Many I-O psychologists are interested in studying aspects of the same fundamental psychological processes of perception, cognition, attitude formation, emotional responsiveness and other interpersonal influences, individual differences, and so forth, that characterize the substance of academic psychology. Organizational application of the knowledge gained may be of lesser interest. Company employees or college students may provide a readily available *convenience sample* of research participants for such investigations depending on the nature of the researcher's employment. In general, they are no more or less appropriate subjects for such investigations than anyone else, and there is no a priori reason to expect them to have any particular interest in the research problem or in participating in the investigation.

II Applied Psychological Research Not Necessarily Intended to Benefit Directly a Particular Organization or the Study Participants

I-O psychologists generally conduct applied research that is aimed at achieving an understanding of the effective functioning of individual employees, supervisor—subordinate dyads, work teams, management committees and larger units, or the organization as a whole. This work may have the potential to advance the field because it is concerned with organizationally relevant theoretical or applied issues, and/or is conducted with appropriate samples of persons in actual work settings. But, even in the case of field research with employees, the study might not be responsive to any specific concerns of those in the organization which serves as the research site and may not be of any direct benefit or even interest to the participants.

III Institutional or Organizational Research Benefitting Primarily the Organization

This refers to research aimed at improving the functioning of the specific organization in which it is carried out—for example, by developing new procedures such as an employee selection testing program or by investigating the causes of an organizational problem such as a high rate of voluntary turnover. The hallmark of this category of research is that, despite the applied setting, the study is not generally intended to benefit the employees (or college students, or other organization members) who participate in it and it is unlikely to provide any direct benefits to them. Typical examples include employees serving as knowledgeable sources of information (so-called subject-matter experts, or SMEs) for a job analysis, or as examinees in a test validation study the results of which will be applied by the organization to the problem of selecting new job applicants.

IV Institutional or Organizational Research Likely to also Benefit the Study Participants

This is research which also (as with category III) is aimed at improving the functioning of the specific organization in which it is carried out, but in which the results of the study can be expected to also benefit the particular participants as well as other organization members. For example, in evaluating the effectiveness of programs such as alternative training techniques, compensation policies or other interventions, the most effective training procedures or pay plan may be implemented throughout the organization, including even those employees who served as controls or in an experimental comparison group during the research.

V Therapeutic Research Intended to benefit Those Who Participate in the Study (and Frequently, by Extension, the Organization as Well)

Sometimes a problem may be identified in a particular subunit of the organization, or for the organization as a whole, that prompts an investigation and implementation of ways of ameliorating the problem or improving the work life of those affected. It may be difficult sometimes to distinguish between those actions which are more properly thought of as *interventions* (i.e., the implementation of changes in policies, programs or practices) and the *research* components of the same undertaking. Projects of this sort include quality of work life improvements such as flextime options or various employee assistance programs; task redesign in accord with the principles and aims of job enrichment or team-building; or the analysis and resolution of interdepartmental conflict.

Source: Based in part on material from the APA (2017) and the federal OHRP (2019).

Most research with human participants in the social and behavioral sciences (e.g., in sociology and anthropology, social and experimental psychology, economics, marketing and consumer behavior, or political science) is of Type I or II, and to a lesser extent, III—meaning that the researcher's interest in conducting the study is theoretically motivated or problem-driven, and it ordinarily does not include benefitting the prospective participants. They are merely representatives by which general scientific principles may be explored or solutions to applied problems sought. Of course, that doesn't preclude the research also having ultimate value for humankind; but, as Shipley (1977) observed, for the most part the social scientist "does not study the individual but the species" (p. 95). That is why methodological issues like representative sampling, external validity and the generalizability of research findings are important. But it is also why ethical issues concerning voluntary participation in research, absence of coercion to participate, informed consent and the wellbeing of research participants are also so profound.

In that context, the applied research represented by Categories IV and V (including some, but not all, institutional research) is of special interest because it holds the promise of benefitting directly those who have participated in it. Assuming there is some overlap between the interests of the organization and those of its individual members, this is one way in which applied organizational research can be characterized as more beneficent than that of our colleagues engaged in a more basic or scientific enterprise. Commensurate with that characterization, an advantage enjoyed by the organizational researcher in I-O psychology engaged in institutional research (Categories III & IV), as well as Type V research, is that employees—and even applicants for employment by the organization—may be assumed to have a conditional obligation to cooperate with such research. That is a reasonable interpretation of the implied social contract between employees or applicants and the employer—assuming that the research serves a justifiable organizational purpose, is not threatening or harmful to the people and does not make egregious demands on them.[2] In my experience, most employees readily accept this obligation when the relevance of the study is evident and it is explained adequately.

Conversely, a corollary of that right we enjoy because of employees' obligations is the duty to see that their obligation is not abused or experienced as coercive. There is, obviously, an inherent conflict between the principle that all research participation should be explicitly voluntary and the existence of a relatively open-ended implicit obligation of workers to participate in legitimate organizational research. Notwithstanding the implied obligation, adherence to the moral principle of respect for persons requires that we treat research participation as genuinely volitional to avoid even the semblance of coercion. This is

2 The *Standards for Educational and Psychological Testing* (AERA, APA, NCME, 2014) indicates that informed consent for testing may be assumed as implied in the case of employment settings (Standard 8.4).

another area in which our ethical prescriptions may put us at odds with organizational policies, and that may need to be made clear to key decision makers so we can "resolve the conflict consistent with the General Principles and Ethical Standards of the Ethics Code" (APA, 2017, Standard 1.03).

An additional abuse of the employees' obligation would be to assume that it extends to their cooperation with our personal research agenda comprised of Category I or II research. Although we may enjoy access to employees who are potential research participants (as a convenience sample), they are not obliged to participate in the conduct of investigations that primarily reflect our individual interests when those are not reflective of the legitimate and reasonable concerns of the organization to which they are obligated. And that is so even if top management has agreed to allow the project to be implemented in their organization. Having made that point, it is also necessary to acknowledge that it is sometimes difficult to differentiate the extent to which a project represents the exploration of our own personal, professional or scientific interests, versus legitimate organizational concerns.

Therefore, it should be kept in mind that most participants in social science research, including I-O psychology, are generally not in it for self-serving reasons. We owe their participation to other situational and/or motivational factors, such as their curiosity about the research, their willingness to cooperate in the interests of science or to enhance the effectiveness of the organization, or to comply with the wishes of an authority figure such as the researcher (who may be a manager, consultant or professor). In addition, they may be persuaded that participation will have some educative value, or they may be prevailed upon by a monetary inducement or a requirement for a college course. The trust that Kimmel (1996) spoke of in this chapter's epigram needs to be a major component of the social contract between ourselves and our research participants. In addition, as practitioners, we need to keep in mind that trust also plays a key role in our relationships with the users, the intended beneficiaries, of our applied research. For example, the confidence of company managers in market researchers was predicted best by the perceived integrity of the researchers (e.g., being seen as having high personal standards) more than by their perceived expertise (Moorman et al., 1993).

The exceptional importance of trust to the research enterprise is attributable to the power inequities between its participants or subjects on one hand and both the researcher and sponsor of the research on the other. Some time ago, Orne (1962) focused on the psychological experiment as a *social relationship* in which "the roles of subject and experimenter are well understood and carry with them well-defined mutual role expectations" (p. 777). Greenberg and Folger (1988) explored further the nature of various roles taken by experimental participants. The participant's or respondent's role is influenced greatly by what Orne called the *demand characteristics* of the experimental situation, including—once the person agrees to participate—a willingness to comply with a very wide range of actions upon request. This high degree of compliance is related to most people's general belief in the value of science, a willingness to accept the legitimacy of the research procedures and authority of the researcher, a desire to abide by the compact made when they agreed to participate, and a well-meaning intention to be a good subject. Orne went on to emphasize the importance of recognizing the potential effects on research participants of the contextual demand characteristics of the experimental situation as distinct from the effects of the experimental variables. Participants respond to the totality of the situation, which includes both sets of cues and stimuli, and responses to the situational context may be responsible for artifactual research findings.

Kelman (1972) presented a more elaborated social systems analysis of the power deficiency of the research subject relative to the researcher and sponsor, and viewed many of the problematic ethical issues in research as reflecting the potentially illegitimate exercise of this power. There are three aspects of the prospective research subject's relative disadvantage or vulnerability:

1. *The person's position in society, in general.* The consequences of this structural determinant may be seen in the preponderance of social science research with children, the old, poor, infirm, addicted, hospitalized or otherwise incarcerated, as well as college sophomores and military personnel.

2. *The person's position within the organization or institution in which the research is carried out.* Thus, more research is conducted with recruits and enlisted personnel than with officers in the military, more with nonexempt employees and low- and middle-level managers than with high-level executives in corporations, more with prison inmates than with correction officers, and more with college freshmen and sophomore members of an introductory psychology subject pool than with seniors. Therefore, special attention has been paid to protecting vulnerable participants such as students in departmental subject pools (Chastain & Landrum, 1999). Those in organizational positions of authority generally define the research problems and provide the resources for its implementation. Moreover, the availability of many of these potential participants may be due to their feeling that they have little prerogative to decline to participate when requested, even indirectly, by those higher up. As noted earlier, the employee's obligation to cooperate with legitimate and reasonable organizational research should not be transformed into a coercive experience.

3. *The person's position within the research situation itself.* As Kelman (1972) noted, "The investigator usually defines and takes charge of the situation on his [sic] own terms and in line with his own values and norms, and the subject has only limited opportunity to question the procedures" (p. 991). This is especially true when the research is carried out in the researcher's facilities (e.g., a college laboratory or a testing room in the Employee Relations department of a corporation), or when the researcher is a high-status

individual who is in another role relationship with the potential participant (e.g., college professor or senior-level manager. Around the same time that the salience of demand characteristics and role relationships in psychological experiments were pointed out by Orne (1962), they provided the very mechanism by which the limits of obedience to authority were famously investigated (Milgram, 1963, 1974).

Due to concern about the asymmetric power relations in scientific research with human participants, great attention has been paid during the past 50+ years to the ethics of behavioral and social science research.[3] This has consisted of assuring voluntary participation and informed consent to participate; eliminating coercive influences; minimizing the deception of participants; and providing debriefing, feedback, and dehoaxing, as well as securing privacy and confidentiality for participants.[4] Surveys of published empirical research in psychology have indicated that research reports rarely describe obtaining informed consent or having provided debriefing or feedback to participants, and in the opinion of some the use of deception remains a problem (Adair et al., 1985; Hertwig & Ortman, 2008a, 2008b; Korn & Bram, 1988; Walsh-Bowers, 1995).

Racialism in Scientific Psychology

This book has not focused on racial issues per se—aside from economic/social justice issues tangentially in Chapter 8—and can reasonably be faulted for that omission. Roberts et al. (2020) remind us that "race plays an important role in how people think, develop, and behave" and so they set out to "document how often psychological research acknowledges this reality and to examine whether people who edit, write, and participate in the research are systematically connected" (p. 1295). They analyzed more than 26,000 empirical research articles from 1974 to 2018 in top-tier cognitive, developmental, and social psychology journals.

Overall, only 5% of the publications highlighted race (fewer than 1% in cognitive);[5] 83% of the journal editors-in-chief were white, and they published 93% of the articles; yet "fewer publications that highlight the role of race in human psychology have been accepted and published by white editors than by

---

3   Also playing a prominent role in the focus on ethical matters, including the establishment of federal regulations for the protection of research participants, was the public's revulsion on learning about several dubious and in some cases unconscionable studies in both medical and social research, such as the Tuskegee study of the long-term effects of syphilis (cf. Kimmel, 1988, 1996, for brief reviews).

4   Most of these issues are equally important in the professional nonresearch activities of I-O psychologists, as well as in research, with the notable exception of deception (and the need for consequent explanations, called *dehoaxing),* which has no acceptable role in professional practice.

5   "Highlighted" meant that race was highlighted in an article's title and/or abstract.

editors of color" (p. 1300); 63% of the articles that highlighted race had first authors who were white. Additional analyses led them to conclude "that the psychological publication process is no less reflective of racial inequality than most of society" (p. 1301). Also, "white participants were more common in publications written by white authors … and less common in publications written by authors of color … . Conversely, participants of color were more common in publications written by authors of color … and less common in publications written by white authors" (p. 1302).

They found that "the psychological publication process is, understandably, subject to the same structural inequities that stratify the rest of society" (p. 1303), and that this lack of racial diversity may have the practical effect of leaving the field of psychology unprepared for an increasingly diverse society. Buchanan et al. (2021) suggest that

> current scientific practices [in psychological science] may serve to maintain white supremacy with significant and impactful consequences … on Black, Indigenous, and other People of Color (BIPOC) populations … . [They go on to] present examples of how epistemic oppression exists within psychological science, including in how science is conducted, reported, reviewed, and disseminated.

They also advance some accountability steps "to ensure that psychological science moves beyond talk and toward action … [to] upend the influence of white su-premacy in psychological science" (p. 1097).

Informed Consent (IC)

Formal Standards[6]

With the partial exceptions of research designs that rely on the collection and analysis of archival or anonymous data or on naturalistic observations of persons in public places, empirical psychological research generally requires the assent and cooperation of the people who participate for us. In fact, it has been suggested

---

6   Throughout the remainder of this chapter and the next, reference will be made from time to time to applicable ethical guidelines originally promulgated by the Office for Protection from Research Risks (OPRR), as appropriate. These primarily consist of the regulations for the *Protection of Human Subjects*, National Institutes of Health, Department of Health and Human Services (1991), the current "Ethical Principles of Psychologists and Code of Conduct" of the American Psychological Association (APA, 2002/2010b/2017), as well as the *Publication Manual of the APA* (2020). The federal regulations may be obtained electronically at several websites, including https://history.nih.gov/research/downloads/45cfr46.pdf. The reader is advised to consult those sources directly for specific requirements.

that we ought to think of our potential participants as another granting agency to which we must apply for necessary resources to implement our proposed research (Rosenthal, 1994).

Psychologists are increasingly concerned with obtaining the informed consent (IC) of those with whom we work. This is, of course, in keeping with the nature of applied research and practice in I-O psychology, in which a project may include elements of both research and practice. Even the seminal Belmont Report recognized this complex reality and concluded that if a multifaceted project included an element of research, that project should undergo review for the protection of human subjects.[7] It should be noted that under federal regulations (45 CFR part 46, "the common rule") any systematic investigation designed to produce generalizable knowledge (as is the case when there is an intention to publish the results) is considered "research."

The principal purpose of obtaining IC from prospective participants in our research or practice is to ensure that they can protect their own interests and exercise autonomy over their own welfare (Greenberg & Folger, 1988). In general, IC may be defined as the collection of procedures by which people choose to participate in a project, such as a research study or organizational intervention, after being apprised of all matters that might reasonably be expected to influence that decision. Box 13.2 presents a summary of the generally acknowledged requirements for obtaining and documenting IC from research participants. It is a condensation of material from the APA (2017) ethical code and the applicable federal regulations governing research with human participants promulgated by the OHRP (2019) and administered locally by institutional review boards (IRBs), as well as generally accepted ethical procedures.[8]

These requirements (as well as those pertaining to privacy, confidentiality, deception, debriefing, etc.) are best understood as reflecting several dimensions of the domain of moral principles noted in earlier chapters: treating people with dignity and respect for their autonomy (so they are free to decide whether to participate in the research and whether to continue their participation); treating them with concern for their well-being and avoiding the infliction of harm (so that if deception or withholding information can be justified by a rigorous review, adequate debriefing will be provided); abiding by principles of justice and fairness (so that people are not coerced into participation by virtue of their lesser social status or other factors); and displaying honesty, integrity and trustworthiness (so that promises made regarding the confidentiality of replies and the

---

7   See the *Belmont Report;* National Commission for the Protection of Human Subjects of Biomedical and Behavioral Research, Department of Health, Education, and Welfare, 1979.

8   OPRR, founded in 1972, was replaced in 2000 by OHRP. A timeline/history of laws in the U.S. related to the protection of human subjects can be obtained at https://history.nih.gov/about/timelines_laws_human.html.

BOX 13.2 GENERAL GUIDELINES FOR INFORMED CONSENT (IC)

1. Although the specific content of the psychologist's communication with prospective research participants or clients may be expected to vary with the situation, it should ordinarily include a description or explanation of the following:

   a. the overall purpose of the project, its benefits and any drawbacks, and the person's role in it, including the required duration of participation. It should also contain a description of whom to contact if any questions or concerns arise about the research;

   b. any adverse features, from the possible inconvenience of a significant time commitment to potential risks or threats to comfort, safety or self-esteem, which might reasonably affect the person's decision to participate. (But refer to discussion re *Deception,* for possible exceptions.)

   c. other aspects of the project that might affect the decision to participate, such as the inability to guarantee anonymity and plans for maintaining the confidentiality of data;

   d. the voluntary nature of participation, and that the person is free to decline to participate or to withdraw from the project (i.e., to revoke his/her decision to participate) at any time, with no adverse consequences. Special care should be taken in this regard, with respect to potential student participants. Or, if there are potential consequences (as there might be for an employee of an organization sponsoring the work), they should be discussed;

   e. when research participation is a course requirement for students, alternative equitable activities should be made available and explained;

   f. if the decision is made to proceed with a study the design of which requires deception or withholding information, or if IC requirements have been waived by an Institutional Review Board (IRB) (see # 7, below) prospective participants should be told, if practicable, that additional information about the study will be provided at a *debriefing* following their participation in the study (or after the conclusion of the entire study);

   g. if a beneficial intervention is to be provided to some persons or groups and not others, the basis for the assignment is explained, as well as the plans, if any, for extending the intervention to those not originally covered. If the design of the study dictates withholding this information from participants at the beginning of the project, it is made clear by debriefing participants afterward.

2. The psychologist should avoid exaggerating the potential benefits of the project, or *hyperclaiming* (Rosenthal, 1994), in order to induce participation.

3. The above content should be communicated in language that is clear, unambiguous and readily understandable to the particular persons addressed.

4. Nothing should be communicated that indicates or suggests that persons waive their legal rights or release the researcher, practitioner or sponsor from liability for negligence.

5. When feasible, opportunities should be provided for persons to ask and have answered any reasonable questions pertaining to the project, making sure the person understands what has been communicated.

6. Ordinarily, written documentation of IC—a signed consent form containing the above information—should be obtained from each participant, who should be provided with a copy, and the original stored securely.

7. For the following sorts of research or projects, obtaining and documenting IC may not be necessary:

    a. studies done under the auspices of state or local governments, designed to study or evaluate public benefit programs;

    b. studies that involve no more than *minimal risk* to participants; the waiver of IC would not adversely affect their rights and welfare; and the research could not be implemented without the waiver;

    c. studies of normal educational practices or programs in educational settings, or routine assessments of organizational practices or effectiveness in other organizations, when participants can not be identified and when disclosure of the data would not place their employability at risk;

    d. studies involving tests, surveys, interviews or observation of public behavior, unless the data are recorded in a manner that permits identification of the participants or if disclosure of data could be damaging to them;

    e. studies involving archival data that are either publicly available or recorded by the researcher in such a way that participants can not be identified;

    f. studies which could not be done unless a waiver of the IC requirements were granted;

    g. when the signed consent form is the only record linking the participant and the research, and a breach of confidentiality would be potentially harmful.

8. If the researcher is associated with an organization that is subject to the federal regulations governing research with human participants, and

hence has an Institutional Review Board (IRB), or the activities are otherwise subject to IRB review (e.g., the results are intended for general dissemination by means of professional publication), it is the IRB and not the researcher which decides on whether the proposed research meets the exceptions noted in No. 7, above, as well as other matters (e.g., whether the research qualifies for expedited review).

Source: Based in part on material from the APA (2017) Ethics Code and the federal OHRP (2019).

potential benefits, discomforts, or risks of participation are fulfilled). Note that, for the most part, these research requirements are based on deontological principles concerning beneficence and justice and the respect of participant autonomy, dignity, and rights, as well as the researcher's corresponding duties, rather than on consequentialist cost/benefit analyses. A major exception concerns the consequentialist approach which is generally taken to the issue of deception (see below).

Some Contested Issues Regarding IC

Many problems have been raised concerning the implementation of IC procedures; the literature on the topic is vast, so I have avoided consideration of IC for medical treatments and biomedical research, psychotherapy, and other forms of clinical practice, and for so-called "vulnerable populations" like children. Also not reviewed are a few potentially relevant sources that might interest the reader, such as whether and how IC is to be obtained when a researcher uses information provided independently by people on the Internet, as in chat rooms or e-mail (American Association for the Advancement of Science, 1999; Childress & Asamen, 1998; Hewson et al., 1996), as well as special concerns regarding student participant pools (Britton, 1979; Chastain & Landrum, 1999; Dalziel, 1996; Scott-Jones, 2000).

Do People Really Understand IC Explanations?

This question has been posed by those who have raised the reasonable point that consent cannot be truly informed if the prospective participants have not understood the IC communication completely and accurately. That is why formal requirements specify that the IC content be articulated in clear, unambiguous language understandable by the particular audience (see Box 13.2). Stanley et al. (1987) reviewed the research in this area and noted that the methodological quality of studies investigating the comprehension and retention of IC information was not high. Nevertheless, they concluded that "despite these flaws, these studies show a general trend: comprehension of consent information is relatively poor" (p. 736). Similar findings were reported later by Mann (1994) who found that a longer consent form (attempting to describe a procedure fully) was understood less well than a shorter form that omitted some relevant details. More recently, Geier et al. (2021) found that making the consent form highly interactive enhanced comprehension so innovations in information technology have led to some researchers beginning to use "dynamic consent" procedures which allow for ongoing consent decisions and communication, which may enhance participant engagement (Prictor et al., 2020). These findings are especially important in light of another conclusion reached by Stanley et al. (1987): Higher levels of comprehension were associated with higher rates of agreement to participate. But a troubling note is introduced by findings indicating that although a sample of undergraduate experimental participants generally described the IC experiences positively, many of them viewed the experiments in which they had participated as too invasive (suggesting that the IC communication was inaccurate and/or incomplete), and only 20% of them viewed the IC process as a decision point at which they could decline to participate (Brody et al., 1997). Congruent with those findings, over 60% of Mann's (1994) undergraduate participants who signed a consent form were under the (mistaken) impression that they had lost their right to sue the researcher, even for negligence.

It seems obvious that considerable attention needs to be paid to the quality of oral and written IC communications. Samples of written consent forms are available for the researcher's use. For instance, the *Principal Investigator's Manual* of my university contains several examples, as does Kimmel (2007). The OPRR *Informed Consent Tips* advises: "Think of the document primarily as a teaching tool not as a legal instrument."[9] Smith et al. (1995) listed a number of factors that might be expected to affect a person's ability to fully understand the information contained in an IC document: (a) relevant demographic factors like age, socioeconomic status (SES) and cultural dialects; (b) physical or cognitive attributes, including memory, literacy and competency, especially if they cause nervousness and distraction; (c) visual or hearing impairments; (d) defensive emotional reactions, such as denial or regression; (e) attributes of the document, such as reading level, use of technical language and typeface; (f) nature and extent of knowledge and beliefs about research; (g) quality and nature of the manner in which the material is presented; and (h) perceived (or actual) coercion and other situational influences. They recommended writing IC documents at no more than seventh- or eighth-grade reading level (even for highly educated participants) and presenting a thorough oral explanation whenever feasible. The communication of IC information should not be treated in a cursory manner but

9   *Informed Consent Tips* is available at: https://www.hhs.gov/ohrp/regulations-and-policy/guidance/informed-consent-tips/index.html

as an important and integral component of research or practice. As Herbert Kelman observed in the Forward to Kimmel's (2007) text:

> It is still too often the case that ethical considerations are treated as afterthoughts or as obstacles to be gotten out of the way so that the researcher's 'real' work can proceed. In short, the ethical dimension has not been fully internalized by the research community. (p. xiv)

Does Obtaining IC Threaten the Validity of Research Findings?

A number of psychologists have raised various methodological objections to the process of obtaining IC: e.g., that it threatens the representativeness of research samples, hence the generalizability of findings; and that it alters the behavior of participants during the course of the study, hence threatening the internal validity of the research.

The Representativeness Problem

Rosenthal and Rosnow (1975, 1991; Rosnow, 1993, 1997) were the ones primarily responsible for raising the issue of the unrepresentativeness of all-volunteer research samples and the attendant potential problems concerning the generalizability of research results. Kimmel (2007) and Smith (1983) presented succinct reviews of the issue—that is, the extent to which compliance with the ethical prescription for voluntary participation via IC conflicts with scientific values for performing methodologically good studies. In other words, the more self-selected the sample of participants (by virtue of being all volunteers), the less likely it is to represent a random sample from the population of interest. The problem is especially acute with respect to therapeutic research in medicine and clinical psychology (Blanck et al., 1992; Tobias, 1997), in which the potential for causing harm due to the erroneous interpretation of artifactual findings is great. But the problem extends even to survey research, in which requiring written IC may reduce the response rate to the survey or to specific items (Lueptow et al., 1977; E. Singer, 1978; Sobal, 1984).

Rosenthal and Rosnow (1991) reported that volunteer research participants, in comparison with nonvolunteers, tend to be more educated, bright, sociable, desirous of approval yet unconventional and nonconforming, arousal seeking, and of higher SES, as well as more likely to be women than men. For I-O psychologists, this can potentially jeopardize the generalizability of test validation research (e.g., studies utilizing validation samples of volunteers from among current employees) and virtually all studies concerned with understanding work motivation or team processes, as well as other areas of interest.

Given the potential threat to sample representativeness, it is not surprising that some procedural alternatives to obtaining IC have been suggested (cf. Smith, 1983, for a summary) and that a great deal of attention has been paid to the issue of recruiting research participants, as well as to the dangers of coercion, deception, and withholding relevant information from recruits. Various inducements to participate have been utilized, from the clearly unethical (e.g., deliberately not informing prospective participants about aversive aspects of the research protocol), to generally accepted and widely used procedures (e.g., offering small monetary payment or gifts, extra course credit for students, and putting forward appealing descriptions of the research and its value). A potential ethical issue concerns the point at which the latter largely acceptable techniques might become unethical and unacceptable. How much money or how expensive a gift is appropriate to offer without it being coercive to those most in need? How much extra course credit is acceptable—one-third of a grade (e.g., from B to B+) or more? When does an ingenuously enthusiastic and positive description of the research become over-selling or hyper-claiming (Rosenthal, 1994)?

> The psychology of recruiting participants for a research protocol is not dissimilar from other social marketing situations. There is a gray line between applying pressure to participate and being a competent recruiter and researcher. The gray area creates the opportunity for many ethical dilemmas.
>
> *(Blanck et al., 1992, p. 963)*

As applied psychologists we should recognize that these issues pertain to excesses in marketing a project not only to prospective participants but to the organizational decision-makers and colleagues whose permission and cooperation is needed to implement it. For example, one could promise or overestimate the likelihood of positive results in advance of some study or minimize the intrusiveness of research procedures to the operations of the organization. Obviously, hyper-claiming of this sort has potentially adverse consequences for the future of the psychologist's relation with the organization and the reputation of the profession.

The Problem of Artifactual Findings

There is some evidence indicating that more fully informed experimental subjects behave differently from less informed subjects in the subsequent experiments in which they are participating (Adair et al., 1985; Greenberg & Folger, 1988). However, these findings are based on a limited domain of behavior such as verbal operant conditioning and the negative aftereffects of noise or crowding. There appears to be little information available regarding how widespread the effect may be; i.e., which behavioral domains might be more or less susceptible. Although the causal explanations are not always clear, in some instances the observed differences among experimental groups seem to be related to whether the participants were provided with substantive information concerning the study, and in others the effect was produced merely by the consent procedure itself without conveying even the nature of the impending experiment. And in some instances, the result seems to be attributable solely to the specific instruction that one is free to withdraw at any time. The latter findings suggest that the effect is not domain specific. However, based on relatively limited research, IC procedures do not appear to have serious effects in written or interview survey research (Singer, 1978; Sobal, 1984) aside from some negative effects on response rates. Response rates to organizational surveys are probably more a function of employees' job satisfaction and opinions regarding how the organization handles the survey data (Rogelberg et al., 2000).

It is not unusual, however, for researchers—including those in I-O psychology—to inform participants about impending procedures (experiment, survey or controlled intervention) in a way that suggests that they believe such biasing effects are likely. That is, information regarding the purpose of the research and some procedures are deliberately withheld (and sometimes mis-information is supplied) presumably because of a belief that making them known to the participants would affect their behavior, hence biasing the results. Misrepresenting the purpose of the research or supplying a false cover story has been the most frequent kind of deception employed in social psychology research (Gross & Fleming, 1982), and an informal survey of three I-O psychology journals indicates that the same is true there (Nicolopoulos, 2002). For example, a survey or simulation study might be described innocuously to prospective respondents as "intended to investigate the ways in which people react to or evaluate various aspects of their jobs and organizations." It might even be described more specifically as "focused on understanding the nature of employee evaluations." It is unlikely, however, to be described forthrightly as concerned with *rater bias*—"investigating whether supervisors evaluate more favorably the performance of workers who are similar to them in sex, age or ethnicity."

The reason for the omission is the belief that "telling subjects the purpose of the study and the procedures to be followed removes their naivete and spontaneity" (Adair et al., 1985, p. 59). In the latter instance, for example, we might anticipate that mentioning our interest in "similarity bias" in ratings could heighten the salience of the demographic attributes of the employees (real or simulated) who are to be rated and alter the participant—raters' evaluations.

However, that concern is based on the implicit assumption that a naive state of relative ignorance regarding the situation one is in (perhaps with some attendant concern or anxiety regarding the research procedures) is the relevant or "natural" state of the human being. This is an assumption that may not always be correct and should not be accepted uncritically. Humans are exceedingly curious and continually seek meaning in their lives, even imparting meaning to situations in which it is not apparent; total ignorance about the situation one is in is not a customary state and is, in fact, a source of anxiety for many. In contrast to the passive or inanimate nature of the objects studied by physical scientists, people are *agentic* and *reflexive* (Howard, 1985; Manicas & Secord, 1983; Smith & Vetter, 1982). That is, we are aware of our surroundings, we generally experience ourselves as the instruments of our own behavior, and we anticipate the future and attempt to shape it. Withholding information from human research participants does not render them malleable experimental tabula rasas. In at least some instances it may simply contribute to the artificiality of a situation that is arguably unlike the real-life circumstances to which results are generalized. More problematic, it could induce a process of "hypothesis-guessing" by participants, leading to artifactual reactions that further threaten the interpretability of the research. Granted, there are research questions that could not readily be investigated without keeping the participants ignorant of the purpose and/or procedures of the study. Accordingly, rather than keeping participants uninformed, researchers sometimes misinform them about key features of the study, thus raising other ethical concerns (see below, regarding deception).

Are IC Requirements Unreasonable?

Especially given that IC communications may not be well understood by research participants and that they have the potential to introduce artifactual elements into research findings, it has been argued that some requirements are unnecessary or enforced too stringently. For example, it would be inherently contradictory and foolish to require signed IC forms from respondents to an innocuous and anonymous questionnaire survey. Adair et al. (1985) and Diener and Crandall (1978) reminded us that the procedure was originally developed with biomedical research in mind; the effects of social and behavioral research generally do not have the same harm potential. In a now famous sardonic remark, M. B. Smith (1976) observed about behavioral science research: "surely temporary boredom is the most common harm" (p. 450). Thus, obtaining IC may unnecessarily complicate risk-free research (Reynolds, 1979). It has also been argued that obtaining formal written IC in an actually stressful experiment may serve to reduce the perceived freedom of participants to withdraw once it has begun and requiring IC in general may seem to shift the responsibility for ethically questionable practices to the participant (Adair et al., 1985). However, it seems reasonably clear that the researcher is never excused from the responsibility of following ethical practices. Moreover, note that many of these concerns arose early in the history of federal regulation of research with human participants when the rules were less flexible than the current versions. The current OHRP (2019) regulations permit IC requirements to be waived and allow for "expedited review" of harmless research.

But a reasonable case can be made that the requirements are more onerous and less flexible than they seem to be. As Ilgen and Bell (2001b) stated, "in practice, institutional review boards (IRBs) often are reluctant to approve exemptions [to informed consent]. Heavy workloads faced by IRBs create a press toward standard operating procedures that, by their very nature, are resistant to exceptions" (p. 1177). Those authors also warn that such lack of flexibility regarding obviously innocuous, minimal-risk organizational research of the sort I have characterized as Type III, IV, or V (see Box 13.1) may serve to encourage disregard for ethical review in general. They may be correct. A review of the empirical research reported in three I-O psychology journals for 1999, 2000, and 2001 found virtually no mention of formal IC procedures and very few indications of what respondents were told prior to the study (Nicolopoulos, 2002). This was confirmed in a survey reported by Ilgen and Bell (2001a), who found that 44% of the authors of field studies published in the *Journal of Applied Psychology* and *Personnel Psychology* acknowledged not having submitted their studies for IRB approval. In addition, although the regulations requiring IRB approval emphasize coverage of "research conducted or supported by any Federal Department or Agency" (§46.103), it also requires that

> Each institution engaged in research that is covered by this policy, with the exception of research eligible for exemption under §46.104, and that is conducted or supported by a Federal department or agency shall provide written assurance satisfactory to the department or agency head that it will comply with the requirements of this policy.
>
> *(OHRP, 2019, §46.103)*

In other words, any research conducted under the auspices of the organization that receives federal support will be expected to comply even if that study is not supported. In practice, therefore, the university-based I-O psychology researcher conducting an organizational study that is likely to not require written IC of participants (cf. Box 13.2, No. 7 b, c, d, and e) nevertheless must submit a description of the proposed study to their university's IRB for such determination. (However, the study probably would qualify for expedited review.)

If that same I-O psychologist is employed not in a university but as an independent consultant or practitioner in a business organization, it might seem that the same study would not receive IRB review: There would be none that had jurisdiction. But as a psychologist and member of the APA, subject to its ethical code, the researcher nevertheless "must consider ... applicable laws and psychology board regulations" (APA, 2017). Moreover, as pointed out by Ilgen and Bell (2001) regarding potentially publishable research, some journals now require documentation of IC procedures for all submissions. If the I-O psychologist does not have a university affiliation (or a collaborator with such) freestanding IRBs exist from which approval may be sought—for a fee, of course.

Anecdotal reports abound of the supposed unreasonableness of IRBs. For example, IRBs sometimes go beyond the ethical aspects of a study to comment on the technical quality of the proposed research design or procedures, and this is frequently viewed as beyond their legitimate mandate. But Rosenthal (1994) made the argument that, given the substantial individual and institutional resources involved in most research endeavors (including participant involvement), doing a poor study that might not justify the internal validity of its findings is a waste, hence an ethical matter (Rosenthal, 1994). Nevertheless, whether most IRBs are comprised of members with the collective expertise to render such valid judgments in the many fields of research in which they are called on to review is a legitimate issue. Consequently, attention is being paid to procedures that might improve the quality and performance of IRBs (Tsan, 2021; Tsan et al., 2020).

Some psychologists have been concerned about the extent to which many of their colleagues view the application of research ethics as merely "an affront to the integrity of sound research" (Blanck et al., 1992, p. 959) or who may "feel burdened by an expanding body of ethical rules and regulations" (Rosnow, 1997, p. 345) that reflect a changing social contract between science and society. They have offered constructive suggestions by which ethical guidelines may be seen as a stimulus to conducting more effective research such as by increasing our understanding of the meaning of our data and by including more representative samples. I think we would also do well to realize that our right to do research, which some of us feel is infringed upon inappropriately by IRBs, is more in the nature of an "entitlement" than a "claim." That is, although we certainly have such a right, invested in our profession by society because of the potentially valuable contributions we can make, there is no correlative duty imposed on any specific others to comply with that right. We need to make our case each time, in the context of the evolving social contract between science and society about which Rosnow (1997) was so concerned.

A review of published research reports in I-O psychology suggests that OHRP requirements are not in fact salient issues in the field. In 1999, 2000 and 2001 there were a total of 46 studies published in the *Academy of Management Journal, Journal of Applied Psychology,* and *Personnel Psychology* that employed intentional deception (Nicolopoulos, 2002).[10] All of the studies were authored or coauthored by people with academic affiliations, yet none of the reports stated that the study had been submitted for review and received IRB approval. A large majority did not mention having obtained IC, and among those that did almost all failed to describe what information had been provided to prospective participants.

Privacy, Anonymity and Confidentiality

As noted earlier, there are several moral bases that justify research respondents' claims of privacy and confidentiality (Bok, 1989; Davison, 1995; Peterson &

10 There were 555 articles published in the three journals over the three years, 475 (86%) of which were empirical studies (i.e., excluding qualitative and quantitative literature reviews, theoretical articles, reanalyses of previously reported data, computer simulations, etc.). Thus, only 9.7% of the empirical investigations employed deception.

Siddle, 1995). In addition to those noted previously, once a provision of confidentiality has been made as part of the IC agreement, we incur an obligation to keep the promise. In addition, we may add the utilitarian reason that it helps establish the relationship of trust between researcher/practitioner and participant without which quality research and effective practice are not likely to result.

Privacy and Anonymity

Part of the ethical justification for providing IC (along with respect for autonomy) is allowing people to maintain their privacy. *Privacy* is generally defined as the right to determine how much information about oneself will be revealed to others, in what form it will be provided, and under what circumstances (Kimmel, 1988; Sieber, 1992). It is enshrined in the United States as a constitutional "right to be let alone" (Melton, 1988). Kimmel (1988) noted that privacy may entail *solitude* (voluntary isolation), or it may be desired even in social situations such as with *intimacy* among small groups or pairs of persons, and *anonymity* (freedom from identification in public settings).

There are four facets of any situation, including a research study, that influence the extent to which a person may consider their privacy violated (Webb et al., 1981). The first of these is most relevant to observational research and concerns how public the location is in which the person's behavior is being studied. For example, one might anticipate managers to be more uneasy about an observational study assessing how time spent in their offices is distributed among various activities than a study observing traffic flow patterns in the executive cafeteria. The second facet is the extent to which the person(s) studied are public figures whose personal and legal expectations concerning privacy may be lower than for others. The third dimension has to do with the anonymity of the research data, or whether the person can be linked directly with the information obtained from or about them. For most research situations maintenance of anonymity is the best guarantee of privacy.

The last facet noted by Webb et al. (1981) is the nature of the information being collected. Thus, a questionnaire survey focusing on personal opinions and attitudes toward one's superior is likely to be more invasive than one focusing on preferences regarding alternative shift work schedules; a questionnaire seeking to assess personal needs for an employee assistance program providing substance abuse treatment is likely to be experienced as still more invasive. Accordingly, workers experienced less invasion of privacy from electronic performance monitoring when the monitoring was limited to only relevant on-task activities (Alge, 2001). I add a fifth dimension to Webb et al.'s list—the identity of the investigator or observer. Although I do not know how the effects of this influence might be manifested, I would anticipate that such attributes as the prestige and status of the researchers and the extent and quality of their personal relationships with participants probably matter. They may interact with other facets such as the nature of the information collected and the degree of confidentiality or anonymity provided, in affecting such outcomes as response rates and the amount, quality, and truthfulness of the information provided.

Whenever the circumstances of research or practice permit, all information should be obtained and stored in a fashion that maintains the anonymity of respondents. It should be the default option for all social and behavioral science research. Some projects require the explicit linking of participants with the information they have provided: For example, longitudinal investigations such as test validation studies in which predictor and criterion scores must be matched, or a study of employee turnover in which antecedent data must be paired with later separation status. Under those circumstances, the confidentiality of the data is obviously limited. *Confidentiality* refers to the right of people to have the information they provide kept private, and to the agreements we make with them concerning what may be done with the data (Folkman, 2000; Sieber, 1992). In the validation and turnover studies just noted, the requirements necessitating the limits on confidentiality are known in advance and should be discussed with participants as part of the IC process. The personal identifiers that link the data sets with the individual employees should be maintained only as long as necessary to provide the linkage, and then they should be destroyed. If the researcher contemplates a follow-up study necessitating the maintenance of personal identifiers, this must be revealed as part of the original IC process.

Another frequently encountered situation in which anonymity may be breached and confidentiality limited involves the mailed or electronically administered survey in which it may be helpful or even necessary to know who has responded and who has not—even if the motive is simply to issue follow-up reminders. Some rather elaborate and ingenious techniques have been developed to preserve the confidentiality or anonymity of respondents in these sorts of situations (Boruch, 1971; Boruch & Cecil, 1982; Campbell et al., 1977)—also, "reminders" can be sent to everyone.

Confidentiality

For the most part, confidentiality is a less salient issue for I-O psychologists (though no less applicable) than it is for clinical, social or personality psychologist researchers who may conduct investigations in which people's intimate, perhaps embarrassing, or even illegal activities may be exposed. Psychotherapists may also be privy to such information, as well as to suicidal or other self-destructive intentions on the part of disturbed clients. And confidentiality may similarly be critical for other applied psychologists who conduct research with vulnerable populations. Researchers and practitioners in these areas must be concerned with the possibility of their data or records being subpoenaed by a court (APA, Committee on Legal Issues, 1996; Melton, 1988). The research and practice of I-O psychologists tend to be restricted to less personal, work-related concerns with "normal" adult populations. Nevertheless, the confidentiality of data may be threatened by organization members who fail to appreciate the ethical requirements under which behavioral research is conducted and the adverse consequences of violating the trust placed in us by participants. Senior managers, citing the obligation of employees to cooperate with institutional research, have been known to adopt the position that "We paid for (or sponsored the collection of) the data, therefore it's ours—all of it, including the identities of the respondents."

This broaches what is, for many applied psychologists, the familiar question "Who is the client?" For example, it is a prominent issue for clinical psychologists who provide healthcare services to individuals in organizations, such as in police departments or the military (Staal & King, 2000; Zelig, 1988). Professional guidelines speak directly to the issue: "The primary responsibility of the psychologist in a professional role is to the client. The psychologist must resolve conflicts of interest between the employer agency and the client on the basis of this responsibility" (APA, 1987, p. 728). That directive is readily interpretable by clinical psychologists in a therapeutic context. Clinicians are trained as health care providers and, quite naturally, are responsible primarily to their clients—even if the setting in which the service is provided is not a private practice but an institution. It is understandable that responsibility to the employing organization is secondary, even if one of the primary purposes might be to ensure that their clients can fulfill their work role responsibilities (e.g., as police officers or soldiers).

The situation for an I-O psychologist is rather different. The focus of our training is on organizational processes, and we are not trained to provide a therapeutic service for individuals or groups (with some exceptions, e.g., organization development specialists trained in psychodynamic process consultation). The just-cited APA (1987) quotation assumes that there is a distinction between "the employer agency" and "the client." However, many I-O psychologists, most obviously those in consultancy roles, believe that the employer is the client. Many also accept that the organization as well as the individuals with whom they work are all clients.

It is instructive to note how those of our colleagues whose professional activities bear some similarity to clinical or counseling practice (i.e., executive coaching) approach this issue.[11] Witherspoon and White (1996) distinguished between the executive or client who is the primary person receiving coaching,

---

11 "Executive coaching involves a skilled outside consultant assigned to an executive on a regular basis for one or more specific functions—improve the executive's managerial skills, correct serious performance problems or facilitate long-term development—often to prepare him or her for a future leadership role or top corporate position" (Witherspoon & White, 1996, p. 125). An informal survey found that the typical executive trainee was "either a high potential employee or a successful employee who had one or two weaknesses. It appears that organizations are using executive coaches primarily to develop effective employees, rather than as a means of improving employees who are having serious problems" (Harris, 1999, p. 39).

and the *customer* or client system, which is the organization that contracts and pays for the coaching service. Although they made this distinction, and they went on to note discussions with the parties in advance regarding whose interests the coach is serving, unfortunately they did not indicate whose interests those are or what their priorities are in the event of conflicts between the two.

The Boundaries of Confidentiality

I have been asked some version of the following question more than occasionally by graduate students in I-O psychology: "In dealing with employees as a practitioner in an organization, when should I treat information as confidential?" As Human Resources professionals we take on advocacy, questioning and modeling roles in the organization with respect to ethical behavior, reflecting its beneficent, justice and virtuous components (see Figure 12.1).[12] Therefore, unless circumstances exist to the contrary and are made clear to the respondent, every nonroutine communication initiated with an employee for the purpose of obtaining information is confidential (and sometimes routine communications are as well). That includes replies to written or web-based questionnaires, individual interviews, team meetings or focus groups, telephone conversations, and so on, whether in connection with a research study or a company-financed intervention project.

There are four types of circumstances in which partial or complete confidentiality might not obtain. The first is when the employee requests it—for example, to "deliver a message" to someone else in the organization. However, one would be prudent to try to find out what that is all about before complying, as it might impact adversely the views of other respondents and one's reputation in the organization. Ordinarily, the request should simply be refused as inconsistent with our ethical obligations. The second circumstance is when the project requires participants to be identified. For example, it is often wise because of potential litigation to document which employees participated in a test validation study; or a summary of survey findings for each work group may need to be supplied to all group members and their managers. On those occasions the planned limitations on confidentiality must be made clear before the employee agrees to participate. The next possibility pertains to the situation in which we become aware through confidential communications (e.g., gratuitous fill-in comments on a questionnaire survey) that someone apparently is seriously disturbed or otherwise seems to need psychological help. The only way to address the problem directly (e.g., encouraging the person to seek professional help) may be to violate confidentiality. Before doing so, however, one would want to be

---

12 Keep in mind that many people are not well informed about the areas of specialization within psychology and to them all psychologists possess therapeutic skills and attendant responsibilities for confidentiality.

very sure of the seriousness and immediacy of the person's disturbance, which might be extremely difficult to ascertain.

Last, we may be told of someone's past or intended wrongdoing or that one employee means to harm another. These are very difficult situations in which our assurances of confidentiality conflict with other ethical principles. Regarding the first example, we are generally in no position to differentiate such unconfirmed information from mere gossip and so should proceed very cautiously. The informant should be encouraged to act directly if possible. With respect to the second illustration, our ethical principles require us to prevent harm, whenever feasible, and it may be that in attempting to do so the identity of the information source cannot effectively be concealed. In fact, psychotherapists are held to have a legal duty to warn a likely victim of violence that overrides their duty to maintain the confidentiality of the client–therapist relationship (Bennett et al., 1990; *Tarasoff v. Board of Regents of the University of California,* 1976). However, it is notoriously difficult even for trained clinicians under favorable conditions to predict a person's dangerousness, and it is unclear whether a psychologist who is not a therapist, even if licensed, is under the same legal obligation. "A serious violation of confidentiality could occur if the researcher inappropriately warns a third party of a potential threat" (Folkman, 2000, p. 52). The I-O psychologist should consult with colleagues and appropriate others before proceeding in such an instance. An experienced organizational consultant points out that because we cannot accurately predict the consequences of violating a commitment to confidentiality, it is a mistake to ever do so (Clayton Alderfer, personal communication, July 2002).

Moral dilemmas frequently involve conflicting ethical principles—for example, an obligation to do good or prevent harm versus the duty to abide by promises of confidentiality. Whichever choice one makes, it should be based on a well-reasoned rationale uninfluenced by self-serving motives or ignoring the issue. (Thus, talking it over with a knowledgeable and trusted colleague is generally a good idea.) Because whichever option one chooses, including doing nothing, entails a breach of one of the operative ethical strictures, one should be as satisfied as possible that the reasons for the breach are good ones.

Methodological Implications of Confidentiality

Just as there is some concern and limited supportive evidence that IC procedures may affect research findings by reducing response rates, introducing sample bias, or influencing the responses of experimental subjects, confidentiality also appears to carry methodological implications. In this instance, however, the threats to research quality appear to be associated with the *absence* of confidentiality. Blank et al. (1992) reviewed a number of studies suggesting that confidentiality promotes more honest disclosures. But the effects may be limited to procedures that focus on personally sensitive material. A meta-analysis of experimental studies failed to support the general hypothesis that assurance of confidentiality improves survey responses, but it did indicate a significant but modest positive effect when the information asked about was sensitive (Singer et al., 1995). Conversely, those authors also noted the existence of several studies that indicated that elaborate assurances of confidentiality had counterproductive effects, perhaps because of arousing respondents' anxiety, perceptions of threat or suspiciousness. Those effects may be limited to relatively innocuous research for which the assurances might seem incongruous, but "we need to know more about the circumstances under which assurances of confidentiality really reassure respondents and about how best to frame such assurances" (Singer et al., 1995, p. 74).

A comparison of personal interviews conducted at home with self-administered questionnaires regarding women's health issues yielded increased judgments of the truthfulness of responses on the questionnaire only when others in the home might have been able to listen in on the interview (Rasinsk et al., 1999), thus confirming the relevance of confidentiality when sensitive information is requested. When the setting was private, there was no difference in judged truthfulness of the interview and questionnaire. The authors speculated "When the respondent agrees to an interview, rather than accepting an obligation to tell the truth on all questions, he or she may interpret the obligation as that of reporting truthfully to questions that pose no threat" (p. 482). Correspondingly, anonymity did not improve the rate of response to a nonsensitive mailed survey over a confidential but not anonymous condition (Groves et al., 1997).

The use of Deception

The focus of this section is on intentional deceit by researchers as an instrumental technique enabling the conduct of research that presumably could or would not be carried out otherwise. In this context I use the following simple definition: deception consists of intentionally misleading research participants about any substantial aspect of a study.[13]

If we accept the ethical primacy of IC, then it stands to reason that we must be concerned by the conclusion that "Prima facie, it appears that informed consent cannot be given by a subject who has been deceived about an important aspect of an experiment or a study" (Clarke, 1999, p. 151). So, if deception precludes genuine IC, and the applicable section of the APA Ethical Principles begins "Psychologists do not conduct a study involving deception … " (Standard 8.07[a]), why—as

---

13 Failing to inform participants about every hypothesis or the design logic is not "substantial." Baumrind (1985) distinguished between intentional and "nonintentional deception" (e.g., failing to disclose every detail about a research study). Because the latter is invariably innocuous in nature or not entirely the researcher's fault (e.g., misunderstandings by participants), nothing seems to be gained by introducing what is essentially an oxymoron.

documented below—does it persist? We will return to this later when we consider the normative ethical arguments.

Deception in I-O Psychology Research

Because of the nature of the field (what we study and where we study it), the use of deception was never as prevalent in I-O psychology as it has been in social psychology. In fact, with a few exceptions from other social science disciplines,

> it is social psychologists who have used deception in research and have raised these techniques to an art form. In no other area of psychology is deception used so extensively, and when it is used in other areas it almost always is a form of social psychology.
>
> *(Korn, 1997, p. 10)*

Accordingly, whereas many reviews have tracked the incidence of deception in social psychology, and the history of its use in that field has been chronicled (Harris, 1988; Herrera, 1997; Hertwig & Ortmann, 2008a; Kimmel, 2001, 2007; Korn, 1997), I am aware of no comparable concern having been expressed about I-O psychology research.

The variables and research problems of interest to the I-O psychologist less frequently require deception, and a smaller proportion of I-O research consists of laboratory experimentation, which is the methodology in which it is most practiced. For example, a social psychologist might be interested in studying the nature and limits of people's honesty. Because it is generally not possible to know where, when, and how people might behave dishonestly in the normal course of their lives (and because, for most, it is a low-incidence event), social psychologists are likely to investigate the problem experimentally, such as by means of "entrapment studies" which "are conducted to investigate moral character by providing opportunities for subjects to engage in dishonest behavior or perform otherwise reprehensible acts" (Kimmel, 1996, p. 151). Conversely, I-O psychologists are more likely to be interested in the extent to which dispositional measures of honesty or employee conscientiousness (so-called "integrity tests") are effective real-life predictors of various facets of job performance or other organizational outcomes (Sackett & Wanek, 1996). If an I-O psychologist was interested in investigating some aspects of (dis)honest behavior in organizations, with employees as research participants, they would not use deceptive methods.

Although serious deception does not seem to be prevalent in I-O psychology or organizational behavior research, it is not unknown—but almost invariably, it has involved experimental studies with student participants. For example, *equity theory* (Messick & Cook, 1983) is a model of work motivation which posits that individuals compare their perception of the ratio of "outcomes" (i.e., rewards) they receive to the "inputs" they provide (e.g., valuable attributes like one's skills, abilities, and educational qualifications, as well as the effort one expends toward job performance), to the perceived outcome/input ratio(s) of significant "comparison other(s)." The model predicts that if the two ratios are perceived as comparable, a psychologically equitable situation exists; otherwise, the individual will experience a sense of inequity and will be motivated to behave in ways designed to achieve equity, such as by adjusting one's "inputs" (e.g., increasing or decreasing the amount of effort expended on the job, depending on the direction of perceived inequity). Among the great deal of research performed by I-O psychologists testing hypotheses based on this model were laboratory studies in which the experimental manipulation consisted of attempting to alter the participants' personal ratio by diminishing their self-perceived inputs to an anticipated (but often bogus) job assignment. This was done by providing fallacious feedback to the participants, indicating that they had performed poorly on a preliminary qualifying task or test, presumably showing that they were not well suited for the impending work assignment—but would be "employed" nonetheless. The experimental manipulation consisted of misinforming participants about their own talents, to have them perceive that their "inputs" to the job were meager. However, this served to potentially threaten their self-esteem, which was not intended: it was an experimental confound.[14] (In some cases they were not even informed in advance that they were participating in an experiment.)

A more recent example is provided in Box 13.3, which reproduces verbatim a very upsetting letter received by the spouse of one of my students, who was the manager of an expensive, trendy (and excellent) restaurant in New York City. His was one of 240 well-known restaurants that received this identical letter addressed personally, in each instance, to the owner. It came from an assistant professor of organizational behavior (OB) at the prestigious business school of an ivy league university in New York City who was attempting to study what has become a popular concern among businesses in recent years, customer service orientation (Hogan et al., 1984).

Aside from the concern one might expect a restaurateur to have for a customer who was sickened by food at their restaurant, one must appreciate the highly competitive and precarious existence of restaurants in New York (even pre-pandemic) and the heightened threat introduced by the mention of the Better Business Bureau and the Department of Health, to understand the potential emotional impact of this letter. And just for good measure, the personal letter was written on the prestigious university's letterhead and was signed by the faculty member (using his real name)—giving himself a pseudo-promotion to professor. By the time about one-fourth of the restaurants had responded, the hoax became

---

14 An experimental confound is an uncontrolled variable that could be responsible for the observed result, rather than the intended independent variable.

BOX 13.3 AN EXAMPLE OF DECEPTION BY CONCEALING THE EXISTENCE OF THE RESEARCH STUDY

Ivy League Business School
Ivy League University
Graduate School of Business
New York City Address

[Addressed to Individual
Restaurant Owners]

Dear _____:

I am writing this letter to you because I am outraged about a recent experience I had at your restaurant. Not long ago, my wife and I celebrated our first anniversary. To commemorate the event we made plans to dine at [restaurant name]. It was a very special occasion for both of us, and we had been looking forward to the evening for some time.

The evening became soured when the symptoms began to appear about four hours after eating. Extended nausea, vomiting, diarrhea, and abdominal cramps all pointed to one thing: food poisoning. It makes me furious just thinking that our special romantic evening became reduced to my wife watching me curl up in a fetal position on the tiled floor of our bathroom in between rounds of throwing up. I am particularly angry because if I had decided to share my meal with my wife, I would have had to see her suffer the same fate as I did that night.

I begrudgingly accept that occasionally these things happen and that even though you take extreme caution to prevent any cases of food poisoning, the inevitable few will break through. Nevertheless, I am still very angry because it was I who fell ill and only I had to endure that pain.

Had all this happened on any other night of the year I probably would not have bothered to complain, but seeing as how this was a special occasion, I felt incensed and therefore believed it was necessary to write you this letter. We had looked forward to experiencing so many good things at your restaurant, but now, all I am experiencing is extreme irritation. Given that it was our anniversary, we will always bitterly remember this occasion despite how much we wish to forget its aftermath.

In short, I am furious about this entire ordeal. Although it is not my intention to file any report with the Better Business Bureau or the Department of Health, I want you, Mr. [Restaurant Owner], to understand what I went through in anticipation that you will respond accordingly.

I await your response.

Sincerely,

Professor [_____], PhD
Ivy League University

undone, much to the embarrassment of the university (Kifner, 2001). The researcher wrote a letter of apology to each recipient—this time on plain non-letterhead paper—acknowledging that "The study was of my own doing and not that of the business school or the university. None of the data collected for the study will be used for publication, and I will not conduct similar studies in the future." A day later, the dean of the business school also wrote to each restaurateur, indicating

> While the professor initiated this research project on his own, he failed to think through the toll this study would take on its recipients ... As a result of this incident I have immediately asked the governing academic committee, the Executive Committee, to put into place procedures and guidelines for empirical research projects so that this will never happen again.

However, as the reader probably recognizes, something is not right here. The researcher's explanation and the dean's letter implied that the professor was either ignorant of the need for IRB approval of research projects or deliberately circumvented the IRB review procedures. Neither seems very likely. Those inferences are complicated still further by the second sentence cited from the dean's letter, indicating that the university supposedly did not at that time have "procedures and guidelines for empirical research projects" (as are promulgated and implemented by an IRB). For a major research university, this cannot have been the case.

There were 46 (of 475 empirical) articles published in *Journal of Applied Psychology, Personnel Psychology,* or *Academy of Management Journal* during 1999, 2000 and 2001 that appeared to use some form of deception (Nicolopoulos, 2002).[15] Most instances seemed relatively innocuous—for example, merely concealing the true purpose of the study to avoid influencing the data, as with studies of rater bias, eyewitness identification, and the investigation of group processes in which the demographic heterogeneity of the group is not revealed as a variable of interest. But there is a sprinkling of studies such as the one that entailed the use of a misleading cover story regarding the purpose of the research, a secret confederate, a bogus role-assignment procedure, *and* false feedback to the participants. The report of this study makes no mention of any debriefing having been provided at its conclusion. Presumably, the editors and reviewers of the journal also did not think it was necessary.

---

15 In comparison with over 50% of the articles published in the *Journal of Experimental Social Psychology* in 2002 (Hertwig & Ortmann, 2008a); 66% in the *Journal of Personality and Social Psychology*, and 66% in the *Journal of Consumer Research* and *Journal of Marketing Research* (both combined), all in 2001–2002 (Kimmel, 2007).

Attributes of Deception Techniques

Types of Deception

Several scholars have described the various deceptive methods that have been used in social and behavioral research, most notably Sieber (1982a; Sieber et al., 1995), Kimmel (2007, 2011) and Korn (1997). It remains a matter of some concern—affecting the ethical conclusions reached (Lawson, 2001). The varieties of deception can be classified by a simple categorization scheme based on two factors: the nature of the researcher's role in the deception (active or passive), and the potential level of risk or harm to participants (minimal or substantial), forming a hypothetical 2×2 matrix.

The researcher may engage in *passive deception* (the failure to reveal everything that should be revealed about the study: i.e., deception by concealment or omission), or *active deception* (affirmatively misleading research participants or candidates about some substantial feature[s] of the research). The assessment of the potential level of risk or harm that participants might experience is generally a subjective judgment that may be easy to make at the extremes but more difficult for studies that fall in the middle of the risk continuum.[16] Physical harms are generally seen as more severe than psychological or emotional harms (Collins, 1989). Additional possibilities involve economic and legal harms and threats to one's dignity (National Research Council, 2003). In addition, the likely severity may vary with such additional factors as the identity of the participants or the research setting. For simplicity, severity can be dichotomized into *minimal risk* versus *substantial risk*. (It is probably prudent to consider any situation that is not clearly of minimal risk to be of substantial risk.)[17] Thus, there are four cells in this taxonomy: passive deceit with minimal risk, passive deceit entailing substantial risk, active deception with minimal risk, and active deception with substantial risk.

The varieties of deception that have been practiced can be summarized conveniently in three categories or content areas, any of which may be represented within each of the four conditions. These include deception regarding (a) the very existence of the study, or when it will begin (or end); (b) the actual purpose of the study or research problem being investigated; and (c) aspects of the study's methodology, procedures or participants. For example, the ivy league OB assistant professor actively deceived the restaurant owners both about the existence of the research project and, by extension, its purpose, by using a bogus

---

16 Degree of risk is a function of the magnitude of potential harm (a product of its intensity and duration) and its probability of occurrence (National Research Council, 2003).

17 "*Minimal risk* means that the probability and magnitude of harm or discomfort anticipated in the research are not greater in and of themselves than those ordinarily encountered in daily life or during the performance of routine physical or psychological examinations or tests" (OPRR, 1991, §46.102[h][1]).

cover story. In contrast, naturalistic or contrived observational studies in which researchers observe people in public venues, such as with the entrapment studies mentioned earlier, simply conceal the existence of an ongoing study. The example I offered earlier of innocuously describing research investigating possible rater bias as ostensibly concerned with merely "understanding the nature of employee evaluations" passively omits mention of the true problem being investigated. This is done in the belief that explaining the true purpose of the study would distort the ratings data collected.

The last content area, in which participants are deceived about some aspect(s) of the research procedures, subsumes a great variety of deceptive maneuvers such as being given false instructions or false information about stimulus materials (e.g., bogus equipment, as in Milgram's, 1963, 1974, obedience study); or fake scenarios in questionnaire studies using supposedly genuine descriptions of people or situations); use of an unacknowledged confederate (or, with increasing frequency in recent years, a "virtual confederate" in the form of a computer) to misinform or mislead; providing erroneous feedback and/or manufactured data about the participant or about others (as with the equity theory studies noted earlier); using a surreptitious staged manipulation in field settings; collecting irrelevant "filler" data; and misinforming the person about when the study will begin—i.e., the participant is unaware the study has already begun, or the relation between two studies is concealed (Sieber, 1982a; 1982b; Sieber et al., 1995).

The Extent of Deception

It is useful to think about the severity or intensity of the deception used or contemplated in a study (Sieber, 1982a, 1982b) because this is something that members of an IRB are frequently called on to assess (National Research Council, 2003). Thus, some instances of deception may be considered mild or innocuous and some extreme (Greenberg & Folger, 1988; Korn, 1997), with others falling in-between. Kimmel (2007) describes "severe deceptions [as] those that create false beliefs about central, important issues related to participants' self-concept or personal behavior. ... [and] mild deceptions [as] those that create false beliefs about relatively unimportant issues peripheral to participants' self-concept" (p. 64).

It is probably true that virtually all behavioral research involves some deception—of the passive sort—insofar as not every aspect of the study, including its theoretical implications, hypotheses under investigation and procedural details, are ever communicated to participants. And generally they do not need to be—from either an ethical or methodological perspective. This is what Baumrind (1985) called *unintentional deception*.

Overall judgments of the severity of deceit are sometimes difficult to make because each may be influenced by aspects of the deception that we have been considering as well as by additional matters such as the content domain of the research, the constructs investigated, and the quality, extent and timing of any dehoaxing and desensitization provided to the participants. If one were to perform a policy-capturing study assessing the relative contribution of the various components of the research to the overall judgment of severity of deception, my guess is that the most important factor would be the perceived potential level of risk or harm to the participants, followed by the adequacy of debriefing. I would also expect that the purpose served by the deception—that is, the researcher's intent—would play an important, perhaps moderating, role in influencing severity judgments. Deception entirely for the purpose of masking the nature of the study in the belief that participants must be naive to manifest the phenomena under investigation is likely to be perceived as less severe (all else being comparable) than deception intended to induce people into participating in a noxious procedure. In recent years the latter tactic has, in fact, been considered unethical: "Psychologists do not deceive prospective participants about research that is reasonably expected to cause physical pain or severe emotional stress" (APA, 2017, Standard 8.07[b]). (Although I cannot recall any research in I-O psychology that came close to causing physical pain or severe emotional stress.)

The Frequency of Deception

As mentioned earlier, social psychologists (and others) have attended rather closely to the incidence of deception in their published research (Adair et al., 1985; Carlson, 1971; Gross & Fleming, 1982; Hertwig & Ortmann, 2008a; Kimmel, 2001, 2007; McNamara & Woods, 1977; Menges, 1973; Nicks et al., 1997; Ortman & Hertwig, 2002; Seeman, 1969; Sieber et al., 1995; Stricker, 1967; Vitelli, 1988). Although inferences regarding a trend are difficult to sustain because of somewhat differing definitions of deception that were used in each of these reviews, most found an increase in deception during the 1950s, 1960s and early 1970s, to a rate well exceeding half of all published studies, and a decline from the late 1970s through the 1980s to below 50%. Sieber et al (1995) reported the beginnings of an upswing in the 1990s, partially confirmed more recently by Hertwig & Ortmann (2008a), whereas Nicks et al. (1997), in a more comprehensive survey, found a continuation of the downward trend. Sieber et al. (1995) make the case that the trend (in both directions) is a function of changes in the frequency of studies published on topics that rarely require deception, such as attribution, environmental psychology, sex roles (gender), sex differences, socialization, and personality, rather than due to changes in the relative popularity of deceptive methodology per se. Nicks et al. agreed in part with that interpretation of the decline in deception but also cited, as did Kimmel (2007), the growing influences of the APA ethical code and federal regulation of research with humans, as well as a decreased emphasis on randomized laboratory experiments and corresponding increase in surveys and field studies. Hertwig and Ortmann (2008b) believe that the APA code has resulted in a decline in the severity of deceptive methods but has not had much effect on its incidence.

Accordingly, Kimmel et al. (2011) observed that "despite significant ethical advances in recent years, including professional developments in ethical review and codifications, research deception continues to be a pervasive practice and contentious focus of debate in the behavioral sciences" (p. 222).

I have found no surveys of the nature or frequency of deception in I-O psychology, suggesting that it is a low-incidence practice and/or has not been perceived as a problem. That is probably attributable to the joint effects of the nature of the constructs studied, the greater proportion of applied field studies in I-O psychology focusing on pragmatic organizational issues, and a correspondingly lower rate of laboratory experimentation with students. As mentioned previously, a review of three I-O psychology journals (*Journal of Applied Psychology, Personnel Psychology* and *Academy of Management Journal*) for three years (1999–2001) estimated the rate of deception at approximately 10% (Nicolopoulos, 2002). The rate of deception in social psychology has been found to be the highest for studies of compliance, conformity, altruism, aggression, equity and dissonance (Gross & Fleming, 1982). Consequently, it is enticing to speculate on what effect might be had on I-O research, including the use of deception, as we branch out to study new topics such as emotions in organizations (Ashforth & Humphrey, 1995; George & Jones, 1996; Lazarus & Cohen-Charash, 2001; Lefkowitz, 2000), some of which may require deceptive experimental mood-induction procedures. For example, Kimmel et al., (2011) use "Manipulating mood in the psychology laboratory" as an instance of their approach to conducting ethically acceptable deception.

Effectiveness and Effects of Deception

Does It Work?

As noted earlier, there is some evidence to suggest that IC procedures may alter the behavior of research participants—more so in experimental than non-experimental studies—thus producing artifactual findings. The primary purpose of deception is experimental control—to maintain the naivete of participants to ensure the internal validity of the research. As I also noted, however, an argument can be made that, for at least some circumstances and/or areas of research, the imposed artificial state of ignorance that constitutes the temporary world of the naive research subject is itself artifactual. Kruglanski (1975) emphasized the active and interpretive nature of humans even while serving as research subjects and that their search for meaning may entail a suspicious questioning of research experiences. In any event, especially given the ethical challenges to the practice, it makes sense to ask whether deception even works.

Kimmel (2007) concluded that his "review of the literature on the effects of deception ... leaves more questions unanswered than answered" (p. 98). Similarly, Hertwig and Ortmann (2008a) found mixed evidence regarding the thesis that deceived participants do not become resentful about having been fooled by researchers. Defenders and critics of deception can point to studies consistent with their point of view .... Undoubtedly, the available empirical evidence does not allow us to finally settle the methodological debate on deception, and there is room for honest differences in evaluating the ultimate impact of deception. (p. 81)

And a few years later, Kimmel et al. (2011) are consistent in concluding "In general, the findings of studies that have examined the key issues associated with the use of deception are anything but clear-cut" (p. 227).

Suspiciousness

In the heyday of deception research Kelman (1970) mused "I have increasing doubts about the effectiveness of deception as a method for social research" (p. 70). In that chapter he not only acknowledged ethical misgivings but pragmatic concern about whether the widespread use of deceptive techniques, especially among college students, was producing experimental subjects who would be preoccupied with trying to figure out what the research is really all about and either acting accordingly or resentfully behaving to the contrary. He reported one student as stating flatly, "Psychologists always lie!" (p. 71). Kelman was worried that...

> ... the experimenter can no longer assume that the conditions that he [sic] is trying to create are the ones that actually define the situation for the subject. Thus, the use of deception, while it is designed to give the experimenter control over the subject's perceptions and motivations, may actually produce an unspecifiable mixture of intended and unintended stimuli that make it difficult to know just what the subject is responding to. (p. 71)

He speculated that the long-term continued use of deception would be self-defeating as there would be more and more sophisticated and/or cynical subjects. As Seeman (1969), voicing similar doubts put it, "In view of the frequency with which deception is used in research we may soon be reaching a point where we no longer have naive subjects, but only naive experimenters" (p. 1026). In other words, the use of deception may actually work to the detriment of the experimental control it is designed to establish. The suspiciousness may be generated directly by participants' firsthand experiences with deception, and/or by indirect secondhand experience, as from campus scuttlebutt among students (Hertwig & Ortmann, 2008a), as with Kelman's student. However, in a more recent large survey of experimental participants, Krasnow et al. (2020) found that "Participants' present suspicion was not clearly related to past experiences of deception" (p. 1175).

Research participants, especially if they are the least bit suspicious, might react to artifactual cues in the experimental situation that suggest to them the existence of a deception. This was illustrated in the aborted restaurant study of consumer service orientation. The hoax was initially suspected and ultimately revealed by several restaurateurs who noted that the letter of complaint failed to mention details that would be expected following such an (actual) episode—for example, the date and time of occurrence and the dish(es) ordered. The fact that no reservation listing or credit card receipt could be found in the professor's name also added to the suspiciousness. The adverse publicity received by this ill-advised study and the potential ramifications to the field of OB are just the sort of consequences about which many critics of deception are concerned (Baumrind, 1985).

It is partly for this reason that the use of deception in experimental economics is virtually banned. Ortmann and Hertwig (2002) have gone so far as to opine that "there is no theory in economics that could not be tested without deception" (p. 125). But Cook and Yamagishi (2008) have suggested that the ability to forswear deception in experimental economics is due to their focus on conscious, rational choice behavior, rather than "a wider range of views that include non-rational, emotional, and heuristic based elements … . of choice or behavior" (p. 216). This is commensurate with Gross and Fleming (1982), Nicks et al. (1997) and Sieber et al. (1995), who believe the incidence of deception is determined primarily by the topics studied.

Although evidence suggests that "direct experience with deception appears to increase participants' expectations of being deceived in future experiments … [it] does not seem to affect participants' beliefs about psychologists' trustworthiness in general" (Ortmann & Hertwig, 2002, p. 121). Those authors could not find any studies focused on evaluating the effects of indirect experiences with deception. Accordingly, there has been for some time a great deal of professional interest regarding the potential suspiciousness of research participants, especially college students. Kimmel (1996, 2001) reviewed the resulting empirical research up through the 1970s and concluded "There has not been a great deal of research on the extent of subjects' suspiciousness in the research setting and the existing studies present something of a mixed bag" (1996, p. 96). However, he acknowledged elsewhere that, regarding applied marketing research, the increase in refusal rates by consumers is in part due to deceptive research practices (Kimmel & Smith, 2001). Greenberg and Folger (1988) agreed that we are insufficiently informed: "In view of the prevalence of deceptive practices … surprisingly little is known about the extent to which subjects are aware of the deceptions employed" (p. 162). Kimmel (1996) reported on studies that found (a) a substantial proportion of research participants who had been debriefed about the true purpose of the study, including student members of a subject pool, leaked crucial information to other potential participants—even those who had agreed to secrecy; and, tending to confirm Kelman's (1970) and Seeman's (1969) concern, (b) over time, the degree of suspiciousness among participants and the proportion of studies reporting suspicious participants were related to the number of deceptive studies reported. Regarding the impact of such suspiciousness on research results, he again found the results inconsistent. Some studies found no differences between the data obtained from suspicious and presumably naive subjects, whereas some studies did. In addition, again reminiscent of Kelman's and Seeman's warnings, some studies have found that prior experience in a deceptive experiment increased suspicions and affected performance in subsequent research.

Some concern over this issue continued through the 1980s and 1990s. For example, Epley and Huff (1998) found that although participants reported little negative reaction to being deceived in an experiment and debriefed about it, after three months they were still more suspicious of experiments than an uninformed group. (The uninformed group was not told about the deception until the three-month follow-up interview.) They acknowledged, however, not knowing whether the long-term suspicions would result in changed behavior in subsequent experiments. Although student participants may be expected to differ in degree of gullibility regarding the deceptions of experimental confederates (Oliansky, 1991), prospective research participants who have been deceived previously in an experiment are more likely to expect it in the future than those who have not (Krupat & Garonzik, 1994). Complicating the situation greatly is the realization that it may be difficult even to assess accurately the extent to which suspiciousness exists. Taylor and Shepperd (1996) found that participants may refuse to divulge in the post-experimental inquiry or manipulation check that they were suspicious of the experimental procedures. This may be the most disquieting aspect of the problem, as it implies an absence or loss of trust in the researcher and the research process. However, more recently Krasnow et al. (2020), as well as Barrera and Simpson (2012) found that deception did not lead to suspiciousness, and suspiciousness did not significantly affect the validity of experimental results.

Proposed Alternatives

Stimulated primarily by the moral ambivalence associated with deception as well as by the ambiguities regarding its efficacy, several methodological substitutes or alternatives have been suggested and tried. This is commensurate with the dictates of the APA (2017) ethical code, which admonishes that "Psychologists do not conduct a study involving deception unless they have determined that the use of deceptive techniques is justified by the study's significant prospective scientific, educational, or applied value and that *effective nondeceptive alternative procedures are not feasible*" (Standard 8.07[a], emphasis added).

Describing these options in detail is beyond the scope of this book, but they have been described or reviewed by Clarke (1999), Cook and Yamagishi (2008), Greenberg and Folger (1988), Kelman (1972), Kimmel (2007), Kimmel et al. (2011), Smith (1983) and others. Evaluations of their efficacy are not particularly encouraging. By far the most frequently implemented and evaluated alternative is *role playing* in which people are fully informed about all pertinent aspects of the study procedures—including the experimental manipulations—and asked to participate as if they were in the actual situation. Kelman (1972) viewed this as just one of a variety of participatory research procedures designed to restructure the ethical nature of the research enterprise.

A similar procedure is that of *role-taking* in which participants imagine themselves in a presented situation without even enacting the role. This has been used, for example, by a colleague of mine to study interpersonal rejection—students read and projected themselves into a realistic scenario. They did not have to actually be placed in a humiliating situation. The major argument against role-based procedures has been that, at best, the results pertain to people's hypothetical or anticipated behavior—i.e., how they think they would behave if they were in a real situation—which is probably subject to social desirability biases (as well as other self-presentation biases), not their likely actual behavior. But this criticism overlooks the corresponding epistemological ambiguities of deception research noted earlier, and perhaps it underestimates the degree to which participant role players may identify with their parts and become emotionally engaged in the circumstances, as occurred in the famous Stanford prison experiments (Haney et al., 1973; Zimbardo et al., 1973).

The array of additional options includes using simple self-report measures (e.g., of past dishonest behaviors, rather than using an entrapment study); obtaining limited IC or forewarning prospective participants that some aspects of the study may not be as they appear to be, but that this will be explained later; and a form of role-playing—structured game-like simulations such as with "mock-jury" research. Other possibilities include "after the fact consent," in which participants' consent is sought after the experiment and debriefing are completed. As a prophylaxis procedure aimed at reducing the severity of deception, the use of *quasi-controls* has been advocated by Orne (1969) and Suls and Rosnow (1981). This consists of having respondents imagine themselves undergoing the research as described (a form of role-taking) and reacting to it before the study is actually conducted with other participants. Alternative research protocols can be explored this way, and the least deceptive one that nevertheless maintains the necessary features of the design can be the one implemented.

Clarke (1999) "examined [these] various proposals which are aimed at reconciling informed consent standards with deceptive practices in the social sciences and found all of them to be inadequate" (p. 161). He proposed an alternative, called *indirect consent*, that entails each potential participant having a trusted confidant who knows them well (a proverbial "Aunt Mabel") who would help them "decide whether or not to participate, without revealing the nature of the deception in the experiment or study" (p. 162). (As a practical matter, he suggested "Perhaps, however, there are institutional equivalents to Aunt Mabel which we can adapt or can set up" (p. 163). I am not aware of any empirical demonstrations of the procedure.

Two things should be kept in mind: (a) the external or ecological validity of information gleaned from most of these methods is controversial, and (b) although they may have been proposed as alternatives to deception, some methods can also be used in conjunction with deception procedures, such as when the true purpose of a simulation study is concealed. The bottom line is the widespread view that among the reasons deception has remained relatively prevalent in social psychology research is that these alternatives have, for the most part, not worked very well (Adair et al., 1985; Christensen, 1988; Clarke, 1999).

Effects on Those Deceived

The moral justifications for the use of deception are consequentialist arguments in which the procedure is condoned if the potential benefits can be seen as outweighing the likely harms. In that context, therefore, the possible adverse effects on research participants of having been deceived is a salient empirical issue. The data from studies investigating the issue are primarily of two sorts: follow-up inquiries of actual research participants who had been deceived, and the reactions of people asked to read descriptions of studies in which participants were deceived (i.e., role-taking).

Smith (1983) and Kimmel (1996) reviewed a great many studies and came away with similar conclusions: "the negative effects of deception appear to be minimal" (Kimmel, 1996, p. 104), and "there is little evidence of harm or long-term negative effects, possibly because most research procedures are not more serious or harmful than everyday life events" (Smith, 1983, p. 316). Moreover, additional studies report similar findings (Epley & Huff, 1998; Fisher & Fryberg, 1994; Schwartz & Gottlieb, 1981; Smith & Berard, 1982; Smith & Richardson, 1983), although some negative reactions have been reported (Lindsay & Adair, 1990; Oliansky, 1991), and even Smith acknowledged "In most studies of participants' reactions, however, there are a few subjects who did not have a good experience" (p. 317). But other reviewers have come away more concerned about the effects on participants (Hertwig & Ortmann, 2001, 2008a, 2008b; Ortmann & Hertwig, 2002).

The general absence of negative reactions to deception (e.g., when former participants report belief in the importance of the research and accept the necessity for using deceit to investigate the problem) is especially noteworthy because the same respondents generally make it clear that they did (or would) not like being stressed, harmed, or embarrassed. Such adverse experiences, not deception per se, are what they object to. Broder (1998) emphasized the distinction that should be maintained between noxious experimental treatments (to be avoided) and the act of deceiving participants (which may be rather benign and presumably unavoidable in order to carry out the research).

Even if most participants are sanguine about having been deceived it would not mean, as noted earlier, that they may not be suspicious of researchers and future research participation. Interestingly, the opinions and attitudes toward the research and one's actual or projected participation in it tend to be more favorable among those who took part in research and were deceived than among those who merely imagined having participated. The reason(s) for that distinction are not clear. It has been explained optimistically as due to the likelihood that deceived (and rather elaborately debriefed) participants are more likely to have found the experience interesting and of educational value. It has also been attributed more negatively to cognitive dissonance reduction (Baumrind, 1985)—that is, evaluating the experience as interesting and worthwhile as a means of justifying one's feelings of embarrassment or shame at having been duped. This would be commensurate with the finding noted earlier that participants may be unwilling to communicate their suspiciousness about the study to the researcher even after it is concluded. Hertwig and Ortmann (2008a) raise "the possibility that those students who do not resent being deceived may be the ones who expect deception as part of the game. Such an expectation can, of course, also jeopardize experimental control" (p. 69).

Baumrind (1985) went on to question the construct validity of participants' post-experimental self-reports as measures of possible harm:

> After all, if self-reports could be regarded as accurate measures of the impact of experimental conditions, we could dispense entirely with experimental manipulation and behavioral measures, substituting instead vivid descriptions of environmental stimuli to which subjects would be instructed to report how they would act. (p. 168)

The Normative Ethical Arguments

The use of deception by researchers is problematic and of great concern to many psychologists, generating considerable debate (Broder, 1998; Kimmel, 1998; Kimmel et al., 2011; Korn, 1998; Ortmann & Hertwig, 1997, 1998). It seems to strike a deadly blow at the ethical heart of the research enterprise—the trust that we ask of our participants. It also appears to be antithetical to our humanistic tradition and to the respect for people's dignity and autonomy that is the spirit of IC. So, when deception is used it is generally because of a belief that

> the phenomena that the psychologist hopes to observe would be destroyed if he [sic] revealed the true purpose of the experiment to his subjects … Without deception, it would be impossible—at least within the limits of our current research technology—to obtain the kind of information that many psychological experiments are designed to produce. (Kelman, 1972, p. 996)

Or, more succinctly, "Certain kinds of deception are necessary to gather certain data in certain settings" (Goode, 1996, p.11). The use of deception represents a particular resolution of a conflict between values: arguably, compromising the concerns of individuals for privacy, self-determination and respect, on behalf of the entitlement rights of the researcher, the profession and society to produce knowledge.

It does seem true, notwithstanding disbelief by some economists, that there are problems that cannot be investigated without using deception. This makes the stakes in the deception debate very high for the field. For example, in studies of incidental learning participants are instructed to respond in some irrelevant way to experimental stimuli not knowing that a memory test of the stimuli will follow. A plausible cover story is necessary to conceal the true nature of the study—otherwise, the learning would be intentional, not incidental. Broder (1998) used this example to make the point that...

> ... the ethical question concerning deception in this research therefore cannot be whether deception is necessary within this research (because it is) but rather whether this research is necessary. This must of course be the topic of public discussion in which psychologists will have to defend their claims about the relevance of their research. But this is the case for every empirical science. (p. 806)

However, the implicit assumption that a bogus cover story creates the uniform psychological reality necessary to permit valid inferences from the results has not gone unchallenged (Baumrind, 1985).

Views on the general matter of deception can be formulated as representing deontological theories concerned with right and wrong and the origins of those judgments, and consequentialist (or utilitarian) theories concerned with the harmful and beneficial effects of actions. Each category contains both rule-based and act-based versions. In all instances, my preference is for normative stances that reflect the meta-ethical position of universalism, meaning that my interests as a researcher do not necessarily take precedence over the best interests of others, including potential research participants.

PRO: The Modified Act-Utilitarian Argument Permitting Deception

The act-utilitarianism model was developed largely by Bentham to render moral reasoning more objective and measurable. He believed that ethical choices should and could be determined not by vague abstractions and metaphysical or religious dictates but by whichever action produces the greatest aggregate good for all those affected by it. The model is afflicted with a host of theoretical, pragmatic and empirical difficulties: How should *good* be defined and by whom? can all the consequences of an action be known? and even if known, they may not all be measurable; and even if known and measurable, they may not be comparable on a common metric to assess the net effects of alternative actions, as required. And even if all that is possible, can it be accomplished in time to be used for decision-making? Utilitarian conclusions also sometimes fly in the face of common and intuitive moral principles like promise-keeping, truth-telling or fulfilling duties and obligations; and finally, the criterion of the greatest overall good ignores the potential injustice of maldistributions of the benefits and costs among individuals and groups.

The predominant view in the social and behavioral sciences—at least the view that is officially codified in numerous ethical statements (e.g., APA, 2002/ 2017)—is essentially an act-utilitarian (consequentialist) argument. It is a modification of the traditional utilitarian position in that it provides a justification for *permitting* deception when certain conditions are met; it does not make deception obligatory under any circumstances—even if that alternative could be shown to yield the greatest good in a particular situation. In that sense, it seems to me that there is an implicit acknowledgment in this position of the morally dubious nature of deception. That interpretation is confirmed by a reading of Standard 8.07 of the APA Code: "Psychologists do not conduct a study involving deception *unless* … " (emphasis added). Standard 8.07 goes on to specify that the permissibility of deception must be justified by the study's "significant prospective scientific, educational, or applied value and that effective nondeceptive alternative procedures are not feasible." Permissibility is also contingent on meeting all the other safeguards against causing harm: review by an IRB, affording as much IC as possible, and extensive debriefing.

In other words, as characterized by two of its critics, deception has been justified by psychologists as a "strategy of last resort" (Hertwig & Ortmann, 2008a, p. 83). But they conclude that it hasn't worked that way, as evidenced by its continued frequent use. They also suggest that the reason "is that the APA rule suffers from a serious design flaw. It leaves the decision of whether deception is justified by its anticipated value to those who stand to benefit from its use" (Hertwig & Ortmann, 2008b, p. 224).

The tacit acknowledgment that deception is, at best, a "necessary evil" that must be justified affirmatively in each individual instance is also reflected in the absence of any other form of supporting ethical rationale from rule-utilitarianism or a deontological approach. Formally, there is no reason why deception could not be justified by a *rule-utilitarian* argument—For example, the scientific and societal benefits of research in general and over the long run could be viewed as outweighing the discomforts or harm to participants which might in some instances be unavoidable, so that only egregious cases of deception need be guarded against. But I am not aware of that argument ever having been made, and I would not support it.

Hypothetically, the decision to proceed with deceptive research is based on a subjective assessment that the degree of harm or extent of costs likely to be associated with its implementation is substantially exceeded by the anticipated benefits. However, it is generally taken for granted that virtually all the costs are borne by the participants, and the benefits mostly accrue to the researcher and to society (and may be impossible to specify), so that review procedures for the protection of human participants are likely to focus almost exclusively on the costs or potential harms (Rosnow, 1997). This is why the empirical debate over the extent to which participants actually have been harmed or offended by being deceived is so spirited. In addition, it has been pointed out that the review process seldom considers the costs and benefits of *not* doing the research, thus failing to acknowledge sufficiently the potential benefits to society that may be lost by not allowing it to be done (Rosenthal & Rosnow, 1984; Rosnow, 1997).

PRO: An Act-Deontological Position Permitting Deception

The difficulties encountered in implementing rule-deontology (e.g., what to do when two or more "absolute" moral principles conflict) led to development of the act-deontological model that allows for the preeminence of some principles over others or permits of some qualifications of a general rule. For example, the absolute prohibition against killing ("Thou shalt not") is excepted by some people in the case of war, or to protect an innocent person's life, or to punish a capital offender. However, when the effects of particular actions are used as a basis for making the qualifications or for choosing among alternatives, the deontological approach takes on some of the trappings of consequentialism.

Kimmel et al. (2011) "advance a normative social contract that identifies conditions under which deception in behavioral science research is or is not morally permissible" (p. 237). Although they couch their proposal in terms of *social contract theory* (a rule-based perspective) I believe it may be better understood, in general, as an act-deontological position. That is, as offering exceptions to a blanket prohibition ("deception is permissible only if ... " or "deception is not permissible unless ... ").

A major drawback of the social-contractarian approach is the potential social power differential between the parties—in this case, a researcher and the prospective participants (cf. John Rawls and "contracts of adhesion" in Chapter 3). That is why Kimmel et al. (2011) offer the model as a hypothetical (not actual) contract, requiring *hypothetical consent* by participants. Indeed, four of the five "principles" that must be met are at the discretion of the researcher. They are: (1) "The use of deception as a last resort, once all alternative procedures are ruled out as unfeasible"; (2) "Researchers using deception increase the scope of informed consent and explicitly forewarn that deception may be used in behavioral science research"; (3) "Researchers anticipate and make allowances for possible vulnerabilities of participants in developing studies that use deception and in seeking informed consent"; (4) "Researchers never expose participants to procedures or risks that they themselves would be unwilling to accept if similarly situated"; and (5) "Research participants cooperate fully and in good faith in research studies they have accepted to participate in." It may be seen that the social contractarian characterization is not apt because the only obligation pertaining to the participants (#5) is not directly pertinent to the issue of deception and could be eliminated with no loss of comprehensiveness. Participants have already agreed to cooperate by virtue of their "informed consent"—while ignorant of the impending deception.

CON: The Rule-Deontological Prohibition

Rule-deontological positions emphasize invariant principles based on such considerations as one's moral duty and respect for people (Kant), contractarian social justice (Hobbes and Rawls), individual rights (Locke), and/or self-realization through social concern or institutional and political reform (Hegel and Marx).

The simplest, most straightforward arguments against the use of deceptive methods are that they are unequivocally wrong, irrespective of whether participants are harmed. They are wrong because they violate our duty to do no harm and to respect the autonomy, dignity and worth of all people by dealing with them truthfully and not treating them instrumentally like "research material" (Veatch, 1987) and/or because they unjustly assign all the costs of the research enterprise to one group. Hypothetically, an *act-deontological* argument could be made against the deception that allowed exceptions under certain circumstances, such as when the anticipated value of the research is high and the severity of deception low (but notice that a consequentialist perspective has sneaked in to make the argument). Presumably, a *rule-deontological* argument could even be made in *favor* of deception if researchers' responsibilities to their profession, society and the advancement of knowledge were seen as uniformly more important than their obligations to research participants. But I have not come across a serious statement of that position—probably because it is antithetical to the very essence of ethical thought.

CON: The Rule-Utilitarian Objection

Mills' "secondary principles" evolved into rule utilitarianism in response to some of the problems noted with act utilitarianism. Rule utilitarianism employs ethical principles based on culturally influenced views of their relative utility for society overall. For example, most cultures have learned that telling the truth is, in general, more culturally adaptive than never knowing when one is being lied to; its utility doesn't need to be assessed in every individual ethically relevant situation. Consequently, rule utilitarianism

> is seen as more consistent with the logic of moral reasoning and the common understanding of morality as a social code, where individuals have convictions about moral obligations and minimum moral standards. Thus,

it is seen as more intuitively plausible and less likely to be at odds with nonconsequentialist reasoning than act–utilitarianism.

(Kimmel, 2001, p. 673)

But because these rules are treated more as guidelines or default options than as absolute standards, the practical advantage gained in decision-making can be offset by a certain degree of indeterminacy in rule-utilitarian analyses. In other words, in contrast to an act-utilitarianism analysis in which one is obliged to act on the most utile option (if it can be determined), several alternative courses of action may be permissible under a rule-utilitarian analysis.

Some protagonists in the deception debate identify the "moral philosophizing" objections to it as exclusively deontological in nature (e.g., Christensen, 1988, p. 669). That overlooks the prevalence of rule-utilitarian objections, such as those articulated most notably by Baumrind (1985). She argued persuasively that the use of deception violates three rules that are of enormous adaptive advantage in western society, thus causing substantial harms to research participants, the profession and society. The first rule is the right of self-determination, which is reflected in the right of research participants to IC. "Thus, subjects have the right to judge for themselves whether being lied to or learning something painful about themselves constitutes psychological harm for them" (p. 167). The second rule consists in the obligation of a fiduciary (the researcher) to protect the welfare of the beneficiary, in this case the research participant. And third is the obligation, especially of a fiduciary like a researcher or professor in relation to students, to be loyal and trustworthy, not undermining the trust offered by the participant/student.

In making the case regarding harms done to participants by deception Baumrind (1985) challenged much of the evidence that has been garnered ostensibly demonstrating that participants do not feel harmed or even wronged by deception if adequate explanation of the need for the process is provided. (A view echoed some years later in the writings of Hertwig and Ortmann.) The evidence, she pointed out, is generally based on superficial questionnaire or interview responses obtained by people not trained clinically to "uncover true feelings of anger, shame, or altered self-image in participants who believe that what they say should conform with their image of a 'good subject'" (p. 168).

She made the argument that the profession is harmed by deception research because social support for behavioral science research is jeopardized when we promote values that conflict with the generally accepted tenets of moral conduct. In fact, the commitment to the truth of the researchers themselves may be undermined. Evidence was reviewed earlier regarding the increased suspiciousness and lack of trust engendered in research participants because of having been deceived. Baumrind warned that such attitudes may generalize to all expert authorities, thus having deleterious effects on society at large (although that seems not to have happened). Her forceful attack on deception is also based on a belief "that the scientific and social benefits of deception research cannot be established with sufficient certitude to tip the scale in favor of procedures that wrong subjects" (p. 170).

Post-Research Procedures: Manipulation Checks, Debriefing, Dehoaxing and Desensitization

Respect and concern for the well-being of research participants should extend beyond the boundaries of the primary data-gathering steps to include what I will generically refer to as *post-research procedures*.[18] The issue is more important than the amount of space that can be devoted to it here. Consequently, the reader is referred to other reviews of the topic (Greenberg & Folger, 1988; Harris, 1988; Kimmel, 1996, 2007; Tesch, 1977) and to extremely helpful procedural protocols provided by experienced researchers (Holmes, 1976a, 1976b; Mills, 1976). The general term post-experimental procedures, or the more inclusive post-research procedures encompasses several activities that are relevant to nonexperimental methods like questionnaire surveys or experience-based learning activities, such as games and simulations, as well as to experiments (Lederman, 1992; Stewart, 1992).

Multiple Aims and Objectives

The researcher-initiated exchanges between investigator and participant following the data-collection phase of a study have three types of objectives: (a) methodological—to check on the efficacy of experimental manipulations, measures and procedures; (b) educational—to inform and educate the participants about the study and the value of behavioral and social science research; and (c) ethical—to reverse any misconceptions due to deception and to ameliorate any adverse consequences as a result of it (Greenberg & Folger, 1988; Harris, 1988; Tesch, 1977). Although those distinctions are still useful in elucidating the different functions that may be going on simultaneously in post-research procedures, in the decades since Tesch first pointed out the distinctions, it has come to be accepted that the educational responsibilities we owe to research participants are also part of our ethical obligations (APA, 2017, Standard 8.08).

The Methodological Functions: Procedural Inquiry, Manipulation Checks and Safeguards against Leakage

These steps are generally applicable to experimental research only, and in contrast with the other purposes of post-research procedures, they are for the benefit of

---

18 I am not entirely happy with the designation of these procedures as occurring "post-research" as it might imply a secondary status to them; but I have not thought of a better term. ("Post data gathering" is awkward, and perhaps misleading when data are collected re the manipulation checks.)

the researcher, not the participants. They mostly involve collecting additional information from the participants, whereas the others primarily entail imparting information (Greenberg & Folger, 1988). The information sought is of three types, all contributing to the establishment of the internal validity of the experimental findings. The first thing ordinarily of interest to the experimenter is a manipulation check to assess whether the independent variable was operative as intended—i.e., did it produce the effects on the participants or create the conditions desired? Suppose, for example, I conduct an experiment investigating the effect of mood state on cognitive information processing—the encoding, storage and retrieval of performance data used in making employee appraisal ratings. If my study entails comparing the evaluations made by people who are frustrated or angry with those who are in a pleasant emotional state (as well as an untreated comparison group), I might have had to create experimental conditions that induce those contrasting moods in different participants before obtaining their ratings data. My ability to interpret the results of the study accurately will depend on my confirmation that they did, in fact, feel frustrated or happy, depending on which experimental treatment they received. I will attempt to find that out from them after they conclude the experimental tasks. (This assumes, of course, that we can rely on such verbal reports. But I may have some pertinent observational data regarding their behavior during the experiment as well.)

The second reason for conducting the inquiry is an assessment of the extent to which the behavior of the participants might have been influenced by extraneous demand characteristics of the research (Orne, 1962). Similarly, if there has been some deception involved (as might very well be necessary in a mood-induction study), the researcher will want to have some idea whether the participants were suspicious about it or accepted the "genuineness" of the situation. Unfortunately, as noted earlier, it is not at all clear whether the experimental participants will be willing to reveal their suspicions (Taylor & Shepperd, 1996) or whether such suspiciousness necessarily impacts their behavior during the experiment (Kimmel, 2007). The third methodological aim—frequently salient in the university subject pool environment—consists of the researcher's attempt to impress on the participants the need to not reveal any features of the study to prospective participants that would invalidate their participation. However, as is the case regarding the communication of their suspicions, the evidence is equivocal that such pledges to secrecy by participants will be kept (Kimmel, 1996). Although it is tempting to simply derogate the trustworthiness of students who leak such information, their behavior may reflect an antipathy resulting from the negative reactions they had to the research enterprise. In any event, it sometimes results in the researcher delaying a full debriefing until after the completion of the study, at which time some students may no longer be available and may, therefore, be left with the recollections and effects of a bad experience. But "if scientific or humane values justify delaying or withholding this information [about the study], psychologists take reasonable measures to reduce the risk of harm" (APA, 2017, Standard 8.08[b]).

The Educational Function: Debriefing

The ubiquitous term *debriefing* derives historically from military usage—in particular, the British Royal Air Force during World War II—in which pilots were briefed at the beginning of a mission and interrogated or debriefed at its conclusion (Harris, 1988). The term was introduced into the language of experimental psychology by Stanley Milgram (1964), and it was ultimately used generically to refer to one or more of several different procedures with rather different objectives (Aronson & Carlsmith, 1968). For example, the term may be used in psychiatry to refer to post-traumatic interventions, such as those offered to victims of the World Trade Center (September 11, 2001) attack, designed to help "promote the emotional processing of traumatic events through the ventilation and normalization of reactions and preparation for possible future experiences" (Bisson & Deahl, 1994, p. 717).

The overall importance of debriefing (in the global sense) is suggested by some findings that most research participants do not find their participation particularly enjoyable or interesting, and the debriefing was not a positive experience (Brody et al., 2000; Lindsay & Adair, 1990). This is a matter of some concern because, in the opinion of some experienced researchers, "the most important determinant of the subject's feeling about the research experience ... is the debriefing" (Smith, 1983, p. 323). In fact, student participants in one survey

> found the experiences to be boring, irrelevant, and a waste of time. In a few cases ... students ... expressed considerable contempt for the entire psychological research endeavor ... . No student ... could say anything intelligible about the experiment's purpose or design.
>
> *(Coulter, 1986, p. 317)*

This appears to have nothing to do with deception or noxious experimental manipulations: "Faculty seem to have underestimated the introductory students' dislike of research participation in apparently innocuous studies" (Lindsay & Adair, 1990, p. 292). Brody et al. (2000) also reported a substantial variability in the content, format and quality of debriefing practices followed by researchers—even within a single university department of psychology. They also noted that the most frequent student complaint was that the information provided during the debriefing was insufficient and unclear. "None of the participants spontaneously mentioned educational value as an outcome of their research participation" (p. 23).

Given the frequently mandatory nature of student participation in research, it seems imperative for both educational and ethical reasons that the research experience be academically justifiable (Coulter, 1986). This is commensurate with the ethical guideline to "provide a prompt opportunity for participants to obtain appropriate information about the nature, results, and conclusions of the research" (APA, 2017, Standard 8.08). At first blush, it might seem that this imperative is significantly less salient for applied research in I-O psychology, which is less likely to involve laboratory experimentation with students and more likely to entail survey procedures with more mature employees. However, even surveys are sometimes long, demanding, boring, mildly invasive or otherwise upsetting; employees may also feel that because of organizational pressures their participation is as mandatory as that of a student in a university subject pool. They too deserve to understand the purpose and potential value of the research (perhaps to the organization or all employees), and they might even be pleased to learn about the nature of their contribution to it.

The Ethical Functions: Dehoaxing and Desensitization

The APA Code, as far back as the 1992 edition, obligated psychologists to explain to participants as early as is feasible any deception that occurred and to "correct any misconceptions that participants may have" (Standards 8.07[c] and 8.08[a]). That process is called *dehoaxing*. Most psychologists accept that appropriate dehoaxing also includes a detailed explanation of why the deception was necessary and a personal apology for having done so (Smith & Richardson, 1983). The 2002 revised code made explicit what many researchers had believed for some time, by adding "When psychologists become aware that research procedures have harmed a participant, they take reasonable steps to minimize the harm" (APA, 2002/2017, Standard 8.08 [c]). That is what is meant by *desensitization* in this context. The distinction between the two related procedures was first made by Holmes (1976a, 1976b).

Holmes (1976a) described the objective of dehoaxing as follows: "the problem is to convince the subjects that the fraudulent information they were given (e.g., that they are seriously maladjusted) was in fact fraudulent and thereby relieve any anxiety engendered by that information" (p. 859). However, the participants may find themselves in a virtual "Catch-22": If they believe the researcher's description of having just deceived them, why should they believe that they are not being deceived again? Perhaps they are being set up for a more complex manipulation involving a deception within a deception (yes, it has been done). Or perhaps they interpret the experimenter's explanation as a benign expression of sympathy, but still untrue, for one who is so "seriously maladjusted."

Despite those difficulties, Holmes (1976a, 1977) found that de-hoaxing could, if done carefully and thoughtfully, effectively eliminate the misinformation participants received attendant upon a research deception. Hollingsworth (1977) was less sanguine about its effectiveness, especially with respect to false feedback about personal qualities, such as one's intelligence or sociability. Some researchers have advocated that experimenters spend as much or more time with participants after the experiment is over as they did during the data collection (Greenberg & Folger, 1988). In response to the possibility that dehoaxing may not be effective—that is, the false beliefs may persist despite debriefing (Holmes, 1976a)—Misra (1992) demonstrated that including "a formal discussion of the belief perseverance phenomenon" as a feature of the dehoaxing enhanced its effectiveness. And Eyde (2000) recommended that participants be reassured that extensive pilot testing had been done to assure that the deception was believable "and that the participant's acceptance of the ruse was not a reflection of the participant's gullibility, but rather of the lab's care and skill in designing the process" (p. 71). Of course, such difficulties would be obviated by a blanket proscription against noxious deceptions. On the other hand, Sommers and Miller (2013) suggest some (innocuous) conditions under which the practice may be omitted.

Among a sample of 46 published studies in I-O psychology that used deception, most did not report providing any debriefing or dehoaxing (Nicolopoulos, 2002). Among those that did, most did not provide any information about its content, including whether the deception was revealed and explained. These are some typical descriptions of the debriefing procedures, quoted in their entirety: "Following this, the experimenter debriefed and thanked the participants"; "Finally, participants were debriefed and dismissed"; "Participants completed a posttask questionnaire, were debriefed, thanked, and allowed to leave"; "Finally, all participants were debriefed and paid"; "After completing the questionnaire, participants were debriefed and dismissed." Just two informative descriptions of appropriate procedures were found. For example,

> Following the exercises, participants completed a post-experimental questionnaire and were debriefed, thanked, and allowed to leave. The debriefing provided information about the purpose of the study and the roles of the confederates, made apologies for the deception, and provided a phone number for participants who had further questions or concerns.

I cannot recall encountering a research study in I-O psychology in which the nature and severity of the deception and potential harm to participants was so great as to warrant desensitization procedures, which Holmes (1976b) defined as "the process of helping the subjects deal with new information about themselves acquired as a consequence of the behaviors they exhibited during the experiment" (p. 868). The classic example, of course, is the majority of Milgram's (1963, 1964, 1974) research participants who, in their (bogus) role of research assistant, discovered that they were compliant enough to obey the authoritative researcher's instructions to administer (bogus but realistic) severe electric shocks to "inefficient learners" who were actually research confederates. Many of them apparently showed quite significant signs of distress during the experiment.[19] Among the many serious matters to be considered in performing research of that nature (unlikely to receive IRB approval today) is the necessary prescreening of prospective participants that would be needed to eliminate any possibility of employing even a single psychologically "fragile subject" (Norris, 1978). In writing about such relatively extreme instances of deception, Baumrind (1985)—in a rather deontological vein—notes that "Effective debriefing does not nullify the wrong done participants by deceiving them and may not even repair their damaged self-image or ability to trust adult authorities" (p. 172).

I think that her summary of the general and educational debriefing protocol developed by Mills (1976) is a fitting conclusion:

> The experiment is explained very gradually and every point reviewed until the subject understands. Subjects are given time to reorganize their perceptions of the experiment and their responses to it, from possible humiliation and discomfort to self-acceptance and, it is to be hoped, sympathetic understanding of the researcher's perspective. Subjects are offered a genuine opportunity to withdraw their data after having received a full explanation of the purposes of the experiment. Moreover, by adding to the investigators' emotional and fiscal costs, painstaking and effective debriefing procedures introduce a noncoercive but persuasive deterrent to investigators who are contemplating deception research.
>
> *(Baumrind, 1985, p. 173)*

Adding Further to the Framework for Ethical Decision Making

38. Adopting a social perspective on the nature of research in I-O psychology emphasizes that most research is conducted to gratify the scientific or professional interests of the researcher and/or to address an organizational problem—as with institutional research. In both cases the employee/participant generally doesn't expect to benefit directly from the enterprise and so they cannot be expected to have any a priori motivation to participate. In addition, the nature of our professional right to do research generally is in the form of an entitlement with no

---

19 In the 1960s, '70s and '80s Milgram's work was vociferously criticized (e.g., Baumrind, 1964, 1985). A little later it was lauded as "groundbreaking" (Elms, 1995) and of "inestimable value, and that *the demonstrable costs were relatively negligible*" (Miller, 1986, emphasis added). A little after that, the "revival" of obedience experiments was criticized as overlooking Milgram's misrepresentations of debriefing procedures, the risks posed, and the harm done to participants (Nicholson, 2011). Additional criticisms have been raised (e.g., Haslam et al., 2015), including the failure of social psychology textbooks to acknowledge the criticisms (Griggs & Whitehead III, 2015).

corresponding responsibility imposed on anyone to comply with it. These conditions are reflected in the ethical prescription that research participation must always be voluntary and not coerced. Nevertheless, it is widely accepted that the implied social contract invoked by employment obligates employees and applicants to cooperate with legitimate and reasonable institutional research (but not with our personal research agenda for which they are simply a convenience sample). Should a conflict arise between these two contradictory expectations, it ought to be resolved by subordinating the employees' implied contractual obligation, in deference to their right to exercise autonomy over their own welfare by refusing to participate.

39. **Deontological principles dominate the ethical strictures governing research participation: treating people with dignity and respect for their autonomy (so they are free to decide whether to participate in the research and whether to continue their participation); having concern for their well-being and avoiding the infliction of harm (so that if deception or withholding information can be justified by a rigorous review, adequate debriefing will be provided); abiding by principles of justice and fairness (so that people are not coerced into participation by virtue of their lesser social status or other factors); and displaying honesty, integrity and trustworthiness (so that promises made regarding the confidentiality of replies and the potential benefits, discomforts or risks of participation are fulfilled).**

40. **Psychologists are responsible for knowing and adhering to the professional, ethical, and legal requirements for research with human participants, such as providing informed consent and confidentiality, irrespective of the work setting and nature of the research (e.g., both basic theoretical research and applied institutional research).**

41. **Intentionally deceiving research participants remains a contentious issue in social, behavioral and biomedical research. Despite the categorical objections of some, the ethical consensus, as articulated in the APA (2017) ethical code, reflects a reluctant act–utilitarian permissibility. "Psychologists do not conduct a study involving deception unless … [it] is justified by the study's significant prospective scientific, educational, or applied value and that effective nondeceptive alternative procedures are not feasible" (Standard 8.07[a]). Moreover, it must be explained to participants "as early as is feasible" (8.07 [c]), and the decision to deceive must be approved by an appropriate review committee, such as an IRB.**

14

SCIENTIFIC INTEGRITY

> How much does a story in the media about research misconduct cost? Nothing? Wrong. It costs millions, maybe billions, of dollars. It leads individuals to stop contributing to foundations that support research … . Misconduct in science creates a breach of trust that threatens the viability of the research enterprise. It puts financial resources at risk and undermines the public's trust in research findings. Perhaps worst of all, it can lead to students deciding that research is not for them.
>
> Michael J. Zigmond and Beth A. Fischer

I wonder if the reader, like myself, has given little thought (at best) to the effects of research misconduct summarized by Zigmond and Fischer (2014), above, prior to reading their admonition. The topic of the responsible conduct of research (RCR) is usually taught encapsulated in scientific terms, with little consideration of wider implications (cf. Figure 14.1). Much of this chapter concerns the factors that give rise to the issue to begin with.

Some psychologists believe that psychology has a serious image problem with the public—that many people are skeptical about the status of psychology as a useful science. (Perhaps the reader has personally encountered such skepticism.) However, those who believe that this is a very recent problem are incorrect. "As the twentieth century wore on, psychological knowledge in-creased enormously, and psychologists assumed respected and influential po-sitions. But somehow the hopes for continuous improvement in the condition of mankind through psychology declined. It became almost naive to assume that what was discovered through research could have much effect on man's [sic] nature or institutions" (Leona Tyler, 1973, p. 1021). A more recent and widely shared systematic discussion of this issue is Lilienfeld's (2012) article in

DOI: 10.4324/9781003212577-17

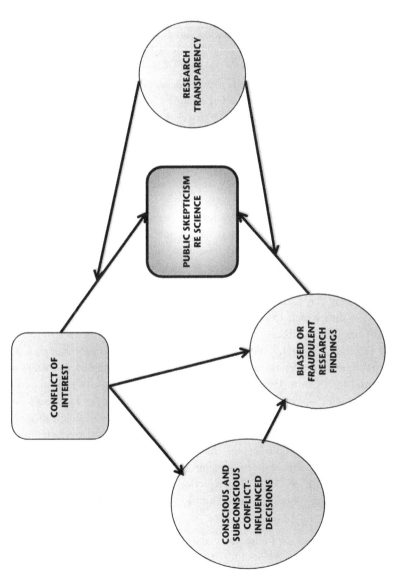

FIGURE 14.1 Potential effects of conflict of interest on research and public opinion

the *American Psychologist*.[1] He examined six common criticisms directed at psychology challenging its scientific basis—although he also presented substantial evidence rebutting each: (a) "Psychology is merely common sense"; (b) "Psychology does not use scientific methods"; (c) "Psychology cannot yield meaningful generalizations because everyone is unique"; (d) "Psychology does not yield repeatable results"; (e) "Psychology cannot make precise predictions"; and (f) "Psychology is not useful to society." He also went on to discuss several potential sources of the public's skepticism. Some of them reflect misunderstandings regarding the nature of psychological science and research, but some relate to "psychology's failure to police itself" (p. 117). Mostly, in that regard, he had in mind "the insinuation of dubious science into much of mental health practice" (p. 118).

The topic was revisited just a few years later by Ferguson (2015), who observed that "Psychology's status as a science is clearly not accepted as a *given* either among policymakers, the general public, or other scientists" (p. 527). He emphasized internal problems within psychological science that might be responsible. To Lilienfeld's discussion of our poor self-policing, Ferguson added a few more reasons that are also relevant to our concerns in this chapter: methodological issues, including questionable research practices, replication (i.e., lack thereof), the problem of null findings, and lack of transparency; and the conflict between social advocacy and science (see chapter 10).

The previous chapter noted that psychology, because of the widespread use of experimental deception techniques, may have a public image problem of another sort, as well: remember the student who volunteered "psychologists always lie!"? And of special import for I-O psychology, let's add consideration of what I have purported to be a corporate/managerialist bias that has adversely affected much of our work in many ways, including our relations with workers. I present all this as the context within which to consider the matter of integrity in the responsible conduct of research (RCR).

In all fairness, however, "the latter half of [the 20th] century has seen an erosion in the perceived legitimacy of science [in general] as an impartial means of finding truth" (MacCoun, 1998, p. 259). Indeed, large numbers of people in the U.S. fought against fluoridation of the public water supply and vaccination of their children against frequent childhood diseases; many reject evolution as an explanatory mechanism in favor of "creationism," as well as the overwhelming evidence of human-caused climate change. Approximately twice as many Americans believe in extra-sensory perception (ESP; 41%) as in nontheological evolution (22%) (Hornsey, 2020). The rejection of science is only sometimes due to misinformation or ignorance; it is "mostly driven by motivated cognition"

---

1 Lilienfeld also reviewed self-criticisms stemming from *within* the field. These have largely been constructive, leading to reforms in the various fields of psychology. But they pertain to rather different issues than the manifestations of public skepticism.

(Lewandowsky & Oberauer, 2016, p. 217). That is, findings are rejected "because the science is in conflict with people's worldviews, or political or religious opinions" (p. 217). Similarly, Hornsey (2020) summarized the research bases of "six psychological roots from which science-skeptical attitudes grow: ideologies; vested interests; conspiracist worldviews; fears and phobias, personal-identity expression; and social-identity needs" (p. 583).

It is not so surprising, therefore, that instances of actual fraud seem confirmatory and become major news (Carey, 2015a; Gross, 2011; Marcus & Oransky, 2015). Researchers have reason to be concerned and as indicated in the epigram to this chapter, there can be substantial consequences. Serious improprieties have been noted in biotechnology, drug research, computer science, other biomedical fields, etc. (Economist, 2013; Shamoo & Resnik, 2009). The combination of (relatively rare) improprieties and (more frequent) mistaken and sloppy publications that require corrective *errata* or complete retractions motivated some researchers to begin keeping systematic track of journal retractions and blogging about it regularly.[2] On the other hand, not everyone believes that all, or even most, retractions are an indication of disintegrity. "A stigma should not be attached to the retraction of a scientific paper … . the rise in retractions over the past few years does not signify a surge in misconduct: on the contrary, it reflects a growing scientific integrity. A growing number of journals are now prepared to publish retractions … . Retractions are therefore more logically and usefully interpreted as evidence for the commitment of editors and scientists to remove invalid results from the literature" (Fanelli, 2014). I believe each retraction needs to be understood independently.

A Succinct Overview: It's All About Validity

All the issues mentioned above reflect the various ways in which, and the extent to which we can legitimately justify the accuracy of the conclusions or knowledge drawn from our research—i.e., their validity. (And as such, it is a very large topic that extends beyond the purview of this volume.) The modern era of such concerns began more than 65 years ago with a focus on the meaningfulness of each individual experiment—its *internal, external, conclusion*, and *construct validity* (Campbell, 1957; Campbell & Stanley, 1963; Cook & Campbell, 1979). And methods are still being elucidated to increase those features (Kenny, 2019).

None of those are achievable if the study findings are not reproducible. *Reproducibility* has been defined authoritatively as "obtaining consistent computational results using the same input data, computational steps, methods, code, and conditions of analysis" (National Academy of Sciences, 2019, p. 1). It is both more fundamental and less ambitious than the better-known *replicability*: "obtaining consistent results across studies aimed at answering the same scientific

2   See http://retractionwatch.com/.

questions, each of which has obtained its own data" (National Academy, 2019, p. 1). Both R's are necessary if science is to achieve the aim of *generalizability*—i.e., "the extent that results of a study apply in other contexts or populations that differ from the original one" (National Academy, 2019, p. 1). A massive demonstration project illustrated that different research teams, even under controlled conditions (e.g., random assignment of participants from the same population; investigation of the same research questions; preregistration of all analyses), produce a variety of results as a function of differences in study design—i.e., a potential lack of replicability (Landy, et al., 2020). (Although this sort of very large-scale project also permits investigation of the potential conditions for generalizability.) All three criteria, beginning with reproducibility, depend on *transparency*: "a study's data and code have to be available in order for others to reproduce and confirm the results" (National Academy, 2019, p. 2). Accordingly, considerable attention has been paid recently to advancing rigorous *reporting standards* for empirical research studies in psychology (Applebaum, et al., 2018; Eich, 2014; Kazak, et al., 2018; Levitt, et al., 2018), as well as for the *metascience* of "evidence synthesis methods" (B.T Johnson, 2021, p. 1)—i.e., literature reviews.

The integrity of scientific research may be threatened by a variety of behaviors that range from intentional, serious misconduct at one extreme (instances of *corruption*, cf. Tables 6.4, 7.1), to well-intended but biased practices at the other. The middle of the continuum is populated by practices and procedures many of which are of questionable propriety, some of which may be questionable only under certain circumstances, as well as innocent conditions such as random (Type I—"false positive") errors that pollute the record. What they all have in common, along with mundane instances of sloppy work or use of incorrect statistical methods, is posing a challenge to the integrity, veracity and utility (i.e., the overall quality) of the scientific product.

One of the best indicators of the quality of science is the replicability of its findings. In fact, "the replication of research findings … and peer review … represent the standard means for guarding against dishonesty and error in science" (Kimmel, 2007, p. 308). Replicability has become quite a salient and contentious issue in psychology—e.g., Ferguson (2015), among many others, refers to "the replication crisis." It has even been aired in the popular press (Carey, 2016; Van Bavel, 2016), sometimes with unsettling implications (Carey, 2015b). But it is an enormous topic, and much of the concern is only related tangentially to our primary topic of ethics, per se.[3] Consequently, this chapter will only consider in passing the issue of replicability and its companion, *publication bias*, which is also related to the over-reliance on *null hypothesis significance testing* (NHST); the primary focus will be on misconduct. Later in the chapter peer review also is considered.

---

3 On June 7, 2022, a google search on "replication in psychology" yielded 36,300,000 results, up from 4,710,000 six years ago; limiting the search to "replication crisis in psychology" yielded 5,560,000 hits, up from just 409,000.

Concern for Scientific Misconduct

According to the federal Office of Research Integrity (ORI) research misconduct did not become a matter of public notoriety until a U.S. congressional sub-committee held hearings in 1981 on then-recent cases of misconduct at four major research centers.[4] This resulted in the passage of some beginning legislation in 1985; explanatory *Guidelines* were published in 1986; and the Final Rule, "Responsibilities of Awardee and Applicant Institutions for Dealing With and Reporting Possible Misconduct in Science," was published in the *Federal Register* in 1989, codified as 42 CFR Part 50, Subpart A; it was updated on May 17, 2005 in the *Federal Register*, as 42 CFR Parts 50 and 93, "Public Health Service Policies on Research Misconduct." (This process of federal legislation having a major impact guiding professional activities ought to be familiar to I-O psychologists of a certain age, based on our experiences following passage of the Civil Rights Acts of 1964 and 1991, Age Discrimination in Employment Act of 1975, Americans with Disabilities Act of 1990, et al.)

In 1989 two offices were opened in the Department of Health and Human Services (DHHS) and National Institutes of Health (NIH) for dealing with research misconduct. In 1992 they were closed, and their functions con-solidated into the ORI. Additional legislation in 1993 established ORI as a separate entity within DHHS, independent of the agencies that fund research. In the mid-1990s ORI began many research and educational programs, in-cluding a study of the consequences of whistleblowing on whistleblowers. By 2000, "The role, mission and structure of the ORI was focused on preventing research misconduct and promoting research integrity principally through oversight, education, and review of institutional findings and recommenda-tions." Accordingly, it currently administers training programs such as for in-stitutions' *research integrity officers* (RIOs), constructs instructional materials and runs seminars for many constituencies including graduate students. It also publishes a newsletter, reports on misconduct findings regarding individuals, and posts regularly on a Twitter account.[5]

Definitions

Research Misconduct: Fabrication, Falsification and Plagiarism (FFP)

Box 14.1 presents the definition of research misconduct promulgated by the ORI of the DHHS. Note that it is defined both narrowly and broadly. It is defined

4   Obtained from < https://ori.hhs.gov/historical-background > on June 7, 2022.
5   In addition to those resources a widely used training program is the Collaborative Institutional Training Initiative (CITI), started in 2000 and is available at https://about.citiprogram.org/.

narrowly as pertaining to just three specific unethical actions: *fabricating* or *falsifying* material and *plagiarizing* the work of others; it specifically excludes honest mistakes or disagreements. This is reiterated in APA's Ethical Code (2017; Standards 8.10 Reporting Research Results, and 8.11 Plagiarism). It is defined broadly because it captures a very wide, inclusive domain of activities and settings. For example: (a) it pertains to not only conducting and reporting research, but also to research proposals or to reviewing the work of others; (b) "research" may even include a demonstration project; and in virtually every discipline that employs empirical research with living (human or animal) participants; (c) "falsification" pertains to not only data, but to anything that renders the research record inaccurate; (d) the "research record" includes any form of communication, in any medium; (e) "plagiarism" includes appropriating even someone's ideas without acknowledging their source; and (f) because "intention" is often difficult to prove, demonstrating that the misbehavior(s) in question was done "knowingly" or "recklessly" is sufficient.

In Table 6.4 and in "Adding Further to the Framework for Ethical Decision Making" at the end of chapter 7 (No. 14), I presented five general paradigms of ethical dilemmas. Two of them seem particularly relevant as potential threats to research integrity. They are *temptation* (contemplating an action in accord with some self-serving motive, goal or ambition that would be unjust, deceitful or cause harm to another), and *coercion* (being pressured to violate ethical standards). For example, in discussing the issue of "HARKing" (see below) Kerr (1998) "believes that most authors who HARK are responding primarily to strong external incentives: to the way the system works" (p. 213).[6] Also in chapter 7 (Table 7.1), I summarized six non-independent constructs illustrating definitional confusion in the study of misconduct in organizations. In our field, intentional violations of research integrity (in an organizational context) as defined above, have been characterized alternatively as *unethical behavior, organizational deviance, corruption, organizational misbehavior,* or as *counterproductive work behavior.*

Thus, it is probably not surprising to learn that I agree with Macrina's (2014) focus on individual values of the scientist, and the core "values of the scientific community" (p. 35) as the bases for the promotion of research integrity. Based on reviewing international publications in the area he generated the following list of characteristics: honesty; trust; fairness; openness; accountability; stewardship; objectivity; accuracy and reliability; impartiality and independence. A similar list compiled by Shamoo and Resnik (2009) overlaps in several instances and adds confidentiality; respect for colleagues, intellectual property, the law, and research subjects; and social responsibility.

---

6 "Strong external incentives" may consist of attractions (temptation), or repulsions (coercion).

BOX 14.1   THE FEDERAL GOVERNMENT'S DEFINITION OF RESEARCH MISCONDUCT AND REQUISITE EVIDENCE

Research Misconduct Defined

Research misconduct is defined as fabrication, falsification, or plagiarism in proposing, performing, or reviewing research, or in reporting research results … .

Research, as used herein, includes all basic, applied, and demonstration research in all fields of science, engineering, and mathematics. This includes, but is not limited to, research in economics, education, linguistics, medicine, psychology, social sciences, statistics, and research involving human subjects or animals.

Fabrication is making up data or results and recording or reporting them.

Falsification is manipulating research materials, equipment, or processes, or changing or omitting data or results such that the research is not accurately represented in the research record.

The research record is the record of data or results that embody the facts resulting from scientific inquiry, and includes, but is not limited to, research proposals, laboratory records, both physical and electronic, progress reports, abstracts, theses, oral presentations, internal reports, and journal articles.

Plagiarism is the appropriation of another person's ideas, processes, results, or words without giving appropriate credit. Research misconduct does not include honest errors or differences of opinion.

Findings of Research Misconduct

A finding of research misconduct requires that:

- There be a significant departure from accepted practices of the relevant research community; and
- The misconduct be committed intentionally, or knowingly, or recklessly; and
- The allegation be proven by a preponderance of the evidence.

From "Federal Research Misconduct Policy," *Federal Register*, Dec. 6, 2000 (Vol. 65, No. 235, p. 76260–76264). Downloaded from https://ori.hhs.gov/federal-research-misconduct-policy, June 7, 2022.

Impact of FFP

Steneck (2006) points out that "fabrication and falsification obviously can have significant impacts on research. A researcher who intentionally publishes fabricated or falsified research results clearly undermines the reliability of the research record and of all decisions and/or relationships based on that research" (p. 62). In contrast he points out that...

> ... . plagiarism has no necessary impact on the reliability of the research record. Results are results, whether or not the person reporting them deserves credit for their discovery. Plagiarism may waste some funds ... . It can also undermine trust between colleagues ... and potentially cause some public harm ... . Therefore ... plagiarism cannot be ignored, but the extent of its impact on research is probably small in comparison to other irresponsible behaviors. (p. 62)

Nevertheless, I would be remiss not to point out that it is considered sufficiently serious by the academic and scientific community to get a publication retracted, a dissertation revoked, a student expelled, or a researcher seriously censured, perhaps dismissed from their position. Any uncovered instance of FFP contributes to the "image problem" noted above.

Additional "Questionable Research Practices" (QRPs)

For at least 30 years it has been recognized that a great many forms of scientific misconduct may be committed that don't necessarily rise (perhaps the more appropriate path is "sink") to the egregious level of FFP (Committee on Science, Engineering and Public Policy, 1992). However, it would be mistaken to think of these as trivial transgressions or as unimportant because of their distorting effects on our science and sometimes contamination of relations within the research community. In fact, some investigators have become convinced that researchers themselves are more concerned about misconduct at this level of "more mundane, everyday problems in the work environment" that seem much more prevalent than serious FFPs (DeVries et al., 2006, p. 43; also, John et al., 2012; Martinson et al., 2005). However, their concern may emanate not simply because of that prevalence, but from the realization that "reproducibility forms the cornerstone of scientific progress ... . [and] researchers have recently begun to investigate questionable research practices (QRPs) as an important cause of low reproducibility" (Linder & Farahbakhsh, 2020, p. 335; see the section on "The Issue[s] of Replication," following).

Focusing on the analysis and reporting of data, Sterba (2006) classifies QRPs as either overt or covert misconduct. Some examples of overt misconduct include dichotomizing continuous data to create significant findings; and cross-validating exploratory data procedures with confirmatory procedures on the same data set (observed in many structural equation modeling studies). Sterba notes that these practices have been denounced in the literature for decades "yet are still quite prevalent" (p. 307). Covert misconduct includes practices such as selectively trimming the data; capitalizing on chance variation in a number of ways (e.g., failing to adjust the Type I error rate when it should be done); and several forms of selective reporting.

An important realization is that many overt procedures are potentially detectable by sophisticated methodologists, but covert procedures are not. Wasserman (2013) has proposed a set of "ethical guidelines for researchers who are post-data collection and beginning their data analysis" (p. 3). Assumptions underlying her work are that the major causes of these practices involve incompetence, carelessness, interpersonal anomalies, inadequate supervision of junior researchers, and/or a work environment that does not support ethical conduct.

Steneck (2006) discusses many QRPs that have been revealed in a variety of surveys. They include (in no particular order): publishing the same data or results in more than one publication; breaking up a study into multiple publications ("salami slicing"); assigning authorship credit inappropriately; inadequate record keeping; changing the order of authors on publications listed in one's c.v.; listing unaccepted papers as "in press" on one's c.v.; inventing bogus publications; granting honorary or ghost authorship; summarizing findings inaccurately in a manuscript's abstract; social and theoretical biases in the publication process (linked to country of origin, institutional affiliation, research orientation); bias in the design, interpretation or reporting of a study for a variety of reasons, including the source of funding; failure to conduct a proper literature review; failure to disclose conflicts of interest, such as involvement in firms whose products are based on one's research; and failing to present data that contradicts one's previous research or theoretical model.

Fanelli (2009) adds: "mining" the data to find a statistically significant relationship that is then presented as the original focus; and selectively publishing only when a study supports one's hypotheses. Ferguson (2015) further adds: stopping data collection only when statistical significance is achieved; selecting only the data analytic strategy that produces significance; convenient exclusion of outliers; convenient inclusion or exclusion of covariates in statistical analyses; and running multiple independent experiments but reporting only those with significant results. DeCoster et al. (2015) include some of those listed above, and include examining different ways of transforming variables, examining the same hypothesis using different analyses or in different subgroups of participants or by using different methods and scrutinizing undesirable findings more closely than desirable findings. Based on focus groups with scientists DeVries et al. (2006) note 11 common misbehaviors; from large-scale surveys Martinson et al. (2005) add 16; and John et al. (2012) list 10 more. Even assuming some overlap, it seems like the list could be endless. Some of those just itemized involve instances of "hypothesizing after the results are known" (HARKing) (Kerr, 1998).

The Deceptive Practice of Post-hoc Hypothesizing (HARKing)[7]

While Kerr (1998), a social psychologist, referred to HARKing, Leung (2011), a management scholar, referred to PPHA ("Presenting Post hoc Hypotheses as A priori," p. 472). They are both concerned about its damaging, potentially unethical aspects, and likely widespread occurrence in psychology and organization studies. In a fascinating and somewhat remorseful *mea culpa*, an unidentified senior scholar admits to having engaged in the practice in order to get published—partly for the benefit of his untenured coauthor—but nevertheless believes that "if any significant part of research is 'secretive' or could be construed as disingenuous or duplicitous, then there are viable grounds for suspecting that *is* unethical" (Anonymous, 2015, p. 216, emphasis in the original).

Kerr presented five versions of HARKing. They all involve "taking the post hoc plausibility of hypotheses into account in deciding what hypotheses to advance in the report's introduction" (p. 198). I will describe briefly the three versions that he reports a sample of 156 behavioral scientists in three disciplines having observed frequently among their colleagues.[8] They are:

i. **Pure HARKing**. Adopting and advancing any plausible hypotheses consistent with known results, especially the current set, even if they were seen as implausible or unanticipated a priori.

ii. **Suppress Loser Hypotheses.** Adopting and reporting only those a priori hypotheses that were confirmed. I.e., suppressing any plausible a priori hypotheses that are contradicted by the data.

iii. **Empirical Inspiration.** Correctly adopting and reporting all hypotheses seen as plausible a priori (even if not confirmed), but also hypotheses not seen as plausible or that were unanticipated a priori. (This seems to be viewed as less severe than ii because there is no suppression of disconfirming evidence.)[9]

---

7   I pay special attention to this issue because of its potential distorting effects on the scientific record, the difficulty of documenting its occurrence, and its relevance to the broader issues of significance testing and replication and psychology's supposed "crisis" in that regard.

8   These are itemized as versions 1, 3 and 5 in the original. Numbers two and four are "Pure HARKing + Straw Man" and "Post Hoc Plausibility + Necessity of Anticipation." In addition to the survey results, Kerr discusses some inferential "circumstantial evidence" of HARKing that may be gleaned from research reports.

9   It is also possible that one might observe some interesting, unexpected finding that is unrelated to the focus of the study (probably less likely in controlled experimentation than in field studies) that can be reported appropriately as such (cf. Lefkowitz, 1994).

Adverse Effects

Kerr (1998) identified 12 "potential costs," or adverse effects on science from HARKing. Note that 9 of the 12 are substantially methodological in nature (that is my characterization, not his). For example: (i) when a theoretically un-anticipated finding is advanced as if it had been hypothesized there is a risk of its being nothing more than a Type I error, so "'theory' is constructed to account for what is, in fact, an illusory effect" (p. 205); similarly, (ii) according to Popper (1972; see chapter 10) science advances by our generating theory-based hypotheses that are testable and disconfirmable. But if the hypothesis has been HARKed based on known results, disconfirmability is precluded; and (iii) if a theoretically plausible hypothesis doesn't pan out and those findings are suppressed, potentially valuable information has been lost.

Some years later, Murphy and Aguinis (2019) distinguished between two forms of HARKing (using a different scheme than Kerr's). Using realistic simulations, they found *cherry-picking* to have somewhat less adverse biasing effects on the conclusions drawn from data analysis than does *question-trolling*. Cherry-picking involves picking out from among alternatives the most advantageous operational measure(s) or sample(s) to yield the desired finding (i.e., there is only one population effect under examination). They explained question-trolling as consisting of "searching through data involving several different constructs, measures of those constructs, interventions, or relationships to find seemingly notable results worth writing about" (p. 1).

I would like to highlight three other "costs" identified by Kerr that are particularly relevant to the aims of this book: (iv) as alluded to in the epigram of this chapter, breaches of trust threaten the scientific enterprise. HARKing "violates a fundamental ethical principle of science: the obligation to communicate one's work honestly and completely" (Kerr, 1998, p. 209). As confessed by Anonymous (2015), duplicity *is* unethical (as well as misleading and potentially wasteful); (v) the acceptance, and perhaps the widespread occurrence of HARKing may contribute to a culture of cynicism and more extensive "fudging"; and perhaps most important, (vi) I share Kerr's special concern for the effect of HARKing on students:

> HARKed articles present a rosy picture—a prescient scientist anticipates and correctly predicts a complex pattern of results. When the student begins work, he or she is likely to discover that nature is only rarely so cooperative: Partial successes and undeniable failures are commonplace. Students react to this discrepancy in many ways. Those who make a situational attribution—that actual science is a lot more difficult and unpredictable than published science—are likely to persist and persevere … . On the other hand, those who make a personal, dispositional attribution—that they lack the imagination or talent to do publishable science—are more likely to give up. (p. 208)

There had not been, to my knowledge, any empirical evidence of the extent of HARKing in I-O psychology until Bosco et al. (2016) used "an indirect methodological approach for assessing HARKing's impact because authors do not describe the process of hypothesis generation in their articles" (p. 710). They analyzed more than 500 effect sizes from published research in *Journal of Applied Psychology* and *Personnel Psychology* (Study 1) and from a published meta-analysis (Study 2). They presumed that "if hypothesized relations are stronger than nonhypothesized relations, the difference is likely due to HARKing" (p. 710). That is what they found overall in both data sets: uncorrected correlations of .20 vs. .09, and .22 vs. .16, respectively. They characterize these differences in effect sizes as "large in relation to typical effects reported" (p. 746) in the field, so that HARKing "poses a potential threat to research results, substantive conclusions, and practical applications" (p. 746).[10]

A recent option offered by some journals with the potential to reduce the incidence of HARKing, is *preregistering* a research manuscript—the design and analysis plan for the research are preregistered in a public, open-access (OA) repository. This is part of the *Open Science Framework* (OSF) that also includes publicly sharing all research materials and all data.[11] (See below.)

Incidence of Misconduct and the Monitoring of RCR

As noted above, scientific misconduct was not a salient public issue until the 1980s. At that time, and in the absence of empirical data, although "informal surveys suggested that irresponsible conduct might be fairly common ... . researchers countered these suggestions by arguing that misconduct could not be widespread since it was kept in check by peer review and self-regulation" (Steneck, 2006, p. 54). Even a generation later, "scientists commonly assert that misconduct in research is rare" (Macrina, 2014, p. 13). Steneck (2006) notes that actual confirmed cases of misconduct by the National Science Foundation and the Department of Health and Human Services are very low— "only 20–30 cases in a typical year"—but that "studies have suggested that researchers do not report the misconduct they know about, thereby undermining the main mechanism for discovering misconduct" (p. 57).

But there are better data. Martinson et al. (2005) surveyed more than 3,000 NIH-funded scientists, asking about self-reported misbehaviors that had been

---

10 However, I believe the conclusion should be taken as tentative at best. The data are indeterminative because of a flaw in the study's logic. One should expect higher effect sizes for hypothesized effects, even if they were all proposed a priori (i.e., with no HARKing), because of researchers having generated the hypotheses based on thorough and useful literature reviews of relevant theory and research. Although, other factors such as "confirmation bias" (MacCoun, 1998) could also play a part.

11 For additional information see https://osf.io/tvyxz/wiki/1.%20View%20the%20Badges/.

judged as serious and likely sanctionable by university compliance officers. "Overall, 33% of the respondents said they had engaged in at least one of the top ten behaviours during the previous three years" (p. 738). These were more often instances of QRPs than FFPs. In a follow-up article Martinson et al. (2006) found that self-reported misbehaviors were positively related to perceived violations of distributive and procedural justice. Scientists who "believe they are being treated unfairly … are more likely to behave in ways that compromise the integrity of science" (p. 51). These findings would be predicted by the Theory of Self-Concept Maintenance noted in chapter 7, in which honest people (in this case, research scientists) may give in to a limited degree of dishonesty, especially when it can be rationalized to not conflict with their positive self-concept. And, indeed, it has been observed that some researchers who had engaged in misconduct "thought they could bend research misconduct rules without actually committing research misconduct" (DuBois, 2014, p. 32).

Fanelli (2009) performed a meta-analysis of 18 studies using self-reports from (mostly biomedical) scientists in response to questions asking whether they have committed or know of a colleague who has committed research misconduct.[12] Approximately 2% acknowledged fabricating, falsifying or altering data; and 14% had personal knowledge of a colleague doing so. Approximately 10% admitted to engaging in QRPs. A later meta-analysis, based on some of the same surveys plus others, and focused on plagiarism, yielded an average of approximately 2% admitting plagiarism and 30% knowing a colleague who had done so (Pupovac & Fanelli, 2015). That analysis also found that the rate at which scientists admit having fabricated or falsified data, or committed plagiarism has declined over time, from 1987–2010, mostly in the U.S.

Koocher and Keith-Spiegel (2010) reported on a survey of almost 2,600 Principal Investigators (PIs) who had received NIH funding from any of 15 federal agencies. Almost 84% of them were aware of or "suspected acts of scientific wrongdoing" (p. 438)! The most frequently reported wrongs were (in descending order): fabrication or falsification; questionable publication practices (e.g., "gift" authorship); plagiarism; creating an unsuitable work environment (e.g., sexual harassment); and incompetence (e.g., inappropriate data analyses).

Promoting Compliance and Transparency

Gross (2016) offered four mechanisms for the prevention of scientific misconduct. The first, and probably most problematic is *whistleblowing*. Based on the belief that "Responding to an allegation of research misconduct tends to be a unique rather than a routine event at most institutions" (ORI, 2014) the Office of Research Integrity

---

12 As misconduct is most often a private act, anonymous self-reporting is used frequently in surveying unethical behavior (cf. Andreoli & Lefkowitz, 2009).

offers website support in "handling misconduct." Also available is a "User-Friendly Guide" to responding to research wrongdoing, prepared by three psychologists (Keith-Spiegel et al., 2010). Self-regulation is one of the rights and responsibilities of a profession (cf. Chap. 9). Therefore, the accepted norm in psychology is to "get involved" if one is aware of wrongdoing (APA Code, 2017. Standard 1.04 Informal Resolution of Ethical Violations). Consequently, one of the valuable features of the "User-Friendly Guide" is the attention it pays to the emotional and interpersonal difficulties and complicated feelings likely to be engendered when contemplating getting involved—either informally (generally recommended at first, if possible) or formally. Koocher and Keith-Spiegel (2010) found that 63% of the PIs they surveyed who reported an incident of observed wrongdoing did take some sort of action, generally informal. An interesting finding is that "Respondents reported lingering misgivings in 40% of cases in which they had direct evidence of wrongdoing but chose not to act. Those feelings sometimes lasted for years" (p. 439).

Gross's (2016) other suggestions involve the RCR training courses offered by the federal government; a call to de-emphasize the number of publications as an important criterion for appointments, tenure, promotion, etc. (in a similar vein, cf. also Luthar, 2017; Sternberg, 2016); and data recording and data sharing (aspects of "Open Science"). Also, as noted earlier, considerable attention has been paid recently to advancing rigorous *reporting standards* for empirical research studies in psychology (Applebaum, et al., 2018; Eich, 2014; Kazak, et al., 2018; Levitt, et al., 2018).

The Issue(s) of Replication

When a psychologist suggests that we have a "problem" concerning replication (or a "replication crisis" or a widespread "failure to replicate") either or both of two things might be meant: one is a normative issue reflecting a paradoxically negative opinion of the value of studies designed to replicate prior research findings. It is paradoxical because it is generally accepted that "repeatability is the primary assurance of the integrity of research data ... . The ability of other investigators to replicate the experiments by following the method in the published report is crucial to the advancement of science" (Shamoo & Resnik, 2009, p. 51).[13] Yet, despite the critical importance of replication, it is widely observed that "Successful replications are unpublishable; journals reject such research saying, 'But we already knew that.' Of course, the failures to replicate are also unpublishable; we all learned that our first week in graduate school ... . The justification for that practice is that 'there are a lot of reasons why a good, published study will fail to replicate'" (Spellman, 2012, p. 58). So, for this first version of the replication problem, "the replication crisis is not a crisis because

13 Psychology's "replication problem" has been associated primarily with experimental, social, and cognitive psychology, but it has received attention vis-à-vis clinical, counseling, and school psychology as well (Tackett, et al., 2017).

some areas of psychology have not been replicated, but rather that the debate over replication has revealed *an academic culture in which a central tenet of science, replicability, does not appear to be universally valued*" (Ferguson, 2015, p. 529, emphasis added). The reader may recall (cf. Chap. 10) that some psychologists have expressed concern for the putative liberal (as opposed to conservative) bias of psychological research. Accordingly, Reinero et al. (2020) investigated whether such a political slant in research findings might be related to the replicability of the findings. It wasn't.

The second meaning of "replication problem" refers to a methodological issue concerning *replicability*—Ferguson's notion that "some areas of psychology have not been replicated"—i.e., it has not been possible to replicate them successfully. This suggests potential problems in the theoretical basis, design, execution, analysis and/or reporting of research; the fault(s) may reside with the original study and/or the replication. In other words, the implicit question concerns the reproducibility of psychological science. Recall that among the public criticisms of psychology reviewed by Lilienfeld (2012) was "psychology does not yield repeatable results."

Psychology seems finally to be attending to the replicability issue, with the promotion of a new type of journal article, a collaborative Registered Replication Report (RRR) (e.g., Holcombe, 2016; Landy et al, 2020; Simons, 2014; Simons et al., 2014). "These reports compile multiple replications of a single effect, conducted by labs throughout the world who all agree to follow a preregistered and vetted protocol. The end result is not a judgment of whether a single replication attempt succeeded or failed—it is a robust estimate of the size and reliability of the original finding" (Simons, 2014, p. 76). Similarly, the organization *Retraction Watch* has initiated "The Pipeline Project" in which multiple labs agree to conduct pre-publication independent replications (PPIRs) of a selected body of work before it is published.[14]

As discussed below, replicability is also related to long-noted problems associated with the emphasis on *null hypothesis significance testing* (NHST). Box 14.2 outlines the interrelationship among all these issues, some of their antecedents and unfortunate effects. The consequences are "disappointing" for researchers, journal publishers and editors, as well as for others who care about the integrity of science and its reputation.

But before proceeding further, it is worth noting the admonition from Nosek et al. (2022) regarding some basics: "*A finding can be reproducible, robust, replicable, and invalid at the same time* … . However, conducting replications can help identify sources of invalidity if those sources of invalidity are present or absent across replications" (p. 723, emphasis added). In the same vein, Vazire et al. (2022) "propose that the credibility revolution in psychology, which has its roots in replicability, can be harnessed to improve psychology's validity more broadly" (p.162).

---

14 See https://osf.io/q25xa/.

BOX 14.2 THE VICIOUS CYCLE OF DISAPPOINTING RESEARCH

1. Academic researchers are under enormous internal and external pressure to publish to obtain tenure, promotion, career success, feelings of self-worth and recognition.
2. The cost of running a journal is very expensive so there are few publication outlets relative to the large number of researchers graduated every year.
3. The journals that do exist are under economic pressure and so restrict page limits available.
4. All of the above results in very low "acceptance rates" for manuscript submissions, especially for the coveted "top-tier" journals (Aguinis et al, 2020). This, of course, exacerbates the pressures and stress on researchers, journal editors and reviewers (the "gatekeepers").[15]
5. To maximize the putative utility of available journal space, preference is afforded to "new" and/or "theoretically meaningful" studies, not to replications of prior published research.
6. For the same reason, preference is also afforded to manuscripts reporting statistically significant findings that support the stated hypotheses—yielding *publication biases*.
7. Researchers, recognizing #5, understandably consider conducting replication studies to be a waste of time and resources and so are not motivated to do so.
8. Researchers, recognizing #6, engage in a variety of procedures, including in some small number of cases, intentional misconduct (fabrication and falsification) and, in a larger number of cases, other questionable research practices—representing *opportunistic biases* and *confirmation bias*. Studies that nevertheless are not "successful" are not submitted for publication—the *file drawer problem*.
9. The questionable research practices surreptitiously (in some cases, unknowingly) inflate Type-I error rates and produce a greater number of statistically significant findings than could be expected based on true effect sizes and the limited statistical power (sample sizes) of most studies.
10. Hence, the corpus of published research is characterized by many Type-I errors, beyond the formal stated risk level ($p < .05$) —i.e., *false positives*.

---

15 The average rejection rate for 65 APA journals in 2021 was 67%. *Journal of Applied Psychology*, at 89%, was tied for the highest (APA, 2022).

11. When attempts are made to replicate published findings they often fail to do so for methodological reasons: insufficient statistical power; or failure to adequately reproduce the original methodology—the *wallpaper effect*.

12. But because of the incidence of false positive findings, even high-quality replications show disappointing rates of replicability, thus reinforcing the pressures and practices enumerated in (1)–(8) and contributing to the negative public image of the scientific enterprise.

Empirical Findings

An informed consideration of the topic must begin with the enormous co-operative study (involving hundreds of coauthors and volunteers in its execution) published by the Open Science Collaboration (OSC) (2015) based on replications of 100 studies from three psychology journals. The motivation for the study was the rationale that "Reproducibility is a defining feature of science, but the extent to which it characterizes current research is unknown ... . Reproducibility is not well understood because the incentives for individual scientists prioritize novelty over replication" (p. 943) (cf. Box 14.2, #5, #7).[16] Moreover, convincing analyses have been made, including in medical research, that in fact "most published research findings are false" (Ioannidis, 2005). And the National Science Foundation (NSF) Directorate for Social, Behavioral and Economic Sciences (2015) expressed concern—not because there was a particular problem in the SBE sciences, but because we are well-suited to understand the problems and develop effective strategies for changing behavior (i.e., research practices).

The great impact and shock waves engendered by the OSC study are a consequence of its information value (a function of its great scope and novelty) and its not very flattering findings. The authors' overall conclusion is that "A large portion of replications produced weaker evidence for the original findings despite using material provided by the original authors, review in advance for methodological fidelity, and high statistical power to detect the original effect sizes" (p. 943). The mean effect size for the replications was approximately half that of the original studies. Only about one-third as many of the replications had statistically significant results (p < .05) as had the originals. The 95% confidence interval of the replication effect sizes contained fewer than half of the original effect sizes. Only 36% to 47% of the studies were successfully replicated (using five different criteria).

Many of the reactions to the study, including articles and op-ed pieces in the lay press (e.g., Barrett, 2015), were critical analyses by psychologists. They often focused

---

16 The authors may have conflated *replication* (testing a prior finding with different data) with *reproducibility* (testing a prior finding with the same data and analysis strategy) (Nosek et al., 2022).

on the difficulties typically encountered in reproducing all the conditions and context of the original studies that might have affected the results—the so-called *wallpaper effect*.[17] But the authors were well aware of the issue and went to some lengths to mitigate it (e.g., contacting the original authors for study materials; having them review the replication plan; archiving everything publicly; et al.). Nevertheless, there are those who still criticize the OSC study because: (a) the replication studies were insufficiently similar to the originals (in some cases using different populations, countries and methods), thus introducing random error; (b) the original studies were not chosen randomly from the three journals; (c) a single replication attempt for each study has insufficient statistical power (cf. RRRs, the Pipeline Project and PPIRs, above); and (d) only 69% of the authors of the original studies endorsed (beforehand) the methodological protocols of the replications, and the replication rate was much higher for those studies (almost 60%) than for the ones not endorsed (15.4%) (Gilbert et al., 2016). Moreover, Patil et al. (2016) found that the results "can be viewed as statistically consistent with what one might expect when performing a large-scale replication experiment … . 77% of the replication effect sizes reported were within a 95% prediction interval calculated using the original effect size" (p. 539). The debate about the OSC study and about replication in general continues within the field (e.g., Landy et al., 2020; Winerman, 2016).

A very recent synthesis of five published replication studies (including the OSC), involving a total of 307 individual replications, yielded rather more favorable findings (Nosek et al., 2022): "64% reported statistically significant evidence in the same direction, with effect sizes 68% as large as in the original studies" (p. 725).[18] Perhaps more important, those authors go on most constructively to discuss "What replicates and what does not?" as well as "Cultural, social, and individual challenges for improving replicability." Space precludes consideration here.

Problems of Statistical Significance Testing, Publication Bias, Opportunistic Bias and Confirmation Bias

Almost all the serious forms of misconduct, HARKing and other QRPs discussed in this chapter are inextricably linked with the norms of scientific publication—e.g., publication decisions by journal editors "favoring studies with positive results over studies with null or negative effects" (de Bruin et al., 2015). The pressure to produce publishable results, especially if one's study has been funded externally, as

---

17 An ironic label, suggesting that research results might differ because they were impacted by extraneous unrecognized minor differences such as (facetiously) the wallpaper design. I-O psychologists are familiar with the notion of *moderator effects*.

18 However, they point out that there was something of a positive bias in the studies because the replication studies were on average 15.1 times as large as the originals, yielding relatively "high [statistical] power to detect a significant effect in the same direction as the original even if the effect size was much smaller in the replication study" (p. 726).

well as the desire for tenure and career advancement, and other "corrupting influences in the current research environment" (Shamoo & Resnik, 2009, p. 55) undoubtedly contribute to the "biased decisions" noted above as QRPs by DeCoster et al. (2015), Fanelli (2009), Ferguson (2015), Kerr (1998), Leung (2011) and Steneck (2006). They are some of the unintended adverse effects of "psychological science's well-known aversion to publishing null results" (Ferguson, 2015, p. 529).

Many of those QRPs can be characterized as providing *opportunistic biases* (DeCoster et al., 2015), which "occur whenever researchers examine multiple analyses before deciding exactly which ones to present as part of a report. The selection process makes it more likely for the researcher to find significant results and larger effect sizes" (p. 499) (cf. Murphy & Aguinis, 2019: cherry-picking and question-trolling). Simmons et al. (2011) refer to these decisions as exercising "researcher degrees of freedom" (p. 1359) and emphasize that the likelihood of observing at least one falsely positive finding "is necessarily greater than 5%" (the customary stated significance level). The result is that *confirmation bias* is facilitated, referring to the observation that a "hypothesis is more likely to be confirmed than disconfirmed irrespective of its truth value" (MacCoun, 1998, p. 269). Unfortunately, there is also evidence from careful reviews of thousands of published articles that scientists play fast and loose with the way in which they report p-values (Krawczyk, 2015; Pritschet et al., 2016). The results are summed up in a famously-titled article from a few years ago, "Why most published research findings are false" (Ioannidis, 2005).

Because of our "aversion to the null" noted above, it can be concluded that virtually all scientific misconduct, questionable practices, and bias (intentional or from ignorance) are motivated by one thing: obtaining (or at least being able to report) statistically significant results that reject the null hypothesis. That is an extraordinary realization because the flaws, limitations and errors of null hypothesis significance testing (NHST) have been known for 50 years or more. Cumming (2014) and Schmidt (1996, 2010) provide informative background and Schmidt shows that the benefits of NHST that most researchers believe to be so are illusory, and the practice "has led to frequent serious errors in interpreting the meaning of data" (1996, p. 120). For example, contrary to popular belief: (i) the significance level of a study *does not* indicate the probability of a study being successfully replicated (the probability of replication is given by the statistical power of the study); (ii) the significance level of a study *does not* indicate the size or importance of a finding (only effect size indices, such as d, do that); and (iii) if a difference or a relation is not statistically significant that *does not* mean that it is zero or essentially zero or due to chance (it simply means that nothing can be concluded; it does not disprove the research hypothesis).

Schmidt (1996) bemoaned that "40 years of logical demonstrations of the deficiencies of significance testing have failed to … convince researchers to abandon the significance test" (p. 127). Fourteen years later he's still chastising us (Schmidt, 2010), and years after that, Cumming (2014) still asked plaintively

"Why is NHST so deeply entrenched?" (p. 11). Fife (2020) responded "Despite passionate and cogent arguments against NHST, several obstacles remain and will remain no matter how red-faced methodologists get" (p. 1055). Exploring the reasons is too far off the topic for us, but I am immediately reminded of Hertwig and Engel's (2016) notion of *deliberate ignorance*—"the conscious choice not to seek or use knowledge (or information) (p. 359)," which can serve as a strategic device. This state of affairs is confirmed by a study demonstrating that published research psychologists "overestimated the power of specific research designs with a small expected effect size, and 95% underestimated the sample size needed to obtain .80 power for detecting a small effect (Bakker et al., 2016, p. 1069).

Schmidt and Cumming each recommended the same solutions. The results of individual studies should be reported in terms of point estimate(s) of the effect size(s) (ES) and their confidence interval(s) (CI). The size of the CI is an index of the precision of estimation. For example, in the present context, a group of studies representing replications of the same research might reveal a low level of "repeatability," as measured by relatively few significant findings, and lead to the abandonment of the research area. But it might also be revealed that almost all the studies, despite variation in their point estimates and low incidence of statistical significance, have confidence intervals that overlap, providing considerable support that there is a true effect. With respect to summarizing and interpreting a body of literature, both authors recommend the use of meta-analysis. Cumming (2014) recommends several additional practices, as well as the use of ESs, CIs and meta-analysis, and refers to them as "The New Statistics" (cf. also Eich, 2014). Shrout and Rodgers (2018) offer several procedural and statistical steps to address all these problems. And Fife (2020) takes a somewhat different, and ambitious, tack and advocates an entire graphic-based eight-step "general statistical-analysis strategy [that] promises to resolve the majority of statistical traps researchers may fall into" (p. 1054).

Open Science

The latest edition of the APA's (2020) *Publication Manual* notes that "most journals require Authors submitting a manuscript for publication to also submit forms affirming their compliance with ethical standards for research and publication and disclosing their conflicts of interest, if any" (p. 11). The form is based on the 15 Standards of the APA Ethical Principles that concern research.[19] The manual also provides a convenient nine-item "Ethical Compliance Checklist" (p. 26) that should be consulted starting in the planning stages of a study.

"Open science practices ... refer to the openness, integrity, and reproducibility of research findings and materials" (Banks, et al., 2019); similarly,

---

19 The form is available at https://www.apa.org/pubs/journals.

"open science ... research practices [are] intended to enhance the rigor and trustworthiness of our science" (Castille et al., 2022); and "open science ... is about making scientific methods, data and findings more accessible ... . Three overarching principles shape open science practices: transparency, sharing, and replication" (Guzzo, et al., 2022); and finally, "open scientific practices... [should] ... provide strong incentives for individual researchers to share data, materials, or their research process" (Eich, 2014). Notwithstanding the worthwhile objectives, the implementation may be slow due to the profusion of challenging practices that have been recommended. In its relatively brief life, the movement has generated a minimum of 24 challenges (Nosek et al., 2015: eight standards of three levels each); plus 21 (Castille et al, 2022: seven standards, three aspects each); and 13 "actionable items" for seven primary stakeholder groups (Banks, et al., 2019), $k = 58$. Even acknowledging some overlap among the recommendations (based on just three sources), it is likely that "the breadth of tactics can be overwhelming and imply an all-or-nothing approach ... that can discourage getting started" (Castille, et al., 2022, p. 459). It is little wonder that those authors recommend selecting just one practice for an individual study, as if one were at a buffet "experienced over multiple visits where different cuisines [practices] are sampled" (p. 459).

A comprehensive approach to promoting an open research culture has been initiated by several organizations, including the APA Board of Scientific Affairs and, most notably, the Center for Open Science.[20] They convened a group of 30 scientists who formed the *Transparency and Openness Promotion* (TOP) Committee (Nosek, et al., 2015), and developed a set of guidelines to counteract "an academic reward system that does not sufficiently incentivize open practices" (p. 1422). As indicated above, the *TOP Guidelines* consist of eight standards. They concern citation standards, data transparency, analytic methods (code) transparency, research materials transparency, design and analysis transparency, preregistration of studies, preregistration of analysis plans, and replication. They are independent modules that can be adopted separately. And they have operationalized three levels of stringency for each, so there can be considerable flexibility in their adoption. As of the end of 2020 over 5,000 journals and organizations had become signatories of the TOP Guidelines and they ceased listing additional ones. Among the most common recommended practices—thought to have potentially ameliorative influences on a host of QRPs, confirmation bias, publication bias, HARKing, opportunistic biases, p-hacking and other distortions of NHST, as well as other corrupting influences—is the preregistration of studies in advance of their implementation and (possible) publication submission. This is thought "to promote a greater focus on the research process ... relative to research outcomes" (Grand

20 Information is available from https://www.cos.io/initiatives/top-guidelines.

et al., 2018; cf. also Toth et al., 2021)—and as noted earlier can also pertain to systematic replication attempts as well as to developmental studies.

Many individual scientific associations have proposed similar (albeit smaller-scale) programs, such as that of the Alliance for Organizational Psychology (2016), comprised of representatives from the International Association of Applied Psychology (IAAP)—Div. 1, the Society for Industrial-Organizational Psychology (SIOP), and the European Association of Work and Organizational Psychology (EAWOP).

For the skeptics (or very cautious) among us, it's worth acknowledging that I-O psychologists have also presented a dramatic and sophisticated description of several ways in which open science practices may be incompatible with the advancement of knowledge "in disciplines founded on connectivity between science and practice" (i.e., applied research) (Guzzo, et al., 2020, p. 3). For example, transparency and data sharing may be precluded by using proprietary methods and protecting participant and organizational anonymity; the exclusive requirement of a priori theory- and hypothesis-formulation and testing will preclude the fruitful use of inductive and abductive methods with "big data" (Guzzo, et al., 2015) using dozens of variables, multiple levels of analysis, many potential moderators, etc., resulting sometimes in "unexpected discoveries, especially when studying social systems such as organizations" (2020, p. 33). Note, however, ethical/justice concerns have also been raised concerning the use of big data (Yankov et al., 2020).

A Philosophical Integration

Going beyond proposed methodological remedies, we have Linder and Farahbaksh (2020) to thank for attempting to shed some systematic philosophical light on the "grey area of justifiable and unjustifiable practices" that separates QRPs from legitimate methods of inquiry (p. 335). They use a deontological, largely Kantian framework focused jointly on two dimensions: (i) the rules, norms and motives that guide the individual researcher's data analytic practices; and (ii) the extent to which those procedures could legitimately be accepted as normative for the field. The first is rooted in Kant's notion of a reasoned and unequivocal good—i.e., *good will*, or moral justification (cf. Chap. 4). In other words, it doesn't matter if one's practices are driven in part by individual-personal career success (achieving publications, tenure, promotion), if they also follow the reasoned dictates of doing one's moral and professional duty. The second focuses on whether those practices also can be accepted as a generalized expectation for the entire field—i.e., the *universalizability* of a *categorical imperative*. Note, however, that is rather in contrast with a more cynical Hobbesian belief that "some questionable practices may constitute the prevailing research norm" (John et al., 2012, p. 524), and when it comes to scientific standards, a "centralized mechanism for vigilance and enforcement" may need to be created (Engel, 2015, p. 361). It is all reminiscent of the aphorism "trust but verify!"

Professional Relations[21]

Chapter 13 began with a consideration of "The Social Nature of the Research Enterprise," emphasizing the several important ways in which "the proper treatment and protection of research participants" reflect interpersonal relations, including an imbalance in status and power, between researchers and their voluntary study participants (primarily college students and company employees). The same realization applies to relations among and between researchers, collaborators, colleagues, advisees, journal editors and reviewers. And the same principles pertain: honesty, trust, fairness, respect and nonmaleficence.

The Rights and Responsibilities of Authorship

As noted earlier, for scholars and researchers publication is the means of obtaining employment, career advancement and long-term success, professional recognition, and self-esteem. (In I-O psychology it may be less true for practitioners.) Many do not think the venerable expression "publish or perish" to be much of an exaggeration, if at all. In recent years, because of growing specialization, subspecialization and interdisciplinary and cross-cultural projects, collaborative studies with multiple authors are more the norm than the exception, thus giving rise to concerns for the proper assignment of publication credit. The primary *right* of researchers is to have their contributions to the research recognized accurately and fairly. In general, one earns the right of authorship by having made a substantial contribution to the study, and the byline credits should "accurately reflect the relative scientific or professional contributions of the individuals involved, regardless of their relative status. Mere possession of an institutional position, such as department chair, does not justify authorship credit" (APA, 2017, Standard 8.12 Publication Credit). That sounds all-well-and-good, but in most instances clarification is necessary. Which "contributions" count? What is their relative importance? And how is that decided?

Shamoo and Resnik (2009) have helpfully enumerated the process of research that can be used as a guide. The components are:

1. Defining problems; 2. Proposing hypotheses; 3. Summarizing the background literature; 4. Designing experiments; 5. Developing the methodology; 6. Collecting and recording data; 7. Providing data; 8. Managing data; 9. Analyzing data; 10. Interpreting results; 11. Assisting in

21 The balance of this chapter owes much to the organization and insights of Francis L. Macrina (2014), Adil E. Shamoo and David B. Resnik (2009), and the authors of individual chapters in Bruce D. Sales and Susan Folkman (2000). One chapter cannot do justice to the thoroughness of those sources, so the interested reader is directed there.

technical aspects of research; 12. Assisting in logistical aspects of research; 13. Applying for a grant/obtaining funding; 14. Drafting and editing manuscripts. (p. 103)

In an academic setting, various of these roles may be carried out by a professor who is the principal investigator (PI), other professor-collaborators, a laboratory manager, graduate students or postdoctoral fellows, undergraduate students, lab assistants or technicians and statistical or equipment consultants. Apportioning credit is primarily a matter of the subjectively judged importance of the component(s) and the amount and quality of the work performed.[22] Given the indeterminacy of the multiple possible solutions to the end product, and the generality of ethical principles like fairness and justice,

> ... it is unlikely that an appeal to ethical principles alone will provide unequivocal resolution [if a] dispute involves differing interpretations of the nature and significance of individual contributions. Consequently, one of the recommendations ... is that individuals involved in collaborative research, including faculty-student collaborations, establish agreement on how research responsibilities will be apportioned and how research credit will be allocated prior to initiating a joint research project.
>
> *(McGue, 2000, p. 75)*

Such an agreement, however, is not set in stone. There are any number of reasons that it may warrant periodic review and revision.

Authorship of a research publication submission also "affirms who accepts responsibility for it" (Macrina, 2014, p. 83). Those responsibilities include agreeing with and being willing to defend the conclusions and interpretations of the study, as well as the order of authorship credit; knowing that it was conducted ethically and reported accurately; and that it is not being considered for publication elsewhere (McGue, 2000).

Peer Review (PR)

Peer review (PR) is a remarkable procedure. Think about it. The determination of whether one's scholarship is worthy of being publicly recognized is based entirely on independent judgments of fellow scholars who may be total strangers. The process depends largely on volunteers, and many researchers are both authors and reviewers. It epitomizes a valuable collaborative social system, creating a de facto

---

22 Obviously, things may be a lot more complicated because of particular research designs and settings such as large-scale multi-component studies, field studies, ongoing longitudinal research programs, et al. Moreover, the same components may differ in importance for different projects.

moral community of interest. Moreover, the system is not merely "valuable," it is indispensable. "It is hard to imagine any reasonable alternative to peer review. Without peer review, researchers would have no way to control the quality of articles or funded research or to promote objective, reliable research—there would be no way to separate the wheat from the chaff" (Shamoo & Resnik, 2009, p. 123). Of course, given all the fallibilities and prejudices of human judgment, there are weaknesses, limitations and ongoing sources of complaint; it can be improved. What social system is perfect? What is remarkable is how relatively well it does work most of the time.

Macrina (2014) suggests that a manuscript review has two functions—to help the editor decide regarding publication, and to contribute to the quality and effectiveness of the published study.

The Domain of PR

Peer reviews occur in at least nine guises. They differ in such matters as context or setting; the specific purpose; structure and formality (e.g., whether a guide or format is provided to be followed); and whether the process is anonymous. But they all involve an evaluation of the quality of a scholar's research product by a peer, and when done responsibly, constructive feedback is provided as well. They occur in circumstances in which the peer(s) may serve in one or more of the following roles:

1. Journal editor or member of an editorial board. One of these will ordinarily be the *corresponding editor* in communication with the author(s) of the submitted manuscript.
2. *Ad hoc* journal reviewer or *referee* who has volunteered to be available and is assigned a manuscript (generally in one's area of expertise) by an editor. These reviews are generally *single-blind* (the reviewer is anonymous) or *double-blind* (both reviewer and author are anonymous—except to the editor).
3. Reviewers of submissions to professional conferences. A similar function to #2 but generally with shorter manuscripts or proposals. And many more to review (anonymously) in a relatively short period of time, so generally briefer critiques.
4. Reviewer of grant proposals, rather than completed manuscripts, as a member of a panel or "study section," on behalf of a government or private funding agency. Identities of the specific reviewers may be confidential even if the panel is known. The applicant is often known because the review includes an evaluation of the applicant's body of related work.
5. Reviewer of research proposals as an identified member of an institutional review board (IRB). In the opinion of many, this differs from #4 in that the review is purportedly confined to potential ethical issues raised by the study

design, not its scientific adequacy; and the board will ordinarily contain members from a variety of disciplines as well as a representative external to the institution.[23]

6. Editor of a volume comprised of chapters or sections written by authors generally invited to do so by the editor. In this guise, the peer reviewer has a clear self-interest in contributing to the quality of submissions.

7. Member of a university departmental appointments, tenure, and promotion committee in which the totality of a colleague/candidate's past scholarly accomplishments are evaluated. Typically, members of the committee are public, and their overall evaluation is known but individual judgments are confidential.

8. Like #7, but as an "outside reviewer," typically in the candidate's disciplinary area but not at the same university. The reviewer may be among those suggested by the candidate and/or be solicited by the university administration. The review is generally, but not invariably, kept confidential.

9. Consultant on behalf of a book publisher, asked to provide an evaluation of a book proposal submitted to the publisher for consideration. The reviewer will ordinarily work in the topic area of the proposal and may have been suggested by the nascent author or chosen by the publisher independently.

Some Issues in the PR Process

As was noted above, "there are weaknesses, limitations and ongoing sources of complaint" concerning PR. Many of these have been elucidated in detail by Macrina (2014) and Shamoo and Resnik (2009), and I have relied on those sources for much of what follows.

How is a reviewer's impartiality assured?

Some potential reviewers may be disqualified because of a role relationship with the author—being at the same institution or having collaborated recently. But the "bottom line" answer to the question is some combination of the reviewer's professional reputation and their personal integrity, sense of responsibility and commitment to the process. As indicated in the next issue, that does not always pertain.

---

23 IRB approval is a prerequisite to ethically conduct a study with human participants and to publish the findings. It is not surprising, therefore, that there has long been much contention surrounding the process (National Research Council, 2003). Kimmel (2007) also reviews many of the issues. And in the opinion of some (e.g., Rosenthal, 1994) "ethics and scientific quality are very closely interrelated. Everything else being equal, research that is of higher scientific quality is likely to be more ethically defensible" (p. 127).

Collegiality and professionalism

As noted above there are two main functions served by reviews (helping the editor's decision-making; helping to improve the manuscript), and "the peer reviewer does not have to be an adversary to do either of those jobs" (Macrina, 2014, p. 108). An experienced author and journal editor recently described six types of reviews/reviewers he has encountered (Ward, 2016). One of them is characterized positively as *Enthusiastic and supportive*. The other five, not so much. They include: *Bitter and twisted* ("… reveals a reviewer's sense of being out of place in their field, a situation with which they are not happy and that comes through in the review"); *In my day* ("… experience is drawn upon to comment on how things are different than they once were. Different not in a good way! … There once was a time … when the field was better …"); *It is all about me* ("… for some reviewers, the review is a chance to showboat, to use it as means of generating citations for their own work"); *Goalpost moving* ("Presented with a revised paper … this review … asks for a second set of revisions based not on the original paper but on the revised paper"); and *Not much to work with* ("Whether they are negative or positive, the content is so minimal that there is relatively little with which to work as an editor … . There is little explanation or justification for the decision").

Conflict of Interest[24]

Reviewers are generally asked to review a manuscript that is related to one's expertise and may even overlap directly with one's own work. The norm of confidentiality notwithstanding there is all sorts of mischief that could be done by one so inclined.[25] For example, the contents of the paper may be useful for the reviewer's own research; criticizing the paper harshly or delaying the review in an untimely fashion might allow the reviewer to publish his/her own research first. These are intentionally corrupt actions. Moreover, similar actions could be taken by third-party others if the reviewer fails to maintain the privileged confidentiality of the process.

Reliability and validity of reviews

I am not alone in having had manuscripts rejected by one journal in the field and accepted by another (and then, in one instance, viewed as important and interesting enough to have been excerpted for another publication). Shamoo and

24 This chapter concludes with a broader discussion of conflicts of interest.
25 Recall the type of ethical dilemma noted as *Paradigm II* in chapter 7, "Temptation: Contemplating an action in accord with some self-serving motive, goal or ambition that would be unjust, deceitful or cause harm to another."

Resnik (2009) review research documenting "significant bias and low agreement of opinions on the same proposal or potential publication … . Some of the biases that can affect peer review include theoretical, conceptual, and methodological disagreements; professional rivalries, institutional biases, and personal feuds" (p. 117–118). Most times the cause(s) of inconsistent reviews are not known. I very recently received two simultaneous reviews of a manuscript I submitted for publication in which one reviewer described it as "beautifully written and documented with excellent points," while the other reviewer wrote that it was "overly long and hyperbolic."

It is also generally recognized that even simple errors are often not caught by reviewers, and that "the process of peer review generally is not designed to detect fabricated and falsified results" (Macrina, 2014, p. 112).

Controversial and/or interdisciplinary work

Certain manuscript submissions are particularly difficult to evaluate. These include new and controversial research, and interdisciplinary studies. The issue re interdisciplinarity is the most straightforward: are there reviewers sufficiently knowledgeable in the combination of areas represented to afford a meaningful review? Assembling a few reviewers, each of whom has expertise in some of the areas, may not be adequate if they fail to appreciate the integrative aspects of the research or its theoretical underpinnings. The different disciplines may even have different evaluative standards for publication. New and controversial work can present an even more difficult set of issues. "Research can be controversial for a number of reasons: it may be highly creative or innovative, it may challenge previously held theories, or it may be interdisciplinary" (Shamoo & Resnik, 2009, p. 118). Those authors go on to discuss the biasing effect of reviewers who are often "established researchers with theoretical and professional commitments, [who] may be very resistant to new, original, or highly innovative ideas or ideas that challenge their own work" (p. 118).

Responsibilities of Reviewers

Based on all the foregoing we can readily infer that a potential reviewer should consider the following before agreeing to a PR assignment. Am I qualified to review this paper, considering its conceptual, design and data-analytic content? Will my schedule allow me to do so in a prompt and timely fashion, in the framework requested? Do I have any potential personal, institutional, theoretical or commercial conflicts of interest that might render giving a fair and objective review difficult? Am I cognizant of and comfortable with the requisite norms of confidentiality, collegiality and professionalism to render an appropriate and constructive evaluation?

Advising and Mentoring

In addition to the explicit course curricula and related activities by which students acquire their knowledge and skills regarding the research enterprise there are the *informal curriculum* and the *hidden curriculum* (Hafferty, 1998). The informal one refers to the unplanned, ad hoc, mostly interpersonal exchanges with faculty that take place daily; the hidden one is the implicit set of influences that I-O psychologists are familiar with under the rubrics of organizational norms, climate and culture. On a different topic, I have written previously about my belief that "these are the two modes ... in which many of our students are implicitly socialized into I-O's corporatist value system" (Lefkowitz, 2014a, p. 41) (cf. Chap. 12). But whether it's a corporatist value system at issue, or the values of performing competent, responsible and ethical research, the socialization process entails our activities as mentors and advisors. (I use *advising* to refer to imparting information about the more formal and structured aspects of fulfilling degree requirements. *Mentoring* is broader and may include some advising, but generally involves many more and more complex matters, as described below.)

Recently, the notion of an *educational pipeline* has been extended from its customary usage in K–12 education, to graduate school, postdoctoral training, and employment for those with a doctorate (Kaslow, et al., 2018). The emphasis has been on the often-neglected transitions between these pipeline stages, "such as selecting psychology as an undergraduate major, applying to and getting accepted into a doctoral program ... , applying and matching with a doctoral internship program, obtaining postdoctoral placement, becoming licensed (if applicable), and securing employment, and possibly subsequent employment" (p. 47). An invaluable and gratifying contribution to this approach has been offered by Jaremka et al. (2020) who attempt to destigmatize the common experiences of repeated rejection, imposter syndrome, and burnout—as "common academic experiences no one talks about" (p. 519).

In discussing the ethical aspects of the mentor-student relationship, Shamoo and Resnik (2009) note the following salient points:

- The relationship is asymmetrical. Mentors have greater power, experience, knowledge, and control over the student.
- Although mentors may depend on their students for research or teaching assistance, students are more dependent on their mentors for everything from education and training to emotional support and job recommendations.
- Students are highly vulnerable so it is possible they can be manipulated or abused.
- As a consequence of all the above, the relationship is reasonably thought of as *fiduciary* in nature, meaning that the primary issue is a moral responsibility for the well-being of the student.

Mentoring Processes[26]

In the context of our focus on RCR, it can be stated simply that the mentor-student relationship is one of the most important (arguably, *the* most important) ways in which newcomers to the field learn and come to appreciate the proper treatment and protection of research participants and the integrity of the scientific enterprise. Tangney (2000) put it very well:

> Researcher-supervisors may be in a special position to help bring to life abstract ethical principles in a way that formal course work may not; ethics training in the context of an ongoing research project has immediate relevance to students. Moreover ... such context-based training in ethics teaches students much about the process of ethical problem solving and decision-making ... . By learning about research ethics through hands-on experience, students can learn to become active ethical agents. (p.98)

Following is a brief enumeration of the ways in which mentoring takes place:

1. Explicit teaching of how to *do* research and *be* ethical, as well as other procedural knowledge.
2. Providing a role-model of *doing* research and *being* ethical.
3. Evaluating and critiquing constructively the student's research, writing and teaching in a manner appropriate to the student's level of professional development.
4. Providing advice and fostering socialization regarding the formal rules and informal norms of collegiality, being a researcher (and/or practitioner) and teacher, attending professional conferences, et al.
5. Promoting the career development of trainees by advising about networking, introducing them to colleagues, coaching interpersonal skills, recommending them for awards, jobs or other forms of recognition, et al.
6. Because of the primacy of the mentor-student relationship, the mentor should be sensitive to potentially difficult aspects of the student's personal life. Faculty differ, however, in the extent to which they tend to "get involved." I believe it is highly contingent—on the particular issues that may arise, the mentor's predisposition in this regard, and the nature and quality of the dyadic relationship.

---

26 Both Macrina (2014) and Shamoo and Resnik (2009) have written extensively about "characteristics of the mentor-trainee relationship," and "important [mentoring] activities," respectively. The description of *mentoring processes* is in part an amalgam of their insights.

7. Taking the lead in developing a relationship with students characterized by mutual respect, trust, open communication, and encouraging increasing levels of responsibility in ways that always have the students' best interests in mind.

Potential Problems in the Mentoring Process

Effective performance of those seven functions entails a mix of competencies that may not have been acquired in the faculty member's own education as a graduate student and post-doctoral Fellow. From an institutional view, therefore, academic departments and programs should not assume that "it will just happen," or that every newly minted Assistant Professor possesses those competencies. There should be an institutional commitment to the process; fortunately, structured guidance is available from the National Academy of Sciences (1997) and National Institutes of Health (2000). Nevertheless, because of a lack of preparation and the asymmetrical nature of the relationship, problems have been known to occur. For example:

*   A student may not be credited fairly for work performed (e.g., as a co-author).
*   A student may be taken advantage of by being given too much work, for the benefit of the mentor.
*   A student may be given misinformation or bad advice.
*   A student may be taken for granted, mistreated, intimidated, discriminated against or harassed in numerous ways.
*   Favoritism may be shown to some student(s) and not others.
*   The mentor may be insensitive to or ignore a student's psychological distress and fail to recommend help.
*   The mentor may fail to monitor the student's performance, and progress, or provide appropriate feedback.
*   The academic department or program may not have provided sufficient and clear appeal procedures for students to use when there is a problem in the relationship.
*   There is general agreement that faculty should "be sensitive to the potential conflicts that may arise in cases in which they have essentially dual roles with student research assistants (e.g., when serving as both employer and faculty evaluator)" (Tangney, 2000, p. 101). In particular, Macrina (2014) believes that "projects in which the mentor has a monetary stake or other compelling interest are not acceptable training experiences" (p. 66). This raises a particularly salient issue for I-O psychologists who simultaneously may be professors, researchers, and consultants to organizations. It is not unusual for graduate students to be given consulting assignments, with the supervision of a faculty advisor—especially when the consulting project is indistinguishable

from bona fide "research" (i.e., it aims in part to produce generalizable knowledge to be published in a scientific journal). In some cases, with respect to some applications, it is highly unlikely for an I-O student to gain such experience any other way. In other words, remuneration notwithstanding, the work assignment legitimately contributes to the education and training of the I-O student. (In fact, the career trajectories envisaged by many I-O students favor full-time professional practice.) Yet, that does not diminish the potential role conflict for the professor, who is both a fiduciary advisor to the student and their boss while serving a paying client—a client whose interests may not be entirely coterminous with those of the student.

Conflict of Interest

This chapter has already touched on a few issues pertinent to a consideration of conflicts of interest (COI). They include, in the order in which they appeared: public skepticism about the integrity of science and scientific research; a rise in the number of journal retractions; establishment in the 1980s of federal legislation and government agencies concerned with research misconduct; QRPs and other biased practices as a consequence of "corrupting influences" in the academic and scientific environment; impartial peer review of colleagues' work, including possible COI; fiduciary nature of the advisor/mentor's relationship with student advisees; and potential conflict when serving as both a faculty advisor and employer of students.

A comprehensive literature review by Bekelman et al. (2003) confirmed that

> financial relationships among industry, scientific investigators, and academic institutions are pervasive. About one fourth of biomedical investigators at academic institutions receive research funding from industry. One study reported that lead authors in 1 of every 3 articles published hold relevant financial interests, while another reported that approximately two thirds of academic institutions hold equity in 'start up' businesses that sponsor research performed by their faculty. (p. 463)

Is that worrisome? Well, in their meta-analysis of eight review articles covering 1,140 original articles in biomedical fields they found a statistically significant relationship between industry financial sponsorship of research and pro-industry study conclusions. Also important because it speaks to potential mediating mechanisms, in their literature review they "found 4 studies that empirically demonstrated that industry preferentially supports trial designs that favor positive results" (p. 463). That is a rather rare instance of documenting a corrupting influence.

In the field of nutrition-related research (206 articles over five years, concerning soft drinks, juice and milk), it was found that "funding source was significantly related to conclusions" (Lesser et al., 2007, p. 41). "For intervention studies, the proportion with unfavorable conclusions was 0% for [studies that had] all industry funding versus 37% for no industry funding (p = 0.009)" (p. 41). And more recently we have learned that our over-concern for the role played by fat, saturated fat, and dietary cholesterol in the etiology of coronary heart disease—and not added dietary sugars—has been due in great measure to the sugar industry trade association's payments to Harvard nutrition researchers in the 1960s (Kearns et al., 2016).

Very illuminating, you might admit, but what has all this to do with I-O psychology? (After all, the potential harm from conflicts of interest in biomedical research, especially clinical trials, would seem much greater than for any I-O research.) Just over 20 years ago Russell et al. (1994) published a meta-analysis of 28 years of criterion-related validation studies (N = 138) from the *Journal of Applied Psychology* and *Personnel Psychology*. They investigated the interesting questions of whether some extraneous factors might be shown to affect observed validity findings—such as "the reason or reasons why a research project was initially conducted," or "the reward structure faced by investigators," or "the original motivation or impetus to conduct a research project" (Pp. 164, 165). They found that (a) "average validities reported by first authors employed in private industry were significantly greater than those reported by first authors employed in academia (.32 vs. .24, p < .001)"; (b) "projects conducted to address some organizational need yielded significantly higher mean criterion-related validities than projects conducted to address some investigator interest (.32 vs. .24, p < .001)"; and (c) "projects conducted to address EEO concerns and augment existing selection system validities both yielded mean validities greater than those found for studies conducted primarily to maximize validity or to test theories: .331 versus .281 and .218, p < .001)" (p. 166).

Russell et al. were primarily interested in the implications of their findings for the conduct of validity generalization studies. But the following observations they made are apt for our purposes: "It appears that original research in personnel selection contains blind spots caused by combinations of investigators' KSAs and reward contexts"; and that "real-world investigators from industry, academia, consulting, and the public sector will probably not decide to conduct identical job analyses, to operationalize criteria the same way, or to use comparable test administration procedures (i.e., make the same judgment calls)" (p. 169). The currently unanswerable question is what the reasons are for that. Might the mediating mechanisms (strategic decisions regarding the design and conduct of one's study and interpretation of the data; possible unconscious biases and motivated distortions) employed by the authors in the Russell et al. validation studies be like those by the authors of the biomedical and nutritional research studies noted above? Is having one's drug evaluation study funded by an industry source with a vested interest in the product being evaluated substantially different than conducting a validation study for compliance with EEO concerns on behalf of the organization subject to legal review?

I don't mean to suggest that there is conscious malfeasance on the part of any of the researchers whose work was meta-analyzed, above—nor could I, without more information about the primary studies. Nor is that necessary to make the point. For example, we know that people harbor unconscious prejudices that they find ego-alien when they learn about them after experiencing feedback from the Implicit Association Test (Banaji & Greenwald, 2013). Similarly, "people may be influenced by financial, personal or other interests even though they are not aware of their effects. People often claim that they would never deliberately allow personal, professional, political, or financial interest to affect their thought processes or behavior" (Shamoo & Resnik, 2009, p. 190). Another example:

> many physicians deny the potential for the receipt of small promotional items to undermine their professional objectivity ... . In fact, researchers have found that the more gifts a physician receives, the more likely he or she is to believe that they do not influence behavior ... . [But reviews] correlated physician-detailer interactions with marked physician preferences for new products that hold no demonstrated advantage over existing ones, a decrease in the prescribing of generics, and a rise in both prescription expenditures and irrational and incautious prescribing.
>
> *(Katz et al., 2003, p. 40).*[27]

That is an example of how COI works.

Figure 14.1 illustrates the potential effects of COI—on the quality of the research record, and on the public perception of the integrity and value of science. An actual conflict of interest that adversely affects the research is mediated by the conflict-influenced actions of the researcher(s) and by other possible effects not attributable to the researcher(s) (such as by the actions of others who are the source of the competing interest). Whether the tainted research findings and the COI itself result in adverse public reactions depends on the widespread availability of that information. In other words, the transparency of the situation (e.g., from news reports or other mass media) moderates the effects of the COI and the tainted findings on public perception.

An essential point to be made (illustrated in Figure 14.1) is that adverse public skepticism may result from the mere *appearance* of a COI, in the absence of any conflict-influenced actions by the researcher(s) and the absence of any taint to the findings. That brings us to a consideration of some definitional issues.

Definitional Matters

Perhaps because of the significant influence of government involvement, there is a high degree of consistency among the experts who have written about COI in

---

27 A "detailer" is a drug (or medical device) company representative who visits physicians' offices, often several times a month

scientific research and academe in general (Bradley, 2014; Kalichman et al., 2016; Korenman, 2006; Sales & Lavin, 2000; Shamoo & Resnik, 2009). What follows is a condensation of their scholarship.

Conflicts of Interest (COI) versus Apparent COI

Essentially, they are the same thing because "the conflict lies in the situation, not in any behavior or lack of behavior of the individual. That means that a conflict of interest is not intrinsically a bad thing" (Korenman, 2006, p. 1). In other words, people don't necessarily act on all their "interests." Bradley (2014) succinctly defines COI as "when an individual exploits, or appears to exploit, his or her position for personal gain or for the profit of a member of his or her immediate family or household" (p. 217). The essence of the situation is that the individual has competing or contradictory interests regarding the same activity (an "interest" is defined as a goal, objective, commitment or value). The classic situation is when the possibility of gaining something of personal value potentially conflicts with the execution of one's responsibilities or duties. It does so by affecting one's thought processes (judgment or decision-making) and/or actions. Guidelines from the Department of Health and Human Services (DHHS) and the National Science Foundation (NSF) focus on significant outside financial interests and require disclosure by researchers funded by the agencies of amounts over $5,000 and $10,000, respectively, received from potentially conflicting sources (Kalichman et al., 2016).

Forms of Conflict

It will be helpful at this point to recall the taxonomy of five forms of ethical challenges or dilemmas I designated at the end of Chapter 7 (cf. #14 of the framework for Ethical Decision making, and Table 6.4). Briefly stated, the five paradigms are: I. The opportunity to prevent harm; II. Self-serving temptation; III. Conflict between competing roles; IV. Conflict between competing values; and V. External coercive pressures. Each of the forms of conflict elaborated in the RCR literature can be understood as an exemplar of one or more of these paradigms.

Conflict of Interest

"A conflict of interest in research exists when the individual has interests in the outcome of the research that may lead to a personal advantage and that might, therefore, in actuality or appearance compromise the integrity of the research" (Korenman, 2006, p. 1). In other words, a temptation for personal gain of some sort exists (Paradigm II) that incentivizes behavior counter to the proper execution of the research—whether or not that occurs. Several situations may be described as such but are rarely if ever discussed in this context in I-O research and/or practice. For example, (a) being asked by an organization to conduct a needs analysis in some area (e.g., supervisor training) for the purposes of preparing a Request for Proposals, to which you will be among the bidders; (b) conducting a validation study of an assessment device or survey instrument that one has developed and copyrighted and markets commercially to clients; (c) being asked to recommend the best comprehensive employee selection system for a particular client's needs, including assessment of a KSA for which you own one among many comparable and available instruments; (d) being asked by a journal editor to review a manuscript that presents evidence in favor of a theory of leadership that is an intellectual competitor of another such theory that you have developed and advanced. The reader probably could suggest others. Bradley (2014) discusses COI in various domains of activity: (a) in the conduct of science (e.g., reviewing others' manuscripts for publication or grant applications for funding); (b) academic conflicts (e.g., when outside entrepreneurial activities benefit from the reputation and/or resources of the academic's university); (c) intramural conflicts (e.g., serving on a tenure review committee); and others.[28]

Conflict of effort or Commitment

Many professionals work long hours and feel stressed and overworked. This often occurs because of having multiple sets of responsibilities, each with associated non-overlapping duties. A university professor may have extensive undergraduate as well as graduate level teaching duties, be conducting a research program, serve on department or university committees or have other administrative responsibilities, advise students, serve on dissertation committees—and especially, perhaps, do a little outside paid consulting as well. The potential for a form of role conflict (Paradigm III), due to the multiple time demands is apparent, and is not necessarily a COI. (It is also possible that the source of some of the demands invokes Paradigm V—external coercive pressures.) The most salient version is when the outside work commitments interfere with performance of aspects of the primary academic employment, thus transforming a mere conflict of effort/ commitment to a COI as well. Many universities have mechanisms in place to limit and document such outside activities.

Conflict of Duty

This may take the form of a substantive role conflict (not based on time pressures) (Paradigm III) and/or a values conflict (Paradigm IV). Again, they are not necessarily

---

28 Bradley (2014), Korenman (2006), and Shamoo and Resnik (2009) each present several case studies.

COIs. For example, a student, for reasons they believe important, might insist on implementing an independent research project in a manner that their professor is virtually certain will be ineffective. Which is the professor's greater duty and more important moral value—to respect the student's autonomy and allow the "growth experience," or to prevent harm and promote what is ostensibly in the student's best interests? (Note that this example invokes Paradigm I, Opportunity to Prevent Harm, as well.)

Conflict of Conscience

This, too, does not involve potential financial or other personal gains, so it is not necessarily a COI. It differs from other conflicts in that it often goes unrecognized by others. Although "deeply held personal beliefs are appropriate determinative factors in individual choices … . [a] dilemma arises when one's personal beliefs are imposed on others … . A conflict of conscience arises when the convictions of an individual are allowed to override scientific merit in reaching a decision" (Bradley, 2014, p. 215, 216). I believe this can be considered a form of values conflict (Paradigm IV). Bradley adds a critical observation: "Quite often there will be differences of opinion on whether a conflict of conscience is viewed in a positive or negative light" (p. 216). For example, should I refuse to accept a human factors consulting assignment aimed at improving the efficient production of a civilian model of the AR-15 assault rifle? Should I (also) refuse to be the chair of a student's dissertation committee, if his on-site factory field research is an investigation of whether some group-process intervention has the same effect? (What have you concluded from chapters 10 and 12 about the role of personal values in psychological research and professional practice?)

Conclusion

The potential problem of COIs, for both individual researchers and for their institutions, was exacerbated in 1980 by a passage at the federal level of the Bayh Dole Act (35 U.S.C.§200– 212).[29] It enabled and encouraged scientists and their non-profit academic institutions to develop profitable financial relationships with industry, exploiting the intellectual property of the universities. Products that were initially developed with the aid of federal research funding led to disclosure requirements of the DHHS or NSF, as noted earlier. This has had the greatest impact on biomedical science, which is why so much of the literature of COI focuses on that domain. Similar disclosure requirements have been implemented in other government settings such as for the

---

29 The legislation is available at http://www.unemed.com/wp-content/uploads/2015/ 06/35-U.S.C.-200-212-Bayh-Dole-Act.pdf.

researchers who are members of the many advisory committees that report to the Food and Drug Administration (FDA).

Although this has not been a particularly salient issue in I-O psychology, I have tried to illustrate by examples the potential relevance of COI in I-O research, practice and in academic settings. As Shamoo and Resnik (2009) observed: "Individuals and institutions have many different duties and interests. Only a hermit could avoid all COIs and apparent COIs" (p. 205).

Adding Further to the Framework for Ethical Decision Making

42. In recent years the veracity of scientific inquiry has been called into question, and public skepticism has included psychology and other social sciences. It is reminiscent of similar issues directed particularly at I-O psychology half a century ago (cf. Chap. 12). While I-O has largely overcome many (not all) of those challenges, psychology is in the midst of major soul-searching and has been initiating constructive enhancements to the openness, transparency and veracity of the scientific enterprise. This has been initiated in part by governmental regulation but also driven by professional self-correction from within the field. To the extent that surveys shed light on misconduct, it seems that serious transgressions are rare and that less serious (but still worrisome) research practices are more common. These include persistent logical and data analytic biases.

43. Replication remains a dynamic and contentious issue, with considerable disagreement about whether it is a problem of "crisis" proportions. It is the heartbeat of science, and the process is affected by ethical, theoretical and methodological shortcomings, but there are no norms of expected repeatability that might serve as objective standards.

44. The honesty, trust, care and respect that must characterize the ethical researcher's relationship with volunteer research participants (cf. Chap. 13) is no less true regarding professional relations among research collaborators, coauthors, research assistants, graduate students and advisees, peer reviewers and others who contribute to maintaining the integrity of the scientific enterprise. This extends also to recognition of the potentially damaging effects of conflicts of interest. These can be anticipated and avoided if appropriate, or managed and disclosed, as is often required.

SECTION IV
Conclusion

15

A MODEL FOR TAKING MORAL ACTION

In this last chapter I present a strategy for approaching, analyzing and resolving ethical issues. It is predicated on a belief that the nearly infinite variety of human interaction virtually guarantees that each of us will at some time be confronted by a problem with moral implications that, on one hand, does not seem to generate a useful intuitive solution, and on the other hand, is not articulated adequately in our professional or organizational codes or casebooks. On such occasions, it is helpful to have an overall strategy and some general guidelines to follow as a path to taking moral action.

The strategy offered here consists of three stages. The first stage refers to the ongoing anticipatory steps that every professional ought to maintain with the objective of preventing or minimizing the occurrence of ethical problems. The second stage is a *predecisional audit* based on a distillation of the 44 summary items or learning points gleaned from the preceding chapters. The third is a re-commended 11-item procedure for *making ethical decisions and taking moral action*, to be implemented following one's personal predecisional audit taking.

But before embarking on a description of those stages it will be useful to briefly revisit a preliminary question. How might one determine when to invoke these (latter two) sets of procedures? That is, how does one know that a problem is ethical or moral in nature? What is the domain of moral action?

The Domain of Moral Action

As derived from normative ethical theories like the ones reviewed in Part I, as well as from the study of moral psychology and moral and social values, a pro-blem is generally considered to have ethical implications if it involves one or more of several dimensions of human interaction that reflect fundamental moral

DOI: 10.4324/9781003212577-19

or ethical principles and that are enshrined as such in formal codes of conduct (e.g., APA, 2017; Canadian Psychological Association [CPA], 2017). Wittmer (2001) noted that two additional elements of an ethical situation are that one is faced with a choice and that one's actions are expected to have significant impact on the welfare of others. Thus, he concluded, "an *ethical situation* is taken to be essentially one in which *ethical dimensions are relevant and deserve consideration in making some choice that will have significant impact on others*" (p. 483).

The function served by the ethical dimensions or moral principles is to guide one's deliberations by providing the criteria with which reasoning and action can be assessed and justified from a moral perspective. As noted throughout this book, however, the principles are abstract and general, so the criteria tend to be vague. Indeed, that is why ethical codes such as that of the APA and the CPA articulate more specific *ethical standards* that reflect the general principles. In addition, the principles contain no intrinsic indication of their relative importance (although not causing physical harm or pain to another is at or near the top of the list of most moral philosophers). Their generality and indeterminate rank order cause difficulty when they indicate conflicting resolutions. Even the best ethical analysis, therefore, will sometimes leave the decision-maker in a quandary; in fact, the use of ethical principles for guidance can make the decision more complex (Newman & Brown, 1996). Even on those occasions, however, the process may nevertheless help sharpen the issues.

Depending on how narrowly or broadly conceived and multifaceted each of the principles is defined, the domain of moral action has been represented by from two meta-dimensions (e.g., Justice and Welfare) to six or seven principles. I have categorized them into five subdomains.

Respect for People

The origins of this subdomain are largely deontological—distinctively Kantian—as well as based on theories of human rights like John Locke's and Hegelian notions of self-realization. It directs our attention to actions that reflect the rights of all persons to be treated with respect and dignity and to be allowed to exercise their rights to privacy or confidentiality, freedom, autonomy and self-expression. We are to view these rights and liberties as *universalizable*—that is, as much applicable to anyone else as to ourselves—and as bounded by corresponding reciprocal obligations. Your autonomy rights (e.g., to pursue your research objectives) do not necessarily extend to the point where they supersede my right to decide whether I wish to participate in that research.

Fairness and Justice

This dimension is informed primarily by ethical theories based on the social contract and by political, sociological and psychological concepts of procedural and distributive justice. It is among the more nebulous of the ethical principles and more subject to interindividual variability in interpretation as a function of one's personal and social values (cf. Skitka & Tetlock, 1993). Being just may be conceived *characterologically* as the essence of virtue. Being *treated justly or fairly* may be viewed in a Kantian sense as having an appropriate balance of rights and duties. *Social justice* refers to the properties of a social system, such as an organization or an entire nation, and is generally defined in terms of a fair distribution of the system's benefits and burdens. Normative ideas of what constitutes appropriate distributive criteria—hence which outcomes are seen as right or wrong—tend to be culturally determined by the nature of the economic and/or political system of a society. For example, in the private sector the American preference is for equity (merit) over equality and need, even to the point of tolerating extreme and dysfunctional disparities in income and wealth. In the public sector, e.g., in the courts, equality is the ideal. Models of social justice from political philosophy help us distinguish between (largely predetermined) outcomes that merely reflect the differential opportunities and degrees of economic and political power between people, versus truly impartial outcomes that can be defended rationally and accepted as fair even by those with vested interests, or by those who haven't fared so well in terms of those outcomes.

Caring: Beneficence

This principle derives from consequentialist moral theory and the empathy-based perspective of an "ethics of care" in moral psychology—especially as reflected in the traditional service ideal of the professions. For example, "providers of I-O psychological services are guided primarily by the principle of promoting human welfare" (APA, Committee on Standards for Providers of Psychological Services, 1981, p. 668). An ethics of care is driven by the meta-principle of *universalism*—that no one's interests, including one's own, counts for more than those of anyone else's unless reasonably justified. But we can expect the universalist standard to be at odds with the reality that we care more for some persons than others. In addition, those to whom we owe some special obligation, duty or responsibility may justifiably make a special claim on our concerns. Consequently, in an organizational setting those special cares and concerns that we feel for friends and certain coworkers may conflict at some point with the universalist norms of fairness as impartiality and equal treatment, or as equity and merit, which are meant to be the primary determinants of our professional behavior toward others. "Playing favorites" is generally frowned upon.

In earlier chapters I pointed out that some deontological (e.g., libertarian rights-based) views focus virtually exclusively on the avoidance of doing harm; doing good is not viewed as a salient ethical obligation. Indeed, calling someone a "do-gooder" is sometimes meant in disparagement. As noted earlier, the classical libertarian position seems an anemic version of morality and an egoistic denial of the adaptive advantages of prosocial, cooperative and communal behavior. Nevertheless, it is reasonable to acknowledge some limitations on the obligation to be beneficent. It even may be difficult to differentiate between moral acts of beneficence and mere socially conventional behavior. There are ambiguous boundaries—between doing the ethically right thing versus merely being polite, and between being unethical versus ("merely") being rude.

The principle of beneficence is especially appropriate in relation to those who help further our own interests (e.g., employees, students, advisees, clients and research participants). This is certainly the case for those who occupy positions of lesser status and power, so we are in a position uniquely capable of providing benefit to them and may even bear some fiduciary duty to do so (Beauchamp & Childress, 1994). In other words, the extent to which one may be expected to do good depends in part on one's social status and on the circumstances of one's role relationships (Newman & Brown, 1996).

Caring: Nonmaleficence

Although this principle shares some intellectual lineage with the subdomain of beneficence, it is not merely the opposite side of the same coin, and so I have listed it separately. Refraining from unjustifiably doing harm is the principle about which there is the greatest consensus among moral philosophers. It differs from the principle of beneficence primarily in its unconditional and non-contingent nature. Whereas the extensiveness of our moral obligations to do good—especially our emotional commitment to it—may be structured and delimited by the nature of our social identity and role relationships, the obligation to not cause harm is generally thought to apply universally. The principle pertains most appropriately and is felt most keenly with respect to those in vulnerable positions; for I-O psychologists, these people are likely to be employees, students, advisees and research participants. It also extends to a wariness against the possibility that third parties might misuse our work to harm others (e.g., individual assessments, survey findings or other information obtained confidentially). The importance or primacy of this principle is suggested in the APA (2017) code of ethics: "When conflicts occur among psychologists' obligations or concerns, they attempt to resolve these conflicts in a responsible fashion that avoids or minimizes harm" (Principle A: Beneficence and Nonmaleficence). In other words, nonmaleficence is to be given deference in the resolution of ethical dilemmas.

Moral Virtue or Character

The sources of this subdomain are many, including classical Greek philosophy, religious teachings, a Kantian sense of duty, as well as psychological considerations regarding the relative consistency of moral behavior and contemporary intuitionist theory. (Almost every theory seems to have a virtue aspect.) Some ethical statements include principles that may be considered facets of this subdomain—for example, *fidelity*, *integrity in relationships*, *scientific integrity*, and *trust* (APA, 2017; CPA, 2017; Smith, 2000). But as noted in chapter 5 there is considerable disagreement in specifying just what attributes qualify as "virtues," and how many there are (cf. Table 5.1). Therefore, rather than singling out specific attributes like those just mentioned and having to justify the exclusion of others, I have opted to emphasize the broader perspective connoted by *moral character*.[1]

Virtue and character are roughly synonymous, referring to relatively stable personality attributes with the same behavioral manifestations. Included in the domain are traditional moral virtues like truthfulness, integrity, and trust, as well as other attributes that have only more recently been construed by moral psychologists: *moral sensitivity* (Rest, 1994), *moral motivation* (Stocker, 1976), *moral emotions* (Thompson, 2009) and *self-sanctions* (Bandura 1991) (cf. Fig. 6.1). Moral virtue differs somewhat from the first four subdomains (respect, justice, beneficence and nonmaleficence) in that rather than simply denoting an ethical principle (i.e., a content domain), it focuses on the locus of moral action—the person—and emphasizes the role played by a moral character in initiating and shaping the process of ethical reasoning and acting. Moral character refers to both a constellation of ethical traits (e.g., honesty and integrity) and to the associated moral motivations that reflect all the ethical principles, including respect for persons, justice, beneficence and nonmaleficence (Shafer-Landau, 2015).

Stage I: Anticipating Problems

A practical approach to professional ethics should emphasize prevention (Pryzwansky & Wendt, 1999). To use an analogy from public health medicine, if moral problem solving represents the "treatment" for a dilemma, this stage consists of maintaining good "moral hygiene" in an ongoing attempt to reduce the incidence of ethical challenges experienced. Canter et al. (1994) presented a seven-step process of ethical decision-making. However, the first six steps are actually preventive in nature and focus on developing and maintaining the knowledge base on which ethical reasoning depends. Those six steps are discussed next, and I have added a seventh.

---

1 The restriction of virtues to those that are moral in nature excludes such traditional and "selfish virtues" as respectability, chastity, perseverance, prudence and fortitude; they fall outside the domain of ethical considerations as customarily defined by moral philosophers. I also use the term virtue without any religious connotations.

1. **Be familiar with relevant ethics codes.** Canter et al. (1994) referred specifically to the code of the APA, but one might also include that of the CPA as well as codes promulgated by other appropriate organizations or groups of professionals, such as the Academy of Management (2022), the Society for Human Resource Management (2014) and even the International Union of Psychological Science (2008). In a similar vein, it is also useful to become familiar with the sorts of ethical problems most likely to be encountered by psychologists in general (cf. APA Annual Reports of the Ethics Committee; Peterson, 1996; Pope &Vetter, 1992); the particular problems associated with one's field (Eyde & Quaintance, 1988; Eyde et al., 1993; Lefkowitz, 2021; Lefkowitz & Watts, 2022; London & Bray, 1980; Lowman, 1991; Lowman et al. 2006); or with specific areas of specialization (e.g., American Statistical Association, 2022; Hollander, 1998; International Taskforce on Assessment Center Guidelines, 2015; Lefkowitz & Lowman, 2017; Loch et al. 1998; Sashkin & Prien, 1996). To the extent that psychologists sometimes blunder into ethical indiscretions due to ignorance (Keith-Spiegel, 1977), familiarizing oneself with these guidelines and maintaining one's awareness of updates and revisions to the codes may provide a degree of immunization. Indeed, "lack of awareness or misunderstanding of an ethical standard is not itself a defense to a charge of unethical conduct" (APA, 2017, p. 2).

2. **Know the applicable state laws and federal regulations (in the U.S.).** This includes a substantial array of regulations and statutes, including state laws regulating the licensing of psychologists and dealing with issues of confidentiality, malpractice, and research with human subjects. Especially pertinent for I-O psychologists are statutes and regulations governing employment practices, such as the Civil Rights Acts of 1964 and 1991, The Equal Pay Act of 1963, the Americans with Disabilities Act of 1990, the Age Discrimination in Employment Act (1967), the Genetic Information Nondiscrimination Act of 2008, and the *Uniform Guidelines on Employee Selection Procedures* (EEOC, CSC, DOL, DOJ, 1978).

3. **Know the rules and regulations of the Institution where you work.** There are two purposes served by this knowledge. The first is rather straightforward, having to do with assuring appropriate and competent professional practice in keeping with the organization's expectations. The second is more problematic and concerns potential issues of person–organization fit. At the broadest level, it is not unusual for professionals to experience values conflicts with respect to the goals and objectives of the organizations in which they are employed, and these may sometimes manifest themselves in specific ethical dilemmas. The operative stance to be adopted is articulated clearly in the standards of the APA (2017) code:

    1.03. Conflicts Between Ethics and Organizational Demands. If the demands of an organization with which psychologists are affiliated or for whom they are working are in conflict with this Ethics Code, psychologists clarify the nature of the conflict, make known their commitment to the Ethics Code, and take reasonable steps to resolve the conflict consistent with the General Principles and Ethical Standards of the Ethics Code. Under no circumstances may this standard be used to justify or defend violating human rights.

Of course, considering this standard, the preferred strategy is to anticipate potential conflicts in advance of their occurrence so that mutually acceptable strategies can be agreed on when circumstances are calm. (See Point 7 of this list.)

4. **Engage in continuing education in ethics.** Canter et al. (1994) enumerated many of the steps that may be taken in this regard: taking courses or workshops in ethics, subscribing to journals that focus on ethical and professional issues, reading books on ethics pertaining to one's area of practice (and research), and attending seminars and workshops such as those at SIOP annual conferences. I add the practice of initiating exchanges with colleagues about ethical issues and promoting the topic at professional conferences, which would have the beneficial effect of increasing the topic's salience.

5. **Identify when there is a potential ethical problem.** One might say that is what much of this book is about—an attempt to heighten the reader's awareness of potential ethical issues by highlighting (among other things) the role played by one's personal attributes, attitudes and values in the definition and approach to such problems. Canter et al. (1994) focused predominantly on clinical practice and the danger of practicing beyond one's professional expertise. The issue of competence certainly pertains beyond clinical practice. But of more general importance is appreciating the varied manifestations of the five ethical principles constituting the domain of moral action, which serve to alert us that we may be facing an ethical challenge.

6. **Learn a method for analyzing ethical obligations in often complex situations.** Canter et al. (1994) recommended the use of a decision-making model of the sort presented below and by Banks, et al. (2022), as the third and final stage of the overall strategy for taking moral action. I believe that the second, predecisional stage is also helpful, and that the value of any decision-making routine is greatly limited without some rudimentary mastery of moral philosophy and the insights of moral psychology or *behavioral ethics*.

7. **Maintain a mind-set of ethical watchfulness.** Several of the foregoing recommendations coalesce around the notion of avoiding ethically ambiguous situations or clarifying them before one gets involved. Pryor's (1989) notion of *ethical watchfulness* seems like a reflection, at least in part, of one's moral sensitivity (Rest, 1994) in the service of minimizing ethical difficulties.

Watchfulness is enabled by staying familiar with the relevant knowledge domain (Points 1–4 of this list), especially with respect to potential conflicts among obligations owed to different parties; adopting an ethical perspective with respect to the evaluation of any suggested new procedures, strategies, or policies (Point 5); and exercising caution and taking time for reflection and/or consultation (Point 6). "The watchful psychologist seeks, where appropriate, to draw on the collective wisdom of the profession" (Pryor, 1989, p. 298). Over the years, some I-O psychologists have thoughtfully enumerated ethical problems that are likely to be encountered by practitioners in the field (Eyde & Quaintance, 1988; London & Bray, 1980; Lowman, 1991; Lowman et al., 2006). And two SIOP-sponsored surveys of its members have yielded hundreds of verbatim descriptions of ethical encounters (Lefkowitz, 2021; Lefkowitz & Watts, 2022) samples of which are in Tables 6.5 and 15.1, and fully available on the SIOP website.

Stage II: A Predecisional Audit—the Framework For Ethical Decision Making

If one encounters a challenging ethical problem despite having taken the foregoing preventive measures, I suggest that the first steps in the solution of the problem might be to review the perspectives embodied in the 44 summary conclusions or learning points derived in the preceding chapters. This stage is still predecisional because the points deal with contextual or background factors—such as orienting information from ethical models, moral psychology and social and political theory. They are meant to prompt reflections about one's own values and those of the organization(s) and institution(s) within which one functions in the belief that in dealing with potential ethical dilemmas it is best to "clarify and refine our values and ethics before we need to draw on them" (Gellermann et al., 1990, p. 88). Many of the learning points are very general in nature, and so they are relevant to a wide array of ethical difficulties but may not be especially pertinent to the problem at hand. The pre-decisional review is meant to sensitize or cue the actor to potentially salient or enlightening matters that could be useful in the decisional stage of ethical reasoning and taking moral action, including nonrational aspects of the process.

Rather than recapitulating the 44 points seriatim, I summarized and integrated them into six groups according to their sources. To enable more convenient reference, I also indicated their original numbering and the chapters in which they were derived.

Learning Points from Ethical Theory (Chaps. 2, 3, 4 and 5)

The nature of ethical principles has historically been framed by a Manichean battle between those who view them as reflections of subjective feelings and

TABLE 15.1 Examples of Academic and Practitioner Ethical Situations Reported in 2019

Form of dilemma or misbehavior	Academic incidents	Practitioner incidents
Opportunity to Prevent Harm	10. A fellow faculty member was asking inappropriately personal questions during faculty search interviews (e.g., what does your father do?) and making inappropriate comments to minority faculty (e.g., you won't just be a token black faculty member). For a while, she could not participate in interviews at all. Later she was permitted to only when there were other faculty members present. She filed a grievance but the sanctions held.	11. Sent out survey to employees with a confidentiality statement around how the data would be used, who would see it and who would have access to it. Senior leader wanted to use the data to identify a group for a follow-up survey even though this what [sic] not how we said the data would be used. Someone else made decision to use the data.
Temptation	12. We conducted a study and did not find any results. We looked for results in other parts of the study and found something interesting. My colleague wanted to publish this study but I thought it slightly [sic] unethical as we had been "fishing" (though we had a good theoretical explanation for what we found and could base it in theory). I suggested to conduct at least one other study to see if the results hold and are thus not arbitrary. My colleague initially wasn't impressed but we conducted more studies with better measures and the results held and everyone was happy.	13. Data had been coded wrong by mistake for a job analysis survey. I discovered my own mistake only after the review of the survey with the client. It affected a portion of the decisions made. If I kept quiet, no one would know. I told my supervisor and a new meeting was scheduled to go over that portion of the survey.
Role Conflict	14. A new faculty member needed a place to stay for a few days and asked a student to provide housing and transportation. This was inappropriate because the student felt he/she could not decline the request. I am not sure it was resolved at all, The event happened and resulted in tension afterward.	15. There was a perceived conflict of interest between a manager and a supplier, where the two had a declared friendship. A third party raised concerns regarding the evaluation of the supplier and awarding of work. Unbeknown to the third party the manager and his immediate directors had already ensured that the supplier reported to and was evaluated by an unconnected party.

(Continued)

TABLE 15.1 (*Continued*)

Form of dilemma or misbehavior	*Academic incidents*	*Practitioner incidents*
Values Conflict	16. Teach a stats class. The textbook was available for free online so I didn't have the students buy it. I'm basically violating copyright.	17. Improper use of measurement/predictive modelling, resulting in recommending people who will be worse at the job. IO team raised that it was a problem, and argued our stance. We were told that this is a value issue and that we will be continuing to build models that suggest clients should hire less intelligent people. No the issue was not resolved satisfactorily
Coercion	18. Before I received tenure, the chair of my tenure committee stopped by my office one day to talk. During this conversation he brought up his role and that the committee largely felt that I was on track toward tenure. He then mentioned that he would appreciate being added to one of the papers that I was planning to submit as a co-author and implied that this could help with his support through my tenure review process. He asked me to think about it and to let him know if that was something that I would be willing to do and left. Following the conversation I spoke with my department chair to let them know what had happened. I let them know that I felt I was meeting all of the tenure requirements at our university and that I did not plan to respond. As such, I wanted to inform them in case this became an issue. I didn't choose to otherwise report this individual or take action to report them but wanted to make sure that my decision to not agree to their request would [sic] lead to retribution. I never	19. When conducting a survey data collection, one of the manager level employees wanted to check each survey and require his subordinates to re-take the survey if they did not pass the attention check questions. I thanked him for supporting the survey, but let him know that we couldn't require participants to take the survey (at all) or re-take them.

followed back up with them; this individual did a softer ask at a later time and I made it clear that I would be happy to potentially collaborate if they had a project that they felt I could contribute to, but that I would not feel comfortable simply adding their name to a paper that I was submitting (and I chose not to otherwise invite them to work on any of my current projects).

| Incivility or Rudeness | 20. Graduate student informed her advisor, in the presence of another faculty member, that she thought the advisor was engaging in "microaggressions." The Advisor and other faculty members listened to the student's concerns and praised her for speaking up. The advisor met with the student afterward and apologized for any actions that were perceived to be microaggressive, or otherwise hurtful. The advisor and the student later created a mentoring compact. The issue was resolved satisfactorily. | 21. A leader made a joke pertaining to the perils of hiring women (e.g., that they take extended parental leave). The woman who prompted the joke was a mid-level subordinate. She spoke with him several days later and expressed why jokes like his could be harmful. He apologized and has since made an effort to be more sensitive regarding gender issues. |
| Corruption | 22. I alerted editors of numerous top IO journals to apparent data and results fabrication. Some acted appropriately but others acted completely unethically. Some of these admitted that the data appeared to be fabricated but said that they could not act out of fear of being sued by the apparent perpetrators. Others told me that the practice of fabrication was so widespread that it would be unfair to single out these particular individuals. One editor informed the perpetrator that I had contacted the journal to express my concerns, resulting in me getting threatening letters and threats to my personal safety. | 23. A senior HR person at [company name omitted for anonymity] took our proposal for a project and sent it to her husband at [company name omitted for anonymity], who copied our proposal, resubmitted it, and got the project. Our ideas, they got the business. |

Source: Reproduced from Lefkowitz, J. & Watts, L. (2022). Ethical incidents reported by industrial-organizational psychologists: A ten-year follow-up. *Journal of Applied Psychology*, 107(10), 1781–1803. Available on-line Nov. 1., 2021. Used by permission. Incidents are numbered seriatim from Table 6.5.

beliefs and those who view them as representations of objective moral facts, including those of divine origin. An unsuccessful attempt at a resolution has been to take one's cues regarding the specification of moral principles from the empirical facts of human behavior—concluding that what is normative statistically (or of high heritability) should be seen as normative morally. But the logic is flawed, and the diversity of human behavior is too great: What *is* does not provide a sufficient justification for what *ought* to be (Point 6, Hume's Law). A useful middle-ground is the emphasis on ethical reasoning (Point 1). We can accept normative prescriptions based on a well-reasoned rationale and the solution to a moral dilemma if it is supported by better arguments than alternative solutions. As psychologists, however, we are well aware of the potential distortions to which rational deliberations are subject, and so we accept the need for exposing those deliberations to others. Similarly, we are also mindful that behavior tends to be influenced by a variety of motives and external influences so that one's moral reasoning and intentions do not invariably lead to the corresponding moral action (Point 4). The study of moral psychology illuminates many of those additional determinants of action.

A rational, analytic approach also provides a middle-ground solution between the idiosyncratic cultural relativist and the cultural universals position regarding ethical standards (Point 5). The middle way posits a certain number of core values that develop in response to the common problems faced by all societies in having to regulate the behavior of its members, but those values may be expressed in a dazzling variety of culturally linked social customs and practices.

Among the important assumptions or meta-issues underlying moral reasoning are universalizability (Points 2, and 9a) and universalism (Points 3 and 9b). That is, in the first instance, the ethical solution to a given situation should be the same irrespective of who is in the situation. Therefore, your recommendation to a colleague is probably not an ethical one if, faced with the same moral dilemma, you would not behave in the way recommended. Second, ethical behavior must mean more than the expression of mere self-interest. Unless reasonably justified (e.g., by duties and obligations one owes to particular others), no person's interests—including one's own—count for more morally than anyone else's. In addition, the essence of ethics and morality is the right treatment of others, generally respecting their dignity, autonomy, and striving for social recognition and self-realization (Points 9c and 9d).

Although some morally enjoined actions such as the proscription against incest might be associated with immediately and intuitively felt emotional reactions (Haidt, 2001), most ethical dilemmas involve competing motives or values conflicts and are more likely to engender rational attempts at a solution. Because most of us are reasonably well socialized, our ethical solutions are not necessarily experienced as being forced upon us against our will, as Kantian notions of doing one's duty seem to imply. Conversely, we may feel pangs of conscience and guilt over the most mundane transgressions. Therefore, although our feelings may be useful introspective clues to what is salient for us, they are not reliable indicators of the moral rectitude of our intentions or actions (Point 8).

The structure of moral reasoning traditionally has taken either a *deontological* or *consequentialist* form, based in the first instance on principles of right and wrong, duty, obligations, rights, or fairness and justice, and in the second case on the balance of anticipated benefit and harm accruing to all those affected by the contemplated actions. However, both forms of normative theory have been subject to extensive criticism; consequently, they have undergone a variety of structural modifications, some of which tend to render them more alike—for example, the development of rule-utilitarianism and act-deontological views (Point 7). For those reasons, and because some problems seem to lend themselves more readily to one form of analysis than the other, it is prudent to be familiar with both perspectives so that we may avail ourselves of the most relevant one.

The perceived theoretical deficiencies of the two traditional normative models have also contributed to a resurgence of virtue theory, adding a third— *aretaic*—model, that focuses on a more holistic view of the moral actor (Point 12). The emphasis is on moral character and personality attributes, moral motivation and intentions, rather than on adhering to abstract principles, of either a deontological or consequentialist sort. It is not without its own deficiencies as well, such as defining and delimiting what should count as a "virtue." Moreover, the three approaches can lead to conflicting conclusions.

Because ethics concerns not only personal convictions and morality, but the regulation of behavior and power relations between and among people, organizations, and economic and social institutions, it is essentially political in nature, as reflected explicitly in the fields of political philosophy and political economy (Point 10). The implied social contract between employee and employer is an example of such, in which each party has a right to expect dutiful, respectful and ethical behavior on the part of the other (Point 11).

Learning Points from the Psychological Study of Moral Behavior (Chaps. 6 and 7)

The fundamental psychological capacities that enable the development of a mature moral perspective (e.g., empathic sensitivity, and an appreciation of the consequences of one's actions) seem to appear early in life in virtually all cultures, suggesting that ethical behavior is among the critically important and indispensable features of human existence. This implies that ethical considerations should be afforded considerable deference in human affairs and not be conceived of as a discretionary afterthought (Point 13). Common paradigms of ethical challenges studied by moral psychologists include: contemplating an action that would harm or wrong another; anticipating someone's being harmed by a third party; having conflicting obligations from two or more role relationships; facing a situation in which two or more of one's important values are in conflict; and experiencing coercive pressure to violate one's standards (Point 14). (cf. Tables 6.4, 6.5, 15.1.)

Notwithstanding the common core of human potentials, these capacities develop into culturally distinctive patterns of ethical concern. For example, in portions of Africa, the Middle East, Southeast Asia, and the Far East, communitarian group-based principles are more salient than the individualistic rights-based conceptions of justice typical in the west (Point 15). And perhaps most important, the study of moral psychology reveals that ethical conduct is certainly no less complex than other varieties of social behavior (Point 16). It is conditioned by developmental and dispositional antecedents with perceptual, cognitive, motivational, and likely innate components; it reflects schema-based reasoning processes as well as other consistencies of personality and character. Yet there are many influences that dispose toward a lack of individual consistency, too: conflicting values and competing objectives; the cognitive and motivational limitations of our "bounded ethicality"; the consequences of prior ethical decisions; contemporaneous social pressures and other contextual influences including organizational norms and expectations (which may themselves be internally inconsistent); and others. Consequently, there is no compelling reason to anticipate that invariably behaving ethically is easy or should be taken for granted.

Learning Points from the Study of Individual and Social Values (Chap. 8)

Values refer to the relative importance with which we view generalized end states (terminal values) or standards of conduct (instrumental values; Point 17). As core aspects of personality, akin to assumptions one takes for granted, they play a directing role in the formation of our specific beliefs, attitudes and actions concerning how things ought to be. Not all values are ethical or moral; those that are pertain to the domain of moral action (Point 19). Particulars of our upbringing such as "national background, social class, family roots, education and life experiences" (Hofstede, 2001, p. 523) result in individual differences in values and in what is perceived as just (Point 21). Consequently, social conflicts frequently involve principled differences among individuals or groups who disagree about the relative priority of such generalized means and/or ends. In a related manner, intrapersonal conflicts, including ethical dilemmas, also often involve competing values. The complexity of social and moral attitudes and action is increased still further by virtue of (a) distinctions between one's espoused (normative) values and one's less conscious experiential (normal) "values in use" and (b) the unattractive role sometimes played by principled values statements as mere post-hoc rhetorical devices for rationalizing discriminatory and/or self-serving motives (Points 18 and 20).

Even though the primary purposes of many societal institutions and individual organizations do not concern moral matters per se, their actions can nevertheless be viewed from an ethical standpoint—i.e., with respect to the principles defining the domain of moral action (Point 24). This seems eminently true in the case of modern business corporations because of the extraordinary influence and power they wield over people's lives. For the same reason, and because of our contributions to those organizations, we should be thinking of social justice issues as concerning matters beyond the narrow concern for perceived organizational justice (Point 23). This recommended perspective invokes consideration of social justice issues concerning the distribution of benefits and burdens throughout society. United States cultural norms and the capitalist free-market economic system predispose to an equity- or merit-based criterion of distributive justice; with few exceptions, it has been demonstrably effective in maximizing the production and aggregation of material wealth for society overall. However, quite a convincing argument can be made for the moral superiority of the distributive justice criteria of equality or need over merit (Point 22). At the least, in keeping with widely accepted ethical principles, justice criteria of need and equality ought to be considered as a means of attenuating the morally dubious extreme distributional inequities of the so-called free-market system.

Learning Points from the Study of Institutional (i.e., Professional, Scientific and Organizational) Values (Chaps. 9, 10 and 12)

The privileges that accrue to members of a profession entail corresponding obligations to the society that has bestowed that status on the occupation. Chief among these is the expectation that professional expertise will be used "to improve the condition of individuals, organizations, and [the entire] society" (APA, 2017, p. 3), not just for the paying clients (Points 25 and 30). A number of likely points of friction between the structural and cultural features as well as the objectives of large organizations and the values and expectations of professionals who may be employed in them have been well-documented. These include, in the case of public corporations, the overriding importance of enhancing shareholder value to the relative neglect of other stakeholder groups. Although there are reasons to anticipate that I-O psychologists may experience less of those sorts of frictions than members of some other professions, those reasons themselves are troubling to the extent that they suggest our failure to embrace the professional service ideal (Point 27). Although the decades-old criticism of I-O psychology as "unscientific" has not been justifiable for quite some time, the charge that the field has not outgrown the organizational, managerial and anti-labor biases that helped account for its success still seems pertinent (Point 35).

Many I-O psychologists consider themselves entirely scientific and objective in their research and practice, by which they frequently mean that those activities are not influenced by any personal or social values—that their work is value-free. This logical positivist tradition adopted from the natural sciences has undergone serious challenges by *postmodern* or *social constructivist* perspectives for more than a generation, even with respect to basic research. The challenge seems more credible with respect to applied research and professional practice. Without necessarily taking sides categorically in this epistemological "culture war," it seems difficult to imagine how one could accept the value-free assumption when many of the constructs and problems we investigate, as well as the goals and objectives of our professional practice, are influenced greatly if not defined entirely by the corporate enterprise and its dominant value structure (Points 28 and 29). That our field's professional values are so commensurate with those of the organizational cultures in which we work tends to render them invisible to many of us so that the field is mischaracterized as value-free (Point 35). It would seem preferable to articulate all the values that get reflected in our work, from whatever sources—as well as those which are not represented or even controverted—to more fully appreciate the consequences and implications of what we do.

A more morally sensitive (Rest, 1986b, 1994) I-O psychology would have to incorporate an explicitly normative perspective to accompany the scientific and instrumental perspectives that dominate the field (Point 36). To the questions "Is it valid?" and "Is it cost-effective?" we need to add "Is it right?" This would encompass a broader system of values to include psychology's humanistic tradition, greater concern for the individual employee to balance our organizational outlook, and a recognition of the extent to which the societal consequences of our work are as germane as is its technical competence. Recent publications in I-O and the growth of professional awareness indicated by the Global Organization for Humanitarian Work Psychology permit a cautiously optimistic outlook in that regard. This transformational enterprise will be supported by those employee-centered human resource specialists, progressive business leaders, management scholars, other psychologists and business ethicists who have already begun it (Point 37).

Learning Points from the Study of Business Values (Chap. 11)

Business is a moral enterprise. That is, the consequences of business activity are very much within the domain of moral action—involving interpersonal behavior and personal decision-making with substantial effects on the well-being of many, and subject to standards of fairness and justice. Its ultimate justification is the utilitarian one of maximizing the aggregate good. Even the fundamental free-market model of economic activity was couched by Adam Smith in terms of the classical liberal moral philosophy of natural rights theory and the assumption of virtuous dealings (Point 31 and 32).

Notwithstanding the general success of the free-market economic model, many contemporary business scholars, social theorists, and others have challenged its adequacy as a moral model and the consequences it fosters. It is viewed as promoting a narrow conceptualization of life's goods, vast and morally indefensible distributional inequities regarding those goods, and egregiously harmful effects based on the excessive pursuit of power and profits (Point 33). An alternative model has been promoted by those critics, involving the notion of corporate social responsibility (CSR) and recognition of multiple stakeholders with legitimate claims on the concerns of the corporation (Point 34). Their objective is to "foster corporate capitalism that is accountable, ethical, and humane" (Epstein, 1999, p. 253). This alternative version of political economy and philosophy does not appear to be represented much in I-O psychology scholarship and practice; thus, the macro-level values that provide the salient context for our normative views are dominated by the profit-maximization–shareholder value perspective.

Learning Points from the Responsible Conduct of Research with Human Participants (Chapters 13 & 14)

Deontological principles dominate the ethical standards governing research participation: treating people with dignity and respect for their autonomy (so they are free to decide whether to participate in the research and whether to continue their participation); having concern for their well-being and avoiding the infliction of harm (so that if deception or withholding information can be justified by a rigorous review, adequate debriefing will be provided); abiding by principles of justice and fairness (so that people are not coerced into participation by virtue of their lesser social status or other factors); and displaying honesty, integrity and trustworthiness (so that promises made regarding the confidentiality of replies and the potential benefits, discomforts, or risks of participation are fulfilled; Point 39).

The bulk of our research, whether basic or applied, is aimed at fulfilling our own intellectual and professional goals and/or organizational objectives; it is not often, like so-called therapeutic research, designed to directly benefit the specific students, employees or others who participate in it for us. Consequently, they have little, if any, moral or social responsibility to comply with our professional desires (Point 38). In other words, to whatever extent we as professionals have a right to conduct the research for which we have been trained, it is more of an "entitlement" than a "claim." Moreover, it is prudent to proceed on that premise notwithstanding that employees have an obligation to cooperate with legitimate organizational research. And it is our responsibility to know and adhere to the professional and ethical standards and government regulations that codify these principles, irrespective of the setting in which the research is conducted (Point 40).

Despite the categorical objections of some, the ethical consensus in psychology regarding the intentional deception of research participants reflects a reluctant act-utilitarian permissibility. "Psychologists do not conduct a study involving deception unless … [it] is justified by the study's significant prospective scientific, educational, or applied value and that effective nondeceptive alternative procedures are not feasible" (APA, 2017, Standard 8.07[a]). And it must be explained to participants "as early as is feasible" (Standard 8.07 [c]). In addition, the decision to deceive must be approved by an appropriate review committee, such as an IRB (Point 41).

Scientific inquiry, perhaps especially in social science, has been viewed with some skepticism by the public. Some of this concern seems undeserved, but some seem to be related to a variety of questionable research practices. The "good news" is that this has been recognized and acknowledged by the research community and is leading to a variety of procedures aimed at enhancing the transparency and veracity of research methods (Point 42). The "bad news" is that the academic environment remains such that HARKing, publication bias, opportunistic biases, and confirmation bias result in unknown but likely high rates of Type I errors in our research literature, rendering the replicability of that research problematic (Point 43). The responsible conduct of research includes concern for the honesty, trustworthiness and respect afforded peers, students and advisees, no less than for our research participants; as well as attending to the potentially corrupting influence of conflicts of interest (Point 44).

Stage III: A Model for Making Ethical Decisions and Taking Moral Action

It seems apparent that decision-making as a general cognitive construct is on a firm theoretical footing and displays consistent individual differences in adults (de Bruin et al., 2020; Parker et al., 2018). But, as pointed out by Banks et al. (2022), *ethical* decision-making involves elements not included in general theoretical models for decision-making, and so it might be reasonably subject to question. In fact, recent work in moral psychology (behavioral ethics) prompts considering a preliminary challenge to the viability of ethical decision-making: I.e., is effective ethical problem-solving necessary and is it even possible?

Is Ethical Problem-Solving Necessary?

It has been a couple of generations since we have known that people can learn and improve their performance while having no recall of the experience (Graf & Schacter, 1985; Schacter, 1987). Further research on what those authors were the first to call *implicit memory* helped clarify "how past learning, operating in ways that bypass conscious awareness, nevertheless shapes conscious judgment and perception (Greenwald & Banaji, 2017, p. 861).[2] That line of research led to the *Implicit Association Test*, used to measure a variety of implicit attitudes, stereotypes

---

2   They take some pains to impress that *implicit* should be given an empirical definition, as reflecting indirect measurement methods, and not necessarily as unconscious processes. (For example, measures of response latency to paired associates as a measure of relative associative strength.)

and biases (Sleek, 2018).[3] All of this can be understood in the context of dual-process models of cognition (Lieberman et al., 2020) discussed in Chapter 7, in which "various nonconscious mental systems perform the lion's share of the self-regulatory burden" (Bargh & Chartrand, 1999, p. 462) including moral behavior.

Some psychologists believe that encountering an ethical problem elicits intuitive emotional reactions in us, based on innate "moral modules" (cf. the social intuitionist model, SIM, Chapter 6 and Table 6.3). Some emphasize the social acquisition early in the life of moral values and attributes such as moral sensitivity as the origins of our intuitive emotional reactions. But irrespective of one's views regarding their source, it may be that adults tend to have an "immediate, pre-reflective response" (Kitchener, 1984, p. 44) to an ethical situation that is based on some mixture of innate reaction, acquired moral values and sensitivity and introjected prior experiences with similar situations. So, is further conscious deliberation, as with ethical decision-making, needed? I believe that there are several reasons to answer in the affirmative. However useful intuitive responses might occasionally be in situations requiring an immediate reaction, even Kitchener acknowledged that they often are not enough and that critical-evaluative processes are often needed. Correspondingly, Weaver et al. (2014) have pointed out that ethics training (as in business schools) needs to account for the challenging task of "trigger[ing] processes that make cognitive reappraisal of intuitions more likely" (p. 118). In other words, even the putative salience of emotional intuitions does not necessarily negate the need for moral reasoning to refine those intuitions adaptively.

In fact, there are several aspects of the intuitionist model itself that explain why the prevalence of moral intuitions should not be [mis]interpreted as eliminating a role for ethical reasoning, judgment, problem-solving--and perhaps more importantly, acquiring the competencies to do it well. First, ethical reasoning is not completely negated in the SIM; the model views moral decision-making as an "iteration of intuitive and reasoned processes [that] happens when people talk about moral issues; [although] it rarely happens in a single head" (Haidt, 2004, p. 285). And we know that people encountering ethical conflicts, ambiguities, temptations and/or external pressures in their research, a professional practice or institutional lives often do confer with trusted colleagues and family members.

Second, the SIM is a descriptive model of how moral judgments seemingly (to some) are made: "It is not a normative or prescriptive claim about how moral judgments ought to be made ... . people following their moral intuitions often

---

3 Similarly, Houwer (2019) and Connor and Evers (2020) recommend portraying *implicit bias* as a behavioral phenomenon, and a feature of situations, respectively, rather than a latent attribute of individuals. This is partly because research findings have "established that IAT-measured attitudes and stereotypes were often either unwelcome to, or explicitly rejected by, research subjects" (Greenwald & Banaji, 2017, p. 866).

bring about nonoptimal or even disastrous consequences" (Haidt, 2001, p. 815). That is likely the reason that "Although the value of the moral intuition perspective has been demonstrated in multiple fields ... , its application in organizational contexts is limited" (Weaver et al., 2014). Approaches based on an intuitionist perspective or "nonrational" decision making model do not appear to offer much systematic help in what to *do* when faced with a realistic ethical dilemma (Rogerson et al., 2011; Weaver et al., 2014; Schminke et al., 2010). As noted in chapter 1 the ultimate purpose of this book is to help raise the quality of moral reasoning and ethical problem-solving.

Third, as pointed out in chapter 7, moral psychologists are generally concerned with explaining moral *judgments* such as good/bad, permissible/forbidden, immoral, guilty, and disgusting. Accordingly, the SIM "focuses on moral judgment and moral thinking rather than on moral behavior" (Haidt & Kesebir, 2010, p. 801). But as professional scientists and practitioners working in complex social organizations, the ethical problems we encounter require solutions—i.e., *taking moral action*—so our focus is on behavioral outcomes.

Fourth, the SIM does suggest circumstances under which moral reasoning and problem-solving may be expected to exhibit preeminence over intuition; and those circumstances characterize the real-life context in which I-O psychology is practiced. They include: (a) situations in which the likely intuitions elicited are "weak" (i.e., relatively mundane ethical problems, not akin to dramatic challenges like "eating one's dead pet dog"; Haidt, 2001, p. 817); (b) when there are "competing intuitions" such as the temptations, value conflicts, role conflicts and coercive pressures comprising typical ethical dilemmas (cf. #14 of "Adding Further to the Framework for Ethical Decision Making," Chap. 7). Some dilemmas are particularly difficult, such as when ethical principles conflict (Pryzwansky & Wendt, 1999; Sales & Lavin, 2000); and (c) when there is "high processing capacity" (i.e., the person involved has the requisite cognitive ability for ethical problem-solving).[4]

So, in conclusion, I agree with Maxwell (2016) that "teaching reasoning skills is compatible with the basic assumptions of the new synthesis in moral psychology [i.e., the role of situational influences and moral intuitions preceding moral judgments]" (p. 82). I will return shortly to the very important explanation he offers as to what accounts for that compatibility.

Is Dependable Ethical Problem-Solving Even Possible?

If we conclude from the above that moral intuitions don't preclude ethical reasoning, and may even require the clarification provided by such, perhaps the thing to

---

4 There would be little reason to write this book if I didn't believe that generally to be true of I-O psychologists.

consider is the accuracy or trustworthiness of those reasoning processes. It is more than ¾ of a century since the political scientist Herbert Simon (1955) revolutionized economics, psychology, management, and cognitive science by revealing the effects of *bounded rationality* and *satisficing* on managerial decision-making.

By now it is well known that in the realm of objective facts our judgments are frequently distorted by simplifying *heuristics* (mental short-cuts) that sometimes are accurate but often lead to mistaken conclusions (Kahneman, 2011; Kahneman et al., 1982; Tversky & Kahneman, 1974). Importantly, Sunstein (2005) pointed out that "People use moral heuristics too—moral shortcuts, or rules of thumb, that lead to mistaken and even absurd moral judgments … . Examples are given from a number of domains … . In all of these contexts, rapid, intuitive judgments make a great deal of sense, but sometimes produce moral mistakes that are replicated in law and policy" (p. 531). (The issues are discussed and debated by 24 commentaries on Sunstein's essay by eminent philosophers, psychologists, legal and business scholars, cognitive scientists, et al.) Similarly, Gigerenzer (2010) argue[s] that *much* (not all) of moral behavior is based on heuristics … . Relying on heuristics in place of optimizing is called *satisficing*" (p. 529, emphasis in original). He goes on to emphasize the mostly neglected role of the social context/environment in shaping moral behavior, along with character and reasoning. (Recall the discussion of "The Disposition vs. Context Issue" in Chap. 5. Virtue Ethics.)

Most important is the question of whether heuristics and biases render moral deliberations infeasible. In chapter 7 it was noted that "prejudices, unconscious biases, heuristics and competing motives often result in our making choices or taking actions that are not at all reflective of our conscious intentions." The book *Blind Spots* (Bazerman & Tenbrunsel, 2011) is premised on the awareness that "our ethical behavior is distinctly different from our expectations" (p. 12). According to them, that is so because we are subjected to the unconscious limitations of both *bounded awareness* and *bounded ethicality*. The former refers to limitations in our awareness and recognition of all the aspects and implications of an ethical problem; the latter to personal biases and other constraints that serve to elevate the salience of our self-interest over other motives ("moral heuristics" in Sunstein's terminology).

Kim et al. (2015) propose that the combination of bounded awareness and ethicality along with realistic limitations on our actions raises serious doubts about "the practical relevance of the moral principles that business ethics theory prescribes. We call this doubt the *Radical Behavioral Challenge*" (p. 341, emphasis added). Their response to RBC is essentially "so what?" (My characterization, not theirs.) They point out that "the impact of bounded ethicality is fixed not by the laws of human nature but by human choice … . There are individuals who, even under stressful conditions, can stop and do what seems most commendable" (p. 349). (For example, some participants in Milgram's (1974) study of obedience to authority did not succumb.).

Apropos of the point being made here is the subtitle of *Blindspots*: "Why we fail to do what's right, and *what to do about it*" (emphasis added). The rapid, intuitive "system 1" or "system s" reactions reflecting our bounded awareness and ethicality are often inadequate. As noted, Haidt (2001) acknowledged, "people following their moral intuitions often bring about nonoptimal or even disastrous consequences" (p. 815). Similarly, Rogerson et al. (2011) indicate that ethical decision-makers "should acknowledge that their initial thoughts might be wrong and refrain from jumping to the first seemingly sufficient solution that occurs to them. Instead, they should actively seek alternative perspectives and consider being a devil's advocate for themselves" (p. 631). In other words, "what to do about it" is that we should consciously and intentionally invoke our deliberative "system 2" or "system c" problem-solving processes to integrate "emotional sensitivity, personal values, contextual forces, and intuitive responses with normative rational analysis in order to aid the often complex and challenging task of making ethical decisions" (Rogerson, et al., 2011, p. 622). And "while it is important for normative theorizing and pedagogy to recognize those impediments [of bounded ethicality], these impediments should not function as a justification for not doing the right thing" (Kim et al., 2015, p. 351–2). Moreover, this approach has been extended to procedures to remedy the effects of bias (including implicit biases) at the societal level (Greenwald et al., 2022).

Prior to the appearance of the first edition of this book in 2003 a number of scholars attempted to provide helpful decision-making models, checklists, flowcharts or decision trees as aids in producing satisfactory and satisfying solutions to moral dilemmas (Canadian Psychological Association, 2000; Cavanagh et al., 1995; Cooper, 1998; Gellerman et al., 1990; Gortner, 1991; Haas & Malouf, 1995; Koocher & Keith-Spiegel, 1998; Lewis, 1991; Nagle, 1987; Newman & Brown, 1996; Sales & Lavin, 2000), and some were reviewed by Nagy (2011), Wittmer (2001) and by Pryzwanski and Wendt (1999).[5] An optimistic appraisal of these procedures is that they not only are helpful with respect to the deliberations at hand, but that repeated use of them for each ethics-related incident will help "fine-tune and shape appropriate responses" (Koocher & Keith-Spiegel, 1998, p. 12), thus providing cumulative improvements in one's ethical problem-solving skills. In fact, it may not be too far-fetched to suggest that guided and practiced striving to do the right thing

---

5   The following section owes much to their work. The models are normative—prescriptive problem-solving aids—and very different from the empirically grounded descriptive or conceptually derived predictive models such as the one in Fig. 6.1 or as illustrated by the Miceli et al. (2001) model predicting whistle-blowing behavior in response to perceived wrongdoing, or that of Thiel et al. (2012) emphasizing managerial "sensemaking."

contributes to becoming more of the right kind of person (and, according to Aristotle, experiencing the ultimate good– flourishing).

But we should take seriously Ladenson's admonition that "in the case of any approach that analyzes the ethical decision-making process primarily in terms of a determinate, well-defined, and ordered sequence of steps, there is a near total lack of fit between subject matter and method" (cited in Gellermann et al., 1990, p. 90). I confess to considerable sympathy with Ladenson's opinion; complex social situations with moral aspects can involve a bewildering mix of antecedent conditions, contrasting interpretations and personal beliefs, competing values and motives, divided loyalties, and contradictory principles and institutional demands. So that, after concluding 14 chapters that attempt to shed some light on those complexities, ending with a normative list of invariant sequential decision-making steps seems simplistic and anticlimactic.[6] The "steps" in the decision-aid should not be viewed literally, to be taken seriatim—or, that the prior one(s) must be "completed" before one can engage the next—or, for that matter, that all of them need occur in every situation. For example, it may seem that at the time one becomes cognizant of a dilemma to be dealt with, one has already implicitly taken several of the "steps" (e.g., implicitly acquired much relevant information). It is not even unusual to begin thinking (perhaps prematurely) of solutions before one has fully articulated the issues. The "steps" should be thought of as highlighting more or less seamless points of an iterative process, as opposed to a discrete linear sequence. Schminke et al. (2010) also called into question the "many traditional approaches to ethical decision-making [that] assume managers engage in a rational, linear decision process when addressing ethical dilemmas" (p. 271).

But that is not a valid justification for demonizing all ethical problem-solving. Maxwell (2016) expressed it more clearly, in justifying the compatibility of teaching ethical problem-solving with the newer empirical findings from moral psychology. They are compatible

> if one regards the rules, steps or procedures that typically feature in models of moral deliberation as an analytic framework for breaking an impasse of uncertainty about an ethical problem—rather than as a kind of algorithm which, when applied to an ethical problem, produces a reliable moral judgment on which to base the ethically right course of action in the circumstances… .

---

6   There is little choice in a print medium, however, but to present them sequentially for didactic purposes. But I have deliberately shied away from referring to them as *steps*, unless in quotes. Two possibilities might be *quasi-steps* or *nascent steps*, but those seem beyond awkward!

> ... the pedagogical role of the sorts of models of ethical deliberation that are common in ethics education (and which are maligned in behavioral ethics for being mis-educational) is not as much to depict real-world ethical reasoning as it is to provide an enabling analytic framework intended to help individuals move forward conceptually when faced with uncertainty about what they should do (pp. 82, 83).

On balance, I believe there is a positive contribution to be made by such moral mnemonics (if they realistically include a role for situational, nonrational and emotional influences, including personal bias) because they focus our attention on the *process* of decision-making and taking moral action, rather than on specific rules or standards. After all, the scant empirical evidence that exists suggests that I-O psychologists "cannot always agree on what behaviors are appropriate, and even when they do agree on what to do, they often disagree on why" (Tannenbaum et al., 1989, p. 234). The view adopted here fits between the preeminence of intuitions on the one hand, and rational models in which emotions play only an irrational antithetical role, on the other hand. It is in keeping with Gaudine and Thorne (2001), who adopt the view that "Emotions should not be ignored as 'irrational biases' to a rational ethical decision process but attention to one's emotions may result in better ethical decisions" (p. 175).

There is no doubt that most complex ethical dilemmas will be comprised of idiosyncratic details at a level of specificity much beyond what can be anticipated and described in this or any other decision model. But the overall process is generalizable even if the particulars of the problems vary. I agree with Tannenbaum et al. (1989), who concluded that "the task of ethics training is to convey ethical reasoning processes ... the ethics reasoning process enables us to generalize to new and unique situations" (p. 234).

The recommended process contains 11 non-discrete (i.e., overlapping) "steps," within four broad, identifiable but not entirely separable phases: problem identification, information gathering, problem analysis and choice, and following through. These should not be taken as akin to an invariant road map; they are meant to provide "an analytic framework for breaking an impasse of uncertainty about an ethical problem."

Problem Identification

1. *Decide Whether the Problem is an Ethical One.*

What is the nature of the difficulty? Do you have a sense that this is more than just a technical problem to be solved or a matter of mere social convention? An ethical problem will generally invoke one or more principles from "The Domain of Moral Action." It may entail the threatened disrespect of some person(s), such as by violating their rights to privacy or autonomy or failing to honor an obligation to them; the potential imposition of unjustified ill effects on some or the distribution of undeserved rewards to others; a temptation to refrain from affording benefit or care to another that one ought to provide; contemplation of the infliction of harm (or of failing to prevent it), especially on those who possess lower social status, fewer resources or less power; or a violation of the moral virtues concerning truthfulness, fidelity, trust, and so on--especially to those with whom we have a fiduciary relationship.

2. *Understand the Structure and Complexity of the Problem.*

What are the key issues and who is affected? As noted earlier (cf. Tables 6.4, 6.5, 15.1), a great many ethical dilemmas can be encompassed in a simple taxonomy consisting of five ethical paradigms (that are not even mutually exclusive): (i) considering harming or wronging another, especially when motivated by self-serving reasons, notwithstanding that there may be some external pressure to do so; (ii) having foreknowledge of someone's harmful intentions to a third party, as when one is privy to an organization's confidential plan to downsize; (iii) having conflicting responsibilities or obligations to two or more people, as occurs frequently among I-O psychologists who are retained by organization decision makers other than the employees with whom they work; (iv) confronting a situation in which two or more important personal values are in conflict—that is, giving expression to one will deny expression of the other(s)—as is the case for the researcher who is disturbed by the realization that his or her research question can only be addressed adequately by means of perpetrating a deception on the experimental participants; and (v) being pressured (e.g., by a coauthor or a client) to violate a standard of professional or personal conduct.

But the essence of the difficulty may have as much to do with the specific persons involved as with the structure of the dilemma. Can you identify all the parties directly involved and the wider array of stakeholders who are potentially affected? They may include individual employees, students, research participants, advisees, or interns; or the issues may involve peers—colleagues, competitors or perhaps a superior; at the macro-level, there may be potential consequences for the client/organization/employer as an entity or for particular employee groups, consumers or shareholders; a salient issue may be the reputation of our profession as a consequence of your actions or impacts on society at large. Last but not least of course, are the implications for oneself. Especially challenging are situations in which the pressure to engage in some ethically questionable activity stems from one's employer or client, so that resisting may have potentially adverse personal consequences. To what extent does the particular "cast of characters" make a difference in your experience of the problem? Would it be the same problem, would there even be a problem, if different persons were involved? That is, would your likely actions be the same? If not, you should explore why that is so and whether the inconsistency can be justified comfortably. For example, the researcher noted in the previous paragraph would probably be less likely to implement deception in a field study with company employees as research participants than with students. Both the structure of the dilemma (e.g., the number of conflicting elements) and the variety of persons affected contribute to the degree of moral complexity with which one is faced.

Initial Information Gathering

3. *Get the Facts.*

To what extent does understanding and addressing the problem depend on factual matters potentially subject to confirmation? It makes little sense to begin a thoughtful process of ethical reasoning if it is likely to be based on incorrect premises. How certain can you be that the circumstances of the problem are as you perceive them? It will be helpful to be able to make clear distinctions between factual matters and one's unconfirmed assumptions (e.g., concerning the antecedent conditions giving rise to the difficulty) or between one's personal beliefs and values that may be invoked. It would probably be a good idea to familiarize yourself with recognizing the cognitive and emotional distortions to which we are susceptible (Banaji & Greenwald, 2013; Kahneman, 2011). One should think in terms of deliberately counteracting our "bounded awareness" (Bazerman & Tenbrunsel, 2011) and avoiding any tendency toward informational biases such as "motivated blindness" (Kim et al., 2015).

Similarly, one needs to think about the degree of certainty associated with one's expectations regarding the anticipated consequences of alternative courses of action (see below). Virtually all ethical decision-making models focus on a consideration of the anticipated consequences associated with the various options being pondered. But how certain can you be of those consequences? Can you rule out your own wish-fulfilling biases? It would be reassuring to consult knowledgeable and trusted others who might provide a consensus on which to base one's judgments.

4. *Assess the Seriousness of the Problem.*

At least as important as the complexity of the problem, likely more so, is its moral intensity, which is determined by the nature of the potential consequences

(Collins, 1989; Jones, 1991). And the most salient consequences are those that are harmful.[7] Most people agree that physical harms (pain, injury and suffering) are the most serious, followed by economic or financial harm, and "mere" emotional or psychological harm—in that order. In the utilitarian tradition of assessing aggregate outcomes, the overall magnitude of the anticipated harms ought to play a key role in one's deliberations. For example, any given harm is magnified by the number of people affected. A moral problem is also likely to be viewed as more intense if the potential consequences have a greater probability of occurring. Therefore, you should begin to think about whether you have enough reliable information to begin mapping out the consequences of your alternative options and their comparative likelihoods of actually happening.

Two other sets of elements are likely to contribute to the felt intensity of the ethical issue. The first are temporal factors, such as whether a decision must be made quickly, affording little time for reflection; and the degree of immediacy with which the consequences follow the action taken. Under conditions of extreme haste, we may be forced to rely on our intuitive "gut reactions" with accompanying feelings of uncertainty about having done the best thing. So, an important early decision is to determine how quickly you must act. But if you know that you tend toward some impulsivity in your choice behavior, be wary of reacting prematurely. A situation in which you know that your actions will initiate ill effects immediately will ordinarily make the dilemma more painful, but that is likely to be an inherent feature of the situation that cannot be changed.

The second set of factors has to do with personal dimensions of the situation, such as the degree of connectedness one has to the person(s) affected, whether more than one person is impacted, or the distinction between harming (or benefitting) an individual versus an impersonal entity such as a corporation. For example, most people are more likely to return an excess refund of the money received from an individual than the same amount received from an insurance company (although some employees may feel as personally responsible to their organization as to a friend).

Problem Analysis and Choice

5.   *Restate the Problem in Ethical Terms.*

The troubling issues will probably have been encountered or presented to you in pragmatic operational (i.e., non-theoretical) terms (e.g., "Should I or should I not

---

7   In this context I use harm as a broad construct extending beyond the two ethical principles of beneficence and nonmaleficence to include adverse effects associated with disrespectful, unjust, hurtful or disloyal actions as well. I.e., the notion is stretched to encompass deontological "wrongs."

do such-and-such?"). Ethical reasoning is facilitated by articulating the problem in ethical terms, which you ought to be able to do based on your identification of the problem and initial information gathering. In fact, this may seem unnecessary (redundant). You will have already realized that the problem is ethical in nature (cf. # 1), involving one or more of the five broad principles constituting the domain of moral action. But there is another possible reason for doing so. Bazerman and Tenbrunsel (2011) suggest that focusing on the abstract moral principles that will be violated by selfish acts you may be contemplating, instead of thinking about the immediate concrete rewards motivating the temptation, makes it more likely for you to do the right thing that you intend.

So, if you've not already done so, it is time to articulate as clearly as possible which ethical principles are involved. Is it that people's rights are being violated or that some are being taken advantage of unfairly? Are you under pressure to violate a promise of confidentiality or to take personnel actions that will be gratuitously hurtful for reasons that you believe are inadequate? Likely, you are conflicted and at least somewhat uncertain about what to do (or else there would not be a problem). What, as precisely as you can identify them, are the causes of the conflict? It may be that circumstances suggest that two or more ethical principles are in opposition, and you will not be able to adhere to one without violating the other. For example, the source of the "pressure" to violate confidentiality may be coming from a sense of responsibility to prevent wrongdoing or harm. Or perhaps the structure of the situation is that you feel justifiably tempted to behave selfishly. (Beware of self-serving bias.) Once the problem has been specified in terms that clearly identify the ethical stakes at risk, you are almost ready to undertake more formal and analytic ethical reasoning—which you no doubt have implicitly begun by now, in any event. But there is a preliminary step that may obviate the need for doing so.

6.   *Is There a Ready Solution? Concession, Compromise, Codes and Consensus.*

Because you now have a pretty good understanding of the ethical issues, you can recognize potential solutions that may be readily available without having to initiate more analytic processes. There are four possibilities. First, you may, however reluctantly, concede that you simply cannot justify going ahead with (or refraining from preventing) a contemplated dubious act based on self-serving motives despite how well rationalized they are or how much "license" you allow yourself, and despite the frustration caused by your concession. I trust that you would not, for example, deceive your IRB by intentionally withholding relevant information, irrespective of how "unreasonable" the committee members seem to be. This is what I think of as a pseudo-dilemma in which one really knows all along what the right thing is to do—and that ultimately you will do it; the conflict primarily reflects one's reluctance, frustration or annoyance at being placed in such circumstances. In these situations, the "concession" is to oneself—more precisely, acting on a moral principle that outweighs whatever the competing motive(s) may be, or acknowledging a "bottom-line" ethical position you are unwilling to violate.

Second, once the ethical issues have been specified clearly, a compromise may more readily be perceived. It might be as straightforward as acknowledging that one of the two or more ethical principles in opposition is significantly more important than the other(s) and should be given deference.

The third possibility harks back to the anticipatory steps outlined earlier as part of Stage I: Be familiar with the ethics codes, applicable laws and regulations, professional standards, relevant organizational policies, and other normative statements of professional proprieties, such as the SIOP-sponsored case illustrations (Lowman et al., 2006) and other sources mentioned earlier in this book. It may just be that the issue distressing you—or a close parallel—is not unique and has been thought through and documented previously by colleagues. (Although it is possible that details of the situation you are in render the written guidelines inapplicable or insufficient.) In addition, I hope that you have available colleagues and friends with whom you can consult on the matter. Despite how vexatious the problem is for you—from your uncomfortable position in the middle of it—it is possible that they will helpfully see the situation as less conflicting. A fourth possibility, therefore, is that a consensus among trusted and knowledgeable colleagues may be all that is needed to resolve the dilemma—if it is acceptable to you. (There is no reason to believe that a colleague's judgments are necessarily less fallible than your own or that there may not be genuine differences between you and colleagues in values and ethical reasoning.)

7. *Acknowledge Your Personal Beliefs, Values and Egoistic Biases as Well as Any External Pressures or Emotional Factors Relevant to the Issues.*

If no ready solution is apparent, you will need to proceed further with more formal ethical reasoning. But before doing so, it is necessary to explore the extent to which your personal perspective, values or even biases play a role in those processes. That may not be as easy and straightforward as I may have made it sound, given the often-implicit nature of our ordinary prejudices and out-group biases (Banaji & Greenwald, 2013; Kim et al., 2015). If, as is often the case, one has a personal stake in the matter at hand, a near-ubiquitous issue will be satisfying oneself that the action taken is not merely a reflection of self-serving motives. As noted in the SIM, "If the principal difficulty in objective moral reasoning is the biased search for evidence …, then people should take advantage of the social persuasion link … and get other people to help them improve their reasoning" (Haidt, 2001, p. 829). In listing the potential options you have and their associated consequences (discussed next), special attention needs to be paid to the ethical justification of those options that further your self-interest. The origin of those forces may include discomforting external pressures from one's client, employer or significant others such as one's boss.

It is also important to reflect on one's system of values, both the normative-espoused values that may be readily accessible, and one's experiential, less conscious "values in use," as well as post-facto "values-justification" processes (cf. chapter 8) that may be expected to impact one's judgment. Our values can be counted on to play a role in how we structure and understand the situation, evaluate the alternatives we construe, and decide on a course of action. Some of the intrapersonal conflicts in ethical decision-making can be attributed to the lack of clarity characterizing most people's understanding of their diverse value system (Brown & Crace, 1996; DiNorcia & Tigner, 2000). Introspectively achieving a greater understanding of one's values and their relative ordering may even, perhaps, prevent reaching a decision that is primarily a post hoc "values justification" rationalization for the expression of egoistic or prejudicial motives.

Building on your understanding of the key issues and who is affected (# 2), a necessary companion process to making more salient one's own preferences and values is the attempt to appreciate the way in which other participants and affected parties experience the situation based on their concerns and motives. This appreciation is a requisite ingredient of the universalist assumption in moral reasoning, yet the circumstances may not be conducive to your finding out directly from other stakeholders what are their interests—hence, requiring your empathic sensitivities to do so.

8. *Enumerate Options and Their Consequences.*

Considering the foregoing seven processes, you should be in a position to generate a list of potential options or alternative courses of action, along with the consequences that may be anticipated from each. Haas and Malouf (1995) suggested that this step should assume the nature of a "brainstorming" process in which emphasis is placed on producing novel and creative potential solutions that attempt to reconcile competing ethical principles. Similarly, Koocher and Keith-Spiegel (1998) advised that alternatives should be developed without regard to their feasibility, utility, riskiness, cost, appropriateness or even their ethicality! Their advice is aimed at maximizing the array of options that can be considered—including the option of doing nothing—to enhance the probability of arriving at the best one. In keeping with that advice, Bazerman and Tenbrunsel (2011) add that people are more likely to choose the ethical option when considering several alternative options, as opposed to considering simply whether to proceed with one (dubious) action.

Koocher and Keith-Spiegel recommended that, in enumerating the consequences anticipated from each option, whenever relevant the "consequences should include economic, psychological, and social costs; short-term, ongoing and long-term effects; the time and effort necessary to effect each decision, including any resource limitations; any other risks, including the violation of individual rights; and any benefits" (p. 14). (In my experience it is unlikely you will be able to fill all the cells in that metaphorical spreadsheet.) As already noted (#2), the specification of consequences should include, to the extent feasible, consideration of the effects on all identifiable stakeholders, and special attention should be paid to the issue of the actual likelihood of occurrence of the anticipated consequences (# 3). This advice is consistent with the exercise of one's moral imagination (Werhane, 1999). Nagy (2011) offers succinct advice in evaluating a hypothetical action: "What could possibly go wrong as a result of this choice, even though the probability is low?" (p. 159).

In addition to the self-reflection and insights promoted in # 7, it is useful at this time also to contemplate the effects of other potentially relevant features of your "personal equation," such as the maturity of your moral character—that is, your degree of moral sensitivity and moral identity—and whether your moral musings tend to be shaped by a particular form of normative thinking. Are you generally dismissive of ethical considerations, frequently viewing them as idealistic and unnecessary intrusions on the real concern for getting things done? Or are moral principles a key element of your self-identity? Do you tend to think in moralistic (deontological) terms of right and wrong that will preempt any utilitarian analysis? If so, your specification of consequences will focus on the ethical principles reflected in the options. Does your moralistic approach permit of any qualifications or exceptions? Or maybe you are something of an ethical pragmatist, more likely to entertain utilitarian considerations of the ways in which people are benefitted and harmed by a contemplated action, in search of maximizing the good or minimizing the hurt? Similarly, do you tend toward optimism or pessimism as a dispositional attribute? Are you inclined to an unhappy or sarcastic cynicism regarding the motives of others? The matters alluded to by these questions may all affect the nature and range of alternatives you contemplate and your projections of their likely consequences, hence your choice of which one(s) to implement.

Moreover, according to Nisan (1990, 1991), our ethical choices at any point in time are affected by previous recent ethical choices we have made, as reflected in the motivational influence of our moral balance. In other words, the generation of alternatives and specification of their likely consequences is not an entirely rational and objective enterprise as is frequently implied by decision-making strategies such as this. Effort and personal insight are required to assure their accuracy in the hopes of arriving at the best solution.

9. *Evaluate and Choose.*

If you have approached the process in a thoughtful manner up to this point, you will probably be able to arrive at a best choice. You may even realize that you have already done so, apparently without "trying." On the other hand, sometimes it is not so easy, because of what Schminke et al. (2010) refer to as "problematic preferences" (p. 284)—i.e., it may not be all that clear where your preferences lie among the alternatives developed. In any event, it is important to accept that it is unlikely to be a perfect choice—that is, one with an absence of negative features and associated misgivings. (If one were available, you probably would not have needed to embark on this process.) Moreover, as noted above (# 7), additional discussion at this time with a knowledgeable and sympathetic colleague, friend, professor or mentor may prove helpful in achieving an accurate assessment of the alternatives.

It has been observed that egocentric motives are more salient at the time of implementing a decision than when involved in the process of evaluating and choosing (Bazerman & Tenbrunsel, 2011). So, they recommend that one anticipate that occurrence by focusing on those self-serving objectives in advance to diminish their later potency.

In evaluating the positive and negative consequences identified with each option, a number of guiding principles are worth keeping in mind: (a) *universalism* or equality of interests—Have I given appropriate consideration to the interests of everyone affected, adequately justifying why the interests of some might legitimately be given greater weight than others?; (b) *right reasoning*—am I sanguine that the reasons substantiating this choice are better than the arguments that favor the other alternatives? Am I satisfied that my own self-interest has not been the major determinative factor? (c) *universalizability*: would I advise anyone else like me in this same situation to do what I am choosing to do? Or does it pass the "family test"? That is, would I be pleased to explain to my family what I am about to do?[8] Answers to those sorts of questions will be influenced by personal attributes like your level of moral identity and degree of moral motivation. In addition, if Nisan's (1990, 1991) notion of moral balance has some validity, that sense of identity will not result in an invariant ethical posture but will reflect a "limited morality" (or "license") in which we permit ourselves to deviate somewhat from the ideal, in response to other influences. The degree of such deviation, however, is itself likely to be limited by the motivation to preserve our moral identity.

For I-O psychologists, organizational influences may play an important part in the decision process, constituting one influential source threatening to upset our moral balance. Organizational ethical culture or a firm's moral atmosphere has an impact on the ethical behavior of employees (Martin & Cullen, 2006). Of particular interest is Jansen and Von Glinow's (1985) observation that organizational reward systems may influence behavior in ways that contradict the dominant espoused ethical norms of the organization, thus establishing counternorms such as "do whatever it takes to get the job done on time." What, if any, organizational precedents, unacknowledged norms, or other social pressures might

8   An alternative formulation is the "*Wall Street Journal* test." I.e., would I be pleased if what I am contemplating appeared on the front page of the *WSJ*?

militate against your decision and need to be anticipated? Bazerman and Tenbrunsel (2011) add that areas in an organization "characterized by uncertainty, time pressure, short-term horizons, and isolation" are fertile ground for generating pressures for unethical behavior (p. 164).

Following Through

10. *Implement the Choice.*

As discussed in the early chapters of this book and illustrated in Fig. 6.1, the implementation of a moral choice into moral action should not be taken for granted. There are many factors that account for the imperfect correlation between intentions and behavior, including implicit biases (Banaji & Greenwald, 2013; Kim et al., 2015). On a more pragmatic note, in some instances one is simply not able to take unilateral action, and implementing a course of action may require the cooperation of others and a very different skill set than was necessary to arrive at the choice (Haas & Malouf, 1995; Newman & Brown, 1996). This is especially liable to be the case for I-O psychology practitioners working in the complex social system of a large corporation. It is not unlike the distinction between the statistical knowledge needed to design a factorial experiment and the wider set of sophisticated knowledge, skills and abilities required to carry it out effectively in an organizational field setting.

After making a tentative decision, the first step in implementation will generally be to discuss the choice with key stakeholders likely to be affected by it and to share that information with as many of those concerned as is feasible (Koocher & Keith-Spiegel, 1998). The focus of the discussion could be twofold: (i) whether there are any hitherto unforeseen difficulties in implementation that were not incorporated in the specification of consequences on which the decision process was based. These may simply be practical problems concerning timing, resources, and the like, or it may be that others are able to envision that your proposed action is an inadequate solution to the dilemma or perhaps raises new problems; and (ii) whether the perspectives and reactions of others provide some insights into the potential biasing or distorting effects of your judgments.

A key consideration at this point is your assessment of whether there are forces like organizational counternorms that may keep you from doing what you have chosen to do. Haas and Malouf (1995) noted what they referred to as "the 'prudence' aspect of this question" (p. 18), having to do with the fact that an ethical choice sometimes comes at a considerable cost to the person implementing the decision. This may be especially true in an organizational context. For example, in comparison with higher-level managers, lower-level managers and supervisors are less likely to believe that their organizations are managed ethically and are more likely to report having had to compromise their personal principles to conform with organizational expectations (Posner & Schmidt, 1987). It has been suggested, however, that subordinates who are at higher levels of cognitive moral development (a la Kohlberg) will be less affected by their supervisors' influence (Wimbush, 1999). Try to be aware of the social sanctions mediated by organizational reward structures, normative expectations, and other indications of valued policies and practices such as leadership and compliance processes (Ciulla, 1998; Peterson, 2001) as these influence your taking moral action.

Also pertinent at this point are your internalized self-sanctions (Bandura, 1986, 1991) associated with aspects of your moral identity. The contemplated satisfaction and enhanced self-respect stemming from the confirmation and enactment of one's moral ideals and the converse self-condemnation anticipated from a failure to live up to them are salient influences for most people—albeit not always successful. Situations in which one is confronted unavoidably with instances of unethical behavior on the part of others (e.g., high-ranking managers) in the organization may be especially threatening. Nielsen (1989) contrasted a number of strategies that can be taken from the standpoint of an individual in *opposition* to the offending parties (e.g., secretly or quietly blowing the whistle within or outside the organization; or anonymously threatening to do so; and conscientiously refusing to implement an unethical policy), with *collaborative solutions* in which people have successfully worked with others to build a more ethical organization. There are difficulties and limitations associated with both sets of strategies.

11. *Evaluation and Review.*

It is important to take the time to ponder the results of your actions—preferably with knowledgeable and trusted colleagues. Guard against a tendency to "reinterpret" one's own questionable behavior as having been more appropriate than it was (Bazerman & Tenbrunsel, 2011). One technique is to use the five ethical principles to evaluate the results. Has the problem been resolved only to yield a new moral dilemma? Might that have been anticipated? It is probably wise to accept that the resolution of ethical problems may not be entirely emotionally satisfying: "resolution is ordinarily an approximate state" (Cooper, 1998, p. 27). Nevertheless, to what extent have your actions met the needs of the situation? Did any stakeholders get the short end of the stick? If so, why? Did the consequences turn out as expected? If not, to what extent is it attributable to having misread the situation initially (#s 2 and 3)? As pointed out in the *Canadian Code of Ethics for Psychologists* (CPA, 2017), at this point one should accept responsibility for the consequences of one's action, correct any negative consequences, and reengage in the decision-making process if the ethical issue is not resolved.

Perhaps most important, what have you learned from this experience that will be useful for the next dilemma encountered? A potential value of engaging in a process such as this is the increased ease with which it may be called on in the future, as well as the structure it provides in recognizing and understanding what might have gone wrong. As Gellermann et al. (1990) noted, "Reflect on the results of your action; clarify your vision and beliefs; refine your values and ethics; and give feedback to your consciousness as a means of heightening your ethical sensitivity and developing your ability to act ethically in the future" (p. 87). It may be unreasonable to expect that you will achieve an entirely satisfactory resolution of every ethical dilemma but producing increasingly skilled efforts to do so should be the objective.

REFERENCES

Abdulsalam, D., Maltarich, M. A., Nyberg, A. J., Reilly, G., & Martin, M. (2021). Individualized pay-for-performance arrangements: Peer reactions and consequences. *Journal of Applied Psychology*, *106*(8), 1202–1223.

Abramson, A. (2021). Cultivating empathy. *Monitor on Psychology*, Nov./Dec., 44–52.

Academy of Management. (2022). Academy of Management code of ethics. Retrieved from https://aom.org/about-aom/governance/ethics/code-of-ethics on June 21, 2022.

Academy of Management Journal. (1999). Special research forum on stakeholders, social responsibility, and performance. *42*(5).

Acemoglu, D., & Restrepo, P. (2018). The race between man and machine: Implications of technology for growth, factor shares, and employment. *American Economic Review*, *108*(6), 1488–1542.

Acemoglu, D., & Restrepo, P. (2019). Automation and new tasks: Haow technology displaces and reinstates labor. *Journal of Economic Perspectives*, *33*(2), 3–30.

Acemoglu, D., & Restrepo, P. (2020). Robots and jobs: Evidence from US labor markets. *Journal of Political Economy*, *128*(6), 2188–2244.

Acemoglu, D., Manera, A., Restrepo, P., Katz, L. F., & Zwick, E. (2020). Does the US tax code favor automation? *Brookings Papers on Economic Activity*, Spring, 231–300.

Ackerman, P. L. (1987). Individual differences in skill learning: An integration of psychometric and information processing perspectives. *Psychological Bulletin*, *102*(1), 3–27.

Adair, J. G., Dushenko, T. W., & Lindsay, R. C. (1985). Ethical regulations and their impact on research practice. *American Psychologist*, *40*, 59–72.

Adams, J. S. (1965). Inequity in social exchange. In I. Berkowitz, (Ed.), *Advances in Experimental Social Psychology*, Vol. 2 (pp. 267–299). New York: Academic Press.

Adams, R. M. (1976). Motive utilitarianism. *The Journal of Philosophy*, *73*, 467–481.

Adler, N. E., Boyce, T., Chesny, M. A., Cohen, S., Folkman, S., Kahn, R. L., & Syme, S. L. (1994). Socioeconomic status and health: The challenge of the gradient. *American Psychologist*, *49*, 15–24.

Adler, S. (2022). Fostering greater DEI in the workplace: The Friday group's recommendations. *The Industrial-Organizational Psychologist*, *59*(3).

Agle, B. R., & Caldwell, C. B. (1999). Understanding research on values in business: A level of analysis framework. *Business & Society, 38,* 326–387.

Aguinis, H., Bradley, K. J., & Brodersen, A. (2014). Industrial-organizational psychologists in business schools: Brain drain or eye opener? *Industrial and Organizational Psychology: Perspectives on Science and Practice, 7*(3), 284–303.

Aguinis, H., Cummings, C. W., Ramani, R., & Cummings, T. G. (2020). "An A is an A": The new bottom line for valuing academic research. *Academy of Management Perspectives, 34*(1), 135–154.

Aguinis, H., & Glavas, A. (2012). What we know and don't know about corporate social responsibility: A review and research agenda. *Journal of Management, 38,* 932–968.

Aguinis, H., & Glavas, A. (2013). Embedded versus peripheral corporate social responsibility: Psychological foundations. *Industrial and Organizational Psychology: Perspectives on Science and Practice, 6*(4), 314–332.

Aguinis, H., & Kraiger, K. (2009). Benefits of training and development for individuals and teams, organizations, and society. *Annual Review of Psychology, 60,* 451–474.

Ahmad, M. G., Klotz, A. C., & Bolino, M. C. (2021). Can good followers create unethical leaders? How follower citizenship leads to leader moral licensing and unethical behavior. *Journal of Applied Psychology, 106*(9), 1374–1390.

Ajzen, I. (1988). *Attitudes, personality, and behavior.* Chicago: Dorsey.

Ajzen, I., & Fishbein, M. (1980). *Understanding attitudes and predicting social behavior.* Englewood Cliffs, NJ: Prentice-Hall.

Akrivou, K., & Sison, A. J. G. (Eds.) (2016). *The challenges of capitalism for virtue ethics and the common good: Interdisciplinary perspectives.* Cheltanham: Edward Elgar.

Akst, D. (2013, Summer). What can we learn from past anxiety over automation? *The Wilson Quarterly.* Retrieved from http://archive.wilsonquarterly.com/sites/default/files/articles/AutomationAnxiety.pdf on May 22, 2016.

Alfano, M. (2016). *Moral psychology: An introduction.* Cambridge, UK: Polity Press.

Alidina, S., Adams, J., Portny, S., Loeb, M., Kindel, S., Zeller, D., Canavor, N., Anthony, R., Boyd, B., & Donaldson, M. C. (n.d.). *Career development all-in-one for dummies.* Hoboken, NJ: John Wiley.

Albee, G. W. (2000). The Boulder model's fatal flaw. *American Psychologist, 55,* 247–248.

Alderfer, C. P. (1998). Group psychological consulting to organizations: A perspective on history. *Consulting Psychology Journal, 50,* 67–77.

Alfano, M. (2016). *Moral psychology: An introduction.* Cambridge, UK: Polity Press.

Alge, B. J. (2001). Effects of computer surveillance on perceptions of privacy and procedural justice. *Journal of Applied Psychology, 86,* 797–804.

Allegretto, S., Jacobs, K., Graham-Squire, D., & Scott, M. E. (2014, Oct.). *The public cost of low-wage jobs in the banking industry.* Berkeley, CA: UC Berkeley Labor Center.

Allen, F. (1952). *The big change.* New York: Harper.

Alliance for Organizational Psychology. (2016). *Memorandum of Understanding on Fostering Ethical, Relevant and Rigorous Research.* Retrieved from http://www.siop.org/userfiles/image/Refresh2016/AOP_2016_MoU.pdf on July 6, 2016.

Allport, G. F. (1954). *The nature of prejudice.* Reading, MA: Addison Wesley.

Almond, B. (1993). Rights. In P. Singer (Ed.), *A companion to ethics* (pp. 259–272). Cambridge, MA: Blackwell.

Alperovitz, G., & Hanna, T. M. (2015, July 23). Socialism, American-style. *The New York Times,* A 3.

Alzola, M. (2015). Virtuous persons and virtuous actions in business ethics and organizational research. *Business Ethics Quarterly, 25*(3), 287–318.

American Association for the Advancement of Science. (1999, June 25). Net news. *Science, 284,* 2051.

American Educational Research Association, American Psychological Association & National Council on Measurement in Education. (2014). *Standards for educational and psychological testing.* Washington, DC: AERA.

American Psychiatric Association. (2000). *Diagnostic and statistical manual of mental disorders* (4th Ed., text rev.). Washington, DC: Author.

American Psychological Association. (1987). Guidelines for conditions of employment of psychologists. *American Psychologist, 42,* 724–729.

American Psychological Association. (1992). Ethical principles of psychologists and code of conduct. *American Psychologist, 47,* 1597–1628.

American Psychological Association. (2000). What does it pay to be a psychologist? *Monitor on Psychology, 31,* 13.

American Psychological Association. (2002). Ethical principles of psychologists and code of conduct. *American Psychologist, 57,* 1060–1073.

American Psychological Association. (2006, July 15). Stereotype threat widens achievement gap. Retrieved from http://www.apa.org/research/action/stereotype.aspx on June 3, 2016.

American Psychological Association. (2008). Mission statement for APA. Retrieved from http://www.apa.org/about/policy/chapter-6.aspx on June 16, 2016.

American Psychological Association. (2010a). 2010 Amendments to the 2002 "Ethical Principles of Psychologists and Code of Conduct". *American Psychologist, 65*(5), 493.

American Psychological Association. (2010b). Ethical principles of psychologists and code of conduct. With the 2010 Amendments Adopted February 20, 2010, effective June 1, 2010. Retrieved from http://www.apa.org/ethics/code/index.aspx

American Psychological Association. (2010c). Salaries in psychology 2009. Report of the 2009 APA salary survey. Retrieved from http://www.apa.org/workforce/publications/09-salaries/index.aspx on May 27, 2016.

American Psychological Association (2022). Summary report of journal operations, 2021. *American Psychologist, 77*(5), 714–715.

American Psychological Association. (2017). *Ethical principles of psychologists and code of conduct.* Washington, DC: Author.

American Psychological Association. (2020). *Publication manual of the american psychological association* (7th Ed.). Washington, DC: Author.

American Psychological Association, Committee on Legal Issues. (1996). Strategies for private practitioners coping with subpoenas or compelled testimony for client records or test data. *Professional Psychology: Research and Practice, 27,* 245–251.

American Psychological Association, Committee on Standards for Providers of Psychological Services. (1981). Specialty guidelines for the delivery of services by industrial/organizational psychologists. *American Psychologist, 36,* 664–669.

American Psychological Association, Ethics Committee. (1988). Trends in ethics cases, common pitfalls, and published resources. *American Psychologist, 43,* 564–572.

American Psychological Society. (1992, February). Human capital initiative: Report of the national behavioral science research agenda committee [Special issue]. APS *Observer.*

American Psychological Society. (1993a, October). Human capital initiative. Report 1: The changing nature of work [Special issue]. APS *Observer.*

American Psychological Society. (1993, December). Human capital initiative. Report 2: Vitality for life: Psychological research for productive aging [Special issue]. APS *Observer*.

American Psychological Society. (1996a, February). Human capital initiative. Report 3: Reducing mental disorders: A behavioral science research plan for psychopathology [Special issue]. APS *Observer*.

American Psychological Society. (1996b, April). Human capital initiative. Report 4. Doing the right thing: A research plan for healthy living [Special issue]. APS Observer.

American Statistical Association. (2022). *Ethical guidelines for statistical practice*. Author. Approved, February.

Americans for Tax Fairness. (2014, April). *Walmart on tax day: How taxpayers subsidize america's biggest employer and richest family*. Washington, D.C.: Author.

Amis, J., Brickson, S., Haack, P., & Hernandez, M. (2021). Taking inequality seriously. *Academy of Management Review*, *46*(3), 431–439.

Anderson, C., & Brion, S. (2014). Perspectives on power in organizations. *Annual Review of Organizational Psychology and Organizational Behavior*, *1*, 67–97.

Anderson, S., Cavanagh, J., Collins, C., Hartman, C., & Yeskel, F. (2000). *Executive excess 2000: Seventh annual CEO compensation survey*. Boston: United for a Fair Economy.

Andreoli, N., & Lefkowitz, J. (2009). Individual and organizational antecedents of misconduct in organizations. *Journal of Business Ethics*, *85*(3), 309–332.

Anonymous. (2015). The case of the hypothesis that never was; Uncovering the deceptive use of post hoc hypotheses. *Journal of Management Inquiry*, *24*(2), 214–216.

Antoni, A., Reinecke, J., & Fotaki, M. (2020). Caring or not caring for coworkers? An empirical exploration of the dilemma of care allocation in the workplace. *Business Ethics Quarterly*, *30*(4), 447–485.

Applebaum, M., Cooper, H., Kline, R. B., Mayo-Wilson, E., Nezu, A., & Rao, S. M. (2018). Journal article reporting standards for quantitative research in psychology: The APA publication and communications board task force report. *American Psychologist*, *73*(1), 3–25.

Appiah, J. K. (2014). "Experimental philosophy". Chapter 2 in C. Luetge, H. Rusch, & M. Uhl (Eds.), *Experimental ethics: Toward an empirical moral philosophy*. New York: Palgrave.

Aquino, K., Freeman, D., Reed II, A., Lim, V. K. G., & Felps, W. (2009). Testing a social-cognitive model of moral behavior: The interactive influence of situations and moral identity centrality. *Journal of Personality and Social Psychology*, *97*(1), 123–141.

Aquino, K., & Reed, H. (2002). The self-importance of moral identity. *Journal of Personality and Social Psychology*, *83*(6), 1423–1440.

Ardichvili, A., Mitchell, J. A. & Jondle, D. (2009). Characteristics of ethical business cultures. *Journal of Business Ethics*, *85*, 445–451.

Argyris, C. (1970). *Intervention theory and method*. Reading, MA: Addison-Wesley.

Argyris, C., & Schon, D. A. (1978). *Organizational learning*. Reading, MA: Addison-Wesley.

Arnold, D. W. (1990). Invasion of privacy: A rising concern for personnel psychologists. *The Industrial-Organizational Psychologist*, *28*(2), 37–39.

Ariely, G., & Mann, H. (2013). A bird's eye view of unethical behavior: Commentary on Trautmann et al. (2013). *Perspectives on Psychological Science*, *8*(5), 498–500.

Aristotle. (1953/2004). *The nicomachean ethics*. London: Penguin Books.

Armstrong, K. (2018). "I feel your pain": The neuroscience of empathy. *Current Directions in Psychological Science*, *31*(1), 29–31.

Arneson, R. (1999). Against Rawlsian equality of opportunity. *Philosophical Studies, 93,* 77–112.

Aronfreed, J. (1994). Moral development from the standpoint of a general psychological theory. In B. Puka (Ed.), *Moral development: A compendium* (Vol. 1, pp. 170–185). New York: Garland.

Aronson, E., & Carlsmith, J. M. (1968). Experimentation in social psychology. In G. Lindzey & E. Aronson (Eds.), *Handbook of social psychology* (rev. ed., Vol. 2, pp. 1–79). Reading, MA: Addison-Wesley.

Aronson, J., Quinn, D. M., & Spencer, S. J. (1998). Stereotype threat and the academic underperformance of women and minorities. In J. K. Swim, & C. Stangor (Eds.), *Prejudice: The target's perspective* (pp. 83–103). San Diego: Academic.

Arrington, R. L. (1998). *Western ethics: An historical introduction.* Malden, MA: Blackwell.

Arthur, W. B. (2011). The second economy. *McKinsey Quarterly,* Oct. Retrieved from from http://www.mckinsey.com/business-functions/strategy-and-corporate-finance/our-insights/the-second-economy on May 22, 2016.

Arvey, R. D., & Zhang, Z. (2015). Biological factors in organizational behavior and I/O Psychology: An introduction to the special edition. *Applied Psychology: An International Review, 64*(2), 281–285.

Ashforth, B. E., Gioia, D. A., Robinson, L. L., & Treviño, L. K. (2008). Introduction to special topic forum: Re-viewing organizational corruption. *Academy of Management Review, 33*(3), 670–684.

Ashforth, B. E., & Humphrey, R. H. (1995). Emotion in the workplace: A reappraisal. *Human Relations, 48,* 97–125.

Ashkansy, N. M., & Dorris, A. D. (2017). Emotions in the workplace. *Annual review of organizational psychology and organizational behavior, 4,* 67–90.

Ashkanasy, N. M., Windsor, C. A., & Treviño, L. K. (2006). Bad apples in bad barrels revisited: Cognitive moral development, just world beliefs, rewards, and ethical decision-making. *Business Ethics Quarterly, 16*(4), 449–473.

Atari, M., Davani, A. M., & Dehghani, M. (2020). Body maps of moral concerns. *Psychological Science, 31*(2), 160–169.

Athanasopoulou, A., & Selsky, J. W. (2015). The social context of corporate social responsibility: Enriching research with multiple perspectives and multiple levels. *Business & Society, 54*(3), 322–364.

Audi, R. (2012). Virtue ethics as a resource in business. *Business Ethics Quarterly, 22*(2), 273–291.

Audi, R., & Murphy, P. E. (2006). The many faces of integrity. *Business Ethics Quarterly, 16*(1), 3–21.

Austin, J., & Villanova, P. (1992). The criterion problem. *Journal of Applied Psychology, 77,* 836–874.

Autor, D. H. (2015). Why are there still so many jobs? The history and future of workplace automation. *Journal of Workplace Perspectives, 29*(3), 3–30.

Ayal, S., Gino, F. Barkan, R., & Ariely, D. (2015). Three principles to REVISE people's unethical behavior. *Perspectives on Psychological Science, 10*(6), 738–741.

B Corporation (2015). Best for the world. Downloaded April 18, 2015 from www.bcorporation.net/

Babalola, M. T., Greenbaum, R. L., Amarnani, R. K., Shoss, M. K., Deng, Y., Garba, O. A., & Guo, L. (2020). A business frame perspective on why perceptions of top management's bottom-line mentality result in employees' good and bad behaviors. *Personnel Psychology, 73*(1), 19–41.

Bachani, J., Blomme, R. J., & Pirson, M. (2018). *Humanistic management: Social entrepreneurship and mindfulness, Vol. II: Foundations, cases and experiences.* New York: Business Expert Press.

Baier, K. (1993). Egoism. In P. Singer (Ed.), *A companion to ethics* (pp. 197–204). Cambridge, MA: Blackwell.

Baker, D., Bivens, J., & Scheider, J. (2019). *Reining in CEO compensation and curbing the rise of inequality.* Washington, DC: Economic Policy Institute, June 4. Retrieved from https://www.epi.org/publication/reining-in-ceo-compensation-and-curbing-the-rise-of-inequality/ Nov. 10, 2021.

Baker, D., & Scheider, J. (2018). *CEO pay still not related to performance.* Economic Policy Institute. Retrieved from https://www.epi.org/blog/ceo-pay-still-not-rekated-to-performance/ on Oct. 11, 2021.

Baker, D. B., & Benjamin, L. T. (2000). The affirmation of the scientist-practitioner: A look back at Boulder. *American Psychologist, 55,* 241–247.

Bakjia, J., Cole, A., & Helm, B. (2010). Job and income growth of top earners and the causes of changing income Inequality: Evidence from U.S. tax return data. Department of Economics Working Paper, 2010-24, Williams College, November.

Bakjia, J., Cole, A., & Helm, B. (2012). Job and income growth of top earners and the causes of changing income inequality: Evidence from U.S. Tax Return Data. Department of Economics Working Paper, Williams College, April.

Bakker, M., Hartgerink, H. J., Wicherts, J. M., & van der Maas, L. J. (2016). Researchers' intuitions about power in psychological research. *Psychological Science, 27*(8), 1069–1077.

Balliet, D. & Van Lange, A. M. (2013). Trust, conflict, and cooperation: A meta-analysis. *Psychological Bulletin, 139*(5), 1090–1112.

Balhttp, P. M. (with 32 others). (2019). Manifesto for the future of work and organizational psychology. *European Journal of Work and Organizational Psychology, 28*(3), 289–299.

Banaji, M. R., & Greewald, A. G. (2013). *Blind spot: Hidden biases of good people.* New York, NY: Delacorte Press.

Bandura, A. (1986). *Social foundations of thought and action: A social cognitive theory.* Englewood Cliffs, NJ: Prentice-Hall.

Bandura, A. (1991). Social cognitive theory of moral thought and action. In W. M. Kurtines, & J. L. Gewirtz (Eds.), *Handbook of moral behavior and development: Vol. 1.* Theory (pp. 45–103). Hillsdale, NJ: Lawrence Erlbaum Associates.

Bandura, A. (1999). Moral disengagement in the preparation of inhumanities. *Personal and Social Psychology Review, 3,* 193–209.

Bandura, A. (2001). Social cognitive theory: An agentic perspective. *Annual Review of Psychology, 52,* 1–26.

Bandura, A. (2016). *Moral disengagement: How people do harm and live with themselves.* New York: Macmillan.

Bandura, A., Barbaranelli, C., Caprara, G. V., & Pastorelli, C. (1996). Mechanisms of moral disengagement in the exercise of moral agency. *Journal of Personality and Social Psychology, 71*(2), 364–374.

Banks, G. C., Field, J. G., Oswald, F. L., O'Boyle, E. H., Landis, R. S., Rupp, D. E., & Rogelberg, .G. (2019). Answers to 18 questions about open science practices. *Journal of Business and Psychology, 34*(3), 257–270.

Banks, G. C., Knapp, D. J., Lin, L., Sanders, C., & Grand, J. A. (2022). Ethical decision-making in the 21st century: A useful framework for industrial-organizational psychologists. *Industrial-Organizational Psychology: Perspectives on Science and Practice, 15*(2), 220–235.

Bannerjee, B. (2021). Modern slavery is an enabling condition of global neoliberal capitalism: Commentary on modern slavery in business. *Business & Society, 60*(2), 415–419.

Bapuji, H. (2015). Individuals, interactions and institutions: How economic inequality affects organizations. *Human Relations, 68*(7), 1059–1083.

Barber, B. (1965). Some problems in the sociology of the professions. In K. S. Lynn (Ed.). *The professions in America* (pp. 15–34). Boston: Houghton Mifflin.

Bargh, J. A., & Chartrand, T. L. (1999). The unbearable automaticity of being. *American Psychologist, 54*, 462–479.

Bar-Hillel, M., & Yaari, M. (1993). Judgments of distributive justice. In B. A. Mellers & J. Baron (Eds.), *Psychological perspectives on justice: Theory and applications* (pp. 55–84). New York: Cambridge University Press.

Baritz, L. (1960). *The servants of power: A history of social science in American industry*. Westport, CT: Greenwood.

Barkema, H. G., Chen, X., George, G., Luo, Y., & Tsui, A., (2015). West meets East: New concepts and theories. *Academy of Management Journal, 58*(2), 460–479.

Barkema, H. C., & Gomez-Mejia, L. R. (1998). Managerial compensation and firm performance: A general research framework. *Academy of Management Journal, 41*, 135–145.

Barkow, J. H., Comides, L., & Tooby, J. (Eds.). (1992). *The adapted mind: Evolutionary psychology and the generations of culture*. New York: Oxford University Press.

Barnett, T. (2001). Dimensions of moral intensity and ethical decision making: An empirical study. *Journal of Applied Social Psychology, 31*(50), 1038–1057.

Barnett, T., & Vaicys, C. (2000). The moderating effect of individuals' perceptions of ethical work climate on ethical judgments and behavioral intentions. *Journal of Business Ethics, 27*, 351–362.

Barney, J. B., & Harrison, J. S. (Eds.) (2020). Special Issue: Stakeholder theory at the crossroads. *Business & Society, 59*(2), 203–383.

Baron, J. (1997). Biases in the quantitative measurement of values for public decisions. *Psychological Bulletin, 122*, 72–88.

Barrera, D., & Simpson, B. (2012). Much ado about deception: Consequences of deceiving research participants in the social sciences. *Sociological Methods and Research, 4*(3), 383–413.

Barrett, L. F. (2015, Sept. 1). Psychology is not in crisis. *The New York Times Op-Ed*, A23.

Barry, B. (1989). *A treatise on social justice: Vol. 1. Theories of justice*. Berkeley, CA: University of California Press.

Barry, B., & Stephens, C. U. (1998). Objections to an objectivist approach to integrity. *Academy of Management Review, 23*, 162–169.

Bartels, L. K., Harrick, E., Martell, K., & Strickland, D. (1998). The relationship between ethical climate and ethical problems within human resource management. *Journal of Business Ethics, 17*, 799–804.

Baruch, Y. (2006). Career development in organizations and beyond: Balancing traditional and contemporary viewpoints. *Human Resource Management Review, 16*, 125–138.

Bauer, R., & Fee, D. H. Jr. (1972). *The corporate social audit*. New York: Russell Sage Foundation.

Baumeister, R. F., Stillwell, A. M. N., & Heatherton, T. F. (1994). Guilt: An interpersonal approach. *Psychological Bulletin, 115*, 243–267.

Baumann-Pauly, D. (2016). Book Review: Corporate Social Responsibility in a Globalizing World. *Business Ethics Quarterly, 26*(1), 137–141.

Baumeister, R. F., Vohs, K. D., & Tice, D. M. (2007). The strength model of self-control. *Current Directions in Psychological Science, 16,* 351–355.

Baumeister, R. F., Tice, D. M., & Vohs, K. D. The strength model of self-regulation: Conclusions from the second decade of willpower research. *Perspectives on Psychological Science, 13*(2), 141–145.

Baumrind, D. (1964). Some thoughts on ethics of research: After reading Milgram's "behavioral study of obedience". *American Psychologist, 19,* 421–423.

Baumrind, D. (1985). Research using intentional deception: Ethical issues revisited. *American Psychologist, 40,* 165–174.

Bazerman, M. H., & Gino, F. (2012, Jan.). Behavioral ethics: toward a deeper understanding of moral judgment and dishonesty. *Harvard Business School Working Knowledge,* HBS Working Paper No. 12-054.

Bazerman, M. H., Messick, D. M., Tenbrunsel, A. E., & Wade-Benzoni, K. A. (Eds.). (1997). *Environment, ethics, and behavior: The psychology of environmental valuation and degradation.* San Francisco: New Lexington.

Bazerman, M. H., & Tenbrunsel, A. E. (2011). *Blind spots: Why we fail to do what's right and what to do about it.* Princeton, NJ: Princeton University Press.

Beauchamp, T. L., & Childress, J. F. E. (1994). *Principles of biomedical ethics* (4th ed.). New York: Oxford University Press.

Bebchuk, L. A., Fried, J. M., & Walker, D. I. (2002). *Managerial power and rent extraction in the design of executive compensation.* (NBER Working Paper No. w9068). Cambridge, MA: National Bureau of Economic Research.

Bebeau, M. J. (1994). Influencing the moral dimensions of dental practice. In J. R. Rest & D. Narvaez (Eds.), *Moral development in the professions* (pp. 121–146). Hillsdale, NJ: Lawrence Erlbaum Associates.

Becker, T. E. (1998). Integrity in organizations: Beyond honesty and conscientiousness. *Academy of Management Review, 23,* 154–161.

Bekelman, J. E., Li, Y., & Gross, C. P. (2003). Scope and impact of financial conflicts of interest in biomedical research. *JAMA, 289*(4), 454–464.

Belar, C. D. (2000). Scientist Practitioner ≠ Science + Practice. *American Psychologist, 55,* 249–250.

Bell, R. (1985). Professional values and organizational decision making. *Administration & Society, 17,* 21–60.

Belman, D. (1992). Unions, the quality of labor relations, and firm performance. In L. Mishel, & P. B. Voos (Eds.), *Unions and economic competitiveness* (pp. 41–107). Armonk, NY: M. E. Sharpe.

Benjamin, L. T. Jr. (2001). American psychology's struggles with its curriculum: Should a thousand flowers bloom? *American Psychologist, 56,* 735–742.

Benjamin, L. T. Jr. (2002). Revisiting psychology's core curriculum. *American Psychologist, 57,* 454–455.

Benjamin, L. T. Jr., & Crouse, E. M. (2002). The American Psychological Association's response to *Brown v. Board of Education:* The case of Kenneth B. Clark. *American Psychologist, 57,* 38–50.

Bennis, W. M., Medin, D. L., & Bartels, D. M. (2010). The costs and benefits of calculation and moral rules. *Perspectives on Psychological Science, 5*(2), 187–202.

Berenson, A. (2002, June 29). Tweaking numbers to meet goals comes back to haunt executives. *The New York Times,* A1, C3.

Berg, J. (1993). How could ethics depend on religion? In P. Singer (Ed.), A *companion to ethics* (pp. 525–533). Cambridge, MA: Blackwell.

Berger, A. (1979). How the press blew three mile island. *The Real Paper*. Quoted in Smith, 2021.

Bergman, M. A., & Jean, V. A. (2016). Where have all the "workers" gone? A critical analysis of the unrepresentativeness of our samples relative to the Labor market in the industrial-organizational psychology literature. *Industrial and Organizational Psychology: Perspectives on Science and Practice, 9*(1), 84–113.

Berkey, B. (2020). The value of fairness and the wrong of wage exploitation. *Business Ethics Quarterly, 30*(3), 414–429.

Berle, Jr. A. A. (1954). *The 20th century capitalist revolution*. New York: Harcourt, Brace and World.

Berle, A. A. Jr., & Means, G. C. (1932). *The modern corporation and private* property. New York: Macmillan.

Bernoulli, D. (1954). Exposition of a new theory on the measurement of risk. *Econometrica, 22*, 23–36. (Original work published 1738)

Bernstein, A., Hadash, Y., Lichtash, Y., Tanay, G. Shepard, K., & Fresco, D. M. (2015). Decentering and related constructs: A critical review and metacognitive processes model. *Perspectives on Psychological Science, 10*(5), 599–617.

Bersoff, D. N. (2008). *Ethical conflicts in psychology* (2nd ed.) Washington, DC: American Psychological Association.

Bertland, A. (2008). Virtue ethics in business and the capabilities approach. *Journal of Business Ethics, 84*, 25–32.

Bettache, K., & Chin, C-Y. (2019). The invisible hand is an ideology: Toward a social psychology of neoliberalism. *Journal of Social Issues, 75*(1), 8–19.

Beu, D., & Buckley, M. R. (2001). The hypothesized relationship between accountability and ethical behavior. *Journal of Business Ethics, 34*, 57–73.

Bevan, W. (1980). On getting in bed with a lion. *American Psychologist, 35*, 779–789.

Bhuyan, N., & Chakraborty, A. (2020). Overcoming the fact-value dichotomy: Rethinking business ethics as a mediating discourse. *Teaching Ethics, 20*(1-2), 113–125.

Bisson, J. I., & Deahl, M. P. (1994). Psychological debriefing and prevention of post-traumatic stress: More research is needed. *British Journal of Psychiatry, 165*, 717–720.

Bivens, J., & Mishel, L. (2013). The pay of corporate executives and financial professionals as evidence of rents in top 1 percent incomes. Economic Policy Institute Working Paper, No 296, June.

Blackburn, R. T., & Fox, T. G. (1983). Physicians' values and their career stage. *Journal of Vocational Behavior, 22*, 159–173.

Blakeney, R., Broenen, R., Dyck, J., Frank, B., Glenn, D., Johnson, D., & Mayo, C. (2002). Implications of the results of a job analyses of I–O psychologists. *The Industrial-Organizational Psychologist, 39*, 29–37.

Blancero, D. M., DelCampo, R. G., & Marron, G. F. (2010). Just tell me! Making alternative dispute resolution systems fair. *Industrial Relations, 49*(4), 524–543.

Blank, P. D., Bellak, A. S., Rosnow, R. L., Rotheram-Borus, M. J., & Schooler, N. R. (1992). Scientific rewards and conflicts of ethical choices in human subjects research. *American Psychologist, 47*, 959–965.

Blanton, H., Jaccard, J., Strauts, E., Mitchell, C., & Tetlock, P. E. (2015). Toward a meaningful metric of implicit prejudice. *Journal of Applied Psychology, 100*(5), 1468–1481.

Blasi, A. (1980). Bridging moral cognition and moral action: A critical review of the literature. *Psychological Bulletin, 88,* 1–45.

Blasi, A. (2009). The moral functioning of mature adults and the possibility of fair moral reasoning. In D. Narvaez, & D. K. Lapsley (Eds.), *Personality, identity, and character: Explorations in moral psychology* (pp. 396–440). New York: Cambridge University Press.

Bledstein, B. J. (1976). *The culture of professionalism: The middle class and the development of higher education in America.* New York: Norton.

Blinder, A. (2015, Dec. 4). Ex-chief of Massey Energy convicted of lesser count in miners' deaths. *The New York Times,* A18.

Blinder, A. (2016, April 7). Mine chief is sentenced in conspiracy over safety. *The New York Times,* A12.

Bloom, P. (2012). Religion, morality, evolution. *Annual Review of Psychology, 63,* 179–199.

Bloom, P. (2017). Empathy, schmempathy: Response to Zaki. *Trends in Cognitive Sciences, 21,* 60–61.

Blum, L. (1987). Particularity and responsiveness. In J. Kagan, & S. Lamb (Eds.), *The emergence of morality* in young children (pp. 306–337). Chicago: University of Chicago Press.

Blumenthal, R. G. (2000, September 4). Capitalist plot? The pay gap between workers and chiefs looks like a chasm. *Barron's,* 10.

Blustein, D. L. (2001). Extending the reach of vocational psychology: Toward an inclusive and integrative psychology of working. *Journal of Vocational Behavior, 59,* 171–182.

Blustein, D. L., Kenny, M. E., Di Fabio, A., & Guichard, J. (2019). Expanding the impact of the psychology of working: Engaging psychology in the struggle for decent work and human rights. *Journal of Career Assessment, 27*(1), 3–28.

Boddy, C. R. (2010). Corporate psychopaths, bullying and unfair supervision in the workplace. *Journal of Business Ethics, 100,* 367–369.

Boddy, C. R. (2011). The corporate psychopaths theory of the global financial crisis. *Journal of Business Ethics, 102,* 25–259.

Boddy, C. R. (2014). Corporate psychopaths, conflict, employee affective well-being and counterproductive work behavior. *Journal of Business Ethics, 121,* 107–121.

Boddy, C. R., Ladyshewsky, R., & Galvin, P. (2010a). Leaders without ethics in globabl business: Corporate psychopaths. *Journal of Public Affairs, 10,* 121–138.

Boddy, C. R., Ladyshewsky, R., & Galvin, P. (2010b). The influence of corporate psychopaths on corporate social responsibility and organizational commitment to employees. *Journal of Business Ethics, 97,* 1–19.

Boddy, C. R., Miles, D., Sanyal, C., & Hartog, M. (2015). Extreme managers, extreme workplaces: Capitalism, organizations and corporate psychopaths. *Organization, 22*(4), 530–551.

Boehm, V. (1980). Research in the "real world": A conceptual model. *Personnel Psychology,* 33, 495–503.

Bok, D. (2009). *Universities in the marketplace: The commercialization of higher education.* Princeton, NJ: Princeton University Press.

Bok, S. (1989). *Secrets.* New York: Pantheon.

Bolinger, D. (1982). *Language: The loaded weapon.* London: Longman.

Bolino, M. C., Klotz, A. C., Turnley, W. H., & Harvey, J. (2013). Exploring the dark side of organizational citizenship behavior. *Journal of Organizational Behavior, 34,* 542–559.

Bolino, M. C., Hsiung, H-H., Harvey, J., & LePine, J. A. (2015). "Well, I'm tired of tryin'!" Organizational citizenship behavior and citizenship fatigue. *Journal of Applied Psychology, 100*(1), 56–74.

Bommer, M., Gratto, C., Gravander, J., & Tuttle, M. (1987). A behavioral model of ethical and unethical decision making. *Journal of Business Ethics, 6,* 265–280.

Bonnefon, J-F., Shariff, A., & Rahwan, I. (2015). Autonomous vehicles need experimental ethics: Are we ready for utilitarian cars? *Science Magazine,* Oct. 13, 1–15.

Boruch, R. F. (1971). Maintaining confidentiality of data in educational research: A systemic analysis. *American Psychologist, 26,* 413–430.

Boruch, R. F., & Cecil, J. S. (1982). Statistical strategies for preserving privacy in direct inquiry. In J. E. Sieber (Ed.), *The ethics of social research: Surveys and experiments* (pp. 207–232). New York: Springer-Verlag.

Bown, H. R. (1953). *Social responsibilities of the businessman.* NY: Harper.

Bowie, N. (2017). *Business ethics: A Kantian perspective,* 2nd Ed. New York: Cambridge University Press.

Boyd, D. (1994). The character of moral development. In B. Puka (Ed.), *Moral development: A compendium* (Vol. 6, pp. 449–477). New York: Garland.

Boyle, B. A., Dahlstrom, R. F., & Kellaris, J. J. (1998). Points of reference and individual differences as sources of bias in ethical judgments. *Journal of Business Ethics, 17,* 517–525.

Boyes, C. (2010). *Career management secrets.* New York: Harper Collins.

Bradley, F. H. (1935). *Ethical studies* (2nd ed.). Oxford, England: Clarendon.

Bradley, S. G. (2014). Competing interests in research. Chap. 7 In F. L. Macrina, *Scientific integrity,* 4th Ed., (pp. 209–241). Wash. D.C.: ASM Press.

Bramel, D., & Friend, R. (1981). Hawthorne, the myth of the docile worker, and class bias in psychology. *American Psychologist, 36,* 867–878.

Brandeis, L. D. (1971). *Business—A profession.* New York: Kelley. (Original work published 1914.)

Brandt, M. J., & Reyna, C. (2015). The chain of being: A hierarchy of morality. *Perspectives on Psychological Science, 6*(5), 428–446,

Brandt, M. J., Reyna, C., Chambers, J. R., Crawford, J. T., & Wetherell, G. (2014). The ideological-conflict hypothesis: Intolerance among both liberals and conservatives. *Current Directions in Psychological Science, 23*(1), 27–34.

Brannick, M. T., & Levine, E. L. (2002). *Job Analysis.* Thousand Oaks, CA: Sage Publications.

Branscombe, N. R., Ellemers, N., Spears, R., & Doosje, B. (1999). The context and content of social identity threat. *Sepsis, Jan,* 35–58.

Bredemeier, B. J. L., & Shields, D. L. L. (1994). Applied ethics and moral reasoning in sport. In J. R. Rest, & D. Narvaez (Eds.), *Moral development* in *the professions* (pp. 173–188). Hillsdale, NJ: Lawrence Erlbaum Associates.

Brief, A., Dukerich, J. M., & Doran, L. I. (1991). Resolving ethical dilemmas in management: Experimental investigations of values, accountability, and choice. *Journal of Applied Social Psychology, 21,* 380–396.

Brien, A. (1998). Professional ethics and the culture of trust. *Journal of Business Ethics, 17,* 391–409.

Brister, E. (2014). Using illustrative case studies: A case in teaching climate ethics. *Teaching Ethics, Spring,* 17–34.

Britton, B. K. (1979). Ethical and educational aspects of participating as a subject in psychology experiments. *Teaching of Psychology, 6,* 195–198.

Brockner, J., Konovsky, M., Cooper-Schneider, R., Folger, R., Martin, C., & Bies, R. (1994). Interactive effects of procedural justice and outcome negativity on victims and survivors of job loss. *Academy of Management Journal, 37,* 397–409.

Brody, J. L., Gluck, J. P., & Aragon, A. S. (1997). Participants' understanding of the process of psychological research: Informed consent. *Ethics & Behavior*, 7, 285–298.

Brody, J. L., Gluck, J. P., & Aragon, A. S. (2000). Participants' understanding of the process of psychological research: Debriefing. *Ethics & Behavior*, 10, 13–25.

Broder, A. (1998). Deception can be acceptable. American *Psychologist*, 53, 805–806.

Bronner, E. (2001, July 15). Posner v. Dershowitz: A famous judge and a famous lawyer scrutinize the Supreme court's role in the presidential election. *The New York Times Book Review*, 11–12.

Bronowski, J. (1960). *The* common *sense of science*. Middlesex, England: Penguin.

Brooks, M. E., Grauer, E., Thornbury, E. E., & Highhouse, S. (2003). Value differences between scientists and practitioners: A survey of SIOP members. *The Industrial-Organizational Psychologist*, 40(4), 17–23.

Brooks, J. N. (1966). *The great leap: The past twenty-five years in America*. New York: Harper & Row.

Brossoit, R. M., Wong, J. R., Robles-Saenz, F., Barber, L. E., Allen, T. D., & Britt, T. W. (2021). Is that ethical? The current state of industrial-organizational psychology graduate training in ethics. *The Industrial-Organizational Psychologist*, 58(3).

Brown, D., & Crace, R. K. (1996). Values in life role choices and outcomes: A conceptual model. *Career Development Quarterly*, 44, 211–223.

Brown, S. L., Brown, R. M., & Penner, L. A. (2011). *Moving beyond self-interest: perspectives from evolutionary biology, neuroscience and the social sciences*. New York: Oxford University Press.

Bruder, M., & Tanyi, A. (2014). How to gauge moral intuitions? Prospects for a new methodology. Chap. 11 in C. Luetge, H. Rusch, & M. Uhl (Eds.). *Experimental ethics: Toward an empirical moral philosophy* (pp. 157–174). Houndmills, England: Palgrave Macmillan.

Buchanan, N. T., Perez, M., Prinstein, M. J., & Thurston, I. B. (2021). Upending racism in psychological science: Strategies to change how science is conducted, reported, reviewed, and disseminated. *American Psychologist*, 76(7), 1097–1112.

Buckle, S. (1993). Natural law. In P. Singer (Ed.), *A companion to ethics* (pp. 161–174). Cambridge, MA: Blackwell.

Buhrmester, M. D., Talaifar, S., & Gosling, S. D. (2018). An evaluation of Amazon's Mechanical Turk, its rapid rise, and its effective use. *Perspectives on Psychological Science*, 13(2), 149–154.

Bullock, H. E., & Quinn, D. M. (2019). Special section: Psychology's contributions to understanding and alleviating poverty and economic inequality. *American Psychologist*, 74(6), 635–697.

Bureau of Labor Statistics, U.S. Department of Labor (2022). *Occupational Outlook Handbook*, Psychologists, at https://www.bls.gov/ooh/life-physical-and-social-science/psychologists.htm, retrieved March 16, 2022.

Burke, R. J. (2015). Flourishing in love and work. Chap. 1 In R. J. Burke, K. M. Page & C. L. Cooper (Eds.), *Flourishing in life, work and careers: Individual wellbeing and career experiences*. Cheltenham, UK: Edward Elgar Publishing.

Burke, R. J. & Cooper, C. L. (Eds.) (2009). *Research companion to corruption in organizations*. Cheltenham, UK: Edward Elgar.

Burke, R. J., Page, K. M. & Cooper, C. L. (Eds.). *Flourishing in life, work and careers: Individual wellbeing and career experiences*. Cheltenham, UK: Edward Elgar Publishing.

Burton, B. K., & Dunn, C. P. (1996). Feminist ethics as moral grounding for stakeholder theory. *Business Ethics Quarterly, 6,* 133–147.

Business & Society. (2000). Revisiting corporate social performance [Special issue]. *39,* 4.

Byrne, Z. S. Hayes, T. L. McPhail, S. M., Hakel, M. D., Cortina, J. M., & McHenry, J. J. (2014). Educating industrial-organizational psychologists for science and practice: Where do we go from here? *Industrial and Organizational Psychology, 7*(1), 2–14.

Callaci, B. (2021, Apr. 13). It's time for labor to embrace antimonopoly. The Forge. Retrieved from https://forgeorganizing.org/article/its-time-labor-embrace-antimonopoly on April 20, 2021.

Cameron, L. D., Brown, P. M., & Chapman, J. G. (1998). Social value orientations and decisions to take proenvironmental action. *Journal of Applied Social Psychology, 28,* 675–697.

Campbell, D. T. (1957). Factors relevant to the validity of experiments in social settings. *Psychological Bulletin, 54*(4), 297–312.

Campbell, D. T., Boruch, R. F., Schwartz, R. D., & Steinberg, J. (1977). Confidentiality-preserving modes of access to files and to interfile exchange for useful statistical analysis. *Evaluation* Quarterly, *1,* 269–300.

Campbell, D. T., & Stanley, J. C. (1963). *Experimental and quasi-experimental designs for research.* Chicago, IL: Rand-McNally.

Campbell, J. P. (1990). The role of theory in industrial and organizational psychology. In M. D. Dunnette, & L. M. Hough (Eds.), *Handbook of industrial and organizational psychology* (2nd ed., Vol. 1, pp. 39–73). Palo Alto, CA: Consulting Psychologists Press.

Campbell, J. P., Daft, R. L., & Hulin, C. L. (1982). *What to* study: *Generating and developing research questions.* Beverly Hills: Sage.

Campion, M. A. (1996). Why I'm proud to be an I/O psychologist. *The Industrial-Organizational Psychologist, 34*(1), 27–29.

Campion, M. A., Adams, E. F., Morrison, R. F., Spool, M. D., Tornow, W. W., & Wijting, J. P. (1986). I/O psychology research conducted in nonacademic settings and reasons for nonpublication. *The Industrial-Organizational Psychologist, 24*(1), 40–43.

Canadian Psychological Association. (2000). *Canadian code of ethics* for *psychologists,* (3rd Ed.). Ottawa, Canada: Author.

Canadian Psychological Association. (2017). *Canadian code of ethics* for *psychologists,* (4th Ed.). Ottawa, Canada: Author.

Canter, M. B., Bennett, B. E., Jones, S. E., & Nagy, T. F. (1994). *Ethics for psychologists: A commentary on the* APA *ethics code.* Washington, DC: American Psychological Association.

Carey, B. (2015a, June 16). Science under scrutiny: A steady increase in study retractions has alarmed journals and researchers. *The New York Times,* D1.

Carey, B. (2015b, Sept. 17). Antidepressant Paxil is unsafe for teenagers, analysis of original data finds. *The New York Times,* A20.

Carey, B. (2016, March 4). Report questioning psychology studies is criticized. *The New York Times,* A3.

Carey, K. (2016, June 22). Private watchdog of for-profit colleges is tested by its federal watchdog. *The New York Times,* A12.

Carlo, G., Pytlikzillig, L. M., Roesch, S. C. & Dienstbier, R. A. (2009). The elusive altruist: The psychological study of the altruistic personality. Chap. 12 In D. Narvaez, & D. K. Lapsley (Eds.), *Personality, identity and character: Explorations in moral psychology* (pp. 271–294). New York: NY: Cambridge University Press.

Carlson, R. (1971). Where is the person in personality research? *Psychological Bulletin, 75,* 203–219.

Carr, S. C. (2007). I-O psychology and poverty reduction: Past, present, and future? *The Industrial-Organizational Psychologist, 45*(1), 43–50.

Carr, S. C., De Guzman, J. M., Eltyeb, S. M., Furnham, A., MacLachlan, M., Marai, L., & McAuliffe, E. (2012). An introduction to humanitarian work psychology. Chapter 1 In S. C. Carr, M. MacLachlan, & A. Furnham (Eds.), *Humanitarian Work Psychology* (pp. 3–33). Basingstoke: Palgrave MacMillan.

Carr, S. C., MacLachlan, M., & Furnham, A. (Eds.) (2012). *Humanitarian work psychology.* UK: Palgrave Macmillan.

Carr, S. C., Parker, J., Arrowsmith, J., Haar, J., & Jones, H. (2017). Humanistic management and living wages: A case of compelling connections? *Humanistic Management Journal, 1*(2), 215–236.

Carr, S. C., Thompson, L. F., Reichman, W., McWha, I., Marai, L., MacLachlan, M., & Baguma, P. (2013, April). Humanitarian work Psychology: Concepts to contributions. *Society for Industrial and Organizational Psychology White Paper Series.* Bowling Green, OH: SIOP, Inc.

Carroll, A. B. (1987). In search of the moral manager. *Business Horizons, 30*(2), 7–16.

Carroll, A. B. (1991). CSP measurement: A commentary for methods for evaluating an elusive construct. In J. E. Post (Ed.), *Research in corporate social performance and policy* (Vol. 12, pp. 385–401). Greenwich, CT: JAI.

Carroll, A. B. (1999). Corporate social responsibility: Evolution of a definitional construct. *Business & Society, 38,* 268–295.

Carroll, A. B. (2021). Corporate social responsibility: Perspectives on the CSR construct's development and future. *Business & Society, 60*(6), 1258–1278.

Carter, R. T. (1991). Cultural values: A review of empirical research and implications for counseling. *Journal of Counseling & Development, 70,* 164–173.

Carter, R. T., Gushue, G. V., & Weitzman, L. M. (1994). White racial identity development and work values. *Journal of Vocational Behavior, 44,* 185–197.

Carton, A. W. (2018). "I'm not mopping the floors, I'm putting a man on the moon": How NASA leaders enhanced the meaningfulness of work by changing the meaning of work. *Administrative Science Quarterly, 63*(2), 323–369.

Cartwright, S., & Cooper, C. L. (1997). *Managing mergers and acquisitions: Integrating people and cultures.* Oxford: Butterworth Heinemann.

Cartwright, S., & Holmes, N. (2006). The meaning of work: The challenge of regaining employee engagement and reducing cynicism. *Human Resource Management Review, 16,* 199–208.

Caruana, R., Crane, A., Gold, S. & LeBaron, g. (2021). Modern slavery in business: The sad and sorry state of a non-field. *Business & Society, 60*(2), 251–287.

Cascio, W. F. (1993). Downsizing: What do we know? What have we learned? *Academy of Management Executive, 7,* 95–104.

Cascio, W. F. (1995). Whither industrial and organizational psychology in a changing world of work? *American Psychologist, 50,* 928–939.

Cascio, W. F. (1998). Learning from outcomes: Financial experiences of 311 firms that have downsized. In M. K. Gowing, J. D. Kraft, & J. C. Quick, (Eds.), *The new organizational reality: Downsizing, restructuring, and revitalization* (pp. 55–70). Washington, DC: American Psychological Association.

Cascio, W. F. (2002). Strategies for responsible restructuring. *Academy of Management Executive, 16,* 80–91.

Cascio, W. F., & Aguinis, H. (2008). Research in industrial and organizational psychology from 1963 to 2007: Changes, choices and trends. *Journal of Applied Psychology, 93*(5), 1062–1081.

Cascio, W. F. & Alegre, R. (2016). How technology is changing work and organizations. In F. P. Morgeson, H. Aguinis & S. J. Ashford (Eds.). *Annual Review of Organizational Psychology and Organizational Behavior, 3,* 349–375.

Cascio, W. F., Young, C. E., & Morris, J. R. (1997). Financial consequences of employment-change decisions in major U.S. corporations. *Academy of Management Journal, 40,* 1175–1189.

Caspi, A., Roberts, B. W., & Shiner, R. L. (2005). Personality development: Stability and change. *Annual Review of Psychology, 56,* 453–484.

Casselman, B. (2021, Oct. 20). Economic gains hobbled as labor market shrinks: Wielding rare leverage to push demands, workers are in no hurry to return. *The New York Times,* A1.

Castile, C. M., Kreamer, L. M., Albritton, B. H., Banks, G. C., & Rogelberg, S. G. (2022). The open science challenge: Adopt one practice that enacts wisely shared values. *Journal of Business and Psychology, 37,* 459–467. Published online, 12 April, 2022.

Castro, B. (Ed.). (1996). *Business and society: A reader in the history, sociology, and ethics of business.* New York: Oxford University Press.

Cavanagh, G. F. (2009). *American business values* (6th ed.). Englewood Cliffs, NJ: Prentice-Hall.

Cavanagh, G. H., Moberg, D. J., & Velasquez, M. (1995). Making business ethics practical. *Business Ethics Quarterly, 5*(July), 399–418.

Ceci, S. J., & Papierno, P. B. (2005). The rhetoric and reality of gap closing: When the "have-nots" gain but the "haves" gain even more. *American Psychologist, 60*(2), 149–160.

Chambers, J. R., Schlenker, B. R., & Collisson, B. (2012).Ideology and prejudice: The role of value conflicts. *Psychological Science, 24*(2), 140–149.

Champion, R. (1985). The importance of Popper's theories to psychology. *American Psychologist, 40,* 1415–1417.

Chan, G. K. Y. (2008). The relevance and value of Confucianism in contemporary business ethics. *Journal of Business Ethics, 77,* 347–360.

Chandler, R. C. (2001). Deontological dimensions of administrative ethics revisited. In T. L. Cooper (Ed.), *Handbook of administrative ethics* (2nd ed., pp. 179–193). New York: Marcel Dekker.

Chapman, A. D. (1981). Value-orientation analysis: The adaptation of an anthropological model for counseling research. *Personnel and Guidance Journal,* 59, 637–642.

Chastain, G., & Landrum, R. E. (Eds.). (1999). *Protecting human subjects: Departmental subject pools and institutional review boards.* Washington, DC: American Psychological Association.

Chen, Z., Hang, H., Pavelin, S., & Porter, L. (2020). Corporate social (ir)responsibility and corporate hypocrisy: Warmth, motive and the protective value of corporate social responsibility. *Business Ethics Quarterly, 30*(4), 486–524.

Chetty, R., Hendren, N., Kline, P., & Saez, E. (2014a). Where is the land of opportunity? The geography of intergenerational mobility in the United States. *Quarterly Journal of Economics, 129*(4), 1553–1623.

Chetty, R., Hendren, N., Kline, P., Saez, E., & Turner, N. (2014b). Is the United States still a land of opportunity? Recent trends in intergenerational mobility. *American Economic Review: Papers & Proceedings, 104*(5), 141–147.

Chia, A., & Mee, L. S. (2000). The effects of issue characteristics on the recognition of moral issues. *Journal of Business Ethics, 27*, 255–269.

Childress, C. A., & Asamen, J. K. (1998). The emerging relationship of psychology and the internet: Proposed guidelines for conducting internet intervention research. *Ethics & Behavior, 8*, 19–35.

Choe-Smith, C. U. (2020). Service learning in philosophical ethics. *Teaching Ethics, 20*(1–2), 91–112.

Choi, I., Nisbett, R. E., & Norenzayan, A. (1999). Causal attribution across cultures: Variation and universality. *Psychological Bulletin, 125*, 47–63.

Christensen, C. M. (1997). *The innovator's dilemma: The revolutionary book that will change the way you do business.* New York: Harper Business.

Christensen, L. (1988). Deception in psychological research: When is its use justified? *Personality and Social Psychology Bulletin, 14*, 664–675.

Chun, R. (2010). Organizational virtue, CSR, and performance. In M. Schminke (Ed.), *Managerial ethics: Managing the psychology of morality.* New York: Routledge.

Church, A. H., & Burke, W. W. (1992). Assessing the activities and values of organization development practitioners. *The Industrial-Organizational Psychologist, 30*, 59–66.

Cialdini, R. B., Brown, S. L., Lewis, B. P., Luce, C., & Neuberg, S. L. (1997). Reinterpreting the empathy-altruism relationship: When one into one equals oneness. *Journal of Personality and Social Psychology, 73*, 481–494.

Ciulla, J. B. (Ed.). (1998). *Ethics, the heart of leadership.* Westport, CT: Praeger.

Clarke, S. (1999). Justifying deception in social science research. *Journal of Applied Philosophy, 16*(2), 151–166.

Clarkson Centre for Business Ethics, University of Toronto. (1999). *Principles of stakeholder management: The Clarkson principles.* Toronto: Author.

Clarkson Centre for Business Ethics, University of Toronto. (2000). *Research in stakeholder theory, 1997–1998: The Sloan Foundation minigrant project.* Toronto: Author.

Clay, R. A. (2000). Why every private practitioner needs a business plan. *Monitor on Psychology, 31*, 48–49.

Clay, R. A. (2016). Celebrating healthy workplaces. *Monitor on Psychology,* May, 43.

Clymer, A. (1999, September 9). Sharp divergence found in views of military and civilians. *The New York Times,* A.20.

Coady, C. A. J. (2009). The Problem of Dirty Hands. In E. N. Zalta (Ed.), *The Stanford Encyclopedia of Philosophy* (Revised July 6, 2009). Downloaded April 27, 2011 from <http://plato.stanford.edu/entries/dirty-hands>

Cober, R., Silzer, R., & Erickson, A. (2009). Practice perspectives: Science-practice gaps in industrial-organizational psychology. *The Industrial-Organizational Psychologist, 47*(2), 103–110.

Coghlan, D., & Brannick, T. (2000). *Doing action research in your own organization.* Thousand Oaks, CA: Sage.

Cohen, A. (2016). *Imbeciles: The supreme court, American eugenics and the sterilization of Carrie Buck.* New York: Penguin Press.

Cohen, A. B. (2015). Religion's profound influences on psychology: morality, intergroup relations, self-construal, and enculturation. *Current Directions in Psychological Science, 24*(1), 7–82.

Cohen, B., & Greenfield, B. (2021, August 1). Men of ice cream, men of principle. *The New York Times,* SR 9.

Cohen, P. (2015a, March 18). Taxes take away, but also give back, mostly to the very rich. *The New York Times*, B 1.

Cohen, P. (2015b, Oct. 13). For-profit colleges fail standards, but get billions. *The New York Times*, A1.

Cohen, R. (2000, October 15). The ethicist: Fair or foul? *The New York Times Magazine*, Sec. 6, 48.

Cohen, R. (2001, September 23). The ethicist: Blood ties. *The New York Times Magazine*, 30–31.

Cohen, R. (2002, April 8). The politics of ethics. *The Nation*, 274, 21–23.

Cohen-Charash, Y., & Spector, P. (2001). The role of justice in organizations: A meta-analysis. *Organizational Behavior and Human Decision Processes*, 86, 278–321.

Colby, A., & Kohlberg, L. (1987). *The measurement of moral judgment* (Vols. 1 & 2). New York: Cambridge University Press.

Cole, D., Sirgy, M. J., & Bird, M. M. (2000). How do managers make teleological evaluations in ethical dilemmas? Testing part of and extending the Hunt-Vitell model. *Journal of Business Ethics*, 26, 259–269.

Colquitt, J. A. (2001). On the dimensionality of organizational justice: A construct validation of a measure. *Journal of Applied Psychology*, 86, 386–400.

Colquitt, J. A., Conlon, D. E., Wesson, M. J., Porter, C. O. L. H., & Ng, K. Y. (2001). Justice at the millennium: A meta-analytic review of 25 years of organizational justice research. *Journal of Applied Psychology*, 86, 425–445.

Colquitt, J. A., Greenberg, J., & Scott, B. A. (2005). Organizational justice: Where do we stand? In J. Greenberg & J. A. Colquitt (Eds.). *Handbook of organizational justice*. Mahwah, NJ: Lawrence Erlbaum Associates.

Colquitt, J. A., Scott, B. A., Rodell, J. B., Long, D. M., Zapata, C. P., Conlon, D. E., & Wesson, M. J. (2013). Justice at the millennium, a decade later: A meta-analytic test of social exchange and affect-based perspectives. *Journal of Applied Psychology*, 98(2), 199–236.

Colquitt, J. A., & Zipay, K. P. (2015). Justice, fairness, and employee reactions. *Annual Review of Organizational Psychology and Organizational Behavior*, 2, 75–99.

Committee on Science, Engineering and Public Policy (U.S.). Panel on Scientific Responsibility and the Conduct of Research. (1992). *Responsible science: Ensuring the integrity of the research process*. Washington, DC: National Academy Press.

Comte-Sponville, A. (2001). *A small treatise on the great virtues: The uses of philosophy in everyday life*. New York: Metropolitan Books/Henry Holt.

Congressional Budget Office (2011). *Trends in the distribution of household income between 1979 and 2007*. Washington, D.C.: Author.

Connor, A. (2001). From brain researcher to social scientist, they all answer to "psychologist". *APS Observer*, 14(1), 1, 8–9, 11.

Connor, P., & Evers, E. R. K. (2020). The bias of individuals (in crowds): Why implicit bias is probably a noisily measured individual-level construct. *Perspectives on Psychological Science*, 15(6), 1329–1345.

Cook, T. D., & Campbell, D. T. (1979). *Quasi-experimentation: Design and analysis issues for field settings*. Boston, MA: Houghton Mifflin.

Cooke, K. S., & Yamagishi, T. (2008). A defense of deception on scientific grounds. *Social Psychology Quarterly*, 71(3), 215–221.

Cooke, R. A., & Rousseau, D. M. (1988). Behavioral norms and expectations. *Group and Organization Studies*, 13, 245–273.

Cooper, C. L., & Locke, E. A. (Eds.). (2000). *Industrial and organizational psychology: Linking theory with* practice. Oxford, England: Blackwell.

Cooper, D., Mokhiber, Z., & Zipperer, B. (2021). *Raising the federal minimum wage to $15 by 2025 would lift the pay of 32 million workers.* Washington, D.C.: Economic Policy Institute, March 9. Retrieved from https://www.epi.org/publication/raising-the-federal-minimum-wage-to-15-by-2025-would-lift-the-pay-of-32-million-workers/, Nov. 15, 2021.

Cooper, T. L. (1998). *The responsible administrator: An approach to ethics for the administrative role* (4th ed.). San Francisco: Jossey-Bass.

Cooper, T. L. (Ed.). (2001). *Handbook of administrative ethics*, 2nd Ed. New York: Dekker.

Copleston, F. (1994). A *history of philosophy: Vol. V. Modern philosophy: The British philosophers from Hobbes to Hume. New* York: Doubleday.

Corkery, M. (2016, Oct. 7). More wrath aimed at Wells Fargo, in a newspaper ad. *The New York Times*, B3.

Corkery, M. & Cowley, S. (2016, Sept. 17). Warned about excesses, then prodded to sell. *The New York Times*, A1, B3.

Corkery, M. & Silver-Greenberg, J. (2015, Nov. 3). When scripture is the rule of law. *The New York Times*, B1, 6-7.

Corkery, M., & Silver-Greenberg, J. (2016, Feb. 22). A nursing home murder and a family's arbitration fight. *The New York Times*, A1, B5.

Cornelissen, G., Bashshur, M. R., Rode, J., & Le Menestre, M. (2013). Rules or consequences? The role of ethical mind-sets in moral dynamics. *Psychological Science, 24*(4), 82–488.

Cortina, L. M., Kabat-Farr, D., Magley, V. J., & Nelson, K. (2017). Researching rudeness: The past, present, and future of the science of incivility. *Journal of Occupational Health Psychology, 22*(3), 299–313.

Costa, P. T. Jr., & McCrae, R. R. (1985). *The NEO Personality Inventory.* Odessa, Fl: Psychological Assessment Resources.

Costanza, D. P., & Finkelstein, L. M. (2015). Generationally based differences in the workplace: Is there a *there* there? *Industrial and Organizational Psychology, 8*(3), 308–323.

Coulter, X. (1986). Academic value of research participation by undergraduates. *American Psychologist, 41*, 317.

Cowan, R. L., & Fox, S. (2015). Being pushed and pulled: A model of US HR professionals' roles in bullying situations. *Personnel Review, 44*(1), 119–139.

Cragg, W., Arnold, D. G., & Muchlinski, P. (2012). Special Issue: Human rights and business. *Business Ethics Quarterly, 22*(1), 1–144.

Crain, A.l., Martinson, B. C., & Thrush, C. R. (2013). Relationship between the survey of organizational research climate (SORC) and self-reported research practices. *Science and Engineering Ethics, 19*, 835–850.

Cramer, M. (2021, July 4). Investigating Amazon, the employer. *The New York Times*, A2.

Cresswell, J., Clifford, S. & Pollack, A. (2015, Dec. 18). FBI arrests C.E.O. vilified for drug costs. *The New York Times*, B6.

Crimston, D. Hornsey, M. J., Bain, P. G., & Bastian, B. (2018). Toward a psychology of moral expansiveness. *Current Directions in Psychological Science, 27*(1), 14–19.

Crocker, J., Canevello, A., & Brown, A. A. (2017), Social motivation: Costs and benefits of selfishness and otherishness. In S. T. Fiske, D. L. Schacter, & S. E. Taylor (Eds.). *Annual Review of Psychology, 68*, 299–325.

Crockett, M. J. (2016). How formal models can illuminate mechanisms of moral judgment and decision making. *Current Directions in Psychological Science, 25*(2), 85–90.

Crompton, R. (1991). Review of M. Burrage & R. Torstendahl (Eds.) Professions in theory and history: Rethinking the study of the professions, and R. Torstendahl & M. Burrage (Eds.) The formation of professions: Knowledge, state and strategy. *Sociology, 25*(1), 147–149.

Cropanzano, R. (1993). *Justice in the workplace:* Approaching *fairness in human resource management.* Hillsdale, NJ: Lawrence Erlbaum Associates.

Cropanzano, R. S., & Ambrose, M. L. (2015). *The Oxford University handbook of justice in the workplace.* New York: Oxford University Press.

Cropanzano, R., Byrne, Z. S., Bobocel, D. R., & Rupp, D. E. (2001). Moral virtues, fairness heuristics, social entities, and other denizens of organizational justice. *Journal of Vocational Behavior, 58,* 164–209.

Cropanzano, R., Goldman, B., & Folger, R. (2003). Deontic justice: the role of moral principles in workplace fairness. *Journal of Organizational Behavior, 24,* 1019–1024.

Cropanzano, R., Massaro, S., & Becker, W. J. (2017). Deontic justice and organizational neuroscience. *Journal of Business Ethics, 144*(4), 733–754.

Cross, B. (2021). Moral philosophy, moral expertise, and the argument from disagreement. *Bioethics, 30*(3), 188–194.

Cugueró-Escofet, N., & Fortin, M. (2014). One justice or two? A model of reconciliation of normative justice theories and empirical research on organizational justice. *Journal of Business Ethics, 124,* 435–451.

Cunningham, P. J., Grossman, J. M., St. Peter, R. F., & Lesser, C. S. (1999). Managed care and physicians' provision of charity care. *Journal of the American Medical Association, 281,* 1087–1092.

Curtis, V., Aunger, R., & Rabie, T. (2004). Evidence that disgust evolved to protect from risk of disease. *Proceedings of the Royal Society of London B, 271,* S131–S133.

Dahnani, L. Y., Beus, J., & Joseph, D. L. (2017). Workplace discrimination: A meta-analytic extension, critique, and future research agenda. *Personnel Psychology, 71,* 147–179.

Dalai Lama. (1999). *Ethics for the new millennium.* New York: Riverhead.

Dalai Lama (2011). *Beyond religion: Ethics for a whole world.* New York, NY: Houghton Mifflin Harcourt.

Dalton, G. (1974). *Economic systems and society.* Kingsport, TN: Kingsport.

Daley, S. (2015, April 26). Speeding in Finland can cost a fortune, if you already have one. *The New York Times International,* 12.

Dalziel, J. R. (1996). Students as research subjects: Ethical and educational issues. *Australian Psychologist, 31,* 119–123.

Damasio, A. R., Harrington, A., Kagan, J., McEwen, B. S., Moss, H., & Shaikh, R. (Eds.). (2001). *Unity of knowledge: The convergence of natural and human science* (Vol. 935). New York: Annals of the New York Academy of Sciences.

Damon, W. (1999). The moral development of children. *Scientific American, 281,* 72–79.

Danley, J. R. (1994). *The role of the modern corporation in a free society.* Notre Dame, IN: University of Notre Dame Press.

Danley, J. R. (2000). Philosophy, science and business ethics: Frederick's new normative synthesis. *Journal of Business Ethics, 26,* 111–122.

D'Andrade, R. (1995). Objectivity and militancy: A debate. I. Moral models in anthropology. *Current Anthropology, 36*(3), 399–408.

Darley, J. M., Messick, D. M., & Tyler, T. R. (2001). *Social influences on ethical behavior in organizations.* Mahwah, NJ: Lawrence Erlbaum Associates.

Davis, G. F. (2016). Can an economy survive without corporations? Technology and robust organizational alternatives. *Academy of Management Perspectives, 30*(2), 129–140.

Davison, G. (1995). The ethics of confidentiality: Introduction. *Australian Psychologist*, 30, 153–157.

Davidson, R. E. (1985). Professional conflicts within organizations. *Sociology and Social Research, 69*, 210–220.

Davis, M. (1994). *Empathy: A social-psychological approach*. Madison, WI: Brown & Benchmark.

Davis, N. A. (1993). Contemporary deontology. In P. Singer (Ed.), A *companion to ethics* (pp. 205–218). Cambridge, MA: Blackwell.

Dawis, R. V. (1991). Vocational interests, values, and preferences. In M. D. Dunnette & L. M. Hough (Eds.), *Handbook of industrial & organizational psychology*, (Vol. 2, pp. 833–871). Palo Alto, CA: Consulting Psychologists Press.

Dawis, R. V., & Lofquist, L. H. (1984). A *psychological theory of work adjustment*. Minneapolis: University of Minnesota Press.

Dawkins, C. E. (2012). Labored relations: Corporate citizenship, labor unions, and freedom of association. *Business Ethics Quarterly, 22*(3), 473–500.

De Bakker, F. G. A., Matten, D., Spence, L. J., & Wickert, C. (2020). Special Issue: Corporations, social responsibility and capitalism. *Business & Society, 59*(7), 1295–1514.

De Bruin, A., Treccani, B. & Della Sala, S. (2015). Cognitive advantage in Bilingualism: An example of publication bias? *Psychological Science, 26*(1), 99–107.

De Bruin, B., Parker, A. M., & Fischoff, B. (2020). Decision-making competence: More than intelligence? *Current Directions in Psychological Science, 29*, 186–192.

Decety, J., & Cowell, J. M. (2014). Friends or foes: Is empathy necessary for moral behavior? *Perspectives on Psychological Science, 9*(5), 525–537.

De Corte, W., Lievens, F. & ackett, P. R. (2007). Combining predictors to achieve optimal trade-offs between selection quality and adverse impact. *Journal of Applied Psychology, 92*, 1380–1393.

DeCoster, J., Sparks, E. A., Sparks, J. C., Sparks, G. G., & Sparks, C. W. (2015). Opportunistic biases: Their origins, effects, and an integrated solution. *American Psychologist, 70*(6), 499–514.

de Waal, F. B. M. (1996). *Good natured: The origins of right and wrong in humans and other animals*. Cambridge, MA: Harvard University Press.

de Waal, F. B. M. (2008). Putting the altruism back in altruism. *Annual Review of Psychology, 59*, 279–300.

Deal, T. E., & Kennedy, A. A. (1999). *The new corporate cultures: Revitalizing the workplace after downsizing, mergers, and reengineering*. Cambridge, MA: Perseus.

Deaux, K., Reid, A., Mizrahi, K., & Ethier, K. A. (1995). Parameters of social identity. *Journal of Personality and Social Psychology, 68*, 280–291.

Deci, E. L., & Ryan, R. M. (1991). Intrinsic motivation and self-determination in human performance. In R. M. Steers, & L. W. Porter (Eds.), *Motivation and work behavior* (5th ed., pp. 44–58). New York: McGraw-Hill.

Deci, E. L., Koestner, R. & Ryan, R. M. (1999). A meta-analytic review of experiments examining the effects of extrinsic rewards on intrinsic motivation. *Psychological Bulletin, 125*(6), 627–668.

Deckop, J. R. (2006). *Human resource management ethics*. Greenwich, CT: Information Age Publishing.

De Cremer, D. Mayer, D. M., & Schminke, M. (2010). Guest Editors' Introduction: On understanding ethical behavior and decision-making: A behavioral ethics approach. *Business Ethics Quarterly, 20*(1), 1–6.

DeGeorge, R. (1987). The status of business ethics: Past and future. *Journal of Business Ethics, 6,* 201–212.

Delaney, A., & Golshan, T. (2021, Oct, 20). Federal unemployment benefits are gone. Businesses still say they can't find workers. Economic Policy Institute. Retrieved from https://www.huffpost.com/entry/federal-unemployment-benefits-hiring_n_616f6f79e4b 005b245c38217?utm_source=Economic+Policy+Institute&utm_campaign=059ca659e5-EMAIL_CAMPAIGN_2021_10_27&utm_medium=email&utm_term=0_e7c5826c50-059ca659e5-58536137&mc_cid=059ca659e5&mc_eid=c3b577356e on Nov. 17, 2021.

DeLeon, L. (1994). The professional values of public managers, policy analysts and politicians. *Public Personnel Management, 23,* 135–152.

Delery, S. F. (2016, Apr. 12). Quoted in N. Popper. Goldman's settlement on mortgages is less than meets the eye. *New York Times,* A1, B3.

Delgado, R., & Stefancic, J. (2001). *Critical race theory: An introduction.* New York: NYU Press.

Demuijnck, G. (2015). Universal values and virtues in management versus cross-cultural moral relativism: An educational strategy to clear the ground for business ethics. *Journal of Business Ethics, 128,* 817–835.

Den Hartog, D. N. (2015). Ethical leadership. *Annual Review of Organizational Psychology and Organizational Behavior, 2,* 409–434.

Den Hartog, & Belschak, F. D. (2012). Work engagement and Machiavellianism in the ethical leadership process. *Journal of Business Ethics, 107*(1), 35–47.

Derber, C. (1998). *Corporation nation: How corporations are taking over our lives and what we can do about it.* New York: St. Martin's Griffin.

Dessler, G. (1999). How to earn your employees' commitment. *Academy of Management Executive, 13,* 58–67.

Deutsch, M. (1969). Socially relevant science: Reflections on some studies of interpersonal conflict. *American Psychologist, 24,* 1076–1092.

Deutsch, M. (1975). Equity, equality, and need: What determines which value will be used as the basis of distributive justice? *Journal of Social Issues, 31,* 137–149.

Deutsch, M. (1985). *Distributive justice.* New Haven, CT: Yale University Press.

DeVries, R., Anderson, M. S., & Martinson, B. C. (2006). Normal misbehavior: Scientists talk about the ethics of research. *Journal of Empirical Research on Human Research Ethics, 1*(1), 43–50.

De Waal, F. (2009). *The age of empathy.* New York: Crown.

Dewey, J. (1929). *The quest for certainty.* New York: Minton, Balch.

Dewey, J. (1939). *Theory of valuation.* Chicago: University of Chicago Press.

Diener, E., & Crandall, R. (1978). *Ethics in social and behavioral research.* Chicago: University of Chicago Press.

Diener, E., & Seligman, M. E. P. (2018). Beyond money: Progress on an economy of well-being. *Perspectives on Psychological Science, 13*(2), 171–175.

Dierdorff, E. C., & Morgeson, F. P. (2013). Getting what the occupation gives: Exploring multilevel links between work design and occupational values. *Personnel Psychology, 66,* 687–721.

Digman, J. M. (1990). Personality structure: Emergence of the five-factor model. *Annual Review of Psychology, 41,* 417–440.

Dik, B. J., Byrne, Z. S., & Steger, M. F. (Eds.). *Purpose and meaning in the workplace.* Washington, DC: American Psychological Association.

Ding, X. P., Wellman, H. M., Wan, Y., Fu, G., & Lee, K. (2015). Theory-of-mind training causes honest young children to lie. *Psychological Science, 26*(11), 1812–1821.

DiNorcia, V., & Tigner, J. (2000). Mixed motives and ethical decisions in business. *Journal of Business Ethics, 25,* 1–13.

Di Nucci, E. (2014). Trolleys and double effect in experimental ethics. Chap. 7 in In C. Luetge, H. Rusch & M. Uhl (Eds.), *Experimental ethics: Toward an empirical moral philosophy* (pp. 80–93). Houndmills, England: Palgrave Macmillan.

Doh, J., Husted, B. W., & Yang, X. (2016). Ethics, corporate social responsibility, and developing country multinationals. *Business Ethics Quarterly, 26*(3), 301–315.

Donaldson, T. (1982). *Corporations and morality.* Englewood Cliffs, NJ: Prentice-Hall.

Donaldson, T. (1989). *The ethics of international business.* New York: Oxford University Press.

Donaldson, T., & Dunfee, T. W. (1994). Toward a unified conception of business ethics: Integrative social contracts theory. *Academy of Management Review, 19,* 252–284.

Donaldson, T., & Preston, L. E. (1995). The stakeholder theory of the corporation: Concepts, evidence, and implications. *Academy of Management Review, 20,* 65–91.

Donaldson, T., & Walsh, J. P. (2015). Toward a theory of business. *Research in Organizational Behavior, 35,* 181–207.

Doris, J. M. (2002). *Lack of character: Personality and moral behavior.* New York: Cambridge University Press.

Doris, J. M. & the Moral Psychology Research Group. (2010). *The moral psychology handbook.* New York, NY: Oxford University Press.

Douglas, H. E. (2009). *Science, policy and the value-free ideal.* Pittsburgh: University of Pittsburgh Press.

Douglas, P. C., Davidson, R. A., & Schwartz, B. N. (2001). The effect of organizational culture and ethical orientation on accountants' ethical judgments. *Journal of Business Ethics, 34,* 101–121.

Drucker, J. (2022, Feb. 23). Leaders want Treasury to examine hiring issue. *The New York Times,* B3.

Druckman, D., & Wagner, L. M. (2016). Justice and negotiation. *Annual Review of Psychology, 67,* 387–413.

Duarte, J. L., Crawford, J. T., Stern, C., Haidt, J. Jussim, L., & Tetlock, P. E. (2015). Political diversity will improve social psychological science. *Behavioral and Brain Sciences, 38,* 1–13.

Dubinsky, A. J., & Loken, B. (1989). Analyzing ethical decision making in marketing. *Journal of Business Research, 19,* 83–107.

DuBois, J. M. (2014). Ethically speaking. Learning from cases of research misconduct. *Monitor on Psychology, 45*(1), 32–33.

Duchon, D., & Drake, B. (2009). Organizational narcissism and virtuous behavior. *Journal of Business Ethics, 85,* 301–308.

Duckett, L. J., & Ryden, M. B. (1994). Education for ethical nursing practice. In J. R. Rest & D. Narvaez (Eds.), *Moral development in the professions* (pp. 51–70). Hillsdale, NJ: Lawrence Erlbaum Associates.

Duckworth, A. L., Gendler, T. S., & Gross, J. J. (2016). Situational strategies for self-control. *Perspectives on Psychological Science, 11*(1), 35–55.

Duff, A., & Cotgrove, S. (1982). Social values and the choice of careers in industry. *Journal of Occupational Psychology, 55,* 97–107.

Dunfee, T. W. (1987). Work-related ethical attitudes: A key to profitability? In S. P. Sethi & C. M. Falbe (Eds.), *Business and society: Dimensions of conflict and cooperation* (pp. 292–310). Lexington, MA: Lexington.

Dunford, B. B., & Devine, D. J. (1998). Employment at-will and employee discharge: A justice perspective on legal action following termination. *Personnel Psychology, 51,* 903–934.

Dunkelberg, J., & Jessup, D. R. (2001). So then why did you do it? *Journal of Business Ethics, 29,* 51–63.

Dunn, J. (2014). Moral development in early childhood and social interaction in the family. Chap. 7 In M. Killen, & J. G. Smetana (Eds.), *Handbook of moral development.* New York: Taylor and Francis Group, 135–159.

Dunnette, M. D. (1984, August). *I/O psychology in the 80s: Fads, fashions, and folderol revisited.* Paper presented at the 92nd Annual Conference of the American Psychological Association, Toronto.

Dunnette, M. D. (1990). Blending the science and practice of industrial and organizational psychology: Where are we and where are we going? In M. D. Dunnette, & L. M. Hough (Eds.), (1990). *Handbook of industrial and organizational psychology* (2nd ed., Vol. 1, pp. 1–27). Palo Alto, CA: Consulting Psychologists Press.

Dunnette, M. D. (2001). Science and practice in applied psychology: A symbiotic relationship. *Applied Psychology: An International Review, 50,* 222–224.

Dunnette, M. D., & Hough, L. M. (Eds.). (1990). *Handbook of industrial and organizational psychology* (2nd ed., Vol. 1). Palo Alto, CA: Consulting Psychologists Press.

Dunnette, M. D., & Hough, L. M. (Eds.). (1991). *Handbook of industrial and organizational psychology* (2nd ed., Vol. 2). Palo Alto, CA: Consulting Psychologists Press.

Dunnette, M. D., & Hough, L. M. (Eds.). (1992). *Handbook of industrial and organizational psychology* (2nd ed., Vol. 3). Palo Alto, CA: Consulting Psychologists Press.

Durkheim, E. (1953). *Sociology and philosophy.* New York: The Free Press. (Original work published 1898)

Durkheim, E. (1956). *The division of labor in society.* New York: The Free Press. (Original work published 1893).

Dutton, J. E., Glynn, M., & Spreitzer, G. M. (2006). Positive organizational scholarship. In J. Greenhaus, & G. Callahan (Eds.), *Encyclopedia of career development* (pp. 641–644). Thousand Oaks, CA: Sage Publications.

Dutton, J. E., Workman, K. M., & Hardin, A. E. (2014). Compassion at work. *Annual Review of Organizational Psychology and Organizational Behavior, 1,* 277–304.

Dwyer, S. (2008). How not to argue that morality isn't innate: Comments on Prinz. Chapter 7.1 In W. Sinnott-Armstrong (Ed.), *Moral psychology. Volume 1: The evolution of morality: Adaptations and innateness* (pp. 407–418). Cambridge, MA: The MIT Press.

Earley, P. C., & Gibson, C. B. (1998). Taking stock in our progress on individualism–collectivism: 100 years of solidarity and community. *Journal of Management, 24,* 265–304.

Eaton, A. A., Grzanka, P. R., Schlehofer, M. M., & Silka, L. (Eds.). Special issue: Public psychology: Engaged science for the 21st century. *American Psychologist, 76*(8).

Eavis, P. (2021, June 13). They're cashing in like never before. *The New York Times,* B1.

Eavis, P. (2022, March 3). A Starbucks votes union in Starbucks's hometown. *The New York Times,* B1.

Economic Innovation Group (2016). *The 2016 Distressed Communities Index.* Washington, DC: Author.

Economic Policy Institute. (2014, Dec. 18). *The top 10 charts of 2014*. Washington, DC: Economic Policy Institute.

Economic Policy Institute. (2015, Dec. 17). *The top charts of 2015*. Washington, DC: Author.

Economic Policy Institute. (2019, Dec. 23). *Top charts of 2019: Thirteen charts that clarify what our economic priorities need to be in 2020*. Washington, DC: Author.

Economic Policy Institute. (2021, April 23). Fact Sheet. Unions help reduce disparities and strengthen our democracy. Retrieved from https://www.epi.org/publication/unions-help-reduce-disparities-and-strengthen-our-democracy/ on Oct. 21, 2021.

Eckensberger, L. H., & Zimba, R. F. (1997). The development of moral judgment. In J. W. Berry, P. R. Dasen, & T. S. Saraswathi (Eds.), *Handbook of cross-cultural psychology* (Vol. 2, pp. 299–338). Boston: Allyn & Bacon.

Economist. (2013, Oct. 19). Problems with scientific research: How science goes wrong. Downloaded from http://www.economist.com/node/21588069/print on April 25, 2016.

Edwards, C. P. (1987). Culture and the construction of moral values: A comparative ethnography of moral encounters in two cultural settings. In J. Kagan & S. Lamb (Eds.), *The emergence of morality in young children* (pp. 123–151). Chicago: University of Chicago Press.

Edwards, C. P. (1993). Culture and the construction of moral values: A comparative ethnography of moral encounters in two cultural settings. In A. Dobrin (Ed.), *Being good and doing* right: *Readings in moral development* (pp. 93–120). Lanham, MD: University Press of America.

Edwards, J. T., Nalbandian, J., & Wedel, K. R. (1981). Individual values and professional education: Implications for practice and education. *Administration & Society, 13*, 123–143.

Edwards, R. (1993). *Rights at work: Employment relations in the post-union era*. Washington, DC: Brookings Institution.

Eich, E. (2014). Business not as usual. *Psychological Science, 25*(1), 3–6.

Eisenberg, N., & Miller, P. A. (1987). Empathy, sympathy and altruism: empirical and conceptual links. In N. Eisenberg & J. Strayer (Eds.), *Empathy and its development* (pp. 292–316). Cambridge, England: Cambridge University Press.

Eisenberger, R., Malone, G. P., & Presson, W. D. (2016). Optimizing perceived organizational support to enhance employee engagement. *Society for Human Resource Management-Society for Industrial and Organizational Psychology Science of HR Series*.

Eiser, J. R. (1987). *The expression of attitude*. New York: Springer-Verlag.

Ekman, P. (2016). What scientists who study emotion agree about. *Perspectives on Psychological Science, 11*(1), 31–34.

Elizur, D., & Sagie, A. (1999). Facets of personal values: A structural analysis of life and work values. *Applied Psychology:* An *International Review, 48*, 73–87.

Ellemers, N., & van Nunspeet, F. (2020). Neuroscience and the social origins of moral behavior: How neural underpinnings of social categorization and conformity affect every day moral and immoral behavior. *Current Directions in Psychological Science, 29*(5), 513–520.

Ellen III, B. P., Alexander, K. C., Mackey, J. D., McAllister, C. P., & Carson, J. E. (2021). Portrait of a workplace deviant: A clearer picture of the Big Five and Dark Triad as predictors of workplace deviance. *Journal of Applied Psychology, 106*(12), 1950–1961.

Elliott, K. C. (2011). Direct and indirect roles for values in science. *Philosophy of Science, 78*(April), 303–324.

Elliott, K. C., & Resnick, D. B. (2014). Science, policy, and the transparency of values. *Environmental Health Prospects, 122*(7), 647–650.

Elliott, P. (1972). *The sociology of the professions.* New York: Herder and Herder.

Elms, A. (1995). Obedience in retrospect. *Journal of social Issues, 51,* 21–31.

Emler, N., & Hogan, R. (1991)Moral psychology and public policy. In W. M. Kurtines & J. L. Gewirtz (Eds.), Handbook of moral behavior and development. Vol. 3. (pp. 69–93). Hillsdale, NJ: Lawrence Erlbaum Associates.

Endrikat, J., deVilliers, C., Guenther, T. W. & Guenther, E. M. (2021). Board characteristics and corporate social responsibility: A meta-analytic investigation. *Business & Society, 60*(8), 2099–2135.

Engel, C. (2015). Scientific disintegrity as a public bad. *Perspectives on Psychological Science, 10*(3), 361–379.

Engel, G. V. (1970). Professional autonomy and bureaucratic organization. *Administrative Science* Quarterly, *15,* 12–21.

England, G. W., & Lee, R. (1974). The relationship between managerial values and managerial success in the United States, Japan, India, and Australia. *Journal of Applied Psychology, 59,* 411–419.

Epley, N., & Huff, C. (1998). Suspicion, affective response, and educational benefit as a result of deception in psychology research. *Personality and Social Psychology Bulletin, 24,* 759–768.

Epstein, E. M. (1999). The continuing quest for accountable, ethical, and humane corporate capitalism: An enduring challenge for social issues in management in the new millennium. *Business & Society, 38,* 253–267.

Epstein, S. (1989). Values from the perspective of cognitive-experiential self-theory. In N. Eisenberg, J. Reykowski, & E. Staub (Eds.), *Social and moral values: Individual and societal perspectives* (pp. 3–22). Hillsdale, NJ: Lawrence Erlbaum Associates.

Equal Employment Opportunity Commission, Civil Service Commission, Department of Labor, and Department of Justice. (1978, August 25). Uniform guidelines on employee selection procedures. *Federal Register, 43*(166), 38290–38315.

Equilar, Inc. (2015). 200 highest-paid CEO's 2016. Retrieved from http://www.equilar.com/reports/38-new-york-times-200-highest-paid-ceos-2016.html on June 8, 2016.

Erikson, E. H. (1964). The golden rule in the light of new insight. In E. H. Erikson (Ed.), *Insight and responsibility: Lectures* on *the ethical implications of psychoanalytic insight* (pp. 219–243). New York: Norton.

Ermann, M. D., & Lundman, R. J. (Eds.). (1996). Corporate *and governmental deviance: Problems of organizational behavior* in contemporary *society* (5th ed.). New York: Oxford University Press.

Escrig-Olmedo, W., Muñoz-Torres J., & Fernandez-Izquierdo, M. A. (2012). Sustainable development and the financial system: Society's perceptions about socially responsible investing. *Business Strategy and the Environment, 22,* 410–428.

Etzioni, A. (Ed.). (1969). *The semi-professions and* their *organization.* New York: The Free Press.

Etzioni, A. (1988). *The moral dimension: Toward a new economics.* New York: The Free Press.

Etzioni, A. (1996). *The new golden rule:* Community *and morality* in *a democratic society.* New York: Basic Books.

Etzioni, A. (2015). *The new normal: finding a balance between individual rights and the common good.* Routledge/Taylor & Francis Group.

Evans, J. (2021). How professionals construct moral authority: Expanding boundaries of expert authority in stem cell science. *Administrative Science Quarterly, 66*(4), 989–1036.

Evans, J., St., B. T. & Stanovich, K. E. (2013). Dual-process theories of higher cognitions: Advancing the debate. *Perspectives on Psychological Science*, *8*(3), 223–241.

Ewing, J., & Tabuchi, H. (2016, July 20). Lawsuits trace Volkswagen's cover-up of cheating all the way to the top. *New York Times*, B1.

Executive compensation scoreboard. (2000, April 17). *Business Week*, pp. 114–142. NYC, NY: Bloomberg Businessweek.

Eyde, L. D. (2000). Other responsibilities to participants. In B. D. Sales, & S. Folkman (Eds.), *Ethics in research with human* participants (pp. 61–73). Washington, DC: American Psychological Association.

Eyde, L. D., & Quaintance, M. K. (1988). Ethical issues and cases in the practice of personnel psychology. *Professional Psychology: Research and Practice*, *19*, 148–154.

Eyde, L. D., Robertson, G. J., Krug, S. E., Moreland, K. L., Robertson, A. G., Shewan, C. M., Harrison, P. L., Porch, B. E., Hammer, A. L., & Primoff, E. S. (1993). *Responsible test use: Case studies for assessing human behavior*. Washington, DC: American Psychological Association.

Fanelli, D. (2009). How many scientists fabricate and falsify research? A systematic review and meta-analysis of survey data. *PLoS ONE*, *4*(5), 1–11.

Falkenberg, L., & Herremans, I. (1995). Ethical behaviours in organizations: Directed by the formal or informal systems? *Journal of Business Ethics*, *14*, 133–143.

Fanelli, D. (2010). Do pressures to publish increase scientists' bias? An empirical support from US states data. *PLoS One*, *5*(4), 1–7.

Fanelli, D. (2014, May 1). Rise in retractions is a signal of integrity. *Nature*, 33.

Fanelli, D., Costas, R., & Larivière, V. (2015). Misconduct policies, academic culture and career stage, not gender or pressures to publish, affect scientific integrity. *PLoS One*, *10*(6), 1–18.

Faraci, D. (2019). Wage exploitation and the nonworseness claim: Allowing the wrong, to do more good. *Business Ethics Quarterly*, *29*(2), 169–188.

Farah, M. J. (2012). Neuroethics: The ethical, legal, and societal impact of neuroscience. *Annual Review of Psychology*, *63*, 571–591.

Farber, H. S., Herbst, D. Kuziemko, I., & Naidu, S. (2021). Unions and inequality over the twentieth century: New evidence from survey data. *Quarterly Journal of Economics*, *136*(3), 1325–1385.

Favaretto, M., De Clereq, E., Gaab, J., & Elger, B. S. (2020). First do no harm: An exploeration of researchers' ethics of conduct in big data behavioral studies. *PLoS ONE*, *15*(11), e0241865, 1–23.

Feather, N. T. (1982). Reasons for entering medical school in relation to value priorites and sex of student. *Journal of Occupational Psychology*, 55, 119–128.

Feather, N. T. (1992). Values, valences, expectations and actions. *Journal of Social Issues*, *48*, 109–124.

Fehr, R., Fullmer, A., & Keng-Highberger, F. T. (2020). How do employees react to leaders' unethical behavior? The role of moral disengagement. *Personnel Psychology*, *73*(1), 73–93.

Fehr, R., Yam, K. C. S., & Dang, C. (2015). Moralized leadership: The construction and consequences of ethical leadership perceptions. *Academy of Management Review*, *40*(2), 182–209.

Feinberg, J. (1984). *Harm to others: The moral limits of the criminal law*. New York: Oxford University Press.

Feinberg, M. R., & Lefkowitz, J. (1962). Image of industrial psychology among corporate executives. *American Psychologist*, *17*, 109–111.

Ferguson, C. J. (2015). "Everybody knows psychology is not a real science:" Public perceptions of psychology and how we can improve our relationship with policy-makers, the scientific community, and the general public. *American Psychologist, 70*(6), 527–542.

Ferguson, L. W. (1962–1965). *The heritage of industrial psychology* (14 pamphlets). Hartford, CT: Finlay.

Ferrell, O. C., Fraedrich, J. & Ferrell, L. (2002). *Business ethics: Ethical decision making and cases.* Boston, MA: Houghton Mifflin Company.

Feyerabend, P. K. (1963). How to be a good empiricist-A plea for tolerance in matters epistemological. In B. Baumrin (Ed.), *Philosophy of science: The Delaware seminar.* (Vol. 2, pp. 3–41). New York: Wiley.

Feyerabend, P. K. (1975). *Against method.* London: Redwood Barn.

Fieser, J. (1996). Do businesses have moral obligations beyond what the law requires? *Journal of Business Ethics, 15,* 457–468.

Fife, D. (2020). The eight steps of data analysis: A graphical framework to promote sound statistical analysis. *Perspectives on Psychological Science, 15*(4), 1054–1075.

Fine, A. D., & van Rooij, B. (2021). Legal socialization: Understanding the obligation to obey the law. *Journal of Social Issues, 77*(2), 367–391.

Finkel, N. J., & Groscup, J. L. (1997). When mistakes happen: Commonsense rules of culpability. *Psychology, Public Policy, and Law, 3,* 65–125.

Fischhoff, B., & Broomell, S. B. (2020). Judgment and decision making. In S. T. Fiske, & D. L. Schacter (Eds.). *Annual Review of Psychology, 71,* 331–355.

Fish, J. M. (2000). What anthropology can do for psychology: Facing physics envy, ethnocentrism, and a belief in "race". *American Anthropologist, 102,* 552–563.

Fisher, C. B., & Fryberg, D. (1994). Participant partners: College students wight the costs and benefits of deceptive research. *American Psychologist, 49,* 417–427.

Fisher, S. R., & White, M. A. (2000). Downsizing in a learning organization: Are there hidden costs? *Academy of Management Review, 25,* 244–251.

Fishman, D. B. (1999). *The case for pragmatic psychology.* New York: New York University Press.

Flanagan, O., Sarkissian, & Wong, D. (2008). Naturalizing ethics. Chap. 1 In W. Sinnott-Armstrong, (Ed.) (2008), *Moral Psychology: Volume I. The evolution of morality: Adaptations and innateness* (pp. 1–25). Cambridge, MA: The MIT Press.

Flanagan, O., & Williams, R. A. (2010). What does the modularity of morals have to do with ethics? Four moral sprouts plus or minus a few. *Topics in Cognitive Science, 2,* 430–453.

Fletcher, J. (1966). *Situation ethics: The new morality.* Philadelphia: Westminster.

Flannery, M. E. (2018). Follow the Money: The School-to-(Privatized)-Prison Pipeline. *NEA Today, 36*(3), 63.

Folger, R., & Lewis, D. (1993). Self-appraisal and fairness in evaluations. In R. Cropanzano (Ed.), *Justice in the workplace: Approaching fairness in human resource management* (pp. 107–131). Hillsdale, NJ: Lawrence Erlbaum Associates.

Folkman, S. (2000). Privacy and confidentiality. In B. D. Sales, & S. Folkman (Eds.), *Ethics in research with human participants* (pp. 49–58). Washington, DC: American Psychological Association.

Forbes, Inc. (1996). *Thoughts on virtue: Thoughts and reflections from history's great thinkers.* Chicago: Triumph Books.

Forbes top CEOs: Corporate America's most powerful people. (2001). *Forbes Magazine* [online serial]. Available: http://www.forbes.com/CEOS

Ford, J. (2001). Call for papers. Academy of Management Review special topic forum. Language and organization. *Academy of Management Review*, 26, 328–330.

Ford, J. (2015). Perspectives on the evolving "business and peace" debate. *Academy of Management Perspectives, 29*(4), 451–460.

Ford, R. C., & Richardson, W. D. (1994). Ethical decision making: A review of the empirical literature. *Journal of Business Ethics, 13*, 205–221.

Fountain, J. W. (2002 January 5). On an icy night, little room at the shelter. *The New York Times*, A1, A9.

Fox, H. R., & Spector, P. E. (2002). Occupational health psychology: I–O psychologists meet with interdisciplinary colleagues to discuss this emerging field. *The Industrial-Organizational Psychologist, 39*, 139–142.

Fox, L., Garfinkel, I., Kaushal, N., Waldfogel, J., & Wimer, C. (2014). *Waging war on poverty: Historical trends in poverty using the supplemental poverty measure.* Working paper 19789. Cambridge, MA: National Bureau of Economic Research.

France, A. (1930). *The red lily.* Chapter 7. London: John Lane—The Bodley Head, Ltd. (First published 1894).

Franke, G. R., Crown, D. F., & Spake, D. F. (1995). Gender differences in ethical perceptions of business practices: A social role theory perspective. *Journal of Applied Psychology, 82*, 920–934.

Frankena, W. K. (1973). *Ethics*, (2nd ed.). Englewood Cliffs, NJ: Prentice-Hall.

Fraser, J. A. (2001). *White-collar sweatshop: The deterioration of work and its rewards in corporate America.* New York: Norton.

Frazer, M. J., & Kornhauser, A. (1986). *Ethics and social responsibility in science education.* Oxford: Pergamon.

Frederick, W. C. (1995). *Values, nature, and culture in the American corporation.* New York: Oxford University Press.

Frederick, W. C. (1999). An Appalachian coda: The core values of business. *Business & Society, 38*, 206–211.

Freeman, R. E., Moriarty, B., & Stewart, L. A. (2009). Ethical leadership. Ch. 8 In R. J. Burke & C. L. Cooper (Eds.), *Research companion to corruption in organizations* (pp. 192–205). Cheltenham, UK: Edward Elgar.

Freeman, R. E., & Phillips, R. A. (2002). Stakeholder theory: A libertarian defense. *Business Ethics* Quarterly, *12*, 331–349.

Frega, R. (2021). Employee involvement and workplace democracy. *Business Ethics Quarterly, 31*(3), 360–385.

Freidson, E. (1973). Professions and the occupational principle. In E. Freidson (Ed.), *The professions and their prospects* (pp. 19–38). Beverly Hills: Sage.

Freidson, E. (1986). *Professional powers: A study of the institutionalization of formal knowledge.* Chicago: University of Chicago Press.

Freidson, E. (2001). *Professionalism: the third logic.* Chicago: University of Chicago Press.

French, W., & Weis, A. (2000). An ethics of care or an ethics of justice. *Journal of Business Ethics, 27*, 125–136.

Freudenheim, M. (2001, July 11). In a shift, an H.M.O. rewards doctors for quality care. *The New York Times*, C1, C4.

Frey, B. F. (2000). The impact of moral intensity on decision making in a business context. *Journal of Business Ethics, 26*, 181–195.

Frey, W. J. (2015). Teaching responsibility: Pedagogical strategies for eliciting a sense of moral responsibility. *Teaching Ethics, 15*(2), 317–336.

Friedman, H. (2002). Psychological nescience in a postmodern context. *American Psychologist, 57*(6-7), 462–463.

Friedman, M. (1970, September 13). The social responsibility of business is to increase its profits. *The New York Times Magazine,* 32–33, 122, 124, 126.

Friedman, M. (1982). *Capitalism and freedom,* (2nd ed.). Chicago: Chicago University Press.

Fritz, C., & Ellis, A. M. (2015). *A marathon, not a sprint: The benefits of taking time to recover from work demands.* Bowling Green, OH: Society for Industrial and Organizational Psychology.

Fritzsche, D. J. (1995). Personal values: Potential keys to ethical decision-making. *Journal of Business Ethics, 14,* 909–922.

Fritzsche, D. J., & Becker, H. (1984). Linking management behavior to ethical philosophy—An empirical investigation. *Academy of Management Journal, 27,* 166–175.

Fudge, R. S., & Schlacter, J. L. (1999). Motivating employees to act ethically: An expectancy theory approach. *Journal of Business Ethics, 18,* 295–304.

Fuller, J., Langer, C., & Sigelman, M. (2022, Feb. 11). Skills-based hiring is on the rise. Downloaded from https://hbr.org/2022/02/skills-based-hiring-is-on-the-rise on Apr. 11, 2022.

Furedy, J. J., & Furedy, C. (1982). Socratic versus sophistic strains in the teaching of undergraduate psychology: Implicit conflicts made explicit. *Teaching of Psychology, 9,* 14–20.

Galen, L. W. (2012). Does religious belief promote prosociality? A critical examination. *Psychological Bulletin, 138*(5), 876–906.

Gambino, R. (1973, November-December). Watergate lingo: A language of non-responsibility. *Freedom at Issue,* 7–9, 15–17.

Gan, C., Guo, W., Chai, Y. & wand, D. (2020). Unethical leadership behavior and employee performance: A deontic justice perspective. *Personnel Review, 49*(1), 188–201.

Garbers, Y., & Konradt, U. (2014). The effect of financial incentives on performance: A quantitative review of individual and team-based financial incentives. *Journal of Occupational and Organizational Psychology, 87,* 102–137.

Gardner, H. (2002, February 22). Good work, well done: A psychological study. *The Chronicle of Higher Education,* Section 2, B7–B9.

Gardner, H., Csikszentmihalyi, M., & Damon, W. (2001). *Good work: When excellence and ethics meet.* New York: Basic Books.

Gasser, M., Butler, A., Waddilove, L., & Tan, R. (2004). Defining the profession of industrial-organizational psychology: *The Industrial-Organizational Psychologist, 42*(2), 15–20.

Gaudine, A. & Thorne, L. (2001). Emotion and ethical decision-making in organizations. *Journal of Business Ethics, 31,* 175–187.

Geertz, C. (1973). *The interpretation of cultures.* New York: Basic Books.

Geier, C., Adams, R. B., Mitchell, K. M., & Holtz, B. E. (2021). Informed consent for online research—Is anybody reading?: Assessing comprehension and individual difference in readings of digital consent forms. *Journal of Empirical Research on Human Research Ethics, 16*(3), 154–164.

Gelfand, M. J., Erez, M. & Aycan, Z. (2007). Cross-cultural organizational behavior. *Annual review of Psychology, 58,* 479–514.

Gellermann, W., Frankel, M. S., & Ladenson, R. F. (1990). *Values and ethics in organization and human systems development: Responding to dilemmas in professional life.* San Francisco: Jossey-Bass.

Gelles, D. (2015, May 17). It's (still) their party: Cry if you want to, but C.E.O.s' paychecks are only getting bigger. *The New York Times*, B1.

Gelles, D. (2016, April 7). The social algorithm. *The New York Times*, F11.

Gelles, D. (2022, May 22). Jack Welch and the rise of C.E.O.s behaving badly. *The New York Times*, B1.

Gelman, R., & Baillargeon, R. (1983). A review of some Piagetian concepts. In J. H. Flavell & E. M. Markman (Eds.), *Handbook of child psychology. Vol. 3: Cognitive development* (pp. 167–230). New York: Wiley.

George, J. M., & Jones, G. R. (1996). The experience of work and turnover intentions: Interactive effects of value attainment, job satisfaction, and positive mood. *Journal of Applied Psychology, 81*, 318–325.

Gerard, H. B. (1983). School desegregation: The social science role. *American Psychologist, 38*, 869–877.

Gergen, K. J. (1985). The social constructionist movement in modern psychology. *American Psychologist, 40*, 266–275.

Gergen, K. J. (1992). Social construction and moral action. In D. N. Robinson (Ed.), *Social discourse and moral judgment* (pp. 9–27). San Diego: Academic.

Gergen, K. J. (1994). Exploring the postmodern: Perils or potentials? *American Psychologist, 49*, 412–416.

Gergen, K. J. (2001). Psychological science in a postmodern context. *American Psychologist, 56*, 803–813.

Gergen, K. J. (2002). Psychological science: To conserve or create? *American Psychologist, 57*, 463–464.

Gergen, K. J., Gulerce, A., Lock, A., & Misra, G. (1996). Psychological science in cultural context. *American Psychologist, 51*, 496–503.

Gewirtz, J. L. (1972). Some contextual determinants of stimulus potency. In R. D. Parke (Ed.), *Recent trends in social learning theory* (pp. 7–33). New York: Academic.

Giacobbe-Miller, J. (1995). A test of the group values and control models of procedural justice from the competing perspectives of labor and management. *Personnel Psychology, 48*, 115–142.

Gibbs, J. C. (1991). Toward an integration of Kohlberg's and Hoffman's moral development theories. *Human Development, 34*, 88–104.

Gibbs, J. C., Basinger, K. S., Grime, R. L. & Snarey, J. R. (2007). Moral judgment development across cultures: Revisiting Kohlberg's universality claims. *Developmental Review, 27*, 443–500.

Gibson, K. (2000). The moral basis of stakeholder theory. *Journal of Business Ethics, 26*, 245–257.

Gigerenzer, G. (2020). Moral satisficing: Rethinking moral behavior as bounded rationality. *Topics in Cognitive Science, 2*, 528–554.

Gilbert, D. T., King, G., Pettigrew, S. & Wilson, T. D. (2016). Comment on "Estimating the reproducibility of psychological science". *Science, 351*(6277), 1037–1038.

Gillespie, R. (1988). The Hawthorne experiments and the politics of experimentation. In J. G. Morawski (Ed.), *The rise of experimentation in American psychology* (pp. 114–137). New Haven, CT: Yale University Press.

Gilliland, S. W., & Hale, J. M. S. (2005). How can justice be used to improve employee selection practices? In J. Greenberg, & J. A. Colquitt (Eds.), *Handbook of organizational justice* (pp. 411–438). Mahwah, NJ: Lawrence Erlbaum

Gilliland, S., Steiner, D., & Skarlicki, D. (Eds.) (2001). *Theoretical and cultural perspectives on organizational justice.* Greenwich, CT: Information Age.

Gilligan, C. (1982). *In a different voice: Psychological theory and women's development.* Cambridge, MA: Harvard University Press.

Gilligan, C., & Wiggins, G. (1987). The origins of morality in early childhood relationships. In J. Kagan & S. Lamb (Eds.), *The emergence of morality in young children* (pp. 277–305). Chicago: University of Chicago Press.

Gini, A. & Green, R. M. (2013). *Ten virtues of outstanding leaders: Leadership and character.* Malden, MA: Wiley-Blackwell.

Gino, F., Schweitzer, M. E., Mead, N. L., & Ariely, D. (2011). Unable to resist temptation: How self-control depletion promotes unethical behavior. *Organizational Behavior and Human Decision Processes, 115,* 191–203.

Gioia, D. (2021). On the road to hell: Why academia is viewed as irrelevant to practicing managers. *Academy of Management Discoveries.* Published online, June 30. Https://doi. org/10.5465/amd.2021.0200

Giovanola, B. (2009). Re-thinking the anthropological and ethical foundation of economics and business: Human richness and capabilities enhancement. *Journal of Business Ethics, 88,* 43–444.

Godwin, K. E., Seltman, H., Almeda, M., Skerbetz, M. D., Kai, S., Baker, R. S., & Fisher, A. V. (2021, March 26). The elusive relationship between time n-task and learning: not simply an issue of measurement. *Educational Psychology,* published online. https://doi.org/10.1080/01443410.2021.1894324

Godwin, L. N. (2015). Examining the impact of moral imagination on organizational decision making. *Business & Society, 54*(2), 254–278.

Gloss, A., Carr, S. C., Reichman, W., Abdul-Nasiru, I., & Oestereich, W. T. (2017). From handmaidens to POSH humanitarians: The case for making human capabilities the business of I-O psychology. *Industrial and Organizational Psychology, 10*(3), 329–369.

Goel, V. & Wingfield, N. (2015, Dec. 2). Facebook chief vows to donate 99% of his shares for charity. *The New Times,* A1.

Goenka, S. N. (1993). Moral conduct, concentration, and wisdom. In S. Bercholz & S. C. Köhn (Eds.), *The Buddha and his teachings* (pp. 96–121). Boston, MA: Shambala.

Goldberg, E. (2021, May 1). At N.Y.U., the Ph.D.s of tomorrow are picketing today. *The New York Times,* A12.

Goldberg, E. (2021, Dec. 11). After mass firing via Zoom, Better.com's C.E.O. is on leave. *The New York Times,* B4.

Goldberg, E. (2022, Jan. 9). No more working for jerks! *The New York Times,* B6.

Golden, L. (2015, April 9). Irregular work scheduling and its consequences. Economic Policy Institute. Retrieved from http://www.epi.org/publication/irregular-work-scheduling-and-its-consequences/ on July 18, 2015.

Goldfinch, A. (2015). *Rethinking evolutionary psychology.* New York: Palgrave MacMillan.

Goldman, B., & Cropanzano, R. (2015). "Justice" and "fairness" are not the same thing. *Journal of Organizational Behavior, 36,* 313–318.

Goldstein, M. (2016, Jan. 21). Congress calls Shkreli to testify on rapid rises in drug pricing. *The New York Times,* B1.

Goldstone, R. L. (2022). Performance, well-being, motivation, and identity in an age of abundant data: Introduction to the "well-measured life." Special Issue of Current Directions in Psychological Science. *Current Directions in Psychological Science, 31*(1), 3–11.

Gonin, M. (2015). Adam Smith's contribution to business ethics, then and now. *Journal of Business Ethics*, *129*, 221–236.

Gonzalez, M. F., Capman, J. F., Oswald, F. L., Theys, E. R., & Tmczak, D. L. (2019). "Where's the I-O?" Artificial Intelligence and machine learning in talent management systems. *Personnel Assessment and Decisions*, *5*(3), Article 5.

Gonzalez, M. F., Liu, W., Shirase, L., Tomczak, D. L., Lobbe, D. E., Justenhoven, R., & Martin, N. R. (2022). Allying with AI? Reactions toward human-based, AI/ML-based, and augmented hiring processes. *Computers in Human Behavior*, Online 5 January.

Goode, E. (1996). The ethics of deception in social research: A case study. *Qualitative Sociology*, *19*(1), 11–33.

Goode, E. (1999, June 1). For good health, it helps to be rich and important. *The New York Times*, A1, A9.

Goode, W. J. (1960). Encroachment, charlatanism, and the emerging profession: Psychology, sociology, and medicine. *American Sociological Review*, 25, 902–914.

Goode, W. J. (1969). The theoretical limits of professionalization. In A. Etzioni (Ed.), *The semi-professions and their organization* (pp. 266–313). New York: The Free Press.

Gooden, R. E. (1993). Utility and the good. In P. Singer (Ed.), A *companion to ethics* (pp. 241–248). Cambridge, MA: Blackwell.

Goodman, L. (2009). The Master List of Virtues. Downloaded on Dec. 4, 2015 from http://beliefcloset.com/wp-content/uploads/2010/05/Virtues-The-Master-List.pdf

Goodman, P. S. (2021, Dec. 11). How supply chain upheaval became a life-or-death threat. *The New York Times*, B1.

Goodstein, L. D. (1983). Managers, values, and organization development. *Group and Organization Studies*, *8*, 203–220.

Gordon, M. E., & Burt, R. E. (1981). A history of industrial psychology's relationship with American unions: Lessons from the past and directions for the future. *International Review of Applied Psychology*, *30*, 137–156.

Gortner, H. F. (1991). *Ethics for public managers*. New York: Greenwood.

Gortner, H. E. (2001). Values and ethics. In T. L. Cooper (Ed.), *Handbook of administrative ethics* (2nd ed., pp. 509–528). New York: Marcel Dekker.

Gorusch, R. L., & Ortberg, J. (1983). Moral obligation and attitudes: Their relation to behavioral intentions. *Journal of Personality and Social Psychology*, *44*, 1025–1028.

Gottschalk, P. (1993). Changes in inequality of family income in seven industrialized countries. *American Economic Review*, *83*, 136–142.

Gould, E. (2016, Sept. 1). Looking at the latest wage data by education level. Working economics blog. Economic Policy Institute. Retrieved from https://www.epi.org/blog/looking-at-the-latest-wage-data-by-education-level/ on Jan. 25, 2022.

Gould, E. (2018, June 22). Two-thirds of adults have less than a four year degree. Economic Snapshot. Economic Policy Institute. Retrieved from https://www.epi.org/publication/two-thirds-of-adults-have-less-than-a-four-year-degree-policymakers-should-work-to-make-college-more-attainable-for-them-but-also-strengthen-labor-protections-that-help-all-workers/ on Jan. 25, 2022.

Gould, E. (2019, Mar. 15). Higher returns on education can't explain growing wage inequality. Working Economic Blog. Economic JPolicy Institute. Retrieved from https://www.epi.org/blog/higher-returns-on-education-cant-explain-growing-wage-inequality/ on Jan. 25, 2022.

Gould, E. (2020, Feb. 20). State of working America wages 2019. Economic Policy Institute. Retrieved from https://www.epi.org/publication/swa-wages-2019/ on Oct. 11, 2021.

Gould, S. J. (1981). *The mismeasure of man.* New York: Norton.

Gowing, M. K., Kraft, J. D., & Quick, J. C. (Eds.). (1998). *The new organizational reality: Downsizing,* restructuring, *and revitalization.* Washington, DC: American Psychological Association.

Grand, J. A., Rogelberg, S. G., Bankis, G. C., Landis, R. S., & Tonidandel, S. (2018). *Perspectives on Psychological Science, 13*(4), 448–456.

Grant, A. M., & Shandell, M. S. (2022). Social motivation at work: The organizational psychology of effort for, against, and with others. In S. T. Fiske & D. L. Schacter (Eds.). *Annual Review of Psychology, 73,* 301–326.

Grant, J. D., & Wagar, T. H. (1992). Willingness to take legal action in wrongful dismissal cases: Perceptual differences between men and women. *Perceptual and* Motor *Skills, 74,* 1073–1074.

Gray, J. (2000). *Two faces of liberalism.* New York: The New Press.

Greenberg, A. E. & Spiller, S. A. (2015). Opportunity cost neglect attenuates the effect of choices on preferences. *Psychological Science Online First,* Nov. 16, 1–11. Downloaded Dec. 1 from <pss.sagepub.com>.

Greenberg, J. (2009). Everybody talks about organizational justice but nobody does anything about it. *Industrial and Organizational Psychology: Perspectives on Science and Practice, 2*(2), 181–195.

Greenberg, J. (2010). *Insidious workplace behavior.* New York: Routledge.

Greenberg, J., & Folger, R. (1988). *Controversial issues in social research methods.* New York: Springer-Verlag.

Greene, C. N. (1978). Identification modes of professionals: Relationship with formalization, role strain, and alienation. *Academy of Management Journal, 21,* 486–492.

Greene, J. D. (2007). Why are VMPFC patients more utilitarian? A dual-process theory of moral judgment explains. *Trends in Cognitive Science, 11*(8), 322–324.

Greene, J. D. (2009). Dual-process morality and the personal/impersonal distinction: A reply to McGuire, Langdon, Coltheart and MacKenzie. *Journal of Experimental social Psychology, 45*(3), 581–584.

Greene, J. D., Sommerville, R. B., Nystrom, L. E., Darley, J. M., & Cohen, J. D. (2001, September 14). An fMRI investigation of emotional engagement in moral judgment. *Science, 293,* 2105–2108.

Greenfield, P. M. (1997). You can't take it with you: Why ability assessments don't cross cultures. *American Psychologist, 52,* 1115–1124.

Greenhouse, L. (2001, March 22). Court says employers can require arbitration of disputes. *The New York Times,* C1, C6.

Greenhouse, S. (1998, March 30). Equal work, less-equal perks: Microsoft leads the way in filling jobs with "permatemps". *The New York Times,* D1, D6.

Greenhouse, S. (2002, June 25). Suits say Wal-Mart forces workers to toil off the clock. *The New York Times,* A1, A18.

Greenhouse, S. (2014, July 16). A push to give steadier shifts to part-timers. *The New York Times,* A1.

Greenhouse, S. (2019). *Beaten down, worked up: The past, present, future of American labor.* New York: Anchor Books/Penguin Random House.

Greenwald, A. G., & Banaji, M. R. (2017). The implicit revolution: Reconceiving the relation between conscious and unconscious. *American Psychologist, 72*(9), 861–871.

Greenwald, A. G., Dasgupta, A. G., Dovidio, J. F., Kang, J., Moss-Racusin, C. A., & Teachman, B. A. (2022). Implicit-Bias remedies: Treating discriminatory bias as a public-health problem. *Psychological Science in the Public Interest, 23*(1), 7–40.

Greller, M. M. (1984). High earnings for I/O psychologists. *The Industrial-Organizational Psychologist, 21*, 55–58.

Grice, S., Sturgis, G., Avery, A., Modeste, R. & Brawley, U. (2021). Diversity, Equity, and inclusion strategies: Using measurement to support your black employees. *SIOP white Paper Series.* Bowling Green, OH: Society for Industrial and Organizational Psychology.

Griffin J. J., & Prakash, A. (2014). Special Issue: Corporate responsibility: Initiatives and mechanisms, Part I. *Business & Society, 53*(4), 463–619.

Griffin, M. A., & Kabanoff, B. (2001). Global vision: The psychology of safety. *The Industrial-Organizational Psychologist, 38*, 123–127.

Griggs, R. A. & Whitehead III, G. I. (2015). Coverage of recent criticisms of Milgram's obedience experiments in introductory social psychology textbooks. *Theory & Psychology, 25*(5), 564–580.

Grijalva, E., & Newman, D. A. (2015). Narcissism and counterproductive work behavior (CWB): Meta-analysis and consideration of collectivist culture, big five personality and narcissism's facet structure. *Applied Psychology: An International Review, 64*(1), 93–126.

Grimshaw, J. (1993). The idea of a female ethic. In P. Singer (Ed.), *A companion to ethics* (pp. 491–499). Cambridge, MA: Blackwell.

Gross, A. E., & Fleming, I. (1982). Twenty years of deception in social psychology. *Personality and Social Psychology Bulletin, 8*, 402–408.

Gross, C. (2011, Dec. 21). Disgrace: On Marc Hauser. *The Nation.* Downloaded from http://www.thenation.com/print/article/165313/disgrace-marc-hauser on Dec. 30, 2011.

Gross, C. (2016). Scientific misconduct. In S. T., Fiske, D. L. Schacter, & S. E. Taylor (Eds.), *Annual Review of Psychology, 69*, 693–711.14

Groves, B. W., Price, J. H., Olsson, R. H., & King, K. A. (1997). Response rates to anonymous versus confidential surveys. *Perceptual and Motor Skills, 85*, 665–666.

Grusec, J. E., Chaparro, M. P., Johnston, M., & Sherman, A. (2014). The development of moral behavior from a socialization perspective. Chap. 6 In M. Killen, & J. G. Smetana (Eds.), *Handbook of moral development.* New York: Taylor and Francis Group, 113–134.

Guba, E. G., & Lincoln, Y. S. (1994). Competing paradigms in qualitative research. In N. K. Denzin & Y. S. Lincoln (Eds.), *Handbook of qualitative research* (pp. 105–117). Thousand Oaks, CA: Sage.

Guimond, S. (1995). Encounter and metamorphosis: The impact of military socialization on professional values. *Applied Psychology: An International Review, 44*, 251–275.

Guion, R. M. (1991). Personnel assessment, selection, and placement. Chap. 6 In M. D. Dunnette & L. M. Hough (eds), *Handbook of industrial and organizational psychology*, 2nd Ed., Vol. 2. Palo Alto, CA: Consulting Psychologists Press.

Guion, R. M. (1998). *Assessment, measurement, and prediction* for personnel *decisions.* Mahwah, NJ: Lawrence Erlbaum Associates.

Gummeson, E. (1999). *Qualitative methods in management research.* Thousand Oaks, CA: Sage.

Gunthorpe, D. L. (1997). Business ethics: A quantitative analysis of the impact of unethical behavior by publicly traded corporations. *Journal of Business Ethics, 16*, 537–543.

Guzzo, R. A., Fink, A. A., King, E., Tonidandel, S., & Landis, R. S. (2015). Big data recommendations for industrial-organizational psychology. *Industrial and Organizational Psychology, 8*(4), 491–508.

Guzzo, R. A., Jette, R. D., & Katzell, R. A. (1985). The effects of psychologically based intervention programs on worker productivity: A meta-analysis. *Personnel Psychology, 38*, 275–291.

Guzzo, R. A., Schneider, B., & Nalbantian, H. R. Open science, closed doors: The perils and potential of open science for research in practice. *Industrial-Organizational Psychology: Perspectives on Science and Practice.* Downloaded June 19, 2022 from https://www.siop.org/Research-Publications/IOP-Journal/IOP-Focal-Articles.

Haas, L. J., & Malouf, J. L. (1995). *Keeping up the good work: A practitioner's guide to mental health ethics* (2nd ed.). Sarasota, FL: Professional Resource Press.

Haber, S. (1991). *The quest for authority and honor in the American professions, 1750–1900.* Chicago: University of Chicago Press.

Habermas, J. (1990). *Moral consciousness and communicative action.* Cambridge, MA: MIT Press.

Hacker, J. S., & Pierson, P. (2016). *American amnesia: How the war on government led us to forget what made America prosper.* New York: Simon & Schuster.

Hackman, J. R., & Oldham, G. R. (1980). *Work redesign.* Reading, MA: Addison-Wesley.

Hadani, M., & Combes, S. (2015). Compementary relationships between corporate philanthropy and corporate political activity: An exploratory study of political marketplace contingencies. *Business & Society, 54*(6), 859–881.

Hafer, C. L., & Bègue, L. (2005). Experimental research on just-world theory: Problems, developments, and future challenges. *Psychological Bulletin, 131*(1), 128–167.

Hafferty, F. W. (1998). Beyond curriculum reform: Confronting medicine's hidden curriculum. *Academic Medicine, 73*(4), 403–407.

Hagstrom, W. O. (1965). *The scientific community.* New York: Basic Books

Haidt, J. (2001). The emotional dog and its rational tail: A social intuitionist approach to moral judgment. *Psychological Review, 108*, 814–834.

Haidt, J. (2003). The emotional dog does learn new tricks: A reply to Pizarro and Bloom (2003). *Psychological Review, 110*(1), 197–198.

Haidt, J. (2004). The emotional dog gets mistaken for a possum. *Review of General Psychology, 8*(4), 283–290.

Haidt, J. (2012). *The righteous mind: Why good people are divided by politics and religion.* New York, NY: Pantheon.

Haidt, J., & Joseph, C. (2004). Intuitive ethics: How innately prepared intuitions generate culturally variable virtues. *Daedalus,* Fall, 55–66.

Haidt, J. & Jussim, L. (2016). Psychological science and viewpoint diversity. *APS Observer, 29*(2), 5–7.

Haidt, J. & Kesebir, S. (2010). Morality. Chapter 22 In S. Fiske, D. Gilbert, & G. Lindzy (Eds.), *Handbook of Social Psychology,* 5th Ed., Vol. 2, (pp. 797–832). Hoboken, NJ: Wiley.

Hakel, M. D. (1988). Introducing the American Psychological Society. *The Industrial-Organizational Psychologist, 26*, 22–24.

Hakel, M. D., Sorcher, M., Beer, M., & Moses, J. L. (1982). *Making it happen: Designing research with implementation in mind.* Beverly Hills: Sage.

Hakim, D., Kessler, A. M., & Ewing, J. (2015). As VW pushed to be No. 1, ambitions fueled a scandal. *The New York Times,* P. 1, 24.

Hakim, D. & Tabuchi, H. (2015, Sept. 24). An industry with an outlaw streak against regulation. *The New York Times,* B1.

Hall, D. T. (1996). Introduction: Long live the career—a relational approach. In D. T. Hall, & Associates (Eds.), *The career is dead—long live the career: A relational approach to careers* (pp. 1–12). San Francisco: Jossey-Bass.

Hall, D. T. (2004). The protean career: A quarter-century journey. *Journal of Vocational Behavior, 65*, 1–13.

Hall, D. T., & Associates. (Eds.). (1996). *The career is dead—long live the career: A relational approach to careers*. San Francisco: Jossey-Bass.

Hall, D. T., Feldman, E. & Kim, N.(2013). Meaningful work and the protean career. Chapter 3 In B. J. Dik, Z. S. Byrne, & M. F. Steger. (Eds.), *Purpose and meaning in the workplace*. Wash., DC: American Psychological Association.

Hall, D. T., & Richter, J. (1990). Career gridlock: Baby boomers hit the wall. *Academy of Management Executive, 4*, 7–22.

Hall, R. T. (1975). *Occupations and the social structure* (2nd ed.). Englewood Cliffs, NJ: Prentice-Hall.

Hamlin, J. K. (2013). Moral judgment and action in preverbal infants and toddlers: Evidence for an innate moral core. *Current Directions in Psychological Science, 22*(3), 186–193.

Hamner, W. C., & Smith, F. J. (1978). Work attitudes as predictors of unionization activity. *Journal of Applied Psychology, 63*, 415–421.

Hanauer, N. & Reich, R. B. (2016, April 21). Help for overworked Americans. *The New York Times*, A29.

Hancock, J. (2019). *Applied humanism: How to create more effective and ethical businesses*. New York: Business Expert Press.

Hancock, P., & Tyler, M. (2001). *Work, postmodernism and organization*. Thousand Oaks, CA: Sage.

Handelsman, M. M., Knapp, S. & Gottlieb, M. C. (2009). Training ethical psychologists: An acculturation model. *Professional Psychology: Research and Practice, 36*(1), 59–65.

Haney, C., Banks, W. C., & Zimbardo, P. G. (1973). Interpersonal dynamics in a simulated prison. *International Journal of Criminology and Penology, 1*, 69–97.

Hare, B. (2017). Survival of the friendliest: Homo Sapiens evolved via selection for prosociality. In S. T. Fiske, D. L. Schacter, & S. E. Taylor (Eds.). *Annual Review of Psychology, 68*, 155–186.

Hare, R. M. (1993). Universal prescriptivism. In P. Singer (Ed.), *A companion to ethics* (pp. 451–463). Cambridge, MA: Blackwell.

Harrington, S. J. (1997). A test of a person-issue contingent model of ethical decision making in organizations. *Journal of Business Ethics, 16*, 363–375.

Harris, B. (1988). Key words: A history of debriefing in social psychology. In J. G. Morawski (Ed.), *The rise of experimentation in American psychology* (pp. 188–212). New Haven, CT: Yale University Press.

Harris, M. (1999). Practice network: Look, it's an I/O psychologist. . . . No, it's a trainer. . . . No, it's an executive coach! *The Industrial-Organizational Psychologist, 36*, 38–42.

Harris, R. J. (1993). Two insights occasioned by attempts to pin down the equity formula. In B. A. Mellers & J. Baron (Eds.), *Psychological perspectives on justice: Theory and applications* (pp. 32–54). New York: Cambridge University Press.

Harrison, D. A., Kravitz, D. A., Mayer, D. M., Leslie, L. M., & Lev-Arey, D. (2006). Understanding attitudes toward affirmative action programs in employment: Summary and meta-analysis of 35 years of research. *Journal of Applied Psychology, 91*, 1013–1036.

Harrison, L. E., & Huntington, S. P. (2000). *Culture matters: How values shape human progress.* New York: Basic Books.

Hart, D., Atkins, R., & Ford, D. (1998). Urban America as a context for the development of moral identity in adolescence. *Journal of Social Issues, 54,* 513–530.

Hart, D. K. (2001). Administration and the ethics of virtue: In all things, choose first for good character and then for technical expertise. In T. L. Cooper (Ed.), *Handbook of administrative ethics* (pp. 131–150). New York: Marcel Dekker.

Hartel, C. E. J. (1998). Vantage 2000: The consequences and distinctiveness of shiftwork. *The Industrial-Organizational Psychologist, 35,* 76–79.

Hartigan, J. A., & Wigdor, A. K. (1989). *Fairness in employment testing.* Washington, DC: National Academy Press.

Hartman, D. F. (2015). Should ethics courses be more practical? *Teaching Ethics, 15*(2), 349–368.

Hartman, E. M. (1998). The role of character in business ethics. *Business Ethics Quarterly, 8*(3), 547–559.

Hartman, E. M. (2008). Socratic questions and Aristotelian answers: A virtue-based approach to business ethics. *Journal of Business Ethics, 78,* 313–328.

Harvey, D. (2005). *A brief history of neoliberalism.* Oxford: Oxford University Press.

Harvey, R. J. (1991). Job analysis. Chap. 2 In M. D. Dunnette & L. M. Hough (Eds.), *Handbook of industrial and organizational psychology,* 2nd Ed., Vol. 2. Palo Alto, CA: Consulting Psychologists Press.

Haslam, S. A., Reicher, S. D., Millard, K., & McDonald, R. (2015). "Happy to have been of service": the Yale archive as a window into the engaged followership of participants in Milgram's "obedience" experiments. *The British Journal of Social Psychology, 54,* 55–83.

Hatch, E. (1983). *Culture and morality: The relativity of values in anthropology.* New York: Columbia University Press.

Hayakawa, S., Tannenbaum, D., Costa, A., Corey, J. D., & Keysar, B. (2017). Thinking more or feeling less? Explaining the foreign-language effect on moral judgment. *Psychological Science, 28*(10), 1387–1397.

Hazer, J. T., & Alvares, K. M. (1981). Police work values during organizational entry and assimilation. *Journal of Applied Psychology, 66,* 12–18.

Hebl, M., Madera, J. M., & Morgan, W. B. (2019). Special issue on reducing discrimination in the workplace: An introduction. *Personnel Assessment and Decisions, 5*(2), i–iii.

Heinze, D., Sibary, S., & Sikula, Sr. A. (1999). Relations among corporate social responsibility, financial soundness, and investment value in 22 manufacturing industry groups. *Ethics & Behavior, 9,* 331–347.

Henrich, J., & Muthukrishna, M. (2021). The origins and psychology of human cooperation. *Annual Review of Psychology, 72,* 207–240.

Herman, J. (2021, August 1). Rethinking the divide over pseudonymity online. *The New York Times,* ST 9.

Herrera, C. D. (1997). A historical interpretation of deceptive experiments in American psychology. *History of the Human Sciences, 10,* 23–36.

Hertwig, R., & Engel, C. (2016). Homo ignorans: Deliberately choosing not to know. *Perspectives on Psychological Science, 11*(3), 359–372.

Hertwig, R., & Ortmann, A. (2001). Experimental practices in economics: A methodological challenge for psychologists. *Behavioral and Brain Sciences, 24,* 383–451.

Hertwig, R., & Ortmann, A. (2008a). Deception in experiments: revisiting arguments in its defense. *Ethics & Behavior, 18*(1), 59–92.

Hertwig, R., & Ortmann, A. (2008b). Deception in social psychological experiments: Two misconceptions and a research agenda. *Social Psychology Quarterly, 71*(3), 222–227.

Herzberg, F. (1966). *Work and the nature of man.* Cleveland, OH: World.

Herzberg, F., Mausner, B., & Snyderman, B. (1959). *The motivation to* work. New York: Wiley.

Hess, D. (2001). Regulating corporate social performance: A new look at social accounting, auditing, and reporting. *Business Ethics Quarterly, 11,* 307–330.

Hessen, R. (1979). *In defense of the corporation.* Stanford, CA: Hoover Institution.

Hewson, C. M., Laurent, D., & Vogel, C. M. (1996). Proper methodologies for psychological and sociological studies conducted via the internet. *Behavior Research Methods, Instruments & Computers, 28,* 186–191.

Heyes, C. (2020). Psychological mechanisms forged by cultural evolution. *Current Directions in Psychological Science, 29*(4), 399–404.

Heyes, C. (2021). Is morality a gadget? Nature, nurture and culture in moral development. *Synthese, 198,* 4391–4414.

Hickey, S., & Cooper, D. (2021). Cutting unemployment insurance benefits did not boost job growth: July state jobs data show a widespread recovery. Working Economics Blog, August 24. Economic Policy Institute.

Highhouse, S. (1999). The brief history of personnel counseling in industrial-organizational psychology. *Journal of Vocational Behavior, 55,* 318–336.

Highhouse, S., & Schmitt, N. W. (Eds.). (2013). A snapshot in time: Industrial-organizational psychology today. In N. W. Schmitt, S. Highhouse, & I. B. Weiner (Eds.), *Handbook of psychology: Industrial and organizational psychology,* 2nd Ed. (pp. 3–13). John Wiley & Sons, Inc.

Hill, R. P. & Rapp, J. M. (2014). Codes of ethical conduct: A bottom-up approach. *Journal of Business Ethics, 123,* 621–630.

Himmelstein, D. U., Woolhandler, S., Hellander, I., & Wolfe, S. M. (1999). Quality of care in investor-owned vs not-for-profit HMOs. *Journal of the American Medical Association, 282,* 159–163.

Hinings, C. R., Thibault, L., Slack, T., & Kikulis, L. M. (1996). Values and organizational structure. Human *Relations, 49,* 885–916.

Hirsch, B. T., & Macpherson, D. A. (2020). Union membership and coverage database from the CPS. Unionstats.com, data compiled from the Current Population Survey, Feb. 24, 2020.

Hirsch, F. (1976). *Social limits to growth.* Cambridge, MA: Harvard University Press.

Hoffman, M. L. (1977). Moral internalization: Current theory and research. In L. Berkowitz (Ed.), *Advances in experimental social psychology* (Vol. 10, pp. 86–133). New York: Academic.

Hoffman, M. L. (1983). Affective and cognitive processes in moral internalization. In E. T. Higgins, D. N. Rubie, & W. W. Hartup (Eds.), *Social cognition and social development: A sociocultural perspective* (pp. 236–274). Cambridge, MA: Cambridge University Press.

Hoffman, M. L. (1988). Moral development. In M. H. Bornstein & M. E. Lamb (Eds.), *Developmental psychology: An advanced textbook* (pp. 497–548). Hillsdale, NJ: Lawrence Erlbaum Associates.

Hoffman, M. L. (1991). Commentary. *Human Development, 34,* 105–110.

Hoffman, M. L. (2000). *Empathy and moral development*. New York: Cambridge University Press.

Hofmann, S. G. (2002). More science, not less. *American Psychologist, 57*, 462.

Hofstede, G. (1980). *Culture's consequences: International differences in work-related values.* Beverly Hills: Sage.

Hofstede, G. (2004). *Culture's consequences: Comparing values, behaviors, institutions, and organizations across nations.* Thousand Oaks, CA: Sage.

Hofstede, G., Hofstede, G. H., & Minkov, M. (2010). *Cultures and organizations: Software of the mind: Intercultural cooperation and its importance for survival* (3rd ed.). New York: McGraw-Hill.

Hofstede, G., Neuijen, B., Ohayv, D. D., & Sanders, G. (1990). Measuring organizational cultures: A qualitative and quantitative study across twenty cases. *Administrative Science Quarterly, 35*, 286–316.

Hogan, R., & Hogan, J. (2001). Assessing leadership: A view from the dark side. *International Journal of Selection and Assessment, 9*(1/2), 40–51.

Hogan, J., Hogan, R., & Busch, C. M. (1984). How to measure service orientation. *Journal of Applied Psychology, 69*, 167–173.

Holcombe, A. O. (2016). Introduction to the registered replication report: Hart & Albarracín (2011). *Perspectives on Psychological Science, 11*(1), 156–157.

Holub, M. (2021). Working with jerks: A manager's perspective. Employment Practices Solutions. Retrieved from http://www.epspros.com/news-resources/white-papers/2021/working-with-jerks-a-managers-perspective.html on July 14, 2021.

Hollander, E. P. (1998). Ethical challenges in the leader-follower relationship. In J. B. Ciulla (Ed.), *Ethics, the heart of leadership* (pp. 49–61). Westport, CT: Praeger.

Hollingsworth, R. (1977). Effectiveness of debriefing. *American Psychologist, 32*, 780–782.

Holmes, D. S. (1976a). Debriefing after psychological experiments: I. Effectiveness of post-deception dehoaxing. *American Psychologist, 31*, 858–867.

Holmes, D. S. (1976b). Debriefing after psychological experiments: II. Effectiveness of post-deception desensitizing. *American Psychologist, 31*, 868–875.

Holmes, D. S. (1977). Valins's postdeception dehoaxing revisited. *American Psychologist, 32*, 385.

Hong, R. Y., Koh, S., & Paunonen, S. V. (2012). Supernumerary personality traits beyond the big five: Predicting materialism and unethical behavior. *Personality and Individual Differences, 53*, 710–715.

Hood, J. M. (1996). *The heroic enterprise: Business and the common good.* New York: The Free Press.

Hopkins, W. E., & Hopkins, S. A. (1999). The ethics of downsizing: Perceptions of rights and responsibilities. *Journal of Business Ethics, 18*, 145–156.

Hornsey, M. J. (2020). Why facts are not enough: Understanding and managing the motivated rejection of science. *Current Directions in Psychological Science, 29*(6), 583–591.

Hoshmand, L. T., & Polkinghorne, D. E. (1992). Redefining the science-practice relationship and professional training. *American Psychologist, 47*, 55–66.

Hosmer, L. T., & Masten, S. E. (1995). Ethics vs. economics: The issue of free trade with Mexico. *Journal of Business Ethics, 14*, 287–298.

Houwer, J. D. (2019). Implicit Bias is behavior: A functional-cognitive perspective on implicit bias. *Perspectives on Psychological Science, 14*(5), 835–840.

Howard, A. (1995). *The changing nature of work.* San Francisco: Jossey-Bass.

Howard, G. S. (1985). The role of values in the science of psychology. *American Psychologist, 40*, 255–265.

Huang, G., Wellman, N., Ashford, S. J., Lee, C., & Wang, L. (2017). Deviance and exit: The organizational costs of job insecurity and moral disengagement. *Journal of Applied Psychology, 102*(1), 26–42.

Hüffmeier, J., & Zacher, H. (2021). The basic income: Initiating the ne3eded discussion in industrial, work, and organizational psychology. *Industrial and Organizational Psychology: Perspectives on Science and Practice, 14*(4), 531–619.

Hughes, E. C. (1965). Professions. In K. S. Lynn (Ed.), *The professions in America* (pp. 1–14). Boston: Houghton Mifflin.

Hulin, C. (2001). Applied psychology and science: Differences between research and practice. Applied *Psychology: An International Review, 50*, 225–234.

Hülsheger, U. R., van Gils, S. & Walkowiak, A. (2020). The regulating role of mindfulness in enacted workplace incivility: An experience sampling study. *Journal of Applied Psychology, 106*(8), 1250–1265.

Hume, D. (1978). *A treatise of human* nature. Oxford, U.K.: Oxford University Press.

Hunt, S. D., & Vitell, S. (1986). A general theory of marketing ethics. *Journal of Macromarketing, 6*, 5–16.

Hunter, S. T. (2012). (Un)ethical leadership and identity: What did we learn and where do we go from here? *Journal of Business Ethics, 107*(1), 79–87.

Huselid, M. A. (1995). The impact of human resource management practices on turnover, productivity, and corporate financial performance. *Academy of Management Journal, 38*, 635–672.

Husted, B. W. (2014). Corporate social responsibility practice from 1800—1914: Past initiatives and current debates. *Business Ethics Quarterly, 25*(1), 125–142.

Huston, A. C. & Bentley, A. C. (2010). Human development in societal context. *Annual Review of Psychology, 61*, 411–437.

Huszczo, G. E., Wiggins, J. G., & Currie, J. S. (1984). The relationship between psychology and organized labor: Past, present, and future. *American Psychologist, 39*, 432–440.

Ilgen, D. R., & Bell, B. S. (2001a). Conducting industrial and organizational psychological research: Institutional review of research in work organizations. *Ethics & Behavior, 11*, 395–412.

Ilgen, D. R., & Bell, B. S. (2001b). Informed consent and dual purpose research. *American Psychologist, 56*, 1177.

Ilgen, D. R., Hollenbeck, J. R., Johnson, M. & Jundt, D. (2005). Teams in organizations: From input-process-output models to IMOI models. *Annual Review of Psychology, 56*, 517–543.

International Labor Organization. (2017). Global estimates of modern slavery: Forced labour and forced marriage. Downloaded from https://www.ilo.org/global/publications/books/WCMS_575479/lang–en/index.htm, March 18, 2022.

International Personnel Management Association. (1990). *IPMA code of ethics*. Alexandria, VA: Author.

International Task force on Assessment Center Guidelines. (2015). Guidelines and ethical considerations for assessment center operations. *Journal of Management, 41*(4), 1244–1273.

International Union of Psychological Science. (2008). Universal Declaration of Ethical Principles for Psychologists, Adopted, July 26.

Ioannidis, J. P. A. (2005). Why most published research findings are false. *PLoS Medicine*, 2(8), 696–701.

Irwin, N. (2016, April 24). Mr. moneybags gets more out of social security. *The New York Times*, A6.

Irwin, N. (2016, June 29). Trump's speech shows the challenge of running on economic nostalgia. *The New York Times*, A17.

Irwin, N. (2021, June 6). "Historic" shift in labor force favors workers. *The New York Times*, B1.

Irwin, N. & Bui, Q. (2016, April 11). Where the poor live in America may help determine life span. *The New York Times*, A1.

Isaac, M. (2015, Sept. 2). Judge rebuffs Uber in ruling on drivers. *The New York Times*, B1.

Israel, M., & Hay, I. (2006). *Research ethics for social scientists: Between ethical conduct and regulatory compliance*. Los Angeles, CA: Sage.

Ivory, D., Protess, B. & Bennett, K. (2016, June 26). When you dial 911 and Wall St. answers. *The New York Times*, A1.

Ivory, D., Protess, B. & Vlasic, B. (2015, May 23). G.M. inquiry is said to find criminal fault. *The New York Times*, B1.

Ivory D. & Tabuchi, H. (2016, Jan. 5). Emails suggest airbag maker boldly rigged data. *The New York Times*, A1.

Jackall, R. (1988). *Moral mazes: The world of the corporate manager*. New York, NY: Oxford University Press.

Jackson, J. C., Castelo, N., & Gray, K. (2020). Could a rising robot work force make humans less prejudiced? *American Psychologist*, 75(7), 969–982.

Jackson, J. P. Jr. (1998). Creating a consensus: Psychologists, the Supreme Court, and school desegregation, 1952–1955. *Journal of Social Issues*, 54, 143–177.

Jacobs, K., Perry, I., & MacGilvary, J. (2015, April). *The high public cost of low wages*. Berkeley, CA: UC Berkeley Labor Center.

Jaffee, S., & Hyde, J. S. (2000). Gender differences in moral orientation: A meta-analysis. *Psychological Bulletin*, 126, 703–726.

James, W. (1907). *Pragmatism: A new name for some old ways of thinking*. New York: Longmans.

Janis, I. (1982). *Victims of groupthink* (2nd ed.). Boston: Houghton Mifflin.

Jansen, E., & Von Glinow, M. A. (1985). Ethical ambivalence and organizational reward systems. *Academy of Management Review*, 10, 814–822.

Jaremka, L. M., Ackerman, J. M., Gawronski, B., Rule, N. O., Sweeny, K., Tropp, L. R., Metz, M. A., Molina, L., Ryan, W. S. & Vick, S. B. (2020). Common academic experiences no one talks about: Repeated rejection, imposter syndrome, and burnout. *Perspectives on Psychological Science*, 15(3), 519–543.

Jawahar, I. M., & McLaughlin, G. L. (2001). Toward a descriptive stakeholder theory: An organizational life cycle approach. *Academy of Management Review*, 26, 397–414.

Jehl, D. (2001, March 25). Regulations czar prefers new path. *The New York Times*, A1, A28.

Jenkins, G. D. Jr., Mitra, A., Gupta, N., & Shaw, J. D. (1998). Are financial incentives related to performance? A meta-analytic review of empirical research. *Journal of Applied Psychology*, 83, 777–787.

Jensen, K., & Silk, J. B. (2014). Searching for the evolutionary roots of human morality. Chap. 22 In M. Killen, & J. G. Smetana (Eds.), *Handbook of moral development* (pp. 475–494). New York: Taylor and Francis Group.

Jensen, L. A. (2020a). *The Oxford handbook of moral development: An interdisciplinary perspective*. Oxford: Oxford University Press.

Jensen, L. A. (2020b). Moral development from paradigms to plurality. Chap. 1 In L. A. Jensen (ed.), *The Oxford handbook of moral development: An interdisciplinary perspective* (pp. 3–6). Oxford: Oxford University Press.

John, L. K., Loewenstein, G., & Prelec, D. (2012). Measuring the prevalence of questionable research practices with incentives for truth telling. *Psychological Science, 23*(5), 524–532.

Johnson, B. T. (2021). Editorial: Toward a more transparent, rigorous, and generative psychology. *Psychological Bulletin, 147*(1), 1–15.

Johnson, M. A. (2021). Making sense of "good" and "bad": A deonance and fairness approach to abusive supervision and prosocial impact. *Business Ethics Quarterly, 31*(3), 386–420.

Jones, G. E., & Kavanagh, M. J. (1996). An experimental examination of the effects of individual and situational factors on unethical behavioral intentions in the workplace. *Journal of Business Ethics, 15*, 511–523.

Jones, H. B. Jr. (1995). The ethical leader: An ascetic construct. *Journal of Business Ethics, 14*, 867–874.

Jones, S. E. (2001). Ethics code draft published for comment. Monitor *on Psychology, 32*(2), 76–89.

Jones, T. M. (1991). Ethical decision-making by individuals in organizations: An issue-contingent model. *Academy of Management Review*, 16, 366–395.

Jones, T. M. (1995). Instrumental stakeholder theory: Synthesis of ethics and economics. *Academy of Management Review, 20*, 404–437.

Jordan, A. E., & Meara, N. M. (1990). Ethics and the professional practice of psychologists: The role of virtues and principles. *Professional Psychology: Research and Practice, 21*, 107–114.

Jorgenson, G. (2006). Kohlberg and Gilligan: Duet or duel? *Journal of Moral Education*, 35(2), 179–196.

Jost, J. T., Banaji, M. R. & BNosek, B. A. (2004). A decade of system justification theory: Accumulated evidence of conscious and unconscious bolstering of the status quo. *Political Psychology, 25*(6), 881

Journal of Applied Psychology (2016). Special section on employee deviance and withdrawal, *101*(4), 463–548.

Judge, T., & Zapata, C. P. (2015). The person-situation debate revisited: Effect of situation strength and trait activation on the validity of the big five personality traits in predicting job performance. *Academy of Management Journal, 58*(4), 1149–1179.

Kagan, J. (1987). Introduction. In J. Kagan, & S. Lamb (Eds.), *The emergence of morality in young children* (pp. ix–xx). Chicago: University of Chicago Press.

Kagan, J. (2018). Three unresolved issues in human morality. *Perspectives on Psychological Science, 13*(3), 346–358.

Kahneman, D. (2011). *Thinking, fast and slow*. New York: Farrar, Straus and Giroux.

Kahneman, D., Slovik, P., & Tversky, A. (1982). *Judgment under uncertainty: Heuristics and biases*. New York: Cambridge University Press.

Kalichman, M., Magnus, P. D. & Plemmons, D. (2016). Conflicts of interest. In *Resources for Research Ethics Education*. Downloaded Aug. 23, 2016 from <http://research-ethics. net/topics/conflicts-of-interest/?print>

Kalleberg, A. L. (2000). Nonstandard employment relations: Part-time, temporary and contract work. Annual *Review of Sociology, 26,* 341–365.

Kalleberg, A. L. (2008). The mismatched worker: When people don't fit their jobs. *Academy of Management Perspectives, 22*(1), 24–40.

Kalleberg, A. L. (2009). Precarious work, insecure workers: Employment relations in transition. *American Sociological Review, 74*(1), 1–22.

Kanfer, R. (2001). I/O psychology: Working at the basic-applied psychology interface. *Applied Psychology: An International Review, 50,* 235–240.

Kanner, A. D., & Kasser, T. (2000). Stuffing our kids: Should psychologists help advertisers manipulate children?, *The Industrial–Organizational Psychologist, 38,* 183–187.

Kant, I. (1785a). Fundamental principles of the metaphysic of morals. Translated by T. K. Abbott (1895). Coppell, TX: Pantianos Classics.

Kant, I. (1785b). *Groundwork of the metaphysics of morals.* Translated by T. K. Abbott. Coppell, TX: Pantianos Classics.

Kaplan, S. (2017). The bigger picture of employee well-being: Its role for individuals, families and societies. SHRM-SIOP Science of HR Series.

Kaplan, S. N. (2012). Executive compensation and corporate governance in the U.S.: Perceptions, facts, and challenges. National Bureau of Economic Research Working Paper No. 18395. Washington, D.C., July 10.

Kaslow, N. J., Bangasser, D. A., Grus, C. L. McCutcheon, S. R., & Fowler, G. A. (2018). Facilitating pipeline progress from doctoral degree to first job. *American Psychologist, 73*(1), 47–62.

Katz, D., Caplan, A. L., & Merz, J. F. (2003). All gifts large and small: Toward an understanding of the ethics of pharmaceutical industry gift-giving. *The American Journal of Bioethics, 3*(3), 39–46.

Katz, D., & Kahn, R. (1978). *The social psychology of organizations* (2nd ed.). New York: Wiley.

Katz, L. F. & Krueger, A. B. (2016, March 29). The rise and nature of alternative work arrangements in the United States, 1995–2015. Retrieved from https://krueger.princeton.edu/sites/default/files/akrueger/files/katz_krueger_cws_-_march_29_20165.pdf, on June 17, 2016.

Katzell, R. A. (1994). Contemporary meta-trends in industrial and organizational psychology. In H. C. Triandis, M. D. Dunnette, & L. M. Hough (Eds.), *Handbook of industrial and organizational psychology* (2nd ed., Vol. 4, pp. 1–89). Palo Alto, CA: Consulting Psychologists Press.

Katzell, R. A., & Austin, J. T. (1992). From then to now: The development of industrial-organizational psychology in the United States. *Journal of Applied Psychology, 77*(6), 803–835.

Kaufman, A., Zacharias, L., & Karson, M. (1995). *Managers vs. owners: The struggle for corporate control in American democracy.* New York: Oxford University Press.

Kaye, D. (2021, June 9). DEI and the many forms of workplace bias. *Employment Practices Solutions, Inc.* Downloaded from http://www/epspros.com/news-resources/white-papers/2021/dei-and-the-many-forms-of-workplace-bias.html on July 14, 2021.

Kaye, L. (2021, May 4). Speak up on social and political issues, employees tell the boss. Retrieved from https://www.tiplepundi.com/story/2021/political-issues-employees/721971, May 5, 2021.

Kazak, A. E. (2018). Editorial: Journal article reporting standards, *American Psychologist, 73*(1), 1–2.

Kearns, C. E., Schmidt, L. A., & Glantz, S. A. (2016). Sugar industry and coronary heart disease research: A historical analysis of internal industry documents. *JAMA Internal Medicine*, Published online September 12, E1–E6.

Kearns, M., & Roth, A. (2020). *The ethical algorithm: Thew science of socially aware algorithm design*. Oxford, UK: Oxford University Press.

Kecharananta, N., & Baker, H. G. (1999). Capturing entrepreneurial values. *Journal of Applied Social Psychology, 29*, 820–833.

Kegan, R. (1993). The evolution of moral meaning-making. In A. Dobrin (Ed.), *Being good and doing right: Readings in moral development*. (pp. 15–35). New York: Latham.

Keita, G. P., & Sauter, S. L. (1992). *Work and well-being: An agenda for the 1990s*. Washington, DC: American Psychological Association.

Keith-Spiegel, P. (1977). Violation of ethical principles due to ignorance or poor professional judgment versus willful disregard. *Professional Psychology: Research and Practice, 8*, 288–296.

Keith-Spiegel, P., & Koocher, G. P. (1985). *Ethics in psychology: Professional standards and cases*. New York: Random House.

Keith-Spiegel, P., Sieber, J. & Koocher, G. P. (2010). *Responding to research wrong-doing: A user-friendly guide*. Available from http://www.ethicsresearch.com/images/RRW_11-10.pdf.

Keith-Spiegel, P., & Whitley, Jr. B. E. (2001). Academic dishonesty [Special issue]. *Ethics & Behavior, 11*(3).

Kelly, Jr. E. W. (1995). Counselor values: A national survey. *Journal of Counseling and Development, 73*, 648–653.

Kelly, G. (1962). *The psychology of personal constructs*. New York: Norton.

Kelley, M. (1983). Values in organizational theory and management education. *Academy of Management Review, 8*, 376–386.

Kelman, H. C. (1970). Deception in social research. In N. K. Denzin (Ed.), *The values of social science* (pp. 65–86). Chicago: Aldine.

Kelman, H. C. (1972). The rights of the subject in social research: An analysis in terms of relative power and legitimacy. *American Psychologist, 27*, 989–1016.

Kelman, H. C. (2021). A responsible psychologist is a responsible citizen. *Journal of Social Issues, 77*, 917–935.

Kendler, H. H. (1993). Psychology and the ethics of social policy. *American Psychologist, 48*, 1046–1053.

Kendler, H. H. (1999). The role of value in the world of psychology. *American Psychologist, 54*, 828–835.

Kennedy, A. A. (2000). *The end of shareholder value: Corporations at the crossroads*. Cambridge, MA: Perseus.

Kennett, J., & Fine, C. (2009). Will the real moral judgment please stand up? *Ethical Theory and Moral Practice, 12*(1), 77–96.

Kenny, D. A. (2019). Enhancing validity in psychological research. *American Psychologist, 74*(9), 1018–1028.

Kenrick, D. T., & Funder, D. C. (1988). Profiting from controversy: Lessons from the person-situation debate. *American Psychologist, 43*, 23–34.

Kensbock, J. M., Alkærsig, L., & Lomberg, C. (2022). The epidemic of mental disorders in business—How depression, anxiety, and stress spread across organizations through employee mobility. *Administrative Science Quarterly, 67*(1), 1–48.

Kerr, N. L. (1998). HARKing: Hypothesizing after the results are known. *Personality and Social Psychology Review*, *2*(3), 196–217.

Kessel, F. (1969). The philosophy of science as proclaimed and *science* as practiced: "Identity" or "dualism"? *American Psychologist*, *24*, 999–1005.

Keynes, J. M. (1964). *The general theory of employment, interest, and money*. New York: Harcourt Brace Jovanovich. (Original work published 1935)

Kidder, R. M. (1995). *How good people make tough choices*. New York: Morrow.

Kifner, J. (2001, September 8). Scholar sets off gastronomic false alarm. *The New York Times*, A1, B2.

Kilburg, R. R. (2012). *Virtuous leaders: Strategy, character, and influence in the 21st century*. Washington, DC: American Psychological Association.

Killen, M., & Smetana, J. G. (Eds.) (2014). *Handbook of moral development*, 2nd Ed. New York: Psychology Press/Taylor & Francis Group.

Kim, B., Moon, J. J., & Kim, E. (2022). Executive migration matters: The transfer of CSR profiles across organizations. *Business & Society*, *61*(1), 155–190.

Kim, K., Kim, M., & Qian, C. (2018). Effects of corporate social responsibility on corporate social performance. *Journal of Management*, *44*, 1097–1118.

Kim, T. W., Monge, R., & Strudler, A. (2015). Bounded ethicality and the principle that "ought" implies "can". *Business Ethics Quarterly*, *25*(3), 341–361.

Kim, T. W., & Routledge, B. R. (2022). Why a right to an explanation of algorithmic decision-making should exist: A trust-based approach. *Business Ethics Quarterly*, *32*(1), 75–102.

Kimball, B. A. (1992). *The "true professional ideal" in America*. Cambridge, MA: Blackwell.

Kimble, G. A. (1984). Psychology's two cultures. *American Psychologist*, *39*(8), 833–839.

Kimmel, A. J. (1988). *Ethics and values in applied social research*. Newbury Park, CA: Sage.

Kimmel, A. J. (1996). *Ethical issues in behavioral research: A survey*. Cambridge, MA: Blackwell.

Kimmel, A. J. (1998). In defense of deception. *American Psychologist*, *53*, 803–805.

Kimmel, A. J. (2001). Ethical trends in marketing and psychological research. *Ethics & Behavior*, *11*, 131–149.

Kimmel, A. J. (2007). *Ethical issues in behavioral research: Basic and applied perspectives*, 2nd Ed. Malden, MA: Blackwell Publishing.

Kimmel, A. J., & Smith, N. C. (2001). Deception in marketing research: Ethical, methodological, and disciplinary implications. *Psychology and Marketing*, *18*, 663–689.

Kimmel, A. J., Smith, N. C. & Klein, J. G. (2011). Ethical decision-making and research deception in the behavioral sciences: An application of social contract theory. *Ethics & Behavior*, *21*(3), 222–251.

King, E., & Gilrane, V. (2015). *Social science strategies for managing diversity: Industrial and organizational opportunities to enhance inclusion*. Bowling Green, OH: Society for Industrial and Organizational Psychology.

King, L. A., & Hicks, J. A. (2021). The science of meaning in life. In S. T. Fiske, & D. L. Schacter (Eds.). *Annual Review of Psychology*, *72*, 561–584.

Kinnane, J. F., & Bannon, M. M. (1964). Perceived parental influence and work-value orientation. *Personnel and Guidance Journal*, *43*, 273–279.

Kirsch, J. A., Love, G. D., Radler, B. T., & Ryff, C. D. (2019). Scientific imperatives vis-à-vis growing inequality in America. *American Psychologist*, *74*(7), -777.

Kish-Gephart, J. J., & Campbell, J. T. (2015). You don't forget your roots: The influence of CEO social class background on strategic risk taking. *Academy of Management Journal*, *58*(6), 1614–1636.

Kish-Gephart, J. J., Harrison, D. A., & Treviño, L. K. (2010). Bad apples, bad cases, and bad barrels: Meta-analytic evidence about sources of unethical decisions at work. *Journal of Applied Psychology*, *95*(1), 1–31.

Kissinger, A. (2016, Feb. 23). So how much do you get paid? *On Labor*. Downloaded May 19, 2016, from <https://onlabor.org/2016/02/23/so-how-much-do-you-get-paid/>

Kitchener, K. S. (1984). Intuition, critical evaluation and ethical principles: The foundation for ethical decisions in counseling psychology. *The Counseling Psychologist*, *12*, 43–55.

Klein, E. (2001). Pro bono: What, why, and how? *The Industrial–Organizational Psychologist*, *38*, 112–113.

Kleining, J. (1996). *The ethics of policing*. New York: Cambridge University Press.

Kluckhohn, C. (1951). Values and value orientations in the theory of action: An exploration in definition and classification. In T. Parsons & E. Shils (Eds.), *Toward a general theory of action* (pp. 388–433). Cambridge, MA: Harvard University Press.

Kluckhohn, F. R., & Strodtbeck, F. L. (1961). *Variations in value orientations*. Evanston, 1L.: Row, Peterson.

Kluver, J., Frazier, R., & Haidt, J. (2014). Behavioral ethics for homo economicus, homo heuristicus, and homo duplex. *Organizational Behavior and Human Decision Processes*, *123*, 150–158.

Knapp, S. (1999). Utilitarianism and the ethics of professional psychologists. *Ethics & Behavior*, *9*, 383–392.

Knapp, S., Handelsman, M. M., Gottlieb, M. C., & VandeCreek, L. D. (2013). The dark side of professional ethics. *Professional Psychology: Research and Practice*, *44*(6), 371–377.

Köbis, N. C., van Prooijen, J-W., Righetti, F. & Van Lange, P. A. M. (2017). The road to bribery and corruption: Slippery slope or steep cliff? *Psychological Science*, *28*(3), 297–306.

Kohlberg, L. (1973). Continuities in childhood and adult moral development revisited. In P. B. Baltes & K. Schaie (Eds.), *Life-span developmental psychology: Personality and socialization* (pp. 179–204). New York: Academic.

Kohlberg, L. (1981). *Essays on moral development: Vol. 1. The philosophy of moral development: Moral stages and the idea of justice*. San Francisco: Harper and Row.

Kohlberg, L. (1984). *Essays on moral development: Vol. 2. The psychology of moral development*. San Francisco: Harper & Row.

Kohlberg, L., Levine, C., & Hewer, A. (1983). Moral stages: A current formulation and a response to critics. In J. A. Meacham (Ed.), *Contributions to human development*, (Vol. 10, p. 174). New York: Karger.

Kohlberg, L., & Ryncarz, R. A. (1990). Beyond justice reasoning: Moral development and consideration of a seventh stage. In C. N. Alexander, & E. J. Langer (Eds.), *Higher stages of human development: Perspectives on adult growth* (pp. 191–207). New York: Oxford University Press.

Kok, P., van der Wiele, T., McKenna, R., & Brown, A. (2001). A corporate social responsibility audit within a quality management framework. *Journal of Business Ethics*, *31*, 285–297.

Kolk, A. (2016). The social responsibility of international business: From ethics and the environment to CSR and sustainable development. *Journal of World Business*, *51*, 23–34.

Koocher, G., & Keith-Spiegel, P. (1998). *Ethics in psychology: Professional standards and cases* (2nd ed.). New York: Oxford University Press.

Koocher, G., & Keith-Spiegel, P. (2010). Peers nip misconduct in the bud. *Nature, 466,* 438–440.

Koopman, J., Lanaj, K., & Scott, B. A. (2016). Integrating the bright and dark sides of OCB: A daily investigation of the benefits and costs of helping others. *Academy of Management Journal, 59*(2), 414–435.

Koppes, L. L. (2002). Using the jigsaw classroom to teach the history of I/O psychology and related topics. *The Industrial-Organizational Psychologist, 39,* 109–112.

Korenman, S. G. (2006). Teaching the responsible conduct of research in humans (RCRH). Chap. 4. Conflicts of interest (COI). Downloaded on Aug. 24, 2016 from <http://ori.hhs.gov/education/products/ucla/default.htm>

Korman, A. K. (Ed.). (1994). *Human dilemmas in* work organizations: *Strategies for re-*solution. New York: Guilford.

Korn, J. H. (1997). *Illusions of reality: A history of deception in social psychology.* Albany, NY: State University of New York Press.

Korn, J. H. (1998). The reality of deception. *American Psychologist, 53,* 805.

Korn, J. H., & Bram, D. R. (1988). What is missing in the method section of APA journal articles? *American Psychologist, 43,* 1091–1092.

Kornhauser, A. (1947). Industrial psychology as management technique and as social science. *American Psychologist, 2*(7), 224–229.

Kornhauser, A. (1949). *Psychology of labor-management relations.* Champaign, IL: Industrial Relations Research Association.

Kornhauser, W. (1962). *Scientists in industry.* Berkeley, CA: University of California Press.

Korten, D. C. (1995). *When corporations* rule *the world.* West Hartford, CT: Kumarian.

Korten, D. C. (1999). *The post-corporate world: Life after capitalism.* San Francisco: Berrett-Koehler.

Kosinski, M., Matz, S. C., Gosling, S. D., Popov, V., & Stillwell, D. (2015). Facebook as a research tool for the social sciences: Opportunities, challenges, ethical considerations, and practical guidelines. *American Psychologist, 70*(6), 543–556.

Kotabe, H. P., & Hofmann, W. (2015). On integrating the components of self-control. *Perspectives on Psychological Science, 10*(5), 618–638.

Kouchaki, M. (2015). Professionalism and moral behavior. *Business & Society, 54*(3), 376–385.

Kouchaki, M. & Wareham, J. (2015). Excluded and behaving unethically: social exclusion, physiological responses, and unethical behavior. *Journal of Applied Psychology, 100*(2), 547–556.

Kożusznik, B. & Glaser, S. (2021). *Hearing the international voices of professionals in industrial, work, and organizational psychology: A declaration of identity.* SIOP Research Publication, March 26.

Kracher, B., & Wells, D. L. (1998). Employee selection and the ethic of care. In M. Schminke (Ed.), *Managerial ethics* (pp. 81–97). Mahwah, NJ: Lawrence Erlbaum Associates.

Kramer, R. M. (1999). Trust and distrust in organizations: Emerging perspectives, enduring questions. *Annual Review of Psychology, 30,* 569–598.

Krasner, L., & Houts, A. C. (1984). A study of the "value" systems of behavioral scientists. *American Psychologist, 39,* 840–849.

Krasnow, M. M., Howard, R. M. & Eisenbruch, A. B. (2020). The importance of being honest? Evidence that deception may not pollute social science subject pools after all. *Behavior Research Methods, 52,* 1175–1188.

Krawczyk, M. (2015). The search for significance: A few peculiarities in the distribution of P values in experimental psychology literature. *PLoS One*, *10*(6), 1–19.

Krebs, D. L. & Denton, K. (2005). Toward a more pragmatic approach to morality: A critical evaluation of Kohlberg's model. *Psychological Review*, *112*(3), 629–649.

Krebs, D. L., Vermeulen, S. C. A., Carpendale, J. I., & Denton, K. (1991). Structural and situational influences on moral judgment: The interaction between stage and dilemma. In W. M. Kurtines, & J. L. Gewirtz (Eds.), *Handbook of moral behavior and development: Vol. 2. Research* (pp. 139–169). Hillsdale, NJ: Lawrence Erlbaum Associates.

Kristiansen, C. M., & Zanna, M. P. (1988). Justifying attitudes by appealing to values: A functional perspective. *British Journal of Social Psychology*, *27*, 247–256.

Kristiansen, C. M., & Zanna, M. P. (1994). The rhetorical use of values to justify social and intergroup attitudes. *Journal of Social Issues*, *50*, 47–65.

Kronzon, S., & Darley, J. (1999). Is this tactic ethical? Biased judgments of ethics in negotiation. *Basic and Applied Social Psychology*, *21*, 49–60.

Krueger, J. I. (2002). Postmodern parlor games. *American Psychologist*, 57, 461–462.

Kruger, D. J. (2002). The deconstruction of constructivism. *American Psychologist*, *57*, 456– 457.

Kruglanski, A. W. (1975). The human subject in the psychology experiment: Fact and artifact. In L. Berkowitz (Ed.), *Advances in experimental social psychology* (Vol. 8, pp. 101–147). New York: Academic.

Krugman, P. (2001, December 11). Laissez not fair. *The New York Times*, A27.

Krupat, E., & Garonzik, R. (1994). Subjects' expectations and the search for alternatives to deception in social psychology. *British Journal of Social Psychology*, *33*, 211–222.

Kuenzi, M., Mayer, D. M., & Greenbaum, R. L. (2020). Creating an ethical organizational environment: The relationship between ethical leadership, ethical organizational climate, and unethical behavior. *Personnel Psychology*, *73*(1), 43–71.

Kuhn, T. (1970). The structure of scientific revolutions (2nd ed.). *International encyclopedia of unified science: Foundations for the unity of science, Vol. 2*. Chicago: University of Chicago Press.

Kuhn, T. (1977). *The essential tension*. Chicago: University of Chicago Press.

Kuhn, T. (1996). *The structure of scientific revolutions* (3rd ed.). Chicago: University of Chicago Press.

Kuhn, T. (2000). *The road since structure*. Chicago: University of Chicago Press.

Kurtines, W. M., Alvarez, M., & Azmitia, M. (1990). Science and morality: The role of values in science and the scientific study of moral phenomena. *Psychological Bulletin*, *107*(3), 283–295.

Kurzban, R., Burton-Chellew, M. N., & West, S. A. (2015). The evolution of altruism in humans. *Annual Review of Psychology*, *66*, 575–599.

Kurzynski, M. J. (1998). The virtue of forgiveness as a human resource management strategy. *Journal of Business Ethics*, *17*, 77–85.

Kymlicka, W. (1993). The social contract tradition. In P. Singer (Ed.), *A companion to ethics* (pp. 186–196). Cambridge, MA: Blackwell.

Kymlicka, W. (2002). *Contemporary political economy: An introduction, 2ⁿᵈ Ed*. Oxford, UK: Oxford University Press.

Lafer, G., & Loustaunau, L. (2020, July 23). *Fear at work: An inside account of how employers threaten, intimidate, and harass workers to stop them from exercising their right to collective bargaining*. Economic Policy Institute. Retrieved from https://www.epi.org/publication/fear-at-work-how-employers-scare-workers-out-of-unionizing/ on Nov. 17, 2021.

Landers, N. (2019). The existential threats to I-O psychology highlighted by rapid technological change. In R. N. Landers (Ed.), *Cambridge Handbook of Technology and Employee Behavior* (pp. 3–21). New York, NY: Cambridge University Press.

Landy, F. J., Barnes, J. L., & Murphy, K. R. (1978). Correlates of perceived fairness and accuracy of performance evaluation. *Journal of Applied Psychology, 63,* 751–754.

Landy, J. F., & Goodwin, G. P. (2015). Does incidental disgust amplify moral judgment? A meta-analytic review of experimental evidence. *Perspectives on Psychological Science, 10,* 518–536.

Landy, J. F. (& 49 coauthors). (2020). Crowdsourcing hypothesis tests: Making transparent how design choices shape research results. *Psychological Bulletin, 146*(5), 451–479.

Lange, D., Bundy, J., & Park, E. (2022). The social nature of stakeholder utility. *Academy of Management Review, 7*(1), 9–30.

Langer, M., Oster, D., Speith, T., Hermanns, H., Kästner, L., Schmidt, E., Sesing, A., & Baum, K. (2021). What do we want from explainable artificial intelligence (XAI)?—A stakeholder perspective on XAI and a conceptual model guiding interdisciplinary XAI research. *Artificial Intelligence, 296,* 103473.

Langlais, P. J., & Bent, B. J. (2014). Individual and organizational predictors of the ethicality of graduate students' responses to research integrity issues. *Science and Engineering Ethics, 20,* 897–921.

Larrick, R. P. (2016). The social context of decisions. *Annual Review of Organizational Psychology and Organizational Behavior, 3,* 441–467.

Latham, G. (2000). The reciprocal effects of science on practice: Insights from the practice and science of goal setting. *Canadian Psychology, 42,* 1–11.

Latham, G. (2001). The reciprocal transfer of learning from journals to practice. *Applied Psychology: An International Review, 50,* 201–211.

Laudan, L. (1984). *Science and values: An essay on the aims of science and their role in scientific debate.* Berkeley, CA: University of California Press.

Laurin, K. (2017). Belief in God: A cultural adaptation with important side effects. *Current Directions in Psychological Science, 26*(5), 458–463.

Lavelle, L. (2000, October 16). CEO pay: The more things change . . . . *Business Week,* (3703), 106–108.

Lawler, E. E. (1971). Thoughts about the future. *Professional Psychology, 2,* 21–22.

Lawler, E. E. III, Mohrman, A. M. Jr., Mohrman, S. A., Ledford, G. E. Jr., & Cummings, T. G. (Eds.). (1985). *Doing research that is useful for theory and practice.* San Francisco: Jossey-Bass.

Lawrence, P. R., & Lorsch, J. W. (1969). *Organization and environment: Managing differentiation and integration.* Homewood, IL: Irwin.

Lawson, E. (2001). Informational and relational meanings of deception: Implications for deception methods in research. *Ethics & Behavior, 11,* 115–130.

Lazarus, R. S., & Cohen-Charash, Y. (2001). Discrete emotions in organizational life. In R. L. Payne & G. L. Cooper (Eds.), *Emotions at work: Theory, research and applications for management* (pp. 45–81). Chichester, England: Wiley.

Lear, R. W. (2000). Compensation obscenity. *Chief Executive, 14,* 14.

Lederman, L. C. (1992). Debriefing: Toward a systematic assessment of theory and practice. *Simulation & Gaming, 23,* 145–160.

Lee, E-S., Park, T-Y. & Koo, B. (2015). Identifying organizational identification as a basis for attitudes and behaviors: A meta-analytic review. *Psychological Bulletin, 141*(5), 1049–1080.

Lefkowitz, J. (1990). The scientist-practitioner model is not enough. *The Industrial-Organizational Psychologist, 28*(1), 47–52.

Lefkowitz, J. (1994). Race as a factor in job placement: Serendipitous findings of "ethnic drift". *Personnel Psychology, 47*(3), 497–514.

Lefkowitz, J. (2000). The role of interpersonal affective regard in supervisory performance ratings: A literature review and proposed causal model. *Journal of Occupational and Organizational Psychology, 73,* 67–85.

Lefkowitz, J. (2003). *Ethics and values in industrial-organizational psychology.* Mahwah, NJ: Lawrence Erlbaum Associates.

Lefkowitz, J. (2004). Contemporary cases of corporate corruption: Any relevance for I-O psychology? *The Industrial-Organizational Psychologist, 42*(2), 21–29.

Lefkowitz, J. (2005). The values of Industrial-Organizational Psychology: Who are we? *The Industrial-Organizational Psychologist, 43*(2), 13 – 20.

Lefkowitz, J. (2006). The constancy of ethics amidst the changing world of work. *Human Resource Management Review, 16,* 245–268.

Lefkowitz, J. (2007a). "Ethics in Industrial-Organizational Psychology Research". In S. Rogelberg, Ed., *The Encyclopedia of Industrial and Organizational Psychology, Vol. 1,* (pp. 218–222). Thousand Oaks, CA.: Sage.

Lefkowitz, J. (2007b). "Ethics in Industrial-Organizational Psychology Practice". In S. Rogelberg, Ed., *The Encyclopedia of Industrial and Organizational Psychology, Vol. 1* (pp. 215–218). Thousand Oaks, CA.: Sage.

Lefkowitz, J. (2007c). Corporate Social Responsibility. In S. Rogelberg, Ed., *The Encyclopedia of Industrial and Organizational Psychology, Vol. 1* (pp. 114–118). Thousand Oaks, CA.: Sage.

Lefkowitz, J. (2008). To prosper, organizational psychology should … expand its values to match the quality of its ethics. *Journal of Organizational Behavior, 29*(4), 439–453.

Lefkowitz, J. (2009a). Promoting employee justice: It's even worse than that! *Industrial and Organizational Psychology, 2*(2), 220–224.

Lefkowitz, J. (2009b). Individual and Organizational Antecedents of Misconduct in Organizations: What Do We [Believe That We] Know, And On What Bases Do We [Believe That We] Know It? Chap. 2 In C. Cooper, & R. Burke (Eds.), *Research Companion to Crime and Corruption in Organizations.* Cheltenham, UK. Northampton, MA: Edward Elgar (pp. 60–91).

Lefkowitz, J. (2010a). Industrial-organizational psychology's recurring identity crises: It's a values issue! *Industrial and Organizational Psychology, 3*(3), 293–299.

Lefkowitz, J. (2010b). Special Section Commentary 1. Can professions contribute to the reduction of world-wide poverty? A case in point: Organizational psychology and pay diversity. *International Journal of Psychology, 45*(5), 371 – 375.

Lefkowitz, J. (2011a). Rating teachers illegally? *The Industrial-Organizational Psychologist, 48*(4), 47–49.

Lefkowitz, J. (2011b). The science, practice and morality of work psychology. *Industrial and Organizational Psychology, 4*(1), 112–115.

Lefkowitz, J. (2011c). Ethics in industrial-organizational psychology. Vol. 2, Chap. I.8, In S. Knapp, L. VandeCreek, M. Gottlieb, & M. Handelsman (Eds.), *APA Handbook of ethics in psychology.* Wash., DC: American Psychological Association.

Lefkowitz, J. (2012a). The impact of practice values on our science. *The Industrial-Organizational Psychologist, 50*(2), 16–22.

Lefkowitz, J. (2012b). From humanitarian to humanistic work psychology: The morality of business. Chap. 5 In S. C. Carr, M. MacLachlan, & A. Furnham (Eds.), *Humanitarian work psychology: Alignment, harmonization and cultural competence.* London, UK: MacMillan, 103–125.

Lefkowitz, J. (2013a). Values of I-O psychology: Another example: What and whom we don't study and what it all suggests about the profession. *The Industrial-Organizational Psychologist, 51*(2), 46–56.

Lefkowitz, J. (2013b). Values and ethics of a changing I-O psychology: A call to (further) action. Chap. 1 In J. B. Olson-Buchanan, L. K. Bryan, & L. F. Thompson (Eds.), *Using I-O psychology for the greater good: Helping those who help others* (pp. 13–42). Society for Industrial and Organizational Psychology, Frontier Series.

Lefkowitz, J. (2014a). Educating I-O psychologists for science, practice and social responsibility. *Industrial and Organizational Psychology, 7*(1), 41–46.

Lefkowitz, J. (2014b). Psychology departments versus business schools: Tempest in a teapot? *Industrial and Organizational Psychology, 7*(3), 311–317.

Lefkowitz, J. (2015). The maturation of a profession: A work psychology for the new millennium. Chapter 18 In I. McWha, D. C. Maynard, & M. ONeill Berry (Eds.), *Humanitarian work psychology and the global development agenda: Case studies and interventions.* Routledge Psychology Press.

Lefkowitz, J. (2016). News flash! Work psychology discovers workers!. *Industrial and Organizational Psychology, 9*(1), 137–144.

Lefkowitz, J. (2017). *Ethics and Values in Industrial-Organizational Psychology,* 2nd Ed (p. 603). New York: Taylor & Francis/Routledge.

Lefkowitz, J. (2019). The conundrum of industrial-organizational psychology. *Industrial and Organizational Psychology: Perspectives on Science and Practice, 12*(4), 473–478.

Lefkowitz, J. (2021). Forms of ethical dilemmas in industrial-organizational psychology. *Industrial and Organizational Psychology: Perspectives on Science and Practice, 14*(3), 297–319.

Lefkowitz, J. (2023). Organizational outcomes: It's not (only) a levels issue. *Industrial and Organizational Psychology: Perspectives on Science and Practice, 15*(3), 432–435.

Lefkowitz, J., & Lowman, R. L. (2017). Ethics of Employee Selection. Chap. 26 In J. L. Farr & N. T. Tippins, (Eds.), *Handbook of Employee Selection,* 2nd ed (pp. 575–598). New York: Routledge/Taylor & Francis Group. (1st ed. Published 2010.)

Lefkowitz, J. & Watts, L. (2022). Ethical incidents reported by industrial-organizational psychologists: A ten-year follow-up. *Journal of Applied Psychology, 107*(10), 1781–1803.

Legros, S., & Cisleghi, B. (2020). Mapping the social norms literature: An overview of reviews. *Perspectives on Psychological Science, 15*(1), 62–80.

Leib, M., Köbis, N., Soraperra, I., Weisel, O., & Shalvi, S. (2021). Collaborative dishonesty: A meta-analytic review. *Psychological Bulletin, 147*(12), 1241–1268.

Leonard, T. C. (2016). *Race, eugenics, and American economics in the progressive era.* Princeton, NJ: Princeton University Press.

Leong, F. T. L. Pickren, W. E., & Vasquez, M. J. T. (2017). APA efforts in promoting human rights and social justice. *American Psychologist, 72*(8), 790.

Leonhardt, D. (2002, April 7). Did pay incentives cut both ways? *The New York Times,* Section 3, pp. 1, 6, 7.

Lerner, J. S., Li, Y., Valdesolo, P., & Kassam, K. S. (2015). Emotions and decision making. *Annual Review of Psychology, 66*, 799–823.

Lerner, M. J. (Ed.). (1975). The justice motive in social behavior [Special issue]. *Journal of Social Issues, 31*(3).

Lesser, L. I., Ebbeling, C. B., Goozner, M., Wypij, D., & Ludwig, D. S. (2007). Relationship between funding source and conclusion among nutrition-related scientific articles. *PLoS Medicine, 4*(1), e5, 0041-0046.

Leung, K. (2011). Presenting post hoc hypotheses as A priori: Ethical and theoretical issues. *Management and Organization Review, 7*(3), 471–479.

Levitt, H. M., Bamberg, M., Creswell, J. W., Frost, D. M. Josselson, R., & Suárez-Orozco, C. (2018). Journal article reporting standards for qualitative primary, qualitative meta-analytic, and mixed methods research in psychology: The APA publications and communications board task force report. *American Psychologist, 73*(1), 26–46.

Lewandowsky, s. & Oberauer, K. (2016). Motivated rejection of science. *Current Directions in Psychological Science, 25*(4), 217–222.

Lewis, C. W. (1991). *The ethics challenge in public service: A problem-solving guide.* San Francisco: Jossey-Bass.

Lewis, D. M., Al-Shawaf, L., Conroy-Beam, D., Asao, K., & Buss, D. M. (2017). Evolutionary psychology: A how-to guide. *American Psychologist, 72*(4), 353–373.

Lewis, T. (2015). The CEO who knowingly sold tainted peanuts that killed 9 people got 28 years in prison. Business Insider, Sept. 22, 2015. Downloaded Sept. 25, 2015 from http://www.businessinsider.com/ceo-who-sold-tainted-peanuts-will-go-to-prison-2015-9.

Li, N. P., van Vugt, M., & Colarelli, S. M. (2018). The evolutionary mismatch hypothesis: Implications for psychological science. *Current Directions in Psychological Science, 27*(1), 38-44.

Lickona, T. (1994). Research on Piaget's theory of moral development. In B. Puka (Ed.), *Fundamental research in moral development* (Vol. 2, pp. 321–342). New York: Garland.

Lilienthal, D. (1953). *Big business: A new era.* New York: Harper.

Lieberman, M. D., Gaunt, R., Gilbert, D. T. & Trope, Y. (2002). Reflexion and reflection: A social cognitive neuroscience approach to attributional inference. In M. P. Zanna (Ed.), *Advances in Experimental social Psychology, Vol. 34* (pp. 199–249). New York: Academic Press.

Lilienfeld, S. O. (2012). Public skepticism of psychology: Why many people perceive the study of human behavior as unscientific. *American Psychologist, 67*(2), 11–129.

Lim, S. & Cortina, L. M. (2005). Interpersonal mistreatment in the workplace: The interface and impact of general incivility and sexual harassment. *Journal of Applied Psychology, 90*(3), 483–496.

Lin, S-H., Ma, J., & Johnson, R. E. (2016). When ethical behavior breaks bad: How ethical leader behavior can turn abusive via ego depletion and moral licensing. *Journal of Applied Psychology, 101*(6), 815–830.

Lind, E. A., & Tyler, T. R. (1988). *The social psychology of procedural justice.* New York: Plenum.

Lindblom. L. (2011). The structure of a Rawlsian theory of just work. *Journal of Business Ethics, 101*(4), 577–599.

Lindblom. L. (2018). In; defense of a Rawlsian fair equality of opportunity. *Philosophical Papers, 47*(2), 235–263.

Linder, C., & Farahbakhsh, S. (2020). Unfolding the black box of questionable research practices: Where is the line between acceptable and unacceptable practices? *Business Ethics Quarterly, 30*(3), 335–360.

Lindsay, R. C. L., & Adair, J. G. (1990). Do ethically recommended research procedures influence the perceived ethicality of social psychological research? Canadian *Journal of Behavioural Science, 22,* 282–294.

Lipartito, K. J., & Miranti, P. J. (1998). Professions and organizations in twentieth century America. *Social Science Quarterly, 79,* 301–320.

Lipsey, M. W. (1974). Research and relevance: A survey of graduate students and faculty in psychology. *American Psychologist, 29,* 541–553.

Lizotte, M-K., & Warren, T. (2021). Understanding the appeal of libertarianism: Gender and race differences in the endorsement of libertarian principles. *Analyses of Social Issues and Public Policy, 21*(1), 640–659.

Llewellyn, E. v. Z., Nei, E., & Rothman (Sr.), S. (2016). Conceptualising the professional identity of industrial or organizational psychologists within the South African context. *SA Journal of Industrial Psychology, 42*(1), xxx

Loch, K. D., Conger, S., & Oz, E. (1998). Ownership, privacy and monitoring in the workplace: A debate on technology and ethics. *Journal of Business Ethics, 17,* 653–663.

Locke, E. A. (Ed.). (1986). Generalizing from laboratory to field settings: Research findings from industrial-organizational psychology, organizational behavior, and human resource management. Lexington, MA: Lexington.

Locke, E. A. (1988). The virtue of selfishness. *American Psychologist, 43,* 481.

Locke, E. A. (2002). The dead end of postmodernism. *American Psychologist, 57,* 458.

Locke, E. A., & Becker, T. (1998). Rebuttal to a subjectivist critique of an objectivist approach to integrity in organizations. *Academy of Management Review, 23,* 170–175.

Locke, E. A., & Woiceshyn, J. (1995). Why businessmen should be honest: The argument from rational egoism. *Journal of Organizational Behavior, 16,* 405–414.

Locke, J. (1988). Two treatises of government. In P. Laslett (Ed.), *Two treatises of government* (pp. 141–428). New York: Cambridge University Press. (Original work published 1689)

Loe, T. W., Ferrell, L., & Mansfield, P. (2000). A review of empirical studies assessing ethical decision making in business. *Journal of Business Ethics, 25,* 185–204.

Lohr, S. (2022a, Jan. 11). Economists point to tech on pay gap. *The New York Times,* B1.

Lohr, S. (2022b, Jan. 17). Requirement for degrees curbs hiring. *The New York Times,* B1.

Lohr, S. (2022c, Feb. 17). Are free-market ideas stale? Some scholars think so. *The New York Times,* B4.

London, M. (Ed.). (1995). *Employees, careers, and job creation: Developing growth-oriented human resource strategies and programs.* San Francisco: Jossey-Bass.

London, M. (1996). Redeployment and continuous learning in the 21st century: Hard lessons and positive examples from the downsizing era. *Academy of Management Executive, 10,* 67–78.

London, M., & Bray, D. W. (1980). Ethical issues in testing and evaluation for personnel decisions. *American Psychologist, 35,* 890–901.

Loomis, E. (2021, April 16). An Amazon union never had a chance. *The New York Times,* A19.

Lounsbury, M. (2002). Institutional transformation and status mobility: The professionalization of the field of finance. *Academy of Management Journal, 45,* 255–266.

Lowman, R. L. (1991). Ethical human resources practice in organizational settings. In D. Bray & Associates. (Eds.), *Working with organizations and their people: A guide to human resources practice* (pp. 194–218). New York: Guilford.

Lowman, R. L. (1993a). *Counseling and psychotherapy of work dysfunctions*. Washington, DC: American Psychological Association.

Lowman, R. L. (1993b). An ethics code for I/O psychology: For what purpose and at what cost? *The Industrial-Organiztional Psychologist*, *31*(1), 90–92.

Lowman, R. L. (Ed.), Lefkowitz, J., McIntyre, R., & Tippins, N. (Assoc. Eds.). (2006). *The ethical practice of psychology in organizations* (2nd ed.) Washington, DC: American Psychological Association.

Lu, H., Liu, X., & Falkenberg, L. (2022). Investigating the impact of corporate social responsibility (CSR) on risk management practices. *Business & Society*, *61*(2), 496–534.

Lubinski, D. (1992). Aptitudes, skills, and proficiencies. Chap. 1 In M. D. Dunnette, & L. M. Hough (Eds.), *Handbook of industrial and organizational psychology*, 2nd Ed., Vol. 3. Palo Alto, CA: Consulting Psychologists Press, Inc.

Lublin, J. S. (1999, April 8). Lowering the bar. *The Wall Street Journal*, R1.

Lueptow, L., Mueller, S. A., Hammes, R. R., & Masters, L. S. (1977). The impact of informed consent regulations on response rate and response bias. *Sociological Methods and Research*, *6*, 183–204.

Luetge, C., Uhl, M., & Rusch, H. (2014). Introduction: Toward an empirical moral philosophy. Chap. 1 In C. Luetge, H. Rusch, & M. Uhl (Eds.). (2014). *Experimental ethics: Toward an empirical moral philosophy* (pp. 1–4). Houndmills, England: Palgrave Macmillan.

Luetge, C., Rusch, H., & Uhl, M. (Eds.) (2014). *Experimental ethics: Toward an empirical moral philosophy*. Houndmills, England: Palgrave Macmillan.

Luria, S. E. (1976). Biological aspects of ethical principles. *Journal of Medicine and Philosophy*, *1*, 332–336.

Luthar, S. S. (2017). Doing for the greater good: What price, in academe? *Perspectives on Psychological Science*, *12*(6), 1153–1158.

Luttwak, E. (1999). *Turbo-capitalism: Winners and losers in the global economy*. New York City: HarperCollins.

Lynn, A. (2021). Why "doing well by doing good" went wrong: Getting beyond "good ethics pays" claims in managerial thinking. *Academy of Management Review*, *46*(3), 512–533.

Lynn, K. S. (Ed.). (1965). *The professions in America*. Boston: Houghton Mifflin.

MacCoun, R. J. (1998). Biases in the interpretation and use of research results. *Annual Review of Psychology*, *49*, 259–287.

Machery, E., & Mallon, R. (2010). Evolution of morality. Chapter 1 In J. M. Doris & the Moral Psychology Research Group. *The moral psychology handbook* (pp. 3–46). New York, NY: Oxford University Press.

MacIntyre, A. (1998). *A short history of ethics* (2nd ed.). Oxford: Routledge Classics.

MacIntyre, A. (2007). *After virtue*, 3rd Ed. London: Duckworth.

Maclagan, P. (1998). *Management and morality*. London: Sage.

Macrina, F. L. (2014). *Scientific integrity: Text and cases in responsible conduct of research*, 4th Ed. Washington, DC: ASM Press.

Mael, F. A. (1991). A conceptual rationale for the domain and attributes of biodata items. *Personnel Psychology*, *44*, 763–792.

Mael, F. A., Waldman, D. A., & Mulqueen, C. (2001). From scientific work to organizational leadership: Predictors of management aspiration among technical personnel. *Journal of Vocational Behavior*, 59, 132–148.

Mahn, K. (2016, Apr. 26). The changing face of socially responsible investing. Forbes. Advisor Intelligence. Retrieved from < http://www.forbes.com/sites/advisor/2016/04/26/the-changing-face-of-socially-responsible-investing/#4eed04a66d09> on June 3, 2016.

Mahoney, M. J. (1976). *Scientist as subject: The psychological imperative*. Cambridge, MA: Ballinger.

Malesic, J. (2021, Sept. 26). Our relationship to work is broken. *The New York Times*, 4R.

Malik, K. (2014). *The quest for a moral compass: A global history of ethics*. Brooklyn, NY: Melville House Publishing.

Malle, B. (2021). Moral judgments. In S. T. Fiske, & D. L. Schacter (Eds.), *Annual Review of Psychology, 72*, 293–318.

Mallory, D., Rupp, D. E., Scott, J. C., Saari, L., Thompson, L. F., Osicki, M., & Sall, E. (2015). Attention all I-O programs: It's time to join the United Nations Global Compact! *The Industrial-Organizational Psychologist, 52*(4), 135–136.

Manicas, P. T., & Secord, P. E. (1983). Implications for psychology of the new philosophy of science. *American Psychologist, 38*, 399–413.

Mann, T. (1994). Informed consent for psychological research: Do subjects comprehend consent forms and understand their legal rights? *Psychological Science, 5*, 140–143.

Mansfield, E. D., & Mutz, D. C. (2013). Us versus them: Mass attitudes toward offshore outsourcing. *World Politics, 65*(4), 571–608.

Mappes, T. A., & Zembaty, J. S. (1997). (Eds.), *Social ethics: Morality and social policy*, (5th ed.). New York: McGraw-Hill.

Marcus, A., & Olansky, I. (2015, May 23). What's behind big science frauds? *The New York Times*, A19.

Marcy, T., & Bayati, A. (2020). How I-O psychology can help in the selection and development of neurodiverse employees. *SIOP White Paper Series*. Bowling Green, OH: Society for Industrial and Organizational Psychology.

Marinescu, I., Ouss, I., & Pape, L-D. (2021). Wages, hires, and labor market concentration. *Journal of Economic Behavior and Organization, 184*, 506–605.

Marinescu, I., & Rathelot, R. (2018). Mismatch unemployment and the geography of job search. *American Economics Journal: Macroeconomics, 10*(3), 42–70.

Marshall, B., & Dewe, P. (1997). An investigation of the components of moral intensity. *Journal of Business Ethics, 16*, 521–530.

Martin, A., & Olson, K. R. (2015). Beyond good and evil: What motivations underlie children's prosocial behavior. *Psychological Science, 10*(2), 159–175.

Martin, K. D., & Cullen, J. B. (2006). Continuities and extensions of ethical climate theory: A meta-analytic review. *Journal of Business Ethics, 69*(2), 175–194.

Martin, K. E. (2015). Ethical issues in the big data industry. *MIS Quarterly Executive, 14*(2), Article 4.

Martinson, B. C., Anderson, M. S., Crain, A. L., & de Vries (2006). Scientists' perceptions of organizational justice and self-reported misbehaviors. *Journal of Empirical Research on Human Research Ethics: An International Journal, 1*(1), 51–66.

Martinson, B. C., Anderson, M. S., & de Vries (2005). Commentary. Scientists behaving badly. *Nature, 435*, 737–738.

Martinson, B. C., Thrush, C. R., & Crain, A. L. (2013). Development and validation of the survey of organizational research climate (SORC). *Science and Engineering Ethics, 19*, 813–834.

Maslow, A. H. (1969). Toward a humanistic biology. *American Psychologist, 24*, 724–735.

Maslow, A. H. (1998). *Toward a psychology of being* (3rd ed.). New York: Wiley.

Mason, E. S., & Mudrack, P. E. (1997). Are individuals who agree that corporate social responsibility is a "fundamentally subversive doctrine" inherently unethical? *Applied Psychology: An International Review, 16,* 135–152.

Mattick, P. (2000, March 26). You've got an attitude. Review of "On the Emotions" by Richard Wollheim. *The New York Times,* Book Review Section, 149, 28.

Maurer, R. (2021, Dec. 20). New York City to Require bias Audits of AI-based type HR Technology. Society for Human Resource Management.

Maxwell, B. (2016). The debiasing agenda in ethics teaching: An overview and appraisal of the behavioral ethics perspective. *Teaching Ethics, 16*(1), 75–90.

May, D. R., Chang, Y. K., & Shao, R. (2015). Does ethical membership matter? Moral identification and its organizational implications. *Journal of Applied Psychology, 100*(3), 681–694.

May, D. R., & Pauli, K. P. (2002). The role of moral intensity in ethical decision making. *Business & Society, 41,* 84–117.

May, K. (1998). Work in the 21st Century: The role of I/O in work–life programs. *The Industrial–Organizational Psychologist, 36,* 79–82.

Mays, V. M. (2000). A social justice agenda. *American Psychologist, 55,* 326–327.

Mazar, N., Amir, O., & Ariely, D. (2008). The dishonesty of honest people: A theory of self-concept maintenance. *Journal of Marketing Research, XLV,* 633–644.

McAdams, D. P. (2009). The moral personality. Chap. 1 In D. Narvaez, & D. K. Lapsley (Eds.), *Personality, identity, and character: Explorations in moral character* (pp. 11–29). New York, NY: Cambridge University Press.

McAdams, D. P., & Pals. K. L. (2006). A new big five: Fundamental principles for an integrative science of personality. *American Psychologist, 61*(3), 204–217.

McCabe, D. M. (1997). Alternative dispute resolution and employee voice in nonunion employment: An ethical analysis of organizational due process procedures and mechanisms—The case of the United States. *Journal of Business Ethics, 16,* 349–356.

McCall, Jr., M. W., & Bobko, P. (1990). Research methods in the service of discovery. In M. D. Dunnette, & L. M. Hough (Eds.), *Handbook of industrial and organizational psychology* (2nd ed., Vol. 1, pp. 381–418). Palo Alto, CA: Consulting Psychologists Press.

McClendon, J. (2006). The consequences and challenges of union decline. Chapter 13 In J. R. Deckop (Ed.), *Human resource management ethics* (pp. 261–281). Greenwich, CN: Information Age Publishing.

McConnell, T. (2018). Moral Dilemmas. In E. N. Zalta (Ed.). *The stanford encyclopedia of philosophy* (Fall 2018 edition). Stanford, CA: The Metaphysics Research Lab, Center for the Study of Language and Information (CSLI), Stanford University. Downloaded from https://plato.stanford.edu/entries/moral-dilemmas/ on December 16, 2018.

McCormack, T., Feeney, A., & Beck, S. R. (2020). Regret and decision-making: A developmental perspective. *Current Directions in Psychological Science, 29*(4), 346–350.

McCullough, M. E., Kilpatrick, S. D., Emmons, R. A., & Larson, D. B. (2001). Is gratitude a moral affect? *Psychological Bulletin, 127,* 249–266.

McElroy, J. C., Morrow, P. C., & Rude, S. N. (2001). Turnover and organizational performance: A comparative analysis of the effects of voluntary, involuntary, and reductionin-force turnover. *Journal of Applied Psychology, 86,* 1294–1299.

McGue, M. (2000). Authorship and intellectual property. Chapter 7 In B. D. Sales, & S. Folkman (Eds.), *Ethics in research with human participants.* Washington, DC: American Psychological Association, 75–95.

McIntyre, L. (2015, Nov. 8). The price of denialism. *The New York Times Sunday Review*, 8.

McKay, R., & Whitehouse, H. (2014). Religion and morality. *Psychological Bulletin, 141*(2), 47–473.

McKee-Ryan, F. M., Song, Z., Wanberg, C. R., & Kinicki, A. J. (2005). Psychological and physical well-being during unemployment: A meta-analytic study. *Journal of Applied Psychology, 90*(1), 53–76.

McKillip, J., & Owens, J. (2000). Voluntary professional certifications: Requirements and validation activities. *The Industrial-Organizational Psychologist, 38*, 50–57.

McKinley, W., Zhao, J., & Rust, K. G. (2000). A sociocognitive interpretation of organizational downsizing. *Academy of Management Review, 25*, 227–243.

McMillan, G. S. (1996). Corporate social investments: Do they pay? *Journal of Business Ethics, 15*, 309–314.

McNamara, J. R., & Woods, K. M. (1977). Ethical considerations in psychological research: A comparative review. *Behavior Therapy, 8*, 703–708.

McNicholas, C., Poydock, M., & Rhinehart, L. (2021, Feb. 9). Why workers need the protecting the right to organize act. Retrieved from https://www.epi.org/publication/why-workers-need-the-pro-act-fact-sheet/?utm_source=Economic+Policy+Institute&utm_campaign=e80e64d55a-EMAIL_CAMPAIGN_2021_09_15_COPY_01&utm_medium=email&utm_term=0_e7c5826c50-e80e64d55a-58536137&mc_cid=e80e64d55a&mc_eid=c3b577356e on Oct. 21, 2021.

McWha-Herman, I., Maynard, D. C., & Berry, M. O. (Eds.). (2015). *Humanitarian work psychology and the global development agenda: Case studies and interventions*. Routledge Psychology Press.

McNicholas, C. Poydock, M., Wolfe, J., Zipperer, B., Lafer, G. & Loustaunau, L. (2019, Dec. 11). Unlawful: U.S. employers are charged with violating federal law in 41.5% of all union election campaigns. Economic Policy Institute. Retrieved from https://www.epi.org/publication/unlawful-employer-opposition-to-union-election-campaigns/ on Nov. 17, 2021.

McWhirter, E. H., & McWha-Hermann, I. (2021). Social justice and career development: Progress, problems, and possibilities. *Journal of Vocational Behavior, 126*.

Meara, N. M. (2001). Just and virtuous leaders and organizations. *Journal of Vocational Behavior, 58*, 227–234.

Meglino, B. M., & Ravlin, E. C. (1998). Individual values in organizations: Concepts, controversies, and research. *Journal of Management, 24*, 351–389.

Meier, B. (2016, February 6). Lawyers suing G.M. now fight each other. *New York Times*, B1.

Mejia, S. (2019). Weeding out flawed versions of shareholder primacy: A reflection on the moral obligations that carry over from principals to agents. *Business Ethics Quarterly, 29*(4), 519–544.

Melé, D. (2009). Integrating personalism into virtue-based business ethics: The personalist and the common good principles. *Journal of Business Ethics, 88*, 227–244.

Melton, G. B. (1988). When scientists are adversaries, do participants lose? *Law and Human Behavior, 12*, 191–198.

Meltzer, H., & Stagner, R. (1980). Industrial organizational psychology: 1980 overview. Epilogue. *Professional Psychology, 11*, 543–546.

Menges, R. J. (1973). Openness and honesty versus coercion and deception in psychological research. *American Psychologist, 28*, 1030–1034.

Merritt, M. W., Doris, J. M. & Harmon, G. (2010). Character. Chap. 11 In J. M. Doris & the Moral Psychology Research Group. (2010). *The moral psychology handbook* (pp. 355–401). New York, NY: Oxford University Press.

Merton, R. K. (1973). *The sociology of science: Theoretical and empirical investigations.* Chicago: University of Chicago Press.

Messick, D. M., & Cook, K. S. (Eds.). (1983). *Equity theory: Psychological and sociological perspectives.* New York: Praeger.

Messick, D. M. (1993). Equality as a decision heuristic. In B. A. Mellers, & J. Baron (Eds.), *Psychological perspectives on justice: Theory and applications* (pp. 11–31). New York: Cambridge University Press.

Meyers, C. (2021). The ethics of ethics centers. Editor's note. *Teaching Ethics, 21*(2), 143–148.

Miceli, M. P., Van Scotter, J. R., Near, J. P., & Rehg, M. T. (2001). Responses to perceived organizational wrongdoing: Do perceiver characteristics matter? In J. M. Darley, D. M. Messick, & T. R. Tyler (Eds.), *Social influences on ethical behavior in organizations* (pp. 119–135). Mahwah, NJ: Lawrence Erlbaum Associates.

Miles, J. R., & Fassinger, .E. (2021). Creating a public psychology through a scientist-practitioner-advocate training model. *American Psychologist, 76*(8), 1232–1247.

Milgram, S. (1963). Behavioral study of obedience. *Journal of Abnormal and Social Psychology, 67,* 371–378.

Milgram, S. (1964). Issues in the study of obedience: A reply to Baumrind. *American Psychologist, 19,* 849.

Milgram, S. (1974). *Obedience to authority.* New York: Harper & Row.

Miller, A. G. (1986). *The obedience experiments: A case study of controversy in social science.* New York, NY: Praeger.

Miller, D. T. (1999). The norm of self-interest. *The American Psychologist, 54,* 1053–1060.

Miller, D. T. & Prentice, D. A. (2016). Changing norms to change behavior. In S. T. Fiske, D. L. Schacter, & S. E. Taylor (Eds.). *Annual Review of Psychology, 67,* 339–362.

Miller, G. (2008). Kindness, fidelity, and other sexually selected virtues. In W. Sinnott-Armstrong (Ed.), *Moral Psychology: Volume I. The evolution of morality: Adaptations and innateness* (pp, 209–243). Cambridge, MA: The MIT Press.

Miller, G. A. (1969). Psychology as a means of promoting human welfare. *American Psychologist, 24,* 1063–1075.

Miller, J. G., Goyal, N., & Wice, M. (2017). A cultural psychology of agency: Morality, motivation, and reciprocity. *Perspectives on Psychological Science, 12*(5), 867–887.

Mills, J. (1976). A procedure for explaining experiments involving deception. *Personality and Social Psychology Bulletin, 2,* 3–13.

Miner, J. B. (1992). *Industrial-organizational psychology.* New York: McGraw-Hill.

Minton, C., Kagan, J., & Levine, J. (1971). Maternal control and obedience in the two-year-old. *Child Development, 42,* 1873–1894.

Mischel, W. (1999). Personality Coherence and dispositions in a Cognitive-Affective Personality System (CAPS) Approach. In D. Cervone & Y. Shoda (eds.). *The coherence of personality: social-cognitive bases of consistency, variability and organization* (pp. 37–60). New York: Guilford Press.

Mischel, W. (2014). *The marshmallow test: Mastering self-control.* New York, NY: Little, Brown & Company.

Mishel, L. (2021a). Growing inequalities, reflecting growing employer power, have generated a productivity-pay gap since 1979. Downloaded from https://www.epi.org/blog/growing-inequalities-reflecting-growing-employer-power-have-generated-a-productivity-pay-gap-since-1979-productivity-has-grown-3-5-times-as-much-as-pay-for-the-typical-worker/ on Oct. 11, 2021.

Mishel, L. (2021b). The enormous impact of eroded collective bargaining on wages. Washington, DC: Economic Policy Institute, April 8. Downloaded from https://www.epi.org/publication/eroded-collective-bargaining/ Nov. 10, 2021.

Mishel, L. (2021c). The enormous impact of eroded collective bargaining on wages. Economic Policy Institute, April 8. Viewed at epi.org/22389.

Mishel, L., Bivens, J., Gould, E., & Shierholz, H. (2012). *The state of working America, 12th Edition.* Ithaca, NY: Cornell University Press

Mishel, L., & Davis, A. (2015, June 21). Top CEOs make 300 times more than typical workers: Pay growth surpasses stock gains and wage growth of top 0.1 percent. *Economic Policy Institute Issue Brief #399*, p. 14.

Mishel, L. & Kandra, J. (2020, Dec. 1). Wages for the top 1% skyrocketed 160% since 1979 while the share of wages for the bottom 90% shrunk. Economic Policy institute. Retrieved from https://www.epi.org/blog/wages-for-the-top-1-skyrocketed-160-since-1979-while-the-share-of-wages-for-the-bottom-90-shrunk-time-to-remake-wage-pattern-with-economic-policies-that-generate-robust-wage-growth-for-vast-majority/, Oct, 13, 2021.

Mishel, L., & Kandra, J. (2021, Aug. 10). CEO pay has skyrocketed 1,322% since 1978. Economic Policy Institute. Retrieved from https://www.epi.org/publication/ceo-pay-in-2020/ on Oct. 11, 2021.

Mischel, W., Shoda, Y., & Mendoza-Denton, R. (2002). Situation-behavior profiles as a locus of consistency in personality. *Current Directions in Psychological Science, 11,* 50–54.

Misra, S. (1992). Is conventional debriefing adequate? An ethical issue in consumer research. *Journal of the Academy of Marketing Science, 20,* 269–273.

Mitchell, M. S., Vogel, R. M., & Folger, R. (2015). Third parties' reactions to the abusive supervision of coworkers. *Journal of Applied Psychology, 100*(4), 1040–1055.

Mitchell, M. S., Reynolds, S. J., & Treviño, L. K. (2020). The study of behavioral ethics within organizations: A special issue introduction. *Personnel Psychology, 73*(1), 5–17.

Mitchell, T. R., Hopper, H., Daniels, D., Falvy, J. G., & Ferris, G. R. (1998). Power, accountability, and inappropriate actions. *Applied Psychology: An International Review, 47,* 497–517.

Mitroff, I. I. (1974). *The subjective side of science:* A philosophical inquiry into *the psychology of the Apollo moon scientists.* New York: Elsevier.

Mitroff, I. I., & Denton, E. A. (1999). *A spiritual audit of corporate America: A hard look at spirituality, religion, and values in the workplace.* San Francisco: Jossey-Bass.

Mittelstadt, B. D., Allo, P., Taddeo, M. Wachter, S., & Floridi, L. (2016). The ethics of algorithms: Mapping the debate. *Big Data & Society,* July-Aug., 1–21.

Mobley, W. H., Griffeth, R. W., Hand, H. H., & Meglino, B. M. (1979). Review and conceptual analysis of the employee turnover process. *Psychological Bulletin, 86,* 493–522.

Mokhiber, R., & Weissman, R. (1999). *Corporate predators: The hunt for mega-profits and the attack on democracy.* Monroe, ME: Common Courage.

Monin, B., Pizarro, D. A., & Beer, J. S. (2007). Deciding versus reacting: Conceptions of moral judgment and the reason-affect debate. *Review of General Psychology, 11*(2), 99–111.

Moore, C., Detert, J. R., Treviño, L. K., Baker, V. L., & Mayer, D. M. (2012). Why employees do bad things: Moral disengagement and unethical organizational behavior. *Personnel Psychology*, *65*, 1–48.

Moore, G. (2008). Re-imagining the morality of management: A modern virtue ethics approach. *Business Ethics Quarterly*, *18*(4), 483–511.

Moore, G. (2012). Virtue in business: Alliance Boots and an empirical exploration of MacIntyre's conceptual framework. *Organization Studies*, *3*(3), 363–387.

Moore, G. (2015). Corporate character, corporate virtues. *Business Ethics: A European Review*, *24*(S2), S99–S114.

Moore, G. (2017). *Virtue at work: Ethics for individuals, managers, and organizations*. Oxford: Oxford University Press.

Moore, G. E. (1903). *Principia ethica*. Cambridge, England: Cambridge University Press.

Moorman, C., Deshpande, R., & Zaltman, G. (1993). Factors affecting trust in market research relationships. *Journal of Marketing*, *57*, 81–102.

Morgenson, G. (2015, May 17). It's (still) their party: Shareholders' votes have done little to curb the festivities. *The New York Times*, B1.

Morgenson, G. (2016a, June 12). When student loans outlive failed schools. *The New York Times*, B1.

Morgenson, G. (2016b, June 9). Gauging the value of a C.E.O. *The New York Times*, B1.

Morgeson, F. P., Aguinis, H., Waldman, D. A., & Siegel, D. S. (2013). Extending corporate social responsibility research to the human resource management and organizational behavior domains: A look to the future. *Personnel Psychology*, *66*, 805–824.

Moriarty, J. (2005). Do CEOs get paid too much? *Business Ethics Quarterly*, *15*(2), 257–281.

Moriarty, J. (2009). How much compensation can CEOs permissibly accept? *Business Ethics Quarterly*, *19*(2), 235–250.

Morris, S. A., & McDonald, R. A. (1995). The role of moral intensity in moral judgments: An empirical investigation. *Journal of Business Ethics*, *14*, 715–726.

Moser, C., Den Hond, F., & Lindebaum, D. (2022). Morality in the age of artificially intelligent algorithms. *Academy of Management Learning & Education*, *21*(1), 139–155.

Motro, D., Spoelma, T. M., & Ellis, A. P. J. (2020). Incivility and creativity in teams: Examining the role of perpetrator gender. *Journal of Applied Psychology*, *106*(4), 560–581.

Mouawad, J., & Jensen, C. (2015, Sept. 22). The wrath of drivers: Volkswagen owners' dismay over diesel deceptions imperils a U.S. comeback. *The New York Times*, B1.

Mueller, D. J., & Wornhoff, S. A. (1990). Distinguishing personal and social values. *Educational and Psychological Measurement*, *50*, 691–699.

Mueller, L. (2011). How I-O can contribute to the teacher evaluation debate: A response to Lefkowitz. *The Industrial-Organizational Psychologist*, *48*(5), 17–21.

Muir (Zapata), C. P., Sharf, E. N., & Liu, J. T. (2022). It's not only what you do, but why you do it. How managerial motives influence employees' fairness judgments. *Journal of Applied Psychology*, *107*(4), 581–603.

Mullen, E., & Monin, B. (2016). Consistency versus licensing effects of past moral behavior. *Annual Review of Psychology*, *67*, 363–385.

Mumby, D. K. (2019). Work: What is it good for? (Absolutely nothing)—a critical theorist's perspective. *Industrial and Organizational Psychology: Perspectives on Science and Practice*, *12*(4), 429–443.

Munsterberg, H. (1913). *Psychology and industrial efficiency*. Boston: Houghton-Mifflin.

Munzer, S. R. (1992). *A theory of property*. New York: Cambridge University Press.

Muris, P., Merckelbach, H., Otgaar, H., & Meijer, E. (2017). The malevolent side of human nature: A meta-analysis and critical review of the literature on the dark triad (narcissism, Machiavellianism, and psychopathy. *Perspectives on Psychological Science, 12*(2), 183–204.

Murphy, K. R. (1993). *Honesty in the workplace*. Pacific Grove, CA: Brooks/Cole.

Murphy, K. R. (2009). Content validation is useful for many things, but validity isn't one of them. *Industrial and Organizational Psychology: Perspectives on Science and Practice, 2*(4), 453–464.

Murphy, K. R. (2021). *How groups encourage misbehavior*. New York: Routledge.

Murphy, K. R., & Aguinis, H. (2019). HARKing: How badly can cherry-picking and question-trolling produce bias in published results? *Journal of Business and Psychology, 34*(1), 1–17.

Murray, B. (2000, February). Can academic values mesh with fiscal responsibility? *Monitor on Psychology*, 46–47.

Murrie, D. C., Boccaccini, M. T., Guarnera, L. A., & Rufino, K. A. (2013). Are forensic experts biased by the side that retained them? *Psychological Science, 24*(10), 1889–1897.

Musser, S. J., & Orke, E. A. (1992). Ethical value systems: A typology. *Journal of Applied Behavioral Science, 28*, 348–362.

Myers, D. G., & Diener, E. (2018). The scientific pursuit of happiness. *Perspectives on Psychological Science, 13*(2), 218–225.

Nadal, K. L. (2017). "Let's get in formation": On becoming a psychologist-activist in the 21st century. *American Psychologist, 72*(9), 935–946.

Nagle, R. J. (1987). Ethics training in school psychology. *Professional School Psychology, 2*, 163–171.

Nagy, T. F. (2005). *Ethics in plain english: An illustrative casebook for psychologists* (2nd ed.) Washington, DC: American Psychological Association.

Nagy, T. F. (2011). *Essential ethics for psychologists: A primer for understanding and mastering core issues*. Washington, DC: American Psychological Association.

Naidoo, L. J. (2020). Maximum classroom capacity: How should we teach ethics in I-O psychology? *The Industrial-Organizational Psychologist, 57*(4).

Nath, S. (2021). The business of virtue: Evidence from socially responsible investing in financial markets. *Journal of Business Ethics, 169*, 181–199.

Nathan, P. E. (2000). The Boulder model: A dream deferred—Or lost? *American Psychologist, 55*, 250–252.

National Academy of Sciences. (1997). *Advisor, teacher, role model, friend: On being a mentor to students in science and engineering*. Washington, DC: National Academies Press.

National Academy of Sciences. (2019). *Reproducibility and replicability in science*. Washington, DC: National Academies Press.

National Commission for the Protection of Human Subjects of Biomedical and Behavioral Research, Department of Health, Education, and Welfare. (1979) *Belmont report: Ethical principles and guidelines for the protection of human subjects of research*. FR Doc. 79–12065. GPO 887–809. Washington, DC: U.S. Government Printing Office.

National Conference of Catholic Bishops. (1986). *Economic justice for all: Catholic social teaching and the U.S. economy*. Washington, DC: United States Catholic Conference.

National Employment Lawyers Association. (2016). Advocacy: Forced Arbitration. Retrieved from https://www.nela.org/index.cfm?pg=mandarbitration on June 29, 2016.

National Human Genome Research Institute. (2015). Cloning fact sheet, June 11, 2015. Downloaded on Sept. 25, 2015 from https://www.genome.gov/25020028.

National Institutes of Health. (2000). *Guide to mentoring and training*. Bethesda, MD: NIH.

National Research Council. (2003). *Protecting participants and facilitating social and behavioral sciences research*. Washington, D.C.: National Academies Press.

National Science Foundation Directorate for Social, Behavioral, and Economic Sciences. (2015, May). *Social, behavioral, and economic sciences perspectives on robust and reliable science*. Washington, DC: Author.

Near, J. P., & Miceli, M. P. (1995). Effective whistle-blowing. *Academy of Management Review, 20*, 679–708.

Neubert, M. J., Wu, C., & Roberts, J. A. (2013). The influence of ethical leadership and regulatory focus on employee outcomes. *Business Ethics Quarterly, 23*(2), 269–296.

Neville, F. (2022). Examining the conflicting consequences of CEO public responses to social activist challenges. *Business & Society, 61*(1), 45–80.

Neville, H. A., Awad, G. H., Brooks, J. E., Flores, M. P., & Bluemel, J. (2013). Color-blind racial ideology: Theory, training, and measurement implications in psychology. *American Psychologist, 68*(6), 455–466.

Newman, A., Round, H., Bhattacharya, S., & Roy, A. (2017). Ethical climates in organizations: A review and research agenda. *Business Ethics Quarterly, 27*(4), 475–512.

Newman, D. L., & Brown, R. D. (1996). *Applied ethics for program evaluation*. Thousand Oaks, CA: Sage.

Newmana, G. E., & Cain, D. M. (2014). Tainted altruism: When doing some good is evaluated as worse than doing no good at all. *Psychological Science, 25*(3), 648–655.

Newton, L. (1982). The origin of professionalism: Sociological conclusions and ethical implications. *Business and Professional Ethics Journal, 1*, 33–43.

New York Academy of Sciences. (1999). *Socioeconomic status and health in industrial nations: Social, psychological and biological pathways*. New York, NY: New York Academy of Sciences, Vol. 896.

Ng, T. W. H., & Feldman, D. C. (2015). Ethical leadership: Meta-analytic evidence of criterion-related and incremental validity. *Journal of Applied Psychology, 100*(3), 948–965.

Ng, T. W. H., Wang, M., Hsu, D. Y., & Su, C. (2020). Changes in perceptions of ethical leadership: Effects on associative and dissociative outcomes. *Journal of Applied Psychology, 106*(1), 92–121.

Nichols, D., & Subramaniam, C. (2001). Executive compensation: Excessive or equitable. *Journal of Business Ethics, 29*, 339–351.

Nicholson, I. (2011). "Torture at Yale"; Experimental subjects, laboratory torment and the "rehabilitation" of Milgram's "obedience to authority." *Theory & Psychology, 21*(6), 737–761.

Nicks, S. D., Korn, J. H., & Mainieri, T. (1997). The rise and fall of deception in social psychology and personality research, 1921 to 1994. *Ethics & Behavior, 7*, 69–77.

Nicolopoulos, V. (2002). [Deception survey of three I/O psychology journals]. Unpublished raw data.

Nielsen, R. P. (1989). Changing unethical organizational behavior. *The Academy of Management Executive, 3*, 123–130.

Nieves, E. (2000, February 20). Many in Silicon Valley cannot afford housing, even at $50, 000 a year. *The New York Times*, A20.

Niles, S. G., & Harris-Bowlsbey, J. *Career development interventions in the 21st century*, 4th Ed. Boston, MA: Pearson.

Nisan, M. (1990). Moral balance: A model of how people arrive at moral decisions. In T. Wren (Ed.), *The moral domain* (pp. 283–314). Cambridge, MA: MIT Press.

Nisan, M. (1991). The moral balance model: Theory and research extending our understanding of moral choice and deviation. In W. M. Kurtines, & J. L. Gewirtz (Eds.), *Handbook of moral behavior and development: Vol. 3. Application* (pp. 213–249). Hillsdale, NJ: Lawrence Erlbaum Associates.

Nisbett, R. E., Peng, K., Choi, I., & Norenzayan, A. (2001). Culture and systems of thought: Holistic vs. analytic cognition. *Psychological Review, 108*, 291–310.

Noddings, N. (1986). *Caring: A feminine approach to ethics and moral education.* Berkeley: University of California Press.

Nogami, G. Y. (1982). Good-fast-cheap: Pick any two: Dilemmas about the value of applicable research. *Journal of Applied Social Psychology, 12*, 343–348.

Nord, W. R. (1982). Continuity and change in industrial/organizational psychology: Learning from previous mistakes. *Professional Psychology, 13*, 942–953.

Norman, R. (1983). *The moral philosophers: An introduction to ethics.* Oxford, England: Clarendon.

Norman, R. (1998). *The moral philosophers: An introduction to ethics* (2nd ed.). Oxford, England: Oxford University Press.

Norris, N. P. (1978). Fragile subjects. *American Psychologist, 33*, 962–963.

Nosek, B. A. (and 38 coauthors). (2015). Promoting an open research culture. *Science, 348*(6242), 1422–1425.

Nosek, B. A. (and 15 coauthors). (2022). Replicability, robustness, and reproducibility in psychological science. In S. T. Fiske & D. L. Schacter (Eds.). *Annual Review of Psychology*, 719–748. San Mateo, CA: : Annual Reviews.

Notturno, M. A. (2000). *Science and the open society: The future of Karl Popper's philosophy.* Budapest, Hungary: Central European University Press.

Nozick, R. (1974). *Anarchy, state, and utopia.* New York: Basic Books.

Nozick, R. (1993). *The nature of rationality.* Princeton, NJ: Princeton University Press.

Nucci, L., & Turiel, E. (1978) Social interactions and the development of social concepts in preschool children. *Child Development, 49*, 400–407.

Nucci, L., & Weber, E. K. (1991). The domain approach to values education. In W. M. Kurtines & J. L. Gewirtz (Eds.), *Handbook of moral behavior and development: Vol. 3. Application* (pp. 251–266). Hillsdale, NJ: Lawrence Erlbaum Associates.

Nussbaum, M. C. (2000). *Women and human development: The capabilities approach.* Cambridge: Cambridge University Press.

Nussbaum, M. C. (2003). Capabilities as fundamental entitlements: Sen and social justice. *Feminist Economics, 9*(2-3), 33–59.

Nussbaum, M., & Sen A. (Eds.) (1993). *The quality of life.* New York: Oxford University Press.

O'Connor, E. S. (1999). The politics of management thought: A case study of the Harvard Business School and the Human Relations School. *Academy of Management Review, 24*, 117–131.

Office for Protection From Research Risks, National Institutes of Health, Department of Health and Human Services. (1991 June 18). Protection of human subjects. Title 45, Code of Federal Regulations, Part 46. [GPO 1992 0-307-551].

Office for Human Research Protections (2019, Jan. 21). Department of Health and Human Services. *Protection of Human Subjects.* Title 45 C.F.R. 46, Revised.

Office of Research Integrity. (2014, Dec. 2). Handling misconduct. Downloaded from http://ori.hhs.gov/print/handling-misconduct on July 13, 2016.

Ogbannaya, D., Daniels, K. & Connolly, S. (2017). *Journal of Occupational Health Psychology, 22*(1), 98–114.

Oishi, S. & Kesebir, S. (2015). Income inequality explains why economic growth does not always translate to an increase in happiness. *Psychological Science, 26*(1), 1630–1638.

Oishi, S., Kushlev, K. & Schimmack, U. (2018). Progressive taxation, income inequality, and happiness. *American Psychologist, 7*(2), 157–168.

Okhuysen, G. A., Lepak, D., Ashcraft, K. L., Labianca, G., Smith, V., & Steensma, H. K. (2013). Introduction to special topic forum. Theories of work and working today. *Academy of Management Review, 38*(4), 491–502.

Olenick, J. Walker, R., Bradburn, J., & DeShon, R. P. (2018). A systems view of the scientist-practitioner gap. *Industrial and Organizational Psychology, 11*(2), xxx

Oliansky, A. (1991). A confederate's perspective on deception. *Ethics & Behavior, 1*, 253–258.

Oliver, B. L. (1999). Comparing corporate managers' personal values over three decades, 1967–1995. *Journal of Business Ethics, 20*, 147–161. One wonders, however, whether inclusion of *legal* concerns as part of the domain contributes to a favorable bias.

Olson-Buchanan, J., Bryan, L. K. & Thompson, L. F. (Eds.) (2013). *Using industrial-organizational psychology for the greater good: Helping those who help others.* New York: Routledge.

O'Neill, O. (1993). Kantian ethics. In P. Singer (Ed.), *A companion to ethics* (pp. 175–185). Cambridge, MA: Blackwell.

Ones, D. S., Dilchert, S., Viswesvaran, C., & Salgado, J. F. (2010). Cognitive abilities. Chapter 12 In J. L. Farr, & N. T. Tippins (Eds.), *Handbook of employee selection.* New York: Routledge.

Open Science Collaboration. (2015). Uncovered Estimating the reproducibility of psychological science. *Science, 349*(6251), 943–951.

Opportunity@Work. (2022). Rise with the stars: Building stronger labor market for STARs, communities, and employers. Downloaded from https://opportunityatwork.org on Jan. 25, 2022.

Opportunity@Work & Accenture (2020). Reach for the STARs: Realizing the potential of America's hidden talent pool. Downloaded from https://opportunityatwork.org/our-solutions/stars-insights/reach-stars-report/ on Jan. 25, 2022.

O'Reilly III, C. A., Chatman, J. A., & Doerr, B. (2021). When "me" trumps "we": Narcissistic leaders and the cultures they create. *Academy of Management Discoveries, 7*(3), 419–450.

Organ, D. W., & Greene, C. N. (1981). The effects of formalization on professional involvement: A compensatory process approach. *Administrative Science Quarterly, 26*, 237–252.

Organ, D. W., & Ryan, K. (1995). A meta-analytic review of attitudinal and dispositional predictors of organizational citizenship behavior. *Personnel Psychology, 48*, 775–802.

Organization for Economic Cooperation and Development. (2016). Education Resources. Downloaded from <https://data.oecd.org/eduresource/teachers-salaries.htm> on June 4, 2016.

Orlitzky, M. Schmidt, F. L., & Rynes, S. L. (2003). Corporate social and financial performance: A meta-analysis. *Organization Studies, 24*(3), 403–441.

Orne, M. T. (1962). On the social psychology of the psychological experiment: With particular reference to demand characteristics and their implications. *American Psychologist, 17*, 776–783.

Orne, M. T. (1969). Demand characteristics and the concept of quasi-controls. In R. Rosenthal, & R. L. Rosnow (Eds.), *Artifact in behavioral research* (pp. 143–179). New York: Academic.

Ortmann, A., & Hertwig, R. (1997). Is deception acceptable? *American Psychologist, 52*, 746–747.

Ortmann, A., & Hertwig, R. (1998). The question remains: Is deception acceptable? *American Psychologist, 53*, 806–807.

Ortman, A., & Hertwig, R. (2002). The costs of deception: Evidence from psychology. *Experimental Economics, 5*, 11–131.

O'Sullivan, J. J., & Quevillon, R. P. (1992). 40 Years later: Is the Boulder model still alive? *American Psychologist, 47*, 67–70.

Oyserman, D. (2017). Culture three ways: Culture and subculture within countries. In S. T. Fiske, D. L. Schacter & S. E. Taylor (Eds.), *Annual Review of Psychology, 68*, 435–463.

Oyserman, D., Coon, H. M., & Kemmelmeier, M. (2002). Rethinking individualism and collectivism: Evaluation of theoretical assumptions and meta-analyses. *Psychological Bulletin, 128*, 3–72.

Oyserman, D., & Swim, J. K. (2001). Stigma: An insider's view. *Journal of Social Issues, 57*, 1–14.

Ozanian, M. D. (2000, May 15). Upward bias. *Forbes Magazine* [On-line serial]. Available: http://www.forbes.com/forbes/2000/0515/6511210a.html

Paakkanen, M., Martela, F., Hakanen, J., Uusitalo, L. & Pessi, A. (2020). Awakening compassion in managers—a new emotional skills interventions to improve managerial compassion. *Journal of Business and Psychology*, published online: 29 Oct. Retrieved from https://link-springer-com.remote.baruch.cuny.edu/search?query=paakkanen%2C+Martela&search-within=Journal&facet-journal-id=10869 Nov. 10, 2021.

Paine, F. T., Deutsch, D. R., & Smith, R. A. (1967). Relationship between family background and work values. *Journal of Applied Psychology, 51*, 320–323.

Paolacci, G., & Chandler, J. (2014). Inside the Turk: Understanding Mechanical @Turk as a participant pool. *Current Directions in Psychological Science, 23*(3), 184–188.

Paolillo, J. G. P., & Vitell, S. J. (2002). An empirical investigation of the influence of selected personal, organizational and moral intensity factors on ethical decision making. *Journal of Business Ethics, 35*, 65–74.

Pappas, S. (2022, Jan. 1). The rise of psychologists: Psychological expertise is in demand everywhere. 2022 Trends Report (Monitor). Downloaded from https://www/apa.org/monitor/2022/01/special-rise-psychologists?utm_medium=email&utm_source+rasa_io on Jan 5, 2022.

Pargament, K. I. (2013). *APA handbook of psychology, religion and spirituality.* Washington, DC: American Psychological Association.

Park, T-Y., Park, S., & Barry, B. (2022). Incentive effects on ethics. *Academy of Management Annals, 16*(1), 297–333.

Parker, A. M., de Bruin, B., Fischoff, B., & Weller, J. (2018). Robustness of decision-making competence: evidence from two measures and an 11-year longitudinal study. *Journal of Behavioral Decision-Making, 31*(3), 380–391.

Parker, M. (Ed.). (1998). *Ethics and organizations.* London: Sage.

Parsons, T. (1937). Remarks on education and the professions. *International Journal of Ethics, 47*, 365–369.

Parsons, T. (1954). *Essays in sociological theory.* New York: The Free Press.

Pastore, N. (1949). *The nature-nurture controversy.* New York: King's Cross.

Patil, P., Peng, R. D., & Leek, J. T. (2016). What should researchers expect when they replicate studies? A statistical view of replicability in psychological science. *Perspectives on Psychological Science, 11*(4), 539–544.

Patterson, D. M. (2001). Causal effects of regulatory, organizational and personal factors on ethical sensitivity. *Journal of Business Ethics, 30*, 123–159.

Paulhus, D. L. & Williams, K. (2002). The dark triad of personality: Narcissism, Machiavellianism, and psychopathy. *Journal of Research in Personality, 36*, 5–8.

Pava, M. L., & Krausz, J. (1997). Criteria for evaluating the legitimacy of corporate social responsibility. *Journal of Business Ethics, 16*, 337–347.

Payne, S. C., Morgan, W. B., & Allen, J. (2015). Revising SIOP's guidelines for education and training: Graduate program director survey results. *The Industrial-Organizational psychologist, 53*(2), 158–161.

Pearl Meyer, & Partners. (2000, August 23). *91% of CEO pay rides on performance.* [Press release]. New York: Author.

Pederson, L. J. T. (2009). See no evil: Moral sensitivity in the formulation of business problems. *Business Ethics: A European Review, 18*(4), 335–348.

Peirce, H. (2012, March 14). The real cost of the 2008 bailouts. Downloaded June 6, 2016 from <http://www.usnews.com/opinion/blogs/economic-intelligence/2012/03/14/the-real-cost-of-the-2008-bailouts>.

Pejovich, S. (1990). *The economics of property rights: Towards a theory of comparative systems.* Dordrecht, The Netherlands: Kluwer Academic.

Pelley, J. L. (2014). Science and policy: Understanding the role of value judgments. *Environmental Health Perspectives, 122*(7), A192.

Pence, G. (1993). Virtue theory. In P. Singer (Ed.), *A companion to ethics* (pp. 249–258). Cambridge, MA: Blackwell.

Penner, L. A., Dovidio, J. F., Piliavin, J. A., & Schroeder, D. A. (2005). Prosocial behavior: Multilevel perspectives. *Annual Review of Psychology, 56*, 365–392.

Perry, R. B. (1963). The definition of value in terms of interest. In P. W. Taylor (Ed.), *The moral judgment: Readings in contemporary meta-ethics* (pp. 72–94). Englewood Cliffs, NJ: Prentice-Hall.

Peterson, C. (1996). Common problem areas and their causes resulting in disciplinary actions. In L. J. Bass, S. T. DeMers, J. R. P. Ogloff, C. Peterson, J. L. Pettifor, R. P. Reaves, T. Retfalvi, N. P. Simon, C. Sinclair, & R. M. Tipton (Eds.), *Professional conduct and discipline in psychology* (pp. 71–89). Washington, DC: American Psychological Association.

Peterson, C., & Park, N. (2006). Character strengths in organizations. *Journal of Organizational Behavior, 27*, 1149–1154.

Peterson, C. & Seligman, M. E. P. (2004). *Character strengths and virtues: A Handbook and Classification.* Washington, DC: American Psychological Association.

Peterson, C. C., & Siddle, D. A. T. (1995). Confidentiality issues in psychological research. *Australian Psychologist, 30*, 187–190.

Peterson, D. R. (1991). Connection and disconnection of research and practice in the education of professional psychologists. *American Psychologist, 46*, 422–429.

Petrick, J. A., & Quinn, J. F. (1997). *Management ethics: Integrity at work.* Thousand Oaks, CA: Sage.

Petriglieri, G., & Petriglieri, J. L. (2010. Can business schools humanize leadership? *Academy of Management Learning & Education, 14*(4), 625–647.

Pettit, P. (1993). Consequentialism. In P. Singer (Ed.), *A companion to ethics* (pp. 230–240). Cambridge, MA: Blackwell.

Pfeffer, J. (1994). *Competitive advantage through people: Unleashing the power of the workforce.* Boston: Harvard Business School Press.

Pfeffer, J. (1998). *The human equation: Building profits by putting people first.* Boston: Harvard Business School Press.

Pfeffer, J., & Sutton, R. I. (2006). *Hard facts, dangerous half-truths and total nonsense: Profiting from evidence-based management.* Boston: Harvard Business School Publishing.

Pfeffer, J., & Veiga, J. F. (1999). Putting people first for organizational success. *The Academy of Management Executive, 13,* 37–48.

Phillips, K. P. (1990). *The politics of rich and poor: Wealth and the American electorate in the Reagan aftermath.* New York: Harper Perennial.

Piaget, J. (1965). *The moral judgment of the child.* New York: Free Press. (Original work published 1932).

Pietraszewski, D., & Wertz, A. E. (2022). Why evolutionary psychology should abandon modularity. *Perspectives on Psychological Science, 17*(2), 465–490.

Piff, P. K., Stancato, D. M., Côté, S., Mendoza-Denton, R., & Keltner, D. (2012). Higher social class predicts increased unethical behavior. *Proceedings of the National Academy of Sciences, 109,* 4086–4091.

Pigden, C. R. (1993). Naturalism. In P. Singer (Ed.), *A companion to ethics* (pp. 421–431). Cambridge, MA: Blackwell.

Piketty, T. (2014). *Capital in the twenty—first century.* Cambridge, MA: Belknap Press of Harvard University Press.

Pinto, J., Leana, C. R., & Pil, F. K. (2008). Corrupt organizations or organizations of corrupt individuals? Two types of organization-level corruption. *Academy of Management Review, 33*(3), 685–709.

Pipes, R. B., Holstein, J. E. & Aguire, M. G. (2005).

Pirson, M. (2015a, Jan. 30). Why study social entrepreneurship? *Humanistic Management Network Research Paper No. 02/15.*

Pirson, M. (2015b). Introduction: Conceptualizing humanistic management as an alternative to managing in a post crisis world. *Human Systems Management, 34,* 1–4.

Pirson, M. (2017). *Humanistic management.* Cambridge, UK: Cambridge University Press.

Pirson, M. Bachani, J., & Blomme, R. J. (2017). *Humanistic management: Foundations, cases and examples.* New York: Business Expert Press.

Pirson, M., Goodpaster, K., & Dierkmeiseir, C. (2016). Human dignity and business. *Business Ethics Quarterly, 26*(4), 465–478.

Pitesa, M., & Thau, S. (2013). Compliant sinners, obstinate saints: How power and self-focus determine the effectiveness of social influences in ethical decision making. *Academy of Management Journal, 56*(3), 635–658.

Pizarro, D. A., & Bloom, P. (2003). The intelligence of the moral intuitions: Comment on Haidt (2001). *Psychological Review, 110*(1), 193–196.

Platt, J. R. (1964, October 16). Strong inference. *Science, 146,* 347–353.

Pless, N. M., Maak, T., & Waldman, D. A. (2012). Different approaches toward doing the right thing: Mapping the responsibility orientations of leaders. *Academy of Management Perspectives, 26*(4), 51–65.

Plötner, M., Over, H., Carpenter, M., & Tomasello, M. (2015). Young children show the bystander effect in helping situations. *Psychological Science, 26*(4), 499–506.

Podsakoff, N. P., Whiting, S. W. Podsakoff, P. M., & Blume, B. D. (2009). Individual- and organizational-level consequences of organizational citizenship behaviors: A meta-analysis. *Journal of Applied Psychology, 94,* 122–141.

Poeppelman, T., Blacksmith, N., & Yang, Y. (2013). "Big data" technologies: Problem or solution? *The Industrial-Organizational Psychologist, 51*(2), 119–126.

Pohler, D., & Schmidt, J. A. (2016). Does pay-for-performance strain the employment relationship? The effect of manager bonus eligibility on nonmanagement employee turnover. *Personnel Psychology, 69*, 395–429.

Pollack, A. (2015, May 12). Profiles in science: The gene editor. *The New York Times*, D1.

Pollack, A., & Goldstein, M. (2016, Feb. 3). Email shows profit drove drug pricing. *The New York Times*, B1.

Pope, K. S., & Vetter, V. A. (1992). Ethical dilemmas encountered by members of the American Psychological Association: A national survey. *American Psychologist, 47*, 397–411.

Popper, K. R. (1972). *Objective knowledge: An evolutionary approach.* Oxford, England: Clarendon.

Porter, E. (2015, April 29). Income inequality is costing the nation on social issues. *The New York Times*, B1.

Porter, E. (2017, Jan. 11). Prisons for profit may cost society. *The New York Times*, B1.

Posner, B. Z., Randolph, W. A., & Schmidt, W. H. (1987). Managerial values across functions: A source of organizational problems. Group and Organization *Studies, 12*, 373–385.

Posner, B. Z., & Schmidt, W. H. (1987). Ethics in American companies: A managerial perspective. *Journal of Business Ethics, 6*, 383–391.

Posner, B. Z., & Schmidt, W. H. (1996). The values of business and federal government executives: More different than alike. *Public Personnel Management, 25*, 277–289.

Post, J. E., Frederick, W. C., Lawrence, A. T., & Weber, J. (1996). *Business and society: Corporate strategy, public policy, ethics* (8th ed.). New York: McGraw-Hill.

Powell, G. N. (1998). The abusive organization. *Academy of Management Executive, 12*, 95–96.

Pratto, F., & Shih, M. (2000). Social dominance orientation and group context in implicit group prejudice. *Psychological Science, 11*, 515–518.

Pratto, F., Sidanius, J., Stallworth, L. M., & Malle, B. F. (1994). Social dominance orientation: A personality variable predicting social and political attitudes. *Journal of Personality and Social Psychology, 67*, 741–763.

Pratto, F., Stallworth, L. M., Sidanius, J., & Siers, B. (1997). The gender gap in occupational role attainment: A social dominance approach. *Journal of Personality and Social Psychology, 72*, 37–53.

Press, E., & Washburn, J. (2000, March). The kept university. *The Atlantic Monthly*, 39–54.

Preston, L. E. (1975). Corporation and society: The search for a paradigm. *Journal of Economic Literature, 13*, 434–453.

Preston, M. & De Graaf, S. (2019). Benefits of socioeconomic diversity to organizations: How organizations can promote and benefit from socioeconomic diversity. *SIOP White Paper Series.* Bowling Green, OH: Society for Industrial and Organizational Psychology.

Price, A. (2017). Assets and wealth. Chap. 2 In M. Leyba (Ed.), *State of the Dream 2017: Mourning in America.* United for a Fair Economy, Jan. 16, 13–15.

Prictor, M., Lewis, M. A., Newson, A. J., Haas, M., Baba, S., Kim, H., Kokado, M., Minari, J., Molnár-Gábor, F., Yamamoto, B., Kaye, J., & Teare, H. J. A. (2020). Dynamic consent: An evaluation and reporting framework. *Journal of Empirical Research on Human Research Ethics, 15*(3), 175–186.

Prilleltensky, I. (1997). Values, assumptions, and practices: Assessing the moral implications of psychological discourse and action. *American Psychologist, 52*, 517–535.

Prinz, J. J. (2008). Is morality innate? Chapter 7 In W. Sinnott-Armstrong (Ed.), *Moral Psychology: Vol. I. The evolution of morality: Innateness and adaptation* (pp. 367–406). Cambridge, MA: Massachusetts Institute of Technology Press.

Prinz, J. J., & Nichols, S. (2010). Moral emotions. Chapter 4 In J. M. Doris & the Moral Psychology Research Group. *The moral psychology handbook* (pp. 111–146). New York, NY: Oxford University Press.

Pritschet, L., Powell, D., & Horne, Z. (2016). Marginally significant effects as evidence for hypotheses: Changing attitudes over four decades. *Psychological Science, 27*(7), 1036–1042.

Proctor, B. D., Semega, J. L., & Kollar, M. A. (2016, Sept. 13). Income and poverty in the United States: 2015. U.S. Census Bureau, Report No. P60-256.

Pryor, R. (1982). Values, preferences, needs, work ethics, and orientations to work: Toward a conceptual and empirical integration. *Journal of Vocational Behavior, 20,* 40–52.

Pryor, R. G. L. (1989). Conflicting responsibilities: A case study of an ethical dilemma for psychologists working in organizations. *Australian Psychologist, 24,* 293–305.

Pryzwansky, W. B., & Wendt, R. N. (1987). *Psychology as a profession: Foundations of practice.* New York: Pergamon.

Pryzwansky, W. B., & Wendt, R. N. (1999). *Professional and ethical issues in psychology: Foundations of practice.* New York: Norton.

Pugh, D. S. (1966). Modern organizational theory: A psychological and sociological study. *Psychological Bulletin, 66,* 235–251.

Pugh, D. S. (1969). Organizational behaviour: An approach from psychology. *Human Relations, 22,* 345–354.

Puka, B. (1991). Toward the redevelopment of Kohlberg's theory: Preserving essential structure, removing controversial content. In W. M. Kurtines, & J. L. Gewirtz (Eds.), *Handbook of moral behavior and development: Vol. 1. Theory* (pp. 373–393). Hillsdale, NJ: Lawrence Erlbaum Associates.

Pupovac, V., & Fanelli, D. (2015). Scientists admitting to plagiarism: A meta-analysis of surveys. *Science and Engineering Ethics, 21,* 1331–1352.

Purzycki, B. B., Pisor, A. C., Apicella, C., Atkinson, Q., Cohen, E., Henrich, J., McElreath, R., McNamara, R. A., Norenzayan, A., Willard, A. K., & Xygalatas (2018). The cognitive and cultural foundations of moral behavior. *Evolution and Human Behavior, 29,* 490–501.

Quesque, F., & Rossetti, Y. (2020). What do theory-of-mind tasks actually measure? Theory and practice. *Perspectives on Psychological Science, 15*(2), 384–396.

Rabin, R. C. (2022, Jan. 11). Heart of a genetically altered pic is transplanted into a human. *The New York Times,* A1.

Rachels, J. (1993). Subjectivism. In P. Singer (Ed.), *A companion to ethics* (pp. 432–441). Hoboken, NJ: Wiley-Blackwell.

Rachels, J., & Rachels, S. (2015). *The elements of moral philosophy* (8th ed.). New York: McGraw-Hill.

Raelin, J. A. (1984). An examination of deviant/adaptive behavior in the organizational careers of professionals. *Academy of Management Review, 9,* 413–427.

Raelin, J. A. (1989). An anatomy of autonomy: Managing professionals. *Academy of Management Executive, 3,* 216–228.

Raelin, J. A. (1994). Three scales of professional deviance within organizations. *Journal of Organizational Behavior, 15,* 483–501.

Rainy, V. (Ed.). (1950). *Training in clinical psychology.* New York: Prentice-Hall.

Ralston, D. A., Gustafson, D. J., Elsass, P. M., Cheung, F., & Terpstra, R. H. (1992). Eastern values: A comparison of managers in the United States, Hong Kong, and the People's Republic of China. *Journal of Applied Psychology*, 77, 664–671.

Rand, A. (1964). *The virtue of selfishness.* New York: Signet.

Rank, M. R., & Hirschl, T. A. (2014). *Chasing the American Dream.* New York: Oxford University Press. About Poverty and the Risk Calculator. Downloaded May 20, 2016 from <http://www.riskcalculator.org/About>

Rasinski, K. A., Willis, G. B., Baldwin, A. K., Yeh, W., & Lee, L. (1999). Methods of data collection, perceptions of risks and losses, and motivation to give truthful answers to sensitive survey questions. *Applied Cognitive Psychology*, 13, 465–484.

Rassenfos, S. E., & Kraut, A. I. (1988). Survey of personnel research departments. *The Industrial–Organizational Psychologist*, 25(4), 31–37.

Rattner, S. (2021, Dec. 22). The year in charts. *The new York Times*, A25.

Rawls, J. (1958). Justice as fairness. *Philosophical Review*, 67, 164–194.

Rawls, J. (1971). *A theory of justice.* Cambridge, MA: Harvard University Press.

Rawls, J. (1999). *A theory of justice.* Revised Edition. Cambridge, MA: Belknap Press of Harvard University Press.

Rawls, J. (2001). *Justice as fairness: A restatement.* Edited byE. Kelly. Cambridge, MA: Belknap Press of Harvard University Press.

Rayman, P. M. (2001). *Beyond the bottom line: The search for dignity at work.* New York: Palgrave.

Reburn, K. L., Moyer, F. E., Knebel, R. J., & Bowler, M. C. (2018). Why is living wage not the minimum wage? *The Industrial-Organizational Psychologist*, 56(1), Summer.

Redding, R. E. (2001). Sociopolitical diversity in psychology: The case for pluralism. *American Psychologist*, 56, 205–215.

Reese, H. W., & Fremouw, W. J. (1984). Normal and normative ethics in behavioral sciences. *American Psychologist*, 39, 863–876.

Rehbein, K., & Schuler, D. A. (2015). Linking corporate community programs and political strategies: resource-based view. *Business & Society*, 54(6), 794–821.

Rehwaldt, J. (2019). Expanding the context of moral decision-making: A model for teaching introductory ethics. *Teaching Ethics*, 19(1), 35–51.

Reich, R. B. (2018). *The common good.* New York: Vintage Books/Random House.

Reichman, W. (Ed.). (2014). *Industrial and Organizational Psychology help the vulnerable: Serving the underserved.* New York: Palgrave/Macmillan.

Reinecke, J., Arnold, D. G., & Palazzo, G. (2016). Qualitative methods in business ethics, corporate responsibility, and sustainability research. *Business Ethics Quarterly*, 26(4), xiii–xxii.

Reinero, D. A., Wills, J. A., Brady, W. J., Mende-Siedlecki, P., Crawford, J. T., & Van Bavel, J. J. (2020). Is the political slant of psychology research related to scientific replicability? *Perspectives on Psychological Science*, 15(6), 1310–1328.

Renouard, C. (2010). Corporate social responsibility, utilitarianism, and the capabilities approach. *Journal of Business Ethics*, 98, 897.

Rest, J. R. (1984). The major components of morality. In W. Kurtines & J. Gewirtz (Eds.), *Morality, moral behavior, and moral development* (pp. 24–40). New York: Wiley.

Rest, J. R. (1986a). *Manual for the defining issues test.* Minneapolis: Center for the Study of Ethical Development, University of Minnesota.

Rest, J. R. (1986b). *Moral development: Advances in research and theory.* New York: Praeger.

Rest, J. R. (1994). Background: Theory and research. In J. R. Rest & D. Narvaez (Eds.), *Moral development in the professions* (pp. 1–26). Hillsdale, NJ: Lawrence Erlbaum Associates.

Rest, J. R., & Narvaez, D. (Eds.). (1994). *Moral development in the professions.* Hillsdale, NJ: Lawrence Erlbaum Associates.

Reynolds, P. D. (1979). *Ethical dilemmas and social science research.* San Francisco: Jossey-Bass.

Reynolds, S. J. (2006a). Moral awareness and ethical predispositions: Investigating the role of individual differences in the recognition of moral issues. *Journal of Applied Psychology, 91*(1), 233–243.

Reynolds, S. J. (2006b). A neurocognitive model of the ethical decision-making process: Implications for study and practice. *Journal of Applied Psychology, 91*(4), 737–748.

Reynolds, T. J., & Jolly, J. P. (1980). Measuring personal values: An evaluation of alternative methods. *Journal of Marketing Research, 17*, 531–536.

Rhee, Y. P., Park, C., & Peterson, B. (2021). The effect of local stakeholder pressure on responsive and strategic CSR Activities. *Business & Society, 60*(3), 582–613.

Rich, M. (2016, May 19). Online school sold as a success, but many fail. *The New York Times*, A1.

Rich, M. (2021, August 6). Japanese tears and apologies over "shameful" silver medals. *The New York Times*, A1.

Rife, A. A., & Hall, R. J. (2015). *Work-life balance.* Bowling Green, OH: Society for Industrial and Organizational Psychology.

Riggs, A. E. (2020). Is or ought? Reactions to violations help children to distinguish norms and regularities. *Journal of Experimental Child Psychology, 194*, 104822.

Rilling, J. K., Gutman, D. A., Zeh, T. R., Pagnoni, G., Berns, G. S., & Kilts, C. D. (2002). A neural basis for social cooperation. *Neuron, 35*, 395–405.

Rips, L. J. (2001). Two kinds of reasoning. *Psychological Science, 12*, 129–134.

Roback, A. A. (1917). The moral issues involved in applied psychology. *Journal of Applied Psychology, 1*(3), 232–243.

Robbins, E., Shepard, J., & Rochat, P. (2017). Variations in judgments of intentional action and moral evaluation. *Cognition, 164*, 22–30.

Roberts, S. O., Bareket-Shavit, C., Dollins, F. A., Goldie, P. D., & Mortenson, E. (2020). Racial inequality in psychological research: Trends of the past and recommendations for the future. *Perspectives on Psychological Science, 15*(6), 1295–1309.

Roberts, S. O., & Rizzo, M. T. (2020). The psychology of American Racism. *American Psychologist, 76*(3), 47–487.

Robertson, D. C. (1993). Empiricism in business ethics: suggested research directions. *Journal of Business Ethics, 12*(8), 58–99.

Robeyns, I. (2005). The capability approach: A theoretical survey. *Journal of Human Development, 6*(1), 93–114.

Robeyns, I. (2016). Capabilitarianism. *Journal of Human Development and Capabilities. 17*(3), 397–414.

Roe, R. A., & Ester, P. (1999). Values and work: Empirical findings and theoretical perspective. *Applied Psychology: An International Review, 48*, 1–21.

Roethlisberger, F., & Dickson, W. J. (1939). *Management and the worker.* Cambridge, MA: Harvard University Press.

Rogelberg, S. G., Luong, A., Sederberg, M. E., & Cristol, D. S. (2000). Employee attitude surveys: Examining the attitudes of noncompliant employees. *Journal of Applied Psychology, 85*, 284–293.

Rogerson, M. D., Gottlieb, M. C., Handelsman, M. M., Knapp, S., & Younggren, J. (2011). Nonrational processes in ethical decision making. *American Psychologist, 66*(7), 614–623.

Rokeach, M. (1973). *The nature of human values*. New York: Macmillan.

Rokeach, M., & Ball-Rokeach, S. J. (1989). Stability and change in American value priorities, 1968–1981. *American Psychologist, 44*, 775–784.

Roman, R. M., Hayibor, S., & Agle, B. R. (1999). The relationship between social and financial performance: Repainting a portrait. *Business & Society, 38*, 109–125.

Ronen, S. (1980). The image of I/O psychology: A cross-national perspective by personnel executives. *Professional Psychology, 11*, 399–406.

Rorty, R. (1979). *Philosophy and the mirror of nature*. Princeton, NJ: Princeton University Press.

Ros, M., Schwartz, S. H., & Surkiss, S. (1999). Basic individual values, work values, and the meaning of work. *Applied Psychology: An International Review, 48*, 49–71.

Rosen, H., & Stagner, R. (1980). Industrial/organizational psychology and unions: A viable relationship? *Professional Psychology, 11*, 477–483.

Rosen, T. H. (1987). Reorganizing to meet the needs of scientific psychology. *The Industrial-Organizational Psychologist, 24*(4), 62–63.

Rosenau, P. (1992). *Postmodernism and the social sciences*. Princeton, NJ: Princeton University Press.

Rosenberg, A. (2016). *Philosophy of social science* (6th ed.). Boulder, CO: Westview Press.

Rosenberg, E. (2021). These businesses found a way around the worker shortage: Raising wages to $15 an hour or more. Downloaded from https://www.adn.com/business-economy/2021/06/10/these-businesses-found-a-way-around-the-worker-shortage-raising-wages-to-15-an-hour-or-more/ on March 17, 2022.

Rosenberg, M. (1957). *Occupations and values*. Glencoe, IL: Free Press.

Rosenfeld, J. (2016, March 1). Pay transparency at work: The great equalizer? *On Labor*. Downloaded May 19, 2016 from https://onlabor.org/2016/03/01/pay-tranparency-at-work-the-great-equalizer/

Rosenfeld, J. (2019). US labor studies in the twenty-first century: Understanding laborism without labor. *Annual Review of Sociology, 45*, 449–465.

Rosenfeld, J. & Denice, P. (2015). The power of transparency: Evidence from a British workplace survey. *American Sociological Review, 80*(5), 1045–1068.

Rosenthal, R. (1994). Science and ethics in conducting, analyzing and reporting psychological research. *Psychological Science, 5*, 127–134.

Rosenthal, R., & Rosnow, R. L. (1975). *The volunteer subject*. New York: Wiley.

Rosenthal, R., & Rosnow, R. L. (1984). Applying Hamlet's question to the ethical conduct of research: A conceptual addendum. *American Psychologist, 39*, 561–563.

Rosenthal, R., & Rosnow, R. L. (1991). *Essentials of behavioral research: Methods and data analysis* (2nd ed.). New York: McGraw-Hill.

Rosnow, R. L. (1993). The volunteer problem revisited. In P. D. Blank (Ed.), *Interpersonal Expectations: Theory, research, applications* (pp. 418–436). New York: Cambridge University Press.

Rosnow, R. L. (1997). Hedgehogs, foxes, and the evolving social contract in psychological science: Ethical challenges and methodological opportunities. *Psychological Methods, 2*, 345–356.

Ross, L., & Nisbett, R. E. (1991). *The person and the situation*. Philadelphia, PA: Temple University Press.

Rothstein, R. (2018). *The color of law: A forgotten history of how our government segregated America*. New York: Liveright/W.W. Norton.

Rothstein, R. (2020, Apr. 14). The coronavirus will explode achievement gaps in education. Working Economics Blog. Economic Policy Institute. Retrieved from https://www.epi.org/blog/the-coronavirus-will-explode-achievement-gaps-in-education/ on Jan. 25, 2022.

Rotolo, C. T., Church, A. H., Adler, S., Smither, J. W., Colquitt, A. L., Paul, K. B., & Foster, G. (2018). Putting an end to bad talent management: A call to action for the field of industrial and organizational psychology. *Industrial and organizational psychology*, *11*(2), 176–219.

Rousseau, D. M. (1985). Issues of level in organizational research. In L. L. Cummings & B. M. Staw (Eds.), *Research in organizational behavior* (Vol. 7, pp. 1–38). Greenwich, CT: JAI.

Rousseau, D. M. (1990). Assessing organizational culture: The case for multiple methods. In B. Schneider (Ed.), *Organizational climate and culture* (pp. 153–192). San Francisco: Jossey-Bass.

Rousseau, D. M. (1995). *Psychological contracts in organizations: Understanding written and unwritten agreements*. Thousand Oaks, CA: Sage.

Rousseau, D. M., & Schalk, R. (Eds.). (2000). *Psychological contracts in employment: Cross-national perspectives*. Thousand Oaks, CA: Sage.

Ruggs, E. N., Law, C., Cox, C. B., Roehling, M. V., Wiener, R. L., Hebl, M. R., & Barron, L. (2012). Gone fishing: I-O psychologists' missed opportunities to understand marginalized employees' experiences with discrimination. *Industrial and Organizational Psychology: Perspectives on Science and Practice*, *6*(1), 39–60.

Ruse, M. (1993). The significance of evolution. In P. Singer (Ed.), A *companion to ethics* (pp. 500–510). Cambridge, MA.: Blackwell.

Russell, J. E. A. (2001). Vocational psychology: An analysis and directions for the future. *Journal of Vocational Behavior*, *59*, 226–234.

Russell, P. S., & Giner-Sorolla, R. (2013). Bodily moral disgust: What it is, how it is different from anger, and why it is an unreasoned emotion. *Psychological Bulletin*, *139*(2), 328–351.

Russell, T. L., Sparks, T. E., Campbell, J. P., Handy, K., Ramsberger, P., & Grand, J. A. (2017). Situating ethical behavior in the nomological network of job performance. *Journal of Business Psychology*, *32*, 253–271.

Ryan, A. M. (1999). SIOP's pro bono initiative. *The Industrial–Organizational Psychologist*, *36*, 135–138.

Ryan, A. M. (2003). Defining ourselves: I-O psychology's identity quest. *The Industrial-Organizational Psychologist*, *41*(1), 21–33.

Ryan, A. M., & Ford, K. J. (2010). Organizational psychology and the tipping point of professional identity. *Industrial and Organizational Psychology: Perspectives on Science and Practice*, *3*(3), 241–258.

Ryff, C. D. (2018). Well-being with a soul: Science in pursuit of human potential. *Perspectives on Psychological Science*, *13*(2), 242–248.

Rynes, S. L., Bartunek, J. M., & Daft, R. L. (2001). Across the great divide: Knowledge creation and transfer between practitioners and academics. *Academy of Management Journal*, *44*, 340–355.

Rynes, S. L., Bartunek, J. M., Dutton, J. E., & Margolis, J. D. (2012). Special topic forum on understanding and creating caring and compassionate organizations. *Academy of Management Review*, *37*(4), 503–733.

Rynes, S. L., Gerhart, B., & Parks, L. (2005). Personnel psychology: Performance evaluation and pay for performance. *Annual Review of Psychology*, *56*, 571–600.

Rynes, S. L., & McNatt, D. B. (2001). Bringing the organization into organizational research: An examination of academic research inside organizations. *Journal of Business and Psychology, 16*, 3–19.

Saari, L. M. (2001). Wider forms of the reciprocal model. *Applied Psychology: An International Review, 50*, 241–244.

Sackett, P. R. (1986). Results of society survey on scientist-practitioner issues. *The Industrial-Organizational Psychologist, 24*(1), 37–39.

Sackett, P. R., Callahan, C., DeMeuse, K., Ford, J. K., & Kozlowski, S. (1986). Changes over time in research involvement by academic and nonacademic psychologists. *The Industrial-Organizational Psychologist, 24*(1), 44–49.

Sackett, P. R., & Larson, J. R., Jr. (1990). Research strategies and tactics in industrial and organizational psychology. In M. D. Dunnette, & L. M. Hough (Eds.), *Handbook of industrial and organizational psychology* (2nd ed., Vol. 1, pp. 419–489). Palo Alto, CA: Consulting Psychologists Press.

Sackett, P. R. & Walmsley, P. T. (2014). Which personality attributes are most important in the workplace? *Perspectives on Psychological Science, 9*(5), 538–551.

Sadler-Smith, E. (2013). Toward organizational environmental virtuousness. *The Journal of Applied Behavioral Science, 49*(1), 123–148.

Sagie, A., Elizur, D., & Koslowsky, M. (1996). Work values: A theoretical overview and a model of their effects. *Journal of Organizational Behavior, 17*, 503–514.

Sagiv, L., & Schwartz, S. H. (1995). Value priorities and readiness for out-group social contact. *Journal of Personality and Social Psychology, 69*, 437–448.

Sagiv, L., & Schwartz, S. H. (2022). Personal values across cultures. In S. T. Fiske, & D. L. Shacter (Eds.), *Annual Review of Psychology, 73*, 517–546.

Sajjadiani, S., Sojourner, A. J., Kammeyer-Mueller, J. D., & Mykerezi, E. (2019). Using machine learning to translate applicant work history into predictors of performance and turnover. *Journal of Applied Psychology, 104*(10), 1207–1225.

Sales, B. D., & Folkman, S. (Eds.). (2000). *Ethics in research with human participants.* Washington, DC: American Psychological Association.

Sales, B. D., & Lavin, M. (2000). Identifying conflicts of interest and resolving ethical dilemmas. In B. D. Sales & S. Folkman (Eds.), *Ethics in research with human participants* (pp. 109–128). Washington, DC: American Psychological Association.

Sampson, E. E. (1977). Psychology and the American ideal. *Journal of Personality and Social Psychology, 35*, 762–782.

Samuelson, P. A. (1993). Altruism as a problem involving group versus individual selection in economics and biology. *American Economic Review, 83*, 143–148.

Sandel, M. J. (2009). *Justice: What's the right thing to do?* New York: Farrar, Straus and Giroux.

Sandel, M. J. (2012). *What money can't buy: The moral limits of markets.* Farrar, Straus and Giroux.

Sandel, M. J. (2020). *The tyranny of merit: What's become of the common good?* UK: Allen Lane.

Sanger-Katz, M., & Schwartz, J. (2015, Sept. 29). Assessing the possible health effects from Volkswagen's diesel deception. *The New York Times*, B1.

Santos, L. R., & Rosati, A. G. (2015). The evolutionary roots of human decision making. *Annual Review of Psychology, 66*, 321–347.

Sargent, J., & Matthews, L. (1999). Exploitation or choice? Exploring the relative attractiveness of employment in the Maquiladoras. *Journal of Business Ethics, 18*, 213–227.

Sarte, J-P. (1945). *Existentialism is a humanism*. English language translation, 2007. New Haven, CT: Yale University Press.

Sarwat, J., Mahmud, A. S. & Papageorgiou, C. (2014). What is Keynesian economics?. *Finance & Development, 51*(3). Downloaded from https://www.imf.org/external/pubs/ft/fandd/2014/09/basics.htm on Nov. 16, 2021.

Sashkin, M., & Prien, E. P. (1996). Ethical concerns and organizational surveys. In A. I. Kraut (Ed.), *Organizational surveys: Tools for assessment and change* (pp. 381–403). San Francisco: Jossey-Bass.

Satariano, A. (2021, March 17). Uber gives U.K. drivers new status and benefits. *The New York Times*, B1.

Satariano, A., & Isaac, M. (2021, Sept. 1). Profit and pain in doing Facebook's dirty work: How Accenture makes millions scrubbing sordid content. *The New York Times*, A1, 17.

Saul S. (2015a, Nov. 16). For-profit college system expected to pay millions. *The New York Times*, A15.

Saul, S. (2015b, Nov. 17). For-profit college chain forgives loans. *The New York Times*, A17.

Savage, L. J. (1954). *The foundations of statistics*. New York: Wiley.

Savas, E. S. (1987). Privatization. In S. P. Sethi, & C. M. Falbe (Eds.), *Business and society: Dimensions of conflict and cooperation* (pp. 270–281). Lexington, MA: Lexington.

Savickas, M. L. (2001). Envisioning the future of vocational psychology. *Journal of Vocational Behavior, 59*, 167–170.

Scanlon, T. M. (1998). *What we owe to each other*. Cambridge, MA: Belknap Press/Harvard University Press.

Schaafsma, S. M., Pfaff, D. W., Spunt, R. P., & Adolphs, R. (2015). Deconstructing and reconstructing theory of mind. *Trends in Cognitive Sciences, 19*, 65–72.

Schäfer, M., Haun, D. B. M., & Tomasello, M. (2015). Fair is not fair everywhere. *Psychological Science, 26*(8), 1252–1260.

Scharding, T. K. (2020). Recognize everyone's interests: An algorithm for ethical decision-making about trade-off problems. *Journal of Business Ethics, 31*(3), 450–473.

Schaubroeck, J. M., Hannah, S. T., Avolio, B. J., Kozlowski, S. W. J., Lord, R. G., Treviño, L. K., Dimotakis, N., & Peng, A. C. (2012). *Academy of Management Journal, 55*(5), 1053–1078.

Scheiber, N. (2015, July 13). Growth in the 'gig economy' fuels work force anxieties. *The New York Times*, A1.

Scheiber, N. (2016, Feb. 3). Solo workers unite to tame their gig jobs. *The New York Times*, A 1.

Scheiber, N. (2021a, Nov. 1). How the pandemic has given workers new leverage. *The New York Times*, B1.

Scheiber, N. (2021b, Dec. 22). Union effort by architects underway. *The New York Times*, B1.

Scheiber, N. (2021c, Dec. 22). Workers at Kellogg ratify new contract, ending their strike. *The New York Times*, B4.

Scheiber, N. (2022, Apr. 11). Starbucks union campaign expands organizing efforts. *The New York Times*, B7.

Scheiber, N. & Isaac, M. (2016, May 11). A guild, short of a union, for New York Uber drivers. *The New York Times*, B1.

Schein, E. H. (1980). *Organizational psychology*. Englewood Cliffs, NJ: Prentice-Hall. (Original work published 1965)

Schein, E. H. (1990). Organizational culture. *American Psychologist, 45*, 109–119.

Schein, E. H. (1996). Career anchors revisited: Implications for career development in the 21st century. *Academy of Management Executive, 10*, 80–88.

Scherbaum, C. A., Goldstein, H. W., Yusko, K. P., Ryan, R., & Hanges, P. J. (2012). Intelligence 2.0: Reestablishing a research program on *g* in I-O psychology. *Industrial and Organizational Psychology: Perspectives on Science and Practice, 5*(2), 128–148.

Scherer, A. G. (2016). Can hypernorms be justified? Insights from a discourse-ethical perspective. *Business Ethics Quarterly, 25*(4), 489–516.

Schilpzand, P., De Pater, I. E., & Erez, A. (2016). Workplace incivility: A review of the literature and agenda for future research. *Journal of Organizational Behavior, 37*, S57–S88.

Schleicher, D. J., & Campion, M. A. (2011). Can I retake it? Exploring subgroup differences and criterion-related validity in promotion retesting. *Journal of Applied Psychology, 96*(5), 941–955.

Schmidt, F. L. (1996). Statistical significance testing and cumulative knowledge in psychology: Implications for training of researchers. *Psychological Methods, 1*(2), 115–129.

Schmidt, F. L. (2010). Detecting and correcting the lies that data tell. *Perspectives on Psychological Science, 5*(3), 233–242.

Schmidt, F. L. (2016). The validity and utility of selection methods in personnel psychology: Practical and theoretical implications of 100 years of research. Unpublished manuscript.

Schmidt, F. L., & Hunter, J. E. (1998). The validity and utility of selection methods in personnel psychology. *Psychological Bulletin, 124*(2), 262–274.

Schminke, M. (1998). The magic punchbowl: A nonrational model of ethical management. In M. Schminke (Ed.), *Managerial ethics: Moral management of people and process* (pp. 197–214). Mahwah, NJ: Lawrence Erlbaum Associates.

Schminke, M. (Ed.). (2014). *Managerial ethics: Managing the psychology of morality.* New York: Routledge.

Schminke, M., Ambrose, M. L., & Noel, T. W. (1997). The effect of ethical frameworks on perceptions of organizational justice. *Academy of Management Journal, 40*, 1190–1207.

Schminke, M., Arnaud, A., & Taylor, R. (2015). Ethics, values, and organizational justice: Individuals, organizations, and beyond. *Journal of Business Ethics, 130*, 727–736.

Schminke, M., & Wells, D. (1999). Group processes and performance and their effects on individuals' ethical frameworks. *Journal of Business Ethics, 18*, 367–381.

Schminke, M., Vestal, A., & Caldwell, J. (2010). A review and assessment of ethical decision making models: Is a garbage can approach the answer? Chap. 13 In M. Schminke, (Ed.), *Managerial ethics: Managing the psychology of morality* (pp. 271–297). New York: Routledge.

Schmitt, M. (2016, June 16). Is the Sanders agenda out of date? *The New York Times*, A23.

Schnall, S., Haidt, J., Clore, G. L. & Jordan, A. H. (2015). Landy and Goodwin (2015) confirmed most of our findings then drew the wrong conclusions. *Perspectives on Psychological Science, 10*, 537–538.

Schneewind, J. B. (1993). Modern moral philosophy. In P. Singer (Ed.), *A companion to ethics* (pp. 147–160). Cambridge, MA: Blackwell.

Schneider, B., Ehrhart, M. G., & Macey, W. H. (2013). Organizational climate and culture. *Annual Review of Psychology, 64*, 361–388.

Schneider, B. & Pulakos, E. D. (2022). Expanding the I-O mindset to organizational success. *Industrial-Organizational Psychology: Perspectives on Science and Practice, 15*(3), in press.

Schneider, J., & Smith, K. (1999). SIOP 1999 member survey results. *The Industrial-Organizational Psychologist, 37*(2), 24–29.

Schriesheim, C. A. (1978). Job satisfaction, attitudes toward unions, and voting in a union representation election. *Journal of Applied Psychology, 63,* 548–552.

Schroeder, T., Roskies, A. L. & Nichols, S. (2010). Moral motivation. Chap. 2 In J. M. Doris & the Moral Psychology Research Group. *The moral psychology handbook* (pp. 72–110). New York, NY: Oxford University Press, .

Schumacher, E. F.(1989). Buddhist Economics. In *Small is beautiful: Economics as if people mattered.* New York: Perennial Library.

Schwab, K. (2000). Neighbors on the same planet [Interview]. *Newsweek, 135*(5), 82.

Schwartz, B. (1990). The creation and destruction of value. *American Psychologist, 45,* 7–15.

Schwartz, S. H. (1992). Universals in the content and structure of values: Theoretical advances and empirical tests in 20 countries. *Advances in Experimental Social Psychology, 25,* 1–65.

Schwartz, S. H. (1994). Are there universal aspects in the structure and contents of human values? *Journal of Social Issues, 50,* 19–45.

Schwartz, S. H. (1996). Value priorities and behavior: Applying a theory of integrated value systems. In C. Seligman, J. M. Olson, & M. P. Zanna (Eds.), *The psychology of values: The ontario dymposium* (Vol. 8, pp. 1–24). Mahwah, NJ: Erlbaum.

Schwartz, S. H. (1999). A theory of cultural values and some implications for work. *Applied Psychology:* An *International Review, 48,* 23–47.

Schwartz, S. H., & Bilsky, W. (1987). Toward a psychological structure of human values. *Journal of Personality and Social Psychology, 53,* 550–562.

Schwartz, S. H., & Bilsky, W. (1990). Toward a theory of the universal content and structure of values: Extension and cross-cultural replications. *Journal of Personality and Social Psychology, 58,* 878–891.

Schwartz, S. H., & Gottlieb, A. (1981). Participants' postexperimental reactions and the ethics of bystander research. *Journal of Experimental Social Psychology, 17,* 396–407.

Schwartz, S. J., Lilienfeld, S. O., Meca, A., & Sauvigné, K. C. (2016). The role of neuroscience within psychology: A call for inclusiveness over exclusiveness. *American Psychologist, 71*(1), 52–70.

Schyns, B. (2015). Dark personality in the workplace: Introduction to the special issue. *Applied Psychology: An International Review, 64*(1), 1–14.

Scott, E. D. (2002). Organizational moral values. *Business Ethics Quarterly, 12*(1), 33–55.

Scott, J. C., Aguinis, H., McWha, I., Rupp, D. E., & Thompson, L. F. (2013). News from the SIOP-United Nations team: SIOP has joined the UN Global Compact and so can you!. *The Industrial-Organizational Psychologist, 50*(4), 65–68.

Scott-Jones, D. (2000). Recruitment of research participants. In B. D. Sales & S. Folkman (Eds.), *Ethics in research with human participants* (pp. 27–34). Washington, DC: American Psychological Association.

Searle, R. H., & McWha-Hermann, I. (2021). "Money's to tight (too mention)": A review and psychological synthesis of living wage research. *European Journal of Work and Organizational Psychology, 30*(3), 428–443.

Seberhagen, L. W. (1993a). An ethics code for I/O psychology: Good behavior at low cost. *The Industrial-Organizational Psychologist, 31*(2), 69–71.

Seberhagen, L. W. (1993b). An ethics code for statisticians—What next? *The Industrial–Organizational Psychologist, 30*(3), 71–74.

Seckel, A. (Ed.). (1987). *Bertrand Russell on ethics, sex, and marriage.* Amherst, NY: Prometheus.

Seeman, J. (1969). Deception in psychological research. *American Psychologist, 24,* 1025–1028.

Securities and Exchange Commission. (2022). SEC Enforcement Actions: FCPA Cases. Retrieved July 8, 2022 from https://www.sec.gov/enforce/sec-enforcement-actions-fcpa-cases.

Seligman, M. E. P. (2002). *Authentic happiness: Using the new positive psychology to realize your potential for lasting fulfillment.* New York, NY: Free Press.

Seligman, M. E. P., & Csikszentmihalyi, M. (Eds.) (2000). Positive psychology [Special Issue]. *American Psychologist, 5*(5), 1.

Seligman, M. E. P., Steen, T. A., Park, T. A., & Peterson, C. (2005). Positive psychology progress: Empirical validation of interventions. *American Psychologist, 60*(5), 410–421.

Sen, A. (2009). *The idea of justice.* Cambridge, MA: Belknap.

Seron, C. (2002). Review of E. Freidson, Professionalism: The third logic. *Contemporary Sociology, 31*(5), 551–552.

Sethi, S. P. (1973). Corporate social audit: An emerging trend in measuring corporate social performance. In D. Votaw & S. P. Sethi (Eds.), *The corporate dilemma* (pp. 214–231). Englewood Cliffs, NJ: Prentice-Hall.

Sethi, S. P. (1999). Codes of conduct for global business: Prospects and challenges of implementation. In The Clarkson Centre for Business Ethics. *Principles of stakeholder management* (pp. 9–20). University of Toronto: Author.

Seyfarth, R. M. & Cheney, D. L. (2012). The evolutionary origins of friendship. *Annual Review of Psychology, 63*, 153–177.

Shafer-Landau, R. (2015). *The fundamentals of ethics* (3rd ed.). New York: Oxford University Press.

Shallow, C., Lliev, R., & Medin, D. (2011). Trolley problems in context. *Judgment and Decision Making, 6*(7), 593–601.

Shalvi, S., Gino, F., Barkan, R., & Ayal, S. (2015). Self-serving justifications: Doing wrong and feeling moral. *Current Directions in Psychological Science, 24*(2), 12–130.

Shamoo, A. E. & Resnik, D. B. (2009). *Responsible conduct of research,* 2nd Ed. New York, NY: Oxford University Press.

Shao, R., Rupp, D. E., Skarlicki, D. P., & Jones, K. S. (2013). Employee justice across cultures: A meta-analytic review. *Journal of Management, 39*(1), 263–301.

Shariff, A. F., Wiwad, D., & Aknin, L. B. (2016). Income mobility breeds tolerance for income inequality: Cross-national and experimental evidence. *Perspectives on Psychological Science, 11*(3), 373–380.

Sharkey, P. (2019). Still stuck in place. Stanford Center on Poverty and Inequality. *Pathways: Locked in Place, Winter,* 14–21.

Shaw, J. D. (2014). Pay dispersion. *Annual Review of Organizational Psychology and Organizational Behavior, 1,* 521–544.

Shaw, J. D. (2015). Pay dispersion, sorting, and organizational performance. *Academy of Management Discoveries, 1*(2), 165–179.

Shih, M., Pittinsky, T. L., & Ambady, N. (1999). Stereotype susceptibility: Identity salience and shifts in quantitative performance. *Psychological Science, 10,* 80–83.

Shih, M., Young, J. J., & Bucher, A. (2013). Working to reduce the effects of discrimination: Identity management strategies in organizations. *American Psychologist, 68*(3), 145–157.

Shipley, T. (1977). Misinformed consent: An enigma in modern social science research. *Ethics in Science and Medicine, 4,* 93–106.

Shklar, J. N. (1990). *The faces of injustice.* New Haven, CT: Yale University Press.

Shostak, A. (1964). Industrial psychology and the trade unions: A matter of mutual indifference. In G. Fisk (Ed.), *The frontiers of management psychology* (pp. 144–154). New York: Harper.

Shrivastava, S., Jones, R., Selvarajah, C., & Van Gramberg, B. (2016). Organisational justice: A Senian perspective. *Journal of Business Ethics, 13*(5), 99–116.

Shrout, P. E., & Rodgers, J. L. (2018). Psychology, science, and knowledge construction: Broadening perspectives from the replication crisis. In S. T., Fiske, D. L. Schacter & S. E. Taylor (Eds.). *Annual Review of Psychology, 69,* 487–510.

Shryack, J., Steger, M. F., Krueger, R. F., & Kallie, C. S. (2010). The structure of virtue: An empirical investigation of the dimensionality of the virtues in action inventory of strengths. *Personality and Individual Differences, 48,* 714–719.

Shweder, R. A., Mahapatra, M., & Miller, J. G. (1987). Culture and moral development. In J. Kagan & S. Lamb (Eds.), *The emergence of morality in young children* (pp. 1–83). Chicago: University of Chicago Press.

Sidanius, J., Pratto, F., & Bobo, L. (1996). *Journal of Personality and Social Psychology, 70,* 476–490.

Sieber, J. E. (1982a). Deception in social research I: Kinds of deception and the wrongs they may involve. *IRB: A Review of Human Subjects Research, 4,* 1–6.

Sieber, J. E. (1982b). Deception in social research III: The nature and limits of debriefing. *IRB: A Review of Human Subjects Research, 6,* 1–4.

Sieber, J. E. (1992). *Planning ethically responsible research.* Newbury Park, CA: Sage.

Sieber, J. E., Iannuzzo, R., & Rodriguez, B. (1995). Deception methods in psychology: Have they changed in 23 years? *Ethics & Behavior, 5,* 67–85.

Sikula, A. F. (1973, January–February). The values and value systems of governmental executives. *Public Personnel Management, 2*(1), 16–22.

Sikula, A., Sr., & Sikula, J. (2001). Employee relations ethics [Special issue]. *Ethics & Behavior, 1*(1).

Silberbauer, G. (1993). Ethics in small-scale societies. In P. Singer (Ed.), *A companion to ethics* (pp. 14–28). Cambridge, MA: Blackwell.

Silver-Greenberg, J., & Corkeery, M. (2015, Nov. 2). A "Privatization of the Justice System." *The New York Times,* B1, 4–5.

Silver-Greenberg J., & Corkery, M. (2016, May 15). Start-ups turn to arbitration in workplace. *The New York Times,* N1.

Silver-Greenberg, J., & Gebeloff, R. (2015). Arbitration everywhere, stacking the deck of justice. *The New York Times,* 1, 22–23.

Silzer, R. F., & Parson, C. (2013). Trends in SIOP membership, graduate education, and member satisfaction. *The industrial-Organizational Psychologist, 50*(4), 119–129.

Simha, A., & Cullen, J. B. (2012). Ethical climates and their effects on organizational outcomes: Implications from the past and prophecies for the future. *Academy of Management Perspectives, 26*(4), 20–34.

Simmons, J. P. Nelson, L. D., & Simonsohn, U. (2011). False-positive psychology: undisclosed flexibility in data collection and analysis allows presenting anything as significant. *Psychological Science, 22*(11), 1359–1366.

Simon, H. A. (1955). A behavioral model of rational choice. *Quarterly Journal of Economics, 69,* 99–118.

Simon, H. A. (1990). A mechanism for social selection and successful altruism. *Science, 250,* 1665–1668.

Simon, H. A. (1993). Altruism and economics. *American Economic Review*, *83*, 156–161.

Simon, L. S., Hurst, C., Kelley, K., & Judge, T. A. (2015). Understanding cycles of abuse: A multimotive approach. *Journal of Applied Psychology*, *100*(6), 1798–1810.

Simons, D. J. (2014). The value of direct replication. *Perspectives on Psychological Science*, *9*(1), 76–80.

Simons, D. J., Holcombe, A. O., & Spellman, B. A. (2014). An introduction to registered replication reports at *Perspectives on Psychological Science*. *Perspectives on Psychological Science*, *9*(5), 552–555.

Simpson, E. L. (1994). Moral development research: A case study of scientific cultural bias. In B. Puka (Ed.), *Moral Development: A Compendium* (Vol. 4). New York: Garland.

Simpson, W. G., & Kohers, T. (2002). The link between corporate social and financial performance: Evidence from the banking industry. *Journal of Business Ethics*, *35*, 97–109.

Sims, R. L., & Keon, T. L. (1999). Determinants of ethical decision making: The relationship of the perceived organizational environment. *Journal of Business Ethics*, *19*, 393–401.

Sims, R. R. (1992). Linking groupthink to unethical behavior in organizations. *Journal of Business Ethics*, *11*, 651–662.

Singelis, T. M., Triandis, H. C., Bhawuk, D., & Gelfand, M. J. (1995). Horizontal and vertical dimensions of individualism and collectivism: A theoretical and measurement refinement. *Cross-Cultural Research: The Journal of Comparative Social Science*, *29*, 240–275.

Singer, E. (1978). Informed consent: Consequences for response rate and response quality in social surveys. American *Sociological Review*, *43*, 144–162.

Singer, E., Von Thurn, D. R., & Miller, E. R. (1995). Confidentiality assurances and response: A quantitative review of the experimental literature. *Public Opinion Quarterly*, *59*, 66–77.

Singer, M., Mitchell, S., & Turner, J. (1998). Consideration of moral intensity in ethicality judgements: Its relationship with whistle-blowing and need-for-cognition. *Journal of Business Ethics*, *17*, 527–541.

Singer, M. S. (2000). Ethical and fair work behavior: A normative-empirical dialogue concerning ethics and justice. *Journal of Business Ethics*, *28*, 187–209.

Singer, P. (Ed.). (1993). *A companion to ethics*. Cambridge, MA: Blackwell.

Singer, P. (1995). *Practical ethics*. New York: Cambridge University Press.

Singer, P. (2011). *Practical ethics* (3rd ed.). New York: Cambridge University Press.

Singer, P. (2015). *The most good you can do: How effective altruism is changing ideas about living ethically*. New Haven, CT: Yale University Press.

Sinnott-Armstrong, W. (Ed.) (2008). *Moral Psychology: Volume I. The evolution of morality: Adaptations and innateness*. Cambridge, MA: The MIT Press.

Sison, A. J. G., & Ferrero, I. (2015). How different is neo-Aristotelian virtue from positive organizational virtuousness? *Business Ethics: A European Review*, *24*(S2), S78 – S98.

Sison, A. J. G., Feraro, I., & Guitián, G. (2016). Human dignity and the dignity of work: Insights from Catholic social teaching. *Business Ethics Quarterly*, *26*(4), 503–528.

Sison, A. J. G., Hartman, E. M., & Fontrodona, J. (2012). *Guest Editors' Introduction*. Reviving tradition: Virtue and the common good in business and management. *Business Ethics Quarterly*, *22*(2), 207–210.

Skarlicki, D. P., Ellard, J. H., & Kelln, B. R. C. (1998). Third-party perceptions of a layoff: Procedural, derogation, and retributive aspects of justice. *Journal of Applied Psychology*, *83*, 119–127.

Skarlicki, D. P., van Jaarsveld, D. D., Shao, R., Song, Y. H., & Wang, M. (2016). Extending the multifoci perspective: The role of supervisor justice and moral identity in the relationship between customer justice and customer-directed sabotage. *Journal of Applied Psychology, 101*(1), 108–121.

Skitka, L. J., Hanson, B. E., Morgan, G. S., & Wisneski, D. C. (2021). The psychology of moral conviction. In S. T. Fiske, & D. L. Schacter (Eds.). *Annual Review of Psychology, 72*, 347–366.

Skitka, L. J., & Tetlock, P. E. (1993). Of ants and grasshoppers: The political psychology of allocating public assistance. In B. A. Mellers, & J. Baron (Eds.), *Psychological perspectives on justice: Theory and applications* (pp. 205–233). New York: Cambridge University Press.

Skitka, L. J., Hanson, B. E., Morgan, G. S., & Wisneski, D. C. (2021). The psychology of moral conviction. *Annual Review of Psychology, 72*, 347–366.

Sleek, S. (2015). How poverty affects the brain and behavior. *Association for Psychological Science, 28*(7), 29–32.

Sleek, S. (2018). The bias beneath: Two decades of measuring implicit associations. *APS Observer, 31*(2), 11–14.

Slovik, P., Fischoff, B., & Lichtenstein, S. (1985). Regulation of risk: A psychological perspective. In R. G. Noll (Ed.), *Regulatory policy and the social sciences* (pp. 239–343). Berkeley: University of California Press.

Smith, A. (1976). *An inquiry into the nature and causes of the wealth of nations.* In E. Cannan (Ed.), Chicago: University of Chicago Press. (Original work published 1776).

Smith, A. (2021, Nov. 30). NLRB regional office orders Amazon to hold another election in Alabama. *SHRM HR Daily Newsletter.*

Smith, B. (2021, Oct. 11). A 1979 fight over ideals is still going on. *The New York Times,* B1, 4.

Smith, B. D., & Vetter, H. J. (1982). *Theoretical approaches to personality.* Englewood Cliffs, NJ: Prentice-Hall.

Smith, C. P. (1983). Ethical issues: research on deception, informed consent, and debriefing. In L. Wheeler & P. Shaver (Eds.), *Review of personality and social psychology* (Vol. 4, pp. 297–328). Beverley Hills: Sage.

Smith, C. P., & Berard, S. P. (1982). Why are human subjects less concerned about ethically problematic research than human subjects committees? *Journal of Applied Social Psychology, 12*, 209–221.

Smith, C. P., & Richardson, D. (1983). Amelioration of deception and harm in psychological research: The important role of debriefing. *Journal of Personality and Social Psychology, 44*, 1075–1082.

Smith, D. L., Cutting, J. C., & Riggs, R. O. (1995). Ensuring subjects' understanding of informed consent. *Research Management Review, 7*, 25–33.

Smith, J. (2021). How neoliberalism embraced human rights. *Jacobin Magazine*, Oct. 8. Retrieved on Dec. 9, 2021, from https://jacobinmag.com/2021/10/neoliberalism-mont-pelerin-society-hayek-mises-human-rights-discourse-market-postcolonialism

Smith, J. K. & Smith, R. L. (2016). Socially responsible investing by universities and colleges. *Financial Management, Winter*, 877–922.

Smith, M. (1993). Realism. In P. Singer (Ed.), *A companion to ethics* (pp. 399–410). Cambridge, MA: Blackwell.

Smith, M. B. (1976). Some perspectives on ethical/political issues in social science research. *Personality and Social Psychology Bulletin, 2*, 445–453.

Smith, M. B. (2000). Moral foundations in research with human participants. In B. D. Sales, & S. Folkman (Eds.), *Ethics in research with human participants* (pp. 3–10). Washington, DC: American Psychological Association.

Smith, R. W., Min, H., Ng, M. A., Haynes, N. J., & Clark, M. A. (2022). A content validation of work passion: Was the passion ever there? *Journal of Business and Psychology*. Published online 25 March, 2022.

Smith, S. S., & Richardson, D. (1983). Amelioration of deception and harm in psychological research: The important role of debriefing. *Journal of Personality and Social Psychology, 44,* 1075–1082.

Smith, V. (1997). New forms of work organization. *Annual Review of Sociology, 23,* 315–339.

Smith, W. J., Wokutch, R. E., Harrington, K. V., & Dennis, B. S. (2001). An examination of the influence of diversity and stakeholder role on corporate social orientation. *Business & Society, 40,* 266–294.

Snarey, J. R. (1985). Cross-cultural universality of social-moral development: A critical review of Kohlbergian research. *Psychological Bulletin, 97,* 202–232.

Snarey, J. R. (1986). The relationship of social-moral development with cognitive and ego development: A cross-cultural study. *Behavior Science Research, 20,* 132–146.

Snell, R. S. (1996). Complementing Kohlberg: Mapping the ethical reasoning used by managers for their own dilemma cases. Human *Relations, 49,* 23–49.

Sobal, J. (1984). The content of survey introductions and the provision of informed consent. *Public Opinion Quarterly, 48,* 788–793.

Sober, E. & Wilson, D. S. (1998). *Unto others: The evolution and psychology of unselfish behavior.* Cambridge: Harvard University Press.

Society for Human Resource Management. (2014). *Code of ethics.* Alexandria, VA: Author. Amended, Nov. 21.

Society for Industrial and Organizational Psychology. (2016). *Guidelines for Education and Training in Industrial-Organizational Psychology.* Bowling Green, OH: Author.

Society for Industrial and Organizational Psychology. (2018). *Principles for the Validation and Use of Personnel Selection Procedures* (5th ed.). Bowling Green, OH: Author.

Society for Industrial and Organizational Psychology. (2021). *SIOP Vision, Mission, Values, and Goals,* updated Feb. 3. Downloaded Apr. 27, 2022 from https://www.siop-org/About-SIOP/Mission.

Society for Industrial and Organizational Psychology. (2022). Downloaded from https://www.siop.org/About-SIOP/Advocacy/Government-relations/Advocacy-Resources Feb. 16, 2022.

Solomon, R. C. (1992). *Ethics and excellence: Cooperation and integrity in business.* New York: Oxford University Press.

Solomon S. D. (2015, March 25). The thorny task of advocating good corporate behavior. *The New York Times,* B3.

Sommers, R., & Miller, F. G. (2013). Forgoing debriefing in deceptive research: Is it ever ethical? *Ethics & Behavior, 23*(2), 98–116.

Sonnentag, S. (2015). Dynamics of well-being. *Annual Review of Organizational Psychology and Organizational Behavior, 2,* 261–293.

Sonnert, G., & Commons, M. L. (1994). Society and the highest stages of moral development. *Politics and the Individual, 4,* 31–55.

Sorenson, J., Ewles, G., & Sasso, T. (2015). What do you hope to contribute to society? Integrating science and practice in graduate education. *The Industrial-Organizational Psychologist, 53*(2), 20–25.

Sorensen, J. E., & Sorensen, T. L. (1974). The conflict of professionals in bureaucratic organizations. *Administrative Science Quarterly, 19*, 98–106.

Sorkin, A. R. (2015). Many on wall street say it remains untamed. *The New York Times*, May 19, 2015, B1, 2.

Soros, G. (1998). *The crisis of global capitalism [open society endangered]*. New York: Public Affairs.

Soros, G. (2000). *Open society [reforming global capitalism]*. New York: Public Affairs.

Spector, P. E. (2002). Employee control and occupational stress. *Current Directions in Psychological Science, 11*, 133–136.

Spector, P. E., & Fox, S. (2005). Concluding thoughts: Where do we go from here? In S. Fox & P. E. Spector (Eds.), *Counterproductive workplace behavior: Investigations of actors and targets*. Washington, DC: American Psychological Association.

Spellman, B. A. (2012). Introduction to the special section: Data, data, everywhere … especially in my file drawer. *Perspectives on Psychological Science, 7*(1), 58–59.

Spence, J. T. (1985). Achievement American style: The rewards and costs of individualism. *American Psychologist, 40*, 1285–1295.

Spencer, S. J., Steele, C. M., & Quinn, D. M. (1999). Stereotype threat and women's math performance. *Journal of Experimental Social Psychology, 35*, 4–28.

Staal, M. A., & King, R. E. (2000). Managing a multiple relationship environment: The ethics of military psychology. *Professional Psychology: Research and Practice, 31*, 698–705.

Stagner, R. (1981a). The future of union psychology. *International Review of Applied Psychology, 30*, 321–328.

Stagner, R. (1981b). Training and experiences of some distinguished industrial psychologists. *American Psychologist, 36*(5), 497–505.

Stagner, R. (1982). Past and future of industrial/organizational psychology. *Professional Psychology, 13*, 892–903.

Stanley, A. (2015, Dec. 21). Hedge-fund billionaire's moral index. *The New York Times*, B1.

Stanley, B., Sieber, J. E., & Melton, G. B. (1987). Empirical studies of ethical issues in research. *American Psychologist, 42*, 735–741.

Stanwick, P. A., & Stanwick, S. D. (1998). The relationship between corporate social performance and organizational size, financial performance, and environmental performance: An empirical examination. *Journal of Business Ethics, 17*, 195–204.

Starik (1995). "Should trees have managerial standing?" Toward stakeholder status for non-human nature. *Journal of Business Ethics, 14*, 207–217.

Stark, A. (2021, July 6). Introducing the SIOP diversifying I-O psychology program. Downloaded from https://www.siop.org/research-Publications/items-of-interest/ArtMID/19366/ArticleID/5742/Curated-Session-and-Event-Lists July 7, 2021.

Starmans, C., & Bloom, P. (2016). When the spirit is willing, but the flesh is weak: Developmental differences in judgments about inner moral conflict. *Psychological Science, 27*(11), 1498–1506.

Statman, M. (2007). Socially responsible investments. *The Journal of Investment Consulting, 8*(2), 17–37.

Stavrova, O., Schlösser, T., & Fetchenhauer, D. (2013). Are virtuous people happy all around the world? Civic virtue, antisocial punishment, and subjective well-being across cultures. *Personality and Social Psychology Bulletin, 39*(7), 927–942.

Steele, C. M. (1997). A threat in the air: How stereotypes shape intellectual identity and performance. American *Psychologist, 52*, 613–629.

Steele, C. M. (1999, August). Thin ice: "Stereotype threat" and black college students. *The Atlantic Monthly, 284*(2), 44–54.

Steele, C. M., & Aronson, J. (1995). Contending with a stereotype: African-American intellectual test performance and stereotype threat. *Journal of Personality* and *Social Psychology, 69*, 797–811.

Steiner, A., & Yancey, G. B. (2013). The knowledge and skills employers desire when hiring an I-O psychologist. *The Industrial-Organizational Psychologist, 51*(1), 53–60.

Steininger, M., Newell, J. D., & Garcia, L. T. (1984). *Ethical issues in psychology.* Homewood, IL: Dorsey. https://credo.stanford.edu/documents/NCSS%202013%20 Executive%20Summary.pdf

Steneck, N. H. (2006). Fostering integrity in research: Definitions, current knowledge, and future directions. *Science and Engineering Ethics, 12*(1), 53–74.

Sterba, S. K. (2006). Misconduct in the analysis and reporting of data: Bridging methodological and ethical agendas for change. *Ethics & Behavior, 16*(4), 305–318.

Stern, P. C., Dietz, T., & Guagnano, G. A. (1998). A brief inventory of values. *Educational and Psychological Measurement, 58*, 984–1001.

Sternberg, R. J. (2016). "Am I famous yet?" Judging scholarly merit in psychological science: An introduction. *Perspectives on Psychological Science, 11*(6), 877–881.

Stevens, B. (2008). Corporate ethical codes: effective instruments for influencing behavior. *Journal of Business Ethics, 78*, 601–609.

Stevenson, B. (2021). Quoted in Casselman, B. (2021, Oct. 20). Economic gains hobbled as labor market shrinks: Wielding rare leverage to push demands, workers are in no hurry to return. *The New York Times*, A1.

Stevenson, C. L. (1944). *Ethics and language.* New Haven, CT: Yale University Press.

Stewart, L. P. (1992). Ethical issues in postexperimental and postexperiential debriefing. *Simulation & Gaming, 23*, 196–211.

Stiglitz, J. E. (2013, Oct. 13). Inequality is a choice. The opinion pages: The great divide. *The New York Times.* Downloaded May 22, 2016 from < http://opinionator.blogs. nytimes.com/2013/10/13/inequality-is-a-choice/>

Stiglitz, J. E. (2015). *The great divide: Unequal societies and what we can do about them.* New York: W.W. Norton & Company.

Stirman, S. W., & Beidas, R. S. (2020). Expanding the reach of psychological science through implementation science: Introduction to the special issue. *American Psychologist, 75*(8), 1033–1037.

Stitch, S., Doris, J. M. and Roedder, E. (2010). Altruism. Chapter 5 in J.M. Doris & the Moral Psychology Research Group. *The moral psychology handbook* (pp. 147–205). New York, NY: Oxford University Press.

Stocker, M. (1976). The schizophrenia of modern ethical theories. *The Journal of Philosophy, 73*, 453–466.

Stokes, G., Mumford, M. D., & Owens, W. A. (1994). *Biodata handbook: Theory, research, and use of biographical information in selection and performance prediction.* Palo Alto, CA: CPP Books.

Stolberg, S. G. (2015, Oct. 17). Tapes portray a coal baron lax on safety. *The New York Times*, A1.

Stone, C. D. (1975). *Where the law ends: The social control of corporate behavior.* New York: Harper Colophon.

Stone-Romero, E. F., & Stone, D. L. (2005). How do organizational justice concepts related to discriminatin and prejudice? In J. Greenberg, & J. A. Colquitt (Eds.), *Handbook of organizational justice*. Mahwah, NJ: Lawrence Erlbaum Associates.

Stricker, G. (1997). Are science and practice commensurable? *American Psychologist, 52,* 442–448.

Stricker, G. (2000). The scientist-practitioner model: Ghandi was right again. *American Psychologist, 55,* 253–254.

Stricker, L. J. (1967). The true deceiver. *Psychological Bulletin,* 68, 13–20.

Strom, S. (2003, Aug. 17). An organ donor's generosity raises the question of how much is too much. *The New York Times.* National Edition, Sec. 1, p. 14.

Strum, S. (1987). *Almost human:* A journey *into the world of baboons.* New York: Random House.

Suedfeld, P., & Tetlock, P. E. (Eds.). (1991). *Psychology and social advocacy.* Washington, DC: Hemisphere.

Sugiura, L., Wiles, R., & Pope, C. (2017). Ethical challenges in online research: Public/private perceptions. *Research Ethics, 13*(3-4), 184–199.

Suhler, C. L., & Churchland, P. (2011). Can innate, modular "foundations" explain morality? Challenges for Haidt's moral foundations theory. *Journal of Cognitive Neuroscience, 23*(9), 2103–2116.

Sullivan, E. V. (1994). A study of Kohlberg's structural theory of moral development: A critique of liberal social science ideology. In B. Puka (Ed.), *Moral development: A compendium* (Vol. 4, pp. 46–70). New York: Garland.

Sullivan, J. L., & Transue, J. E. (1999). The psychological underpinnings of democracy: A selective review of research on political tolerance, interpersonal trust, and social capital. Annual *Review of Psychology, 50,* 625–650.

Sullivan, S. E., & Baruch, Y. (2009). Advances in career theory and research: A critical review and agenda for future exploration. *Journal of Management, 35*(6), 1542–1571.

Suls, J. M., & Rosnow, R. L. (1981). The delicate balance between ethics and artifacts in behavioral research. In A. J. Kimmel (Ed.), *Ethics of human subject research* (pp. 49–54). San Francisco: Jossey-Bass.

Sun, W., & Ding, Z. (2021). Is doing bad always punished? A moderated longitudinal analysis on corporate social irresponsibility and firm value. *Business & Society, 60*(7), 1811–1848.

Sunstein, C. (2005). Moral heuristics. *Behavioral and Brain Sciences,* 28, 531–573.

Sverke, M., & Hellgren, J. (2002). The nature of job insecurity: Understanding employment uncertainty on the brink of a new millennium. *Applied Psychology:* An *International Review, 51,* 23–42.

Swanson, D. L. (1999). Toward an integrative theory of business and society: A research strategy for corporate social performance. *Academy of Management Review,* 24, 506–521.

Swigart, K. L., Anantharaman, A., Williamson, J. A., & Grandey, A. A. (2020). Working while Liberal/Conservative: A review of political ideology in organizations. *Journal of Management, 46*(6), 1063–1091.

Szasz, T. S. (1970). *Ideology and insanity.* New York: Doubleday.

Tabuchi, H. (2016a, May 4). Takata airbag recall is said to double, expanding by 35 million. *The New York Times,* B1.

Tabuchi, H. (2016b, Aug. 27). The quest to save a few dollars per airbag led to a deadly crisis. *The New York Times,* A1.

Tackett. K. L. Lilienfeld, S. O., Paatrick, C. J., Johnson, S. L., Krueger, R. F., Miller, J. D., Oltmanns, T. F., & Shrout, P. E. (2017). It's time to broaden the replicability conversation: Thoughts for and from clinical psychology science. *Perspectives on Psychological Science*, *12*(5), 742–756.

Tangney, J. (2000). Training. Chapter 8 In B. D. Sales, & S. Folkman (Eds.), *Ethics in research with human participants* (pp. 97–105). Washington, DC: American Psychological Association.

Tangney, J. P., Stuewig, J., & Mashek, D. J. (2017). Moral emotions and moral behavior. *Annual Review of Psychology*, *58*, 345–372.

Tannenbaum, S. I., Greene, V. J., & Glickman, A. S. (1989). The ethical reasoning process in an organizational consulting situation. *Professional Psychology: Research and Practice*, *20*, 229–235.

Tarasoff v. Board of Regents of the University of California, 17 Cal. 3d 425, Cal. Rptr. 14, 551 P.2d 334 (1976)

Tavallali, C., Reswow, S., & White, J. (2018). 7 questions and answers about AI and I-O. *The Industrial-Organizational Psychologist*, *56*(1).

Tavernese, S. (2016, Feb. 13). Life spans of the rich leave the poor behind. *The New York Times*, A1.

Taylor, J., & Pagliari, C. (2018). Mining social media data: How are research sponsors and researchers addressing the ethical challenges? *Research Ethics*, *14*(2), 1–39.

Taylor, P. Kochhar, R., Fry, R., Velasco, G., & Motel, S. (2011, July 26). *Wealth gaps rise to record highs between whites, blacks and Hispanics*. Washington, DC: Pew Research Center.

Tawney, R. H. (1920). *The acquisitive society*. New York: Harcourt, Brace & Howe.

Taylor, F. W. (1911). The *principles of scientific management*. New York: Harper.

Taylor, K. M., & Shepperd, J. A. (1996). Probing suspicion among participants in deception research: Comment. *American Psychologist*, *51*, 886–887.

Ten Brinke, L., Liu, C. C., Keltner, D., & Srivastava, S. B. (2016). Virtues, vices, and political influence in the U.S. Senate. *Psychological Science*, *27*(1), 85–93.

Tesch, F. E. (1977). Debriefing research participants: Though this be method there is madness to it. *Journal of Personality and Social Psychology*, *35*, 217–224.

Tessler, B. (2013). Workadvance: Testing a new approach to increase employment advancement for low-skilled adults. *mdrc Policy Brief*, June. Available from http://.mdrc.org/sites/default/files/WorkAdvance_Brief.pdf.

Tetlock, P. E. (1992). The impact of accountability on judgment and choice: Toward a social contingency model. In M. P. Zanna (Ed.), *Advances in Experimental Social Psychology*, (Vol. 25, pp. 331–377). New York: Academic.

Tetlock, P. E., & Mitchell, G. (1993). Liberal and conservative approaches to justice: Conflicting psychological portraits. In B. A. Mellers, & J. Baron (Eds.), *Psychological perspectives on justice: Theory and applications* (pp. 234–255). New York: Cambridge University Press.

Thau, S., Derfler-Rozin, R., Pitesa, M., Mitchell, M. S., & Pillutla, M. M. (2015). Unethical for the sake of the group: Risk of social exclusion and pro-group unethical behavior. *Journal of Applied Psychology*, *100*(1), 98–113.

The Economist. (2021, Oct. 21). Striketober: American workers take to the picket lines. Retrieved from https://www.economist.com/united-states/striketober-american-workers-take-to-the-picket-lines/21805726?utm_source=Economic+Policy+Institute&utm_campaign=059ca659e5-EMAIL_CAMPAIGN_2021_10_27&utm_medium=email&utm_term=0_e7c5826c50-059ca659e5-58536137&mc_cid=059ca659e5&mc_eid=c3b577356e on Nov, 17, 2021.

The New York Times Magazine. (2020, Sept. 13). Greed is good. Except when it's bad.

Thoma, S. (1994). Moral judgments and moral action. In J. R. Rest, & D. Narvaez (Eds.), *Moral development in the professions* (pp. 199–212). Hillsdale, NJ: Lawrence Erlbaum Associates.

Thoma, S., Rest, J. R., & Barnett, R. (1986). Moral judgment, behavior, decision making, and attitudes. In J. R. Rest (Ed.), *Moral development: Advances in theory and research* (pp. 133–175). New York: Praeger.

Thomas, K. & Pollack, A. (2016, March 22). Shake-up at Valeant signals end of an era. *The New York Times*, B1.

Thomas, L. (1993). Morality and psychological development. In P. Singer (Ed.), *A companion to ethics* (pp. 464–475). Cambridge, MA: Blackwell.

Thompson, M. N. & Dahling, J. J. (2019). Employment and poverty: Why work matters in understanding poverty. *American Psychologist, 74*(6), 673–684.

Thompson, R. A. (2009). Early foundations: Conscience and the development of moral character. Chap. 7 In D. Narvaez & D. K. Lapsley (Eds.). *Personality, identity and character: Explorations in moral psychology* (pp. 159–184). New York: NY: Cambridge University Press.

Thorne, L., & Saunders, S. B. (2002). The socio-cultural embeddedness of individuals' ethical reasoning in organizations (cross-cultural ethics). *Journal of Business Ethics, 35*, 1–14.

Thun, B., & Kelloway, E. K. (2011). Virtuous leaders: Assessing character strengths in the workplace. *Canadian Journal of Administrative Science, 28*, 270–283.

Tiberius, V. (2008). The nativism debate and moral philosophy: Comments on Prinz. Chapter 7.2 In W. Sinnott-Armstrong (Ed.), *Moral psychology. Volume 1: The evolution of morality: Adaptations and innateness* (pp. 419–426). Cambridge, MA: The MIT Press.

Tiberius, V. (2015). *Moral psychology: A contemporary introduction.* New York, NY: Routledge.

Tiffin, J. (1956). How psychologists serve industry. *Personnel Journal, 36*(10), 372–376.

Timmermans, S. (2008). Professions and their work: Do market shelters protect professional interests? *Work and Occupations, 35*(2), 164–188.

Tippins, N. T., Oswald, F. L., & McPhail, S. M. (2021). Scientific, legal, and ethical concerns about AI-based personnel selection tools: A call to action. *Personnel Assessment and Decisions, 7*(2), Article 1.

Tjeltveit, A. C. (1999). *Ethics and values in psychotherapy.* London: Routledge.

Tittenbrun, J. (2014). *Concepts of Capitalism: The commodification of social life.* New Brunswick, NJ: Transaction Publications.

Tobias, J. S. (1997). BMJ's present policy. *British Medical Journal, 314*, 1111–1114.

Tomasello, M. & Vaish, A. (2013). Origins of human cooperation and morality. *Annual Review of Psychology, 64*, 231–255.

Tomprou, M., & Lee, M. K. (2022). Employment relationships in algorithmic management: A psychological contract perspective. *Computers in Human Behavior*, Available online 23 August. 126, 1–12.

Toth, A., Banks, G. C., Mellor, D., O'Boyle, E. H., Dickson, A., Davis, D. J., DeHaven, A., Bochantin, J. W. & Borns, J. (2021). Study preregistration: An evaluation of a method for transparent reporting. *Journal of Business and Psychology, 36*(4), 553–571.

Toulman, S. (1973). *Human understanding.* Chicago: University of Chicago Press.

Trautman, S. T., van de Kuilen, G., & Zeckhauser, R. J. (2013). Social class and (un) ethical behavior: A framework, with evidence from a large population sample. *Perspectives on Psychological Science, 8*(5), 487–497.

Treaster, J. B. (2001, Dec. 28). U.S. sues Allstate, whose agents cite age discrimination. *The New York Times*, A1.

Treviño, L. K. (1986). Ethical decision making in organizations: A person-situation interactionist model. *Academy of Management Review, 11,* 601–617.

Treviño, L. K., den Nieuwenboer, N. A., & Kish-Gephart, J. J. (2014). (Un)ethical behavior in organizations. *Annual Review of Psychology, 65,* 635–660.

Triandis, H. C. (1995). *Individualism and collectivism*. Boulder, CO: Westview Press.

Triandis, H. C., Dunnette, M. D., & Hough, L. M. (Eds.). (1994). *Handbook of industrial and organizational psychology* (2nd ed., Vol. 4). Palo Alto, CA: Consulting Psychologists Press.

Trinker, R., Tyler, T. R., & Goff, P. A. (2016). Justice from within: The relations between a procedurally just organizational climate and police organizational efficiency, endorsement of democratic policing, and officer well-being. *Psychology, Public Policy, and Law, 22*(2), 158–172.

Trougakos, J. P., Beal, D. J., Cheng, B. H., Hideg, I., & Zweig, D. (2015). Too drained to help: A resource depletion perspective on daily interpersonal citizenship behaviors. *Journal of Applied Psychology, 100*(1), 227–236.

Tsan, M-F. (2021). Improvingk the quality and performance of institutional review boards in the U.S.A. through performance measurements. *Journal of Empirical Research on Human Research Ethics, 16*(5), 479–484.

Tsan, M-F., Ling, B., Feske, U., Zickmund, S., Stone, R., Sonel, A., Arnold, R. M., Fine, M., & Hall, D. E. (2020). Assessing the quality and performance of institutional review boards: Levels of initial reviews. *Journal of Empirical Research on Human Research Ethic, 15*(5), 407–414.

Tsui, A. S., & Enderle, G. (2018). Income inequality in the United States: Reflections on the role of corporations. *Academy of Management Review, 43* (1), 156–168.

Tsui, A. S., Pearce, J. L., Porter, L. W., & Tripoli, A. M. (1997). Alternative approaches to the employee-organization relationship: Does investment in employees pay off? *Academy of Management Journal, 40,* 1089–1121.

Tsutsui, K., & Lim, A. (Eds.). (2015). *Corporate social responsibility in a globalizing world*. Cambridge, UK: Cambridge University Press.

Turiel, E. (1983). *The development of social knowledge: Morality and convention*. Cambridge, England: Cambridge University Press.

Turiel, E., Killen, M., & Helwig, C. (1987). Morality: It's structure, functions and vagaries. In J. Kagan & S. Lamb (Eds.), *The emergence of morality in young children* (pp. 155–243). Chicago: University of Chicago Press.

Turiel, E., Smetana, J. G., & Killen, M. (1991). Social contexts in social cognitive development. In W. M. Kurtines, & J. L. Gewirtz (Eds.), *Handbook of moral behavior and development: Vol. 2. Research* (pp. 307–332). Hillsdale, NJ: Lawrence Erlbaum Associates.

Tversky, A., & Kahneman, D. (1974). Judgment under uncertainty: Heuristics and biases. *Science, 185,* 1124–1131.

Twenge, J. M., Haidt, J., Blake, A. B., McAllister, C., Lemon, H. & Le Roy, A. (2021). Worldwide increases in adolescent loneliness. *Journal of Adolescence*, in press.

Tyler, L. (1973). Design for a hopeful psychology. *American Psychologist, 28,* 1021–1029.

Uchitelle, L. (2001, August 5). Now, the pink slip is all in a day's work. *The New York Times*, A1, A11.

Uchitelle, L. (2002, January 20). The rich are different. They know when to leave. *The New York Times*, Section 4, 1, 5.

Uglietta, J. (2018). Middle theory in professional ethics. *Teaching Ethics*, *18*(2), 161–169.

Uhlmann, E. L., Pizarro, D. A., & Diermeier, D. (2015). A person-centered approach to moral judgment. *Perspectives on Psychological Science*, *10*(1), 72–81.

Ullman, A. (1985). Data in search of a theory: A critical examination of the relationships among social performance, social disclosure, and economic performance. *Academy of Management Review*, *10*, 540–577.

Umphress, E. U., & Bingham, J. B. (2011). When employees do bad things for good reasons: Examining unethical pro-organizational behaviors. *Organization Science*, *22*(3), 621–640.

Umphress, E. E., Bingham, J. B., & Mitchell, M. S. (2010). Unethical behavior in the name of the company: The moderating effect of organizational identification and positive reciprocity beliefs on unethical pro-organizational behavior. *Journal of Applied Psychology*, *95*(4), 769–780.

Unger, R. K. (1983). Through the looking glass: No wonderland yet! (The reciprocal relationship between methodology and models of reality). *Psychology of Women Quarterly*, *8*, 9–32.

United Nations (1948). Universal declaration of human rights. *General Assembly resolution 217A*(III), Dec. 10.

United Nations (2015). The millennium development goals report. Retrieved from http://www.un.org/millenniumgoals/2015_MDG_Report/pdf/MDG%202015%20rev%20(July%201).pdf, June 27, 2016.

United Nations Development Programme. (2000). *Poverty report 2000: Overcoming human poverty*. New York: Author.

United Nations Development Programme. (2015). *Human Development Report 2015*. New York: Author.

United Nations Development Programme. (2020). *Human Development Report 2020*. New York: Author.

United Nations Development Programme. (2021). *The 2021 global multidimensional poverty index (MPI)*. New York: Author.

United States Congress (1977/1998). Foreign Corrupt Practices Act. 15 U.S.C., Secs. 78dd-1, et seq.

U.S. Bureau of Labor Statistics. (2014). Fastest growing occupations. Occupational outlook Handbook. Retrieved from http://www.bls.gov/ooh/print/fastest-growing.htm, on Jan. 22, 2014.

U.S. Department of health and Human Services. (2019). Subpart A of 45 CFR Part 46: *Basic HHS Policy for Protection of Human Subjects*. As revised Jan. 19, 2017, and amended on Jan. 22, 2018 and June 19, 2018. (Effective Jan. 21, 2019).

Van Bavel, J. (2016, May 29). Why do so many studies fail to replicate? *The New York Times Sunday Review*, 10.

Van Buren, H. J. III. (2000). The windingness of social and psychological contracts: Toward a theory of social responsibility in downsizing. *Journal of Business Ethics*, *25*, 205–219.

Van Lange, P. A. M. (2015). Generalized trust: Four lessons from genetics and culture. *Current Directions in Psychological Science*, *24*(1), 71–76.

van Vugt, M. (2017). Evolutionary psychology: theoretical foundations for the study of organizations. *Journal of Organization Design*, *6*(9),

van Vugt, M., Hogan, R., & Anderson, N. (2008). Leadership, followership, and evolution: Some lessons from the past. *American Psychologist*, *63*(3), 182–196, van Wensveen, L. (2005). Cardinal environmental virtues: A neurobiological perspective. In R. Sandler, & P. Cafaro, (Eds.), *Environmental virtue ethics* (pp. 173–194). Lanham, MD: Rowman and Littlefield.

Van Zant, A. B., & Moore, D. A. (2015). Leaders' use of moral justifications increases policy support. *Psychological Science, 26*(6), 934–943.

Vardi, Y. (2001). The effects of organizational and ethical climates on misconduct at work. *Journal of Business Ethics, 29*, 325–337.

Vardi, Y., & Weitz, E. (2016). *Misbehavior in organizations: A dynamic approach,* 2nd Ed. New York: Routledge.

Vasquez, M. J. T. (2012). APA Presidential Address. Psychology and social justice: why we do what we do. *American Psychologist, 67*(5), 337–346.

Vazire, S., Schiavone, S. R., & Bottesini, J. G. (2022). Credibility beyond replicability: Improving the four validities in psychological science. *Current Directions in Psychological Science, 31*(2), 162–168.

Veatch, R. M. (1987). *The patient as* partner. Bloomington: Indiana University Press.

Verbruggen, M., & Sels, L. (2008). Can career self-directedness be improved through counseling? *Journal of Vocational Behavior, 73*, 18–327.

Veselka, V. (2022, Jan. 16). These workers went on strike to save lives. *The New York Times,* 4–5.

Victor, B., & Cullen, J. B. (1988). The organizational bases of ethical work climates. *Administrative Science Quarterly, 33*, 95–119.

Viswesvaran, C., & Ones, D. (2002). Examining the construct of organizational justice: A meta-analytic evaluation of relations with work attitudes and behaviors. *Journal of Business Ethics, 38*, 193–203.

Vitelli, R. (1988). The crisis issue assessed: An empirical analysis. *Basic and Applied Social Psychology, 9*, 301–309.

Volz, K. G., & Hertwig, R. (2016). Emotions and decisions: Beyond conceptual vagueness and the rationality muddle. *Perspectives on Psychological Science, 11*(1), 101–116.

Vosburgh, R., Stage, V., Hendrickson, V., Kohn, H., King, S., Guidry, B., & Zito, E. (2021). 2021 membership survey. *The Industrial-Organizational Psychologist, 58*(4), 23–24.

Vredenburgh, D., & Brender, Y. (1998). The hierarchical abuse of power in work organizations. *Journal of Business Ethics, 17*, 1337–1347.

Waclawski, J., & Church, A. H. (2000). The 2000 SIOP Member survey results are in! *The Industrial-Organizational Psychologist, 38*(1), 59–68.

Waddock, S. A., & Graves, S. B. (1997). Quality of management and quality of stakeholder relations: Are they synonymous? *Business & Society, 36*, 250–280.

Wade, N. (2001a, May 3). Genome feud heats up as academic team accuses commercial rival of faulty work. *The New York Times,* A15.

Wade, N. (2001b, May 18). Link between human genes and bacteria is hotly debated by rival scientific camps. *The New York Times,* A17.

Wade, N. (2015a, Mar. 20). Scientists seek ban on method of editing the human genome. *The New York Times,* A1, 17.

Wade, N. (2015b, Dec. 4). Scientists call for moratorium on editing of human genome. *The New York Times,* A1, 12.

Wagner, R. K. (1997). Intelligence, training, and employment. *American Psychologist, 52*, 1059–1069.

Wagner, V. (2014). Explaining the Knobe effect. Chap. 6 In C. Luetge, H. Rusch, & M. Uhl (Eds.), *Experimental ethics: Toward an empirical moral philosophy* (pp. 6–79). Houndmills, England: Palgrave Macmillan.

Wahn, J. (1993). Organizational dependence and the likelihood of complying with organizational pressures to behave unethically. *Journal of Business Ethics, 12,* 245–251.

Waldo, D. (2001). Lessons for employers in a slowing economy. *The Industrial-Organizational Psychologist, 39*(1), 50–51.

Walker, C. R., & Guest, R. H. (1952). *The man on the assembly line.* Cambridge, MA: Harvard University Press.

Walker, J. E., Tausky, C., & Oliver, D. (1982). Men and women at work: Similarities and differences in work values within occupational groupings. *Journal of Vocational Behavior, 21,* 17–36.

Walker, L. (1984). Sex differences in the development of moral reasoning: A critical review. *Child Development, 55,* 183–201.

Walker, R. (2015). Closing the deal after a lost job. *The New York Times,* B8.

Wallace, J. E. (1995). Organizational and professional commitment in professional and nonprofessional organizations. *Administrative Science Quarterly, 40,* 228–255.

Walsh, M. W. (2000, November 3). Court considers if employer can force pledge not to sue. *The New York Times,* A1.

Walsh-Bowers, R. (1995). The reporting and ethics of the research relationship in areas of interpersonal psychology, 1939–1989. *Theory & Psychology, 5,* 233–250.

Walter, F., Lam, C. K., van der Vegt, G. S., Huang, X., & Miao, Q. (2015). Abusive supervision and subordinate performance: Instrumentality considerations in the emergence and consequences of abusive supervision. *Journal of Applied Psychology, 100*(4), 1056–1072.

Walters, B., Hardin, T., & Schick, J. (1995). Top executive compensation: Equity or excess? Implications for regaining American Competitiveness. *Journal of Business Ethics, 14,* 227–234.

Walzer, M. (2006). Terrorism and just war. *Philosophia, 34,* 3–12.

Wang, H., Tong, L., Takeuchi, R., & George, G. (2016). From the editors—corporate social responsibility: An overview and new research directions. *Academy of Management Journal, 59*(2), 534–544.

Wang, Y., Xu, S., & Wang, Y. (2020). The consequences of employees' perceived corporate social responsibility: A meta-analysis. *Business Ethics: A European Review, 29*(6), 471–496.

Wang, Y., Wang, G. Chen, Q., & Li, L. (2017). Depletion, moral identity, and unethical behavior: Why people behave unethically after self-control exertion. *Consciousness and Cognition, 56,* 186–198.

Wang, Z., Xing, L., Xu, H., & Hannah, S.T., (2021). Not all followers socially learn from ethical leaders: The roles of followers' moral identity and leader identification in hte ethical leadership process. *Journal of Business Ethics, 170,* 449–469.

Waples, E. P., Antes, A. L., Murphy, S. T., Connely, S., & Mumford, M. D. (2009). A meta-analytic investigation of business ethics instruction. *Journal of Business Ethics, 87*(1), 133–151.

Ward, K. (2016). Towards a typology of academic peer review styles. *Urban Geography, 37*(5), 651–654.

Warneken, F. (2018). How children solve the two challenges of cooperation. In S. T. Fiske, D. L. Schacter, & S. E. Taylor (Eds.), *Annual Review of Psychology, 69,* 205–229.

Warren, D. E., Gaspar, J. P., & Laufer, W. S. (2014). Is formal ethics training merely cosmetic? A study of ethics training and ethical organizational culture. *Business Ethics Quarterly, 24*(1), 85–117.

Wartzman, R. (2017). *The end of loyalty: The rise and fall of good job in America.* New York: Public Affairs.

Wasserman, R. (2013). Ethical issues and guidelines for conducting data analysis in psychological research. *Ethics & Behavior, 23*(1), 3–15.

Waters, L., Hall, D. T., Wang, L., & Briscoe, J. P. (2015). Protean career orientation: a review of existing and emerging research. Chap. 12 In R. J. Burke, K. M. Page, & C. L. Cooper (Eds.), *Flourishing in life, work and careers: Individual wellbeing and career experiences.* Cheltenham, UK: Edward Elgar Publishing.

Watson, G. W., Shepard, J. M., & Stephens, C. U. (1999). Fairness and ideology: An empirical test of social contracts theory. *Business & Society, 38,* 83–108.

Watts, L. L., Medeiros, K. E., Mulhearn, T. J., Steele, L. M., Connelly, S., & Mumford, M. D. (2017). Are ethics training programs improving? A meta-analytic review of past and present ethics instruction in the sciences. *Ethics & Behavior, 27*(5), 351–384.

Wayne, L. (1999, November 14). Flat tax goes from 'snake oil' to G.O.P. tonic. *The New York Times,* A1, A30.

Weaver, G. R., Reynolds, S. J., & Brown, M. E. (2014). Moral intuition: Connecting current knowledge to future organizational research and practice. *Journal of Management, 40*(1), 100–129.

Weaver, G. R., Treviño, L. K., & Cochran, P. L. (1999). Corporate ethics programs as control systems: Influences of executive commitment and environmental factors. *Academy of Management* Journal, *42,* 41–57.

Webb, E. J., Campbell, D. T., Schwartz, R. D., Sechrest, L., & Grove, J. B. (1981). *Nonreactive measures in the social sciences* (2nd ed.). Boston: Houghton-Mifflin.

Weber, J. (1993). Exploring the relationship between personal values and moral reasoning. *Human Relations, 46,* 435–463.

Weber, J. (1996). Influences upon managerial moral decision-making: Nature of the harm and magnitude of consequences. *Human Relations, 49,* 1–22.

Weber, J. (2022). Exploring the relationship of variant degrees of national economic freedom to the ethical profiles of millennial business students in eight countries. *Business & Society, 61*(2), 47–495.

Wegner, D. M., & Wheatley, T. (1999). Apparent mental causation: Sources of the experience of will. *American Psychologist, 54,* 480–492.

Weick, K. E. (1995). *Sensemaking in organizations.* Thousand Oaks, CA: Sage.

Weinberg, C. R. (2000, September). CEO compensation: How much is enough? *Chief Executive Magazine,* 3, (159), 48–63.

Weise, K., & Scheiber, N. (2021, Apr. 17). Why workers chose Amazon over a union. *The New York Times,* A1.

Weise, K., & Scheiber, N. (2022, April 2). Amazon workers on staten island give unions a surprise win. *The New York Times,* A1.

Weiss, D. (2015) Privatization and its discontents: The troubling record of privatized prison healthcare. *University of Colorado Law Review, 86*(2). 725.

Weiss, A., Staes, N., Pereboom, J. J. M., Inoue-Murayama, M., Stevens, J. M. G., & Eens, M. (2015). Personality in bonobos. *Psychological Science, 26*(9), 1430–1439.

Weiss, H. W., & Rupp, D. E. (2011). Experiencing work: An essay on a person-centric work psychology. *Industrial and Organizational Psychology: Perspectives on Science and Practice, 4*(1), 83–97.

Wellman, H. M. (2014). *Making minds: How theory of mind develops.* New York, NY: Oxford University Press.

Welsh, D. T., Ordóñez, L. D., Snyder, D. G., & Christian, M. S. (2014). The slippery slope: How small ethical transgressions pave the way for larger future transgressions. *Journal of Applied Psychology, 100*(1), 114–127.

Werhane, P. H. (1999a). *Moral imagination and management decision-making.* New York: Oxford University Press.

Werhane, P. H. (1999b). Justice and trust. *Journal of Business Ethics, 21*, 237–249.

Werhane, P. (2018). Book review. *Business ethics: A Kantian perspective,* 2nd Ed., by Norman Bowie. New York: Cambridge University Press. *Business Ethics Quarterly, 28*(1), 110-113.

Werhane, P. H., & Radin, T. J. (1996). Employment practices in the contemporary American workplace. In W. W. Gasparski, & L. V. Ryan (Eds.), *Human action in business: Praxiological and ethical dimensions* (pp. 417–433). New Brunswick, NJ: Transaction.

Wesche, J. S., & Sonderegger, A. (2021). Repelled at first sight? Expectations and intentions of job-seekers reading about AI selection in job advertisements. *Computers in Human Behavior.* Available online, 25 June.

Wessler, S. F. (2016, June 15). Federal official ignored years of internal warnings about deaths at private prisons. *The Nation.*

Westermann-Behaylo, M. K., Van Buren III, H. J., & Berman, S. L. (2016). Stakeholder capability enhancement as a path to promote human dignity and cooperative advantage. *Business Ethics Quarterly, 26*(4), 529–555.

Western, B., & Rosenfeld, J. (2011). Unions, norms, and the rise in U.S. wage inequality. *American Sociological Review, 76*(4), 513–537.

Whetstone, J. T. (2001). How virtue fits within business ethics. *Journal of Business Ethics, 33*, 101–114.

White, T. I. (1993). *Business ethics: A philosophical reader.* Upper Saddle River, NJ: Prentice Hall.

Whiten, W. (2017). Social learning and culture in child and chimpanzee. In S. T. Fiske, D. L. Schacter, & S. E. Taylor (Eds.), *Annual Review of Psychology, 68*, 129–154.

Whitman, D. S., Caleo, S., Carpenter, N. C., Horner, M. T., & Bernerth, J. B. (2012). Fairness at the collective level: A meta-analytic examination of the consequences and boundary conditions of organizational justice climate. *Journal of Applied Psychology, 97*, 776–791.

Wicks, A. C. (1995). Albert Schweitzer or Ivan Boesky? Why we should reject the dichotomy between medicine and business. *Journal of Business Ethics, 14*, 339–351.

Wicks, A. C., Gilbert, D. R., Jr., & Freeman, R. E. (1994). A feminist reinterpretation of the stakeholder concept. *Business Ethics Quarterly, 4*, 475–497.

Wilburn, K. M., & Wilburn, H. R. (2014). Demonstrating a commitment to corporate social responsibility not simply shared value. *Business & Professional Ethics Journal, 33*(1), 1–15.

Wiley, C. (1998). Reexamining perceived ethics issues and ethics roles among employment managers. *Journal of Business Ethics, 17*, 147–161.

Wilgoren, J. (2001, June 13). Education study finds U.S. falling short: Teachers are found not benefitting in era of economic expansion. *The New York Times,* B1.

Wilkie, D. (2015, August 19). Is the annual performance review dead? Downloaded from https://www.shrm.org/hrdisciplines/employeerelations/articles/pages/performance-reviews-are-dead.aspx, August 20, 2015.

Wilkins, D. B. (1996). Redefining the "professional" in professional ethics: An inter-disciplinary approach to teaching professionalism. *Law and Contemporary Problems, 58,* 241–258.

Wilkinson, R., & Pickett, K. (2009a). *The spirit level: Why more equal societies almost always do better.* London: Allen Lane.

Wilkinson, R., & Pickett, K. (2009b). Income inequality and social dysfunction. *Annual Review of Sociology, 35,* 493–511.

Williams, O. F. (2000). *Global codes of conduct: An idea whose time has come.* Notre Dame, IN: University of Notre Dame Press.

Wilson, E. O. (2000). *Sociobiology: The new synthesis, twenty-fifth anniversary edition.* Boston: Harvard University Press. (Original work published 1975)

Wilson, V. (2020, Nov. 21). Racism and the economy: Focus on employment. Economic Policy Institute. Retrieved from https://www.epi.org/blog/racism-and-the economy-fed/ on Oct. 11, 2021.

Wimbush, J. C., Shepard, J. M., & Markham, S. E. (1997a). An empirical examination of the multi-dimensionality of ethical climate in organizations. *Journal of Business Ethics, 16,* 67–77.

Wimbush, J. C., Shepard, J. M., & Markham, S. E. (1997b). An empirical examination of the relationship between ethical climate and ethical behavior from multiple levels of analysis. *Journal of Business Ethics, 16,* 1705–1716.

Winerman, L. (2016, June). How much of the psychology literature is wrong? *Monitor on Psychology,* 14–17.

Winston, A. S. (2011). Value neutrality and *SPSSI*: The quest for policy, purity, and legitimacy. *Journal of Social Issues, 67*(1), 59–72.

Witherspoon, R., & White, R. P. (1996). Executive coaching: A continuum of roles. *Consulting Psychology Journal: Practice and Research, 48,* 124–133.

Wittmer, D. P. (2001). Ethical decision-making. In T. L. Cooper (Ed.), *Handbook of administrative ethics* (2nd ed., pp. 481–507). New York: Marcel Dekker.

Wolf, R. N., & Ozehosky, R. J. (1978). Industrial psychology: In need of a learned lawyer? *Professional Psychology, 9*(2), 178–182.

Wolff, J. (2005). Economic Justice. Chapter 17 In H. LaFollette (Ed.), *The Oxford Handbook of Practical Ethics* (pp. 433–458). New York: Oxford University Press.

Wong, A. (2022, Jan. 8). Columbia's student workers end strike after deal. *The New York Times,* A14.

Washington, D. C., & Wong, D. (1993). Relativism. In P. Singer (Ed.), *A companion to ethics* (pp. 442–450). Cambridge, MA: Blackwell.

Woo, V., Lall-Trail, S., & Islam, S. (2021). Delivering on DEI: An analysis of coursework and research in graduate programs. Downloaded from https://www.siop.org/research-Publications/items-of-interest/ArtMID/19366/ArticleID/5742/Curated-Session-and-Event-Lists Jan. 7, 2022.

Wood, A. (1993). Marx against morality. In P. Singer (Ed.), *A companion to ethics* (pp. 511–524). Cambridge, MA: Blackwell.

Woodward, A. L. (2009). Infants' grasp of others' intentions. *Current directions in Psychological Science, 18,* 53–57.

Wooldridge, A. (2000, March 5). Come back, company man! *The New York Times Magazine, 149,* 82–83.

Wooler, S. (1985). Let the decision maker decide!: A case against assuming common occupational value structures. *Journal of Occupational Psychology, 58,* 217–227.

Workplace Fairness (2016). Our Rights Arbitration Agreements. Retrieved from https://www.workplacefairness.org/forced-arbitration-agreements, on June 29, 2016.

Wowak, A. J., Mannor, M. J., & Wowak, K. D. (2015). Throwing caution to the wind: The effect of CEO stock option pay on the incidence of product safety problems. *Strategic Management Journal, 36,* 1082–1092.

Wyld, D. C., & Jones, C. A. (1997). The importance of context: The ethical work climate construct and models of ethical decision making—An agenda for research. *Journal of Business Ethics, 16,* 465–472.

Wynn, K., Bloom, P., Jordan, A., Marshall, J., & Sheskin, M. (2018). Not noble savages after all: Limits to early altruism. *Current Directions in Psychological Science, 27*(1), 3–8.

Yam, K. C., Fehr, R., Keng-Highberger, F. T., Klotz, A. C., & Reynolds, S. J. (2015). Out of control: A self-control perspective on the link between surface acting and abusive supervision. *Journal of Applied Psychology, 100*(2), 292–301.

Yankov, G. P., Wexler, B., Haidar, S., Kumar, S., Zheng, J., & Li, H. (2020). Algorithmic justice. *SIOP White Paper Series.* Bowling Green, OH: Society for Industrial-Organizational Psychology.

Yao, J., Lim, S., Guo, C. Y., Ou, A. Y., & Ng, J. W. X. (2022). Experienced incivility in the workplace: A meta-analytic review of its construct validity and nomological network. *Journal of Applied Psychology, 107*(2), 193–220.

Yates, S. Q. (2016, Aug. 18). Phasing out our use of private prisons. Posted in: Office of the Deputy Attorney General. Downloaded Aug. 25, 2016 from <https://www.justice.gov/opa/blog/phasing-out-our-use-of-private-prisons>

Yenney, S. L., & American Psychological Association Practice Directorate. (1994). *Business strategies of a caring profession: A practitioner's guidebook.* Washington, DC: American Psychological Association.

Yong, J. C., Li, N. P., & Kanazawa, S. (2021). Not so much rational but rationalizing: Humans evolved as coherence-seeking, fiction-making animals. *American Psychologist, 76*(5), 781–793.

Zacher, H., & Rudolph, C. W. (2020). Individual differences and changes in subjective wellbeing during the early stages of the Covid-19 pandemic. *American Psychologist, 76*(1), 62.

Zacher, H., & Rudolph, C. W. (2022). Intraprofessional political disagreement and occupational identification. Unpublished manuscript.

Zajonc, R. B. (1980). Feeling and thinking: Preferences need no inferences. *American Psychologist, 35,* 151–175.

Zaki, J. (2017). Moving beyond stereotypes of empathy. *Trends in Cognitive Sciences, 21,* 59–60.

Zaman, R., Jain, T. Smaara, G. & Jamali, D. (2022). Corporate governance meets corporate social responsibility: Mapping the interface. *Business & Society, 61*(3), 690–752.

Zelig, M. (1988). Ethical dilemmas in police psychology. *Professional Psychology: Research and Practice, 19,* 336–338.

Zelizer, V. A. (1983). *Morals and markets: The development of life insurance in the United States.* New Brunswick: Transaction Publishers.

Zhang, Y., He, B., Huang, Q., & Xie, J. (2020). Effects of supervisor bottom-line mentality on subordinate unethical behavior. *Journal of Managerial Psychology, 35*(5), 419–434.

Zhong, C-B. (2011). The ethical dangers of deliberative decision making. *Administrative Science Quarterly, 56,* 1–25.

Zickar, M. J. (2001). Using personality inventories to identify thugs and agitators: Applied psychology's contribution to the war against labor. *Journal of Vocational Behavior, 59*(1), 149–164.

Zickar, M. & Gibby, R. E. (2007). Four persistent themes throughout the history of I-O psychology in the United States. In L. Koppes (Ed.), *Historical perspectives in industrial and organizational psychology* (pp. 61–80). Mahwah, NJ: Erlbaum.

Zietsch, B. P., Westberg, L., Santtila, P., & Jern, P. (2015). Genetic analysis of human extrapair mating: heritability, between-sex correlation, and receptor genes for vasopressin and oxytocin. *Evolution and Human Behavior, 36*(2), 130–136.

Zigmond, M. J. & Fischer, B. A. (2014). Foreward: teaching responsible conduct responsibly. In F. L. Macrina, *Scientific integrity: Text and cases in responsible conduct of research*, 4th Ed. Washington, DC: ASM Press.

Zimbardo, P. G., & Haney, C. (2020). Continuing to acknowledge the power of dehumanizing environments: Comment on Haslam et al. (2019) and Le Texier (2019). *American Psychologist, 75*(3), 400–402.

Zimbardo, P. G., Haney, C., Banks, W., & Jaffe, D. (1973, April 8). The mind is a formidable jailer: A Pirandellian prison. *The New York Times Magazine*, 38–60.

Zimmer, C. (2015, Oct. 20). Gene editing takes a big leap. *The New York Times*, D4.

Zimmer, C. (2021, July 24). Scientists have finally filled in all the gaps in the human genome. *The New York Times*, A17.

Zipkin, A. (2000, October 18). Getting religion on corporate ethics: A scourge of scandals leaves its mark. *The New York Times*, C1, C10.

Zipperer, B., Cooper, D., & Bivens, J. (2021). A $15 minimum wage would have significant and direct effects on the federal budget. Washington, DC: Economic Policy Institute. Retrieved from https://www.epi.org/publication/a-15-minimum-wage-would-have-significant-and-direct-effects-on-the-federal-budget/ on Nov 10, 2021.

INDEX

Note: **Bold** page numbers refer to tables and *italic* page numbers refer to figures.

Made in the USA
Monee, IL
17 November 2024

70342250R00374